Children's
Writers'
& Artists'
YEARBOOK
2022

Other Writers' & Artists' title

Writers' & Artists' Guides to . . . Series
The best advice on how to write and get published

Writing for Children and YA by Linda Strachan
Getting Published by Alysoun Owen
How to Hook an Agent by James Rennoldson
How to Write by William Ryan
Self-publishing by a team of self-publishing experts

The Organised Writer: How to stay on top of all your projects and never miss a deadline by Antony Johnston

'Antony has uncovered a secret I wish I'd learned twenty years ago;
writing benefits way less from inspiration than from sound process.'
Merlin Mann

'I'm a messy-brained writer. *The Organised Writer* helped me
to tidy-up, and improved my working life on a daily basis.'
Kieron Gillen

NEW in July 2021
Writers' & Artists' Yearbook 2022

'...the first place I turned to' *Peter James*

You can buy copies from your local bookseller or online at
www.writersandartists.co.uk/shop

Children's Writers' & Artists' YEARBOOK 2022

EIGHTEENTH EDITION

The essential guide for children's writers and artists
on how to get published and who to contact

B L O O M S B U R Y

LONDON · OXFORD · NEW YORK · NEW DELHI · SYDNEY

BLOOMSBURY YEARBOOKS
Bloomsbury Publishing Plc
50 Bedford Square, London, WC1B 3DP, UK
29 Earlsfort Terrace, Dublin 2, Ireland

BLOOMSBURY YEARBOOKS, WRITERS' & ARTISTS' and the Diana logo are
trademarks of Bloomsbury Publishing Plc

This edition published 2021

A catalogue record for this book is available from the British Library

ISBN: eBook 978-1-4729-8284-1; PB 978-1-4729-8285-8

2 4 6 8 10 9 7 5 3 1

Typeset by DLxml, a division of RefineCatch Limited, Bungay, Suffolk
Printed and bound in Great Britain by CPI Group (UK) Ltd, Croydon, CR0 4YY

To find out more about our authors and books visit www.bloomsbury.com and sign up for our
newsletters.

Writers' & Artists' team
Editor Alysoun Owen
Assistant editor Eden Phillips Harrington
Articles copy-editor Virginia Klein
Listings editors Lisa Carden, Rebecca Collins, Eden Phillips Harrington
Editorial assistance Lauren MacGowan; Sophia Blackwell (poetry)
Production controller Ben Chisnall

About the *Yearbook*

The Editor welcomes readers to this edition of the *Children's Writers' & Artists' Yearbook.*

In the opening to this year's *Foreword* on page xi, M. G. Leonard writes that for her the prospect of becoming a published author seemed very much out of reach: 'as daunting as climbing Mount Everest'. But, as she goes on to describe and as her bestselling books attest, she *did* reach the summit. Her words and those of the other writers who have contributed to the 70-plus articles in this book should prove that, although there are challenges, it is possible to find an audience for your writing. This *Yearbook* is here to be your Sherpa. It exists to share experiences, advice and support with writers for children and teens across all ages, genres and formats. In addition, it provides up-to-date contact details for thousands of individuals across organisations and companies in the media industries who might help you as you develop your writing and start to seek representation from a literary or illustration agent, or as you explore ways to get your work noticed.

New articles this year span a wide range of forms and markets, from *Writing poetry for children* by Rachel Rooney (on page 213) to *The learning curve: writing for the children's educational market* by Rachel Bladon (page 111). If you are writing fiction, take a look at Anna Wilson's piece on *Finding your voice and point of view* (page 70) for advice on which voice to adopt in your narrative (first, second or third person?). Award-winning novelist Christopher Edge's *Plotting and pace in your middle-grade adventure* (page 153) and *World-building in your fantasy fiction* by L.D. Lapinski (page 160) also offer inspirational insights. If you are keen to self-publish your book, Jenny Bowman recommends that you select an editor to help you: see *How to hire a freelance editor* on page 200. Sophie Clarke introduces us to *The life and works of a literary scout* on page 242, while in the *Money, tax and benefits* section (starting on page 435) and in *Copyright and contracts* (from page 425) onwards, you will find brand-new pieces on the financial and legal aspects of the writing life.

Whether you are just starting out as a writer, whether you want to develop your work in new directions or are looking to consolidate your knowledge, whether you are keen to research the most appropriate agent or publisher to submit your work to, or to discover how to write for stage, screen or magazines – there's sure to be something between these pages for you.

Alysoun Owen, Editor

⚠ During the preparation of this *Yearbook*, the impacts of the 2020–21 coronavirus were still being felt. Some of the articles allude to this. The lockdowns and associated social distancing and uncertainties have necessarily impacted on live events such as literary festivals, award ceremonies, poetry and theatre performances, face-to-face creative writing courses, and much more besides. We have included updated listings for these as we do every year in consultation with the companies and organisations themselves, though are aware that many will not be going ahead in their current form. Some of the information in this year's *Yearbook* will be subject to greater change than usual as a result.

Contents

Praise for the *Yearbook*

'Takes the great advice that's in this *Yearbook*.'
David Almond

'[An] impressive raft of advice and notes on every aspect of the business.'
Quentin Blake

'Riffle these pages and turn your dream into an ambition.'
Frank Cottrell Boyce

'To find your way as a children's author, *CWAYB* should be your first port of call.'
Sarah Crossan

'Between the covers of this book is
everything you need to know to get published.'
Julia Donaldson

'Contains a wealth of essays, articles and advice.'
Frances Hardinge

'Stuffed full of useful facts to help you get writing (and drawing).'
Liz Pichon

'Whenever people ask me about how to get their work for children
published ... the first words to come out of my mouth are always:
Children's Writers' & Artists' Yearbook.'
Michael Rosen

'A goldmine of invaluable information.'
Francesca Simon

'Filled with practical and creative advice.'
William Sutcliffe

'I wish you all the luck in the world. Don't be a ninny
like me, practically giving up at the first rejection.
Consult the excellent *Children's Writers' & Artists' Yearbook.*'
Jacqueline Wilson

More than a book

The Writers & Artists **website** (www.writersandartists.co.uk) provides free content and support to writers.

You will find hundreds of **articles** on the writing and publishing process, regular **writing competitions**, and a **community** space to share your work or ask questions about the entire creative process. Features, such as being able to annotate and bookmark pages, can be accessed by creating your **free user account.** As a registered member of the Writers & Artists community, you will receive – straight to your dashboard – exclusive discounts on books, events and editing services and regular content to match your particular interests.

You can find details of our range of **editing services** as well as our **writing courses** and **workshops** (face-to-face and online), including **Manuscript Submission** Masterclasses and one-day **How to Get Published** events.

Our **Listings subscription** offers you access to the entire database of contacts in the latest edition of the *Writers' & Artists' Yearbook* and of this *Yearbook*, as well as hundreds of additional online-only entries.

Whatever your needs, we hope that Writers & Artists resources, whether delivered in an ebook, print, online or at our events, will provide you with the information, advice and inspiration you are looking for.

Short story competition

The annual *Writers' & Artists' Yearbook* Short Story Competition offers published and aspiring writers the chance to win a place on an Arvon residential writing course (worth £850). In addition, the winner's story will be published on the Writers & Artists website.

To enter the competition, submit a short story (for adults) of no more than 2,000 words, on any theme by 11 February 2022 to waybcompetitions@bloomsbury.com. For full details, terms and conditions, and to find out more about how to submit your entry, visit www.writersandartists.co.uk/competitions.

You can find details of competitions for children's writing under *Children's book and illustration prizes and awards* on page 384.

ARVON runs creative writing courses and retreats from three writing houses in the UK, each in a beautiful rural location. Published writers lead week-long or short residential courses. Covering a diverse range of genres, from poetry and fiction to screenwriting and non-fiction, Arvon courses have provided inspiration to thousands of people at all stages of their writing lives. You can find out more and book a course online at www.arvon.org.

Foreword

M. G. Leonard

To me, the feat of becoming a published author was as daunting as climbing Mount Everest … people say they want to do it but the odds of getting to the top are slim and the probability of getting hurt is high. Few people try and even fewer succeed.

Stage One of my ascent was to have the *idea* for my book – and it crawled into my brain on six legs with an exoskeleton and two pairs of wings. My story was going to be about beetles, an ecological entomological adventure, and so I enthusiastically began researching the bugs – which I thought would take a couple of weeks but actually took six years, because there are over 400,000 known species of beetle and I hadn't known that.

Stage Two was to *write* the book. During this time, I bought the *Writers' & Artists' Yearbook* and put it on a shelf beside my desk. I would flick through the pages inhaling the smell of an industry I longed to be a part of. Foolishly, I didn't read it. Including false starts and real-life obstacles to creativity, like getting divorced and being a single working mum, it took me four years to complete a draft of my manuscript.

Finally, I was moving to Stage Three of the climb – getting an agent! I'd fantasised about finding my literary best friend, the Clyde to my Bonnie, who would belay for me on the toughest part of the ascent – submitting to publishers. But then I got the fear. What if I sent my book to every single agent in the *Writers' & Artists' Yearbook* and they all hated it? I would crash to earth, a failure (cue sad music). I chose procrastination as my avoidance technique: I took the *Yearbook* and went through every agent, putting the ones I thought looked good (all of them) into a spreadsheet; I typed out all their details into columns (there was absolutely no need to do this), including their submission preferences. Then one day I'd completed my long list of possible agents … there was nothing else I could do other than submit.

At this point, I must confess that I presumed my book about a 13-year-old boy and a sentient giant rhinoceros beetle was for adult readers. I have no defence for this other than I thought: I am an adult, the story came out of my brain, so it must be for adults. As you might guess from this assumption, I hadn't got a clue about how the publishing industry worked. Despite spending a large percentage of my life in libraries and bookshops, I hadn't considered the categories books are sorted into or where my story might fit amongst them. I hadn't thought about what happened after you got an agent. I figured my agent would tell me that. This was an error.

I submitted to four agents on my list. Three rejected me with no feedback. I added a column to my spreadsheet in which to put insults about agents who rejected me. The fourth agent asked for the full manuscript and I sent all 120,000 words of it to them, only to receive a swift reply telling me my book was middle grade (I didn't know what this meant) and that they only represented adult fiction and YA (I didn't know what this meant either). They informed me a middle-grade debut shouldn't exceed 60,000 words and politely suggested I do some market research and edit my book accordingly.

I fell to the ground with a sickening thud. But I'm not a quitter, and a year later, on maternity leave, I began submitting again. This time I'd bought a copy of the *Children's*

Writers' & Artists' Yearbook and focused my attention on understanding the rock face I was climbing. I read the whole book, cover to cover, learning about the business and drawing courage from author essays about their journey to publication. It's rare to find a book that's as useful as it is inspiring, but this book is essential reading for aspiring children's authors. Equipped with new knowledge, I began my second ascent, able to see the hand- and footholds that others had used before me.

Once again, I submitted to four agents; once again, three of them rejected me. One said a book on beetles wouldn't sell. Another was rude about my protagonist. I was rude about both of them in my spreadsheet. However, I took on board the agent's concerns about my protagonist and revised my opening chapters. The fourth agent requested my full manuscript. I submitted my 60,000-word book, with a more likeable protagonist, and held my breath … Eventually, I was rewarded with a real-life phone call! Unfortunately, I had a six-month-old baby, so it went to voicemail.

I can still remember repeatedly listening to that voicemail. It was surreal, like getting a message from the other side. The agent said they liked my beetle book and that I could write, but that the manuscript needed work; it had a flabby fourth act and a problematic ending. They told me to call the Golden Egg Academy. This was not the news I'd been hoping for, but it was a crevice into which I could insert my fingers and heave myself a little further up the mountainside. At the Golden Egg Academy, I discovered I'd written a middle-grade book with a YA ending and got a lesson in story structure. I edited my book again. Finally, I had a manuscript fit for submission, and the Golden Egg Academy helped me find both my agent and my first publishing deal.

My journey to publication would have been easier and quicker if I'd read the *Children's Writers' & Artists' Yearbook* before I began my epic climb, but I got here in the end. So, dear climber, put this book in your backpack and don't just smell it, read it from cover to cover. Heed the advice you're given, only be rude in spreadsheets, and don't give up. See you at the top.

M. G. Leonard is the bestselling, award-winning writer of children's books *Beetle Boy* (2016), *Beetle Queen* (2017) and *Battle of the Beetles* (2018), published by Chicken House, the *Adventures on Trains* series with Sam Sedgman (Macmillan Children's 2020-22) and *Twitch* (Walker Books 2021). Her books have been translated into 40 languages and *Beetle Boy* is being developed as a live-action series for TV. *Beetle Boy* won the Branford Boase Award (2017), and was shortlisted for the Waterstones Children's Book Award and longlisted for the Carnegie Medal. *The Highland Falcon Thief* (Macmillan Children's 2020), the first in the *Adventures on Trains* series, won the Books Are My Bag Readers Award 2020 for Children's Fiction and the Children's Fiction Book of the Year 2021 in the British Book Awards.

Books
Spotting talent

Publishers and literary agents are not looking for what *they* like but for what children will like. Chicken House publisher Barry Cunningham famously accepted the manuscript of the first *Harry Potter* book which – as everyone knows – turned out to be the first of an international bestselling series. He explains here what he is looking for when he reads a new manuscript.

I'm a fan: I love reading and I love great stories. For many years I travelled with Penguin the length and breadth of the country – on tours with authors like Roald Dahl, to schools with the Puffin Book Club or to lonely writers' festivals. It was during this time that I learnt the most important part of my trade – how children react to the books they love, the authors that they adore, and how they put up with the material that they are coerced into reading. Reluctant readers indeed!

At Chicken House, we love to celebrate new author – and discover new voices for young readers – through our *Times*/Chicken House Children's Fiction Competition for unpublished writers. We're on the lookout for original ideas, a fresh voice, a diverse range of entries and stories that children will love. More on this later.

First steps

All publishers get streams of brown envelopes – especially, like divorces, after Christmas or the summer holidays – when writers finally feel something must be done with that story they've been working on.

So, how do you get your manuscript read by a publisher? Firstly, find out what the publisher wants: A sample? The complete manuscript? Perhaps, like us, they only accept submissions through specific avenues – for us, it's *The Times*/Chicken House Children's Fiction Competition. For most editors, first on the reading list are the submissions from agents, manuscripts recommended by other authors or by someone whose judgement they trust. So, if you know someone who knows someone, use the contact.

Next, know a little about the list you are submitting to: look at their catalogue or read some of their books. Let publishers know how much you like their publications (we all like those sorts of comments!) and how you think your novel might sit with the rest of their titles.

Then, write a short snappy synopsis – a page will do (I've had some that are as long as half the novel itself!). It should tell the publisher what the book is about, its characters and why they should read it. Also include a little bit about you, the author. Don't forget that. It can be almost as important as anything else in these days of marketing and personality promotion (no, you don't *have* to have had an exciting job, but it does give an impetus to read on …).

I worked with a very famous editor in my first job who was talking one day about her regular advice to first-time writers. Her advice began with a simple question: 'Have you thought of starting at Chapter 2?' Strangely, I find myself repeating this regularly. Often I find the first chapter is tortured and difficult, before the writer relaxes into the flow of the story in Chapter 2. And often things improve if we start straight into the action, and come back and explain later. But more importantly, first novels often fail because the editor doesn't get past a poor opening section. Beginnings are crucial, because I know children won't persevere if the story has a poor start, either.

So what am I looking for?

Back to the heart of things … There are writers who know a lot about children – they might be teachers or parents – so does this mean they can write more relevantly for young people? There are authors who know nothing about modern children, don't even really like children – does this mean they will never understand what a child wants? There are 'crossover' books that don't appear to be for real children at all. There are books with children in them that aren't children's books. Confused?

To me it's simple. Books that really work for children are written from a child's perspective through an age-appropriate memory of how the author felt and dreamed and wondered. The best children's writers carry that childhood wonder, its worry and concern, or even its fear and disappointment, around with them. They have kept the child within alive – so writing is not a professional task of storytelling for tiny tots but a simple glorious act of recreating the excitement of childhood.

That's part one of what you need. Part two, in my view, is a concentration on your audience. I've worked with adult writers too and there is a difference here. Children's authors are creating for a distinctly different readership – they need to think in a more *humble* way than if their work was for their contemporaries. What I mean is that they have to be mindful of how their work will impact on children. Characters must have convincing voices, descriptions must be good enough for children to visualise, and authors must be aware of things like children's attention span when it comes to detailed explanations.

But perhaps even more important is an awareness of the emotional effect of a story on a child. We must always remember their hunger for hope and a bright tomorrow, the closeness and importance of relationships – how easily a world can be upset by parents, or loss of an animal or a friend – and the way in which action really does speak to children, for fantasy and adventure is part of the process of literally growing an imagination.

(If all this means nothing to you, and writing for children is just another category, then I don't think you should bother. That's not to say all this should operate consciously in the mind of the new writer – but that's what a publisher seeks, and that's what I'm looking for.)

Categories and concepts

Everyone has read about the older children's market, and its lucrative crossover into the kind of children's book that adults buy for themselves. I think this will continue to be a growing phenomenon – but the best books in the field will still be clear in their intent: not looking 'over their shoulder' at adults, but true to themselves and their subjects.

I'm sure fantasy will continue to hold a firm following – but with the best books based around character and not simply wild lands and strange people. Historical fiction is poised for a comeback for older children – showing the rich material and heritage we have in our shared everyday culture, as well as the 'big battles' of yore.

At last all kinds of young adult fiction has found a firm market and any number of clear voices: hard-edged, romantic, comic, or a wild mixture of all three! Both here and in the USA, the 13–18 age group is firmly established as a permanent adjunct to the children's market, buying for themselves thrillers, dystopian adventures and books that speak to crises and concerns.

But my favourite category is the most neglected – real stories and novels for 7–9 year-olds. This was once the classic area of children's books, with the biggest names and the greatest longevity of appeal. Sadly, it has become the haunt of derivative series and boring chapter books. But there are clear signs of revival, with bestselling stories for this age group and the slightly older 9–12 category coming thick and fast. It's a great area for new talent; Chicken House has enjoyed many runaway bestsellers in this category, including *The Girl of Ink & Stars* by Kiran Millwood Hargrave (winner of the Waterstones Children's Book Prize) and *Asha & the Spirit Bird* by Jasbinder Bilan (winner of the Costa Book Award).

Picture books have had a great revival – seeing off the apparent challenges of apps and new technology to reassert the love of a beautifully-produced picture story, so I expect more innovations coming here. The success of cartoon novels and graphic story treatments for older readers has shown how story and illustration can work together in amusing and stimulating ways, enticing those who are looking for something a little bit different.

Language and setting

It's often said that, like exams, children's books are getting easier, that the language is getting 'younger' while the plots are getting more sophisticated. I don't think this is true. Certainly, for all markets, dialogue is more important than ever – and less time is taken in description. Children are used to characters who say what they mean, and whose motivations and subtleties emerge in speech. But largely I think this makes for more interpretation and imagination. Descriptions now concentrate on setting and atmosphere, rather than telling us authoritatively what the hero or heroine feels. All to the good in my view, and something new writers for children should absorb.

Also welcome in contemporary children's books is the freeing up of the adult! These characters are no longer confined to small walk-on parts and 'parental' or 'villainous' roles. Nowadays, adults in children's novels are as well drawn as the children, sometimes as touchingly vulnerable people themselves. But as in life, the most potent and frightening image in any children's book remains the bad or exploitative parent.

International scope

Children's literature is truly one of our most glorious 'hidden exports'. British writers continue to be very successful around the world, particularly in the USA and Europe. It is worth remembering this – while setting is not so important as inspiration, obviously UK-centred plots, regional dialogue and purely domestic issues, if not absolutely necessary, are best avoided. But there is no need either – like a creaky old British film – to introduce 'an American boy' or mid-Atlantic slang to your work to appeal to another audience. This seldom works and is often excruciating!

The marketplace

The market still remains delightfully unpredictable. It is hopeless to look at last year's trends and try to speculate. The sound and timelessly good advice is to find your own voice and, above all, to write from the heart. If you can touch what moved you as a child or still moves the child within you, then there's your 'market appeal'. Whether it's aboard the frigate of your imagination or in the quieter but equally dangerous seas of the lonely soul, skill and inspiration will win you your readership.

So, if you're up to the challenge, we'd love to read your story. *The Times*/Chicken House Children's Fiction Competition is an annual competition – so if you've missed the deadline this year, never fear. The prize is a £10,000 publishing contract with Chicken House, and every short- and longlisted writer will receive an editorial report on how to make their story the best it can possibly be.

Oh, and finally, don't give up - as I once said to a certain young woman about a boy called Harry …

Barry Cunningham OBE was the editor who originally signed J.K. Rowling to Bloomsbury Children's Books. He now runs his own publishing company, Chicken House (see page 14), specialising in introducing new children's writers to the UK and USA. Notable recent successes include James Dashner, Cornelia Funke, M. G. Leonard, Kiran Millwood Hargrave, Jasbinder Bilan, Maz Evans and Lucy Christopher. Chicken House and *The Times* jointly run an annual competition to find new writers; visit www.chickenhousebooks.com or see page 393. Barry was awarded an OBE in 2010 for services to publishing.

Breaking down the market: where does your book sit?

Author, editor and book packager Jasmine Richards provides a breakdown of the established market categories used by publishers and booksellers, to help budding authors know where their own work might fit in.

Writing for children is big business. Around 10,000 children's books are published every year in the UK. Publishers and agents are saying that children's books are having a renaissance. That's despite the fact that, ten years ago, some in the industry were pronouncing the death of the printed book for young readers. We now know that parents are worried about screen time and its effects. Parents want their children to turn pages rather than swipe left. To tell the truth, adults still seem to prefer reading printed text also. There is something comforting and nourishing about the physical book and that realisation is why sales of that format will continue to increase.

So, if the children's market is so buoyant, why is it so hard to get published? The fact is, the children's market is a very established and mature business, and competition is ferocious. It also has some very big players who have a lot of the market share. Amazingly, the two biggest-selling authors of 2019 were children's authors. David Walliams' sales totalled more than £19.1m and Julia Donaldson's £14m. According to *The Bookseller* both Walliams and Donaldson achieved landmark total sales last year, with Walliams surpassing £100m since he was first published in 2008 and Donaldson topping £150m.

Thrown into the mix, you also have celebrity fiction from musicians, TV personalities, YouTubers and sports stars. Then you have the perennial children's classics that book buyers return to again and again because they are excellent stories that stand the test of time. Established adult writers have also entered the marketplace, creating books for young adults and increasing their range of readers downwards. Finally, you have several well-established series each written by a team of writers on a rapid publishing cycle (such as the *Rainbow Magic* and *Beast Quest* series). There are an awful lot of books on the shelves and, for a new book to go on, another will have to come off. Obviously, there is infinite space online – but that doesn't help with discoverability.

In this fiercely competitive market, publishers are looking for exceptional books – novels that will stand out in this crowded arena and grab, not just the readers' attention, but also the attention of all the gatekeepers who will encounter the book before it even reaches the bookshop. A new book needs to convince sales directors selling in and also the head buyers at the main book chains, planning their offering. The book will need to be able to hold its own; it needs to be 'sticky' or, in other words, memorable and really easy to pitch. People in the industry love books, but the bottom line is that publishing is a business. Each book needs to have the potential to perform, if it is going to be published and if it is going to stay in print.

So, what can an author do to give themselves the best chance? Well – write a great story! A story with characters that readers will care about. A plot that turns the pages for the reader. A world that feels real and rich. A children's author must produce all those things, but it would be wise for them also to master an understanding of the market so they can appreciate the universe their book will operate in. There are a few ways to do this:

• Attend writing conferences or children's book events put on by people like SCBWI (see page 356) where you'll see people in the industry talking about what they are buying and why.

• Spend lots of time in bookshops and see what kind of books are on the table tops or in promotion.

• Keep an eye on what novels are winning key children's book awards or getting a lot of reviews in the print media.

• Read publications like *The Bookseller* to see what is happening in the world of publishing.

• Follow authors, book publicists, agents, booksellers and editors on social media to see what they are saying about the industry.

• It's also worth visiting libraries or talking to teachers about what books kids are reading.

• Most importantly, chat to children and ask what they are enjoying about the books they're reading. Their answers might surprise and inspire you.

Authors also need to get an understanding of the age ranges of children's books, a sense of word lengths for each of those age brackets, and some of the other features that are unique to certain parts of the market. Editors, including this one, can be a bit reticent when it comes to defining word counts. There is a good reason for this caginess. Books are works of art. They are an author's creative endeavour and thus not something that will always sit neatly in predefined categories. Still, if a book is going to sit outside some of the established norms when it comes to word count, then that needs to be for a good reason.

There are also some practical considerations to do with word counts; the bigger the book, the more it costs to print, after all, but there are set price points at the different age ranges. For instance, a middle-grade book will normally have a higher price point than a book for a 5–7 year-old and the middle-grade book can take a heftier page count because the publisher can charge more for that book.

You also need to consider the reading stamina of the children at the different age ranges. If an author writes a 70,000-word book for a 7–9 year-old, when the average is 10,0-00–15,000 words, then they are asking an awful lot of that reader. That's not to say that some readers won't be up to the task, but is that extended word count really serving the story well? Is it giving the book its best chance of being published? Is it giving the child reader the best reading experience? The guidelines provided below are just that: a guide – the average word count for the different age ranges of books – but there will always be exceptions. Ultimately, a story should be as long or as short as it *needs* to be.

Picture books

Golden rule: keep picture book text short! Remember, the pictures will do a lot of the telling in the story. The best picture books really take advantage of that fact. Picture books are often split out into two categories:

Books for age 0–2. These will not have many words at all (300 words or fewer) but they will have very strong images that tend to relate to the everyday and familiar rather than more fantastical settings or themes.

Books for 2–5 year-olds (although older children will still get a lot out of picture books and will be reading these alongside first chapter books). These books are on average between 300 and 1,500 words, but some books might just be one word! Although short, these books need to have definite story beats, and twists and turns that will delight both the adult reader and child listener. They should explore the experiences and possible feelings that young children may be dealing with for the first time. The best picture books are those where a kind of magic happens in that space between the images and the text, and in which that interplay brings new meaning. The picture book should be a pleasure to read out loud, with rhythm but not necessarily rhyme – as this could have an impact on how well the book sells internationally. Rhyme can be pretty tricky to make work in translation, although not impossible!

Printing a book in full colour is not cheap; the publishing house that commissions the title needs to be sure that they will achieve co-editions with overseas publishers to keep printing costs down and make the book profitable. When writing a picture book, it is worth keeping the 32-page format front and centre – this roughly works out at 24 pages or 12 spreads in which to tell the story. The narrative needs to offer ample opportunity for illustration, but that does not mean the author should dictate what these illustrations might be. It is a collaboration. Part of the publisher's role in the process of publishing a picture book is to find the perfect pairing of author and illustrator.

Younger readers

Books for readers aged 5–7. These tend to have shorter sentences and simpler diction. Some may feature chapters, and illustration can either be in colour or in black-and-white. They average between 500 and 4,000 words.

Books for readers 7–9. These are on average between 10,000 and 15,000 words but can be longer. Readers at this age will have a bit more confidence and may be devouring a lot of series fiction and enjoying the fact that they are reading whole novels. The age of the protagonists in these books will tend to be at the top end of the actual readership or perhaps even older.

Middle-grade fiction or core readers

Novels for 9–12 year-olds will be significantly longer than the previous category and average at about 30,000-40,000 words. A novel can be much longer for this age range, especially if it is a fantasy title. Whatever the number, the words should serve the story and ensure that it is being delivered in the optimal way. If the novel is going to be 80,000 words that can work, but there should be a very good reason for it.

Generally, readers in this age range have a lot more stamina. They will identify strongly with the hero, so a close third-person perspective or first-person narrative can work very well here. The protagonist tends to be aspirational and so often they are aged around 13. Readers in this age range can deal with more complex stories and themes, but a more challenging style choice might be off-putting.

Books for teenagers and YA

Books for readers aged 12+ can be anything from 30,000 words upwards. There is series fiction for teenagers, but the idea of author as the main brand is perhaps something teenagers identify with more commonly, rather than a series title. Teenagers are interested in exploring big ideas, regardless of the genre, and an author can take a few more risks with the style choice or perspective in order to help get those big ideas across.

The protagonists in these books tend to be teenagers rather than 20+ year-olds. There is also a burgeoning category – called NA or New Adult – of books which feature protagonists in their early 20s. In the UK this age range has not become firmly fixed as yet, but may well do in the future.

Jasmine Richards is an author who has written over a dozen books for children and teenagers. Her most recent novel, *Keeper of Myths*, is published by HarperCollins Children's Books in the US. She is also the co-creative on the *Aziza's Secret Fairy Door* series published by Macmillan. She has over 15 years' worth of publishing experience having worked at Puffin, Working Partners and Oxford University Press as an editor and story developer. In 2019 Jasmine founded Storymix: The Inclusive Fiction Development Studio (www.storymix.co.uk), which creates series with protagonists of colour for publishers. Storymix also supports and incubates writers from minority ethnic backgrounds and offers a pathway into being published. She's always looking for talented writers and illustrators to work with. Her author website is www.jasminerichards.com and you can follow her on Facebook and Twitter @JRichardsAuthor and @storymixstudio.

See also...
• *What are children's publishers looking for?*, page 9

What are children's publishers looking for?

Editorial director Rebecca Hill highlights the key ingredients that combine to produce a children's book that will inspire the passion of an editor, publishing team and readers. She urges writers to focus on their craft, knowing that a great book relies on a great story, one with its own fully developed world that captures the reader from start to finish.

Stories! Each year publishers send thousands of books out into the world, into the hands of eager children, so how can you make sure your story gets to the top of a publisher's pile? Every editor is a fan of reading, but the truth is we get sent more material than we can hope to acquire. What we are all looking for when we open up a new manuscript is a story that allows us to do what we love best ... *read.*

It really is that simple. What I'm looking for when I start a story is to be that writer's biggest fan. The books we publish at Usborne have all given me that feeling of wanting to shout about them from the rooftops: 'Listen to this sentence, everybody! Turn the page and gasp, dear reader ... Hide under the covers and tremble, if you dare dive into this one.' Stepping into a world that is thoroughly developed, and has characters that live and breathe, is a feeling unlike any other. So, if a book can hook me in and make me laugh, make me cry, affect me more than anything else I've read that week, I know that's the one to be passionate about. And passion is what every editor needs – first at an editorial meeting, then at an acquisition meeting and at every available opportunity after that, until that book ends up on a bookseller's table.

As an editorial director, when I'm building Usborne's list I'm always aware of providing a book for every reader. After all, there are lots of tastes that need catering for. But it is essential to see a company's passion for each and every book – from the very first editorial meeting when a submission is discussed. That is exactly what is needed to make a book a success because, beyond the editor's door, a whole team of people will need to love and champion a book: the cover designer, the sales teams, the publicist, the rights team and the marketing department. Without company-wide passion a book could disappear, but with it a book will fly, because we come together to become its superfans.

But before editors even start reading a story and becoming superfans, we make judgements based on your **title**. The title is the crucial 'first sell' of your book to the reader; I can't emphasise enough that a title needs to work hard, and you need to work hard on making it right. As publishers, we are not looking for a set of clumsily arranged buzz words – *The Secrets of the Forbidden Girl in the Magical Dragon Kingdom with Unicorns* – but we are looking for a title that tells us what kind of book you are writing. Strong titles should shine a light on something about your novel, be that the character, the tone or the central interest. Great titles should make us want to know what your book is about. Great titles should make us want to read on.

After the title, the **start** of your story is essential. I so often find myself getting distracted from the story in front of me by a plot that doesn't quite know where it is heading, or a character that doesn't leap out from the pages to ensure I don't return to the demands of office life. Make sure your opening is as strong and grabby as you can make it, without throwing the whole of the kitchen sink in there. Openings are the reason we carry on but, more importantly, they are the reason *children* carry on reading, and that is who we, as editors, are always thinking of when we read. Child readers are harsher than any editor, so make sure you work on making your opening as perfect as you can get it. That prologue – do you actually need it? Where should the first chapter start? Often the story gets going just before your inciting incident, so make *that* the kicking off point!

And carry that **guiding light**; ask yourself, what was it that made you want to write this book? What idea? What theme? What was it you wanted to say? What is it you want children to feel? Make sure you keep those things with you when writing and editing, and keep coming back to them, because what editors want to see, when looking for books to acquire, is authors who are in control of their material; authors who understand how their world is built and understand who their characters are; authors who will tell me at some stage of the editing process: *No, no! My character would never do that, but they would do this instead.*

Always, always think about your **audience**. The children's book market is split into age groups, and you need to be aware of what works for those categories – what content is appropriate, what subjects appeal and what word counts are expected.

Then there's the **ending**: this is another area that I often work hard on with authors. Plan where you want your story to go, and what message and emotion you want to leave the reader with. Make sure that when we finish your book we want to thrust it straight into someone else's hands to read!

But how do publishers *really* decide what to publish?

There are many important things for a publisher to consider when acquiring a book. Will children love it? Will international publishing partners want to buy the rights? Does the author have many more stories to tell? If it is a series, how quickly can the author write the next book? Does this book fit the type of publishing house that we are? Is this something that is missing on our list, or is it something that the competition is doing well with? I always hope the answer to all of these questions is 'Yes', but the truth is, my mind is set when I'm about a third of the way through a book – because by then I have fallen in love with the story.

After that comes the editing, the positioning, the building up of the campaign, the writing of sales material, the development of a cover... These things all combine to help make a great story into a great book. Great stories will always find readers, because stories make us who we are, and help us to become what we want to be.

So, how *do* you make sure your book gets to the top of the editor's pile? Focus on your craft! When the market is ever-changing, do publishers really know what trend is coming next? Can we look into a crystal ball and see what will become a bestseller? I'll let you into a secret here: the answer is no and ...erm... no. But I do know a good story, as soon as it arrives on my desk. I open it up, settle down, and then I read, and read and read – doing what every editor loves best. All I want is a story that won't let me stop reading.

Rebecca Hill is fiction editorial director at Usborne Books. She was named Editor of the Year at the British Book Awards 2019, the first children's editor ever to win this coveted prize. Rebecca has acquired and published bestselling authors Holly Bourne, Peter Bunzl, Sophie Anderson and P.G. Bell alongside award-winning titles such as *After the Fire* by Will Hill, winner of the 2018 YA Book Prize, and *Kick* by Mitch Johnson, winner of the Branford Boase Award 2018.

Children's book publishers UK and Ireland

There are changes to listings in this section every year. We aim to provide a comprehensive list of publishing imprints, the name or brand under which a specific set of titles are sold by a publisher. Any one publisher might have several imprints. The imprint usually appears on the spine of a book. Imprints are included either under a publisher's main entry or in some cases as entries themselves. Information is provided in a way that is of most use to a reader. The listings that follow are updated by the Writers' & Artists' editors based on information supplied by those listed.

*Member of the Publishers Association or Publishing Scotland
†Member of Publishing Ireland, the Irish Book Publishers' Association
‡Member of the Independent Publishers Guild

Books

Alanna Max

38 Oakfield Road, London N4 4NL
email info@alannamax.com
website www.alannamax.com
Publisher Ken Wilson Max, *Editor-At-Large* Anna McQuinn

Children's picture books. See website for submissions guidelines. Founded 2012.

Amgueddfa Cymru – National Museum Wales‡

Cathays Park, Cardiff CF10 3NP
tel 029-2057 3235
email post@museumwales.ac.uk
website www.museumwales.ac.uk
Twitter @AmgueddfaBooks
Head of Publishing Mari Gordon

Books based on the collections and research of Amgueddfa Cymru for adults, schools and children, in both Welsh and English. Founded 1907.

Andersen Press Ltd*

20 Vauxhall Bridge Road, London SW1V 2SA
tel 020-7840 8703 (editorial) / 020-7840 8701 (general)
email anderseneditorial@penguinrandomhouse.co.uk
website www.andersenpress.co.uk
Managing Director Mark Hendle, *Publisher* Klaus Flugge, *Directors* Philip Durrance, Joëlle Flugge, Libby Hamilton (editorial picture books), Sue Buswell (editorial picture books), Charlie Sheppard (editorial fiction), Liz White (rights)

A leading children's publisher of picture books, fiction for 5–8 and 9–12 years and young adult fiction. Successes include the *Elmer* series by David McKee, the *Little Princess* series by Tony Ross, *Who's in the Loo?* by Jeanne Willis and Adrian Reynolds, *The Lonely Beast* by Chris Judge, *Out of Shadows* by Jason Wallace and *Liar & Spy* by Rebecca Stead. Will

consider unsolicited MSS. Include sae if response required. For novels, send three sample chapters and a synopsis only. No poetry or short stories. Do not send MSS via email. Founded 1976.

Arcturus Publishing Ltd

26–27 Bickels Yard, 151–153 Bermondsey Street, London SE1 3HA
tel 020-7407 9400
email info@arcturuspublishing.com
website www.arcturuspublishing.com
Editorial Manager Joe Harris (children's)

Children's non-fiction, including activity books, reference, education, practical art, geography, history and science. No unsolicited MSS. Founded 1993.

Aurora Metro‡

67 Grove Avenue, Twickenham TW1 4HX
tel 020-3261 0000
email info@aurorametro.com
website www.aurorametro.com
Facebook www.facebook.com/AuroraMetroBooks
Twitter @aurorametro
Managing Director Cheryl Robson

Adult fiction, young adult fiction, biography, drama (including plays for young people), non-fiction, theatre, cookery and translation. Submissions: send synopsis and three chapters via our website: www.aurorametro.com/contact-us/submit-your-work/. Runs a biennial competition for women novelists (odd years): Virginia Prize For Fiction. Entry fee for submission of either adult or young adult novel. See website: www.aurorametro.com/VirginiaPrize. Imprints include Aurora Metro Books and Supernova Books. Founded 1996.

Award Publications Ltd

The Old Riding School, The Welbeck Estate, Worksop, Notts. S80 3LR
tel (01909) 478170

Books

email info@awardpublications.co.uk
Facebook www.facebook.com/awardpublications
Twitter @award_books
Instagram @award.books

Publishes picture story books, fiction, early learning, information and activity books from birth to 12. No unsolicited material. Please refer to social media sites for details of submission windows. Founded 1972.

b small publishing limited
website www.bsmall.co.uk
Managing Director Catherine Bruzzone, *Publisher* Sam Hutchinson

Activity books and foreign language learning books for 2–12 years. Written in-house. No unsolicited MSS. Founded 1990.

Badger Learning*
Oldmedow Road, King's Lynn, Norfolk PE30 4JJ
tel (01553) 816083
email info@badgerlearning.co.uk
website www.badgerlearning.co.uk
Publisher Sarah Capon

Educational publishing for pupils and teachers across the curriculum, from KS3–KS5. Specialists in publishing teen fiction and books for children 7+ who are struggling or reluctant readers. Range covers high interest age/low reading age titles. Series include *Teen Reads, YA Reads, Papercuts, Between the Lines, Strange Town, Snow-Man, The League of Enchanted Heroes, Full Flight, First Flight* and *Graphic Novels*. Email for submission guidelines. Founded 2001.

Barbican Press Ltd‡
tel (07507) 554731
email martin@barbicanpress.com
website https://barbicanpress.com
Twitter @barbicanpress1
Instagram @barbicanpress
Directors Martin Goodman (managing); James Thornton

An independent micro-publisher. The list includes poetry, drama, writing for children, translations and compelling non-fiction, including issues-driven memoir and vivid tales of maritime communities. LGBTQI+ friendly. Founded 2009.

Barrington Stoke*
18 Walker Street, Edinburgh EH3 7LP
tel 0131 225 4113
email info@barringtonstoke.co.uk
website www.barringtonstoke.co.uk

Fiction for reluctant, dyslexic or under-confident readers: fiction for children 8–12 years with a reading age of 8+, fiction for teenagers with a reading age of 8+, fiction for 8–12 years with a reading age of below 8, fiction for teenagers with a reading age of below 8, non-fiction for children 8–14 years with a reading age

of 8+, graphic novels. Resources for readers and their teachers. No unsolicited MSS. All work is commissioned from well-known authors and adapted for reluctant readers. Founded 1998.

Big Picture Press
Suite 1.07 The Plaza, 535 Kings Road, London SW10 0SZ
tel 020-3770 8888
email hello@templarco.co.uk
website www.templarco.co.uk, www.bonnierbooks.co.uk
Twitter @BigPicturePress
Editorial Director Katie Haworth

Big Picture Press books publishes non-fiction and illustrated gift books. First publications include Mizielinski's *Maps* and Katie Scott's *Animalium*. Focusing on visual presentation, Big Picture Press collaborates with artists such as Chris Wormell (*Planetarium*) and Ximo Abadia (*The Speed of Starlight*). Big Picture Press is an imprint of Bonnier Books UK (page 13).

Bloomsbury Publishing Plc*‡
50 Bedford Square, London WC1B 3DP
tel 020-7631 5600
website www.bloomsbury.com
Chief Executive & Founder Nigel Newton

Bloomsbury Publishing is a leading independent publishing house with authors who have won the Nobel, Pulitzer and Booker Prizes, and is the originating publisher and custodian of the Harry Potter series. Bloomsbury has offices in London, New York (page 40), New Delhi, Oxford and Sydney (page 31). MSS must normally be channelled through literary agents, with the exception of academic and professional titles. Founded 1986.

BLOOMSBURY CONSUMER DIVISION
Managing Director Ian Hudson
Imprints include: Absolute Press, Bloomsbury Activity Books, Bloomsbury Children's Books, Bloomsbury Circus, Bloomsbury India, Bloomsbury Press, Bloomsbury Publishing, Bloomsbury USA, Bloomsbury USA Children's Books, Head of Zeus, Raven Books.

Bloomsbury Children's Books
Publishing Director & International Editor-in-Chief Rebecca McNally, *Publishing Director* Sharon Hutton (non-fiction), *Head of Fiction* Ellen Holgate, *Editorial Directors* Zoe Griffiths (fiction), Saskia Gwinn (non-fiction)
Authors include J.K. Rowling, Louis Sachar, Neil Gaiman, Sarah J. Maas, Sarah Crossan and Brian Conaghan. No complete MSS; send a synopsis with three chapters.

Bloomsbury Education
Head of Education Helen Diamond, *Editorial Director* Hannah Rolls (educational fiction, poetry & digital resources), *Senior Commissioning Editor* Hannah Marston (education – CPD)

Publishes around 75 print titles per year: educational fiction, children's poetry, teacher's books, apps and digital platforms. Imprints include Bloomsbury Education, Andrew Brodie and Featherstone Education. No submissions by email. Look at recently published titles and catalogues to gauge current publishing interests. Much of the list is educationally focused and publishes in series. Allow 8–10 weeks for a response.

Bonnier Books UK*

Victoria House, Bloomsbury Square,
London WC1B 4DA
tel 020-377 0888
email hello@bonnierbooks.co.uk
website www.bonnierbooks.co.uk
Ceo Perminder Mann, *Managing Director* Kate Parkin (adult trade), *Managing Director* Jane Harris (children trade)

Bonnier Books UK is owned by Bonnier Books, a family-owned company headquartered in Sweden. Bonnier Books is a top-15 world publisher. Publishes across a wide variety of genres for different ages. From crime to reading group fiction; memoir to self-help; activity to reference. Publishers of twelve imprints: adult trade (Zaffre, Manilla Press, Blink Publishing, John Blake); Children's trade (Piccadilly Press (page 25), Hot Key Books (page 19), Templar (page 29), Big Picture Press (page 12), Studio Press (page 28)). Founded 2015.

The Book Guild Ltd

14 Priory Business Park, Wistow Road, Kibworth, Leics. LE8 0RX
tel 0800 999 2982
email info@bookguild.co.uk
website www.bookguild.co.uk
Facebook www.facebook.com/thebookguild
Twitter @BookGuild
Directors Jeremy Thompson (managing), Jane Rowland (operations)

Offers traditional and partnership publishing arrangements, with all titles published being funded or co-funded by The Book Guild Ltd (does not offer self-publishing). MSS accepted in fiction, children's and non-fiction genres, please see the website for details. The Book Guild is part of parent company Troubador Publishing Ltd. Founded 1996.

Boxer Books Ltd

email info@boxerbooks.com
website www.boxerbooks.com

No unsolicited MSS in any form unless via a recognised agency. Publishes innovative baby board books, picture books, young fiction and stunning story collections. Founded 2005.

Bright Red Publishing*

Mitchelston Drive Business Centre,
Mitchelston Drive, Kirkcaldy KY1 3NB

tel 0131 220 5804
email info@brightredpublishing.co.uk
website www.brightredpublishing.co.uk
Facebook www.facebook.com/BrightRedBooks
Twitter @_BrightRed
Instagram @bright_red_publishing
Directors John MacPherson, Alan Grierson

Educational publishing for Scotland's students and teachers. Founded 2008.

Brilliant Publications Ltd*‡

Unit 10, Sparrow Hall Farm, Edlesborough, Dunstable LU6 2ES
tel (01525) 222292
email info@brilliantpublications.co.uk
website www.brilliantpublications.co.uk
Facebook www.facebook.com/Brilliant-Publications-340005555138
Twitter @Brilliantpub, @BrillCreative
Managing Director Priscilla Hannaford

Creates easy-to-use educational resources, featuring engaging approaches to learning, across a wide range of curriculum areas, including English, foreign languages, maths, art and design, thinking skills and PSHE. No children's picture books, non-fiction books or one-off fiction books. See Guidelines for Authors on website before sending proposal. Founded 1993.

The British Museum Press

Great Russell Street, London WC1B 3DG
tel 020-3073 4946
email publicity@britishmuseum.org
website www.britishmuseum.org/commercial/british-museum-press
Head of Publishing Claudia Bloch

Award-winning illustrated books for children, young readers and families, inspired by the famous collections of the British Museum. Titles range across picture books, activity books and illustrated non-fiction. Founded 1973.

Burning Chair Publishing*

61 Bridge Street, Kington HR5 3DJ
email info@burningchairpublishing.com
website www.burningchairpublishing.com
Facebook www.facebook.com/BurningChairPublishing
Twitter @Burning_Chair
Directors Simon Finnie, Peter Oxley

Burning Chair is an independent publishing company based in the UK but covering readers and authors across the globe. Welcomes unsolicited young adult fiction submissions (from authors direct as well as through agents) in the following genres: mystery, thriller, suspense, crime, action and adventure, science fiction, fantasy, paranormal, horror, historical fiction. No postal or email submissions. See the submissions page:

www.burningchairpublishing.com/submissions. Founded 2018.

Buster Books
16 Lion Yard, Tremadoc Road, London SW4 7NQ
tel 020-7720 8643
email enquiries@mombooks.com
website www.mombooks.com/buster
Facebook www.facebook.com/BusterBooks
Twitter @BusterBooks
Instagram @buster_books

Reference, activity, board and picture books for 0+ years. Publishes approx. 60 titles a year. Buster's publications include puzzle books, including the *Clever Kids* series, and a wide selection of children's illustrated non-fiction, colouring, drawing, sticker, activity and picture books. Titles range from enlightening books such as *Rise Up, A Day in the Life of a Poo, a Gnu and You* and *Dr Maggie's Grand Tour of the Solar System* to quirky books such as *How Many Spots Has a Cheetah Got?*, *The Dinosaur Department Store* and *My Unicorn and Me*. Bestselling colouring books include the *I Heart Colouring* series and *The Amazing Book of Beasts*. No unsolicited MSS. Founded 1985.

Cambridge University Press*‡
University Printing House, Shaftesbury Road, Cambridge CB2 8BS
tel (01223) 358331
email information@cambridge.org
website www.cambridge.org
Facebook www.facebook.com/CambridgeUniversityPress
Twitter @CambridgeUP
Chief Executive Peter Phillips; *Managing Directors* Mandy Hill (academic), Paul Colbert (ELT), Rod Smith (Cambridge Education)

For children: curriculum-based education books and software for schools and colleges (primary, secondary and international). ELT for adult and younger learners. Founded 1534.

Campbell – see Pan Macmillan

Candy Jar Books
Mackintosh House, 136 Newport Road, Cardiff CF24 1DJ
tel 029-2115 7202
email submissions@candyjarbooks.co.uk
website www.candy-jar.co.uk/books
Facebook www.facebook.com/CandyJarLimited
Twitter @Candy_Jar
Head of Publishing Shaun Russell

Non-fiction and fiction for children aged 7+. Will consider unsolicited MSS. Check website for submission details. Founded 2010.

Cassava Republic Press‡
9 Eri Studio C11, Mainyard Studios, 94 Wallis Road, London E9 5LN
email info@cassavarepublic.biz
website https://cassavarepublic.biz/
Facebook www.facebook.com/CassavaRepublic
Twitter @cassavarepublic
Instagram @cassavarepublicpress

Publishes contemporary Black and African writing. Founded in Abuja, Nigeria, 2006 by Bibi Bakare-Yusuf and Jeremy Weate, with the aim of bringing high-quality fiction and non-fiction for adults and children to a global audience. Has offices in Abuja and London. Founded 2006.

Caterpillar Books – see Little Tiger Group

Catnip Publishing Ltd
320 City Road, London EC1V 2NZ
tel 020-7138 3650
email editorial@catnippublishing.co.uk
website www.bouncemarketing.co.uk/publisher/catnip-publishing
Twitter @catnipbooks
Managing Director Robert Snuggs

New and previously published titles from picture books to teen fiction. Acquires new titles from overseas publishers, reissues out-of-print titles by top authors and commissions original fiction for 7–9 years, 9–12 years and young adult readers. Publishes 15–20 books a year. Recently published books by Pippa Goodhart, Jason Beresford, Berlie Doherty, Sarah Baker, Sophie Plowden, Joan Lingard, Keris Stainton and Anne Booth. Will only consider agented submissions. Founded 2005.

CGP
Coordination Group Publications, Broughton House, Broughton-in-Furness, Cumbria LA20 6HH
tel (01229) 715753
email ewt@cgpbooks.co.uk
website www.cgpbooks.co.uk

Educational books centred around the National Curriculum, including revision guides and study books for KS1, KS2, KS3, GCSE and A level. Subjects include maths, English, science, history, geography, ICT, computer science, psychology, business studies, economics, religious studies, design and technology, PE, music, French, German, Spanish, sociology, 11+, 13+ and functional skills. On the lookout for top teachers at all levels, in all subjects. Potential authors and proofreaders should email the external writing team with their name, subject area, level and experience, plus contact address, ready for when a project comes up in their subject area. Founded 1996.

Chicken House
2 Palmer Street, Frome, Somerset BA11 1DS
tel (01373) 454488
email hello@chickenhousebooks.com
website www.chickenhousebooks.com
Twitter @chickenhsebooks

Managing Director & Publisher Barry Cunningham, *Deputy Managing Director* Rachel Hickman

Fiction for ages 7+ and young adult. No unsolicited MSS. Successes include James Dashner (the *Maze Runner* series), Cornelia Funke (*Inkheart* and *Dragon Rider* series) and Kiran Millwood Hargrave (*The Girl of Ink & Stars*). See website for details of *Times/ Chicken House Children's Fiction Competition* for unpublished writers. Founded 2000.

Child's Play (International) Ltd
Ashworth Road, Bridgemead, Swindon, Wilts. SN5 7YD
tel (01793) 616286
email office@childs-play.com
website www.childs-play.com
Facebook www.facebook.com/ChildsPlayBooks
Twitter @ChildsPlayBooks
Chairman Adriana Twinn, *Publisher* Neil Burden

Children's educational books: board, picture, activity and play books; fiction and non-fiction. Founded 1972.

Christian Education
5/6 Imperial Court, 12 Sovereign Road, Birmingham B30 3FH
tel 0121 472 4242
email anstice.hughes@christianeducation.org.uk
website https://shop.christianeducation.org.uk/, www.retoday.org.uk
Facebook www.facebook.com/RETodayServices
Twitter @IBRAbibleread

Incorporating RE Today Services and International Bible Reading Association. Publications and services for teachers and other professionals in religious education including *REtoday* magazine, curriculum booklets and classroom resources. Also publishes bible reading materials. Founded 2001.

Cicada Books*
Unit 9, 6 Cliff Road, Cliff Road Studios, London NW1 9AN
email info@cicadabooks.co.uk
website www.cicadabooks.co.uk
Twitter @cicadabooks
Instagram @cicadabooks

Publishes a few titles a year. Specialises in highly-illustrated books for adults and children. Founded 2009.

Colourpoint Creative Ltd†
Colourpoint House, Jubilee Business Park, 21 Jubilee Road, Newtownards, Co. Down BT23 4YH
tel 028-9182 6339 (within UK) / +353 (0)48 91846339 (Republic of Ireland)
email sales@colourpoint.co.uk
website www.colourpoint.co.uk
Twitter @colourpointedu
Commissioning Editor Wesley Johnston, *Marketing* Jacky Hawkes

Textbooks for Northern Ireland CCEA board. Educational textbooks for KS3 (11–14 years), KS3 Special Needs (10–14 years), GCSE (14–16 years) and A-Level/undergraduates (age 17+). Not primary. Subjects include, but not limited to, biology, business studies, chemistry, English, geography, history, HE, ICT, Irish, life and health sciences, LLW, MVRUS, PE, physics, politics, technology and design, science and RE. Short queries by email. Full submission in writing including details of proposal, sample chapter/ section to show ability to connect with target age group, qualification/experience in the subject, full contact details and return postage. Textbooks, workbooks and electronic resources all considered. Founded 1993.

Cranachan Publishing*
Blacksheep Croft, 52 North Galson, Isle of Lewis HS2 0SJ
tel (01851) 850700
email hello@cranachanpublishing.co.uk
website www.cranachanpublishing.co.uk
Twitter @cranachanbooks
Instagram @cranachanbooks
Publisher & Founder Anne Glennie

A small independent publisher based on the Isle of Lewis, focusing exclusively on high-quality children's fiction for 9 to 12 years (Pokey Hat imprint) and young adult fiction for teens and 12 years+ (Gob Stopper imprint) with a Scottish flavour. Also publishes educational resources for teachers. Founded 2015.

Cranthorpe Millner Publishers
Nine Hills Road, Cambridge CB2 1GE
tel 020-3441 9212
email kirsty.jackson@cranthorpemillner.com
website www.cranthorpemillner.com
Facebook facebook.com/CranthorpeMillner
Twitter @CranthorpeBooks
Instagram @CranthorpeMillner
Directors Kirsty Jackson (managing), David Hahn (chairman)

Titles include fiction and non-fiction: memoir, celeb autobiographies, history, science fiction, young adult, historical fiction, crime/thriller, literary fiction. Founded 2018.

Crown House Publishing Ltd‡
Crown Buildings, Bancyfelin, Carmarthen SA33 5ND
tel (01267) 211345
email books@crownhouse.co.uk
website www.crownhouse.co.uk
Facebook www.facebook.com/CrownHousePub
Twitter @CrownHousePub
Instagram @crownhousepub
Directors David Bowman (managing), Karen Bowman

Award-winning independent publisher specialising in the areas of education, coaching, business training and development, leadership, NLP, hypnotherapy, psychotherapy, self-help and personal growth. The list includes the Independent Thinking Press imprint, which brings into print the words of some of the UK's most inspiring and entertaining educational speakers and practitioners. Founded 1998.

Independent Thinking Press
email books@independentthinkingpress.com
website www.independentthinkingpress.com

Publishes CPD books and resources for teachers and school leaders. The list includes books on business, training and development, coaching, health and wellbeing, NLP, hypnosis, counselling and psychotherapy and a range of children's books.

Dinosaur Books Ltd
tel 020-7737 6737
email info@dinosaurbooks.co.uk
website www.dinosaurbooks.co.uk
Twitter @dinosaurbooksco
Director Sonya McGilchrist

Based in London. Submissions by email only: submissions@dinosaurbooks.co.uk. Website as above. Publishing chapter books for children aged 5–14. Founded 2014.

DK*
One Embassy Gardens, 8 Viaduct Gardens, London SW11 7BW
tel 020-7139 2000
website www.dk.com
Ceo Carston Coefeld

A member of the Penguin Random House (page 25) division of Bertelsmann, publishing highly visual books for adults and children: travel, licensing, children's, reference, education, gardening, food and drink. Founded 1974.

Dorling Kindersley – see DK

Dref Wen
28 Church Road, Whitchurch, Cardiff CF14 2EA
tel 029-2061 7860
website www.drefwen.com
Directors Roger Boore, Anne Boore, Gwilym Boore, Alun Boore, Rhys Boore

Welsh language publisher. Original, adaptations and translations of foreign and English language full-colour picture story books for children. Also activity books, novelty books, Welsh language fiction for children 7–14 years, teenage fiction, reference, religion, audiobooks and poetry. Educational material for primary and secondary school children in Wales and England, including dictionaries, revision guides and Welsh as a Second Language. Publishes approx. 50 titles a year and has 450 in print. No unsolicited MSS. Phone first. Founded 1970.

The Educational Company of Ireland
Ballymount Road, Walkinstown, Dublin D12 R25C, Republic of Ireland
tel +353 (0)14 500611
email info@edco.ie
website www.edco.ie
Ceo Martina Harford

Educational (primary and post-primary) books in the Irish language. Publishes approx. 60–70 titles each year and has 600–700 in print. Ancillary materials include digital resources, concrete resources and CDs. A member of the Smurfit Kappa Group plc. Founded 1910. Submissions to: amolumby@edco.ie. Please include: a brief description of the project's scope and content; table of contents; sample chapter and biographical details. Allow three months for response. Founded 1910.

Educational Explorers (Publishers)
Unit 5, Feidr Castell Business Park, Fishguard SA65 9BB
tel (01348) 874890
website www.cuisenaire.co.uk
Directors J. Hollyfield

Educational. Recent successes include: mathematics: *Numbers in Colour with Cuisenaire Rods*; languages: *The Silent Way*; literacy, reading: *Words in Colour*; educational films. No longer accepting MSS. Founded 1962.

Electric Monkey – see HarperCollins Publishers

Everything With Words Ltd
16 Limekiln Place, London SE19 2RE
tel 020-8771 2974
email info@everythingwithwords.com
website www.everythingwithwords.com
Managing Director & Publisher Mikka Bott

Children's fiction for ages 5 to young adult. Publishes innovative, quality fiction. Accepts unsolicited MSS. Founded 2016.

Faber and Faber Ltd*‡
Bloomsbury House, 74–77 Great Russell Street, London WC1B 3DA
tel 020-7927 3800
website www.faber.co.uk
Twitter @FaberChildrens
Publisher Leah Thaxton (children's)

High-quality picture books, general fiction and non-fiction, drama, film, music, poetry. For children: fiction for 5–8 and 9–12 years, teenage fiction, poetry and some non-fiction. Authors include T.S. Eliot, Ted Hughes, Philip Ardagh, Justin Fletcher, Harry Hill, Betty G. Birney, Francesca Simon, Karen McCombie, Jennifer Gray, Mackenzie Crook, Natasha Farrant. Founded 1929.

Fairlight Books Ltd‡

Summertown Pavilion, 18–24 Middle Way, Oxford OX2 7LG
email submissions@fairlightbooks.com
website www.fairlightbooks.co.uk/submissions/
Facebook www.facebook.com/FairlightBooks
Twitter @fairlightbooks
Instagram @fairlightbooks

A small publishing house specialising in literary fiction, particularly novellas (the Fairlight Moderns) and online short stories. Founded in 2017.

CJ Fallon

Ground Floor, Block B, Liffey Valley Office Campus, Dublin D22 X0Y3, Republic of Ireland
tel +353 (0)16 166400
email editorial@cjfallon.ie
website www.cjfallon.ie
Executive Directors Brian Gilsenan (managing), John Bodley (financial)

Educational textbooks. Founded 1927.

Farshore Books – see HarperCollins Publishers

David Fickling Books

31 Beaumont Street, Oxford OX1 2NP
tel (01865) 339000
website www.davidficklingbooks.com
Publisher David Fickling, *Publishing Director* Liz Cross

Independent publisher of picture books, novels and non-fiction for all ages, as well as graphic novels, with a focus on brilliant storytelling and world-class illustration. Currently not accepting unsolicited MSS submissions. Founded 1999.

Fine Feather Press

The Coach House, Elstead Road, Farnham, Surrey GU10 1JE
tel 07968 607981
email enquries@finefeatherpreess.com
website www.finefeatherpress.com
Facebook www.facebook.com/finefeatherpress
Twitter @NatureActivity
Contact Andrea Pinnington

Illustrated children's books focusing on the natural world. Founded 2011.

Firefly Press Ltd*

25 Gabalfa Road, Llandaff North, Cardiff CF14 2JJ
email hello@fireflypress.co.uk
website www.fireflypress.co.uk
Facebook www.facebook.com/FireflyPress
Twitter @fireflypress
Publisher Penny Thomas, *Editor* Janet Thomas, *Marketing & Publicity Manager* Megan Farr, *Commercial Director* Robin Bennett, *Sales & Marketing Manager* Simone Greenwood

Award-winning publisher of quality fiction for ages 5 to 19. Founded 2013.

Fisherton Press

email general@fishertonpress.co.uk
website www.fishertonpress.co.uk
Facebook www.facebook.com/FishertonPress
Twitter @fishertonpress
Director Ellie Levenson

A small independent publisher producing picture books for children under 7. Not currently accepting proposals but illustrators are welcome to send links to a portfolio. Founded 2013.

Floris Books*

2A Robertson Avenue, Edinburgh EH11 1PZ
tel 0131 337 2372
email floris@florisbooks.co.uk
website www.florisbooks.co.uk
Facebook www.facebook.com/FlorisBooks
Twitter @FlorisBooks
Commissioning Editors Sally Polson, Eleanor Collins

Children's activity books, novels, board and picture books. Approx. 60 titles each year. Founded 1978.

Kelpies

website www.discoverkelpies.co.uk

Contemporary Scottish fiction – picture books (for 3–6 years), young readers series (for 6–8 years) and novels (for 8–15 years). Recent successes include *The Nowhere Emporium* by Ross MacKenzie and *There Was a Wee Lassie Who Swallowed a Midgie* by Rebecca Colby. See website for submission details.

Galore Park Publishing Ltd*

Carmelite House, 50 Victoria Embankment, London EC4Y 0DZ
tel 020-7873 6412
website www.galorepark.co.uk

Educational textbooks and revision guides for students studying at independent schools. *So You Really Want To Learn* range of textbooks for children 11+ and *Junior* range for children 8–10 years. Courses include Latin, French, English, Spanish, maths and science. Founded 1999.

Gardner Education Ltd

Unit 2, Aston Way, Middlewich, Cheshire CW10 0HS
tel 0845 230 0775
email education@gardnereducation.co.uk
website www.gardnereducation.co.uk
Managing Director Stuart Withers

A specialist supplier of primary and secondary literacy books to schools and parents. Range includes book banded publications, dyslexia friendly texts, Accelerated Reader and Catch Up Literacy approved titles, books tailored for struggling and reluctant readers and a massive selection of titles to cater for all primary and secondary reading preferences. Founded 1999.

Books

GL Assessment

1st Floor Vantage London, Great West Road,
Brentford TW8 9AG
tel 020-8996 3333
email info@gl-assessment.co.uk
website www.gl-assessment.co.uk
Chairman Philip Walters

Independent provider of tests, assessments and
assessment services for education. Aims to help
educational professionals to understand and
maximise the potential of their pupils and students.
Publishes assessments for the 0–19 age group, though
the majority of its assessments are aimed at children
5–14 years. Testing and assessment services include
literacy, numeracy, thinking skills, ability, learning
support and online testing. Founded 1981.

W.F. Graham

2 Pondwood Close, Moulton Park,
Northampton NN3 6RT
tel (01604) 645537
email books@wfgraham.co.uk
website www.wfgraham.co.uk

Activity books including colouring, dot-to-dot, magic
painting, puzzle, word search and sticker books.

Neil Griffiths Consultancy

Willow Cottage, 26 Purton Stoke, Swindon SN5 4JF
tel 07976 574627
email neil@cornertolearn.co.uk
website www.cornertolearn.co.uk
Publisher/International Trainer Neil Griffiths

Training books and learning materials aimed at
teachers and parents with young children. Imprint:
Red Robin Books (picture books):
www.redrobinbooks.com. Founded 2008.

Guppy Publishing Ltd‡

Bracken Hill, Cotswold Road, Oxford OX2 9JG
tel 07884 068983
email bella@guppybooks.co.uk
website www.guppybooks.co.uk
Facebook www.facebook.com/guppybooks
Twitter @guppybooks
Instagram @guppypublishing
Director Bella Pearson

Publishing children's and young adult fiction for ages
5 to 18. Illustrated books for newly emerging readers,
fiction for middle-grade readers and novels for
adults. Poetry, prose, graphic novels. Original,
thought-provoking, literary, publishing 8 to 10 titles
each year that inspire and entertain young readers.
Founded 2019.

Hachette Children's Group*

Carmelite House, 50 Victoria Embankment,
London EC4Y 0DZ
email hcg.editorial@hachettechildrens.co.uk
website www.hachettechildrens.co.uk
Facebook www.facebook.com/hachettekids

Ceo Hilary Murray Hill, *Senior Trade Publisher* Ruth
Alltimes, *Trade Publisher* Emma Blackburn,
Education Publisher Paul Rockett

Hachette UK*

Carmelite House, 50 Victoria Embankment,
London EC4Y 0DZ
tel 020-3122 6000
website www.hachette.co.uk
Ceo David Shelley

Part of Hachette Livre SA since 2004. Hachette UK
group companies: Hachette Children's Group (see
above), Hachette Ireland, Hachette Australia
(page 31), Hachette New Zealand, Headline Book
Publishing, Hodder Education Group, Hodder &
Stoughton, Hodder Faith, Little, Brown Book Group,
John Murray, Orion Group, Octopus Group.
Founded 1986.

Happy Yak

The Old Brewery, 6 Blundell Street, London N7 9BH
tel 020-7000 8084
website www.quartoknows.com/words-pictures
Associate Publisher Rhiannon Findlay

A children's imprint of the Quarto Group, Inc.
(page 26). Happy Yak publishes pre-school, picture
books and illustrated non-fiction for children aged
0–7 years, with a focus on fun, accessible content and
contemporary illustration. Founded 2021.

HarperCollins Publishers*

The News Building, 1 London Bridge Street,
London SE1 9GF
tel 020-8741 7070
Alternative address Westerhill Road, Bishopbriggs,
Glasgow G64 2QT
tel 0141 772 3200
website www.harpercollins.co.uk
Ceo Charlie Redmayne, *Executive Publishers* Oliver
Malcolm, Kimberly Young, *Managing Director* Kate
Elton

For adults: fiction (commercial and literary) and
non-fiction. Subjects include history; celebrity
memoirs; biographies; popular science; mind, body &
spirit; dictionaries; maps and reference. All fiction
and trade non-fiction must be submitted through an
agent. Owned by News Corporation. Founded 1817.

Farshore Books

website www.farshore.com
Executive Publisher Cally Poplak

Children's fiction, young adult (Electric Monkey),
picture books, non-fiction (Red Shed), novelty and
gift, and licenced books. Fiction authors include:
Michael Morpurgo, Laura Ellen Anderson, Andy
Stanton, Lemony Snicket, Holly Jackson, Michael
Grant and David Levithan. Picture Book authors
include: Matt Lucas, Julia Donaldson and Chris
Packham. Books published under licence include
Winnie-the-Pooh, Thomas the Tank Engine, Mr.

Men and Minecraft. Visit website to see current policy on manuscript submissions. Previously known as Egmont UK, acquired by HarperCollins Publishers 2021.

Harper Collins Audio

Group Digital Director Joanna Surman, *Editorial Director* Fionnuala Barrett

Publishes various audio formats. Leading publisher of trade fiction and non-fiction audiobooks for children and adults, as well as standalone audio projects. Publishes in excess of 700 audiobooks each year.

HarperCollins Children's Books

Executive Publisher Ann-Janine Murtagh

Activity books, novelty books, pre-school brands, picture books, pop-up books and book and CD sets. Fiction for 5–8 and 9–12 years, young adult fiction and series fiction; film/TV tie-ins. Publishes approx. 265 titles each year. Picture book authors include Oliver Jeffers, Judith Kerr and Emma Chichester Clark, and fiction by David Walliams, Michael Morpurgo, David Baddiel and Lauren Child. Books published under licence include *Dr Seuss*, *Bing*, *Twirlywoos* and *Paddington Bear*. No unsolicited MSS: only accepts submissions via agents.

Hawthorn Press*‡

1 Lansdown Lane, Stroud, Glos. GL5 1BJ
tel (01453) 757040
email info@hawthornpress.com
website www.hawthornpress.com
Director Martin Large

Publishes books and ebooks for a more creative, peaceful and sustainable world. Series include *Early Years*, *Steiner/Waldorf Education*, *Crafts*, *Personal Development*, *Art and Science*, *Storytelling*. Founded 1981.

Head of Zeus - Zephyr

Clerkenwell House, 5–8 Hardwick Street, London EC1R 4RG
tel 020-7253 5557
email hello@headofzeus.com
website www.headofzeus.com
Facebook www.facebook.com/headofzeus/
Twitter @_ZephyrBooks
Chairman Anthony Cheetham, *Publishing Director* Fiona Kennedy

Children's imprint. Acquired by Bloomsbury 2021 (page 12). Founded 2002.

Hogs Back Books Ltd

34 Long Street, Devizes, Wilts. SN10 1NT
tel (01483) 506030
email enquiries@hogsbackbooks.com
website www.hogsbackbooks.com
Director & Commissioning Editor Karen Stevens

Children's picture books and teenage fiction. Welcomes texts and submissions from illustrators but cannot return material without prior arrangement. Founded 2009.

Hopscotch

St Jude's Church, Dulwich Road, London SE24 0PB
tel 020-7501 6736
email orders@hopscotchbooks.com
website www.hopscotchbooks.com
Associate Publisher Angela Morano Shaw

A division of MA Education. Teaching resources for primary school teachers. Founded 1997.

Practical Pre-School Books

Early years teacher resources.

Hot Key Books

Victoria House, Bloomsbury Squre, London WC1B 4DA
tel 020-3770 8888
email hello@hotkeybooks.com
website www.hotkeybooks.com,
www.bonnierbooks.co.uk
Twitter @HotKeyBooksYA
Executive Publisher Emma Matthewson

Hot Key Books publishes books targeted at teen and older readers, some of which appeal to an adult audience. Hot Key Books is an imprint of Bonnier Books UK (page 13). Founded 2012.

Igloo Books Ltd

Cottage Farm, Mears Ashby Road, Sywell, Northants NN6 0BJ
tel (01604) 741116
email customerservices@igloobooks.com
website www.igloobooks.com
Twitter @igloo_books

Children's: fiction (adult), licensed books, novelty, board, picture, activity books and education. Not currently accepting submissions. Founded 2005.

Imagine That Publishing Ltd

Marine House, Tide Mill Way, Woodbridge, Suffolk IP12 1AP
tel (01394) 386651
email customerservice@imaginethat.com
website www.imaginethat.com
Facebook www.facebook.com/ImagineThatPublishing
Twitter @imaginethatbook
Instagram @imaginethatbook
Chairman Barrie Henderson, *Managing Director* David Henderson

Children's activity books, novelty books, picture books, reference, character, gift books and early learning books. Founded 1999.

Top That

Books plus kits.

Willow Tree

Picture books and chapter fiction.

IWM (Imperial War Museums) Publishing

Lambeth Road, London SE1 6HZ
tel 020-7416 5000
email publishing@iwm.org.uk
website www.iwm.org.uk
Facebook www.facebook.com/iwm.london
Twitter @I_W_M

IWM tells the stories of people who have lived, fought and died in conflicts involving Britain and the Commonwealth since 1914. IWM Publishing produces a range of books drawing on the expertise and archives of the museum. Books are produced both in-house and in partnership with other publishers. Founded 1917.

Jolly Learning Ltd*‡

Tailours House, High Road, Chigwell, Essex IG7 6DL
tel 020-8501 0405
email info@jollylearning.co.uk
website www.jollylearning.co.uk
Director Christopher Jolly

Educational: primary and English as a Bilingual Language. The company is committed to enabling high standards in the teaching of reading and writing. Publishes approx. 25 titles each year and has 300 in print. Recent successes include *Jolly Phonics Extra*, *My Jolly Phonics* and *Jolly Dictionary*. Imprint: Jolly Phonics. Unsolicited MSS are only considered for add-ons to existing products. Founded 1987.

Miles Kelly Publishing

Harding's Barn, Bardfield End Green, Thaxted, Essex CM6 3PX
tel (01371) 832440
email hello@mileskelly.net
website www.mileskelly.net
Director Gerard Kelly

High-quality illustrated non-fiction and fiction titles for children and family: activity books, board books, story books, picture books, poetry, reference, posters and wallcharts. Age groups: preschool, 5–10, 10–15, 15+. Founded 1996.

Kelpies – see Floris Books

The King's England Press

111 Meltham Road, Lockwood, Huddersfield, West Yorkshire HD4 7BG
tel (01484) 663790
email sales@kingsengland.com
website www.kingsengland.com

Poetry collections for both adults and children plus history books. Successes include *The Spot on My Bum: Horrible Poems for Horrible Children* by Gez Walsh, *Revudeville* and *Turned Out Nice Again* by Deborah Tyler-Bennett and *Jordan's Guide to British Steam Locomotives* by Owen Jordan. Also publishes

reprints of Arthur Mee's *The King's England* series of 1930s guidebooks and books on folklore, and local and ecclesiastical history, plus children's and adult fiction. See website for guidelines. However, currently not accepting new unsolicited proposals. Founded 1989.

Kings Road Publishing

Victoria House, Bloomsbury Squre, London WC1B 4DA
tel 020-770 3888
email hello@bonnierbooks.co.uk
website www.bonnierbooks.co.uk
Facebook www.facebook.com/KingsRoadPublishing
Ceo Perminder Mann, *Managing Director* Ben Dunn, *Head of Children's Publishing* Lisa Edwards

Part of Bonnier Books UK (page 13). The children's imprints are Studio Press (page 28), Weldon Owen, which includes it's new sub imprint 20 Watt, and Templar Publishing (page 29), which contains Big Picture Press (page 12). They focus on illustrated non-fiction, picture books, novelty titles, activity books, fiction and family reference. Submissions to be sent to the address above indicating which imprint they are addressed to. Founded 2015.

Knights Of*

97 Granville Avenue, Brixton Village, London SW9 8PS
website https://knightsof.media
Twitter @_KnightsOf
Managing Director Aimée Felone, *Editorial Director* Eishar Brar, *Creative Director* Marssaié Jordan

Children's commercial fiction publisher, championing authors and illustrators from diverse backgrounds. Founded 2016.

Kube Publishing Ltd

Markfield Conference Centre, Ratby Lane, Markfield, Leics. LE67 9SY
tel (01530) 249230
email info@kubepublishing.com
website www.kubepublishing.com
Managing Director Haris Ahmad

Formerly the Islamic Foundation. Books on Islam and the Muslim world for adults and children. Founded 2006.

Ladybird Books

80 Strand, London WC2R 0RL
tel 020-7010 3000
email ladybird@penguinrandomhouse.co.uk
website www.ladybird.co.uk

Ladybird publishes books across a wide range of formats for children aged from birth to 7 years. They include tactile books for babies, nursery rhymes, classic fairy tales and reading schemes, alongside licensed character publishing. Part of Penguin Random House UK (page 25). Founded 1867.

Leckie*

Dipford House, Queens Square Business Park,
Huddersfield Road, Honley, Holmfirth HD9 6QZ
email leckiescotland@harpercollins.co.uk
website www.leckiescotland.co.uk

Leckie has been publishing educational books
specially for Scotland for more than thirty years. Now
part of the Collins family, Leckie publishes resources
for over twenty subjects in secondary – and it has
recently expanded its publishing into primary,
publishing maths and health & wellbeing for the
primary Curriculum for Excellence. Founded 1989.

Frances Lincoln

74–77 White Lion Street, London N1 9PF
tel 020-7284 9300
email reception@frances-lincoln.com
website www.quartoknows.com/Frances-Lincoln
Publisher Andrew Dunn

Imprint of The Quarto Group (page 26). Illustrated,
international co-editions: gardening, architecture,
environment, interiors, photography, art, walking
and climbing, design and landscape, gift, children's
books. Founded 1977.

Frances Lincoln Children's Books

The Old Brewery, 6 Blundell Street, London N7 9BH
tel 020-7700 6700
email katie.cotton@quarto.com
website www.quartoknows.com/Frances-Lincoln-
Childrens-Books
Facebook www.facebook.com/Quartokids
Twitter @QuartoKids
Publisher Katie Cotton

Imprint of The Quarto Group (page 26). Illustrated
children's books: arts and the great outdoors, as well
as visual storytelling, cultural diversity.
Founded 1983.

Lion Hudson Ltd‡

Box 202, 266 Banbury Road, Summertown,
Oxford OX2 7DL
tel (01865) 302750
email info@lionhudson.com
website www.lionhudson.com
Managing Director Suzanne Wilson-Higgins

Bible story retellings, prayer books, picture
storybooks, illustrated non-fiction and information
books on the Christian faith and world religions. Also
specialises in gift books, occasion books, seasonal
books for Christmas and Easter and bible activity
books. Children's submissions: hardcopy with sae if
return required. Founded 1971.

Lion Fiction

Historical fiction, mystery, fantasy and heart-
warming tales with meaning, from authors with a
Christian world-view.

Lion Scholar

Bible related reference works for the serious reader or
first year undergraduate.

Little Door Books

email submissions@littledoorbooks.co.uk
website www.littledoorbooks.co.uk
Twitter @littledoorbooks

Award-winning independent publisher specialising in
children's books. Publishes four or five books a year.
Not currently accepting unsolicited MSS.
Founded 2016.

Little Tiger Group

1 Coda Studios, 189 Munster Road,
London SW6 6AW
tel 020-7385 6333
email contact@littletiger.co.uk
website www.littletiger.co.uk
Group Publishing Director Thomas Truong, *Publisher*
Jude Evans, *Commissioning Editors* Sally Polson,
Eleanor Collins

Religion; philosophy; holistic health; organics; mind,
body & spirit; crafts; parenting. Children's books:
board, picture books, activity books. See website for
submission details. Acquired by Penguin Random
House (page 48) in 2019. Founded 1987.

Caterpillar Books

email contact@littletiger.co.uk
website www.littletiger.co.uk/imprint/caterpillar-
books
Editorial Director Pat Hegarty

Books for children, including novelty board and
picture books.

Little Tiger Press

email contact@littletiger.co.uk
website www.littletiger.co.uk
Publisher Jude Evans, *Editorial Director* Eleanor
Farmer

Children's picture books, board books and novelty
books for preschool–7 years. See website for
submissions guidelines. Founded 1987.

Stripes

email contact@littletiger.co.uk
website www.littletiger.co.uk/imprint/stripes-
publishing
Editorial Director Ruth Bennett

Fiction for children aged 6–12 years and young adult.
Quality standalone titles and series publishing in all
age groups. Will consider new material from authors
and illustrators; see website for guidelines.
Founded 2005.

360 Degrees

email contact@littletiger.co.uk
website www.littletiger.co.uk/special/360degrees
Editorial Director Pat Hegarty

Non-fiction novelty for children aged 5–12 years. Founded 2015.

LOM ART
16 Lion Yard, Tremadoc Road, London SW4 7NQ
tel 020-7720 8643
email enquiries@mombooks.com
website www.mombooks.com/lom
Facebook www.facebook.com/MichaelOMaraBooks
Twitter @OMaraBooks
Managing Director Lesley O'Mara, *Publisher* Philippa Wingate

Illustrated non-fiction for children and adults. Publishes approx. 10 titles a year. Titles include *Fantomorphia*, *Maybe the Moon*, *The Van Gogh Activity Book* and *Life Lessons From My Cat*, plus a range of artist-led drawing, colouring and picture book titles. Unable to guarantee a reply to every submission received, but the inclusion of a sae is necessary for submission to be returned. Imprint of Michael O'Mara Books Ltd. Founded 2015.

Longman – see Pearson UK

Mabecron Books ltd
3 Briston Orchard, St Mellion, Saltash, Cornwall PL12 6RQ
tel (01579) 350885
email ronjohns@mabecronbooks.co.uk
website www.mabecronbooks.co.uk
Twitter @mabecronbooks

Award-winning publisher. Produces beautiful children's picture books and books with a Cornish or west country subject. Linked to bookshops in Falmouth, St Ives and Padstow. Founded 1998.

McGraw-Hill School Education*
8th Floor, 338 Euston Road, London NW1 3BH
tel (01628) 502730
email helpme@mheducation.com
website www.mheducation.co.uk
Facebook www.facebook.com/UKSchoolsMHE
Twitter @UKSchoolsMHE

Educational publisher for primary and secondary education in English, maths, science, humanities and other subject areas, including intervention and learning support. Founded 1888.

Magic Cat Publishing‡
125–127 Mare Street, London Fields, London E8 3SJ
email marketing@magiccatpublishing.co.uk
website www.magiccatpublishing.co.uk
Instagram @magiccatpublishing
Directors Jenny Broom, Rachel Williams

Magic Cat is a small, independent children's publisher. Publishes family-focused non-fiction and gift books that celebrate the art of storytelling. Editors and designers are the heart of the business. Founded 2019.

Mantra Lingua Ltd
Global House, 303 Ballards Lane, London N12 8NP
tel 020-8445 5123
email info@mantralingua.com
website https://uk.mantralingua.com/
Facebook www.facebook.com/Mantralingua
Twitter @mantralingua
Managing Director R. Dutta

Publishes bilingual picture books and educational resources for UK, US, Swedish and German audiences. Looking for illustrators with ability to draw diverse racial faces and authors and story-tellers with ability to interpret or imagine modern city lives. Commission and royalty based relationships with print runs covering between 10 and 15 language editions. Translators and audio narrators, tel: 0845 600 1361. Founded 2002.

Marshall Editions Children's Books
The Old Brewery, 6 Blundell Street, London N7 9BH
tel 020-7812 8633

Publishes beautifully illustrated and engaging books for children. Includes a natural world list, which has expanded into new subject areas, such as cookery, art, craft, film and technology. Part of the Quarto Group, Inc. (page 26).

Maverick Books
Studio 3A, City Business Centre, 6 Brighton Road, Horsham, West Sussex RH13 5BB
tel (01403) 256941
email submissions@maverickbooks.co.uk
website www.maverickbooks.co.uk
Facebook www.facebook.com/Maverick-Childrens-Books
Twitter @maverickbooks
Managing Director Steve Bicknell, *Editor & Designer* Kimara Nye

Publishes titles across the formats of board books, picture books, early readers, graphic reluctant readers, junior fiction and activity books. Has a strong ethos of championing new authors and emerging illustrators, with a big emphasis on supporting them once their book is published. For submissions, please see submissions page on website. Founded 2009.

Kevin Mayhew Ltd
Fengate Farm, Rattlesden, Suffolk IP30 0SZ
tel (01449) 737978
email info@kevinmayhew.com
website www.kevinmayhew.com
Director Barbara Mayhew

Christianity: prayer and spirituality, pastoral care, preaching, liturgy worship, children's, youth work, drama, instant art, educational. Music: hymns, organ and choral, contemporary worship, piano and instrumental, tutors. Greetings cards: images, spiritual texts, birthdays, Christian events, musicians, general occasions. Read submissions section on website before sending MSS/synopses. Founded 1976.

The Mercier Press[†]

email info@mercierpress.ie
website www.mercierpress.ie
General Manager Deirdre Roberts

Books for adults and children. Subjects include Irish literature; folklore; history; politics; humour; current affairs; health; mind, body & spirit; general non-fiction. Founded 1944.

Moonlight Publishing

Garden House at Vine House, Chapel Square, East Hendred Oxon OX12 8JN
email info@moonlightpublishing.co.uk
website https://moonlightpublishing.co.uk/

An independent, family-run company specialised in illustrated information books for children aged 4 to 10. Founded 1980.

Nobrow Books

27 Westgate Street, London E8 3RL
tel 020-7033 4430
email info@nobrow.net
website https://nobrow.net/
Twitter @NobrowPress

Publishes picture books, illustrated fiction and non-fiction and graphic novels. Nobrow Books aims to combine good design and storytelling, quality production value and environmental consciousness. Founded 2008.

Flying Eye Books

email info@nobrow.net
website www.flyingeyebooks.com
Twitter @FlyingEyeBooks

Children's imprint. Focuses on the craft of children's storytelling and non-fiction. Founded 2013.

Nosy Crow*[‡]

14 Baden Place, Crosby Row, London SE1 1YW
tel 020-7089 7575
email hello@nosycrow.com
website www.nosycrow.com
Managing Director Kate Wilson, *Editorial Director* Camilla Reid, *Head of Fiction* Kirsty Stansfield, *Head of Picture Books* Louise Bolongaro, *Head of Non-Fiction* Rachel Kellehar, *Head of Sales & Marketing* Catherine Stokes, *Commercial Director* Adrian Soar

Award-winning children's books and apps, children's publisher for The National Trust and The British Museum. IPG Children's Publisher of the Year 2012, 2013, 2016, 2017 and 2020; IPG Independent Publisher of the Year 2016; BIA Children's Publisher of the Year 2017 and 2019; BIA Independent Publisher of the Year 2020 and Queen's Award for International Trade 2019. Founded 2010.

The O'Brien Press Ltd[†]

12 Terenure Road East, Rathgar, Dublin D06 HD27, Republic of Ireland
tel +353 (0)1 4923333
email books@obrien.ie
website www.obrien.ie
Directors Michael O'Brien, Ivan O'Brien, Kunak McGann

Children: picture books; fiction for all ages; illustrated fiction for ages 3+, 5+, 6+, 8+ years, novels (10+ and young adult): contemporary, historical, fantasy. Non-fiction. Adult non-fiction: biography, politics, history, travel, food & drink, true crime, sport, humour, reference. Adult fiction, crime (Brandon). No poetry or academic. Unsolicited MSS (sample chapters only), synopses and ideas for books welcome – submissions will not be returned. Founded 1974.

Old Barn Books[‡]

Warren Barn, Bedham Lane, Fittleworth, West Sussex RH20 1JW
tel (01798) 865010
email ruth@oldbarnbooks.com
website www.oldbarnbooks.com
Facebook www.facebook.com/oldbarnbooks
Twitter @oldbarnbooks
Instagram @oldbarnbooks

Independent publisher of picture books and fiction for children up to 14 years old and the occasional gift book for adults. Interested in the natural world and promoting empathy. Strong line in Aussie MG fiction. No unsolicited submissions at present. Founded 2015.

Otter-Barry Books Ltd[‡]

Little Orchard, Burley Gate, Herts. HR1 3QS
tel (01432) 820915
email info@otterbarrybooks.com
website www.otterbarrybooks.com
Twitter @otterbarrybooks
Publisher Janetta Otter-Barry

Publishes high-quality illustrated books for children aged from baby to 11+. Authors and illustrators include Jackie Morris, Joseph Coelho, Chitra Soundar, Petr Horáček and Ken Wilson-Max. Founded 2015.

Oxford University Press*

Great Clarendon Street, Oxford OX2 6DP
tel (01865) 556767
email enquiry@oup.com
website www.oup.com
Ceo Nigel Portwood, *Global Academic Business Managing Director* David Clark, *Managing Director, Oxford Education* Fathima Dada, *Managing Director, ELT Division* Peter Marshall

Archaeology, architecture, art, belles lettres, bibles, bibliography, children's books (fiction, non-fiction, picture), commerce, current affairs, dictionaries,

Books

drama, economics, educational (foundation, primary, secondary, technical, university), encyclopedias, ELT, electronic publishing, essays, foreign language learning, general history, hymn and service books, journals, law, medical, music, oriental, philosophy, political economy, prayer books, reference, science, sociology, theology and religion; educational software; *Grove Dictionaries of Music & Art*. Trade paperbacks published under the imprint of Oxford Paperbacks. Founded 1478.

Children's and Educational Division

Managing Director, Oxford Education Fathima Dada, *Sales, Marketing & Operations Director* Richard Hodson, *Business & Strategy Director* Rod Theodorou, *Dictionaries Publisher* Vineeta Gupta, *Director, Digital & Home/School Services* Simon Tanner-Tremaine, *Director, Secondary* Clare Varlet-Baker, *Publishing Director, International* Elspeth Boardley, *Director, Primary* Jane Harley, *Managing Director of Asia Education* Adrian Mellor

Picture books, fiction, poetry and dictionaries. Authors include Tim Bowler, Gillian Cross, Julie Hearne and Geraldine McCaughrean.

Pan Macmillan

6 Briset St, Farringdon, London EC1M 5NR
tel 020-7014 6000
email publicity@macmillan.com
website www.panmacmillan.com
Managing Director Anthony Forbes Watson

Novels, literary, crime, thrillers, romance, science fiction, fantasy and horror. Autobiography, biography, business, gift books, health and beauty, history, humour, natural history, travel, philosophy, politics, world affairs, theatre, film, gardening, cookery, popular reference. No unsolicited MSS except through Macmillan New Writing. Founded 1843.

Campbell

Early learning, pop-up, novelty, board books for the preschool market.

Macmillan Children's Books

Imprint for Macmillan's children's books composed of two divisions: Macmillan Under 6s and Macmillan Over 6s.

Two Hoots

Illustrated children's books.

Tor

Science fiction and fantasy published in hardback and paperback.

Patrician Press

12 Lushington Road, Manningtree CO11 1EF
tel 07968 288651
email patricia@patricianpress.com
website www.patricianpress.com

Facebook www.facebook.com/patricianpress,
www.facebook.com/puddingpress
Twitter @PatricianCom
Publisher Patricia Borlenghi

Paperback and digital publisher of fiction and poetry. Publisher of children's books under the imprint Pudding Press. Founded 2012.

Pavilion Children's Books‡

43 Great Ormond Street, London WC1N 3HZ
tel 020-7462 1500
website www.pavilionbooks.com
Publisher Neil Dunnicliffe

Children's books: from picture books to illustrated fiction, non-fiction and classics. Part of Pavilion Books Company Ltd. Submissions via an agent only. Successes include *The Story of the Little Mole* by Werner Holzwarth, *The King Who Banned the Dark* by Emily Haworth-Booth, *The Journey Home* by Fran Preston-Gannon and *War Game* by Michael Foreman. Founded 2005.

Pearson UK*

Edinburgh Gate, Harlow, Essex CM20 2JE
tel 0845 313 6666
email schools@longman.co.uk
website www.pearsoned.co.uk
Ceo Andy Bird

Consists of five divisions: Virtual Learning, Higher Education, English Language Learning, Workforce Skills and Asessment and Qualifications. Founded 1998.

Harcourt

Educational resources for teachers and learners at primary, secondary and vocational level. Provides a range of published resources, teachers' support and pupil and student material in all core subjects for all ages. Imprints: Ginn, Heinemann, Payne-Gallway, Raintree, Rigby.

Longman

Educational: primary and secondary. Primary: literacy and numeracy. Secondary: English, maths, science, history, geography, modern languages, design and technology, business and economics, psychology and sociology.

Penguin Longman

ELT.

York Notes

Literature guides for students.

Penguin Longman – see Pearson UK

Penguin Random House Children's UK*

One Embassy Gardens, 8 Viaduct Gardens, London SW11 7AY
tel 020-7139 3000

Books

website www.penguin.co.uk
Managing Director Francesca Dow, *Publishing Director* Amanda Punter (Puffin Fiction, non-fiction, licensing & picture books), *Publishers* Ruth Knowles (Puffin Fiction, non-fiction & licensing), Ben Horslen (Puffin Fiction), Lara Hancock (Puffin, picture books, partnerships & illustrated non-fiction), *Publishing Director* Shannon Cullen (Ladybird trade, licensing & education), *Publisher* Kate Heald (Ladybird education & international), *Licensing & Consumer Products Director* Susan Bolsover (Penguin Ventures), *Art Director* Anna Billson

Part of Penguin Random House UK (see below). Children's paperback and hardback books: wide range of picture books, board books, gift books and novelties; fiction; non-fiction, popular culture, digital and audio. Preschool illustrated developmental books for 0–6 years; licensed brands; children's classic publishing and merchandising properties. No unsolicited MSS or original artwork or text. Imprints: Ladybird, Puffin, Penguin. Founded 2013.

Penguin Random House UK*
One Embassy Gardens, 8 Viaduct Gardens,
London SW11 7AY
tel 020-7840 8400
website www.penguin.co.uk
Directors Markus Dohle (Ceo Penguin Random House), Tom Weldon (Ceo Penguin Random House UK)

Penguin Random House UK group companies which publish books for children: Penguin Random House Children's UK (see above). Founded 2013.

Phaidon Press Ltd
Regent's Wharf, All Saints Street, London N1 9PA
tel 020-7843 1000
email enquiries@phaidon.com
website www.phaidon.com
Editorial Director Tracey Smith

Visual arts, lifestyle, culture and food. Founded 1923.

Piccadilly Press
Victoria House, Bloomsbury Squre,
London WC1B 4DA
tel 020-3770 8888
email hello@piccadillypress.co.uk
website www.piccadillypress.co.uk,
www.bonnierbooks.co.uk
Twitter @PiccadillyPress
Executive Publisher Emma Matthewson *Senior Commissioning Editor* Felicity Alexander

Publishes fun, family-orientated stories in any genre. Titles can be standalone stories or part of a series and use design and illustration that is integral to the content when appropriate. Publishes in hardback, paperback, ebook and audio formats. Publishes books primarily for readers aged 5–12 years. Piccadilly Press is an imprint of Bonnier Books UK (page 13). Founded 1983.

Poolbeg Press Ltd
123 Grange Hill, Baldoyle, Dublin D13 N529, Republic of Ireland
tel +353 (0)18 063825
email info@poolbeg.com
website www.poolbeg.com
Directors Kieran Devlin, Barbara Devlin

Children's and teenage fiction. Also adult popular fiction, non-fiction, current affairs. Imprints: Poolbeg, In a Nut Shell. Founded 1976.

Priddy Books
Chancery House, 53–64 Chancery Lane,
London WC2A 1QT
tel 020-7418 5515
website www.priddybooks.com
Publisher Roger Priddy

Specialises in baby/toddler and preschool books: activity books, board books, novelty books, picture books. Founded 2000.

Prim-Ed Publishing
Marshmeadows, New Ross, Co. Wexford Y34 TA46, Republic of Ireland
tel 0851 440075
email marketing@prim-ed.com
website www.prim-ed.com
Managing Director Seamus McGuinness

Educational publisher specialising in copymasters (photocopiable teaching resources) for primary school and special needs lower second level pupils. Books written by practising classroom teachers. Founded 1993.

Puffin – see Penguin Random House Children's UK

Pure Indigo Ltd
Publishing Department, 17 The Herons, Cottenham, Cambridge CB24 8XX
tel 07981 395258
email ashley.martin@pureindigo.co.uk
website www.pureindigo.co.uk/publishing
Commissioning Editor Ashley Martin

Pure Indigo Publishing develops innovative junior series fiction. All titles are available in both print and digital formats and are distributed internationally with select partners. The company also develops software products that complement the product range. The junior series fiction titles are developed in-house and on occasion authors and illustrators are commissioned to complete project-based work. For consideration for commissions visit the website. Founded 2005.

Pushkin Press*
71–75 Shelton Street, London WC2H 9JQ
email books@pushkinpress.com
website www.pushkinpress.com
Facebook www.facebook.com/PushkinPress

Twitter @pushkinpress
Publisher Adam Freudenheim, *Deputy Publisher* Laura Macaulay, *Commissioning Editor* Daniel Seton

Having first rediscovered European classics of the 20th century, Pushkin now publishes novels, essays, memoirs, children's books (Pushkin's Children's) and everything from timeless classics to the urgent and contemporary. Imprints: Pushkin Press, Pushkin Children's Books, Pushkin Vertigo, ONE. Founded 1997.

The Quarto Group, Inc.
The Old Brewery, 6 Blundell Street, London N7 9BH
tel 020-7700 9000 / 020-7700 8066
email dan.rosenberg@quarto.com
website www.quarto.com
Chairman Peter Read

The Quarto Group is a leading global illustrated book publisher and distribution group. It is composed of three publishing divisions: Quarto International Co-editions Group; Quarto Publishing Group USA; and Quarto Publishing Group UK; plus Books & Gifts Direct (a direct seller of books and gifts in Australia and New Zealand) and Regent Publishing Services, a specialist print services company based in Hong Kong. Quarto has nine children's imprints across its three publishing divisions; these are: Quarto International Co-editions Group (Quarto Children's Books, QED Publishing (above), Ivy Kids, small world creations, Happy Yak (page 18), Marshall Children's Books (page 22)), Quarto Publishing Group UK (Wide Eyed Editions (page 30), Frances Lincoln Children's Books (page 21)) and Quarto Publishing Group US (Walter Foster Jr.). Founded 1976.

Ransom Publishing Ltd*
Unit 7, Brocklands Farm, West Meon GU32 1JN
tel (01730) 829091
email ransom@ransom.co.uk
website www.ransom.co.uk
Directors Jenny Ertle (managing), Steve Rickard (creative)

Children's fiction and non-fiction, phonics and school reading programmes, and books for children and adults who are reluctant or struggling readers. Range covers high interest age/low reading age titles, quick reads and reading schemes. Series include *Alpha Stars, Reading Stars Phonics and Book Bands, Reading Stars Plus, Neutron Stars, Pick Your Path, Tales from the Pitch, Boffin Boy, PIG* and *Dark Man*. Not accepting any unsolicited submissions at this time. Founded 1995.

Raven Books
Publishes fiction for children aged 8–14 years.

Really Decent Books
156 Newbridge Road, Bath BA1 3LE
tel (01225) 334747

email info@reallydecentbooks.co.uk
website www.reallydecentbooks.co.uk
Facebook www.facebook.com/reallydecentbooks
Twitter @ReallyDecent
Publisher Phil Dauncey

Independent publisher of books for babies, toddlers and children. Founded 2012.

Red Bird Publishing
Kiln Farm, East End Green, Brightlingsea, Colchester, Essex CO7 0SX
tel (01206) 303525
email info@red-bird.co.uk
website www.red-bird.co.uk
Publisher Martin Rhodes-Schofield

Innovative children's activity packs and books produced with a mix of techniques and materials such as Glow in the Dark, Mirrors, Stereoscopic 3D, Moiré and other optical illusions. Authors are specialists in their fields. Activity books, novelty books, picture books, painting and colouring books, teaching books, posters, hobbies, nature and the environment, science. Age groups: preschool, 5–10, 10–15. No unsolicited MSS. Founded 1998.

Rockpool Children's Books Ltd
6 Kitchener Terrace, Ferryhill, Co. Durham DL17 8AX
tel 07711 351691
email stuarttrotter3@gmail.com
website www.rockpoolchildrensbooks.co.uk
Facebook www.facebook.com/RockpoolChildrensBooks/
Twitter @rockpooltweets
Instagram @rockpool_childrens_books
Publisher & Creative Director Stuart Trotter

Print-on-demand picture books, packager, co-editions, 'All About Picture Books' school visits, illustration. POD: www.rockpool.alburybooks.com. Founded 2006.

Ruby Tuesday Books Ltd‡
6 Newlands Road, Tunbridge Wells, Kent TN4 9AT
tel (01892) 557767
email shan@rubytuesdaybooks.com
website www.rubytuesdaybooks.com
Twitter @RubyTuesdaybk
Publisher & Author Ruth Owen, *All Sales & Rights* Shan White

Publisher of children's books. Founded 2008.

SAGE Publishing*‡
1 Oliver's Yard, 55 City Road, London EC1Y 1SP
tel 020-7324 8500
email info@sagepub.co.uk
website www.sagepublishing.com
Facebook www.facebook.com/SAGEPublishing
Twitter @SAGE_Publishing
Instagram @sage_publishing

Independent company that disseminates journals, books and library products for the educational, scholarly and professional markets. Founded 1965.

Salariya Book Company Ltd*‡
Book House, 25 Marlborough Place,
Brighton BN1 1UB
tel (01273) 603306
email salariya@salariya.com
website www.salariya.com,
www.youwouldntwantto.be
Facebook www.facebook.com/theSalariya
Twitter @theSalariya
Instagram @salariyabooks
Managing Director David Salariya

Children's art, picture books, fiction and non-fiction. Imprints: Book House, Scribblers, Scribo. No unsolicited MSS. Founded 1989.

Scallywag Press Ltd*
10 Sutherland Row, London SW1V 4JT
tel 07910 278462
email publisher@scallywagpress.com
website www.scallywagpress.com
Facebook www.facebook.com/scallywagpress
Twitter @scallywagpress
Contact Sarah Pakenham

Aims to publish works by talented newcomers as well as established authors and illustrators. Currently not accepting unsolicited MSS. Founded 2018.

Schofield & Sims Ltd*
Unit 11, The Piano Works,
113–117 Farringdon Road, London EC1R 3BX
tel (01484) 607080
email editorial@schofieldandsims.co.uk
website www.schofieldandsims.co.uk

Educational: nursery, infants, primary; posters. Founded 1901.

Scholastic Ltd*
Euston House, 24 Eversholt Street,
London NW1 1DB
tel 020-7756 7756
website www.scholastic.co.uk
Chairman M.R. Robinson, *Co-Group Managing Directors* Catherine Bell, Steve Thompson

Children's fiction, non-fiction and picture books, education resources for primary schools. Owned by Scholastic Inc. Founded 1964.

Chicken House
See page 14.

Scholastic Children's Books
tel 020-7756 7761
email submissions@scholastic.co.uk
website www.scholastic.co.uk
Twitter @scholasticuk

Fiction Publisher Lauren Fortune, *Non-Fiction Publisher & Licensing* Elizabeth Scoggins, *Editorial Director, Illustrated Books* Felicity Osborne

Activity books, novelty books, picture books, fiction for 5–12 years, teenage fiction, series fiction and film/TV tie-ins. Recent successes include *Tom Gates* series by Liz Pichon, *Horrible Histories* by Terry Deary and Martin Brown, *His Dark Materials* by Philip Pullman, *The Hunger Games* by Suzanne Collins, and picture books by Julia Donaldson and Axel Scheffler including *Stick Man, Zog, Tiddler, The Highway Rat* and the *Wonkey Donkey* by Craig Smith and Katz Cowley. Imprints: Scholastic, Alison Green Books. No unsolicited MSS. Unsolicited illustrations are accepted, but do not send any original artwork as it will not be returned.

Scholastic Educational Resources
Book End, Range Road, Witney, Oxon OX29 0YD
tel (01993) 893456
Publishing Director Robin Hunt

Professional books, classroom materials, home learning books and online resources for primary teachers, and GCSE support material.

Scripture Union
Trinity House, Opal Court, Fox Milne,
Milton Keynes MK15 0DF
tel (01908) 856000
email hello@scriptureunion.org.uk
website www.scriptureunion.org.uk
Director of Ministry Development (Publishing) Terry Clutterham

Christian books and bible reading materials for people of all ages; educational and worship resources for churches; adult fiction and non-fiction; children's fiction and non-fiction (age groups: under 5, 5–8 years, 8–10 years and youth). Publishes approx. 40 titles each year for children/young people and has 200–250 in print. Recent successes include the *Bible Storybook* series and *Essential 100* by Whitney Kuniholm. Scripture Union works as a charity in over 120 countries and publishes in approx. 20. Will not consider unsolicited MSS. Founded 1867.

SEN Press Ltd
1 Necton Road, Wheathampstead AL4 8AT
tel (01582) 833205
email info@senpress.org
website www.senpress.org
Publisher Janie Nicholas

Literacy and life skills resources for ages 14–19 with special needs. Founded 2003.

Simon & Schuster UK Ltd*
222 Gray's Inn Road, London WC1X 8HB
tel 020-7316 1900
email enquiries@simonandschuster.co.uk
website www.simonandschuster.co.uk
Facebook www.facebook.com/simonschusterUK

Twitter @simonschusteruk
Directors Ian Chapman (Ceo), Rachel Denwood (managing), Ali Dougal (publishing), Helen Mackenzie Smith (editorial, picture books), Jane Griffiths (editorial, fiction)

Children's and young adult fiction, picture books, novelty, pop-up and licensed character. Founded 1986.

Smart Learning

Unit 2, Aston Way, Middlewich, Cheshire CW10 0HS
tel (01423) 206 200
email admin@smart-learning.co.uk
website www.smart-learning.co.uk

High-quality teaching and learning resources for both teachers and children – from Foundation Stage through to KS3. Publishes software and books to enhance the teaching and learning of ICT, phonics, literacy, PSHE and citizenship and English. Founded 2012.

SRL Publishing Ltd

email admin@srlpublishing.co.uk
website www.srlpublishing.co.uk
Facebook www.facebook.com/srlpublishing
Twitter @srlpublishing
Instagram @srlpublishing

Award-winning, climate-positive publisher. Titles range from young adult, new adult, contemporary fiction and crime/thriller to non-fiction including autobiographies and cooking books. Founded 2014.

Stacey Publishing Ltd

14 Great College Street, London SW1P 3RX
tel 020-7221 7166
email info@stacey-international.co.uk
website www.stacey-international.co.uk
Founder Tom Stacey

Illustrated books for children 3–12 years. Publishers of the Musgrove series. Founded 1974.

Strident Publishing Ltd

22 Strathwhillan Drive, Hairmyres, Glasgow G75 8GT
tel (01355) 220588
email info@stridentpublishing.co.uk
website www.stridentpublishing.co.uk
Executive Director Keith Charters

Fiction for children 7–18 years: 7+ years: 'timeless classic' feel; 9+ years: general; teen: general, but especially contemporary social realism; young adult/ adult crossover: high-quality, accessible, (often edgy) literature. Publishes approx. 15 books a year. Renowned for taking provocative young adult titles and for the energetic marketing of all of its titles. Works closely with authors who present in schools/at festivals. Email proposed blurb together with the first three chapters and covering letter stating why book is likely to appeal to readers. Founded 2005.

Stripes – see Little Tiger Group

Studio Press

Victoria House, Bloomsbury Square, London WC1B 4DA
tel 020-3770 8888
email hello@studiopressbooks.co.uk
website www.studiopressbooks.co.uk, www.bonnierbooks.co.uk
Twitter @StudioPress
Executive Director Helen Wicks

Studio Press presents trend, brand and celebrity-led publishing to both the children's and adult market in the UK and seeks to capture current trends in social media, gaming, film, art and design. With a diverse range of formats, including fiction, non-fiction, picture books, gift, humour and activity, Studio Press showcases a range of books with key licensing partners including Disney, The Beano and high-profile authors including Rochelle Humes and Professor Steve Peters. Studio Press is an imprint of Bonnier Books UK (page 13). Founded 2015.

Sweet Cherry Publishing*‡

Unit 36, Vulcan Business Complex, Vulcan Road, Leicester LE5 3EF
tel 0116 253 6796
email info@sweetcherrypublishing.com
website www.sweetcherrypublishing.com
Facebook www.facebook.com/sweetcherrypublishing
Twitter @sweetcherrypub
Director A. Thadha

Children's series fiction specialist. Children's picture books, novelty books, gift books, board books, educational books and fiction series for all ages. Also welcomes young adult novels, trilogies or longer series. Likes to publish a set of books as a box set or in a slipcase. See website for submission guidelines. Founded 2011.

Tarquin Publications

Suite 74, 17 Holywell Hill, St Albans AL1 1DT
tel (01727) 833866
email info@tarquinbooks.com
website www.tarquinbooks.com

Mathematical models, puzzles, codes and logic and paper engineering books for intelligent children. Publishes 7–8 titles each year and has 103 in print. Recent successes include Magic Moving Images and Mini Mathematical Murder Mysteries. Do not send unsolicited MSS. Send a one-page proposal of idea. Founded 1970.

Taylor & Francis Group*

2 and 4 Park Square, Milton Park, Abingdon, Oxon OX14 4RN
tel 020-7017 6000
email enquiries@taylorandfrancis.com
website https://taylorandfrancis.com/
Ceo Annie Callanan, Managing Director (Taylor & Francis Books) Jeremy North

Academic and reference books, including education. Imprints include CRC Press, Europa, Garland Science, Psychology Press, Routledge, Spon and Taylor & Francis. Founded 1988.

Focal Press

Animation, audio, film, gaming, music technology, photography and theatre.

Templar Books

Victoria House, Bloomsbury Square, London WC1B 4DA
tel 020-3770 8888
email hello@templarco.co.uk
website www.templarco.co.uk, www.bonnierbooks.co.uk
Twitter @templarbooks
Editorial Director Katie Haworth

Publishes illustrated children's non-fiction, picture books, fiction, gift and novelty books for all ages. Templar is an imprint of Bonnier Books UK (page 13). Founded 1978.

Three Hares Publishing

2 Dukes Avenue, London N10 2PT
tel 020-8245 8989
email submissions@threeharespublishing.com
website www.threeharespublishing.com
Facebook www.facebook.com/threeharespublishing
Twitter @threeharesbooks
Publisher Yasmin Standen

Submissions are open for children's and young adult books. No picture books. The children's list is currently expanding. Interested in discovering new talent. Visit website for submission guidelines – email submissions only. Founded 2014.

Tiny Owl Publishing Ltd

6 Hatfield road, London W4 1AF
email info@tinyowl.co.uk
website www.tinyowl.co.uk
Facebook www.facebook.com/tinyowlpublishing
Twitter @TinyOwl_Books
Publisher Delaram Ghanimifard

An independent publisher of global children's literature. Publishes high-quality picture books for children 3–11 years. Aims to promote diversity and human rights values. Founded 2015.

Tiptoe Books

United House, North Road, London N7 9DP
tel 020-7520 7600
email enquiries@amberbooks.co.uk
website www.tiptoebooks.co.uk
Chairman Stasz Gnych

Illustrated non-fiction, multi-volume sets, calendars and sticker books for children of all ages. Subjects include history, ancient civilisations, the natural world, fantasy and general reference. Opportunities for freelancers. Children's books imprint of Amber Books Ltd.

Trigger Publishing

The Foundation Centre, Navigation House, 48 Millgate, Notts. NG24 4TS
tel (01636) 600825
email enquiries@triggerpublishing.com
website www.triggerpublishing.com
Facebook www.facebook.com/triggerpub
Twitter @triggerpub
Instagram @triggerpub
Publisher Jo Lal, *Managing Editor* Rachel Gregory

Independent publisher dedicated to mental health welfare, publishes for both adults and children. Founded 2016.

Troika*

Troika Books Ltd, Well House, Green Lane, Ardleigh, Colchester, Essex CO7 7PD
tel (01206) 233333
email info@troikabooks.com
website www.troikabooks.com
Publisher Martin West, *Rights* Petula Chaplin, *Publicity, Marketing & Editorial* Roy Johnson, *Sales* Saltway Global

Publishes picture books, poetry and fiction for all ages, with an emphasis on quality, accessibility and diversity. Recent fiction authors include Savita Kalhan, John Harvey and Miriam Halahmy. Poetry list includes Zaro Weil, Jay Hulme, Sue Hardy-Dawson, Shauna Darling Robertson, Hilda Offen, Coral Rumble, Neal Zetter, Roger Stevens, Dom Conlon, Ed Boxall and Brian Moses. Founded 2012.

Usborne Publishing Ltd‡

Usborne House, 83–85 Saffron Hill, London EC1N 8RT
tel 020-7430 2800
email mail@usborne.co.uk
website www.usborne.com
Directors Peter Usborne, Jenny Tyler (editorial), Andrea Parsons, Nicola Usborne

An independent, family business which creates engaging, innovative books for curious children of all ages. Including baby, preschool, novelty, activity, non-fiction and fiction. Looking for high-quality imaginative children's fiction. No unsolicited MSS. Founded 1973.

Wacky Bee Books*

Shakespeare House, 168 Lavender Hill, London SW11 5TG
tel 020-7801 6300
email hello@wackybeebooks.com
website www.wackybeebooks.com
Facebook www.facebook.com/wackybeebooks
Twitter @wackybeebooks
Director Louise Jordan

Publishing books with a buzz for children 3–12 years. Picture books for 3+, early readers for 5–7, general fiction for 8–12 years. Submission enquiries by email to submissions@wackybeebooks.com. Founded 2014.

Walker Books Ltd*‡

87 Vauxhall Walk, London SE11 5HJ
tel 020-7793 0909
website www.walker.co.uk
Facebook www.facebook.com/walkerbooks
Twitter @walkerbooksuk
Directors Karen Lotz, Ian Mablin (non-executive), Roger Alexander (non-executive), Angela Van Den Belt, Jane Winterbotham, Alan Lee, Mike McGrath, John Mendelson, Hilary Berkman

An independent company with a global reach, publishing activity books, novelty books, picture books, fiction for 5–8 and 9–12 years, young adult fiction, series fiction, film/TV tie-ins, plays, poetry, digital and audio. Publishes approx. 300 titles each year and has 2,000 in print. Continuing successes include the *Alex Rider* series by Anthony Horowitz, *Chaos Walking* by Patrick Ness, *Maisy* by Lucy Cousins, *Where's Wally?* by Martin Handford, the *Mortal Instruments* series by Cassandra Clare and a wide range of award-winning novels and picture books by other authors and illustrators. Imprint: Walker Books, Walker Studio and Walker Entertainment. Write to the editor, enclosing return postage, and allow six months for response. Founded 1980.

Welbeck Publishing Group

20 Mortimer Street, London W1T 3JW
tel 020-7612 0400
email enquiries@welbeckpublishing.com
website www.welbeckpublishing.com

No unsolicited MSS; synopses and ideas welcome, but no fiction or poetry. Founded 1992.

Mortimer

Children's entertainment, licensing and gaming.

Welbeck Flame

Associate Publisher *Felicity Alexander*
Children's fiction.

Wide Eyed Editions

The Old Brewery, 6 Blundell Street, London N7 9BH
tel 020-7700 6700
website www.quartoknows.com/Wide-Eyed-Editions

Imprint of the Quarto Group, Inc. (page 26). Creates original non-fiction for children and families and believes that books should encourage curiosity about the world, inspiring readers to set out on their own journey of discovery. Founded 2014.

Y Lolfa Cyf

Talybont, Ceredigion SY24 5HE
tel (01970) 832304
email ylolfa@ylolfa.com
website www.ylolfa.com
Director Garmon Gruffudd, *Editor* Lefi Gruffudd

Welsh language books and English books of Welsh and Celtic interest, popular biographies and sports books. Founded 1967.

ZigZag Education

Unit 3, Greenway Business Centre, Doncaster Road, Bristol BS10 5PY
tel 0117 950 3199
email submissions@publishmenow.co.uk
website www.zigzageducation.co.uk,
www.publishmenow.co.uk
Development Director John-Lloyd Hagger, *Strategy Director* Mike Stephens

Secondary school teaching resources: English, maths, ICT, geography, history, science, business, politics, P.E., media studies. Founded 1998.

ZooBooKoo International Ltd

4 Gurdon Road, Grundisburgh, Woodbridge, Suffolk IP13 6XA
tel (01473) 735346
email karen@zoobookoo.com
website www.zoobookoo.com

Designer/manufacturer of ZooBooKoo Original Cube Books, multi-level educational folding cube books. Recent successes include *World Football, Human Body, Kings and Queens, French Phrases* and *United Kingdom*.

ZunTold

email elainebous@gmail.com
website https://zuntold.com/
Facebook www.facebook.com/zuntoldbooks
Twitter @zuntold
Instagram @zuntold_books
Director Elaine Bousfield

Publishes new fiction for children and young people and young adults. Also supports young people in their own writing. Interested in middle grade fiction (9–12), teens, young adults and crossover fiction. Agent submissions please send a copy of synopsis and the first three chapters. Submissions opened for authors without an agent in June (for young adult, new adult, cross over fiction) and in December for middle grade. Please note, we do not work with picture books. Founded 2016. Publishing from 2018.

Children's book publishers overseas

Listings are given for children's book publishers in Australia (below), Canada (page 32), France (page 35), Germany (page 35), Italy (page 36), the Netherlands (page 36), New Zealand (page 37), South Africa (page 37), Spain (page 39) and the USA (page 39).

AUSTRALIA

*Member of the Australian Publishers Association

ACER Press*
19 Prospect Hill Road, Private Bag 55, Camberwell, VIC 3124
tel +61 (0)3 9277 5555
email proposals@acer.org
website www.acer.org/au

Publisher of the Australian Council for Educational Research. Produces a range of books and assessments including professional resources for teachers, psychologists and special needs professionals. Founded 1930.

Allen & Unwin Pty Ltd*
83 Alexander Street, Crows Nest, NSW 2065
Postal address PO Box 8500, St Leonards, NSW 1590
tel +61 (0)2 8425 0100
website www.allenandunwin.com
Chairman Patrick Gallagher, *Ceo* Robert Gorman, *Publishing Director* Tom Gilliatt, *Publishing Director* Lou Johnson (Murdoch Books), *Publishing Director* Eva Mills (books for children and young adult)

Fiction for children 5–9 and 10–13 years, teenage fiction, series fiction and narrative non-fiction. Also adult/general trade books, including fiction and broad-ranging non-fiction. Imprints include: Allen & Unwin, Albert Street Books, Inspired Living, Crows Nest, House of Books, Murdoch Books. Submission guidelines: will consider unsolicited MSS (but not picture book texts). Will only accept MSS through their electronic Friday Pitch system. Founded 1990.

Bloomsbury Publishing Pty Ltd*
Level 6, 387 George Street, Sydney, NSW 2000
tel +61 (0)2 8820 4900
email au@bloomsbury.com
website www.bloomsbury.com/au
Facebook www.facebook.com/bloomsburypublishingaustralia
Twitter @BloomsburySyd
Managing Director Liz Bray

Supports the worldwide publishing activities of Bloomsbury Publishing: caters for the Australia and New Zealand territories. Bloomsbury Publishing Plc founded 1986.

Cengage Learning Australia*
Level 7, 80 Dorcas Street, South Melbourne, VIC 3205

tel +61 (0)3 9685 4111
website www.cengage.com.au
Ceo Michael Hansen

Educational books. Founded 2007.

Hachette Australia Pty Ltd*
Level 17, 207 Kent Street, Sydney, NSW 2000
tel +61 (0)2 8248 0800
email auspub@hachette.com.au
website www.hachette.com.au
Ceo Louise Sherwin-Stark

General, children's: picture books, fiction for children 5–8 and 9–12 years, teenage fiction and series fiction. Accepts MSS via website. Founded 1971.

HarperCollins Publishers (Australia) Pty Ltd Group*
Postal address PO Box A565, Sydney South, NSW 1235
tel +61 (0)2 9952 5000
website www.harpercollins.com.au

Literary fiction and non-fiction, popular fiction, children's, reference, biography, autobiography, current affairs, sport, lifestyle, health/self-help, humour, true crime, travel, Australiana, history, business, gift, religion. Founded 1989.

Little Hare Books*
(imprint of Hardie Grant Egmont)
Ground Floor, Building 1, 658 Church Street, Richmond, VIC 3121
tel +61 (0)3 8520 6444
email info@hardiegrantegmont.com.au
website www.hardiegrant.com.au/egmont/our-books/little-hare

Publishes high-quality children's books in Australia and New Zealand. Check website for details of when submissions are accepted. Founded 2010.

McGraw-Hill Australia Pty Ltd*
Level 2, 82 Waterloo Road, North Ryde, NSW 2113
Postal address Private Bag 2233, Business Centre, North Ryde, NSW 1670
tel +61 (0)2 9900 1800
email cservice_sydney@mcgraw-hill.com
website www.mcgraw-hill.com.au

Educational publisher: higher education, primary education and professional (including medical, general and reference). Division of the McGraw-Hill Companies. Founded 1964.

32 Books

New Frontier Publishing*

48 Ross Street, Glebe, NSW 2037
tel +61 (0)2 9660 4614
email info@newfrontier.com.au
website www.newfrontier.com.au
Director Sophia Whitfield

Aims to uplift, educate and inspire through its range of children's books. Activity books, board books, picture books, middle-grade fiction, dictionaries, textbooks. Caters for children 2–12 years. Unsolicited MSS accepted. Understanding of existing list crucial. Downloadable submissions pack available via website. Founded 2002.

Pan Macmillan Australia Pty Ltd*

Level 25, 1 Market Street, Sydney, NSW 2000
tel +61 (0)2 9285 9100
email pan.reception@macmillan.com.au
website www.panmacmillan.com.au
Directors Cate Paterson (publishing), Katie Crawford (sales), Tracey Cheetham (publicity & marketing)

Commercial and literary fiction; children's fiction, non-fiction and character products; general non-fiction; sport. Founded 1843.

Penguin Random House Australia Pty Ltd*

Sydney office Level 3, 100 Pacific Highway, North Sydney, NSW 2060
tel +61 (0)2 9954 9966
email information@penguinrandomhouse.com.au
Melbourne office 707 Collins Street, Melbourne, VIC 3008
website www.penguinrandomhouse.com.au
Ceo Julie Burland, *Publishing Director* Justin Ratcliffe, *Group Publishing Director* Nikki Christer, *Publishing Director, Penguin Young Readers* Laura Harris, *Publicity Director* Karen Reid

General fiction and non-fiction; children's, illustrated. MS submissions for non-fiction accepted, unbound in hard copy addressed to Submissions Editor. Fiction submissions are only accepted from previously published authors, or authors represented by an agent or accompanied by a report from an accredited assessment service. Imprints: Arrow, Bantam, Ebury, Hamish Hamilton, Knopf, Michael Joseph, Penguin, Viking, Vintage and William Heinemann. Subsidiary of Bertelsmann AG. Founded 2013.

University of Queensland Press*

PO Box 6042, St Lucia, QLD 4067
tel +61 (0)7 3365 7244
email reception@uqp.com.au
website www.uqp.com.au

Founded 1948.

R.I.C. Publications Pty Ltd

5 Bendsten Place, Balcatta, WA 6021
tel +61 (0)8 9240 9888
website www.ricpublications.com.au

Educational publisher specialising in blackline master or copymasters and student workbooks for schools and homeschoolers. Founded 1986.

Rhiza Edge

PO Box 302, Chinchilla, QLD 4413
tel +61 (0)7 3245 1938
email editor@rhizaedge.com.au
website www.rhizaedge.com.au
Facebook www.facebook.com/rhizaedge
Commissioning Editor Emily Lighezzolo

Aims to publish relatable, issue-based stories for today's young adult readers, ranging from books with a light, humorous touch through to deeper, more challenging tales. Imprint of Wombat Books (below). Founded 2018.

Scholastic Australia Pty Ltd*

76–80 Railway Crescent, Lisarow, Gosford, NSW 2250
tel +61 (0)2 4328 3555
website www.scholastic.com.au
Chairman David Peagram

Children's fiction and non-fiction. Founded 1968.

Wombat Books*

PO Box 302, Chinchilla, QLD 4413
tel +61 (0)7 3245 1938
email wombat@wombatbooks.com.au
website www.wombatbooks.com.au
Facebook www.facebook.com/wombatbooks
Publisher Rochelle Manners, *Editor & Publicity Coordinator* Emily Lighezzolo

An independent publisher of children's picture books and books for early readers. Always on the lookout for the next story to be shared. Young adult and adult imprint: Rhiza Edge (above). Founded 2009.

CANADA

*Member of the Canadian Publishers' Council
†Member of the Association of Canadian Publishers

Annick Press Ltd†

388 Carlaw Avenue, Suite 200 Toronto, ON M4M 2T4
tel +1 416-221-4802
email annickpress@annickpress.com
website www.annickpress.com
Owner/Director Rick Wilks, *Office Manager* Asiya Awale

Preschool to young adult fiction and non-fiction. Approximately 25% of books are by first-time authors. Founded 1975.

Dundurn Press†

1382 Queen St E, Toronto, ON M4L 1C9
tel +1 416-214-5544

email submissions@dundurn.com
Publisher Kirk Howard

Young adult fiction. Founded 1972.

Fitzhenry & Whiteside Ltd

195 Allstate Parkway, Markham, ON L3R 4T8
tel +1 800-387-9776
email bookinfo@fitzhenry.ca
website www.fitzhenry.ca
Ceo Sharon Fitzhenry

Fiction and non-fiction (social studies, visual arts, biography, environment). Publishes ten picture books, five early readers/chapter books, six middle novels and seven young adult books each year. Approximately 10% of books are by first-time authors. Emphasis is on Canadian authors and illustrators, subject or perspective. Will review MS/illustration packages from artists. Submit outline and copy of sample illustration. For illustrations only, send samples and promotional sheet. Responds in three months. Samples returned with sase. Founded 1966.

HarperCollins Publishers Ltd*

22 Adelaide Street West, 41st Floor, Toronto, ON M5H 4E3
tel +1 416-975-9334
email hcOrder@harpercollins.com
website www.harpercollins.ca
President & Publisher Jonathan Burnham

Literary fiction and non-fiction, history, politics, biography, spiritual and children's books. Founded 1989.

Kids Can Press Ltd†

25 Dockside Drive, Toronto, ON M5A 0B5
tel +1 416-479-7000
email customerservice@kidscan.com
website www.kidscanpress.com
Editorial Director Yvette Ghione

Middle grade/young adult fiction and non-fiction. Publishes 16–22 picture books, 8–12 young readers, 10–18 middle readers and 2–3 young adult titles each year. Recent successes include *Virginia Wolf* by Kyo Maclear and Isabelle Arsenault, Melanie Watt's award-winning *Scaredy Squirrel* series, *If the World Were a Village* by David J. Smith – part of the CitizenKid series – and the *Binky the Space Cat* books. Publishers of *Franklin the Turtle* and *Elliot Moose* characters. Approximately 10–15% of books are by first-time authors. Submit outline/synopsis and between two and three sample chapters. For picture books, submit complete MS. Responds in six months. Only accepts MSS from Canadian authors. Fiction length: picture books – 1,000–2,000 words; young readers – 750–1,500 words; middle readers – 10,000–15,000 words; young adult – over 15,000 words. Non-fiction length: picture books – 500–1,250 words; young readers – 750–2,000 words; middle readers – 5,000–15,000 words. Founded 1973.

McGraw-Hill Ryerson Ltd*

145 Kings Street West, Suite 1501, Toronto ON M5H 1J8
tel +1 800-565-5758
website www.mheducation.ca

Educational and trade books. Founded 1972.

Nelson Education*

1120 Birchmount Road, Toronto, ON M1K 5G4
tel +1 416-752-9448
website www.nelson.com
President & Ceo Steve Brown

Educational publishing: school (K–12), college and university, career education, measurement and guidance, professional and reference, ESL titles. Division of Thomson Canada Ltd. Founded 1914.

Oberon Press

145 Spruce Street, Ottawa, ON K1R 6P1
tel +1 613-238-3275
email oberon@sympatico.ca
website www.oberonpress.ca

General fiction, short stories, poetry, some biographies, art and children's. Only publishes Canadian writers. Founded 1985.

Orca Book Publishers†

1016 Balmoral Road Victoria, BC V8T 1A8
tel +1 800-210-5277
email orca@orcabook.com
website www.orcabook.com

Books for children and young adults. Will consider MSS from Canadian writers only. No submissions by fax or email. See website for submission guidelines. No poetry. Founded 1984.

Pearson Canada*

26 Prince Andrew Place, North York, ON M3C 2T8
tel +1 800-361-6128
website www.pearson.com/ca/en.html
Ceo Dan Lee

Academic, technical, educational, children's and adult, trade. Founded 1998.

Penguin Random House Canada Ltd*

320 Front Street West, Suite 1400, Toronto, ON M5V 3B6
tel +1 416-364-4449
website www.penguinrandomhouse.ca
Ceo Kristin Cochrane

Literary fiction, commercial fiction, memoir, non-fiction (history, business, current events, sports), adult, teen and young readers. No unsolicited MSS; submissions via an agent only. Imprints: Allen Lane Canada, Anchor Canada, Appetite by Random House, Bond Street Books, Doubleday Canada, Emblem, Hamish Hamilton Canada, Knopf Canada, McClelland & Stewart, Penguin Canada, Penguin

Teen, Portfolio Canada, Puffin Canada, Random House Canada, Seal Books, Signal, Strange Light, Tundra Books, Viking Canada, Vintage Canada. Subsidiary of Penguin Random House. Founded 2013.

Pippin Publishing Corporation

PO Box 242, Don Mills, ON M3C 2S2
tel +1 416-510-2918
email arayner@utphighereducation.com
website www.utppublishing.com

ESL/EFL, teacher reference, adult basic education, school texts (all subjects), general trade (non-fiction) – acquired by University of Toronto Press in 2014 (see below). Founded 1995.

Red Deer Press

195 Allstate Parkway, Markham, ON L3R 4T8
tel +1 800-387-9776
email rdp@reddeerpress.com
website www.reddeerpress.com
Publisher Richard Dionne, *Children's Editor* Peter Carver

Literary fiction, science fiction, non-fiction, children's illustrated books, young adult fiction, teen fiction. Publishes books that are written or illustrated by Canadians and that are about or of interest to Canadians. Imprint: RJS (Robert J. Sawyer) Books (science fiction). Publishes 14–18 new books a year. Children's picture books MSS from established authors with a demonstrable record of publishing success are preferred. Currently accepting new MSS. Founded 1975.

Ronsdale Press†

3350 West 21st Avenue, Vancouver, BC V6S 1G7
tel +1 604-738-4688
email ronsdale@shaw.ca
website www.ronsdalepress.com
Facebook www.facebook.com/ronsdalepress
Twitter @ronsdalepress
Director Ronald B. Hatch

Ronsdale is a Canadian publisher based in Vancouver with some 290 books in print. Not currently accepting picture books. Founded 1988.

Scholastic Canada Ltd*

175 Hillmount Road, Markham, ON L6C 1Z7
tel +1 800-268-3860
email custserv@scholastic.ca
website www.scholastic.ca
Facebook www.facebook.com/ScholasticCanada
Twitter @scholasticCDA
Instagram @scholasticcda
Art Director Andrea Casault

Serves children, parents and teachers through a variety of businesses including Scholastic Reading Club and Book Fairs, Scholastic Education, Classroom Magazines, Trade and Éditions Scholastic.

Publishes recreational reading for children and young people from preschoolers to teens and educational materials for kindergarten to Grade 8 in both official languages. Its publishing focus is on books by Canadians. Wholly owned subsidiary of Scholastic Inc. Scholastic Canada is currently interested in reviewing unpublished material by writers from underrepresented communities, including Black writers, Indigenous writers, writers of colour, writers with disabilities, LGBTQIA2S+ writers and writers who identify with other marginalized groups. Canadian artists may submit electronic samples of their work along with their website/contact information to the art director. Never send originals. Please see website for submission guidelines. Founded 1920.

University of Toronto Press

800 Bay Street, Mezzanine, Toronto, ON M5S 3A9
tel +1 416-978-2239
email publishing@utpress.utoronto.ca
website www.utorontopress.com
Vice President, Book Publishing Lynn Fisher, *Editor* Natalie Fingerhut

Imprints include: Aevo UTP; New Jewish Press; Rotman-UTP Publishing. Publishers of non-fiction, monographs, textbooks and academic books, ESL/EFL, teacher reference, adult basic education and school texts. Founded 1901.

Tundra Books

320 Front Street West, Suite 1400, Toronto, ON M5V 3B6
tel +1 416-364-4449
email submissions@tundrabooks.com
email art@tundrabooks.com
website www.penguinrandomhouse.ca/imprints/TU/tundra-books
Facebook www.facebook.com/tundrabooks
Twitter @TundraBooks
Publisher Tara Walker

Publisher of high-quality children's picture books and novels, renowned for its innovations. Publishes books for children to teens. Imprints: Penguin Teen Canada, Puffin Canada, Tundra Books. A division of Penguin Random House Canada Ltd. Founded 1967.

Whitecap Books Ltd†

209–314 West Cordova Street, Vancouver, BC V6B 1E8
tel +1 800-387-9776
website www.whitecap.ca
Facebook www.facebook.com/whitecapbooks
Twitter @whitecapbooks
Ceo Sharon Fitzhenry

Diverse list features books on food, wine, gardening, health and well-being, regional history and regional guidebooks. Market expanded into the United States through Midpoint Books. Submissions must be sent by mail. Full details can be found on website. Founded 1977.

FRANCE

l'école des loisirs

11 rue de Sevres, 75006 Paris
tel +33 (0)1 4222 9410
email edl@ecoledesloisirs.fr
website www.ecoledesloisirs.fr
Managing Director Louis Delas

Specialises in children's literature from picture books to young adult fiction. Founded 1965.

Flammarion

87 quai Panhard et Levassor, 75647 Paris
tel +33 (0)1 4051 3100
website https://editions.flammarion.com
Ceo Gilles Haéri

Leading French publisher. Children's imprints include: Albums du Père Castor, Castor Poche, Tribal, Etonnants Classiques, GF – Flammarion, Chan – OK. Founded 1875.

Père Castor

Children's Publisher Céline Dehaine

Children's picture books, junior fiction, activity books, board books, how-to books, comics, gift books, fairy tales, dictionaries and records and tapes. Covers 0–16 years.

Gallimard Jeunesse

5 rue Gaston Gallimard, 75328 Paris
tel +33 (0)1 4954 4200
website www.gallimard-jeunesse.fr
Children's Publisher Hedwige Pasquet

Publisher of high-quality children's fiction and non-fiction including board books, novelty books, picture books, pop-up books. Founded 1911.

Hachette Livre/Gautier-Languereau

53 rue Jean Bleuzen, 92170 Vanves
tel +33 (0)1 4392 3030
website www.gautier-languereau.fr
Director Sarah Koegler, *Editor Director* Brigitte Leblanc

One shots picture books for children. Imaginative stories for children aged from 2 to 10 years. Illustrated books, pop ups, laser dye-cut books, books with CD. Major illustrators: Antoine Guilloppé, Hélène Druvert, Rébecca Dautremer, Philippe Jalbert, Amanda Minazio, Aurelia Fronty. Publishes approximately 55 titles each year. Will consider unsolicited MSS. Allow four months for response. Contacts on website. Founded 1885.

Kaléidoscope

11 rue de Sèvres, 75006 Paris
tel +33 (0)1 4544 0708
website www.editions-kaleidoscope.com
Children's Publisher Isabel Finkenstaedt

Specialises in up-market picture books for children 0–6 years. Founded 1989.

Editions Sarbacane

35 rue d'Hauteville, 75010 Paris
tel +33 (0)1 4246 3727
email e.beulque@sarbacane.net
website www.editions-sarbacane.com

High-quality activity books, board books, picture books and young adult fiction, fiction for children from preschool age to adult.

Le Sorbier

25 boulevard Romain Rolland, 75014 Paris
tel +33 (0)1 4148 8000
website www.editionsdelamartiniere.fr

High-quality picture books for children up to 10 years and illustrated reference books for 9–12 years. Imprint: De La Martinière Jeunesse.

GERMANY

Carlsen Verlag

Postfach 50 03 80, 22703 Hamburg
tel +49 (0)40 398040
email info@carlsen.de
website www.carlsen.de
Directors Renate Herre, Joachim Kaufmann

Children's picture books, board books and novelty books. Illustrated fiction and non-fiction. Teenage fiction and non-fiction. Publishes both German and international authors including Stephenie Meyer, J.K. Rowling and Philip Pullman. Publisher of the *Harry Potter* series. Imprint: Chicken House Deutschland. Age groups: preschool, 5–10, 10–15, 15+. Unsolicited MSS welcome but must include a sae for return. Do not follow up by phone or post. For illustrations, submit no more than three colour photocopies and unlimited b&w copies. Founded 1953.

dtv Verlagsgesellschaft mbH & Co. KG

Tumblingerstraße 21, 80337 Munich
tel +49 (0)89 38167282
email verlag@dtv.de
website www.dtvjunior.de
Facebook www.facebook.com/dtvVerlag
Twitter @dtv_verlag
Children's Publishing Director Susanne Stark

Fiction and non-fiction for children, teenagers and young adults. Authors include Kate DiCamillo, Kevin Brooks, Colleen Hoover, Sarah J. Maas, Libba Bray, Eva Ibbotson, Sarah Dessen. Founded 1971.

Bold

Young general fiction. Authors include: Hank Green, Atticus, K.A. Tucker. Founded 2018.

Books

Carl Hanser Verlag

Vilshofener Straße 10, 81679 Munich
tel +49 (0)89 998300
email info@hanser.de
website www.hanser-literaturverlage.de
Facebook www.facebook.com/HanserLiteraturverlage
Twitter @hanserliteratur
Instagram @hanserliteratur, hanser.hey
Children's Publisher Saskia Heintz

High-quality hardback books for all ages from
preschool to young adults. Board books, picture
books, fiction and non-fiction. Age groups: 3–10,
10–15, 15+. Founded 1993.

Ravensburger Buchverlag

Robert-Bosch-Straße 1, 88214 Ravensburg
tel +49 (0)751 860
email buchverlag@ravensburger.de
website www.ravensburger.de

Activity books, novelty books, picture books, fiction
for children 5–8 and 9–12 years, teenage fiction,
series fiction and educational games and puzzles.
Publishes approx. 450 titles each year and has 1,500
in print. Will consider unsolicited MSS for fiction
only. Allow two months for response. Founded 1883.

ITALY

De Agostini Editore

Via Giovanni da Verrazano 15, 28100 Novara
tel +39 02-380861
website www.deagostini.it
Publisher Annachiara Tassan

Illustrated and children's books. Founded 1901.

Edizioni Arka srl

Via Milano 73/75, 20010 Cornaredo Milan
tel +39 02-4818230
email daisy.zonato@edizioniel.it
website www.arkaedizioni.it
Publisher Ginevra Viscardi

Picture books and some general fiction for preschool
children and children up to 10 years.

Edizioni El/Einaudi Ragazzi/Emme Edizioni

Via J. Ressel 5, 34018 San Dorligo della Valle TS
tel +39 040-3880311
email edizioniel@edizioniel.it
website www.edizioniel.com
Children's Publisher Orietta Fatucci

Activity books, board books, picture books, pop-up
books, non-fiction, novels, poetry, fairy tales, fiction.
Age groups: preschool, 5–10, 10–15, 15+.

Giunti Editore S.p.A.

Via Bolognese 165, 50139 Florence
tel +39 055-50621
email info@giunti.it
website www.giunti.it
President Sergio Giunti

Activity books, board books, novelty books, picture
books, colouring books, pop-up books and some
educational textbooks. Founded 1841.

Arnoldo Mondadori Editore S.p.A. (Mondadori)

Via Mondadori 1, 20090 Segrate, Milan
tel +39 02-75421
email stampalibri@mondadori.it
website www.mondadori.it

Activity books, board books, novelty books, picture
books, painting and colouring books, pop-up books,
how-to books, hobbies, leisure, pets, sport, comics,
poetry, fairy tales, education, fiction and non-fiction.
Age groups: preschool, 5–10, 10–15, 15+.
Founded 1907.

Adriano Salani Editore S.p.A.

Via Gherardini 10, 20145 Milan
tel +39 02-34597624
email info@salani.it
website www.salani.it
Children's Publisher Simona Scandellari

Picture books, how-to books, comics, gift books,
fiction, novels, poetry, fairy tales. Age groups:
preschool, 5–10, 10–15, 15+. Founded 1862.

THE NETHERLANDS

Lemniscaat BV

Vijverlaan 48, 3062 HL Rotterdam
tel +31 10-2062929
email info@lemniscaat.nl
website www.lemniscaat.nl
Publisher Jesse Goossens

Well-known independent children's book publishers
based in the Netherlands, publishing picture books,
juvenile novels and young adult literature.
Lemniscaat has its own list of titles in the
Netherlands, China, Italy and the USA.
Founded 1963.

Rubinstein Publishing

Prinseneiland 43, 1013 LL Amsterdam
tel +31 20-4200772
email info@rubinstein.nl
website www.rubinstein.nl
Children's Publisher Mascha de Vries

Independent publisher specialising in audiobooks for
children. Also produces novelty books.
Founded 1985.

Van Goor/Van Holkema & Warendorf

PO Box 23202, 1100 DS Amsterdam
tel +31 20-2364200

website www.de-leukste-kinderboeken.nl,
www.bestofyabooks.nl

High-quality picture books, learn-to-read books,
middle grade and (literary) fiction and non-fiction,
young adult. Founded 2009.

NEW ZEALAND

*Member of the New Zealand Book Publishers'
Association*

Cengage Learning New Zealand*
Unit 4B, Rosedale Office Park, 331 Rosedale Road,
Albany, North Shore 0632
Postal address PO Box 33376, Takapuna,
North Shore 0740
tel +64 (0)9 415 6850
Vice President, Higher Education Paul Petrulis, *Vice
President, Schools* Nicole McCarten

Educational books. Founded 2007.

Edify Ltd*
Level 1, 39 Woodside Avenue, Northcote,
Auckland 0627
tel +64 (0)9 972 9428
email mark@edify.co.nz
website www.edify.co.nz
Ceo Adrian Keane

Edify is a publishing, sales and marketing business
providing its partners with opportunities for their
products and solutions in the New Zealand
educational market. Exclusive representatives of
Pearson and the New Zealand based educational
publisher, Sunshine Books. Founded 2013.

Gecko Press*
PO Box 9335, Marion Square, Wellington 6141
tel +64 (0)4 801 9333
email office@geckopress.com
website www.geckopress.com
Publisher Julia Marshall

Children's books: picture books, junior fiction and
non-fiction. Translates and publishes award-winning
children's books from around the world. Selects
books strong in story, character, illustration and
design. See website for submission guidelines.
Founded 2005.

HarperCollins Publishers (New Zealand) Ltd*
Unit D, 63 Apollo Drive, Rosedale, Auckland 0632
tel +64 (0)9 443 9400
email publicity@harpercollins.co.nz
Postal address PO Box 1, Shortland Street, Auckland
1140
website www.harpercollins.co.nz

General literature, non-fiction, reference, children's.
HarperCollins New Zealand does not accept

proposals or MSS for consideration, except via the
Wednesday Post portal on its website. Founded 1989.

McGraw-Hill Book Company New Zealand Ltd
Level 8, 56–60 Cawley Street, Ellerslie, Auckland 1005
Postal address Private Bag 11904, Ellerslie,
Auckland 1005
tel +64 (0)9 526 6200
website www.mcgraw-hill.com.au

Educational publisher: higher education, primary and
secondary education (grades K–12) and professional
(including medical, general and reference). Division
of the McGraw-Hill Companies. Always looking for
potential authors. Has a rapidly expanding publishing
programme. See website for author's guide.
Founded 1974.

New Zealand Council for Educational Research
Box 3237, Education House, 178–182 Willis Street,
Wellington 6140
tel +64 (0)4 384 7939
email david.ellis@nzcer.org.nz
website www.nzcer.org.nz
Publishing Manager David Ellis

Education, including educational policy and practice,
early childhood education, educational achievement
tests, Māori education, schooling for the future,
curriculum and assessment. Founded 1934.

Penguin Random House New Zealand Ltd*
Private Bag 102 902, North Shore, Auckland 0745
tel +64 (0)9 442 7400
email publishing@penguinrandomhouse.co.nz
website www.penguinrandomhouse.co.nz
Facebook www.facebook.com/
PenguinBooksNewZealand
Publishing Director Debra Millar, *Head of Publishing*
Claire Murdoch

Adult and children's fiction and non-fiction.
Imprints: Penguin, Vintage, Black Swan, Godwit,
Viking, Puffin Books. Part of Penguin Random
House. Founded 2013.

SOUTH AFRICA

Member of the Publishers' Association of South Africa

Cambridge University Press, Africa*
Lower Ground Floor, Nautica Building,
The Water Club, Beach Road, Granger Bay,
Cape Town 8005
tel +27 (0)21 773 0147
email capetown@cambridge.org
website www.cambridge.org
Publishing Director Johan Traut

Textbooks and literature for sub-Sahara African countries, as well as primary reading materials in 28 African languages. Founded 1534.

Educat Publishers Pty Ltd
4 Clifford Street, Ottery, Cape Town
tel +27 (0)21 697 3669
email takeeducat@gmail.com
website www.educat.co.za

Educational products including science and maths, product designs for schools and retail, as well as mass markets. Age groups: preschool, 5–10, 10–15, 15+.

Human & Rousseau
12th Floor, Naspers, 40 Heerengracht,
Roggebaai 8012
tel +27 (0)21 406 3033
email nb@nb.co.za
website www.humanrousseau.com

General Afrikaans and English titles. Quality Afrikaans literature, popular literature, general children's and youth literature, cookery, self-help. Founded 1959.

Best Books
Education.

Macmillan Education South Africa
4th Floor, Building G, Hertford Office Park,
90 Bekker Road, Vorna Valley, Midrand 1685
tel +27 (0)11 731 3300
Postal address Private Bag X19, Northlands 2116
website www.macmillan.co.za
Managing Director Preggy Naidoo

Educational titles for the RSA market. Founded 1843.

NB Publishers (Pty) Ltd*
PO Box 879, Cape Town 8000
tel +27 (0)21 406 3033
email nb@nb.co.za
website www.nb.co.za

General: Afrikaans fiction, politics, children's and youth literature in all the country's languages, non-fiction. Imprints: Tafelberg, Human & Rousseau, Queillerie, Pharos, Kwela, Best Books and Lux Verbi. Founded 1950.

New Africa Books (Pty) Ltd
Unit 13A, Athlone Industrial Park,
10 Mymoena Crescent, Cape Town 7764
tel +27 (0)21 467 5860
email info@newafricabooks.co.za
Postal address PostNet, Suite 144, Private Bag X9190, Cape Town 8000

New Africa Books, incorporating David Philip Publishers, is an independent publishing house. Currently publishes fiction and non-fiction for adults, picture books for children and comics for young adults in all South African languages. Founded 1971.

Oxford University Press Southern Africa*
Vasco Boulevard, N1 City, Goodwood,
Cape Town 7460
tel +27 (0)21 596 2300
email oxford.za@oup.com
Postal address PO Box 12119, N1 City,
Cape Town 7463
website www.oxford.co.za
Managing Director Hanri Pieterse

Oxford University Press is one of the leading educational publishers in South Africa, producing a wide range of quality educational material in print and digital format. The range includes books from Grade R to Grade 12, as well as TVET textbooks, textbooks, school literature, dictionaries and atlases. Committed to transforming lives through education by providing superior quality learning material and support. Founded 1586.

Pearson South Africa*
4th Floor, Auto Atlantic Building,
Corner Hertzog Boulevard and Heerengracht Boulevard, Cape Town 8001
Postal address PO Box 396, Cape Town 8000
tel +27 (0)21 532 6008
email pearsonza.enquiries@pearson.com
website https://za.pearson.com/

Pearson South Africa provides learning materials, technologies and services for use in schools, TVET colleges, higher education institutions and in home and professional environments. Founded 2010.

Shuter and Shooter Publishers (Pty) Ltd*
110 CB Downes Road, Pietermaritzburg,
KwaZulu-Natal 3201
tel +27 (0)33 846 8700
email sales@shuters.com
Postal address PO Box 61, Mkondeni, KwaZulu-Natal 3212
website www.shuters.co.za
Ceo Primi Chetty

Core curriculum-based textbooks for use at foundation, intermediate, senior and FET phases. Supplementary readers in various languages; dictionaries; reading development kits, charts. Literature titles in English, isiXhosa, Sesotho, Sepedi, Setswana, Tshivenda, Xitsonga, Ndebele, isiZulu and Siswati. Founded 1925.

Via Afrika Publishers
11th Floor, 40 Heerengracht, Cape Town 8001
Postal address PO Box 5197, Cape Town 8001
tel +27 (0)21 406 3528
email customerservices@viaafrika.com
website www.viaafrika.com
Ceo Christina Watson

Educational materials for South African schools and FET colleges, for all learning areas and subjects at all grades/levels: in all official languages of South Africa. Imprints: Acacia, Action, Afritech, Afro, Atlas, Bateleur Books, Collegium, Idem, Juta/Gariep, KZN Books, Nasou; Stimela, Van Schaik (literature), Via Afrika. Founded 1949.

SPAIN

Grupo Anaya
C/Juan Ignacio Luca de Tena 15, 28027 Madrid
tel +34 913 938 800
website www.anaya.es
Managing Director Carlos Lamadrid

Non-fiction: education textbooks for preschool–15+.

Editorial Cruilla
C/Roger de Llúria 44, 4th, 08009 Barcelona
tel +34 902 123 336
email editorial@cruilla.cat
website www.cruilla.cat

Activity books, novelty books, fiction for children 5–8 and 9–12 years, teenage fiction and poetry. Publishes approx. 120–130 titles each year. Recent successes include *El Vaixell de Vapor* (series), *Vull Llegir!* and *Molly Moon Stops the World/Molly Moon's Incredible Book of Hypnotism.* Subsidiary of Ediciones SM. Founded 1984.

Destino Infantil & Juvenil
Carrer de Llull 51, 60–4A, 08005 Barcelona
email info@librosdelzorrorojo.com
website www.librosdelzorrorojo.com
Children's & Young Adult Director Marta Bueno Miró

Fiction for children 6–16 years. Picture books, pop-up books, fiction and some unusual illustrated books.

Libros del Zorro Rojo
Carrer de Llull 51, 60–4A, 08005 Barcelona
email info@librosdelzorrorojo.com
website https://novedades.librosdelzorrorojo.com/
Editorial Director Fernando Diego García

Small independent publisher specialising in children's and young adult books. Main focus is picture books for young children and classics with high-quality illustrations for young readers. Founded 2004.

Editorial Libsa
Calle de San Rafael 4, 28108 Alcobendas/Madrid
tel +34 916 572 580
email libsa@libsa.es
website www.libsa.es
President Amado Sanchez, *Children's Books Editor* Maria Dolores Maeso

Publisher and packager of highly-illustrated mass market books: activity books, board books, picture books, colouring books, how-to books, fairy tales.

Penguin Random House Grupo Editorial
Luchana 23, 1A, 28010 Madrid
tel +34 915 358 190
website www.penguinrandomhousegrupoeditorial. com

Preschool activity, novelty and picture books through to young adult fiction. Also a packager and printer. Part of Penguin Random House. Children's imprints include: Beascoa, Nube de Tinta, Montena. Founded 2013.

Beascoa
Character publishing, including Disney and Fisher-Price.

Nube de Tinta
Provides novels to a broad range of readers from young adult to adult who share a love of reading.

Montena
Contemporary literary fiction including fantasy.

Vicens Vives SA
Avenida Sarriá 130–132, 08017 Barcelona
tel +34 932 523 700
email rrhh@vicensvives.es
website www.vicensvives.com

Activity and novelty books, fiction, art, encyclopedias, dictionaries, education, geography, history, music, science, textbooks, posters. Age groups: preschool, 5–10, 10–15, 15+.

USA

Member of the Association of American Publishers Inc.

Abingdon Press
2222 Rosa L. Parks Boulevard, Nashville, TN 37228
tel +1 800-251-3320
website www.abingdonpress.com
Facebook www.facebook.com/AbingdonPress
Twitter @AbingdonPress
President & Publisher Neil Alexander

General interest, professional, academic and reference, non-fiction and fiction, youth and children's non-fiction and Vatican Bible School; primarily directed to the religious market. Imprint of United Methodist Publishing House with tradition of crossing denominational boundaries. United Methodist Publishing founded 1789.

Harry N. Abrams, Inc.
195 Broadway, 9th Floor, New York, NY 10007
tel +1 212-206-7715
email abrams@abramsbooks.com
website www.abramsbooks.com

Art and architecture, photography, natural sciences, performing arts, children's books. Imprints include: Abrams, Abrams Appleseed, Abrams Books for

Books

Young Readers, Abrams ComicArts, Abrams Images, Abrams Noterie, Abrams Press, Amulet Books, Amulet Paperbacks, The Overlook Press, Cameron Books. Founded 1949.

Abrams Books for Young Readers
tel +1 212-519-1200
website www.abramsyoungreaders.com
Fiction and non-fiction: picture books, young readers, middle readers, young adult. For picture books submit covering letter and complete MS, for longer works and non-fiction send query and sample chapter with sase.

Aladdin Paperbacks – see Simon & Schuster
Children's Publishing Division

All About Kids Publishing
PO Box 159, Gilroy, CA 95021
tel +1 408-337-1152
email lguevara@allaboutkidspub.com
website www.allaboutkidspub.com
Publisher Mike G. Guevara, *Editor* Linda L. Guevara

Fiction and non-fiction picture books and chapter books. Recent successes include *Don't Let the Dead Bugs Bite!* by Stephen Zmina (picture book) and *Cold Waves, Cold Blood* by Patrick Doherty (teen novel). See website for submission guidelines. Founded 2000.

Atheneum Books for Young
Readers – see Simon & Schuster Children's Publishing Division

Avon – see HarperCollins Publishers

Barefoot Books
23 Bradford Street, Concord, MA 01742
tel +1 617-576-0660
email publicity@barefootbooks.com
website www.barefootbooks.com
Facebook www.facebook.com/barefootbooks
Twitter @BarefootBooks
Editorial Director Emma Parkin

Currently not accepting MS submissions or queries. Accepts illustrator samples via mail only. Please mail samples (no original artwork) for the attention of the editor. Recent successes include *Mindful Kids* by Whitney Stewart, illustrated by Mina Braun; and *The Barefoot Book of Children* by Kate DePalma and Tessa Strickland, illustrated by David Dean (3–7 years, picture book). Length: 500–1,000 words (picture books), 2,000–3,000 words (young readers). US branch founded 1998.

Bick Publishing House
75 Mungertown Road, Madison, CT 06443
tel +1 203-605-0341
email bickpubhse@aol.com
website https://bickpubhouse.com/

Adults: health and recovery, living with disabilities, wildlife rehabilitation. Non-fiction for young adults: philosophy, psychology, self-help, social issues, science. Founded 1993.

Bloomsbury Publishing USA*
1385 Broadway, New York, NY 10018
tel +1 212-419-5300
email Contact-USA@bloomsbury.com
website www.bloomsbury.com/us
Executive Director Adrienne Vaughan

Supports the worldwide publishing activities of Bloomsbury Publishing Plc: caters for the US market. For submission guidelines see: www.bloomsbury.com/us/authors/submissions/. Established in 1998 as an American subsidiary of Bloomsbury Publishing Plc. Founded 1986.

The Blue Sky Press – see Scholastic, Inc.

Boyds Mills & Kane
19 West 21st Street, #1201, New York NY10010
email info@bmkbooks.com
website www.boydsmillsandkane.com
Facebook www.facebook.com/BMKbooks
Twitter @kanepress

Activity books, picture books, fiction, non-fiction and poetry for 18 years and under. Publishes 80 titles each year. Will consider both unsolicited MSS and queries. Send to above address and label package 'Manuscript Submission'. Looking for middle grade fiction with fresh ideas and subject matter, and young adult novels of real literary merit. Non-fiction should be fun and entertaining as well as informative, and non-fiction MSS should be accompanied by a detailed bibliography. Interested in imaginative picture books and welcomes submissions from both writers and illustrators. Submit samples as b&w and/or colour copies or transparencies; submissions will not be returned. Include sase with all submissions. Send art samples to above address and label package 'Art Sample Submission'. Founded 1991.

Boyds Mills Press
Publishes a wide range of high-quality fiction and non-fiction titles for young readers.

Calkins Creek Books
US history and historical fiction.

Kane Press
Publisher of illustrated titles for children ages 3 to 11.

Wordsong
Poetry.

Calkins Creek Books – see Boyds Mills & Kane

Candlewick Press
99 Dover Street, Somerville, MA 02144
tel +1 617-661-3330

email bigbear@candlewick.com
website www.candlewick.com
President & Publisher Karen Lotz, Creative Director & Associate Publisher Chris Paul, Executive Editorial Director & Associate Publisher Liz Bicknell, Editorial Director & Director of Editorial Operations Mary Lee Donovan

Books for babies through teens: board books, picture books, early readers, first chapter books, novels, non-fiction, novelty books, poetry, graphic novels. Publishes 70 picture books, 40 middle readers and 30 young adult titles each year. Founded 1991.

Candlewick Entertainment
Group Editorial Director Joan Powers
Media-related children's books, including film/TV tie-ins.

Charlesbridge Publishing
9 Galen Street, Watertown, MA 02472
tel +1 617-926-0329
email development@charlesbridge.com
website www.charlesbridge.com

Fiction and non-fiction board books, picture books and middle grade books for preschool–14 years. Young adult novels for readers 14+. Dedicated to diversity and new voices across genres. Non-fiction list specialises in nature, concept, history and science. Publishes roughly 60% non-fiction, 40% fiction. Send full MSS; no queries. Responds to MSS of interest. For illustrations, send query with samples, tearsheets and résumé. Founded 1980.

Chicago Review Press
814 North Franklin Street, Chicago, IL 60610
tel +1 312-337-0747
email frontdesk@jpg.com
website www.chicagoreviewpress.com
Publisher Cynthia Sherry

General publisher. Non-fiction activity books for children. Imprint Zephyr publishes professional development titles for teachers. Interested in hands-on educational books. See website for submission guidelines. Founded 1973.

Chronicle Books*
680 Second Street, San Francisco, CA 94107
tel +1 415-537-4200
email hello@chroniclebooks.com
website www.chroniclebooks.com,
www.chroniclebooks.com/titles/kids-teens
Facebook www.facebook.com/chroniclekidsbooks
Twitter @ChronicleKids
Instagram @chroniclekidsbooks
Chairman & Ceo Nion McEvoy, Publisher Christine Carswell

Traditional and innovative children's books. Looking for projects that have a unique bent – in subject matter, writing style or illustrative technique – that

will add a distinctive flair. Interested in fiction and non-fiction for children of all ages as well as board books, decks, activity kits and other unusual or 'novelty' formats. Publishes 60–100 books each year. Also for adults: cooking, how-to books, nature, art, biographies, fiction, gift. For picture books submit MS. For older readers, submit outline/synopsis and three sample chapters. No submitted materials will be returned. Response approx. three months. Founded 1967.

Clarion Books – see Houghton Mifflin Harcourt

Clear Light Books
823 Don Diego, Santa Fe, NM 87505
tel +1 505-989-9590
website www.clearlightbooks.com

For adults: art and photography, cookbooks, ecology/environment, health, gift books, history, Native America, Tibet, Western Americana. Non-fiction for children and young adults: multicultural, American Indian, Hispanic. Looking for authentic American Indian art and folklore. Send complete MS with sase.

David C Cook
4050 Lee Vance View, Colorado Springs, CO 80918
tel +1 719-536-0100
website www.davidccook.com
Ceo Cris Doornbos

Christian education resources for preschool to teenagers. Founded 1875.

Cooper Square Publishing
4501 Forbes Boulevard, Suite 200, Lanham, MD 20706
tel +1 301-459-3366

Part of the Rowman & Littlefield Publishing Group (page 49). Founded 1949.

Dawn Publications
12402 Bitney Springs Road, Nevada City, CA 95959
tel +1 800-545-7475
email chris@deep-books.co.uk
website www.dawnpub.com
Publishers Carol Malnor, Bruce Malnor

Dedicated to inspiring in children a deeper understanding and appreciation for all life on Earth. The aim is to help parents and teachers encourage children to bond with the Earth in a relationship of love, respect and intelligent cooperation, through the books published and the educational materials offered online. Recent successes include: Why Should I Walk? I Can FLY!, Scampers Thinks Like a Scientist, Over on a Desert: Somewhere in the World, He's Your Daddy: Ducklings, Joeys, Kits, and More, I Am the Rain, Paddle Perch Climb, Tall Tall Tree, Daytime Nighttime, Baby on Board, There's a Bug on My Book, A Moon of My Own. See website for submission guidelines. Dawn Books is an imprint of Sourcebooks eXplore, the children's non-fiction division of Sourcebooks. Founded 1979.

Dial Books – see Penguin Young Readers

Tom Doherty Associates, LLC

120 Broadway, 22nd Floor, New York, NY 10271
tel +1 212-388-0100
email enquiries@tor.com
website www.torforgeblog.com
Facebook www.facebook.com/tordotcom
Twitter @tordotcom

Fiction and non-fiction for middle readers and young adults. Publishes 5–10 middle readers and 5–10 young adult books each year. Successes include *Hidden Talents, Flip* by David Lubar (fantasy, 10+ years), *Briar Rose* by Jane Yolen (fiction, 12+ years), *Strange Unsolved Mysteries* by Phyllis Rabin Amert (non-fiction). For adults: fiction – general, historical, western, suspense, mystery, horror, science fiction, fantasy, humour, juvenile, classics (English language); non-fiction. For both fiction and non-fiction, submit outline/synopsis and complete MS. Responds to queries in one month; MSS in six months for unsolicited work. Fiction length: middle readers – 30,000 words; young adult – 60,000–100,000 words. Non-fiction length: middle readers – 25,000–35,000 words; young adult – 70,000 words. For illustrations, query with samples to Irene Gallo, Art Director. Responds only if interested. Imprints: Tor Books, Forge Books, Orb Books, Starscope, Tor Teen. Founded 1980.

Forge

Publishes general fiction, both contemporary and historical; thrillers, mysteries and suspense novels; westerns and Americana; military fiction and non-fiction.

StarScape

Award-winning science fiction and fantasy for middle grade readers ages 10 and up (grades 5 and up), published in hardback and paperback. All titles are age- and theme-appropriate. Some editions include reader's guides and other supplemental materials.

Tor

Science fiction and fantasy published in hardback and paperback.

Tor Teen

website www.torteen.com
Science fiction and fantasy for children 12+ years.

Doubleday – see Penguin Random House

Dover Publications, Inc.

31 East 2nd Street, Mineola, NY 11501
tel +1 516-294-7000
website https://store.doverpublications.com/
Facebook www.facebook.com/doverpublications
Twitter @doverpublications

Activity books, novelty books, picture books, fiction for children 5–8 and 9–12 years, teenage fiction, series fiction, reference, plays, religion, poetry, audio and CD-Roms. Also adult non-fiction. Publishes approx. 150 children's titles and has over 2,500 in print. Successes include *Easy Noah's Ark Sticker Picture, How to Draw a Funny Monster* and *Pretty Ballerina Sticker Paper Doll*. Will consider unsolicited MSS but write for guidelines. Founded 1941.

EDCON Publishing Group

30 Montauk Boulevard, Oakdale, NY 11769–1399
tel +1 631-567-7227
email info@edconpublishing.com
website www.edconpublishing.com

Supplemental instructional materials for use by education professionals to improve reading and maths skills. Includes early reading, *Classics* series, *Easy Shakespeare*, fiction and non-fiction, reading diagnosis and vocabulary books. Founded 1970.

Eerdmans Publishing Company

4035 Park East Court SE, Grand Rapids, MI 49546
tel +1 616-459-4591
website www.eerdmans.com
President & Publisher Anita Eerdmans

Independent publisher of a wide range of religious books, from academic works in theology, biblical studies, religious history and reference to popular titles in spirituality, social and cultural criticism and literature. Founded 1911.

Eerdmans Books for Young Readers

website www.eerdmans.com/Pages/YoungReaders/EBYR-About.aspx

Picture books, biographies, and middle reader fiction and non-fiction. Publishes 18–22 books a year. Seeks MSS that are honest, wise and hopeful but also publishes stories that delight with their storyline, characters or good humour. Stories that celebrate diversity, stories of historical significance and stories that relate to current issues are of special interest. Accepts unsolicited submissions. Send to Acquisitions Editor; responds in four months only to submissions of interest. For illustrations, send photocopies or printed media and include a list of previous illustrated publications. Send to Art Director. Samples will be kept on file; they will not be returned.

Encyclopaedia Britannica Inc.

325 North La Salle Street, Suite 200, Chicago, IL 60654-2682
tel +1 312-347-7159
email contact@eb.com
website www.britannica.com

Encyclopedias, reference books, almanacs, videos and CD-Roms for adults and children 5–15+ years. Founded 1999.

Enslow Publishers, Inc.

101 West 23rd Street, Suite 240, New York, NY 10011
tel +1 800-398-2504
email customerservice@enslow.com
website www.enslow.com
President Mark Enslow, *Vice President & Publisher*
Brian Enslow

Provides fiction and non-fiction content across the K-12 space. Aims to inspire readers to become lifelong learners. Founded 1976.

Evan-Moor Educational Publishers

18 Lower Ragsdale Drive, Monterey, CA 93940
tel +1 800-714-0971
email marketing@evan-moor.com
website www.evan-moor.com
Founder & Ceo William E. Evans

Educational materials for parents and teachers of children (3–12 years): activity books, textbooks, how-to books, CD-Roms. Subjects include maths, geography, history, science, reading, writing, social studies, art and craft. Publishes approx. 50 titles each year and has over 500 in print. Less than 10% of books are by first-time authors. Query or submit outline, table of contents and sample pages. Responds to queries in two months; MSS in four months. See website for submission guidelines. For illustrations, send résumé, samples and tearsheets to the Art Director. Primarily uses b&w material. Founded 1979.

Farrar Straus Giroux Books for Young Readers

175 Fifth Avenue, New York, NY 10010
website https://us.macmillan.com/publishers/farrar-straus-giroux#FYR

An imprint of Macmillan Children's Publishing Group. Books for toddlers through to young adults: picture books, fiction and non-fiction for all ages, and poetry (occasionally). Publishes 70 hardcover originals plus ten paperback reprints each year and has approx. 500 titles in print. Submission details: Approx. 10% of books are by first-time authors. No unsolicited MSS. Founded 1946.

Flux

2297 Waters Drive, Mendota Heights, MN 55120
tel +1 888-917-0145
email publicity@northstareditions.com
email submissions@northstareditions.com
website www.fluxnow.com
Facebook www.facebook.com/FluxBooks
Twitter @FluxBooks
Managing Editor Mari Kesselring

From their very first young adult novels in 2006, Flux set out to be different. Consistently provocative, independently alternative and striving to find unique voices that unsettle, surprise, inform and ignite. See website above for submission guidelines. Accepts electronic submissions only. Flux is an imprint of North Star Editions, Inc.

Flux Books (imprint)

email submissions@northstareditions.com
website www.fluxnow.com

Young adult: fiction for ages 12+ in all genres. Seeks to publish authors who see young adult as a point of view rather than a reading level. Looks for edgy, challenging books that try to capture a slice of teenage experience. Particularly interested in books that tell the stories of young adults in unexpected or surprising situations around the globe. Flux is an imprint of North Star Editions, Inc.

Free Spirit Publishing

6325 Sandburg Road, Suite 100, Golden Valley, MN 55427
tel +1 612-338-2068
email help4kids@freespirit.com
website www.freespirit.com
Facebook www.facebook.com/freespiritpublishing
Twitter @freespiritbooks
President Judy Galbraith

Award-winning publisher of non-fiction materials for children and teens, parents, educators and counsellors. Specialises in self-help materials for kids and teens which empower young people and promote positive self-esteem through improved social and emotional health. Topics include self-esteem and self-awareness, stress management, school success, creativity, friends and family, peacemaking, social action and special needs (i.e. gifted and talented, children with learning differences). Publishes approx. 18–22 new products each year, adding to a backlist of over 200 books and posters. Free Spirit authors are expert educators and mental health professionals who have been honoured nationally for their contributions on behalf of children. Founded 1983.

Fulcrum Publishing

4690 Table Mountain Drive, Suite 100, Golden, CO 80403
tel +1 303-277-1623
website www.fulcrum-books.com

Publishes a wide variety of educational non-fiction texts and children's books, also books and support materials for teachers, librarians, parents and elementary through middle school children. Subjects include: science and nature, literature and storytelling, history, multicultural studies and Native American and Hispanic cultures. Founded 1965.

Gale Cengage Learning*

27500 Drake Road, Farmington Hills, MI 48331–3535
tel +1 248-699-4253
website www.gale.com

Education publishing for libraries, schools and businesses. Serves the K–12 market with the following imprints: Blackbirch Press, Greenhaven Press, KidHaven Press, Lucent Books, Sleeping Bear Press, UXL. Founded 1954.

Greenhaven Press
353 3rd Avenue, Suite 255, New York, NY 10010
website https://greenhavenpublishing.com/

High-quality non-fiction resources for the education community. Publishes 220 young adult academic reference titles each year. Successes include the *Opposing Viewpoints* series. Approx. 35% of books are by first-time authors. No unsolicited MSS. All writing is done on a work-to-hire basis. Send query, résumé and list of published works. Founded 1970.

KidHaven Press
Non-fiction references for younger researchers.

Lucent Books
Non-fiction resources for upper-elementary to high school students. Successes include *Women in the American Revolution* and *Civil Liberties and the War on Terrorism*. No unsolicited MSS. Query with résumé.

Sleeping Bear Press
email sleepingbearpress@cengage.com
website www.sleepingbearpress.com

High-quality picture books.

Gibbs Smith
tel 801-544-9800
email info@gibbs-smith.com
website www.gibbs-smith.com

A Utah-based publisher. Its trade and special interest division publishes home reference, cookbook and children's titles. The Gibbs Smith Education division is the nation's leading publisher of state history programs. All unsolicited queries, submissions and correspondence should be via email. Due to the number of submissions received, the policy is to respond only to projects the company wishes to explore. Founded 1969.

Greenhaven Press – see Gale Cengage Learning

Gryphon House, Inc.
PO Box 10, 6848 Leon's Way, Lewisville, NC 27023
tel +1 800-636-0928
website www.gryphonhouse.com

Early childhood (0–8 years) resource books for teachers and parents. Looking for books that are developmentally appropriate for the intended age group, are well researched and based on current trends in the field, and include creative, participatory learning experiences with a common conceptual theme to tie them together. Send query and/or a proposal. Founded 1971.

Hachai Publishing
527 Empire Boulevard, Brooklyn, New York, NY 11225
tel +1 718-633-0100
email info@hachai.com
website www.hachai.com

Jewish books for children 0–8+ years. Welcomes unsolicited MSS. Specialises in books for children 2–4 years and 3–6 years. Looking for stories that convey the traditional Jewish experience in modern times or long ago, traditional Jewish observance and positive character traits. Founded 1988.

Hachette Book Group*
1290 Avenue of the Americas, New York, NY 10104
tel +1 212-364-1100
website www.hachettebookgroup.com

Divisions: Grand Central Publishing; Hachette Audio; Hachette Nashville; Little, Brown and Company; Little, Brown and Company Books for Young Readers; Orbit; Perseus Books; Yen Press. Imprints: Grand Central: Forever; Forever Yours; Goop Press; Twelve; Vision. Hachette Nashville: Center Street; FaithWords; Worthy Books. Hachette Books: Little, Brown and Company: Back Bay Books; Jimmy Patterson; Little, Brown Spark; Mulholland Books; Voracious. Little, Brown Books for Young Readers: LB Kids; Poppy. Orbit: Redhook. Perseus Books: Avalon Travel; Basic Books; Black Dog & Leventhal; Bold Type Books; Hachette Books; Hachette Go; Moon Travel; Rick Steves Running Press; PublicAffairs; Seal Press. Founded 1996.

Handprint Books
413 Sixth Avenue, Brooklyn, New York, NY 11215–3310
tel +1 718-768-3696
email info@handprintbooks.com
website www.handprintbooks.com
Publisher Christopher Franceschelli

A range of children's books: picture and story books through to young adult fiction. Imprints: Handprint Books, Ragged Bears, Blue Apple. Welcomes submissions of MSS of quality for works ranging from board books to young adult novels. For novels, first query interest on the subject and submit a 7,500-word max. sample. Accepts MSS on an e-submission basis only, sent as attachments in a word processing format readily readable on a PC. Artwork should be sent as small jpgs; artists' website addresses may also be submitted. No series fiction, licensed character (or characters whose primary avatar is meant to be as licences), 'I-Can-Read'-type books, or titles intended primarily for mass merchandise outlets. Founded 2000.

HarperCollins Publishers*
195 Broadway, New York, NY 10007
tel +1 212-207-700

website https://corporate.harpercollins.com/us
President & Ceo Brian Murray

Adult fiction (commercial and literary) and non-fiction. Subjects include biography, business, cookbooks, educational, history, juvenile, poetry, religious, science, technical and travel. Imprints: Avon, Avon Inspire, Avon Red (mass market romance); Broadside Books (conservative non-fiction); Custom House (thought-provoking non-fiction); Day Street Books; Ecco (distinguished fiction and non-fiction); Harper Books (best-selling fiction and non-fiction); Harper Business; Harper Design (popular culture and the arts); Harper Luxe; Harper Perennial; Harper Voyager (science fiction); Harper Wave (health and wellness); HarperAudio; HarperCollins 360; HarperOne (spirituality); Morrow Gift; William Morrow; Witness. No unsolicited material; all submissions must come through a literary agent. Founded 1817.

History Compass LLC
25 Leslie Road, Auburndale, MA 02466
tel +1 617-332-2202
email info@historycompass.com
website www.historycompass.com

The history of the USA presented through the study of primary source documents. Successes include *Get a Clue!* (grades 2–8) and *Adventures in History* series (grades 4–8). Other series include *Perspectives on History* (grades 5–12+) and *Researching American History* (8–15 year-olds and ESL students). Also historical fiction for younger readers. Founded 1990.

Holiday House, Inc.*
120 Broadway, New York NY10271
tel +1 212-646 5025
email submissions@holidayhouse.com
website www.holidayhouse.com

General fiction for children. Publishes 35 picture books, ten young reader, 15 middle reader and eight young adult titles each year. Recent successes include *Lafayette and the American Revolution* by Russell Freedman. Approx. 20% of books are by first-time authors. Send entire MS. Only responds to projects of interest. Will review MS/illustration packages from artists: send MS with dummy and colour photocopies. Founded 1935.

Henry Holt Books for Young Readers
175 Fifth Avenue, New York, NY 10010
website https://us.macmillan.com/henryholt/
Vice President & Publisher Laura Godwin

Imprint of Macmillan Children's Publishing Group. Publishes picture books, chapter books, middle grade titles and young adult titles. Founded 1866.

Houghton Mifflin Harcourt*
3 Park Avenue, Floor 19, New York, NY 10016
tel +1 212-598-5730
website www.hmhco.com

Reference, fiction and non-fiction for adults and young readers. Also educational content and solutions for K-12 teachers and students. Founded 1832.

Houghton Mifflin Harcourt Books for Young Readers
website www.hmhbooks.com

Picture books, fiction, poetry and non-fiction for children, preschool through high school. Recent successes include *The Testing* by Joelle Charbonneau and *Sleep Like a Tiger* by Mary Logue and illustrated by Pamela Zagarenski. Imprint: Clarion Books. For fiction, submit complete MS. For non-fiction, submit outline/synopsis and sample chapters. Responds only if interested. For illustrations, query with samples (colour photocopies and tearsheets). Responds in four months.

Houghton Mifflin Harcourt/Clarion Books
Picture books, fiction, poetry and non-fiction for children, preschool through to high school. Recent successes include *Mr. Wuffles!* by David Wiesner. For fiction and picture books, send complete MS. For non-fiction, send query with up to three sample chapters. Founded 1965.

Hunter House Publishers
4507 Charlotte Ave, Suite 100, Nashville, TN 37209
tel +1 615-255-2665
email submissions@turnerpublishing.com
website www.hunterhouse.com

Imprint of Turner Publishing Company. Non-fiction books on children's physical, mental and emotional health, including books for tweens and children's life skills and activity books (games, classroom and fitness activities) for use by parents, teachers, youth leaders, camp counselors and coaches. Imprint of Turner Publishing Company. Founded 1978.

Hyperion Books for Children*
237 Park Avenue, New York, NY 10017
tel +1 212-633-4400
website www.hyperionbooks.com

Board and novelty books, picture books, young readers, middle grade, young adult, non-fiction (all subjects at all levels). Recent successes include *Don't Let the Pigeon Drive the Bus*, written and illustrated by Mo Willems, *Dumpy The Dump Truck* series by Julie Andrews Edwards and Emma Walton Hamilton (3–7 years) and *Artemis Fowl* by Eoin Colfer (young adult novel, *New York Times* bestseller). Imprints include Michael di Capua Books, Jump at the Sun, Volo. Approx. 10% of books are by first-time authors. Only interested in submissions via literary agents. For illustrations, send résumé, business card, promotional literature or tearsheets to be kept on file to Art Director. Founded 1990.

Illumination Arts Publishing
PO Box 1865, Bellevue, WA 98009
tel +1 425-968-5097

email liteinfo@illumin.com
website www.illumin.com
Editorial Director John Thompson

Picture books. Publishes books to inspire the mind, touch the heart and uplift the spirit. Successes include *The Right Touch*. Length: 300–1,500 words. Founded 1987.

Impact Publishers Inc.

5674 Shattuck Avenue, Oakland, CA 94609
tel +1 805-466-5917
email customerservice@newharbinger.com
website www.newharbinger.com/imprint/impact-publishers

Psychology and self-improvement books and audio tapes for adults, children, families, organisations and communities. Imprint of New Harbinger Publications. Only publishes non-fiction books which serve human development and are written by highly respected psychologists and other human service professionals. Rarely publishes authors outside of the USA. See website for guidelines. Founded 1970.

Incentive Publications by World Book

180 N. LaSalle, Suite 900, Chicago, IL 60601
tel +1 888-482-9764
website https://incentivepublications.com/

Produces supplemental resources for student use and instruction and classroom management improvement materials for teachers. Specializes in supplemental resources for middle grade students and teaching strategies for grades K–12. More than 300 titles are available. Send a letter of introduction, table of contents, a sample chapter and sase for return of material. Acquired by World Book in 2013. Founded 1969.

Jolly Fish Press

2297 Waters Drive, Mendota Heights, MN 55120
tel +1 888-417-0195
email publicity@jollyfishpress.com
email submit@jollyfishpress.com
website www.jollyfishpress.com
Facebook www.facebook.com/JollyFishPress
Twitter @JollyFishPress
Managing Editor Mari Kesselring

Jolly Fish Press is dedicated to promoting exceptional, unique new voices in middle grade fiction and jumpstarting writing careers. See website above for submission guidelines. Accepts electronic submissions only. Jolly Fish Press is an imprint of North Star Editions, Inc. Founded 2011.

Just Us Books, Inc.

395 Pleasant Valley Way, Suite B, West Orange, NJ 07052
tel +1 973-672-7701
email info@justusbooks.com
website https://justusbooks.com/
Publishers Cheryl Hudson, Wade Hudson

Publishers of Black-interest books for young people, including preschool materials, picture books, biographies, chapter books and young adult fiction. Focuses on Black history, Black culture and Black experiences. Imprint: Sankofa Books. Currently accepting queries for young adult titles, targeted to 13–16 year-old readers. Work should contain realistic, contemporary characters, compelling plot lines that introduce conflict and resolution, and cultural authenticity. Also considers MSS for picture books and middle reader chapter books. Send a query letter, 1–2pp synopsis, a brief author biography that includes any previously published work, plus an sase. Founded 1988.

Kaeden Books

PO Box 16190, Rocky River, OH 44116
tel +1 800-890-7323
email info@kaeden.com
website www.kaeden.com

Educational publisher specialising in early literacy books and beginning chapter books. Accepts samples of all styles of illustration but is primarily looking for samples that match the often humorous style appropriate for juvenile literature. Send samples, no larger than 8.5 x 11ins to keep on file. Seeking beginning chapter books and unique non-fiction MSS (25–3,000 words). Vocabulary and sentence structure must be appropriate for young readers. No sentence fragments. See website for complete guidelines. Founded 1986.

Kane Press – see Boyds Mills & Kane

KidHaven Press – see Gale Cengage Learning

Alfred A. Knopf – see Penguin Random House

Lee & Low Books, Inc.

95 Madison Avenue, Suite 1205, New York, NY 10016
tel +1 212-779-4400
email general@leeandlow.com
website www.leeandlow.com
Editorial Director Cheryl Klein, *Senior Editor* Jessica Echeverria, *Tu Books Publisher* Stacy Whitman

Children's book publisher specialising in multicultural literature that is relevant to young readers. The company's goal is to meet the need for stories that children of colour can identify with and that all children can enjoy and which promote a greater understanding of one another. Focuses on fiction, non-fiction and poetry for children 5–12 years, and for middle graders and young adults ages 13–18. Of special interest are realistic fiction, historical fiction and non-fiction with a non-white protagonist, a distinct voice or unique approach. Does not consider folktales or animal stories. Offers two writing contests per year for debut picture book writers and novelists. Writers of colour and/or of

Native nations are especially encouraged to submit. Imprints: Lee & Low, Bebop Books, Tu Books, Children's Book Press, Shen's Books. Please visit www.leeandlow.com/writers-illustrators to see current guidelines and needs. Potential authors will be contacted by email or phone within six months if interested. Founded 1911.

Lerner Publishing Group

1251 Washington Ave, Nr Minneapolis, MN 55401
tel +1 800-328-4929
email info@lernerbooks.com
website www.lernerbooks.com
Publisher Adam Lerner

Independent publisher of high-quality children's books for K–12 schools and libraries: picture books, fiction for children 5–8 and 9–12 years, teenage fiction, series fiction and non-fiction. Subjects include biography, social studies, science, sports and curriculum. Publishes approx. 300 titles each year and has about 1,500 in print. Imprints and partners include: Anderson Press USA; Big & Small; Carolrhoda Lab; Creston Books; Darby Creek; ediciones Lerner; First Avenue Editions; Full Tilt Press; Gecko Press USA; Graphic Universe; Hungry Tomato; JR Comics; Kane Press; Kar-Ben Publishing; Lantana Publishing; LernerClassroom; Lerner Digital; Lerner Publications; Live Oak Media; Lorimer Children & Teens; Maverick Arts; Millbrook Press; Quarto Library; Red Chair Press; StarBerry Books; Twenty-First Century Books; We Do Listen Foundation; and Zest Books. Details can be found on the website: https://lernerbooks.com/Pages/Our-Imprints#imprints. No unsolicited submissions for any imprint. Founded 1959.

Little, Brown & Company

1290 Ave of the Americas, New York, NY 10104
tel +1 212-364-1100
email lbpublicity.Generic@hbgusa.com
website www.littlebrown.com
Facebook www.facebook.com/littlebrownandcompany
Twitter @littlebrown

General literature, fiction, non-fiction, biography, history, trade paperbacks, children's. Founded 1837.

Jimmy Patterson
website www.littlebrown.com/imprint/little-brown-and-company/jimmy-patterson
Publishes James Patterson's *Middle School Years* series and other books by the same author and other popular writers of middle grade fiction.

Little, Brown Spark
Publishes books for young people and adults that spark ideas, feelings and change. Looking for authors who are experts and thought leaders in the fields of health, lifestyle, psychology and science.

Lucent Books – see Gale Cengage Learning

Margaret K. McElderry Books – see Simon & Schuster Children's Publishing Division

McGraw-Hill Professional*

2 Penn Plaza, 12th Floor, New York, NY 10121
tel +1 212-904-2000
website www.mhprofessional.com

Macmillan Publishers, Inc.

120 Broadway, New York, NY 10271
tel +1 646-307-5151
email press.inquiries@macmillanusa.com
website https://us.macmillan.com

Publishers: Celadon Books; Farrar, Straus and Giroux; Flatiron Books; Henry Holt and Co.; Macmillan Children's Publishing Group; Macmillan Audio; St. Martin's Publishing Group; and Tor/Forge. Macmillan Publishers is based in New York City. Founded 1843.

Marshall Cavendish Benchmark

99 White Plains Road, Tarrytown, NY 10591
email marketing@mceducation.com
website www.mceducation.com/mce-intl

Non-fiction books for young, middle grade and young adult readers. Subjects include: American studies, the arts, biographies, health, mathematics, science, social studies, history, world cultures. Imprint of Marshall Cavendish Corporation. Non-fiction subjects should be curriculum-related and are published in series form. Length: 1,500–25,000 words. Send synopsis with one or more sample chapters and sample table of contents. Founded 1968.

Marshall Cavendish Children's Books

99 White Plains Road, Tarrytown, NY 10591
email marketing@mceducation.com
website www.mceducation.com/mce-intl

Picture books and novels for middle grade and teens. Does not accept submissions via email. Imprint of Marshall Cavendish Corporation. Founded 1968.

Mitchell Lane Publishers, Inc.

2001 S.W. 31st Avenue, Hallandale, FL 33009
tel +1 800 223 3251
email customerservice@mitchelllane.com
website www.mitchelllane.com
President Phil Comer

Non-fiction titles for young readers, middle readers and young adults. Founded 1962.

Mondo Publishing*

980 Avenue of the Americas, New York, NY 10018
tel +1 888-886-6636
email info@mondopub.com
website www.mondopub.com

Classroom materials and professional development for K–5 educators. Part of Carnegie Learning. Founded 1986.

Thomas Nelson Publisher

PO Box 141000, Nashville, TN 37214
tel +1 800-251-4000
email publicity@thomasnelson.com
website www.thomasnelson.com

Bibles, religious, non-fiction and fiction general trade books for adults and children. Acquired by HarperCollins in 2012. Founded 1798.

NorthSouth Books

600 Third Avenue, 2nd Floor, New York, NY 10016
tel +1 917-210-5868
website www.northsouth.com
Publisher Herwig Bitsche, *Associate Publisher* Andrew Rushton, *Editor* Beth Terrill

Successes include *The Rainbow Fish* by Marcus Pfister, *Little Polar* by Hans de Beer, *Wonderment* by Lisbeth Zwerger, *Lindbergh: The Tale of a Flying Mouse* by Torben Kuhlmann, *Mr. Squirrel and the Moon* by Sebastian Meschenmoser, *The Green Sea Turtle* by Isabel Mueller and *Surf's Up* by Kwame Alexander and Daniel Miyares. Publishes 100 titles a year. Publishes fresh, original, fiction and non-fiction with universal themes that could appeal to children 3–8 years. Accepting picture book submissions from US authors and illustrators. Guidelines on submissions: accepts picture book MSS (1,000 words or less); typically does not acquire rhyming texts (although have been exceptions for simple/original text); authors do not need to include illustrations; illustrators to send sample sketches in pdf or jpg form. Submit via email: submissionsnsb@gmail.com. Founded 1961.

Orchard Books – see Scholastic, Inc.

The Overlook Press

141 Wooster Street Suite 4B, New York, NY 10012
tel +1 212-673-2210
website www.overlookpress.com
Facebook www.facebook.com/overlookpress
Twitter @overlookpress

Non-fiction, fiction, children's books (*Freddy the Pig* series). Imprints: Ardis Publishing, Duckworth. Imprint of Abrams. Founded 1971.

Richard C. Owen Publishers, Inc.

PO Box 585, Katonah, NY 10536
tel +1 914-232-3903
website www.rcowen.com
Publisher Richard C. Owen

Books for grades K–6. All work must be submitted as hard copy. Books for young learners: Seeks high-interest stories with charm and appeal that children 5–7 years can read by themselves. Interested in original, realistic, contemporary stories, as well as folktales, legends and myths of all cultures. Non-fiction content must be supported with accurate facts. Length: 45–1,000 words. Also beginning chapter books up to 3,000 words.

Pearson Education*

One Lake Street, Upper Saddle River, NJ 07458
tel +1 201-236-7000
email communications@pearsoned.com
website www.pearsoned.com

Educational secondary publisher of scientifically researched and standards-based instruction materials for today's Grade 6–12 classrooms with a mission to create exceptional educational tools that ensure student and teacher success in language arts, mathematics, modern and classical languages, science, social studies, careers and technology, and advanced placements, electives and honors. Part of the Curriculum Division of Pearson Education, Inc. Founded 1966.

Pearson Scott Foresman

One Lake Street, Upper Saddle River, NJ 07458
tel +1 201-236-7000
website www.pearsonschool.com

Elementary educational publisher. Teacher and student materials: reading, science, mathematics, language, arts, social studies, music, technology, religion. Its educational resources and services include textbook-based instructional programmes, curriculum websites, digital media, assessment materials and professional development. Part of the Curriculum Division of Pearson Education. Founded 1896.

Pelican Publishing

400 Poydras Street, Suite 900, Gretna, LA 70130
tel +1 504-684-8976
email editorial@pelicanpub.com
website www.pelicanpub.com
Publisher & President Christen Thompson

Children's books. Also art and architecture books, biographies, holiday books, local and international cookbooks, motivational works, political science, social commentary, history, business. Send a query letter, outline if chapter book, résumé and sase. No queries or submissions by email. No unsolicited MSS for chapter books. Most young children's books are 32 illustrated pages when published; their MSS will be 1,100 words maximum. Proposed books for middle readers (8+ years) should be at least 90pp. Brief books for readers under 9 years may be submitted in their entirety. Founded 1926.

Penguin Random House*

1745 Broadway, New York, NY 10019
tel +1 212-782-9000
website www.penguinrandomhouse.com
Ceo Madeline McIntosh

With 300 independent imprints and brands, more than 15,000 new print titles and close to 800 million print, audio and ebooks sold annually, Penguin Random House is the world's leading trade book publisher. The company was formed on July 1, 2013, and is owned by Bertelsmann. Like its predecessor companies, Penguin Random House is committed to publishing adult and children's fiction and non-fiction print editions, and is a pioneer in digital publishing. Its book brands include storied imprints such as Doubleday, Viking and Alfred A. Knopf (USA); Ebury, Hamish Hamilton and Jonathan Cape (UK); Plaza & Janés and Alfaguara (Spain); and Sudamericana (Argentina); as well as the international imprint DK. Founded 2013.

Penguin Young Readers*

1745 Broadway, New York, NY 10019
tel +1 212-366-2000
website www.penguin.com/children
President Jen Loja

Penguin Young Readers is one of the leading children's book publishers in the USA. The company owns a wide range of imprints and trademarks including Dial Books, Dutton, Grosset & Dunlap, Kathy Dawson Books, Kokila, Nancy Paulsen Books, Penguin Workshop, Philomel, Puffin, G.P. Putnam's Sons, Razorbill, Speak, Viking and Frederick Warne. Penguin Young Readers is also the proud publisher of perennial brand franchises such as the *Nancy Drew* and *Hardy Boys* series, *Peter Rabbit, Corduroy, The Very Hungry Caterpillar, Llama Llama, Mad Libs, Last Kids On Earth, Who Was?*, Roald Dahl, Jacqueline Woodson, S.E. Hinton and John Green among many others. Penguin Young Readers is a division of Penguin Group LLC, a Penguin Random House company. Founded 1935.

Puffin – see Penguin Young Readers

Simon Pulse Books – see Simon & Schuster Children's Publishing Division

Quarto Publishing Group – Walter Foster Publishing Jr.

26391 Crown Valley Parkway, STE 220, Mission Viejo, CA 92691
tel +1 949-380-7510
email karen.julian@quarto.com
website www.quartoknows.com/Walter-Foster-Jr
Group Publisher Anne Landa, *Senior Managing Editor* Karen Julian

Imprint of The Quarto Group. Instructional art books for children and adults. Also art and activity kits for children. A division of Quarto Publishing Group US. Founded 1976.

Random House Children's Books*

1745 Broadway, New York, NY 10019
tel +1 212-782-9000
website www.rhcbooks.com,
www.randomhouse.com/teachers
President & Publisher Barbara Marcus

Random House Children's Books is the world's largest English-language children's trade book publisher. Creates books for preschool children through young adult readers, in all formats from board books to activity books to picture books, graphic novels, novels and non-fiction. Imprints: Dragonfly, Ember, Laurel-Leaf, Little Golden Books, Make Me A World, Princeton Review, Random House Books for Young Readers, Random House Graphic, Rodale Kids, Schwartz & Wade Books, Sylvan Learning, Wendy Lamb Books, Yearling Books. Part of Penguin Random House (page 48). Founded 1925.

Razorbill – see Penguin Young Readers

Roaring Brook Press

120 Broadway, New York, NY 10271
tel +1 646-600-7861
website https://us.macmillan.com/publishers/roaring-brook-press/
Publisher Jennifer Besser

Picture books, chapter books, novels and graphic novels in fiction and non-fiction for young readers, ages 0 to 18. Publishes about 70 titles a year. Awards for titles include: 2014 Michael L. Printz Award, the 2013 and 2020 Robert F. Sibert Medals, the 2009 Pura Belpre Medal and two Pura Belpre Honor awards, three Coretta Scott King awards, the 2011, 2004 and 2003 Caldecott Medals, seven Caldecott Honor awards and a Newbery Honor award, among many others. Division of Holtzbrink Publishers. Part of Macmillan Children's Publishing Group. Does not accept unsolicited MSS or submissions in print or digital. Recent Publications: *Born to Fly* by Steve Sheinkin, *Rebel* by Marie Lu, *Fry Bread* by Kevin Noble Maillard and Juana Martinez-Neal, *Be Kind* by Pat Zietlow Miller and Jen Hill, *Moxie* by Jennifer Mathiue, *All the Impossible Things* by Lindsay Lackey, *I Wanna Be Where You* Are by Kristina Forest, *Black is a Rainbow Color* by Angela Joy and Ekua Holmes, the Stella Diaz series by Angela Dominguez and *Jane Against the World* by Karen Blumenthal. Founded 2002.

Rowman & Littlefield

4501 Forbes Boulevard, Suite 200, Lanham, MD 20706
tel +1 301-459-3366
email customercare@rowman.com
website www.rowman.com
Facebook www.facebook.com/rowmanuk
Twitter @rowmanuk
President & Ceo James E. Lyons

Rowman & Littlefield is an independent publisher specialising in academic publishing in the humanities and social sciences, government and official data and educational publishing. Founded 1925.

Running Press Book Publishers

2300 Chestnut Street, Suite 200, Philadelphia, PA 19103

tel +1 215-567-5080
email perseus.promos@perseusbooks.com
website www.runningpress.com

General non-fiction, science, history, children's fiction and non-fiction, cookbooks, pop culture, lifestyle, illustrated gift books, Miniature Editions. Imprints: Running Press, Running Press Miniature Editions, Running Press Kids, Running Press Adults. Member of the Perseus Books Group. Recent successes include *You Are a Badass* by Jen Sincero, *Ripe* by Cheryl Sternman Rule, *Cats in Hats* by Sara Thomas and *Slow Beauty* by Shel Pink. Founded 1972.

Running Press Kids

Picture books, activity books, young adult fiction. Recent successes include the *Doodles* series.

Sasquatch Books

1904 Third Ave, Suite 710 Seattle, WA 98101
tel +1 206-467-4300
email custserv@sasquatchbooks.com
website www.sasquatchbooks.com

Independent press, located in downtown Seattle. The mission is to seek out and work with gifted writers, chefs, naturalists, artists and thought leaders in the Pacific Northwest and bring their talents to a national audience. Publishes a variety of non-fiction books, as well as children's books under the Little Bigfoot imprint. Are happy to consider queries and proposals from authors and agents for new projects that fit into the company's West Coast regional publishing programme. Founded 1986.

Scholastic, Inc.*

557 Broadway, New York, NY 10012
tel +1 212-343-6100
email news@scholastic.com
website www.scholastic.com
Facebook www.facebook.com/scholastic
Twitter @scholastic

Scholastic is the world's largest publisher and distributor of children's books and a leader in education technology and children's media. Divisions: Scholastic Trade Publishing, Scholastic Book Clubs, Scholastic Book Fairs, Scholastic Education, Scholastic International, Media, Licensing and Advertising. Imprints include: Arthur A. Levine Books, The Blue Sky Press, Cartwheel Books, Chicken House, David Fickling Books, Graphix, Orchard Books, Point, PUSH, Scholastic en español, Scholastic Focus, Scholastic Licensed Publishing, Scholastic Nonfiction, Scholastic Paperbacks, Scholastic Press and Scholastic Reference. In addition, Scholastic Trade Books includes Klutz, a highly innovative publisher and creator of 'books plus' for children. Founded 1920.

Scholastic Trade Books, Children's Book Publishing

Award-winning publisher of original children's books. Publishes over 600 new titles a year including bestselling brands such as *Harry Potter, Captain Underpants, The Hunger Games, Clifford The Big Red Dog, I Spy* and *The Magic School Bus*.

Scholastic Education*

557 Broadway, New York, NY 10012
tel +1 212-343-6100
website www.scholastic.com

Educational publisher of research-based core and supplementary instructional materials. A leading provider in reading improvement and professional development products, as well as learning services that address the needs of the developing reader – from grades pre-K to high school. Publishes 32 curriculum-based classroom magazines used by teachers in grades pre-K–12 as supplementary educational materials to raise awareness about current events in an age-appropriate manner and to help children develop reading skills. Scholastic Education has also developed technology-based reading assessment and management products to help administrators and educators quickly and accurately assess student reading levels, match students to the appropriate books, predict how well they will do on district and state standardised tests and inform instruction to improve reading skills. Founded 1923.

Scholastic Library Publishing

90 Sherman Turnpike, Danbury, CT 06816
tel +1 203-797-3500
website www.scholastic.com

Online and print publisher of reference products.

Simon & Schuster Children's Publishing Division*

1230 Avenue of the Americas, New York, NY 10020
tel +1 212-698-7200
website www.simonandschuster.com/kids
President & Publisher Jon Anderson

Preschool to young adult, fiction and non-fiction, trade, library and mass market. Imprints: Aladdin Paperbacks, Atheneum Books for Young Readers, Beach Lane Books, Little Simon, Margaret K. McElderry Books, Salaam Reads, Simon & Schuster Books for Young Readers, Simon Pulse, Simon Spotlight, Paula Wiseman Books. More details on some of the imprints are given below. Division of Simon & Schuster, Inc. Founded 1924.

Aladdin Books

Vice-President & Publisher Valerie Garfield

Publishes commercial middle grade fiction with an emphasis on adventure, fantasy and humor. Accepts query letters with proposals for middle grade series and single-title fiction, middle grade and commercial non-fiction. Send MS for the attention of the Submissions Editor.

Atheneum Books for Young Readers

Vice-President & Publisher Justin Chanda

Picture books, chapter books, mysteries, biography, science fiction, fantasy, graphic novels, middle grade and young adult fiction and non-fiction. Covers preschool–young adult. Publishes 20–30 picture books, 4–5 young readers, 20–25 middle readers and 10–15 young adult books each year. Approximately 10% of books are by first-time authors. No unsolicited MSS. Send query letter only. Responds in one month.

Margaret K. McElderry Books

Vice-President & Publisher Justin Chanda

Picture books, easy-to-read books, fiction (8–12 years, young adult), poetry, fantasy. Covers preschool to young adult. Publishes 10–12 picture books, 2–4 young reader titles, 8–10 middle reader titles and 5–7 young adult books each year. Approximately 10% of books are by first-time authors. No unsolicited MSS. Fiction length: picture books – 500 words; young readers – 2,000; middle readers – 10,000–20,000; young adult – 45,000–50,000. Non-fiction length: picture books – 500–1,000 words; young readers – 1,500–3,000 words; middle readers – 10,000–20,000 words; young adult – 30,000–45,000 words. Responds in three months. Samples returned with sase.

Simon & Schuster Books for Young Readers

Vice President & Publisher Justin Chandu

Publishes a wide range of contemporary, commercial, award-winning fiction and non-fiction that spans every age of children's publishing. No unsolicited MSS. Send query letter only. Responds in two months. Seeking challenging and psychologically-complex young adult novels; also imaginative and humorous middle grade fiction.

Paula Wiseman

email paulawiseman@simonandschuster.com
Vice-President & Publisher Paula Wiseman

Publishes award-winning and bestselling books, including picture books, novelty books and novels. The imprint focuses on stories and art that are childlike, timeless, innovative and centered in emotion. Approx. 10% of books are by first-time authors. Submit complete MS. Length: picture books – 500 words; others standard length. Considers all categories of fiction. Will review MS/illustration packages from artists. Send MS with dummy.

Sleeping Bear Press – see Gale Cengage Learning

Sourcebooks, Inc.

P.O. Box, 4410, Naperville, IL 60567-4410
website www.sourcebooks.com
Editorial Director Todd Stocke, *Editorial Director, Sourcebooks & Sourcebooks Landmark* Shana Drehs, *Editorial Director, Sourcebooks & Poisoned Pen Press* Anna Michels, *Editorial Director, Sourcebooks Fire &*

Sourcebooks Kids Steve Geck, *Editorial Director, Sourcebooks eXplore (non-fiction)*, Kelly Barrales-Saylor, *Editorial Director, Sourcebooks Casablanca* Deb Werksman

A leading independent publisher with a wide variety of genres including fiction, romance, children's, young adult, gift/calendars and college-bound. E-commerce businesses include *Put Me In the Story*, the number one personalised books platform. Imprints include: Cumberland House, Dawn Publications, Little Pickle Press, Poison Pen Press, Simple Truths, Sourcebooks, Sourcebooks Casablanca, Sourcebooks Fire, Sourcebooks Kids, Sourcebooks Landmarks. Founded 1987.

Sourcebooks Kids

Publishes notable fiction and non-fiction projects including board books, picture books, chapter books and middle-grade works with the hope of engaging children in the pure fun of books and the wonder of learning new things.

Sterling Publishing Co., Inc.

1166 Avenue of the Americas, 17th Floor, New York, NY 10036
tel +1 212-532-7160
email editorial@sterlingpublishing.com
website www.sterlingpublishing.com
Executive Vice-President Theresa Thompson

Adult non-fiction and children's board books, picture books and non-fiction. Subsidiary of Barnes & Noble. Founded 1949.

Flashkids

Workbooks and flash cards for preschool, elementary and middle school students.

Sterling Children's Books

Non-fiction: crafts, hobbies, games, activities, origami, optical illusions, mazes, dot-to-dots, science experiments, puzzles (maths/word/picture/logic), chess, card games and tricks, sports, magic. Non-fiction: Write explaining the idea and enclose an outline and a sample chapter. Include information and a résumé with regard to the subject area and publishing history, and sase for return of material. No email submissions. Send submissions FAO Children's Book Editor.

Teacher Created Resources

12621 Western Ave, Garden Grove, CA 92841
tel +1 800-662-4321
email custserv@teachercreated.com
website www.teachercreated.com

Educational materials. See website for guidelines. Founded 1977.

Viking – see Penguin Young Readers

Walker Books US

99 Dover Street, Somerville, MA 02144
tel +1 617-661-3330
website www.walkerbooksus.com,
www.candlewick.com
Facebook www.facebook.com/CandlewickPressBooks
Directors Susan Van Metre (editorial), Maria
Middleton (art)

Great storytelling and instant reader appeal in fiction,
graphic novels and illustrated non-fiction. Titles
range from young adult to picture books, with
emphasis on middle grade and young adult works.
Walker Books US is a division of Candlewick Press
(page 40). Founded 2017.

Weigl Publishers Inc.

276 5th Ave, Suite 704 #917, New York, NY 10001
tel +1 866-649-3445
email linda@weigl.com
website www.weigl.com

Educational publisher: children's non-fiction titles.
Successes include *The AV2 Collection*
(av2books.com). Founded 1979.

Albert Whitman & Company

250 South Northwest Highway, Suite 320,
Park Ridge, Illinois, IL 60068
tel +1 847-581-0033
email mail@awhitmanco.com
website www.albertwhitman.com

Books that respond to cultural diversity and the
special needs and concerns of children and their
families (e.g. divorce, bullying). Also novels for
middle grade readers, picture books and non-fiction
for children 2–12 years. Send to
submissions@awhitmanco.com. For submissions
guidelines see website. Founded 1919.

Paula Wiseman – see Simon & Schuster
Children's Publishing Division

Wordsong – see Boyds Mills & Kane

Workman Publishing Company*

225 Varick Street, New York, NY 10014
tel +1 212-254-5900
email info@workman.com
website www.workman.com
Publisher & Editorial Director Susan Bolotin

General non-fiction for adults and children.
Calendars. Founded 1968.

World Book, Inc.

233 North Michigan Avenue, Suite 2000, Chicago,
IL 60601
tel +1 800-975-3250
email international@worldbook.com
website www.worldbook.com
Facebook www.facebook.com/WorldBook
Twitter @worldbookinc

EA leading publisher of authoritative, age-
appropriate and reliable print and digital educational
and reference materials for children and adults.
Committed to creating educational products that
meet the highest standards aiming to inspire a
lifelong love of learning. Trade companies include
children's book publisher Bright Connections Media
and Incentive Publications which specialises in
supplemental resources for children and teachers.
Founded 1917.

WorthyKids

6100 Tower Circle, Suite 210, Franklin, TN 37067
email IdealsInfo@hbgusa.com
website www.worthypublishing.com
Facebook www.Facebook.com/worthykidsbooks

An imprint of Hachette Book Group. Picture books
and board books for young children (1–8 years).
Email to request submission guidelines. Digital
submissions not accepted. Due to the large volume of
submissions, the company only responds to those
that are of interest to the publishing program.
Potential authors should become familiar with
current books before submitting. Agents welcome.
Founded 1944.

Yen Press

Hachette Book Group, 1290 Avenue of the Americas,
New York, NY 10104
email yenpress@hbgusa.com
website www.yenpress.com
Facebook www.facebook.com/yenpress
Twitter @yenpress

Graphic novels and manga in all formats for all ages.
Currently not seeking original project pitches from
writers who are not already working with an
illustrator. For submission guidelines see under
Contact on website. Division of Hachette Book
Group (page 44). Founded 2006.

Children's audio publishers

Many of the audio publishers listed below are also publishers of print and electronic books.

Audible

email bizdev_uk@audible.co.uk
website www.audible.co.uk
Twitter @audibleuk

Producer and seller of digital audio entertainment, including fiction and non-fiction audiobooks for adults and children. Publishers interested in exploring business opportunities with Audible may email the address above, or find out more about turning print books into audiobooks at www.acx.com. Founded 1995; acquired by Amazon 2008.

Audiobooks.com

email acquisitions@audiobooks.com
website www.audiobooks.com
Facebook www.facebook.com/audiobookscom
Twitter @audiobooks_com

Subscription audiobook service, offering a wide range of fiction and non-fiction genres, as well as some children's titles. Publishers interested in having their titles included in the company's library may get in touch via the email address above.

Barrington Stoke – see page 12

BookBeat

email info@bookbeat.com
website www.bookbeat.com/uk
Twitter @BookBeatUK

Digital streaming service for adult and children's audiobooks across a variety of fiction and non-fiction genres. Monthly subscription model. Owned by Bonnier. Founded 2017.

Canongate Audio Books

14 High Street, Edinburgh EH1 1TE
tel 0131 557 5111
email support@canongate.co.uk
website www.canongate.co.uk
Twitter @canongatebooks

Classic children's literature such as *Just William*, *Billy Bunter* and *Black Beauty*; also adult, classic and contemporary literary authors. Founded 1991 as CSA Word; acquired by Canongate 2010.

Cló Iar-Chonnacht Teo

Cheardlann, Spiddal, Co. Galway, Republic of Ireland
tel +353 (0)91 593307
email eolas@cic.ie
website www.cic.ie
Twitter @CloIarChonnacht

Ceo Micheál Ó Conghaile, *General Manager* Deirdre Ní Thuathail

Predominantly Irish-language children's books with accompanying audio of stories/folklore/poetry. Established 1985.

Dref Wen

28 Church Road, Whitchurch, Cardiff CF14 2EA
tel 029-2061 7860
website www.drefwren.com
Directors Roger Boore, Anne Boore, Gwilym Boore, Alun Boore, Rhys Boore

Welsh-language and dual-language children's books. Founded 1970.

The Educational Company of Ireland

Ballymount Road, Walkinstown, Dublin D12 R25C, Republic of Ireland
tel +353 (0)1 4500611
email info@edco.ie
website www.edco.ie
Chief Executive Martina Harford

Irish language CDs. Trading unit of Smurfit Kappa Group – Ireland. Founded 1910.

HarperCollins Publishers

The News Building, 1 London Bridge Street, London, SE1 9GF
tel 020-8285 4016
website www.harpercollins.co.uk
Twitter @HarperCollinsUK
Senior Audio Editors Jessica Barnfield, Rebecca Fortuin, Tanya Hougham

Publishers of award-winning fiction and non-fiction audiobooks for adults and children. Founded 1990.

W. F. Howes Ltd

Unit 5, St George's House, Rearsby Business Park, Gaddesby Lane, Rearsby, Leicester LE7 4YH
tel (01664) 423000
email info@wfhowes.co.uk
website www.wfhowes.co.uk

Independent audiobook publisher. Also large-print publisher and digital-services provider to libraries. Releases c. 80 new and unabridged audiobooks monthly. Works with authors/agents directly and a range of large UK publishers, including Penguin Random House and HarperCollins. Founded 1999; UK subsidiary of RBMedia.

Kobo

website www.kobo.com/gb/en
Twitter @kobo

Audiobook streaming service, for a monthly fee. Offers fiction, non-fiction, adult, children's and YA titles.

Macmillan Digital Audio

20 New Wharf Road, London N1 9RR
tel 020-7014 6000
email audiobooks@macmillan.co.uk
website www.panmacmillan.com
Publishing Director, Audio Rebecca Lloyd

Children's titles include *The Gruffalo* by Julia Donaldson and Axel Scheffler. Also adult fiction, non-fiction and autobiography. Founded 1995.

Naxos AudioBooks

5 Wyllyotts Place, Potters Bar, Herts. EN6 2JD
tel (01707) 653326

email info@naxosaudiobooks.com
website www.naxosaudiobooks.com
Twitter @NaxosAudioBooks
Managing Director Anthony Anderson

Recordings of classic literature, modern fiction, non-fiction, drama and poetry. Founded 1994.

Penguin Random House UK Audio (Children's)

Penguin Studios, One Embassy Gardens, Nine Elms Lane, London SW8 5BL
website www.penguinrandomhouse.co.uk
Studio Manager Kate MacDonald

Contemporary and classic literature for younger listeners. Authors include Malorie Blackman, Charlie Higson, Roald Dahl and Eoin Colfer.

Children's book packagers

Many illustrated books are created by book packagers, whose particular skills are in the areas of book design and graphic content. In-house editors match up the expertise of specialist writers, artists and photographers who usually work on a freelance basis.

Aladdin Books Ltd

PO Box 53987, London SW15 2SF
tel 020-3174 3090
email sales@aladdinbooks.co.uk
website www.aladdinbooks.co.uk

Full design and book packaging facility specialising in children's non-fiction and reference. Founded 1980.

Nicola Baxter

16 Cathedral Street, Norwich NR1 1LX
tel (01603) 766585 / 07778 285555
email nb@nicolabaxter.co.uk
website www.nicolabaxter.co.uk
Director Nicola Baxter

Full packaging service for children's books in both traditional and digital formats. Happy to take projects from concept to finished work or supply bespoke authorial, editorial, design, project management or commissioning services. Produces both fiction and non-fiction titles in a wide range of formats, for babies to young adults, and experienced in novelty books and licensed publishing. Founded 1990.

Bender Richardson White

PO Box 266, Uxbridge, Middlesex UB9 5NX
tel (01895) 832444
email brw@brw.co.uk
website www.brw.co.uk
Directors Lionel Bender (editorial), Kim Richardson (sales & production), Ben White (design)

Design, editorial and production of activity books, non-fiction and reference books. Specialises in non-fiction: natural history, science, history and educational. Writers should send a letter and synopsis of their proposal. Opportunities for freelancers. Founded 1990.

Brown Bear Books Ltd

Unit 1/D, Leroy House, 436 Essex Road, London N1 3QP
tel 020-3176 8603
website www.windmillbooks.co.uk
Children's Publisher Anne O'Daly

Specialises in high-quality illustrated reference books and multi-volume sets for trade and educational markets. Opportunities for freelancers. Imprint of Windmill Books. Founded 1967.

John Brown Group – Children's Division

10 Triton Street, Regents Place, London NW1 3BF
tel 020-7565 3000

email andrew.hirsch@johnbrownmedia.com
website www.johnbrownmedia.com
Director Chris Dicey (business development)

Creative development and packaging of children's products including books, magazines, teachers' resource packs, partworks, CDs and websites. Founded 2000.

Global Blended Learning Ltd

Singleton Court, Wonastow Road, Monmouth NP25 5JA
tel (01993) 706273
email info@hlstudios.eu.com
website www.globalblendedlearning.com

Primary, secondary academic education (geography, science, modern languages) and co-editions (travel guides, gardening, cookery). Multimedia (CD-Rom programming and animations). Opportunities for freelancers. Founded 1985.

Graham-Cameron Publishing & Illustration

59 Hertford Road, Brighton BN1 7GG
tel (01273) 385890
email enquiry@gciforillustration.com
Alternative address The Art House, Uplands Park, Sheringham, Norfolk NR26 8NE
tel (01263) 821333
website www.gciforillustration.com
Partners Helen Graham-Cameron, Duncan Graham-Cameron

Offers illustration and editorial services for picture books, information books, educational materials, activity books, non-fiction and reference books. Illustration agency with 37 artists. Do not send unsolicited MSS. Founded 1985.

Hart McLeod Ltd

14A Greenside, Waterbeach, Cambridge CB25 9HP
tel (01223) 861495
email jo@hartmcleod.co.uk
website www.hartmcleod.co.uk
Director Joanne Barker

Primarily educational and general non-fiction with particular expertise in illustrated books, school texts, ELT and electronic and audio content. Opportunities for freelancers and work experience. Founded 1985.

Hawcock Books

242 Bloomfield Road, Bath BA2 2AX
tel (07976) 708720

website www.hawcockbooks.co.uk
Twitter @DavidHawcock

Designs and produces highly creative and original pop-up art and three-dimensional paper-engineered concepts. Most experience is in developing, providing editorial assistance, printing and manufacturing pop-up books and novelty items for the publishing industry. Also undertakes demanding commissions from the advertising world for model-making, point-of-sale and all printed three-dimensional aspects of major campaigns.

Little People Books

The Home of BookBod, Knighton, Radnorshire LD7 1UP
tel (01547) 520925
email littlepeoplebooks@thehobb.tv
website www.littlepeoplebooks.co.uk
Directors Grant Jessé (production & managing), Helen Wallis (rights & finance)

Packager of audio, children's educational and textbooks, digital publications. Parent company: Grant Jessé UK.

Orpheus Books Ltd

6 Church Green, Witney, Oxon OX28 4AW
tel (01993) 774949
email info@orpheusbooks.com
website www.orpheusbooks.com, www.Q-files.com
Executive Directors Nicholas Harris, Sarah Hartley

Produces children's books and ebooks for the international co-editions market: non-fiction and reference. Orpheus Books are the creators of Q-files.com, the online educational resource for schools and libraries. Founded 1993.

The Puzzle House

Ivy Cottage, Battlesea Green, Stradbroke, Suffolk IP21 5NE
tel (01379) 384656

email puzzlehouse@btinternet.com
website www.thepuzzlehouse.co.uk
Partners Roy Preston, Sue Preston

Editorial service creating crossword, quiz, puzzle and activity material for all ages. Founded 1988.

Toucan Books Ltd

The Old Fire Station, 140 Tabernacle Street, London EC2A 4SD
tel 020-7250 3388
website www.toucanbooks.co.uk

International co-editions; editorial, design and production services. Founded 1985.

David West Children's Books

11 Glebe Road, London SW13 0DR
tel 020-8876 1405
email lynn@davidwestbooks.com
website www.davidwestchildrensbooks.com
Proprietor David West, *Partner* Lynn Lockett

Packagers of highly illustrated children's non-fiction books. Specialises in science, art, geography, history, sport and flight. Produces 20 titles each year. Opportunities for freelancers. Founded 1986.

Working Partners Ltd

9 Kingsway, 4th Floor, London WC2B 6XF
tel 020-7841 3939
email enquiries@workingpartnersltd.co.uk
website www.workingpartnersltd.co.uk
Managing Director (Working Partners & Director of IP Creation, Coolabi Group) Chris Snowdon

Children's and young adult fiction series: animal fiction, fantasy, horror, historical fiction, detective, magical, adventure. Recent successes include *Rainbow Magic*, *Beast Quest* and *Warriors*. Unable to accept any MSS or illustration submissions. Pays advance and royalty; retains copyright on all works. Selects writers from unpaid writing samples based on specific brief provided. Always looking to add writers to database: to register details visit website. Founded 1995.

Children's bookshops

The bookshops in the first part of this list specialise in selling new children's books and are good places for writers and illustrators to check out the marketplace. Most of them are members of the Booksellers Association and are well known to publishers. A list of secondhand and antiquarian children's bookshops follows. Independent Booksellers Week usually takes place each year in June or July, but may be affected by ongoing coronavirus restrictions, so please check online for up-to-date opening information.

The Alligator's Mouth

2A Church Court, Richmond, Surrey TW9 1JL
tel 020-8948 6775
email info@thealligatorsmouth.co.uk
website www.thealligatorsmouth.co.uk
Facebook www.facebook.com/alligatorsmouth
Twitter @alligatorsmouth

Independent children's bookshop stocking works for all ages from babies to teenagers. Runs regular story-time sessions, book clubs and author events. Nominated for Children's Bookseller of the Year in *The Bookseller* Industry Awards 2018.

Bags-of-Books

1 South Street, Lewes BN7 2BT
tel (01273) 479320
email bagsofbooks@bags-of-books.co.uk
website https://bags-of-books.co.uk
Twitter @BagsofBooks
Instagram @bagsofbookslewes
Proprietor Rachel Givertz

Independent children's bookshop situated within a 16th-century building. Extensive selection of fiction and non-fiction from babies up to age eighteen. Hosts author visits and runs a books-for-schools programme.

Bert's Books

email bert@bertsbooks.co.uk
website https://bertsbooks.co.uk/
Facebook www.facebook.com/BertsBooks/
Twitter @BertsBooks
Founder Alex Call

Online bookshop with a focus on diversity. Offers books in monthly bundles, including young adult titles. Founded 2019.

Blackwell's Children's Bookshop

Blackwell's Bookshop, 50 Broad Street, Oxford OX1 3BQ
tel (01865) 333694
email oxford@blackwell.co.uk
website https://bookshop.blackwell.co.uk/bookshop/home
Facebook www.facebook.com/blackwellbooks

Stocks over 10,000 titles for children of all ages and holds a regular events programme including author visits to schools. The children's department is at the back of the ground floor of Blackwell's flagship bookshop in central Oxford.

The Blue House Bookshop

10 Bootham, York YO30 7BL
tel (01904) 927838
email karen@thebluehousebookshop.co.uk
website https://thebluehousebookshop.co.uk
Facebook www.facebook.com/bluehousebookshop
Twitter @bookishkids
Instagram @thebluehousebookshop
Proprietor Karen Walker

Independent children's bookshop in the historic heart of York. Offers a range of fiction and non-fiction to young readers. Customers can 'Book a Browse', whereby up to six people can visit the shop exclusively (available after 5pm on weekdays and Sunday afternoons). Supporter of the Yorkshire Dales Millennium Trust. Founded 2019.

The Book Burrow @ Aardvark Books & Café

The Bookery, Manor Farm, Brampton Bryan, Bucknell SY7 0DH
email aardvaark@btconnect.com
website www.aardvark-books.com
Twitter @AardvarkEthel
Proprietors Sheridan and Sarah Swinson

Book and play space with a castle, enchanted forest, pirate cabin and princess seat. Extensive range of books, mostly new but some secondhand and rare. Children's events throughout the year. BA member.

Book Corner

24 Milton Street, Saltburn-by-the-Sea TS12 1DG
tel (01287) 348010
email jenna@bookcornershop.co.uk
website www.bookcornershop.co.uk
Facebook https://en-gb.facebook.com/Book-Corner-Saltburn-1506322029595573/
Twitter @BookCornerShop
Proprietor Jenna Warren

Independent bookshop with dedicated children's section, stocking books for all ages from babies to young adults. Also stocks fiction and non-fiction for adults, and hosts author visits.

The Book House
93 High Street, Thame, Oxon OX9 3HJ
tel (01844) 213032
email office@thebookhousethame.co.uk
website www.thebookhousethame.co.uk
Instagram @the_book_house
Proprietor Brian Pattinson

Specialises in children's books alongside a wide range of titles for all ages. Established in the community for over 45 years, the Book House holds its own literary festival every October.

The Book Nook
First Avenue, Hove BN3 2FJ
tel (01273) 911988
email info@booknookuk.com
website www.booknookuk.com
Twitter @booknookhove
Proprietors Vanessa Lewis, Julie Ward

Specialist children's bookshop set in a child-friendly environment with author events, daily story-time, café and pirate ship. Named Children's Bookseller of the Year at *The Bookseller* Industry Awards 2015 and 2018.

Booka Bookshop and Café
26–28 Church Street, Oswestry, Shrops. SY11 2SP
tel (01691) 662244
email hello@bookabookshop.co.uk
website www.bookabookshop.co.uk
Facebook www.facebook.com/bookabookshop
Twitter @bookabookshop
Proprietors Carrie and Tim Morris

Independent bookshop and café offering a wide range of books, cards and gifts. Hosts a regular programme of author talks and signings, organises themed events, runs bookclubs and works with schools and the local library. Named Independent Bookshop of the Year at *The Bookseller* Industry Awards 2015.

Bookbugs and Dragon Tales
41 Timberhill, Norwich NR1 3LA
tel (01603) 964022
email leanne@bookbugsanddragontales.com
website https://bookbugsanddragontales.com
Facebook www.facebook.com/Bookbugs-and-Dragon-Tales-683095175486432
Twitter @Bookbugsdragon1
Instagram @bookbugsdragontales
Proprietors Dan and Leanne Fridd

Independent bookshop offering a wide range of books and events for children and their families. An events space that hosts bookclubs, classes and other interactive opportunities is also available. Founded 2019.

Bookworm Ltd
1177 Finchley Road, London NW11 0AA
tel 020-8201 9811

email bookworm1@btconnect.com
website www.thebookworm.uk.com

Independent children's bookshop catering for all ages, from babies to young adults. Also supplies books to schools. Hosts author visits and holds regular story-time sessions.

The Broadway Bookshop
6 Broadway Market, London E8 4QJ
tel 020-7241 1626
email books@broadwaybookshophackney.com
website www.broadwaybookshophackney.com
Proprietor Jane Howe

General independent bookshop specialising in literary fiction with a strong selection of children's books for all ages.

Browns Books For Students
22–28 George Street, Hull HU1 3AP
tel (01482) 325413
email enquiries@brownsbfs.co.uk
website www.brownsbfs.co.uk
Facebook www.facebook.com/BrownsBFS
Twitter @BrownsBFS

Supplies any book in print to schools, colleges and international schools. Full school servicing of books on request.

Chicken & Frog
30 Crown Street, Brentwood, Essex, CM14 4BA
tel (01277) 230068
email info@chickenandfrog.co.uk
website https://chickenandfrog.com
Twitter @chickenandfrog
Proprietors Jim and Natasha Radford

Independent children's bookshop and tuition centre. Weekly rhythm and rhyme, creative writing and handwriting sessions.

The Children's Bookshop – Hay-on-Wye
Toll Cottage, Pontvaen, Hay-on-Wye, Herefordshire HR3 5EW
tel (01497) 821083
email sales@childrensbookshop.com
website www.childrensbookshop.com
Twitter @childrnsbkshop
Proprietors Judith and Colin Gardner

Second-hand and antiquarian children's books.

Children's Bookshop (Huddersfield)
37–39 Lidget Street, Lindley, Huddersfield, West Yorkshire HD3 3JF
tel (01484) 658013
email hello@childrensbookshuddersfield.co.uk
website www.childrensbookshuddersfield.co.uk
Twitter @Lindley_Books
Contact Nicola Lee

Independent bookshop stocking a wide selection of titles for children, from picture books to YA. Also offers services to schools.

Children's Bookshop (Muswell Hill)
29 Fortis Green Road, London N10 3HP
tel 020-8444 5500
email admin@childrensbookshoplondon.co.uk
website www.childrensbookshoplondon.com
Facebook www.facebook.com/
ChildrensBookshopLondon
Twitter @childrensbkshop
Instagram childrensbookshoplondon

Specialist children's bookshop. Stocks approximately 12,000 titles and 25,000 books for children from babies to teenagers. Also offers services for schools and individuals. Founded 1974.

DRAKE The Bookshop
27 Silver Street, Stockton-on-Tees TS18 1SX
tel (01642) 909970
email books@drakethebookshop.co.uk
website www.drakethebookshop.co.uk
Twitter @drakebookshop
Proprietors Richard Drake, Melanie Greenwood

Independent bookshop with strong children's offering, as well as events and initiatives aimed at young readers and schools. The shop runs three children's book groups (Teen Readers, High-Rise Readers and Young Bookworms) and offers a selection of dyslexia-friendly titles. Founded 2015.

ebb & flo bookshop
12 Gillibrand Street, Chorley, Lancs. PR7 2EJ
tel (01257) 262773
email info@ebbandflobookshop.co.uk
website www.ebbandflobookshop.co.uk
Facebook www.facebook.com/ebbandflobookshop
Twitter @ebbandflobooks
Proprietor Diane Gunning

Small independent bookshop stocking books for children and adults, plus toys, cards and gifts. Supplies books to local schools, including library restocks and topic boxes. Organises author visits. Hosts a weekly story-time for preschool children as well as regular author events and holiday workshops.

The Edinburgh Bookshop
219 Bruntsfield Place, Edinburgh EH10 4DH
tel 0131 447 1917
email mail@edinburghbookshop.com
website www.edinburghbookshop.com
Facebook www.facebook.com/EdinBookshop
Twitter @EdinBookshop
Proprietor Marie Moser

Named UK Children's Bookseller of the Year at *The Bookseller* Industry Awards 2014, Scottish Independent of the Year 2014, 2015 and 2018. Events programme includes author visits, book clubs and a twice-weekly story-time for the under 5s. Founded 2007.

Far from the Madding Crowd
20 High Street, Linlithgow EH49 7AE
tel (01506) 845509
email sally@maddingcrowdlinlithgow.com
website www.maddingcrowdlinlithgow.com
Facebook www.facebook.com/Far From The Madding Crowd Linlithgow
Twitter @Furtherfrom

Independent bookshop with eclectic range of titles, including children's and preschool. Free story-telling every Saturday at 11am in the Bothy. Strong influence from Scottish publishers.

Ginger and Pickles
51 St Stephen Street, Edinburgh EH3 5AH
tel 0131 285 8069
email hello@gingerandpicklesbookshop.com
website www.gingerandpicklesbookshop.com
Facebook www.facebook.com/
gingerandpickleschildrensbookshop
Instagram @gingerandpicklesbookshop

Independent children's bookshop catering for young readers from birth to teenage years. Also offers professional advice to schools on stocking and ordering key titles. Currently preparing events programme and a schools department. Founded 2020.

Glowworm Books & Gifts Ltd
Unit 2, 5 Youngs Road, East Mains Industrial Estate, Broxburn, West Lothian EH52 5LY
tel (01506) 857570
website www.glowwormbooks.co.uk

Specialises in supplying books for children, especially those who find reading difficult due to physical or special educational challenges.

Golden Hare Books
68 St Stephen Street, Edinburgh EH3 5AQ
tel 0131 225 7755
email mail@goldenharebooks.com
website www.goldenharebooks.com
Twitter @GoldenHareBooks
Owner Mark Jones

Independent bookshop, nominated for Children's Bookseller of the Year in *The Bookseller* Industry Awards 2018 and 2019. Named Independent Bookshop of the Year at the British Book Awards 2019. Events include regular Sunday story sessions for children, book groups and author events.

Harbour Bookshop
2 Mill Street, Kingsbridge, Devon TQ7 1ED
tel (01548) 857233
email hello@harbourbookshop.co.uk
website www.harbourbookshop.co.uk
Twitter @HarbourBookshop
Proprietor Jane Fincham, *Manager* Louise Sanders

Books

Well-established independent bookshop with an extensive range of children's books for all ages. Next-day delivery available. Also works with primary and secondary schools and holds children's book events and celebrations.

Heath Educational Books

Willow House, Willow Walk, Whittaker Road, Sutton, Surrey SM3 9QQ
tel 020-8644 7788
email orders@heathbooks.co.uk
website www.heathbooks.co.uk
Proprietor Richard Heath

Supplies books to schools and teachers throughout Europe. Large showroom.

Jacqson Diego Story Emporium

444 London Road, Westcliff on Sea, Essex SS0 9LN
tel (01702) 344262
email stories@jacqsondiego.com
website www.jacqsondiego.com
Facebook www.facebook.com/JacqsonDiego
Twitter @jacqsondiego

Independent bookshop offering fiction and non-fiction for children and young people. Regular events include bookclubs. Also runs bespoke book-related services for schools and nurseries, including author visits, library audits, consultancy and workshops. A member of the Booksellers Association.

Madeleine Lindley Ltd

Book Centre, Broadgate, Broadway Business Park, Chadderton, Oldham OL9 9XA
tel 0161 683 4400
email books@madeleinelindley.com
website www.madeleinelindley.com
Twitter @teacher_books

Supplies books to schools and nurseries, provides information services and runs open days and training courses for teachers. Hosts author/publisher events for teachers and children.

The Mainstreet Trading Company

Main Street, St Boswells, Scottish Borders, TD6 0AT
tel (01835) 824087
email info@mainstreetbooks.co.uk
website www.mainstreetbooks.co.uk
Facebook www.facebook.com/
Mainstreet.Trading.Company
Twitter @mainstreethare
Instagram mainstreethare
Proprietors Rosamund and Bill de la Hey

General bookshop with a particular focus on children's books. Named Independent Bookseller of the Year at the *The Bookseller* Industry Awards 2012. Winner of Britain's Best Small Shop 2018.

Moon Lane Ink CIC

300 Stanstead Road, London SE23 1DE
tel 020-3489 7030

email info@moonlaneink.co.uk
website www.moonlaneink.co.uk
Facebook www.facebook.com/moonlaneink/
Twitter @moonlaneink
Instagram @moonlaneink

Community-interest company dedicated to raising equality in children's books; equality of access, representation and roles in the publishing industry. In addition to a bookshop, runs enterprise workshops for children as well as a range of events. Founded 2018.

Nickel Books

9 Merlin Close, Sittingbourne ME10 4TY
tel 07731 152089
email enquiries@nickelbooks.co.uk
website www.nickelbooks.co.uk
Twitter @NickelBooks
Instagram @nickelbooks
Proprietor Andrea Don

Mail-order, school books supply, visits, fairs, fetes and events. Specialises in children's books, from birth to teenage; also books for parents.

Norfolk Children's Book Centre

Church Lane, Alby, Norwich NR11 7HB
tel (01263) 761402
email marilyn@ncbc.co.uk
website www.ncbc.co.uk
website https://uk.bookshop.org/shop/norfolkcbc
Facebook www.facebook.com/
norfolkchildrensbookcentre
Twitter @NorfolkCBC
Instagram @NorfolkCBC

Independent bookshop established for over 35 years, specialising in books for children and teachers. Offers storytelling and school booksales within East Anglia, and nationwide conference book displays and mail order. Other specialties include school library assessment and rejuvenation, and topic-based approval collections.

Octavia's Bookshop

24 Black Jack Street, Cirencester, Glos. GL7 2AA
tel (01285) 650677
email info@octaviasbookshop.co.uk
website www.octaviasbookshop.co.uk
Twitter @octaviabookshop
Proprietor Octavia Emanuel

Independent bookshop in which more than half the stock is dedicated to children's titles, from buggy books to teen fiction and classics. Book groups are available for children aged six upwards. Named Children's Independent Bookseller of the Year at the *The Bookseller* Industry Awards 2013.

The Oundle Bookshop

13 Market Place, Oundle, Peterborough PE8 4BA
tel (01832) 273523

Books

email oundlebookshop@colemangroup.co.uk
website www.colemans-online.co.uk/oundle-bookshop.html

General bookshop with extensive children's selection.

Owl and Pyramid
10 Fore Street, Seaton EX12 2LA
tel (01297) 598030
email owl.pyramid@yahoo.com
website www.owlandpyramid.co.uk
Facebook www.facebook.com/owlpyramid
Twitter @OwlPyramid

Independent children's bookshop stocking fiction and non-fiction for young readers from babies to teenagers. Also runs four book clubs for different age groups. Small but growing section of adult fiction and non-fiction. Founded 2014.

Peters Ltd
120 Bromsgrove Street, Birmingham B5 6RJ
tel 0121 666 6646
website www.peters.co.uk
Facebook www.facebook.com/Petersbooksbirmingham
Twitter @petersbooks
Instagram @petersbooks

Specialist supplier of children's books and library furniture to schools, nurseries, academies and public libraries, with a book and furniture showroom, online ordering facilities and ten specialist children's librarians. Also provides a library design and installation service and book-related promotional material. Peters are sponsors of the CILIP Carnegie and Kate Greenaway Shadowing Awards, and also host regular professional development events for teachers and librarians, featuring speakers, authors and illustrators.

Pickled Pepper Books
10 Middle Lane, Crouch End, London N8 8PL
tel 020-3632 0823
email info@pickledpepperbooks.co.uk
website www.pickledpepperbooks.co.uk
Twitter @pickledbooks
Proprietors Urmi Merchant, Steven Pryse

Family-run specialist children's bookshop with a café and weekly programme of events for under 5s including story-times, art and craft, music groups, Spanish and French sing-alongs and NCT coffee mornings. After-school events include book groups for 9–12 year olds and teens' creative writing and illustration clubs. The bookshop also hosts regular interactive author events, as well as innovative theatre and puppet shows. Founded 2012.

The Rocketship Bookshop
5 Bridge Street, Salisbury SP1 2ND
tel (01722) 237172

email info@rocketbookshop.co.uk
website https://rocketshipbookshop.co.uk
Facebook www.facebook.com/rocketshipbookshop
Twitter @rshipbshop
Instagram @rocketshipbooks

Independent bookshop catering predominantly for children and young people, although a specially curated selection of adult titles is also available. Open Monday to Saturday; purchases may also be made via the online shop.

Round Table Books
97 Granville Avenue, Brixton Village, London SW9 8PS
website www.roundtablebooks.co.uk
Twitter @booksround
Director Layla Hudson

Inclusive children's bookshop, launched by the Knights Of, independent children's publisher, which champions authors and illustrators from diverse backgrounds. Founded 2019.

Seven Stories – see page 359

Seven Stories Bookshop
30 Lime Street, Ouseburn Valley, Newcastle upon Tyne NE1 2PQ
tel 0300 330 1095
email bookshop@sevenstories.org.uk
website www.sevenstories.org.uk
Twitter @7StoriesBooks
Manager Billiejo Carlisle

Independent children's bookshop and part of the National Centre for Children's Books. School accounts are available, as is advice on library stock.

Simply Books
228 Moss Lane, Bramhall, Cheshire SK7 1BD
tel 0161 439 1436
email enquiries@simplybooks.info
website www.simplybooks.info
Twitter @simplybooksNo1

Independent bookshop with strong children's selection, as well as regular events and reading groups for adults and children readers.

Storytellers, Inc.
7 The Crescent, St Anne's on Sea, Lytham St Anne's, Lancs. FY8 1SN
tel (01253) 781690
email info@storytellersinc.co.uk
website www.storytellersinc.co.uk
Twitter @storytellersinc
Proprietors Carolyn Clapham, Katie Clapham

Independent bookshop with dedicated children's section. Monthly book clubs for junior and adult readers plus a bi-monthly poetry group for adults. Supplies books to local schools. Regional winner

(North) in the Independent Bookshop of the Year category at *The Bookseller* Industry Awards 2015.

Tales On Moon Lane

25 Half Moon Lane, London SE24 9JU
tel 020-7274 5759
email info@talesonmoonlane.co.uk
website www.talesonmoonlane.co.uk
Twitter @talesonmoonlane
Proprietor Tamara Macfarlane

Specialist children's bookshop which runs yearly children's literature festivals in February and October, as well as weekly story-telling sessions for preschool children.

Through the Wardrobe Books

2 Nettleton Road, Mirfield, West Yorks. WF14 9AA
email hello@throughthewardrobebooks.co.uk
website www.throughthewardrobebooks.co.uk
Facebook www.facebook.com/throughthewardrobebooks
Twitter @WardrobeBooks
Founders Leanne Yeomans, Samantha Ward

Specialist children's and young adults bookshop. Open Monday to Saturday. Founded 2019.

West End Lane Books

277 West End Lane, London NW6 1QS
tel 020-7431 3770
email info@welbooks.co.uk
website www.welbooks.co.uk
Twitter @WELBooks

Independent family-owned bookshop, carrying fiction and non-fiction books and stationery. Offers twice-weekly story-time sessions for preschool children. Hosts regular author talks and book groups, and also offers a children's personal shopper service.

Winstone's Hunting Raven Books

10 Cheap Street, Frome, Somerset BA11 1BN
tel (01373) 473111
email winstonebooks3@gmail.com
Facebook www.facebook.com/HuntingRavenBooks
Twitter @HuntingRavenBks
Proprietor Wayne Winstone, *Manager* Tina Gaisford-Waller

Long-established independent bookshop with extensive range of books and gifts for all ages and a strong children's section. Holds events and signings throughout the year.

South-West Independent bookshop of the year. Other Winstone's bookshops can be found in Sidmouth (http://winstonebooks.co.uk/sidmouth) and Sherborne (https://winstonebooks.co.uk/sherborne).

BOOKSELLERS FOR COLLECTORS

Blackwell's Rare Books

48–51 Broad Street, Oxford OX1 3BQ
tel (01865) 333555
email rarebooks@blackwell.co.uk
website www.blackwell.co.uk/rarebooks
Facebook www.facebook.com/blackwellrare
Twitter @blackwellrare

Deals in early and modern first editions of children's books, among other subjects.

Bookmark Children's Books

Fortnight, Broad Hinton, Swindon, Wilts. SN4 9NR
tel (01793) 731693
email leonora.f.smith@gmail.com
Contacts Leonora Smith, Anne Excell

Mail-order bookseller, specialising in books for collectors, ranging from antiquarian to modern. A wide range of first editions, novelty and picture books, chap-books, ABCs, annuals, etc. Also a selection of vintage toys, games, greetings cards and illustrated postcards, dolls and nursery china. Book-search service available within this specialist area. Member of PBFA, exhibiting at PBFA book fairs in London, Bristol, York, Bath and Oxford. Established 1973.

Henry Sotheran Ltd

2–5 Sackville Street, Piccadilly, London W1S 3DP
tel 020-7439 6151
email rh@sotherans.co.uk
website www.sotherans.co.uk
website https://sotherans.co.uk/blogs/latest-posts
Facebook www.facebook.com/sotherans
Twitter @Sotherans
Instagram @sotherans_piccadilly
Contact Rosie Hodge

Large showroom with hundreds of important children's books spanning two centuries, specialising in first editions and illustrated works by pivotal artists. Opening hours: Mon–Fri 9.30am–6pm. Two specialist catalogues issued annually, available free on request.

Stella & Rose's Books

Monmouth Road, Tintern, Monmouthshire, NP16 6SE
tel (01291) 689755
email enquiry@stellabooks.com
website www.stellabooks.com
Twitter @stellarosebooks

Specialists in rare, out-of-print children's and illustrated books, also carrying a large and varied general stock (over 25,000 books in stock). Stock available for sale via website. Specialist lists issued regularly. Open 10.00am–5.00pm seven days a week. Single items or collections purchased. Founded 1991.

Books, sites and blogs about children's books

These listings include some of the best print and online resources about children's books for readers, writers and illustrators.

BOOKS

The Oxford Companion to Children's Literature

Edited by Daniel Hahn
Published by Oxford University Press (2015, 2nd edn)
ISBN 978-0-1987-1554-2

An indispensable reference book for anyone interested in children's books. Over 900 biographical entries deal with authors, illustrators, printers, publishers, educationalists and others who have influenced the development of children's literature. Genres covered include myths and legends, fairy tales, adventure stories, school stories, fantasy, science fiction, crime and romance. This book is of particular interest to librarians, teachers, students, parents and collectors.

The Reading Bug – and how you can help your child to catch it

by Paul Jennings
Published by Penguin Books (2004)
ISBN 978-0-1413-18400

Paul Jennings is a well-known children's author. This book explains, in his unique humorous style, how readers can open up the world through a love of books. He cuts through the jargon and the controversies to reveal the simple truths, which should enable adults to infect children with the reading bug.

Sticks and Stones: The Troublesome Success of Children's Literature from Slovenly Peter to Harry Potter

by Jack Zipes
Published by Routledge (2002)
ISBN 978-0-4159-38808

Jack Zipes – translator of the Grimm tales, teacher, storyteller and scholar – questions whether children ever really had a literature of their own. He sees children's literature in many ways as being the 'grown-ups' version' – a story about childhood that adults tell kids. He discusses children's literature from the 19th century moralism of Slovenly Peter (whose fingers get cut off) to the wildly successful *Harry Potter* books. Children's literature is a booming market but its success, this author says, is disguising its limitations. *Sticks and Stones* is a forthright and engaging book by someone who clearly cares deeply about what and how children read.

1001 Children's Books You Must Read Before You Grow Up

Edited by Julia Eccleshare
Published by Cassell Illustrated (2009)
ISBN 978-1-8440-36714

This aims to provide an introduction to the best of children's literature, ranging from international classics to contemporary writers. Reviews of each book are accompanied by line drawings and artwork from the books themselves. A number of authors including Michael Morpurgo and Jacqueline Wilson also write about their favourite books. The reviews are ordered according to the book's publication date, from past to present, and age range of the reader.

The Ultimate Book Guide

Edited by Leonie Flynn, Daniel Hahn and Susan Reuben
Published by A&C Black (2009)
ISBN 978-1-4081-04385

Over 600 entries covering the best books for children aged 8–12, from classics to more recently published titles. Funny, friendly and frank recommendations written for children by their favourite and best-known authors including Anthony Horowitz, Jacqueline Wilson, Celia Rees, Darren Shan, David Almond and Dick King-Smith. Plus features on the most popular genres.

The Ultimate First Book Guide

Edited by Leonie Flynn, Daniel Hahn and Susan Reuben
Published by A&C Black (2008)
ISBN 978-0-7136-73319

Comprehensive reference to help children aged 0–7 with their first steps into the world of books. Covers board books and novelty books, through to classic and contemporary picture books, chapter books and more challenging reads. It includes recommendations and features from top authors and experts in the field of children's books, including former Children's Laureate Michael Rosen, Tony Bradman, Malachy Doyle and Wendy Cooling. There are also special features on a variety of topics and themed lists, and a

Books

selection of cross-references to other titles children may enjoy.

The Ultimate Teen Book Guide
Edited by Daniel Hahn and Leonie Flynn
Published by A&C Black (2010, 2nd edn)
ISBN 978–1–4081–04378

Listings of over 700 books that might interest teenage readers, recommended and reviewed by authors such as Melvin Burgess, Anthony Horowitz, Meg Cabot, Eoin Colfer and Philip Pullman. Reviews cover the classics to cult fiction, and graphic novels to bestsellers, and each is cross-referenced to other titles as suggestions of what to read next. The book also contains essays on areas of teenage writing including *Race in Young Adult Fiction* by Bali Rai and *Off the Rails* by Kevin Brooks. There are also the results of a national teen readers' poll, plus reviews from teen readers.

ONLINE

Armadillo
www.armadillomagazine.co.uk

An online magazine about children's books, including reviews, interviews, features and profiles. New issues are posted at the end of March, June, September and December. It was founded in 1999 by author Mary Hoffman as a review publication for children's books.

BBC Bitesize
www.bbc.co.uk/bitesize

Information about UK schools' curriculum. Useful for those wishing to write for educational publishers but also for keeping abreast of curricular topics.

The Bookbag
www.thebookbag.co.uk

A UK-based website focused on great reviews about children's books, there are also booklists and information about book awards, as well as articles and author interviews.

Books for Keeps
http://booksforkeeps.co.uk

Featuring a quarterly online magazine for children's books including book reviews and features.

The Bookseller
www.thebookseller.com

A magazine for the publishing industry, sharing news on author deals, book launches and industry features to subscribers. Some content is available for free, including the fortnightly *Chapter and Verse: The Art of Selling Children's Books* podcast.

BookTrust
www.booktrust.org.uk

Dedicated children's reading charity, this is a useful site for professionals working with young readers. Information on events, prizes, books, authors, etc.

BookTrust Great Books Guide
www.booktrust.org.uk/books-and-reading/our-recommendations/great-books-guide/

BookTrust's independent annual 'pick of the best' in children's paperback fiction published in the previous calendar year. It is designed to help parents and those interested in children's reading to select books for children, from babies to teenagers.

Branford Boase Award
www.branfordboaseaward.org.uk

The website for the annual children's book award dedicated to debut children's writers and their editor. Includes a writing competition for young people.

CBBC
www.bbc.co.uk/cbbc

Website of the CBBC channel with games, activities and news for children.

The Children's Book Council
www.cbcbooks.org

The Children's Book Council in the USA is dedicated to encouraging literacy and the enjoyment of children's books. The website includes reviews of children's books published in the USA, forthcoming publications and author profiles. A good site for checking out the US marketplace.

Children's Laureate
www.booktrust.org.uk/what-we-do/childrens-laureate

Official website of the Children's Laureate with resources and activities for children.

Children's Literature
http://childrenslit.com/

US website of the Children's Literature Comprehensive Database (CLCD), a subscription database with over 100,000 reviews of children's books. Plus links to US author and illustrator websites.

CILIP Carnegie & Kate Greenaway Medals
http://carnegiegreenaway.org.uk

This website follows the only UK children's book award where the winners are selected by specialist children's librarians. The website includes a 'shadowing' area for schools to leave their comments about the books, plus interviews with shortlisted authors.

The Federation of Children's Book Groups

http://fcbg.org.uk/

The FCBG runs an annual children's book award, judged by children, and a network of local groups for those interested in finding out more about children's books and authors. See page 362.

Good Reads for Children

www.goodreads.com/genres/childrens

The Amazon-owned website supports consumer reviews about books for children that can be researched by categories including middle grade and picture books, etc.

The Horn Book

www.hbook.com

US website hosting *The Horn Book Guide Online*, a comprehensive, fully searchable database of over 70,000 book titles and reviews for children and young adults. Also includes a regular newsletter sharing an interview with an author or illustrator, *Authors & Illustrators talk with Roger*, and and a monthly e-newsletter for parents, *Notes from the Horn Book*.

House of Illustration

www.houseofillustration.org.uk

The brainchild of author and illustrator Quentin Blake, the House of Illustration celebrates all forms of illustration, runs regular talks and events and supports schools-based activities.

National Literacy Trust

www.literacytrust.org.uk

The organisation is focused on developing literacy among adults and children and its website documents its activities. See page 364.

Picture Book Den

http://picturebookden.blogspot.com

An independent website created by professional children's authors based in the UK and Ireland where they share their passion for picture books, with blogs on getting published and creating picture books.

ReadingZone.com

https://readingzone.com

A magazine-style website, created with Arts Council support, dedicated to children's books including monthly book reviews by teachers and librarians as well as children, chapters to download, author interviews, news, activities and a regular newsletter. There are distinct areas for teachers, librarians, families, children and teenagers.

Scottish Book Trust

www.scottishbooktrust.com

Information on books for children of all ages in Scotland plus a national programme of events with children's writers: author tours, festivals, writing competitions and exciting activities.

Seven Stories

www.sevenstories.org.uk

The Seven Stories National Centre for Children's Books, based in Newcastle, provides regular events and exhibitions dedicated to children's literature which are highlighted on its website. See page 359.

The Story Museum

www.storymuseum.org.uk

Stories from around the world to watch, hear, read and tell.

Toppsta

https://toppsta.com/

A children's book review website that invites children and adults to review books for children and teenagers.

Words & Pictures

www.wordsandpics.org

The online magazine of SCBWI, a worldwide organisation of writers and illustrators of children's books, with advice on writing, illustrating, news, blogs and activities. See page 356.

Who Next ... ?

www.whonextguide.com

Writers of children's fiction are listed with suggestions of other authors who write in a similar way, together with key book and series titles. There is a small annual subscription fee for accessing the information.

World Book Day

www.worldbookday.com

Providing a range of resources for children and teenagers, from writing and illustration masterclasses to quizzes, activities and reading ideas.

Inspiring writers

Making a writer

Sarah Crossan describes what led her to take her writing seriously, put her secret dream of being a writer into practice and – with time and resolve – achieve her goal.

I never thought a person like me could be a writer. I was an incredibly ordinary child, have become an even more ordinary adult and believed many untruths about writing and writers. Firstly, I didn't come from a family connected to the literati, which I perceived as a major problem, though at the time I probably hadn't even come across the word 'literati'. Secondly, I wasn't privately educated and didn't have anything close to a BBC newsreader's accent – grand drawback. Finally, and perhaps most importantly, I didn't own a serious-looking scarf. You know the ones. All proper artists own them.

When I went to university, to study Philosophy and Literature, my fears about what went into making a writer were compounded as I carefully stalked the creative writing students: they all seemed aloof, important and occasionally sad, hanging out in the humanities building, wearing oversized jumpers and, yes, their scholarly scarves.

After my undergraduate degree, convinced writing wasn't for me (and secretly hating all those creative writing students who'd spent three years smugly impersonating Margaret Atwood), I went off to study teaching. It was a way to make books a part of my daily life. And I was actually really good at it. The students fell in love with words and sentences, with poems and novels. I even convinced a class of hardened Shakespeare haters (one of whom offered to steal my car for £50 so I could pick up the insurance money!) to perform scenes from *Romeo and Juliet*, as well as partake in some Renaissance dancing. I loved teaching – my job was about books and kids, words and relationships.

Then came an afternoon that changed everything – a lesson that had an outcome missing from my planning notes. I was teaching poetry, encouraging students to write about their dreams, their hopes, how they saw their lives developing. I believed in those kids. I knew they could be anything they wanted to be if they just puffed out their chests and did some hard work. They wrote wonderful poems. They wrote moving poems. And then, at the end of the lesson, one child put up his hand and asked a question: 'Have you always wanted to be an English teacher, Miss?'. Now, a more sensitive person might have read some subtext into this, namely *'Why are you a teacher, Miss? You're terrible at your job.'* But I don't think that's what he meant. He genuinely wanted to know whether or not I'd lived my dreams, so shyly I explained that, as well as being a teacher, I wanted to be a writer, a poet and a novelist, but that I didn't think I quite had what it took. The boy frowned, as did a few other students, and angrily replied, 'Well you have a bit of cheek then, don't you, telling us to live our dreams when you haven't even done it yourself. Have you even tried?'

Despite being young, I was a strict teacher; I never tolerated rudeness, but in that moment I was dumbstruck – because he was right. Who was I to lecture them on bravery and risk when I had never taken myself nor my own desires seriously? Instead of asking him to leave the room, where I could speak to him about his tone of voice, I quietly said, 'You're right. I've been too afraid to try.'

On the basis of that very bald conversation, I applied to go back to university and study creative writing – which I did the very next year, annoying the head teacher who had to find a replacement for the next academic year at short notice.

And so I began to write. And I began to take my writing seriously. Rather than going to the cinema when friends asked, I started to say, 'Sorry, I can't. I'm writing.' When they seemed irritated by my resolve, I didn't care. If I wanted to achieve my dream of writing for a living, I had to believe in myself, otherwise no one else would. I found a way out of my shame and into a pattern of work that I loved.

That doesn't mean a contract came quickly; it didn't. It was another ten years of graft and fine-tuning my skills before I found an agent, listed in the *Writers' & Artists' Yearbook* in the children's section, who seemed to fit the bill. I sent her my book and astonishingly she took me on within days. We are still together, for better or for worse, and when I start to flounder and find myself wondering if I should pack it all in, she reminds me that I don't need anything to succeed except a dash of self-belief and a bit of hard work. Oh, and my serious writerly scarf, of course. Everyone needs one of those!

Sarah Crossan is the award-winning author of the young adult novel *One* (Bloomsbury 2015) which won the CILIP Carnegie Medal, the YA Book Prize, the CBI Book of the Year award and the CLiPPA Poetry Award in 2016. Also published by Bloomsbury, her books *The Weight of Water* (2011) and *Apple and Rain* (2014) were both shortlisted for the CILIP Carnegie Medal. Sarah's other children's novels are *Breathe* (2012), its sequel *Resist* (2013), *We Come Apart* (co-authored with Brian Conaghan 2017) and the free verse novel *Moonrise* (2017), which was shortlisted for the Costa Children's Book Award, the YA Book Prize and the CBI Book of the Year Award. Her latest books are *Toffee* (Bloomsbury 2019) and a free verse novel for adults *Here is the Beehive* (Bloomsbury Circus 2020). Sarah was Laureate na nÓg, the Irish Children's Laureate, from 2018-20.

Finding your voice and point of view

Anna Wilson looks at the importance of finding your own distinctive voice as a writer and at the impact and technical considerations involved in choosing a particular point of view to tell your story. She shows how much this choice of viewpoint influences your reader's perceptions, enabling you to 'be the director of your own movie'.

When, as a teenager, I asked someone what it would take to become a writer, they said rather grandly, 'You need to find your voice'. This felt like an important pronouncement, so I nodded sagely, having absolutely no idea what they meant or how I was going to be able to do this for myself. I thought that finding my voice must go hand in hand with having a Muse, or Inspiration, or Life Experience. These were all things I had read that writers should have – and all things which seemed far out of reach to a grammar school kid living in suburbia, where the most exciting thing ever to happen was when Deirdre-next-door got ideas above her station and had a conservatory built.

What I didn't realise was that, to be a writer, I didn't need to do anything other than to write, and I had been doing that ever since I could pick up a pencil. I still have some of my early scribbles – drawings of people, mostly, to whom I would chatter endlessly, creating conversations and adventures for them; these soon morphed into cartoons influenced by my love of the *Beano*, and from there I started writing my own 'proper stories'. By the time I had reached my early teens I had already filled innumerable notebooks with angsty thoughts and records of what I had been up to at school and elsewhere. And I was becoming conscious, through my obsessive reading, that 'becoming a writer' was something that I could aspire to. Yet how to achieve this? How on earth was I to 'find my voice'?

We all have a voice. And if we all started out doing as the great scriptwriter Russell T. Davies does – 'writing how you speak', each of us would soon see our own voice appearing on the page straight away. One of the first mistakes emerging writers tend to make (I include my younger self in this) is that they try too hard to nail down a voice, and end up writing something that rings false. Looking back at my journals, I can see I had a distinctive voice emerging then: the cadence and rhythm of my writing is 100% me, and it has found its way into so much of my children's fiction via characters who bear a striking resemblance to that bored suburban kid who lived in her head and dreamed of better things.

In writerly terms, 'voice' is the combination of **what** is said and **how** it's said. Anyone reading this will be able to think immediately of books with a voice so real it leaps off the page and keeps on talking inside your head long after you've stopped reading. I am thinking of Lauren Child's *Clarice Bean* series (1999–) or Louise Rennison's inimitable Georgia Nicolson in her teen books such as *Angus, Thongs and Full-Frontal Snogging* (Piccadilly Press 1999) or McKay Tambo in Alex Wheatle's *Crongton Knights* trilogy (Little, Brown 2017–). In picture books, voice will come through as strongly in the illustrations as it does in the text. Think of the way the mouse looks out from the pages of *The Gruffalo* (Macmillan 1999); Axel Scheffler's illustrations make sure that the mouse is saying as much with his eyes as Julia Donaldson's words have him say with his mouth.

Much of what constitutes voice will come down to 'point of view', which can often be another minefield. In fact, this seems to get emerging writers into more of a tangle than almost any other technical issue, and it's certainly something that I struggle with every single time I sit down to write a new book. Should I write in the first person and thereby show the whole story through one immutable lens? Should I step back and have an omniscient narrator who can move silently and god-like through my story and have a finger in every pie, a foot in every room, an eye in every meeting-place? Or should I choose one character to take my reader through the story, but keep a pace behind them by writing in third person whilst also staying close to their experiences? In other words, where am I allowing the narrator to stand? From which point of view am I allowing my reader to see things?

All books are written by people, about people – even when they're apparently about animals: any child reading *The Gruffalo* will recognise the power of the mouse's cunning over the other animals' fear and stupidity, and thus the mouse is really a human in disguise. And any being, human or otherwise, can perceive certain things through their senses – and not perceive others. As visual animals we talk about 'view', but good writing in fact uses all the senses, not only sight. Therefore, 'point of view' will necessarily include all the senses. We can't physically see behind our own heads, but we can smell the bakery behind us. We can't see someone six floors up, but we might hear, from the open window, the music they are playing. In writing, as in the rest of life, this idea of what a particular being can and can't perceive widens to include how they understand it, how it makes them feel, what else they know about the world, what they think of it all, what they say, and – crucially – what they don't say about it. All of this is point of view.

When I was writing my *Vlad the World's Worst Vampire* series (Stripes Publishing 2017–), I wanted to keep close to Vlad's experiences. He was going out into the human world for the first time and discovering that it was very different from the terrifying pictures his parents had painted of it. I wanted the reader to see things through his eyes and to taste human food as he tasted it, to see human school and human relationships as he saw them. I therefore chose to write the stories in 'close third', rather than from the perspective of an all-seeing, all-knowing, distant third-person narrator. I could have chosen first person, of course, but I rejected this as I didn't want to use such a limited viewpoint that my reader had only Vlad's voice in their heads. Also, as this is a series for confident young readers who are just becoming adept at reading alone, I didn't want to stray too far from the storytelling voice that they would be used to from most picture books and early readers. So I had many considerations in mind when choosing this 'close third' point of view.

However, I knew there were some things to be aware of in choosing this slightly limited viewpoint: the reader could only ever know what Vlad knew, could only ever see what Vlad saw; and I risked letting him stay in his thoughts too long if I left him on his own for any length of time. This led to me to invent a character who was nearly always with him – his pet bat, Flit. Flit acted like Vlad's own conscience, helping him work through problems or challenging him when he was about to do something stupid (pets can be useful like that in children's fiction, even if they don't actually speak!).

A final note on point of view: whichever voice you choose, and from whichever standpoint you prefer to allow your characters to speak, try to 'vary the camera angles' in your writing. By this I mean, don't always be showing your reader an intense close-up where we are so inside the character's head that we have lost sight of what is going on outside it – this can be a very claustrophobic experience for the reader. Equally, don't swamp the reader with continual long 'wide-angle' shots that give pages and pages of scene-setting;

Books

these can take the reader away from the action and from what the characters are thinking, saying and doing in the moment. Think of yourself as the director of your own movie, particularly when it comes to editing. Ask yourself: has my character spent too long walking down that path wondering what they are going to have for dinner? Or: has the narrator spent too long sitting in a car looking out of the window on the way to their auntie's, taking in the scenery and describing the whole, boring journey beat by beat? Remember that the reader needs to see only the things that matter. Think of how a director uses 'jump-cuts' to move us from one scene to the next. As the American writer Colum McCann says in his wonderful book *Letters to a Young Writer* (Random House 2017):

> It is a good trick to assume that you have a number of changeable lenses. Be fish-eye. Be wide-angle. Be telephoto. Zoom in. Zoom out. Distort. Sharpen. Divide. Imagine yourself into the actual camera. Find the words that are glass and shutter both.

It's all about the degree to which we are inside a character's head. And the choice of which 'person' we choose to write in, or which point of view we choose, will have an impact on how close in we are, right from the off. In first person we are clearly right in the thick of things – we are, as McCann says, 'glass and shutter both'. In third person, there is an immediate element of detachment, but there are degrees of closeness too; you only have to think of how Hilary Mantel writes from the point of view of Thomas Cromwell in *Wolf Hall* (Fourth Estate 2009) to see that 'he' can easily transubstantiate into 'I'.

If all this sounds like too much, and you still have no idea how to find your voice or which point of view is right for your work in progress, step away from the manuscript and give yourself a little exercise to loosen things up. Think yourself into your main character's shoes. If you've been writing in the first person, swap to third – close or omniscient, it's up to you. If you've been using third person, swap to first. Now have a think about a scene that you're struggling to inject some energy into; maybe your character is too much in their head, or they seem to be taking an age to get from A to B and frankly, even you, their creator, is feeling pretty bored with them now. Flip the point of view and see what happens. Has it brought you closer to a character you were struggling to bring alive on the page? Has it given you a perspective that has shown your character in a startling new light? Do you prefer this new piece written from this point of view, or has your writing become stodgier? Why do you feel the way you do about these shifts of perspective?

Above all, have fun! It is in constantly trying things for size that we improve and grow as writers. And it is in playing around like children chattering to their first made-up scribbled pictures, that we learn to find our voice.

Anna Wilson is the author of over 50 books for children, including novels, non-fiction, poems, short stories, picture books and early readers. Her books include *The Parent Problem* (2016) and *The Family Fiasco* (2017), both published by Macmillan Children's, and *Spook-tacular Surprise* (Stripes Publishing 2019), the latest in her *Vlad the World's Worst Vampire* series. Her most recent picture book for children is *The Wide, Wide Sea* (Nosy Crow 2021). She produces an annual children's almanac *Nature Month-by-Month* (Nosy Crow/National Trust). Anna runs creative workshops and is a tutor for the London LitLab and the Arvon Foundation. She will be an RLF Fellow at Exeter University from 2022. See her website www.annawilson.co.uk for more information and read her blog on acwilsonwriter.wordpress.com. Follow her on Twitter @acwilsonwriter.

Notes from a Children's Laureate

Anthony Browne was the Children's Laureate 2009–11. Here he shares his passion for picture books and explains the importance of the Shape Game to develop the act of looking.

It was a long road to becoming the Children's Laureate but I believe it all started with the Shape Game, a simple drawing game that my brother and I thought we'd invented when we were young. I have spoken of this game to children all over the world, and they've made me realise that its prevalence in my own childhood was by no means unique. Children everywhere have invented their own versions of the Shape Game. It has certainly been a very important part of my career, for I have played it in every book I've made.

The rules are very simple: the first person draws an abstract shape; the second person, ideally using a different coloured pen, transforms it into something. It seems that all children love this game and are very good at it – far better than adults are. It is an unfortunate part of growing up that we lose a great deal of contact with our visual imagination. The wonder with which we look at the world diminishes, and this inhibits both our inclination to draw (most adults give up entirely) and also our ability to draw with any real creative value.

Even though the Shape Game is great fun to play, I believe it also has a serious aspect. Essentially, the game is about creativity itself. Every time we draw a picture, or write a story, or compose a piece of music, we are playing the Shape Game. When children ask me (and they always do) where I get my inspiration from, I tell them it's from the same place that they get theirs – from things that happened to me when I was a boy, or things that happened to my own children, from other people's stories, from films, from paintings or from dreams. There are so many sources of inspiration. Everything comes from somewhere else, and when we create something we're transforming our own experience into a picture, a book or perhaps a piece of music. We are playing our own Shape Game.

In my early years my father was the landlord of a pub near Bradford and apparently I used to stand on a table in the bar and tell stories to customers about a character called Big Dumb Tackle (whoever he was). I spent much of my childhood playing sport, fighting and drawing with my older brother and then studied graphic design in Leeds. While I was at art college my father died suddenly and horrifically in front of me, and this affected me hugely. I went through a rather dark period which didn't sit very happily with the world of graphic design. After leaving college I dabbled rather unsuccessfully in the advertising world then heard about a job as a medical artist and thought that it sounded interesting – it was. I worked at Manchester Royal Infirmary for three years painting delicate watercolours of grotesque operations. It taught me a lot more about drawing than I ever learned at art college, and I believe it taught me how to tell stories in pictures. I thought that it was probably time to move on when strange little figures started appearing in these paintings – and so began a career designing greetings cards. I continued to do this for many years working for the Gordon Fraser Gallery.

Gordon Fraser became a close friend and taught me a lot about card design which was to prove very useful when I started doing children's books. I experimented with many styles and many subjects, from snowmen to dogs with big eyes to gorillas. I sent some of my designs to various children's book publishers and it was through one of these that I met Julia MacRae who was to become my editor for the next 20 years. She taught me much of what I know about writing and illustrating children's books.

In 1976 I produced *Through the Magic Mirror*, a strange kind of book in which I painted many of the pictures before I wrote the story. I followed this with *A Walk in the Park*, a story I was to revisit 20 years later with *Voices in the Park*. Probably my most successful book is *Gorilla*, and it was around the time it was published in 1983 that I was badly bitten by a gorilla whilst being filmed for television at my local zoo.

I have published 50 books and been very lucky to win awards for some of these – the Kate Greenaway Medal twice (page 387) and the Kurt Maschler 'Emil' three times. In 2000 I was awarded the Hans Christian Andersen Medal (page 384), which is an international award and the highest honour a children's writer or illustrator can win, and I was the first British illustrator to receive it. My books have been translated into 28 languages. My illustrations have been exhibited in many countries – USA, Mexico, Venezuela, Colombia, France, Korea, Italy, Germany, Holland, Japan and Taiwan – and I've had the pleasure of visiting these places and working with local children and meeting other illustrators.

In 2001–02 I worked at Tate Britain with children using art as a stimulus to inspire visual literacy and creative writing activities. It was during this time that I conceived and produced *The Shape Game*.

In 2009 I was appointed Children's Laureate. In this capacity, my aim was to encourage more children to discover and love reading, focusing particularly on the appreciation of picture books, and the reading of both pictures *and* words. I strongly believe that picture books are special – they're not like anything else.

Sometimes I hear parents encouraging their children to read what they call 'proper' books (that's books without pictures) at an earlier and earlier age. This makes me sad, as picture books are perfect for sharing, and not just with the youngest children. As a father, I understand the importance of the bond that develops through reading and talking about picture books with your child. I believe the best picture books leave a tantalising gap between the pictures and the words, a gap that's filled by the reader's imagination, adding so much to the excitement of the book. Picture books are for everybody at any age, not books to be left behind as we grow older.

I also try to encourage the act of looking. Research has shown that visitors to art galleries spend an average of 30 seconds looking at each painting, and considerably more time reading the captions. It's an unfortunate element of growing up that we can lose a great deal of contact with our visual imagination, and by encouraging children – and adults – to play the Shape Game I hope this will change.

In the best picture books the pictures contain clues; they tell you what characters are thinking or how they're feeling. By reading these clues we get a far deeper understanding of the story. In the UK we have some of the best picture book makers in the world, and I want to see their books appreciated for what they are – works of art.

In spite of my concerns about the state of the market for picture books, I am optimistic about the future. I realise now more than ever that I am incredibly lucky to love what I do. Straight after finishing art college I was disheartened because it seemed inevitable that in order to make a living from art I would have to make massive compromises. The experience of doing those advertising jobs made any dreams I once had seem futile. I was getting paid, but the fun of drawing had been taken away. I retrieved some of the fun when

I was a medical illustrator, and I enjoyed making many of the card designs, but it wasn't until I discovered picture books that I learned it was possible to have as much fun with a paintbrush as I had done as a child *and* get paid for it. This is what I love most about my job. What I do now is exactly what I did then: tell stories and draw pictures. Nothing much has changed, not even my approach. Drawing was always my favourite thing to do, and you could say that my career is comparable to other little boys growing up and being paid to play with Lego or dress up as cowboys.

I am also extremely lucky that I have been able to continue 'playing' for a living for so long. I could never stop drawing. Even if I was to give up doing it for a living I would carry on drawing for pleasure. But doing it for a living *is* doing it for pleasure, so there really is no reason to stop!

Anthony Browne was the Children's Laureate 2009–11. His first book, *Through the Magic Mirror*, was published in 1976 and the classic, *Gorilla*, in 1983 won many awards, including the Kate Greenaway Medal and the Kurt Maschler Award. He has published a number of titles featuring the character Willy, the chimp. His other books include *Zoo*, *Alice's Adventures in Wonderland*, *Voices in the Park*, *Bear's Magic Pencil* and *Me and You*. In 2000 he was the first British illustrator to win the Hans Christian Andersen Award for his services to children's literature. *The Shape Game* was based on his experiences as Illustrator in Residence at Tate Britain in London 2001–2. His most recent book, *Little Frida*, was published by Walker Books in 2019.

See also...
- *Notes from Jacqueline Wilson, page 76
- *Who do children's authors write for?*, page 99
- *Writing books to read aloud*, page 104
- *Notes from the first Children's Laureate*, page 284

Notes from Jacqueline Wilson

Jacqueline Wilson shares her first experience of becoming a writing success.

I knew I wanted to be a writer ever since I was six years old. I thought it would be the most magical job in the world. You could stay at home by yourself and write stories all day long.

I loved making up stories. I had a serial story permanently playing in my head. I used to mutter the words, acting each imaginary character in turn, but I soon learnt that this made people stare or giggle. I mastered the art of saying the words silently, experiencing all sorts of extraordinary adventures internally, while I sat staring seemingly blankly into space. No wonder I was nicknamed Jacky Daydream at school. My Mum thought I wasn't all there, and was forever giving me a shake and telling me not to look so gormless. She laughed at me when I confided that I wanted to be a writer. 'Don't be so daft, Jac! Who on earth would want to read a book written by *you?*' she said.

She had a point. I was a totally unexceptional little girl, shy and anxious, barely able to say boo to a goose. My Mum wanted a daughter like Shirley Temple. She even permed my wispy hair to try to turn it into a cloud of golden ringlets. I ended up looking as if I'd been plugged into a light socket. I couldn't sing like Shirley, I couldn't tap dance like Shirley, and although I could recite long poems with dutiful expression I got so nervous performing I once wet myself on stage.

I didn't *want* to perform, well, certainly not in public. I would act out my stories enthusiastically whenever I was by myself, but I was a total shrinking violet in front of other people. I wasn't the life and soul of the party at school. I didn't clamour to have my friends round to play. I preferred playing elaborate imaginary games all by myself.

I saw a writing career as a wonderful grown-up version of these games. I suppose in a way it *is* – but I had no idea what it's *really* like to be a children's author. I don't think I've had a quiet day at home writing my book for weeks!

I suppose it used to be like that long ago. I've been writing children's books for nearly 50 years. For the first 20 years very few people had ever heard of me. I wrote several books a year for a whole variety of publishers. They were published, and if I hunted high and low I occasionally saw one title in a bookshop down at the end of the Ws. I got a few pleasant reviews, and I was stocked in libraries, but that was about it. I've got copies of my first 40 books and they're all first editions – because they didn't go into any other editions. Publishing was so different in those days. You were kept on lists even if your books barely covered their advances – although eventually my first publisher told me they didn't see the point in buying any more of my books because they were never ever going to be popular.

I was upset, of course, but I felt their remarks were justified. I wrote about lonely imaginative children, all of them odd ones out. I thought that only odd children themselves would want to read them. I was worried that I'd never find another publisher but very luckily for me I was taken on by Transworld (now Penguin Random House). I had the idea of writing a story about a fierce little kid in a children's home desperate to be fostered. I decided to tell it as if this child herself was writing her own life story. I wanted her to have a contemporary, quirky kind of name. Something like … Tracy Beaker.

I knew I wanted the book to have lots of black and white illustrations as if Tracy herself had drawn them. I wanted several to a page, even in the margins. David Fickling was my editor then and he's always been very open to suggestions. 'Brilliant!' he said, rubbing his hands. 'I think I know just the chap too. He's done some wonderful illustrations for poetry books. His name's Nick Sharratt. Let's all meet.'

So Nick and I met in the publishing offices. We were both very shy at first. Nick seemed lovely and very talented but I wasn't quite sure he was wacky enough for Tracy-type illustrations. Then I needed to bend down to get a pen out of my handbag on the floor. I saw Nick's socks peeping out from his trouser hem – astonishingly bright canary yellow socks. I knew everything was going to be fine the moment I saw those amazing socks. In fact it became a running joke between us and I'd buy him ever more zany spotty stripy socks all colours of the rainbow.

We've worked on so many books together now and it's been just as magical as I'd hoped – but not at all as I'd imagined. I don't stay home all by myself and write my books. I have a beautiful book-lined study but I'm hardly ever in it. Most days I do my writing on trains or in the back of cars, scribbling frantically in my notebook on my way to endless meetings and events. I'm lucky enough to be able to write happily in these rather distracting conditions, though it's sometimes embarrassing if the train is crowded. I write in the first person, and my lovely Italian notebooks look like private journals. If a business man glances from his *Daily Telegraph* to my notebook, God knows what he thinks if he reads my fictional teenage girl musing; *I so fancy the boy I saw on the bus. How will I ever get to go out with him?*

People often ask me why I think my books have been so successful. I think there are several reasons, apart from sheer luck. They look great, with Nick's fantastic covers, and his lively black and white illustrations inside break up the text and make it less forbidding for inexperienced readers. I care passionately about language and play little word games with my readers, though I try to write in an immediate colloquial style through my child narrators. My publishers promote my books with energy and commitment. However, I believe the *real* secret of my success is the fact that I started doing many school and library visits early on, talking about my books. In fact I don't think there's a single county in the UK where I haven't given a talk.

I vividly remember my very first talk to a small docile group of Year 7s in a secondary school. I was so nervous I could barely eat breakfast beforehand. I hoped I acted like a reasonably competent sociable adult but inside I was still that shy little girl, terrified of performing. However, I could see the whole point of giving talks to children. It was a wonderful way of introducing them to the delights of reading in general, and to my own books in particular! That was why I was willing to put myself through this torture.

I didn't really know what to talk *about*. It seemed like terrible showing off simply talking about myself and my own work. I ended up reading an extract from Daisy Ashford's *The Young Visiters* to show that children could very occasionally have their work published, and then reading an extract from *Jane Eyre*, which had been my favourite book when I was 12. I realised soon enough that this was completely the wrong approach. The children thought Daisy Ashford bizarre and *Jane Eyre* boring. They only livened up when I changed tack and talked about what I'd been like when I was young. I started to relate to them properly, and found I could tell them funny stories about myself as an earnest teenager, my experiences as a very junior journalist, and then chat to them about my latest book and how it came to be written.

I learnt how to give a talk – but it was a long time before I actually *enjoyed* doing it. I still got very fussed and anxious about it, and I hated it if I couldn't win every child over. After a while you learn that there will be an occasional kid who will give everyone a hard time. You just have to do your best and try to interest all the others. I slogged round several schools and libraries up and down the country every single week – and I learnt so much. This is where children's authors are so lucky. We can meet so many of our readers and find out what they like – and what they don't.

I only go to individual schools and libraries now as special favours to friends, but I still do many talks at festivals. Once you do something enough times you get so used to it you simply can't find it scary. I never get the slightest bit nervous now, even if I've got an audience of hundreds. I had to perform in the garden of Buckingham Palace in front of the Queen and 3,000 children and even that wasn't too worrying. It's just part of my job and I find it great fun.

But I got it right when I was six years old. The *most* magical part of being a writer is staying at home by myself and writing stories all day long.

Jacqueline Wilson DBE has sold over 40 million books in the UK, and has won many major awards. She was the Children's Laureate 2005–7 and was made a Dame for services to literature in 2008. In 2018 she revisited her *Tracy Beaker* series, with *My Mum Tracy Beaker*, which was shortlisted in the UK Author Category in the National Book Awards. This was followed by *We Are The Beaker Girls* in 2019 and adapted for television by CBBC in 2021, breaking their record for most successful launch ever with 2.1 million streams. Last year was marked by the coming-of-age novel *Love, Frankie* and the launch of a film adaptation of Jacqueline's E. Nesbit retelling *Four Children and It*. In 2021, Doubleday will publish another historical novel, *The Runaway Girls*, as well as a contemporary retelling of another E. Nesbit classic titled *The Primrose Railway Children*. Her website is www.jacquelinewilson.co.uk.

See also...
• *Who do children's authors write for?*, page 99

A word from J.K. Rowling

J.K. Rowling shares her first experience of becoming a writing success.

I can remember writing *Harry Potter and the Philosopher's Stone* in a café in Oporto. I was employed as a teacher at the language institute three doors along the road at the time, and this café was a kind of unofficial staffroom. My friend and colleague joined me at my table. When I realised I was no longer alone I hastily shuffled worksheets over my notebook, but not before Paul had seen exactly what I was doing. 'Writing a novel, eh?' he asked wearily, as though he had seen this sort of behaviour in foolish young teachers only too often before. '*Writers' & Artists' Yearbook*, that's what you need,' he said. 'Lists all the publishers and … stuff', he advised before ordering a lager and starting to talk about the previous night's episode of *The Simpsons*.

I had almost no knowledge of the practical aspects of getting published; I knew nobody in the publishing world, I didn't even know anybody who knew anybody. It had never occurred to me that assistance might be available in book form.

Nearly three years later and a long way from Oporto, I had almost finished *Harry Potter and the Philosopher's Stone*. I felt oddly as though I was setting out on a blind date as I took a copy of the *Writers' & Artists' Yearbook* from the shelf in Edinburgh's Central Library. Paul had been right and the *Yearbook* answered my every question, and after I had read and reread the invaluable advice on preparing a manuscript, and noted the time-lapse between sending said manuscript and trying to get information back from the publisher, I made two lists: one of publishers, the other of agents.

The first agent on my list sent my sample three chapters and synopsis back by return of post. The first two publishers took slightly longer to return them, but the 'no' was just as firm. Oddly, these rejections didn't upset me much. I was braced to be turned down by the entire list, and in any case, these were real rejection letters – even real writers had got them. And then the second agent, who was high on the list purely because I liked his name, wrote back with the most magical words I have ever read: 'We would be pleased to read the balance of your manuscript on an exclusive basis … '.

This piece was written for the very first edition of the *Children's Writers' & Artists' Yearbook*, published in 2004.

J.K. Rowling OBE CH is best known as the author of the seven *Harry Potter* novels (Bloomsbury), published between 1997 and 2007. The series has sold over 500 million copies worldwide, been translated into over 80 languages and made into eight blockbuster films. In 2016 J.K. Rowling collaborated with playwright Jack Thorne and director John Tiffany to create a stage play, *Harry Potter and the Cursed Child*, which is now playing in London, the USA and Australia. In the same year, she made her screenwriting debut with the film *Fantastic Beasts and Where to Find Them*. Inspired by the original companion volume, it was the first in a series of new adventures featuring wizarding world magizoologist Newt Scamander. The second, *Fantastic Beasts: The Crimes of Grindelwald*, was released in 2018, and the third instalment is due out in November 2021. J.K. Rowling also writes novels for adults. *The Casual Vacancy* (Little, Brown), was published in 2012 and adapted for television in 2015. Under the pseudonym Robert Galbraith, she is the author of the '*Strike*' crime series. There are five books in the series so far: *The Cuckoo's Calling* (2013), *The Silkworm* (2014), *Career of Evil* (2015), *Lethal White* (2018) and *Troubled Blood* (2020), all published by Little, Brown. The books have been adapted for television by the BBC and HBO.

If at first you don't succeed...

Frances Hardinge describes the steps she took, as a hopeful young writer, to brave rejection, persevere and grow in confidence, and the friends and resources that helped her find where her writing belonged and gain that first momentous book contract.

I was in my teens when I bought my first copy of the *Writers' & Artists' Yearbook*. Back then, the *Children's Writers' & Artists' Yearbook* didn't exist. But in those days I wasn't an adult writing children's fiction, I was a teenager trying my hand at adult fiction.

Buying the book felt significant – a little intimidating, in fact. I sensed that I was making a promise to myself. I wouldn't keep my stories safely hidden away. I would send them off to be judged, and expose my fragile, iridescent bubble-dreams to the jagged edges of the real world. In effect, I had *bought* some of my cowardly excuses into non-existence: '*I can't send my work off, I don't know where to start!*'; '*I don't know what to send, or where!*'. Well, now I did.

And whenever I let schoolwork or other commitments eat up all my time, I'd spot the *Yearbook* on my shelf, fire-engine red. A silent, insistent reminder of my promise to myself. A gentle but much-needed boot in the rear.

I meticulously typed out my stories on the roaring, ill-tempered electric typewriter I'd bought from my sister for five pounds. Every time I made an error and had to perform Tipp-Ex surgery, I agonised over it and considered typing the whole page again.

And all the while I was gripped by a crippling fear that my first submission might be my only chance, and that if I messed it up badly all would be lost. The submissions editor would look coldly at my clunkiest metaphor, or scowl at my Tipp-Ex, and then stride away to the dark chamber where the editor collective kept the Terrible Tome of Authors We Must Never Publish. They would add my name to the list, and from that moment all my other submissions would be doomed. Prospective editors would consult the book, see my name in blood-red letters, shake their heads and throw my manuscript in the bin.

Only after a few trembling submissions did I start to suspect that the Terrible Tome didn't actually exist. Rejection slips arrived in the post, but didn't bring the apocalypse with them. Occasionally there was an actual rejection letter. (My favourite of these effectively said: 'We rather liked your story, and we wish we knew what it was about.') Eventually I realised that I had nothing to lose but the cost of two stamps and a spoonful of pride. If I was turned down it didn't matter. All that mattered was that I kept trying.

By my twenties, I was subscribing to *Writers' News* and *Writing Magazine* to supplement the *Yearbook*. I now typed my stories on a little Franken-puter that my boyfriend had cobbled together from parts of discarded, elderly computers. My friends and I set up a small writers' group, which gave me a regular deadline to keep me writing. With their feedback I became more confident, and less precious about editing my work.

And one day, after sending a short story to a little independent magazine, I received an answer that wasn't a 'no'. This was the first in a series of 'not-no' responses. However, when I received my first book contract a few years later, it was thanks to my good friend Rhiannon Lassiter. She realised something I hadn't – that my peculiar dark fairy tales were actually children's fiction. Rhiannon persuaded me to try writing a children's novel, then wrested my first five chapters from my unwilling hands and marched off with them to her editor.

The *Children's Writers' & Artists' Yearbook* would have been invaluable to me as a young, aspiring children's writer, if I'd had the sense to realise that that was what I was. The latest editions of the *Yearbook* are even richer and more useful than those I bought in my teens and twenties, with more information on agents, prizes, courses, conferences, digital publishing and self-publishing, and a wealth of essays, articles and advice.

Even now, when I look at the *Writers' & Artists' Yearbook*, I still recall everything it symbolised for me. It looks too heavy for the shelf, packed to the binding with hunger, trepidation, determination and hope. It's still a little intimidating. Opportunities often are.

Frances Hardinge is the award-winning author of *Fly by Night* (Macmillan Children's Books 2005), winner of the 2006 Branford Boase Award, and of *Twilight Robbery* (Macmillan Children's Books 2011), shortlisted for the *Guardian* Children's Fiction Prize. Her other books include *Gullstruck Island* (Macmillan Children's Books 2009), *A Face Like Glass* (Pan Macmillan Children's 2012), *Cuckoo Song* (Pan Macmillan 2014), which won the Robert Holdstock Award for Best Novel at the British Fantasy Awards 2015, and *The Lie Tree* (Macmillan Children's Books 2015), which won the Costa Book of the Year 2015 award, the 2016 UKLA Book Award (12–16 category), the 2016 *Boston Globe* Horn Book Fiction Award and the 2016 *Los Angeles Times* Young Adult Literature Prize. *The Lie Tree* was also shortlisted for the Independent Booksellers Week Award 2015, the *Guardian* Children's Fiction Prize 2015 and the 2016 Carnegie Medal. Her latest book is *Deeplight* (Macmillan 2019). She was nominated for the 2021 Astrid Lindgren Memorial Award.

Parent your inner child: what kind of writer are you?

Lucy van Smit explores how to thrive as a writer in uncertain times and how to overcome anxiety, self-doubt and self-criticism. She explains how to apply four key principles of parenting to help you understand, boost and nurture your inner writer.

Your shadow is what you don't know about yourself

Heads up, I'm a dyslexic author who didn't know I had ADHD until after publication. And what should have been the best of times became months of Dark Nights, until my shiny, writerly soul forced me to stop and listen to my life. Luckily, I did, before a virus flipped our world inside out.

What has this to do with your writing career?

As a debutante author, I wish I'd seen overwhelm coming. I was unprepared for the anxiety that infected me and my writing friends. Do you struggle to soothe yourself when fear, rejection, procrastination and writer's block strike? Writers need to be able to regulate their emotions. Here's the kicker: maybe you don't see yourself as anxious? I didn't. I am cheerful, friendly, witty, clever, spiritual; I love life. And I'm tough. Really tough. After all, I'd been a successful TV producer who made documentaries on famous authors. I survived ten miscarriages, the stillbirth of our darling Luke; I'm an expert at getting a seriously dyslexic boy through pushy London day schools; a wife of 30 years … an artist … a writer … top friend … a great mother (something I didn't learn growing up – sorry Mum, but you were rubbish).

Pre-publication oblivion

Neuro-diversity shines at outwitting problems. In TV, I applauded myself for working 20-hour days, in the Philippines living on chocolate and orange juice for six weeks – classic shadow, ADHD behaviour. What you admire is often what kills you. Niceness disguises suppressed feelings. Overworking is labelled success.

Speed forward a decade or three, in the run-up to publication; already an insomniac, I had several nights a week with no sleep. I still didn't get it. Eventually, at the awesome age of 60, it occurred to me that my insomnia, since childhood, was anxiety. My niece sniggered when I told her my revelation. The thing is, unlike you lovelies, we didn't have the word 'anxiety' when I was growing up. We self-medicated with alcohol and distraction; from love affairs to careers.

Older, wiser, I read more. Energy Medicine (yes, my teenage son scoffed too, until the virus), Yoga, Flow Psychology, Nutrition, Spirituality, Podcasts, Writing Workshops. Bought loads more books. The arrogance of a conceptual brain – you try everything … except talking to your intuitive self.

When *Writers'* & *Artists'* asked me for a YA workshop

I wanted to share skills from the Family Links Parenting Programme I ran at my son's school. Its focus is emotional intelligence for otherwise cerebral, articulate, ambitious parents, whose kids behaved in mystifying ways. Who knew rebellion is a child's response to feeling powerless? What if procrastination is rebellion against our powerlessness in the publishing industry? There are four principles of parenting which are useful to apply to writers:

1. Know yourself

I am so busted. Did you know that Socrates ridiculed you if you studied any subject before you took the time to have a good hard look at yourself? In his *Four Quartets*, T.S. Eliot got it: 'We shall not cease from exploration./And the end of all our exploring./ Will be to arrive where we started./And know the place for the first time.' To be a good author, you need to know what makes you tick.

What don't you know about yourself?

As writers, not knowing your shadow shows up in blurting out mean words to yourself, or sabotaging your dreams by never finishing that book.

Mystical, archetypal patterns of power help me decode the excuses I make. What archetype is pulling *your* strings? Are you playing your Victim card? Your Prostitute card; negotiating survival on any terms? We all share four Survival Archetypes. For example, everyone has a Child Archetype – but which one? The Nature Child? The Wounded Child? The Abandoned Child? When we are unconscious, we abandon ourselves. Writers often abandon their own voice: you write what others want; you rate others' approval above your own. This is central in understanding young adults; teenagers often abandon themselves to fit in with their peers. It was the core theme for my debut YA novel, *The Hurting* (Chicken House 2018). Abandoned as a baby by her mother, Nell abducts baby Ulv Pup to win a boy's approval. Redemption comes when her greatest flaw becomes her greatest strength; Nell must choose between the damaged Lukas, the love of her life, or saving the abandoned baby from wolves on his wild Norwegian mountain.

You know the power of words

… but do you notice how you speak to yourself? For instance, using words like 'blame', 'I don't deserve this' or 'I'm entitled' is the language of your Victim Archetype. Author Caroline Myss advises editing shame words out of your vocabulary. And Goethe knew that, once you 'decide', the universe steps in behind you. Intention is everything.

Are you a conceptual or an intuitive writer?

Know your inner writer. Are you an intuitive or a conceptual one? We veer towards one or the other, and ignorance is an obstacle to getting your work to a publishable standard. Have you ever been told your writing is beautiful, and wondered why you're not signed? Do your characters sing off the page with originality? Do agents love, love, love your voice, but don't snap you up?

Maybe, often, it's because the promise of your voice sputters out. Your story rambles; agents give up, confused. Somehow your right brain can't seem to fix your story problem; you add more events to add a bit of structure, only to make the narrative flat, linear. You struggle with the dynamics of drama, conflict. But everyone loves your characters, you wail. You brought them to life. They're so real. Of course. You poured your soul into them. But still … your story doesn't sell.

A conceptual writer is the exact opposite

You've read every writing craft book going. You can hit the Inciting Incident on page one – hey, you can hit it in the opening paragraph. You can write a mesmerising Hook. You nail your story in a 25-word logline (one-sentence summary) and have all those important beats, conflict, climax, rising tension, a great ending. You know exactly what happens to your protagonist at Midpoint. You know her 'flaw' and her basic 'need'. But you don't get snapped up. Why? Maybe, often, agents don't care enough about your characters. Readers don't feel for them, because *you* didn't feel anything when you wrote them. You can't access emotion from your left brain.

We tend to play to our strengths and hide weaknesses, which makes them worse. Learn to use both sides of your brain, but not at the same time. This is why you don't stop to edit when you write your first draft. Editing is a left-brain activity. Switching between two brain hemispheres is a skillset every writer can learn.

Screenwriting guru, Corey Mandell, calls the process 'creative integration'. He advocates an arduous training; conceptual writers are not allowed to structure or plot, for months! Intuitive writers must stop creating dialogue (ouch) until you can crack structure. I don't buy Mandell's theory that your *corpus callosum*, the bit facilitating communication between brain hemispheres, can't work them both at the same time, nor that it takes ages to re-train writers. Practice builds neural pathways, so write. Stop avoiding what you don't like to do – outlining, for instance. Think of it as eating your greens as a kid. A little goes a long way, and there are new tools to help. My favourite tool is 'energy medicine' – brilliant for connecting both sides of your brain, fast. It works by crossing and strengthening the energy pathways in your body. I practise Donna Eden's Daily Energy Routine (https://edenenergymedicine.com/donnas-daily-energy-routine) before I start to write. It calms even a bonkers brain like mine.

Music is another activity that uses both parts of the brain simultaneously. Conceptual writers, try meditating before you start: dance, create a sacred space, breathe, focus on your body, set an intention that tunes you into your creative right brain. You know, by the language you use, which part of the brain you are firing.

As a general principle, intuitive writers do best if they outline first. Keep it simple. Sketch, map it out, just so you know where you're going. Think … what is best for your story? Best for your characters? And best for you to write? When that all aligns, it feels like flow … fun! But conceptual writers, hold off planning. Play first, and discover your characters, before you work on your brilliant plot. Make us *care* first.

2. Empathy

To be a good parent, you need the ability to empathise with your child and put yourself in their shoes. Pixar have a formula to enable conceptual writers to write emotion for their protagonist:

$$EC = EM\,(R+P^2) +H +A +ES +(MS)$$

Don't panic … it's easier than it looks!

To create Empathy (EM) with your reader you need to find the Emotional Core (EC) of your character. What drives them? Fear? Love of a sister? Pixar creates empathy through Recognition (R) of heaping obstacles, so we pity the Protagonist (P^2), makes them Human (H) and gives them a skill for us to Admire (A), like bravery. Also create high Emotional Stakes (ES) … what happens if your protagonist fails? The final element (MS) stands for Meaning: the 'why' of your story. Make readers care what happens to your characters and empathise with what they desperately want or need.

3. Appropriate expectations

The third principle of good parenting. Do you have Appropriate Expectations of your inner writer? (What? … I hear you say.) How long have you been writing? Ten years? Two? Do you assume your inner writer should behave with the maturity of your chronological age – even if you've only been writing for a year or two?

Inappropriate Expectations cause a lot of unnecessary stress. Would you say to a toddler, 'Get up, you Dummy!' when they fall down? But you say that to yourself all the time. There's a reason why Enid Blyton locked her kids away – so she could write. And why Barbara Hepworth dumped her triplets on friends – so she could sculpt. Do you work? Do you have a young family? Or elderly parents? Do you have Appropriate Expectations of what you can get done … or of where you think your writing career should be? My simple rule is: if you are stressed, your expectations are inappropriate. As a writer, have compassion for yourself. Rest.

4. Positive discipline

Finally, in parenting terms, Positive Discipline means praise. We praise children in order to focus on what they are doing right. Good teachers praise. Constant self-criticism doesn't help you perform better or love writing more. We forget how to praise ourselves. Practise. Praise your inner writer for showing up. Praise switches off that constant inner critic that says you're not good enough at this writing malarkey.

You can't praise and criticise yourself at the same time. So praise yourself – when you think like a writer, when you read as a writer, when you sit down to write. We don't compare our children, so don't compare yourself to published authors. Praise yourself for just being you, not for doing more or achieving more. Success will happen naturally, joyfully. Play more. Fun breeds success.

While it's useful to think of parenting your inner writer child, don't take it as an excuse to baby yourself, to have unlimited duvets days, or to 'snowflake', as my teenage son calls it. Writing needs a lot of self-discipline to sit down and write. When it gets tough, finish what you have started. Breathe. Exercise. Play. Know what kind of writer you are before you even think about getting published. I promise that knowing yourself better helps you write better. And when you do send your work out, don't wait to hear back; write something new, don't wait for approval. End of story.

Former TV producer and artist, **Lucy van Smit** won the Bath Children's Novel Award with her debut novel, *The Hurting* (Chicken House 2018), pitched as 'Nordic Noir Wuthering Heights'. Lucy's latest project is *A Writer's Journal Workbook*, publishing in January 2022 (Bloomsbury). Lucy has a BA Hons in Fine Art and a Distinction in her MA in Creative Writing. See http://lucyvansmit.com for more information, and follow Lucy on Twitter and Instagram @Lucyvansmit.

How stories shape you as a writer

Patrice Lawrence reflects on how she found her voice through the stories she read.

I'm writing this in rather unexpected circumstances. I had originally planned a few paragraphs about my love of reading and how privileged I feel now that my own books are on the shelves of libraries and shops and in the hands of readers. I do still feel incredibly privileged, but as we're coming to understand the long-term global impact of the covid-19 virus, it's impossible not to reflect further.

Like many full-time writers, I smiled knowingly in the early days of the pandemic lockdown. Stay inside? That's what we do anyway, isn't it? Hanging around in our pyjamas, staring mystically into space and occasionally tapping a laptop. But, actually, for me that's just a small part of the story. Many of my books are set in London – a city crammed full of history. If I look up, I see Hercules taming horses on the Royal Mews, a pterodactyl on the Natural History Museum and angels on the Apollo Theatre. When I look down, I see clay pipe stems on the Thames foreshore and fragments of pottery that were held by hands hundreds of years ago. So many stories, waiting to be collected and assembled. London also – usually – vibrates with the clamour of many different voices. There are moments of drama happening everywhere. And when I'm not eavesdropping and scribbling notes, I'm visiting schools, learning from the children and young people I write for and about. But not now.

It is an uncertain, frightening time, but what has become clear is the absolute importance of stories. Writers and illustrators have been sharing their stories online; children and young people encouraged to tell their own tales. Struggling to write or even read fiction, I've lost myself in audiobooks, finding comfort in books being read to me.

Stories, though, have shaped me for as long as I can remember. I'm part of the first generation of Caribbean-heritage people to be born in the UK. I have lived in households that were often different from those around me – multi-ethnic, or lone parent, or in a private foster arrangement. I've never lived in a family where we're all the same colour. I was a passionate reader from very young, but there were never stories featuring families like mine.

I started writing. I wrote and illustrated stories about a giant purple rabbit for my toddler brother. I delivered my Year 7 history homework about the Saxons in rhyming couplets (thank you, Mr Mann, for the A). When I was 13, I hit pay dirt when my poem published in the *Brighton Evening Argus* earned me a £1 postal order. At sixth-form college, my 1980s version of *The Wizard of Oz* was performed on stage, complete with Michael Jackson-esque Thriller zombies with releasable arms!

During my 20s, I fell in love with short stories. I managed to get a couple of stories published in teenage romance magazines, greatly helped by the *Writers' & Artists' Yearbook*; I'd read every listing for UK magazines, every detail of every agent, and wondered how on earth I could ever be part of that world. As a young person growing up in Sussex suburbia, it seemed impossible.

Three things happened that inadvertently propelled me into the world of children's publishing. Firstly, I moved to London in my late 20s to be a mature student at Goldsmiths' College. London seemed unfathomable and terrifying for a long time, but gradually I realised I was inside an endless whorl of stories and started noting down vignettes and ideas. Prompted by one of those scraps, I submitted a short story to a competition for unpublished writers and it was included in a high-profile anthology. Although it was adult writing, my characters were teenagers and it led me to my wonderful agent, Caroline Sheldon.

Secondly, I joined a writing group. It is brutal and empowering and, through critiquing and being critiqued, I am an infinitely better writer. We support, commiserate and even run continual professional development sessions to up our game. Last of all, and most important for me, I found my voice. At that time there were no working-class, multi-ethnic British families in children's books – and only a few in adult books. I internalised the message that I was not allowed to write from my own perspective.

Then, one winter afternoon in 1999, I turned on the TV and discovered Malorie Blackman. It was the BBC adaptation of her novel *Pig Heart Boy* (Doubleday 1997). A story about a black family who weren't the Cosbys or in *The Fresh Prince of Bel-Air*? A story set in England? A door opened for me and I stepped through … and eventually wrote *Orangeboy* (Hodder Children's Books 2016). It was shortlisted for the Costa Children's Award and won other prizes. But, do you want to know a secret? It was the fifth book I'd actually written. It took a while!

So, keep at it. Write. Find your voice. Keep improving and, like me, you'll get there.

Patrice Lawrence is an award-winning writer of fiction both for adults and children. Her first book, *Orangeboy* (Hodder Children's Books 2016), was shortlisted for the Costa Children's Book Award and won *The Bookseller* YA Prize and Waterstones Prize for Older Children's Fiction. Her second book, *Indigo Donut* (2017) won the Crimefest YA Prize and was one of *The Times'* top children's books in 2017. *Rose, Interrupted* was published by Hodder in July 2019. All three books have been nominated for the Carnegie Medal. *Eight Pieces of Silva* (Hachette Children's Books) was published in August 2020.

Books

My way into a different world

Sally Green describes how, in middle life, she found herself hooked on the creative process of writing and, by applying hard work and good advice, made her way into the world of the professional writer.

I remember the beginning of my writing career quite clearly. It was a sunny afternoon in June 2010, I was 48 years old and doing housework and I had an idea for a story. I'd never written anything before (no diary, no dabbling in short stories, no childhood dreams of being an author), but what did I have to lose other than a few hours of my time? Anything had to be more interesting than hoovering, and no one would ever read the story but me, so I sat down and wrote.

At school I'd learnt the basics of grammar and punctuation, but I always felt inhibited about my writing and that I lacked imagination. Now I realize that everyone has imagination, but being brave and comfortable enough to risk expressing it is the hard thing. By June 2010 schoolgirl inhibitions were a distant memory, although learning wasn't, as the previous year I'd begun to study Social Sciences with the Open University. Because of the OU course I had developed the habit of writing – I had to produce regular assignments and I enjoyed closing the door on the outside world and immersing myself in a new topic. I loved the process of putting ideas and words together and creating something, even if it was only a rather poor essay on politics.

So that June afternoon, with no more essays to write, I repeated the procedure but instead of an essay I began a short story about a girl who didn't know that she was a witch. I didn't have much of a plan – I just wrote, and I continued the next day and the next. After two weeks of this I had to admit to myself that the story wasn't that short; in fact I was probably writing a novel, and it was now taking up all my time. I was hooked. Possibly I was in love too – with my characters. I was obsessed with them, thinking about what they'd do and how, and why. I carried on writing and by September 2010 my story was complete and definitely not short (136,000 words). It wasn't atrocious but there were things wrong with it, though I wasn't even sure what those things were (the narrative point of view was jumping all over the place). I was desperate to improve and so I switched my OU course to Creative Writing, studying hard and all the while working on my manuscript.

I never really believed I'd be a published writer – it seemed less likely than winning the lottery – but I believed in my story. I wanted to try to get it published, but I had a problem: I didn't know a thing about the publishing world. However, I had heard about the *Writers' & Artists' Yearbook* and I found a rather battered copy at my local library. As soon as I started leafing through it I knew I'd found a book I could trust. I devoured its advice. It became my Bible, a source of knowledge and comfort. It was my way into a different world – the world of the professional writer.

I decided to try the traditional route of getting an agent who would then help me find a publisher, and so I listed the agents who accepted manuscripts for YA books, googled them and chose a few I thought might be interested in my story. I submitted to eight agents and within a few months received five brief replies saying 'No' (though the non-replies were fairly clear No's too). However, one reply was different: it was still a 'No', but the agent said she liked my writing style though the story 'didn't have the necessary edge for today's market'. I was delighted. OK – it was a rejection, but an agent from a prestigious London literary agency liked my writing style! I was over the moon. Better yet, I was fired up – I knew I could do edgy better than most people, and I knew that I could improve on the manuscript that I'd sent out. My mindset, once I decided I'd try to get published, was that I would write at least three novels before I'd give up, so starting again didn't daunt me. I gave myself a year to rewrite the story and immediately set to work. Best of all, I'd been released from the cage that I hadn't realised I was still in; I'd been told to be edgy, and to do that I had to let go of my writing inhibitions and make the story mine.

A year later I was back in the library with the *Writers' & Artists' Yearbook*, following its advice about covering letters and synopses (much better advice than the, often American, tips I'd seen online) for what turned out to be my first published novel.

I would have been lost without *Writers' & Artists' Yearbook* to guide me, and I'm delighted there is now this *Children's Writers' & Artists' Yearbook*. It's a wonderful resource – it's *the* resource for writers.

Sally Green is the author of an internationally acclaimed trilogy of young adult fantasy novels, *Half Bad* (2014), *Half Wild* (2015) and *Half Lost* (2016), published by Penguin. *Half Bad* (2014), which was Sally's debut novel, was named Waterstones Best Book for Teenagers 2015 and was shortlisted for the YA Book Prize 2015 and for the 2015 Branford Boase Award. Sally's latest fantasy series published by Penguin includes, *The Smoke Thieves* (2018), *The Demon World* (2019) and *The Burning Kingdoms* (2020).

See also...
● *Writing for the teenage market,* page 295

How do you do it?

After more than two decades as a published author William Sutcliffe has only one answer to the often-asked question 'How do you do it?'. He shares the most important piece of advice he has to offer and reminds writers to enjoy every step of the long journey they are embarking upon.

In the 23 years that I have been writing and publishing books I have been to scores of literary events, both as a speaker and an audience member. If I had to agglomerate all the questions I've heard put to authors into one overarching meta-question, it would be this: 'How do you do it?'. Sadly, my agglomerated meta-answer to that question would have to be 'I don't know.' Every published writer frequently gets asked for advice, and most of them have only one truly essential tip to offer: buy the *Writers' & Artists' Yearbook*. The key turning point in every professional writer's life is when writing shifts from being a hobby or a dream into a source of income. For making that transition, this book is the Bible.

To get published, you don't have to know someone; you don't have to know someone who knows someone; you don't have to live in Hampstead; and you don't need a degree in English literature. You do, however, need to understand that publishing is a business and that, like every other business, it operates in a way that seems obvious and transparent to insiders, but is opaque and confusing to outsiders. This is what makes the *Writers' & Artists' Yearbook* an essential reference book for everyone who hopes to make a living as a writer. Trying to get published without it is like setting off on a hike without a map.

When put to a writer, the question 'How do you do it?' can mean two things. If it means 'How do you get published?', you are holding the answer in your hands right now. Not everyone who hopes to find a publisher will achieve that, not by a long shot, but if you want to give your work in progress the best possible chance of finding an agent and ultimately a publisher, all the answers you need are right here. Of course, the other thing that question often means is 'How do you write a good book?'; and for that one, there are no clear-cut answers. Moreover, when it comes to key questions such as getting started, editing, plotting, characterisation and getting unstuck when you are stuck, for every writer there is a different solution. There is a right and a wrong way to make a submission to an agent; there isn't a right and a wrong way to write a novel. Everyone finds their own method.

The fascinating essays in this volume contain a wealth of experience from many of Britain's finest children's authors. You will find Jacqueline Wilson on 20 years of perseverance before her big breakthrough; J.K. Rowling on rejection letters; Michael Rosen analysing who children's writers write for; and many more fascinating pieces. None of these essays will tell you how to write like those authors, but they will open your thoughts onto how you should write – how to get your personality onto the page; how to tell a unique story in an original way; how to navigate your own path through the craft of writing. These essays are the second-best resource there is for hearing the secrets of good children's writing. The best resource, of course, is the novels themselves.

Read them. Read them once as a reader, then again as a writer – which is to say with the eyes of a hyena. Pull the books to pieces. Think about the word choices, the structure, the characterisation, the pacing, the world-building. Read the books you love ruthlessly and critically. Read the books you don't love in the same way, and hone your sense of where your literary taste sits. There is no objective scale of good and bad. You need to make your own. This gimlet-eyed reading is essential, because only when you have done it to others will you be able to do it to your own prose. To write for children you have to tap into a playfulness in your imagination, but when it comes to editing and rewriting you have to be brutal. Any word or sentence that isn't doing a useful job has to go.

This book is filled with practical and creative advice for writers at every stage of a writing career, but I would like to leave you with the simplest and most important advice there is: enjoy it. When you write, pour yourself into the work. Think of the blank page not as a scary place but as a path to freedom. Writing can take you anywhere. If you really apply yourself to the task, whether you get published or not, that journey will be worthwhile.

William Sutcliffe writes for adults, young adults and children and is the author of 12 novels, including three titles in his *Circus of Thieves* series, published by Simon & Schuster Children's: *Circus of Thieves and the Raffle of Doom* (2014), *Circus of Thieves on the Rampage* (2015) and *Circus of Thieves and the Comeback Caper* (2016). His YA books are *The Wall* (2014) which was shortlisted for the CILIP Carnegie Medal, *Concentr8* (2016), shortlisted for the YA Book Prize, *We See Everything* (2017), *The Gifted, The Talented and Me* (2019) and *The Summer We Turned Green* (2021), all published by Bloomsbury. William's novels for adults include the international bestseller *Are You Experienced?* (Hamish Hamilton 1997), *New Boy* (Penguin 1996), *Bad Influence* (Hamish Hamilton 2004) and *Whatever Makes You Happy* (Bloomsbury 2008), which was adapted into a Netflix film with the new title, *Otherhood*, in 2019. He is also a screenwriter. His work has been translated into 28 languages.

A jobbing writer's lot

Joanna Nadin describes the challenges, rewards, satisfaction and financial sense of taking on a variety of work, in different genres and for different ages, in order to make a successful and creative living from writing.

Nineteen years ago, I was called into the office of my soon-to-be agent, Sarah Molloy – an agent I'd found in the pages of the *Writers' & Artists' Yearbook*, a dog-eared and annotated copy from our local library. There, in a small, book-lined office, at the top of a skew-whiff staircase on St Martin's Lane in London, I was given two sage, salient pieces of advice: (1) don't cut off your hair, and (2) don't give up your day job until your advance is three times your salary.

The first I ignored and had my Shirley Temple curls shaved defiantly short. The second I have followed doggedly, and it has served me well. Firstly, it has kept me financially safe. I was working in politics at the time and, though hardly in the higher echelons, paid comfortably enough that no advance to this date has ever come close to one year's salary. Secondly, it denied me false hope, which I fear is all too prevalent in a world whose stock-in-trade is fiction and fairy tales.

What Sarah said made it patently clear to me that, if I wanted to make a living from writing, banking all my hopes on one big hitter was a fool's errand. For one thing, those deals are almost as rare as a ticket to a chocolate factory. For another, if they are laid on the table they may turn out to be a poisoned chalice, piling on pressure that a new and possibly novice writer doesn't need: if you don't earn your advance out, your publisher may view you as a disappointment. On top of which, the next advance, if you get one, is almost certain to be a lot smaller.

Debut novelists can be particularly prone to these 'golden hellos'; who wouldn't turn down a life-changing cheque, after all? But what I have found is that it can pay, in the long run, to work on building a reputation as a reliable freelancer. 'Be good, be nice, be on time,' I was once told by another clever fellow. And that is exactly what I try to be – working with both my agents (my style and savings adviser Sarah retired eventually) to find a variety of work that keeps me busy, and keeps the big, bad wolf from the door.

I write for all ages – from picture book up to adult – and across genres too. Alongside my own original trade fiction, I write for specialist publishers on school reading programmes, conjuring up exciting adventures for early readers or retelling traditional tales with a contemporary twist. These deals are often arranged by the publishers directly with authors (usually those who have worked with them on trade titles) rather than through agents, but they are also something I ask to be actively put forward for by my agent. They do usually require working within strict subject guidelines and to strict word counts – sometimes as few as 50 words – and with limited lexicons as well. I see this not simply as a challenge, but also as an opportunity to help hone my storytelling and make it spare and succinct – a skill that can be put to excellent use elsewhere. On top of which, while initial advances for these deals are low, if there are royalties in the contract, these can mount up quickly as books are sold in class-size packs and around the world, meaning you earn out fast and earn several times your advance within five years.

Thanks to a Finnish publishing deal that brought me to the attention of a games company out there, I've written tie-in novels under another name. These are on a flat fee basis, and were agreed after a synopsis and sample chapters met approval. But these hoops proved worth it for me, financially and creatively. While, again, this can mean your characters are already painted and your parameters set before you even begin to think about plot (since the people and world you're being paid to play with is likely to have featured in prequels, a film, a TV series or, as in my case, a gaming app), I saw this as an opportunity to be freed of that part of the process.

I ghostwrite, too, working on a ten-book fiction series with the Olympian Sir Chris Hoy – a collaboration that has inspired and stretched my imagination, as I've helped to bring someone else's distinct vision and mission to life. Aimed at 5-8 year-olds, the *Flying Fergus* series (Piccadilly) has been a process of intense toing and froing between Chris and I as we conjure up the ideas, bringing our editor in once I've sketched them out on paper. Working in this way requires you to park your ego to an even greater extent than the usual editorial process, accepting that you may not even get your own darlings in the text in the first place to kill them off! But it is enormously rewarding, and having someone else come up with storylines in such a long-running series is almost a relief.

I also co-wrote the YA novel *Everybody Hurts* (Atom 2017) with Anthony McGowan, each of us taking one side of the story and playing ping-pong with chapters in a giant game of consequences. This requires patience – again, an effacing of one's own ego – as well as the ability to handle a complete curveball, when your partner decides to take the tale not just left-field but completely out of the park!

Finally, I've written three-minute-long TV scripts for puppet worms, presenting the links between programmes on the kids' TV channel Nickelodeon. The invention required to bring to life all-singing, all-dancing, but ultimately armless annelids is not to be underestimated.

I am, to all extents and purposes, a writer for hire, willing and able to turn my hand to most things. It helps, of course, that I have a background in journalism and politics. Not only did these worlds teach me to write tight copy to tighter deadlines, they also taught me never to work for nothing, and that writers' block is a luxury afforded only to those who don't use words to pay their bills. That's not to say writing isn't sometimes difficult, but it is never impossible.

The relative anonymity of my past employment has also served to satisfy me that these books aren't in some way worth less because they're series, or because my name isn't on the cover. They still allow me to flex my writing muscle, to show off (and, importantly, improve) my skills, and to plunder the soup of story that swirls in my head. This approach hasn't precluded commercial or critical success either. There have been awards, TV deals, places on bestseller lists, if only for a week or two.

Eighty-seven books later, and I'm still not J.K. Rowling or Jacqueline Wilson; you may not even have heard of me. But, do you know what? That's fine. Because, for the last decade, I've earned a living doing what I love – which is a rare privilege in itself.

Working like this does have its drawbacks – you have to be disciplined, organised and able to multitask, including switching between stories on a daily basis at times. And I still haven't entirely given up the day job, at least for one day a week. While I am passionate about publishing, it is a precarious profession and, besides, I am as happy writing scripts and speeches as I am short series or standalone thrillers. I also now hold a PhD in Creative Writing, I lecture on the acclaimed Masters course at Bath Spa University, I give workshops at festivals and events around the country, I visit schools. In other words, I have made words – rather than one or two books – my career. A career that allows me to spend days, weeks, months on end exploring new worlds, playing dress up and let's pretend, trying on new lives for size.

I am a jobbing writer, and I can't think of a better way to live.

Joanna Nadin worked as a journalist and in politics before becoming an award-winning writer. She has written more than 80 books for children, teenagers and adults including the Carnegie-nominated YA novel *Joe All Alone* (Little, Brown 2015), which is now a BAFTA-winning and Emmy-nominated BBC drama series. Joanna lectures in Creative Writing at Bath Spa University. Her latest book for adults is *The Talk of Pram Town* (Mantle 2021), and her latest series for children is *The Worst Class in the World* (Bloomsbury 2020). For more information visit her website https://joannanadin.com. Find her on Facebook @joannanadinauthor and Twitter @joannanadin.

Writing and translating children's fiction

Clémentine Beauvais explains the special satisfaction, pleasure and value to be found in translation, with its concentrated focus on language. She urges all writers to use translation to develop and re-energise their reading and writing skills.

This article is about writing children's fiction and translating children's fiction, and the peculiar kinds of pleasure and knowledge that arise when you do both. Let's start by stating the obvious: there shouldn't be any stark distinction between 'writing' and 'translating' children's fiction. Translating is an act of writing. Some translators actually prefer to call themselves 'writers of translations'. As Kate Briggs puts it beautifully, translated texts 'come to us twice-written'. Aren't we lucky, as readers of translations, that not just *one*, but *two* writers, gave their time and applied their talent to that text?

I was a children's writer long before I became a literary translator, and these days I spend roughly half of my time doing 'my' writing and half of my time translating – namely, redoing someone else's writing. Many people are surprised that I would choose to halve what they see as my 'real writing' time, a thought which you could well translate as: 'Surely translation is something you only do when you can't *really* write?'

My view, of course, is that you should translate only if you can *really* write. And only if you can *really* read. And the more you do it, the more it transforms your writing and reading. I want to convince you that if you wish to be a writer, you should *absolutely* write translations. Even if you don't speak another language fluently. Even though it will never bring you fame or money. Even if no one ever reads your translations. Translate. Do it for yourself, for your writing. Do it as a secret pleasure. Do it as a way of learning to write and read better. Here's why.

Translating is writing, rewriting and rewiring your writing

Translating forces you to focus on language, and only on language. I shiver to write this, because of course there's no such thing as 'only' language: it is literally the *only* stuff literature is made of. But when you write a whole novel, you need to keep a million things in mind at the same time: narrative structure, characterisation, audience considerations, chapter length, ideological aspects, the logistics of seriality. And that's even before the editorial dance starts.

When you're translating, you have one task: language. The story's in place, the characters are there; you have a global view of them, in their finished form. Your task is to focus on the words, and to make sure that, in the target language, each of them does the job of propping up this whole fictional world. By 'each of them' I do mean each word, and this is why translating is close to the purest kind of writing: rarely in one's writerly life does one get the luxury of 'angsting' so much over every single word. You think about every word at least twice – in the source language, and in the target one – when the equivalence is obvious. But it seldom is. So you think of each word many times. It is precision work, a series of micro-decisions, adjusting and tweaking language. That's your only job and it's a colossal one.

Doing so will show you two things that are crucial to developing your writing. Firstly: you are never an expert in your native language. All my qualms about writing in English collapsed when I realised I was working from an erroneous assumption – that I knew French. French fails me just as often as English does. We can never write perfectly in any language, nor even approach perfection. Those little failures of language, of any language, are literature.

Secondly: translating changes your writing by forcing you out of your writerly reflexes. My writerly self is lazy. There are certain character types, certain places, certain genres or certain voices it doesn't write because it can't be bothered to venture out of its comfort zone. And my writerly self is ignorant – it doesn't write about things it doesn't know. My translating self cannot afford such whimsicality. It needs to write a text full of those things my writerly self usually avoids or simply doesn't know about. When I translated Sarah Crossan's *Moonrise* (Bloomsbury Children's 2017), I had to write a whole novel about the American prison system; I ended up having, effectively, written it. I never knew anything about it before; I have now learnt not just facts but a way of writing them. Translating is one of the most enlightening acts of writing you can do, because it forces you into the writerly reflexes and comfort zones of someone else.

And it changes your writing, of course, because there's no way you can survive the experience and not acquire new practices, a new way of looking at structure, at character, at style. It inspires you and re-energises your writing. It gives you a glimpse of what your writing-from-scratch could be like if you tried out something entirely different.

Translating is reading, rereading and learning to read

At the same time, translating is also an act of reading – arguably one of the most reverent, attentive and generous acts of reading. I was, so to speak, a professional reader before I became a translator – as an academic specialising in children's fiction – and those skills are evidently useful when reading-for-translation; it's helpful to be able to notice and name the literary devices, and know roughly what the equivalent ones would be in the other language. For instance, I know that an iambic pentameter in English is like the French twelve-footed alexandrin; both are the classic, solemn rhythms at which the hearts of those cultures beat.

Those reading skills, however, are activated not just for analysis and description, but in close relation with writerly decisions. If I'm looking for equivalence of *effect*, the TaDAM TaDAM TaDAM TaDAM TaDAM of my English iambic pentameter could become the tadadadadaDAM tadadadadaDAM of the French alexandrin. It is equivalently lulling, pleasant and familiar. But wait – perhaps I want my French reader to feel that English beat, to be slightly puzzled by that poetic rhythm from beyond the sea? And there I'll wrench my French into an awkward five-footed line.

I decide. I'm in charge. When you're reading-for-translation, you're exercising your critical reading skills and making that interpretation matter for writing. Thus translating teaches you a special kind of reading practice. You read with the eyes of a critic and a creator. Of course, all writers should read as widely as possible in their chosen genres and beyond, but when we say this we generally mean that they should do this for their own edification and/or for pleasure. Reading for translation adjusts a different kind of lens to your readerly eye; this is active reading, in the sense of reading activated by the writing that must come next.

So when I translated Meg Rosoff's minuscule novel *Moose Baby* (Barrington Stoke 2013), I needed to understand how she packed so much humour in so little space, and it was a free lesson in the mechanics of humour in literature. I learned to spot exactly where funny dwells, at the level of sentence, paragraph, page. But it was no academic exercise; none of this would have mattered unless I also thought about where to reinject that humour in the French rewriting. This is more than close reading – it's intimate reading: you reread the same sentence many times, holding in your head analytical considerations of literary devices, writerly considerations of effect and your own sensitivity as a reader. In so doing, you learn to read better, and more precisely, as you start to develop a sense for the composition and aesthetics of even the tiniest units of text.

So go away and translate

So please: go away and translate. If you're lucky enough to have another language, use it for your writing. Write translations. Pick a book you love in the other language and translate it into your own. Not for money, not for networking, not for any kind of profitability as measured by normal standards. No one will thank you for it; you probably won't be paid for it. But it will teach you so much about reading and writing. It will teach you the amazing focus on language that only translating can afford – the aesthetic epiphanies brought about by the most minute of tweaks; the fact that so much in a good piece of literature depends on the right word; character, plot and the way words pull them in this direction or that. The intense attention to words is a lesson you'll never learn better than when translating.

If you are unlucky enough to be monolingual, learn another language. I'm serious – do it. How can you claim to see what your own language can do if you can't watch it from the vantage point of another? All writers, if they really care about words and language – which is the stuff their work is made of, and therefore a professional requirement – should yearn to feel that estrangement, that distancing which brings understanding, knowledge and the destabilising sense that you can't say everything in your own language.

Careful – I'm not saying 'go away and become bilingual'. Fun fact: not all translators are fluent in the languages they translate *from*. Many can't actually hold a conversation. Translating is an act of writing and reading, not dazzling everyone with your perfect accent. Anyway, even bilinguals don't speak two languages perfectly. Even monolinguals don't speak their one language perfectly. Learn another language precisely, *because you'll never speak it perfectly*.

Start small. Pick up a picture book in whatever language you did at school, ages ago. Translate a few lines, painstakingly, using dictionaries and the internet. From that ugly literal translation, make a beautiful literary one. There you go. It's at the same time much more and much less difficult than it sounds.

People are awed by translators because they think 'they're really good at languages', whereas they should really be awed by thinking 'they're really good at writing'. You're good at writing, and that's all that matters: go and write translations. The more you do it, the more you'll develop that superpower and the better you'll write and the better you'll read. And one day you, too, will join that underground league of people who secretly think: 'Hey, writers. We know our stuff … *and* yours. Here we are, in your writing, taking your words, making them our words. No one's read you like we have. No one's rewritten you like we have. You are mine now.'

Clémentine Beauvais is a Senior Lecturer in English in Education at the University of York. She is also a writer for children and young adults in French, and a literary translator from English to French. Her books written in English include the *Sesame Seade Mysteries* series (Holiday House), *The Royal Babysitters* series (Bloomsbury Children's), *Piglettes* (Pushkin Press 2017, self-translated from the French) and *In Paris With You* (Wednesday Books 2019, translated by Sam Taylor). Her translation of J.K. Rowling's latest children's book, *The Ickabog* was published in French as *L'Ickabog* (Gallimard 2020). She is also the French translator of Sarah Crossan, Elizabeth Acevedo and some works by Meg Rosoff. For more information visit www.clementinebeauvais.com/eng.

Who do children's authors write for?

When writing a children's book, who is an author really writing for? Michael Rosen shares his thoughts on this question and suggests what an author needs to take into account when writing.

People who can write for children don't come with a same format personality or a made-to-measure range of skills. We aren't people who can be easily categorised or lumped together. In part, this is because the world of children's books is constantly changing, starting out from a very diverse base in the first place. This derives from the fact that the world children inhabit is changing and indeed that there is a recognition within the children's books milieu that books are for everyone, not just one small section of the population.

In a way, this means that this is a great time to be writing or illustrating children's books. But that comes with a warning: diverse and changing – yes – but within a set of conventions (I won't say 'rules') and formats. Quite often, people who have written some stories or poems for children ask if I would take a look at them. Sometimes, the first problem that I can see with what they've written is that it doesn't 'fit in'. Or, another way of putting it, the writer hasn't taken a look at what's out there in the bookshops and schools and thought: how can I write something that could go alongside that book, or fit the same niche that that particular book occupies?

But what about artistic freedom? What about the rights of the writer to write about anything? Two things in response to that: nothing can stop you writing about anything you want to, however you want to. But there's no point in kidding ourselves that writing is really 'free'. We all write with our 'reading heads' on. That's to say, we write with the words, sentences, pages, chapters, plots, characters, scenes of the books we've read. If you say to yourself, 'I want to write a novel' or 'I want to write a picture book text', you're only doing so because your mind is full of novels or picture book texts. They are the 'already written' or the 'already read' material we write with. This affects everything we write, right down to the shape and structure of what we write, the tone we hit in the passages we write, the kinds of dialogue and thoughts we put into the writing. A crude analogy here is cooking. We cook with the ingredients that we are given. But more: if we say, we are going to make a cake, there is an understood outcome of what that will be (the cake), and an agreed set of ingredients that can arrive at that understood outcome. So, in a way, we not only cook with appropriate and given ingredients, we also cook with an understood outcome in mind. It has a shape, a smell and a taste that we expect the moment someone says, 'Here is a cake'. Our memory of past cakes prepares our mind and taste for what is to come. This set of memories of past writing and reading is what is in our mind as we write and indeed in the minds of the child readers as they sit down to something they can see is a book. These are what are known as the 'intertexts' we read and write with – memories of past texts.

Secondly, I would say that if you're interested in being published, then you have to look very, very closely at what publishers publish. This means looking at books not only from the point of view of what they say and how they say it. It also means looking at what kind of book it is and inquiring whether there are other books like it. How would you categorise it? This line of questioning puts into your mind a sense of format, of shape, of outcome to guide you as you write. Another analogy: an architect who is asked to design a house knows that he or she has to create rooms that are high enough and large enough for people to live in, that there is a basic minimum of kitchen and bathroom, there is a door to get in and out of, and so on. If it fulfils these conditions, we will call it a house – and not a factory, or a warehouse, say. It's a great help sometimes to look at books from an architect's point of view: what is particular to a book that makes it work? Ask yourself, how did the writer reveal what was coming next? Or, how did the writer hold back and conceal what was coming next? (Writing is a matter of revealing and concealing!) How did the writer arouse your interest? Was it an invitation to care about the people or creatures in the story? Or was it more to do with events or happenings? Or both? Did the book announce itself as being of a particular genre: thriller, historical fiction, comedy, etc? How did it do that? What are the requirements of that genre? Or is it a hybrid?

If all this sounds too technical let me introduce you to someone: the child. If you say to yourself, I'm going to write for children, then even as you say this, you're putting an imagined child (or children) into your mind. This is what literary theorists call 'the implied reader'. We do this in several ways. There might be a real child we know. Robert Louis Stevenson wrote *Treasure Island* largely as part of his relationship with his stepson, Lloyd. But even though we might say, 'RLS wrote it for Lloyd', this doesn't really explain things. What Stevenson was doing, possibly without knowing it, was keeping a mental map of Lloyd's speech and personality in his mind, so as he wrote, he had his version of Lloyd in his head monitoring, guiding and censoring what he was writing.

There is no single way of importing the implied child reader into your head. Some writers do it from memory, connecting with the child they once were and using that version of themselves to guide them in what they write and how they write it. They use memories of what they liked to read, how they themselves spoke and thought and perhaps wrote, when they were a child. Others immerse themselves in the company of children – their own, their grandchildren, nephews and nieces or children in playgroups, nurseries or schools. And some do it by immersing themselves so thoroughly in children's books that they pick up the implied child reader from the actual books. And of course, it's possible to work in a combination of all of these ways. What I don't think you can do is ignore them all.

In fact, what you write can't avoid an implied reader. That may seem odd, because you might say that you had no one in mind when you wrote this or that. The reason you can't avoid it is because the language we use comes already loaded up with its audience. So, if I write, 'Capitalism is in crisis', this is a phrase that implies an audience that first of all understands English, then understands the words 'capitalism', 'crisis' and the phrase 'in crisis'. But more than that, it's an audience that wants to read something like that and is, in a sense, hungry or prepared and sufficiently 'read' to want to read such a sentence – or, more importantly, to go on wanting to read what comes next. If I write, 'My Dad was attacked by a banana …' then I'm already positioning the reader to think about someone who is a child and that child is telling something a bit absurd or possibly funny, perhaps the beginning of a family anecdote or family saga. It's also a 'tease', in that a reader who 'gets it', will know that bananas don't attack anyone. It implies a reader who knows that. In other words, the 'implied reader' is 'inscribed' into what we write. In a way, these implied readers are stuck to the words, phrases, sentences, plots and characters we write.

This means that as we write – and when we go back over what we've written – we need to think about the implied reader we've put there. Who is the child who is going to 'get it'? Who is the child who won't? What kind of children are we talking to? What aspects of those implied children's minds and childhoods are we talking to? The fearful person in the child? The envious one? The yearning one? The lonely one? The greedy one? And so on.

A last thought: we talk of 'writing for children'. To tell the truth, I don't think we do just write for children. I think we write as a way for adults to join the conversations that adults have with adults, adults have with children, children have with children – on the subject of what it means to be a child and live your life as a child. Because it's literature, this conversation often comes in code, with ideas and feelings embodied in symbols (teddy bears, giants, etc), it arouses expectations and hopes (what's coming next?) and because it's literature that children can and will read, it often comes along according to predictable outcomes (getting home, getting redeemed, being saved) that remove the obstacles to unhappiness and imperfection that the story began with, and so on. Nevertheless, children's literature has a magnificent history of saying important things to many people, often in a context where adults are caring for children. I think that's a good thing to attempt.

Michael Rosen has been writing since he was 16 and published his first book in 1969. As an author and by selecting other writers' works for anthologies he has been involved with over 200 books. His most recent books are *On The Move: Poems About Migration* (Walker Books 2020) and *Many Different Kinds of Love: A story of life, death and the NHS* (Random House 2021). He was the Children's Laureate 2007–9 and has an MA and a PhD in Children's Literature. He is Professor of Children's Literature at Goldsmiths, University of London, where he co-devised and co-teaches the MA in Children's Literature. His website is www.michaelrosen.co.uk.

See also...
● *Spotting talent*, page 1

Writing for different genres and markets

Books

Writing books to read aloud

Bestselling author Anne Fine looks at why and how books are read aloud to children.

The first thing to say about writing books to read aloud is that they should be as much of a pleasure to read alone silently as any other story. Indeed, at first it's difficult to see where any differences might lie. Certainly when it comes to stories for the very young we tend to have a picture in our heads of the exhausted parent inviting the child to 'clean your teeth, hop into bed, and I'll read you a story'. And since all days are long for a parent, nobody wants their offspring to be worked into a frenzy all over again. So, in the classic bedtime stories for the younger child, there's very often a softer humour and a gentler tone, and a satisfactory and fulfilling ending.

And for the older child, there often isn't.

So, same old story really. No rules (or having to face the fact that rules appear to be there only for some other writer to irritate you intensely by making a fortune breaking them). But there are always the basic guidelines.

Keep things as simple as they can be for your particular story. With picture books you can of course assume that the child is propped up beside the reader, sharing each illustration as it comes along. But by the time the child is six, maybe they would prefer to snuggle down and shut their eyes to listen. So do you really have to take half a dozen sentences to describe the rigging, and the number and nature of the sails, and exactly how the ship was armed? Couldn't you just refer to it as 'the most magnificent galleon that ever sailed the seas' and leave it at that? After all, if those cannon ever come to be fired, we'll hear about it later.

Listeners are easily distracted. One minute they're all ears; the next, they're actually more interested in tracking the progress of a fly across the ceiling. Of course they're not going to admit they've lost the thread of the story, in case the parent snatches the opportunity to suggest they're too tired to listen and makes for the door, or the teacher decides it's time to move on to the workbooks. But their attention does stray. So it is best to try (as ever) to order your tale so you can start at the beginning and move on in sequence, steering clear of flashbacks.

On this matter of keeping things simple, does it sound mad to say that plots can be overrated? And never more so than in books designed to be read aloud to the young. In my own very short chapter book, *It Moved!*, Lily takes a stone in for Show and Tell and claims it sometimes moves, and we just get to see who in the class believes her and who doesn't, and how they all react over a day of watching it. In the *Stories of Jamie and Angus*, Jamie is an amiable child of about four in a perfectly normal household. His favourite soft toy is a little Aberdeen Angus bull. In the first story, Angus ends up in the washing machine when he's supposed to be 'dry clean only'. In another, the pair sort out the books in their bedroom according to their own rather strange shelving preferences. In yet another, they do little more than draw 'angry eggs'. The stories almost couldn't be more plain and domestic, and yet we still run through joy, misery, jealousy, anxiety, distress, fear, empathy, generosity, self-sacrifice, fury, resentment – the entire mercurial gamut of preschool emotions. So do be confident that, especially for the very young, a tremendous amount can be forged from what seems, at first sight, not very much at all. With writing – just as with practically everything else in life – it's not what you do but the way that you do it.

Children, like adults, have to *care* about what's being read. We adults tend to ask the 'Can I be *bothered* with these people?' question before returning a book, half-read, to the library. It's a test even harder to pass when you're writing for young ones. Remember Robert Browning:

> *If you want your songs to last*
> *Base them on the human heart*

because children love to identify with someone or something in the story – it doesn't really matter what. It could be another child, or a puppy, or even a lost pebble. But they do have to care. So perhaps it's best to make sure that, all the way through, your listener knows what your character (or puppy, or pebble) is feeling. And make sure that these are thoughts and emotions they will recognise. A child of six isn't 'disappointed that the weather is unpleasant'. It's all far more immediate. He feels the tears pricking because his socks are wet and his woolly hat is itching and his coat's too tight under his armpits. Ever heard them moan?

Joan Aiken once remarked that anyone who writes for the young 'should, ideally, be a dedicated semi-lunatic'. But you can go too far. The problem is one of differing – and shifting – levels of sophistication. What makes one child hoot with laughter will cause another to sneer, and there is in any case an entirely undefinable line between cashing in on a child's acceptance of the unlikely or the magical, and offering them something they think of as simply being 'stupid'. You might, for example, get away with the idea that the horse the child rescued from its cruel owner is being secretly kept in the garage, only to find your young readers baulking at the suggestion that Mum could walk in to fetch a screwdriver and not even notice it.

Avoid being arch. Of course there are differing levels at which many shared books can be read. The older reader often gets a sly chuckle out of things that sail right over the head of somebody smaller. But the joke does usually have to be at least potentially inclusive, so that, the tenth time around, out comes the thumb, down comes the chubby hand to stop you turning the page, and out comes the question: 'Daddy was just teasing them, really, wasn't he?' 'Mum *really* wanted to get back to reading the paper, didn't she?' In the benighted language of the National Curriculum, the child's already 'drawing inferences from text' (or, as we used to call it back in the good old days, 'reading').

Does it help to read your work aloud to children to see how it goes down? Not really, no. For one thing most children are notoriously polite and gentle with people they love, or strangers who come into class. And the sheer joy of having their opinions canvassed can send them haywire. One says, 'I liked this bit!' You beam, and all the other hands shoot up. 'I liked that bit!' 'And I liked that bit!' Everyone wants to have a go at the pleasure of shouting out to the visitor.

So trust your own judgement. You are the writer, after all. Try reading it aloud to an imaginary son or daughter or class. You'll soon notice which bits you're rushing through because they're tiresome, and which of the sentences you're tripping over because they're too clumsy or long. You'll realise that, yes, you *can* put that rather ambitious word into a story for four year-olds because the very context and the way in which it will be read out will make its meaning transparent.

Are there some subjects best avoided in books to be shared between adults and children? Again, it's hard to say. Some parents will read anything the child demands. Others, like teachers, will beach up on things like 'pottymouth' poetry ('Well, *you* just said bogey! And you just said poo *twice!*'). Or books that appear to encourage the child to relish – or, worse, be amused by – cruelty and the infliction of pain. I watched as at least 30 parents with small children trooped out of a book fair when one enthusiastic author read out a passage from one of his history books about red hot pokers being driven up people's bottoms. (I wondered, frankly, why the others stayed.) He may justifiably argue that he's sold hundreds of thousands of copies, but I would guess that few of them have been read aloud by squeamish parents to imaginative children before the lights go out. So use your sense.

What about *how* a book is read aloud? Should that make a difference to how you write it? I don't see how it can. After all, some readers treat the words in the old-fashioned way, and simply speak them with intelligence and inflections sympathetic to the meaning. They read, in short, as if it were a *book*. Others go half-mad, acting out every sentence, doing all the voices in different accents, shouting the yells and whispering the quiet bits. They treat the pages in front of them pretty well as a script for a stage performance. Like every other author whose work has been professionally recorded, I've shuddered through one actor's butchering of my work with his frantic showing off, and also been startled to find tears pricking as another has used her skills to mine a poignancy I had forgotten about or never even realised was there. It's their own voice that most writers hear in their head as they put down the words, so go along with that.

And that's the root of all writing, when it comes down to it. Your own voice. Children are strange. Ralph Waldo Emerson defined them as 'curly dimpled lunatics'. They assume that they're immortal. (Why else do adults have to step in so smartly and often, simply to keep them alive?) And children are at one with eternity. (When did you last see a nine-year-old glance at a clock and say, 'My God! It's three already! And I've got nothing done!') Their lives may change immeasurably. See how the language of their stories has moved so seamlessly over the centuries from tumbledown cottages in dark forests, through secret gardens and kind governesses, to the babysitter and the stepbrother. But in their essential nature – however individual and various those natures may be – children have barely changed at all.

So the successful children's authors will always be those who can best make their work chime in with the child's capacity to understand and enjoy it. And since, like Walt Whitman, all children 'contain multitudes', that gives the writer enormous scope to get it very, very wrong or very, very right.

Anne Fine OBE, FRSL is one of the best-known and most popular writers for children of all ages and was Children's Laureate 2001–3. She has twice won both the Carnegie Medal and the Whitbread Children's Book of the Year Award and at the Galaxy British Book Awards has twice been voted Children's Author of the Year. She has also won the *Guardian* Children's Fiction Prize and dozens of other awards in the UK and abroad. Her work is translated into more than 45 languages. Her latest book for older readers is *Shades of Scarlet* (David Fickling Books 2021) and for younger readers, *A Remarkable Ear* (Barrington Stoke 2020). Anne also writes for adults. Her website is www.annefine.co.uk.

Finding new readers and markets

Tom Palmer shows how, by seeking out unexpected working partnerships, a children's author can open up mutually rewarding and productive markets and draw in new young readers.

I have managed to make a living as a full-time children's author for 14 years. As everyone who has tried it knows, it is not easy to earn enough money to live on from being a writer. You're forever in fear. Forever asking yourself questions … How long will people want to buy your books? Will school events dry up as finances tighten and the political landscape changes? There is little respite, even if you are living the dream. Which I am.

That's why I spend a lot of time trying to think of ways I can attract interest to my books, so that people will continue to buy and borrow them. And so schools will keep paying me to visit. One of the most successful ways I have found to do this is to *give*.

Looking for partnerships

There are a lot of organisations, charities and companies who would benefit from working with a children's author. But who are they? What can you give them? And, what can they give you? I have developed relationships with several organisations – large and small – giving and taking. In partnership. As a result of those partnerships, I have boosted my longevity as a children's author.

Each partnership is different and each evolves in its own unpredictable way. But it usually starts with a series of questions that I ask myself, and which I suggest you ask *yourself*. Here is a plan of action:
• Think about what you've written. List subjects, settings, themes, ideas. And dig deep. Text your friends and family. Your readers. Ask them what *they* think you write about.
• Now look at your list. Are there natural partners for your work? (For instance, Beatrix Potter might have chosen the RSPCA, a pet shop chain or *Animals & You* magazine. Or she might not.)

> ### How to approach potential partners
>
> 1 The more you know about the possible partner the better. That includes researching the right person to contact.
> 2 Offer to do as much of the set-up and admin work as you can. They are likely to be under massive time-pressure with their job already.
> 3 When you meet for the first time, try to make it open and creative. Set it up as a thinking/sharing session, not just a blast of ideas from you.
> 4 You probably have to be willing to give first, to do stuff for free to demonstrate that your partnership could help them. Then, as your relationship evolves, the balance will tip back in your favour.

• Suss out one or more partners whose work is linked to what you write about. Again, stretch it. Brainstorm; be creative. Have ideas that are stupid. Cross them out. Have more. There might be one that fits.
• Think carefully about those potential partners. Go to their website. Watch them. What do they do? What do they want to achieve? Can you help them?
• Now think about what you could ask for from *them*. How can they help you to promote your books? Or, how can your link with them help you to promote your books?

Case studies

Over the last decade I have worked successfully with the RAF Museums, England Rugby, the Premier League, Divine Chocolate, Leeds Schools Library Service, Leeds United, the

Anne Frank Trust and many others. Below are three different examples. They could help you see how to identify suitable partners that fit the writing and themes of your own books.

Fair trade chocolate

I was writing a book about football and fair trade for Puffin. It's called *Off Side* and includes storylines relating to the trafficking of young African footballers and to fair-trade cocoa bean farming. I needed help to write it. A lot of help. From people who knew about football and chocolate in Africa.

So I did a bit of research. In fact, my wife did. She came up with Divine Chocolate who work with fair-trade farmers so that the likes of us can give them a fair wage for what they farm. I identified the Right to Dream football academy in Ghana. They look after gifted young child footballers and help protect them from being exploited by corrupt football agents. I contacted both, suggesting that I could help raise awareness of what they do. Could they explain it to me? Could they help me research and write a meaningful book? They said they could.

I went to Ghana at my own expense. I saw everything I needed to see. It was amazing. When I got home I promoted Divine and Right to Dream and the great work they do through writing my story. And my book continues to sell well because it was properly researched and I knew what I was talking about. Job done.

But relationships evolve. When *Off Side* was published, Divine wanted me to tell the story of how fair trade makes a difference. They gave me a PowerPoint. I used it as part of my talk in schools. I did this for free, of course. But it enhanced my school events, made them more meaningful. As a result, more schools wanted to book me to go in and talk to their pupils, meaning my book became better known in schools with fair-trade status and beyond. More book sales. More paid school events. And the raising of awareness of very important issues.

Ask yourself:
– *Does my book deal with an issue or a cause?*
– *Which charity or campaign group might be interested in working with me?*
– *How can I help that cause through my book and events?*

The Royal Air Force

I was writing a series about children going back in time to fly famous RAF aeroplanes. I approached three organisations to ask if they'd like to work with me. Two did not reply. The RAF Museums did.

The RAF Museums have some amazing artefacts in their collections at Hendon and Cosford: tiny kite-like planes from the First World War; terrifying giants like the Vulcan bomber. But the RAF Museums are always looking for ways to bring those planes to life. For ways to tell the story behind them, and about the men and women who flew them. That was what they needed. A way of telling more stories. That's what I could give.

I volunteered to do a school event for them for free, to see if we could work together. It was a success, and they offered to pay me for the next one. Six months later, they had a new exhibition called 'First World War in the Air'. They asked me how we could work together to tell a story about the pilots. One of their exhibits is of the possessions of a 19-year-old pilot, Kevin Furniss, who was killed on his second sortie. His gloves. His shaving equipment. His Bible. His pipe. Letters home. These items were poignant enough on their

Books

own, but I suggested writing a story about Furniss using those objects before his fateful flight. The museum then used the story in schools to attract visitors. And I was paid for the story.

Now I am the museum's Children's Writer in Residence. I do four school and public events a year for them, based around the three important planes from their collections that I have since – with their help – written books about: the Sopwith Camel; the Spitfire; and the Eurofighter Typhoon. My book is on sale in their shops. They promote my events and books to the many RAF and aeroplane interest groups that they work with. We bring schools into their museum and run writing workshops based around their aircraft and artefacts.

Ask yourself:
– *Is there subject matter in my books that relates to a museum, gallery, festival, interest group?*
– *Which ones should I research and what might they be interested in from me?*
– *How could I or my book help them?*
– *Can we work together?*

England Rugby

I had a trilogy of rugby stories published in 2015 by Barrington Stoke (*Rugby Academy: Combat Zone*; *Rugby Academy: Dead Locked*; and *Rugby Academy: Surface to Air*). We timed their publication to tie in with the Rugby World Cup, hosted in the UK that year.

I contacted the education people at England Rugby, the RFU, in the hope that I could apply for money to create literacy interventions. With the RFU as a partners, I'd have a good chance. I suggested that the RFU and I apply for money to tour an event at the library near each of the 13 Rugby World Cup venues. I also suggested a set of literacy resources linking rugby to reading for pleasure and writing. And I said that I could write a live story to be read in schools as the Rugby World Cup was on. Would they be interested?

They were. My ideas met their needs because the RFU are keen to get into schools. They want to use the interest in the game to encourage children to read and write. They want to spread the culture of their five core values. And they want to start more rugby teams in schools to help create players for the future. So they offered to pay for it all direct, with no need to apply for funding.

I now work regularly with the RFU, performing events, creating resources and writing stories that they publish on their website. This has led to my *Rugby Academy* series becoming very well-known in rugby circles. Which goes a long way to explaining how all three sold out their advance within a year of publication.

Ask yourself:
– *Is there an activity or interest at the centre or on the margins of my book?*
– *Does a national or regional body administer that interest?*
– *Who can I work with? Who would be interested in my book?*

Working with partners has been a massive boon for my career. If I had not sought out those partners, I think that my full-time writing career may well have ground to a halt. In addition, I have been able to promote the joys of reading for pleasure to children and families I might not have reached without the help of those partners. And that is deeply satisfying and very much on my agenda. One downside could be that – in always working with partners – I am a slave to *their* agenda. I try to overcome that by making sure the books I write with partners always meet whatever my obsession of the moment is. Also, the good money I make from working with partners buys me time to write other work that is 100% what I want to do.

Tom Palmer is the author of fifty books for children, including three Puffin football series, *Football Academy*, *Foul Play* and *The Squad*. *Foul Play* was shortlisted for the 2008 Blue Peter Book Award. His other books – published by Barrington Stoke – include *Ghost Stadium* (2013), the *Rugby Academy* series (2015) and *Armistice Runner* (2018) and *D-Day Dog* (2019), which both won the UK Children's Book Award in 2019 and 2020. His newest books include *After the War* (2020) and *Arctic Star* (2021), both published by Barrington Stoke, and three books in a rebooted *Roy of the Rovers* series published by Rebellion (2018–21). Tom is Children's Writer in Residence at the RAF Museum and Leeds United FC. Tom was awarded the Ruth Rendell Award for his contribution to literacy in 2019. Find out more at http://tompalmer.co.uk, and follow him on Twitter @tompalmerauthor.

The learning curve: writing for the children's educational market

Rachel Bladon shares her experience of writing children's educational books and describes the appeal and value of this sector, with its broad range of content and skills, and the satisfying creative challenges and rewards it offers a writer.

Any kind of children's writing involves putting yourself in a young person's shoes and viewing the world through their eyes – that is one of the key attractions and challenges of working for this age group. But for writers like me, who are pitching our stories at the educational rather than trade market, there are quite a lot of extra considerations to take on board. It's not just a question of how old your readers are likely to be, but also what level they are working at, what kind of setting they are learning in, and above all, if you write for international markets, where in the world they are.

Children's educational publishing takes many forms. There are textbooks for every subject in UK schools, of course, plus a multitude of extra resources in print, digital and audio format; and, as any parent who's had to support their child with reading will know, there's also an abundance of literacy schemes out there. Then there's the home-learning market, and the sector I have ended up in: ELT (English Language Teaching) publishing, with its vast array of materials for the world's 1.5 billion English language learners.

The appeal of the role

Having your name on a textbook probably doesn't give quite the same hit a writer gets from seeing their lovingly crafted children's story make its way onto the shelves of a bookshop. But for me, this highly market-driven kind of publishing has always had a draw. I'd started out as a writer of information books with a well-known children's publisher, and it was a fun and vibrant place to work. I would sit at my desk writing a children's guide to beginner's German, of which I spoke not a word, while colleagues around me emerged occasionally from heaps of wool, crepe paper, straws and plasticine to write the next spread of a bestselling craft guide or a children's book on science experiments. I loved making a living from crafting words, surrounded by a buzz of creativity, but there was something missing for me in this desk-based existence, and in the broadness and freedom of the brief – which amounted to whatever notes you scribbled down during a short, white-knuckled meeting at the start of every project with the formidably capricious director, in his office on the top floor.

When I became aware of the thriving publishing industry that exists around ELT, something I'd got a qualification in and spent a year earning money from in France when fresh out of university, I realized I'd found something that really appealed to me. What better than travelling the world (and I really did), observing classes, talking to teachers and trying to get under the skin of a different country's education system, then coming home and writing books that would one day be used in those classrooms to help children learn English and thus access a wider world? I became an editor in children's ELT publishing at first, so not officially writing – but the authors of the books I was editing were often teachers with a reputation in their respective countries who had little writing experience, so there was always a lot of rewriting involved. Once I had a family and decided to go freelance, it was easy to make the hop across from editing into actually writing myself. I've always relished, and still do, the many different elements of my role: needing to understand the particular market I'm writing for; applying a particular methodology to the structure of the material; and researching and creating a wide range of content – from topical texts about issues of the moment, 'realia' (concocted newspaper articles, etc used to expose learners to 'real English') and self-contained stories to activities, exercises and tests, as well as scripts for audio and video (and now, of course, digital) components. And then there's the visual side: with the complexity of a textbook and its many constituent parts, the design is absolutely key, so collaborating closely with designers, artists, picture researchers and photographers is an essential part of the job.

Cultural sensitivities

As an ELT author and xenophile, one of the things I love most about writing for international markets is what you learn about the different cultures you are tailoring your materials for. There was a furore in the British press a few years ago when it was unearthed that we in the ELT world abide by a code of taboos called PARSNIPs, which denotes the various things we avoid at all times in our writing: Politics, Alcohol, Religion, Sex, Narcotics, 'Isms' (such as Communism), and Pork. In actual fact, there's a host of other things that we steer clear of, and in the course of my career I've been asked to avoid everything from ghosts and magic to aardvarks and crows. I never got to the bottom of what it is about aardvarks that makes them off-limits, but fortunately that particular taboo has never constrained me too greatly!

Critics have said that, by keeping these things out of our books, we're sanitising them and stifling opportunities for debate, discussion and the broadening of minds. But, while I would draw the line at anything that ventured into the realm of censorship, it has always seemed obvious to me that in books that are going to be used in the classroom, cultural sensitivity is essential. Partly this is a commercial necessity: in many countries, textbooks won't sell unless they are included in approved ministry lists, and anything that's seen as breaching cultural norms is not going to make the grade. But it also seems to be common sense, if you're creating a book for students in another part of the world, to show respect for their culture. In the same way that we'd be unlikely to show a child spitting in the street or smoking in a UK textbook, so teachers in China don't want to see pets in the kitchen (which they consider unhygienic), and a class of children in the Middle East will balk at a picture of someone showing the soles of their feet.

Graded readers

These days, I generally find myself writing for a global market that might typically include Brazil, Poland, Spain, Italy, Japan and Egypt. I've wiggled my way down into a particularly narrow niche in the world of ELT, writing 'graded readers' for students who are learning English. These are simplified storybooks, with the language and vocabulary carefully controlled so that an English language learner can read them fluently, at any level from beginner to advanced, consolidating and expanding their language skills as they do. One of the best things for me about writing graded readers is the freedom to write across different literary genres, and for a wide range of age groups. I've written everything from original fiction for pre-schoolers and adaptations of modern and classic titles for children aged 6-12, to non-fiction for teens and young adults – and in the past few years my smorgasbord of writing work has included new stories based around the TV characters *Dora the Explorer* and *Paw Patrol*, a book about the life and diaries of Anne Frank, an adaptation of the story of Don Quixote, and a young person's guide to the global issues of the 21st century.

For the 'grading' itself, I have a syllabus and vocabulary list on my desk at all times, bespoke for every different series; these tell me exactly what language I can and can't use at any particular level. Some writers might find it limiting and frustrating to work within such constraints, but I love the extra challenge, and I often feel there's something of the cryptic crossword about it – you think of the word that you need to convey a particular thought or idea, but if it doesn't fit your other criteria (in this case the syllabus) you then have to find some other way of saying what you want … it gives the brain a good stretch. The grading comes very much on top of all the requisites for any piece of storytelling; our number one priority is to engage and captivate the reader, so – as for all good stories – the prose needs to be sharp, the dialogues need to flow naturally, the characters have to jump out of the page, and there needs to be a clearly defined story arc. For adaptations, which are a big component of the graded reader library, there are the added challenges of deciding what from the original can be cut or condensed, and of trying to retain the author's original voice in simplified form.

The value and rewards

Writing for children in any format is intrinsically rewarding, of course, but a definite advantage of educational publishing is that the benefits are quantifiable. Research into the effectiveness of graded readers has shown what a huge impact they can have on language learning, and I've been really humbled on the occasions when I've actually seen my books in use in the classroom – this is quite a powerful reminder of the need to get things right and to put together the very best story you possibly can, in the hope of engaging a disaffected student or passing on the tiny nugget that might ignite something in a young mind.

Educational writing is also a lot easier to find a way into than the trade market, I think, especially if you're coming from a teaching background. Most practising teachers are too busy or exhausted to write new materials and, unless you have teaching experience or are a very engaged parent, you're unlikely to have a clear picture of what kind of resources are needed – or might work well – in a classroom setting. So if you do have the background, and the ideas, and are able to get them down on paper well, publishers might be very interested in what you can offer, particularly if you have some standing in your segment of the educational sector. There's also the advantage that sales can be quite substantial, because schools will usually buy class sets; this means every adoption might mean an order of tens or even hundreds of copies, still more if it's made by a big educational chain. Royalties are quite hard to come by these days, at least in the ELT world, but if you can secure them they're likely to hold up reasonably well. The world's bestselling ELT course-book, *Headway* (Oxford University Press), has sold more than 70 million copies, and is still going strong in its fifth edition!

Some might see educational writing for schools as the poor cousin of children's fiction, but I've found it a field with plenty of scope for creativity, in which you can foster a broad range of writing skills and dip your toe into other sides of the publishing process, like marketing and design. If, like Nelson Mandela, you believe that education is 'the most powerful weapon which you can use to change the world', you might just feel that as an educational writer, you're doing something that has value too.

Rachel Bladon is an EFL editor and writer, the author of more than 80 graded readers for adults and children, including *White Fang* (Macmillan Readers 2008), *Mulan* (Oxford Classic Tales 2017) and *The Life and Diaries of Anne Frank* (Oxford Bookworms 2018), winners of the ERF (Extensive Reading Foundation) Language Learner Literature Award. She is Series Editor of the *Oxford Bookworms Library*. For more information see www.linkedin.com/in/rachelbladon.

Writing adventures in the real world: children's non-fiction

Isabel Thomas explores the exciting world of children's non-fiction, and shares her tips for writing the perfect pitch.

Why write non-fiction?

Children's non-fiction is so much more than 'books with facts'. It's a different way for writers to reach young readers, to take them on a journey that makes them laugh, or cry, or bubble over with enthusiasm. It inspires children to explore their world – and to change it.

Recent years have seen an exciting renaissance in the genre. Dozens of new children's non-fiction imprints have been launched, and publishers are investing in lavish illustrations and large formats. Bookshops and libraries have reconfigured their shelves to make space for titles big enough to dive into. Children's non-fiction titles appear in bestseller charts, award shortlists and festival programmes. Readers – and their families – are demonstrating a huge appetite for bold and beautiful adventures in the real world.

It's an exciting time to be writing and illustrating children's non-fiction, and the scope for creativity is huge. I've written picture books, graphic texts and biographies where text and illustrations play together on the page. I've created educational books for libraries and classrooms, activity books packed with paper engineering, and hands-on crafts and experiments.

A good children's non-fiction book is nothing like a textbook. It's an opportunity to tell a complete story that helps children connect bite-sized facts with the bigger picture.

Where do I begin?

Find something that excites YOU, and then work out the best way to pass that excitement on to young readers. For me, it's science and nature.

My first book was about blue and purple foods. Educational non-fiction is often published in series, and the mainstream colours had already been covered! As debuts go it was low key. But it gave me the confidence to offer my services as a science writer to other publishers. Finding your niche is useful in winning that first commission, but it's not enough to know your subject area in depth. To make a topic irresistible to children, you need to know your readers too.

Spend time with children and immerse yourself in their world. Not just literature, but TV, films, apps and playground trends. Children's non-fiction competes with all of these things. I volunteer as a school governor and STEM Ambassador, roles that keep me in touch with curriculum change, and the influences that shape children's lives. I also read at libraries and run school events. 160 books into my career, I've become an expert in thinking like an eight-year-old.

Finding your angle

The value of a non-fiction book lies not just in the information delivered – which must of course be accurate and up-to-date – but in the way it's presented. How will you hook your reader, so that your book educates *and* entertains? Play with ideas, make connections and take your readers on a journey. It might be through humour, adventure or quirky details. Or it might be by making a complex topic simple enough to give a child that 'wow' moment.

An original angle is essential if your book is to stand out on a crowded shelf. Instead of listing facts about space, weave them into an alien's guide to the solar system, or a book of rocket science for beginners. If you're writing about life cycles, how about a zookeeper's handbook, or a hypothetical battle of lion versus tiger?

Developing your idea

At this point, a fiction author would write the first draft, ready to polish to perfection. The advice for non-fiction is rather different: don't write the book!

Children's non-fiction is usually a team effort, combining the author's ideas with those of talented editors, illustrators and designers to create something extraordinary. Unless you are pitching a picture book, there is usually no need to write the entire manuscript up front. Instead, develop a proposal and a few sample spreads, and make these as polished as you can. Once your idea has been commissioned, the editor will work with you to refine the approach, perfect the pacing of content and finalise the text features.

Don't forget to visit bookshops and libraries as you develop your idea. Holding the latest children's non-fiction books in your hands is much more revealing than looking at covers online. Get a feel for the typical extent and word count for each age group. How will you build knowledge and understanding over 48, 64 or 96 pages? Will you write a picture book with 20 words per page, or a reference book with 200? Read as many examples as you can to absorb the language level. Make a note of the page features that non-fiction writers use to break up the text into manageable chunks.

Writing a proposal – dos and don'ts

Children's non-fiction authors work with publishers in several different ways. The first will be familiar if you already write fiction. Pitch an original idea and negotiate an advance and royalty. Some non-fiction authors work with literary agents; others, like me, pitch directly to publishers and use the excellent Society of Authors (see page 349) for advice on contracts. When I worked as a non-fiction commissioning editor, I was equally happy to hear from both.

Editors also come to me with a subject in mind and ask for a text treatment – a fresh new approach that will work for their market. In this case, the remuneration may be a one-off fee, higher than the advance for a similar title. Either way, my first task for each new title is to write a concise and engaging proposal to make the case for my idea.

Begin with an **overview** that showcases your style and tone. It should be good enough to become the back-cover blurb (and it often does). Follow this attention-grabbing introduction with a longer **description**. Explain why the book is timely, perfect for the target age group and why you are the best person to write it. There's no need to send the whole manuscript (unless you are writing a short picture book). Instead provide a **breakdown of the structure**, showing how you build engagement and understanding. Finally, include two or three pages of **sample text** to bring the idea to life.

DO:
• **Explain why you are pitching to this publisher.** Visit bookshops and scour catalogues, including the rights catalogues that publishers produce for book fairs. Find out what makes their books special. Then show why your idea and their list are a perfect match.

• **Come up with an attention-grabbing title** that hints at both subject matter and approach. Humorous and irreverent or lyrical and atmospheric? Hands-on activities or narrative adventure?

• **Point out anything that might drive sales**, such as anniversaries, curriculum links or exhibitions. Remember to work at least 18-24 months ahead – illustrated non-fiction takes around a year to journey from manuscript to shelf.

• **Showcase your voice.** Ten years ago, children's non-fiction often had a formal tone, edited to match house style. Today, a unique voice will help you stand out.

DON'T:

• **Claim that there is no competition**. More often than not, this points to a lack of research. Competition can prove that a topic is in demand. Publishers will always offer books on dinosaurs, space and animals, and are hungry for creative new approaches to these popular themes. Compare your idea to existing titles – ideally successful ones! Explain why your approach will be different (and better).

• **Include illustrations.** Unless you're an author-illustrator, it's the publisher's role to find an illustrator that the audience will love (often, but not always, with your approval). Instead, note down ideas about the type of illustrations you think would work well, as part of your overall vision for the book.

• **Mention how much your family and friends like the idea.** Publishers get many proposals saying 'tested on my kids'. It's better to present the skills and experience that make you an expert in your subject area or target audience – or both!

Writing the book – three golden rules

1. Research is key

One of the best things about writing for a living is the chance to dive into a subject. You might be writing for ten-year-olds, but you'll need to understand your topic in much greater depth. To avoid introducing errors, track down original sources. If you read an interesting article, find the original research too. Better still, interview the author. Insist on two sources for every fact (and never make one of those sources Wikipedia). And be warned – when you're interviewing stuntwomen, scientists or astronauts, job envy is an occupational hazard!

2. Play on the page

Hooking the audience doesn't end with a creative angle. Every page, paragraph and sentence must work hard to weave in the information you'd like to cover, while keeping readers engaged.

Make good use of text features, such as infographics, charts, text boxes and quotes. They can help you to bring interesting facts to the fore, enticing a reader to explore the rest of the page. They also help to pace the flow of information, making complex topics or arguments easier to follow.

Resist the temptation to include everything. First drafts are often double the length of the final text, and the real work comes in deciding what to leave out.

3. Think visually

Illustrations are a key ingredient in children's non-fiction. Sourcing these illustrations (whether buying photographs or commissioning illustrators) is the job of the publisher. But briefing them is the job of the author.

Think like an art director – how will information be broken up into chunks and displayed on the page? What diagrams will help you to explain a difficult concept? Will you include cartoons and visual jokes? An information book might need simple photo briefs, while a graphic text demands detailed descriptions of every panel. Create a wish list, to be realized by a talented illustrator and designer.

Building a writing career

Children's non-fiction authors develop valuable skills: the ability to carry out in-depth research, to write at just the right level for a certain age group, and to build a story that educates and entertains. These skills are in demand outside book publishing – by companies, charities and organisations that want to create outreach resources, by children's magazines, museums and science centres, and by producers of educational websites, blogs and vlogs. Writing other types of non-fiction content helps you keep your voice and ideas fresh. It can also be another way to reach your audience if you have an idea that's close to your heart, but find that there is no commercial demand for it in book form.

As a non-fiction author, you are well placed to **design and run events** linked to your writing. For example, pitch yourself to local schools, museums and festivals; run craft sessions in bookshops and libraries; help children unleash their own non-fiction writing power in an interactive workshop. Events are a direct way to keep in touch with your readers, and you'll come away with dozens of ideas for new books.

Nothing beats the feeling of discovering something wonderful for the first time. Whether I'm writing a biography, an activity book or a picture book, I aim to give readers the same feeling. If I can encourage children to pick up a book, think 'wow', and keep reading, I know I've done a good job. But if they read something that encourages them to close the book, head outside and explore the world ... well, then I know I've done a *great* job.

Where will your next non-fiction adventure take you?

Isabel Thomas has written more than 160 non-fiction titles for young audiences, published by Bloomsbury, Oxford University Press, Penguin Random House, Laurence King, Collins, Pearson, DK, Rising Stars, Raintree, QED, Curious Fox and Wren & Rook in the UK, and translated into more than 30 languages around the world. Her narrative non-fiction picture book *Moth: An Evolution Story* (Bloomsbury 2019) was awarded the 2020 AAAS Subaru Prize for Excellence in Science Books. Isabel's most recent publications include *Scientists* (DK 2021), *Fox: A Circle of Life Story* (Bloomsbury 2020), and *Exploring the Elements* (Phaidon 2020), which was a *New York Times* and Waterstones Book of the Year. Find out more at www.isabelthomas.co.uk and follow her on Twitter @isabelwriting and Instagram @isabelthomasbooks.

See also...
• *Finding new readers and markets,* page 107

Overnight success

Lauren St John describes how she became an overnight success after 20 years of writing and being published.

I was ten when I first decided to become a novelist. At the time we were living on a farm in what was then Rhodesia and books were in short supply. When I did get a new *Famous Five*, Nancy Drew or Black Stallion novel, I'd devour it so quickly and feel so bereft when I reached the end that quite often I'd simply turn it over and start again.

One day, a visitor presented me with a box of secondhand books, among which was a novel written by a 13-year-old. The idea that a teenager could become a published author blew me away. I set to work at once writing a book about a sheep and a snake in a woodpile. I'd heard that it was important to write what you know and I had a string of adopted lambs. Added to which, the woodpile in our garden practically writhed with snakes – most of them poisonous.

The other thing I'd heard about publishers was that your manuscript needed to be typed. To this end, I had my mum take me to the nearest farm we could find that had a typewriter. There, I spent a busy afternoon working my way through a bottle of Tipp-Ex and filling a wastepaper basket with crumpled balls of paper. I never managed to type a single perfect page and that was the thing that defeated me. Publishers, I'd heard, were only interested in perfection.

By the time I turned 11, my principle goals were fame and saving animals. I didn't really care how I became famous and I didn't see lack of talent as a bar of any kind, especially if I achieved my number one ambition: becoming a pop star like Olivia Newton-John. Depending on the day of the week, I also wanted to become an Academy award-winning actress, an artist, an Olympic gold medal-winning eventer or a vet. English was my best subject but I didn't want to become a journalist like the career guidance counsellor advised because I thought journalists were quite horrible.

The funny thing was, I had a brief foray into most of these careers. Having left school at 16 (school, I'd decided, was interfering with my success) and had a couple of months at an art school in Cape Town, I announced to my parents that I wanted to move to the UK to become a pop singer. Until this point I'd led a fairly sheltered life on our farm and at a girl's boarding school (government, not private) and most sane adults would have fallen about laughing before saying a categorical: 'Are you out of your mind? Absolutely not!' End of story.

Fortunately, my parents are just the right side of crazy. My dad is a farmer and ex-soldier who's survived ambushes, snake bites, being gored by a bull and attacked by a crocodile, so very little fazes him. He essentially shrugged and said it was fine if that's what I wanted to do. His main concern was that I didn't starve. My mum is a big believer in the following of dreams, so her response was: 'Here's an air ticket and a little pocket money. Bon voyage!'

By the age of 18 I'd spent a year working as a veterinary nurse in Maidenhead, Berkshire, waitressed and had a fleeting stint teaching horse-riding in Sussex. I'd also tried writing another novel. Having decided that songwriting was the way forward, I was back on the farm in Zimbabwe, riding my horse and working on my singing when my mum called (my parents were now divorced). 'There's a journalism course starting at Harare Polytechnic tomorrow,' she said, 'and you're going to be on it.'

My protests were in vain. When I was accepted onto the course, I grudgingly agreed to try it for two weeks. 'If I don't like it,' I told her, 'I'm quitting.'

In fact, I loved it. Few of our lecturers ever showed up, subjects such as sociology were started then aborted without explanation (I left college able to type only 25 words a minute because our typing teacher quit after two weeks and was never replaced) and our photography studies took place without cameras.

Once, we were taken on a rural reporting assignment where the only food available was goat curry. We slept on mud floors and the communal showers had no curtains. And yet I've never laughed more or learned more than I did that year. It remains one of the best experiences of my life. My diploma is not (in my opinion) worth the paper it's printed on, and yet my time at Harare Polytechnic taught me two things that I believe are critical for any writer:

• **Discipline.** You can write like Dostoevsky but if you can't deliver the goods when you're meant to deliver them, you're going to make a lot of people cross and mess up many production schedules.

• **The danger of preconceptions.** The ability to read people is a critical skill in a writer, as is psychological insight, but more important still is the capacity to have an open mind and the curiosity to look beneath the surface. The flashy, showy people, the beautiful ones, are rarely as interesting as the quiet ones sitting in the corner. As the *Desiderata* says, 'Listen to others, even the dull and the ignorant, for they too have their story.' The same applies to places and to stories.

It was while I was at college that I became obsessed with golf. By the time I graduated, three months later, I was so in love with it that I refused to get a real job. I spent the best part of a year working part-time for a shady promotions company. The director and I spent every available hour playing golf. The following March, with my 20-year-old brain turning slowly to mush, I decided that if I did have to work for a living I'd become a golf journalist. So I hopped on a plane with enough money for one month's rent and moved to London.

A white giraffe out of the blue

How I got from there to becoming a children's author is a long story. Suffice to say that it's taught me that no experience is ever wasted. Veterinary nursing, midnight feasts at boarding school, spending a decade on the PGA men's tour seeing the world and talking to Tiger, hanging out with musicians in Nashville, childhood dreams of becoming a pop singer or winning the Badminton Horse Trials – it all comes in handy if you're an author, especially if you write for children.

People often ask me where I get my ideas, but the truth is that until I wrote *The White Giraffe* I'd never had a single decent plot idea for a novel in my life. Not one. And I'd been trying to dream one up since I was ten.

The White Giraffe itself came out of the blue. At the time I was struggling to find work. I'd spent eight years working as golf correspondent to the *Sunday Times*, as well as writing music features for other newspapers and eight well-received non-fiction books. Yet most of those books were out of print and when it came to convincing editors to take my stories, I couldn't get arrested. I knew I'd hit rock bottom when, desperate for money and fresh out of confidence, I wrote a piece on spec for *Your Cat* magazine and they turned it down. I call it my 'Your Cat' moment. I was forced to sell my flat because I couldn't pay the mortgage. I was fast coming to the conclusion that I'd have to give up writing and find a real job.

In 2005, I was on my way to do some Christmas shopping when, out of nowhere, an image of a girl riding a giraffe popped into my head. When I was a teenager we lived for six years on a farm and game reserve where we actually had a pet giraffe (along with warthogs, a goat, eight horses, eight cats, six dogs and the occasional python) and I thought, 'Wouldn't it be the coolest thing on earth if you could actually ride a giraffe?' And right there on the street the whole story came into my head, including the girl's name, Martine.

I envisioned *The White Giraffe* as a picture book and decided that one day, when I retired, I'd have a tinker with it. But I found I couldn't stop thinking about it. In January, I attempted the first chapter. To my astonishment, it was effortless. The images that poured into my mind were so vivid it was like watching a movie.

After that, I couldn't stop writing. The best part was that, throughout the whole process, I couldn't shake the feeling that the story was being gifted to me. Each day when I sat down to write, I had the strongest sensation that all I had to do was listen for the words. As a consequence, if a name or a plot twist came to me, I used it, no matter how bizarre.

I had the first draft completed in a month. It was 20,000 words long and, as numerous rejections testified, it needed more work done on it. I was prepared to accept that it was probably quite bad, but because of the way the story had come to me I was convinced that it had something special about it. I had a policy. If I disagreed with an editor's criticism of it, I ignored it. If I thought they had a valid point, I did my best to make the suggested changes. If two or more people disliked something in the book, I would concede that they might be right. Yet nothing I did seemed to make a difference. When my agent at the time told me the book was unpublishable, I was devastated.

Eighteen months, 20,000 more words and a change of agent later, four publishers wanted the book. In the meanwhile, I'd written a synopsis for my memoir, *Rainbow's End*, which was bid for by five publishers in the UK, three in the USA and two in the Netherlands. Hamish Hamilton in the UK and Simon & Schuster in the USA bought *Rainbow's End* and Orion gave me a four-book deal for the *White Giraffe* series. After nearly 20 years of trying, I was an 'overnight' success!

Ten children's books on, I'm still pinching myself. Every day I do the short distance commute from my bed to my computer and moments later I'm having an adventure. I might be escaping a volcano with Laura Marlin, saving the Amazon jungle with an ant named Anthony or riding at Badminton, but whatever it is it'll be fun.

I've learned to trust my imagination and the strange process by which stories come to me, out of nowhere and fully formed. *Dead Man's Cove*, the first Laura Marlin mystery, for instance, came to me after I read an article on the singer Laura Marling and thought that Laura Marlin would be a good name for a girl detective. At the time I was reading a book on modern day slavery and the two things coalesced in my imagination. The conservation themes in my *White Giraffe* series were inspired by my African childhood and my work rescuing leopards and dolphins with the wildlife charity, Born Free.

After decades without a solitary book idea, I now find enormous joy in thinking up plots. If you're stuck for ideas, remember that life is infinitely stranger than fiction. There is a wealth of potential bestsellers in every newspaper. A news story about a stowaway could be turned into a novel about a girl whose father works at the airport who rescues a boy. A story about a jungle plane crash could be turned into a girl's own adventure story about the lone survivor of a crash who has to cross the Amazon with a mongrel dog to make it to safety.

Finding *your* 'overnight' success

My number one piece of advice to would-be children's authors is to put the finding of an agent or publisher at the bottom of your priority list. I meet a staggering number of people who've barely written a chapter and yet are utterly obsessed with how to write a query letter and marketing strategies for their books. Trust me when I tell you that none of those things matter if you can't tell a good story.

Concentrate on writing the best book you can. Write from the heart, write for the love of it and write with passion. Contrary to popular belief, publishers and agents are desperate to find great novels. If you follow the advice above, there's no reason at all that yours can't be one of them. Remember that practice makes perfect. Write, write, write. If you value quality of plot and prose over marketing strategies and have faith and perseverance, chances are you will find your book a home.

Then, like me, you'll be an 'overnight' success!

Lauren St John is the author of the multi award-winning children's series published by Orion Children's that includes *The White Giraffe* (2007), *Dolphin Song* (2008), *The Last Leopard* (2009), *The Elephant's Tale* (2010) and *Operation Rhino* (2015). *Dead Man's Cove*, the first book in her *Laura Marlin Mysteries* series, won the 2011 Blue Peter Book of the Year Award and was shortlisted for the Children's Book of the Year. Her bestselling *The One Dollar Horse* series (Orion 2012) has been followed by *The Glory* (Orion 2015). She has also written eight non-fiction adult books, including *Hardcore Troubadour: The Life & Near-Death of Steve Earle* and *Rainbow's End*, a memoir of her childhood in Zimbabwe. *The Snow Angel*, a standalone children's novel for Head of Zeus, was published in 2017. *Kat Wolfe Investigates*, the first in a new middle-grade mystery series, was launched by Macmillan Children's Books in 2018 followed by *Kat Wolfe Takes the Case* (2019) and *Kat Wolfe on Thin Ice* (2021). *Wave Riders*, a standalone sailing mystery, was published in 2021.

See also...

Keeping going: the ups and downs of being a published writer

Theresa Tomlinson shares the emotional and creative highs and lows, opportunities and hurdles an author may encounter during a long writing career. She tracks the course of her career – through finding and losing a trusted editor, writing fiction for children, adults and YA, and moving from traditional publishing to self-publishing.

Books

As a child I had no ambitions to write, but I loved reading and delighted in magical escapes to Narnia. I failed the eleven-plus, and rather struggled at my convent boarding school, but discovered I had some facility for drawing and painting. I spent two years at Hull Art College but left without completing my graphic design course. Unsure of what to do next, I trained to be an infant teacher and it was in that role that I discovered the sheer joy of storytelling (in those days both children and teachers could look forward to a blissful story session at the end of each day).

Later, as the mother of three young children, I started to put together simple picture books, initially focusing on the artwork rather than the words. As time passed the stories grew longer; my interest in the artwork faded and I began to write somewhat obsessively. Visits to the local library provided huge inspiration as I discovered new and exciting children's writers; it was almost like finding a new version of Narnia. Discovering Jane Gardam was a revelation – not only did I love her humour, sensitivity and clear writing style, but I recognised many of the settings based on the part of the north-east coast where I grew up. I knew every street, garden and house in the background of *A Long Way from Verona* (Abacus 1997), heard familiar cadences in the dialogue and experienced once again the familiar tang of steelworks built close to the sea. I began to feel that I, too, had stories to tell.

Having discovered a local writers' workshop, tutored by Berlie Doherty, I settled to work more seriously as a writer; five years of hard work followed, including three inspiring Arvon courses. There were many rejections, but things started to look up when I was awarded a Yorkshire Arts Bursary to help me finish a book in progress – *The Flither Pickers* (1987) – stories of fishing families set on the north-east coast, along with an offer of publication from John Killick of the Littlewood Press, based at Hebden Bridge. Although it was a limited print run, it meant that I had a well-produced example of my work to send to publishers. Fairly soon after that I got my first (modest) offer from a London publisher – for a magical children's story set in the industrial seaside village that I had lived in as a child. The offer came from Julia MacRae, a highly respected publisher with her own imprint within Walker Books and – best of all – she was Jane Gardam's publisher! I was thrilled.

Over the next 20 years, with the support of Julia and my fabulous editor, Delia Huddy, I flourished. One book followed another. Historical themes appealed to me and were appreciated by schools. Julia MacRae moved to Random House and took me with her, though happily Walker Books continued to publish my younger-age 'time-slip' books, which allowed modern children to slip magically back through time to experience an earlier period. I was hugely encouraged when *Riding the Waves* (1990) a more modern novel, set on the north-east coast, was recommended for the Carnegie Medal and my young adult novels were translated into several languages and sold in the USA. I was regularly shortlisted for the Sheffield Children's Book Award (Michael Palin memorably turned his back on me and folded his arms when I was called up onto the stage twice in an award ceremony!); it was such good fun.

Publishing contracts were now becoming rather complicated for me to deal with, so I looked for an agent; persuading Caroline Walsh of David Higham to take me on turned out to be one of the best things I ever did. Educational publishers were asking for more historical time-slip stories and when again one of these, *Meet Me By The Steelmen* (1997), was shortlisted for the Carnegie Medal, I thought my future was secure ... But then gradually things started to change: schools became short of funds and invitations to visit grew scarce, ebooks appeared on the scene and time-slip stories seemed to fall out of favour. However, I still had the backing of my editor and a sympathetic agent.

For some time I had longed to use Anglo-Saxon Whitby as a setting for a story so, having moved to Whitby, I set out to write a trilogy of YA mystery/adventures with Hild's famous monastery as the setting. The research process was sheer pleasure and it was inspiring to be living in sight of the location. *Wolf Girl* (Corgi Children's 2006) was the first book completed and we had almost finished the editing process when my editor Delia suddenly died. The book was published but it didn't sell widely and Random House concluded that readers were not interested in Anglo-Saxon settings, but by then I had become passionately interested in the period; my bookshelves were filled with studies of food, clothing, language and crafts of the time – I'd persuaded my husband that our travels must include Sutton Hoo, West Stow Anglo-Saxon village, Durham, Bede's World (now Jarrow Hall), Yeavering, Bamburgh Castle and Lindisfarne.

By then, fortunately, trying to earn a living by writing had become less of a priority, but it was a depressing time; I almost considered giving up altogether. A few months of ignoring the computer, though, made me realise that it would be even more depressing not to write; for my own wellbeing, I needed to do it. Hearing that Whitby had a writers' group, I went to join them. It was like starting at the beginning again, and there was something rather exciting about that.

I couldn't let my Anglo-Saxon obsession go and began work on an adult murder mystery with the same setting as my YA book and with a theme somewhat similar to Ellis Peters' Cadfael series, but with a 7th-century half-pagan herb-wife, rather than a monk. Creating a much older protagonist was something I'd wanted to try for a while and the character of Fridgyth was already present in *Wolf Girl*, waiting to step forward into the limelight. Whitby Writers Group provided practical criticism and friendly encouragement and my pleasure in writing returned. A difficult decision had to be made when the manuscript was completed: whether to try to get it published traditionally or go down the self-publishing route. I talked it through with my agent and it became clear that, although I'd had some success as a children's writer, that wouldn't mean much when tackling the competitive, adult, historical crime fiction market. Even acceptance by a traditional publisher might mean waiting years for publication.

I was then in my 60s and felt time might be running out, so I decided to experiment with self-publishing. My agent negotiated a contract with Acorn Independent Press. They provided discerning editing, and I enjoyed having lots of input into the cover design. The book was well produced as a print-on-demand (POD) and ebook edition and Acorn helped with marketing and distribution. *A Swarming of Bees* (2012) was put forward for an Amazon promotion and within a few weeks it reached number three in the historical bestsellers chart – I was briefly placed between Hilary Mantel and C.J. Sansom and couldn't have been happier. I recovered my costs fairly quickly and local bookshops still sell copies at a steady pace, which I supply them with.

I set about writing a sequel and I also had a straightforward historical novel published, *The Tribute Bride* (2014), this time with a 6th-century setting. Self-publishing seemed to be working for me, so I began to look at my backlist of out-of-print titles. Two of my short novels, *The Flither Pickers* and *The Herring Girls*, focusing on the harsh lives of the fishing families of the north-east coast, were published in a paperback edition in 2017, illustrated with atmospheric Victorian/Edwardian photographs by Frank Meadow Sutcliffe. York Publishing Services (www.yps-publishing.co.uk) produced the book and it was a real benefit to be able to discuss the project face to face before agreeing to go ahead and at any point during the production process. YPS produced a Kindle version that displays the photographs beautifully and the books are selling steadily in local shops. YPS suggested an initial print run of 250 copies and I'm now into my second run.

However, self-publishing hasn't been all plain sailing. When the manuscript for my 'herb-wife' sequel was finished, Acorn were happy to put the book together but had decided to withdraw from providing marketing services. Once again, my agent came to the rescue: Caroline negotiated a rather different contract with Acorn, and David Higham Agency agreed to take on the setting up and management of a Kindle version and POD facility themselves. *Queen of a Distant Hive* (2017) was produced and has gathered positive reviews – not least from fellow historical writers. I sense that there is more interest in the Anglo-Saxon period now and I have discovered a good community of support out there, especially from those writing in a similar genre. Bloggers invite me to appear as their guest and provide reviews – Annie Whitehead (http://anniewhiteheadauthor.co.uk), Helen Hollick (https://discoveringdiamonds.blogspot.com) and Carla Nayland (http://carlanayland.blogspot.com) are three active examples.

I haven't entirely given up on traditional children's publishing and am working on a YA novel set in Victorian Whitby. At the age of 72 my ambitions are modest. I have a small pension, a supportive husband and a loyal agent – it's a privileged position to be in. I'm grateful simply to be able to sit down at my computer and still spend a few magical hours in Narnia – or any other time or place that I fancy.

Theresa Tomlinson is known for her YA and children's historical novels, particularly those set on the north-east coast of England. Her books include *The Flither Pickers* (1987), *Summer Witches* (1991), the *Forestwife* trilogy – *The Forestwife* (1993), *Child of the May* (1998) and *Path of the She-Wolf* (2000), five *Time Slip* adventures including the republication of *Meet Me By the Steelmen* (Award Publications Ltd 2019), which was followed by a sequel, *Forged in Steel*, shortlisted for the 2021 Sheffield Children's Book Award. Theresa's other books include the *Troy and the Warrior Women* series – *The Moon Riders* (2002) and *The Voyage of the Snake Lady* (2004). Her latest book is *Dark Fortune* (The Old Print Workshop 2021). Theresa has been shortlisted twice for the Carnegie Medal and for the Sheffield Children's Book Award. For more information and Theresa's blog, see www.theresatomlinson.com.

See also...
• *Writing historical novels*, page 146

How to write a picture book

Tessa Strickland highlights the enduring value of picture books, both educational and emotional, for young children in today's world, and offers advice for writers wishing to engage in the child's world on the process, practices, qualities and skills they will need to succeed.

A picture book is a child's first theatre. It's likely to be the first time a child experiences the drama of storytelling as the spoken word, accompanied by glorious illustration and skilful design. As on a theatre stage, several disciplines come together. The result is an art form whose impact on the imagination can extend well beyond childhood. I remain inspired by my favourite childhood picture books, among them Golden MacDonald's evocative Hebridean story *The Little Island* (Doubleday 1946), Kay Thompson's badass heroine *Eloise* (Simon & Schuster 1955) and Barbara Cooney's Caldecott-winning 1959 version of *Chanticleer and the Fox* (Crowell 1958). Decades later, the picture books that were my own children's favourites still take pride of place on the shelves of my family library.

Picture books are not just about entertainment: they play a crucial role in establishing basic literacy skills, emotional intelligence, acquisition of language, appetite for learning and enjoyment of art. Of course, the child is not reading the text, it is being read to her. But as she listens, she knows that the adult reader is decoding those curious black marks that run along the page. She knows too that these marks, these words, are the key to what is happening in the illustrations. So, the heart of the picture book is this marriage between the text and the illustration – each depends on the other.

Where to start

The starting point is the story. Picture books are short (publishers typically require a text of less than 1,000 words), so it's dangerously easy to think that they are easy to write. In fact, the opposite is the case. Writing a picture book presents the same challenges as writing a poem. Your aim is to achieve a sense of balance and harmony between the story as music and as meaning. Small children will experience the storytelling as sound first, sense later. As long as the sound of the language is congruent with its meaning, they will happily let themselves be carried along by the emotional momentum of the narrative.

If you want to have a go at picture book writing, it is a very good idea to spend dedicated time with children under five. You may have children of your own; you may teach in an early-years setting; you may simply like the idea of storytelling for this enthusiastic and receptive age group. Consider volunteering to read aloud at your local preschool, primary school or library. This will help you to get a sense of what stories the children enjoy listening to AND what kind of stories you most enjoy telling. Notice what the children are doing and saying when they play (children come into the world knowing instinctively that play is work. This is how they learn, and their interactions reveal their major interests and preoccupations).

As well as engaging with the child's world, try to remember what you felt like as a child. Get these feelings into your storytelling. This will make your writing authentic. Children see straight through sentimentality, yet an alarming number of adults shy away from the intensities and terrors of childhood and try to sugar-coat it. This won't work.

Practice and peer groups

Write as often as you can. If it's not possible for you to write every day (for many of us, it isn't), then choose at least a couple of hours a week and make this your personal, uninterruptable writing time. Writing is a craft and, like any craft, the more you practise, the better you get. Look for a supportive writing group – the excellent Society of Children's Book Writers & Illustrators (see page 356) has many local chapters and there are also all kinds of courses online and masterclasses at literature festivals (see *Children's writing courses and conferences*, page 403). Peer support groups can be transformative and you will learn a lot, not only about your potential as a writer but also about how to give and receive feedback. Very few of us can write to please everyone. So, like any professional writer, one of your challenges will be how to decide what to retain because you instinctively believe that it works, and what to revise or discard based on other people's feedback.

Finding your thread

Aristotle was right when he said that a story needs a beginning, a middle and an end. When you have an idea for a story, you may be surprised by how difficult it is to start, to get a beginning that really *is* a beginning.

Once you *have* started, it can be tricky to tell the story you thought you were going to tell. Don't worry! This is a good sign. Writing is a creative act. Your characters may well take on lives of their own and decide they are going to get up to all kinds of antics you had not predicted. Be prepared to fool around for a good many drafts, to get to know the characters you are writing about, to give them a back story. The back story won't necessarily appear on the page, but by creating it you will ground your narrative and make it more convincing than it would otherwise be.

Some writers start with their characters and go from there. What ages are they? What are their strengths and weaknesses, likes and dislikes? What do they need or crave? Try writing about two strongly contrasting characters: exaggerate their traits and explore the different ways in which they communicate. You may surprise yourself, and if you do this in a group, you will be fascinated by the different ways in which this one-to-one exchange can be unpacked.

Other writers prefer to start with a situation and then decide who they are going to conjure up to resolve it. This is also a sound strategy and every good story needs a problem. If your characters live in a trouble-free dream world or a happy-ever-after hedgerow, your readers are going to be bored and unconvinced, because life is not like this. So, to engage your young audience, you need a situation which quickly becomes problematic. Then you need a way of resolving the problem that is transformative for your main character. The problem may be internal (for example, your character may be afraid of something) or it may be external (for example, a storm is coming). And you may well find that solving one problem leads to another ... learning how to find your thread AND hold onto it will require you to redraft and redraft.

Staying true to life

The infant's journey from birth to the age of five is the most formative in its entire life. As babies grow into toddlers and then into children, they live among giants, with adults and perhaps older siblings, looming above them and exerting tremendous power. This is why stories about larger-than-life characters resonate so powerfully in young children's minds.

There is something of a trend in contemporary children's publishing to avoid scaring children. In my view, this is a mistake. Fear and rage, pain and sorrow are as familiar to children as cornflakes at breakfast. They are often scared or infuriated and by hearing stories in which scary things happen and are successfully dealt with, they learn that there are ways of navigating and mastering their feelings. Often, successful children's writers tackle these feelings through symbol and metaphor; territory in which most children are naturally at ease.

Using humour

One of the most valuable resources in the picture book writer's toolkit is humour. It is like medicine, and it can take many forms: it may be dry; it may be quiet; it may be outrageous. Understatement can go a long way with children. By contrast, irony and sarcasm tend to be too sophisticated for little ones. So, if you are using humour, keep it straightforward. It can be tempting, as the writer, to introduce layers of tongue-in-cheek humour that are evident to the adult, who is also, after all, the one who is likely to have paid for the book in the first place, and this can be wonderful. Just be careful that it is not at the expense of the child for whom you are writing.

Writing in verse

Aspiring writers can find themselves utterly bewildered by conflicting advice about whether or not to write in verse. My experience both as a publisher and as a writer is that verse is hugely popular. However, it's a common misperception among beginners that verse means no more than having a rhyme scheme. To write in verse, you need to have an ear for metre and for the relationship between metre, tone and meaning. The rhyme is secondary. It is certainly valuable in all kinds of ways – children and adults alike take enormous pleasure in guessing and remembering the word that completes a rhyming couplet, and unexpected rhymes are particularly delightful. But without a convincing metre, verse becomes flat-footed. If you want to write in verse, read and decode the masters, and be prepared to do a lot of re-writing to get it right. One false note will kill your endeavour.

Going to market

You have been diligently writing for a year or two and you now have three or four manuscripts you are happy with. It is time to gird your loins and pitch your work to an agent or a publisher. It is certainly not essential to have an agent, but if you do go this route, a good agent will know what different publishers are looking for and be able to negotiate terms on your behalf. Also, the UK children's publishing industry is a small world. Agents who do well on behalf of their clients do so because they keep up to date on changing trends and know who is looking for what.

You don't need to find an illustrator; the publisher will do this. You just need to have a selection of short manuscripts that are skillfully crafted, that surprise and delight the editor who will read them first and that show you have a distinctive voice. Before you make your submissions, check what is on the market and make sure someone else hasn't already had your idea (you will be surprised by how often this happens). Check the agent's or publisher's website, so that you have a sense of what kind of taste they have and what their successes are.

Be professional. Follow the agent's or publisher's submission guidelines and keep your cover letter brief. You will not help your cause by saying that your children or grandchildren love your writing. Of course they do, but they are not the ones taking the commercial risk.

Persist. Many of the most successful picture book writers have endured years of rejection. They have succeeded not only because they are talented but also because they have been prepared to work very hard and to persevere.

The international picture book market

Picture books are expensive to develop. This is one of the reasons why only a few new picture books appear on UK publishers' lists each year. The expense of sourcing and commissioning artwork, then paying for full-colour origination and printing, quickly runs well into five figures. To recover this investment, UK publishers typically seek out publishing partners overseas, from the USA to China. Economies of scale mean that the more copies a publisher prints, the lower the unit cost. Because the UK market is a small one, publishers here usually seek to sell co-edition licences to as many partners as possible before they go to press.

This process takes time. So, do not give up your day job! The period between having your manuscript accepted and seeing it in the world as a printed book can be anything between one and three years.

Writing in a Global Pandemic

The coronavirus pandemic has drastically changed all of our lives. This includes the lives of everyone involved in children's literature: writers, designers, publishers, printers, educational suppliers, librarians, booksellers, teachers. It's been a year that has brought great suffering for many. For those of us fortunate enough not to have been left jobless or to have lost loved ones, it has been a time of adaptation and reflection. For many - including me - it has prompted a lot of soul-searching about what matters most and what kind of future we want for ourselves and our children. The enforced seclusion of lockdown has not all been gloom and doom. Numerous parents and carers of small children have turned to picture books as fantastic resources for storytelling, sharing and discussion. Publishers with a strong online presence have flourished, often magnificently supported by booksellers who have risen to the challenge of selling in new ways. Those publishers whose sales have to date been more through the shops of public spaces such as art galleries, museums and airport shops have fared less well. There's definitely a sense that we are caught in the wheels of massive change. And because shipping has slowed down, there is a bit of a backlog in many publishers' calendars. However, I have been commissioned to write four picture books in the past year and it's been an enormous pleasure to witness more and more emergent picture book writers secure their first, second or third contracts. As we start to move out of our third UK lockdown and step into summer, I am glad that sales of children's picture books have held there own and I am optimistic that they will continue to do so!

Tessa Strickland is the co-founder and advisory editor of independent children's publisher Barefoot Books. As Stella Blackstone, she has also written many internationally acclaimed picture books. She now runs a private psychotherapy and mentoring practice and leads the picture book writing programme for the Golden Egg Academy (www.goldeneggacademy.co.uk).

Writing short stories for children

Julia Green describes the power and the pleasure of a well-written children's short story, and its essential attributes. She encourages aspiring short story writers to read, study, practice, experiment and to aim high.

Primary School. I'm maybe eight or nine. We're reading a short story in class, from an ancient hardback collection of stories and poems illustrated with line drawings, with a faded blue and green cover. I can't remember the title of the anthology, but I do remember one story, about a lonely man making sand sculptures on the beach – Weymouth, in my memory. And the atmosphere – slightly melancholy, a sense of loss, the way that I often felt as a child when it was time to leave the beach – the tide coming in, late afternoon, the beach emptying out. The man walks away, the sea washes in and erases the sculptures… Later on, aged 13 or 14, in an English lesson we read Ted Hughes' short story *The Rain Horse*, which is all atmosphere – a field, the rain, the threatening horse, a young man's sense of terror.

Why have these particular short stories stayed in my mind over so many years, out of all the others we read as children? Perhaps it's the strong sense of place, the use of vivid detail to create a landscape and a moment in time through the appeal to all the senses. And a strong *feeling*: sadness, sense of loss, fear. It's partly in what is *not said*; an effective short story doesn't waste words. It leaves a space for the reader to imagine, to fill in the gaps. We enter into the story world, stay a short time, and leave again – but as a reader, we're left with the sense that something has changed forever. We've glimpsed something, felt something, of lasting significance. The short story as 'an arrow in flight', as the Irish writer Mary Lavin described it.

We are talking here about **the short story as a form in itself**; not a short book for children, like a picture book, or an illustrated story for young children which is short in length but is in essence a short novel – though much of what I am saying here would apply to these forms of story, too. And we are thinking of the **audience** as children aged from about four, when a child might be listening to the story being read aloud rather than reading for themselves, to about 12. Publishers and booksellers classify readers older than that as 'teen' or 'young adult' rather than children. It is helpful for a new writer to be aware of this. Writing for a four- or five-year-old is obviously very different from writing for someone of 9-12 years. Think about how appropriate the theme or experiences and emotions in your story would be for the age group you want to write for. Alternatively, first write the story you want to write, and *then* think about that question of audience. The problem for many new or unpublished writers is a mismatch between the style/language/content of the story and the age and interest of the 'audience': the child reader. Of course there are many notable exceptions to this, but as a *beginner writer* it's helpful to think about making the age of your main character just a little older than the age of your readers. You will need to be aware of the language and style, too, to make it appropriate for the intended audience.

If you want to write short stories for children, the important thing, of course, is to *read* many! Immerse yourself in the form. You might reread stories you enjoyed as a child, to re-experience them with your adult 'writer' mind, namely reading as-a-writer, alert to the way the story has been written. Examine closely: 1) the language, the way words and sentences work, how much or little description there is, how dialogue is used, how much or how little 'action' or 'plot'; 2) the pace (how quickly do things move along?); 3) what the story is actually 'about'; 4) the form of the short story, studying this is the best way of learning how to do it yourself (not so that you write in exactly the same way – we can only ever write authentically as ourselves – but to help you think about the different options open to you, and the tools of your trade). Make notes for yourself in a notebook.

Read contemporary short stories for children, too, to see what is being published now. Fashions change. Haunt bookshops and libraries. Look at anthologies of short stories published for children, such as *Moonlight Magic* (Stripes 2016) or *My Kind of School* (A&C Black 2008), edited by Tony Bradman; collections for different age groups, such as *The Puffin Book of Stories for Five-Year-Olds* (Penguin 1996) edited by Wendy Cooling, or *Funny Stories for 5-Year-Olds* (Pan Macmillan 2016), edited by Helen Paiba. These contain stories by different writers, new and old.

Read collections of short stories by individual authors, too. These are usually by established authors (it is very rare for a brand-new writer to have a collection of stories accepted for publication):

– Nicola Davies' *Up on the Hill* (Walker 2008) consists of three separate short stories about children who live in the country.

– Michael Morpurgo wrote a memorable collection, published as *The White Horse of Zennor and other stories* (Mammoth 1982).

– Leila Berg's wonderful *Little Pete Stories* (Methuen) for very young children written in the 1950s were groundbreaking in their time for the way she showed 'real' children, feeling strong emotions including anger.

– Emma Carroll's *When We Were Warriors* (Faber 2019) contains three short stories linked to her popular historical novels for children.

– David Almond's collection *Counting Stars* (Hodder Children's 2000) illustrates the richness of the short story form in the hands of a master storyteller. These layered, rich, strange and beautiful stories are based on his childhood in Felling in the North-East of England and transcend the usual publishing boundaries of 'age groups'. Almond wrote them before he wrote the prize-winning *Skellig* (Hodder Children's 1998), but they weren't published until after he was established as a successful novelist for young people.

Read these stories and then, as a 'writing exercise' in your writing notebook (of course you have one of these!), take real incidents or experiences from your own childhood as the material for a short story, so as to get in touch with the real, raw emotions of childhood and to help you find an authentic voice in your writing. (Note: this might end up as a short story *'about* childhood' as distinct from a story *'for* children', two subtly different things.)

One of the great satisfactions of writing a short story is that sense of having the complete story in your hand, so you can 'see' it all at once, with its beautiful, honed shape. You can polish and perfect it, and learn much that will help you with all your writing, particularly about precision and brevity, voice and tone, and about the significance of endings. Aim high. Only the very best writing is good enough for children.

As children's writers, we have other things to consider as well as mastery of the short form. A contemporary short story for children is likely to be commissioned by an editor, via an agent, on a particular theme, to be published alongside other stories by other writers on that same theme. For example, I have been asked to write stories about children and animals suitable for several 'winter' anthologies, about the experience of primary school and on the theme of friendship for children of primary school age (up to age 11). The challenge is to write a story that will be original and different enough from the others in the collection, that will appeal to the age group, be accessible, reflect the diversity of the world we live in and be enjoyable and engaging. The story needs to feel complete, to give the reader that satisfaction of a happy (or happy/hopeful *enough*) ending. It needs to take the reader into its world and introduce the main character (in my case always a child) swiftly and immersively, and to do this within a word limit (in these examples, 1500 words).

So, like a novel but in very condensed form, the story has to establish a character, a setting and a situation. It must take the reader on some kind of 'journey' with ups and downs, as the character does things (takes certain actions) to try to resolve the 'situation' (problem/issue). And then it must swiftly reach an ending – in such a way that the situation you established at the beginning is either resolved or changed in some way. You might ask yourself these questions:
– What does my character want?
– What do they DO, to try to get it?
– How does it all work out? (Do they get what they wanted ... or something else, unexpected?)

In a story for children, it is usually a good idea to put the child at the centre of the action, to make them ACTIVE (rather than passive, having things done TO them). **Write from the child's perspective**. Find a voice that feels fresh and authentic and contemporary. Experiment with first person or close-up third person as a way of bringing your child reader close to the action. Children want to immerse themselves in the story.

I write realistic stories, but a short story might be in any genre: fantasy, science fiction, supernatural, funny, historical. It can be a good way to **try out something new**, in terms of style or genre, before committing to a longer project. And some ideas just come as 'short'; you know that's the form they need to take. After I'd written a commissioned short story about a girl and a seal pup, I went on to write a novel, *Seal Island* (OUP 2014). The short story had led me into a longer story in a similar setting with a similar central character, but with more incidents, more characters, more developed themes and the longer time-frame that a novel allows.

When we are learning, nothing we write is ever wasted, whether it gets published or not. We write first and foremost for ourselves. **Practising the short story form will improve all your writing.** There are short story competitions which can give you the benefit of a deadline, and sometimes a subject or theme, too. Having the constraints of a word count can be strangely liberating. Set yourself a deadline, a word count, and a subject, and see what magic happens. The mind plays games. A character will arrive, and a place – all stories have to happen somewhere – and before you know it, the story will start to emerge. Keep asking questions: *What if...? Supposing she....* Write it, one word, one sentence at a time. Write the first draft, fast. Then – cut, cut, cut! Polish. Make it beautiful. Make it the best story it can be. Write the story only *you* can write.

Julia Green is the author of more than 20 novels and short stories for young people. She is Emeritus Professor in Writing for Young People at Bath Spa University. She founded and until 2019 was Course Director of the MA Writing for Young People, which has launched the careers of more than 65 writers for children and young adults. Her most recent novels for children are *The House of Light* (2019) and *The Children of Swallow Fell* (2020), both published by OUP Children's. She is currently writing a collection of short stories, a new novel and a picture book. For more information see www.julia-green.co.uk.

Writing ghostly stories

Cornelia Funke describes the adventure of writing ghost stories for children. She highlights the questions writers can ask themselves when creating in this genre and considers how scary the stories can be for children.

I am not sure whether I liked ghost stories as a child. I know that at some point I loved Oscar Wilde's *Ghost of Canterville* (and now think it is the most touching ghost story ever told). But the first one I remember was written by a German, Otfried Preussler, whose *Satanic Mill* is an unforgettable tale: Preussler's ghosts were bowling with their own heads, as far as I recall.

Different types of ghosts

The funny ghosts who try to be scary and are not scary at all. We meet them in fairy tales, myths and Hollywood movies. They are slimy and loud, easily frightened by human heroes and, of course, are the most obvious choice for a ghost story written for children.

The first ghost I wrote about was that kind of ghost: Hugo, an ASG (Averagely Spooky Ghost), to be precise. I created him when an editor friend asked me many years ago to write a ghost story for 8–12 year-olds (don't we love it when publishers put our audience in cleanly separated boxes?). The story became a series of books, *Ghosthunters*, about a boy who is very afraid of ghosts but becomes a famous ghost hunter, with the assistance of the ASG. I had immense fun writing about COHAGs (Completely Harmless Ghosts), FOFIFOs (Foggy Fug Ghosts) and GHADAPs (Ghosts with a Dark Past). Interestingly, with every book my ghosts became darker and scarier.

My young readers became quite obsessed with the series and sent me lots of suggestions for ghost types. I heard from teachers that boys who despised reading had stolen *Ghosthunters* books from their tables to secretly devour them. My stories invited readers to play with fear – to make fun of it, hunt it, destroy it.

Ghosts are perfect for that. They are the impersonation of our greatest fears – the fear of the night, of death and what may await us on the other side. Not only that – they impersonate guilt, redemption, sadness that can't even be cured by death, they can bear witness to unspeakable crimes and the inescapable heritage of the past.

Heavy themes.

Nothing suitable for children?

Oh yes, they are. All of them.

Children take life very seriously. Life, death, pain, loss … they still face the big questions, because they haven't learned to look away. We can develop quite a skill in that as grown-ups. Children want to look at the dark because they know that what they fear becomes even more frightening when they turn their back on it or lock it away.

Young readers often don't have emotional memories attached to the themes of death, loss and guilt, which makes them much tougher when they play with them. But they've heard about them, the great monsters waiting … and they love to encounter them on the safe grounds of a printed page. As for the children who do know – we so easily forget that many know quite a lot about death and loss, even guilt – they long for stories that help them to cope with the dark by asking questions about it or maybe even give meaning to it. For them, stories can be both shelter and comfort, without looking away, and ghosts can be the perfect travel companions into realms that know about pain and fear.

It was a long journey through life for me between *Ghosthunters* and *Ghost Knight*. During that period, I learned some things about death and loss, about human nature, good and evil – all this apart from the fact that I had always been completely obsessed with knights. (*The Once and Future King* by T.H. White is still my favourite book).

Serious ghosts

The ghosts I found for *Ghost Knight* were not funny. If you intend to write a ghost story that walks on the darker side of this genre I recommend that you find your heroes in real places. Children love the enchantment of fiction that makes them discover reality. The ghosts I found in Salisbury, Lacock and Kilmington were human, and shadows of ourselves. They take my young readers on a journey into their own future as grown ups, but they also tempt them to travel into the past, to Salisbury Cathedral, Lacock Abbey and Kilmington Graveyard. These are all places where they can touch and breathe times gone and lost and follow in the steps of those who have lived before them.

I will never forget the reading I did at Salisbury Cathedral late at night, surrounded by children and parents. It took place, of course, next to the tomb of William Longespee, the man who had inspired my ghostly hero and incarnated my dreams about knights, and who at the same time allowed me to bow to what Oscar Wilde taught me about the sadness of ghosts.

Writing a ghost story

So, as you see, a ghost story is not just a ghost story. Maybe that is especially true for one written for children. There are so many paths to take. A good story always starts with the right questions. Ghost stories like to hide from us, dress themselves in a dozen veils. In readings I always try to explain this by comparing them to a labyrinth. Each one is full of traps and surprises, full of characters that hide between the hedges and love to jump at the poor writer who is trying to find his way through. There are whispers. A story likes to keep its secrets, but it also likes to be chased, found out, hunted and tamed. So it teases you by giving you hints and wrong tracks. And there you are, a pen in your hand (well, as in my case, you may write using a computer), a Moleskine notebook under my arm (well, once again, you may just carry your laptop … be careful though, there's nowhere to plug in in the labyrinth). You are stumbling down the narrow paths, looking for the one that is exactly right – the one that won't be so long and windy that it bores your readers to death; the one that shows all the secrets, all the characters hiding and whispering … It is the greatest adventure to find the heart of a story. And it's true storyline. Of course this endeavour is especially scary when you are looking for a ghost story! You may only find out after turning several corners that you are dealing with a scary ghost. Did I give you the impression that you choose whether it will be funny or scary? I apologise. The story chooses, once you enter its labyrinth. So make sure you ask the right questions before you decide on the one you enter. What do you want the labyrinth to grow for you?

Do you want your readers to love the ghost whose story you'll tell? Do you want them to pity it? Or fear it? Once again – you may answer all these questions and then find that a completely different story emerges. It has happened to me. Many times.

What age group do you intend to tell your story for? Once again, this is a good question and it needs to be asked. But be ready to change your answer if the story demands it.

The setting. Once you've decided on where the story will be set it will be hard to change it, especially if you choose an existing location. With an imagined one you leave most decisions to the labyrinth (which can be interesting!). With a real place, you walk in with a map, with your research and knowledge guiding you. A real place, with all its history, can be like a bag of provisions for your writer's journey. It can be your main character, all the food you need. It will tell you about landscapes, weather, buildings – even characters – and your readers will be able to follow your tracks in their own world, making a wonderful adventure. I still receive photos showing children in Venice who have followed the tracks of my book, *The Thief Lord*. And I heard about a boy who knelt in front of Longespee's tomb in Salisbury Cathedral after meeting him in *Ghost Knight*.

Oh – one more question: who will you be? The hero? Somebody who watches him/her and all the others, a narrator who knows everything? The god of the story? (Well, ghosts don't accept these gods but try, if you want to.) Most likely, you will be all of them. That's the joy of being a writer. You can live a thousand lives and take a thousand shapes.

Yes, go and write ghost stories! And write them for children! Even the dark ones, soaked in tragedy and the shadows of death – maybe those especially. Children are the most magical audience. They slip into a story like a fish into water. Without hesitating. Without asking how deep it is and where you got it from. They will travel the past on their printed wings. They will face their fear of gravestones and shadows moving in the dark. They will consider the possibility that life may not end in death and wonder why it scares them to see proof of it. They'll remember those who came before them and may even get a glimpse at the never-ending circle of life. And if all that gets too scary, just let them chase the ghosts – to save the good ones and send the bad ones to hell.

Hurrah for ghost stories!

Cornelia Funke (pronounced Foon-ke) is a multiple award-winning author of children's fiction and has sold over 20 million copies of her books worldwide. She was brought to the attention of Barry Cunningham at Chicken House (see page 14) when a young German girl living in England asked him why her favourite author's books were not available in English. Chicken House published her latest title at that time in English translation, *The Thief Lord* (2006) and it stayed at No. 2 on the *New York Times* bestseller list for 25 weeks. It was followed by the *Dragon Rider* series, the *Inkheart* trilogy, *Ghosthunter* series and the *Reckless* series. The fourth installment in the Reckless series, *Silver Tracks*, is published in Autumn 2021 (Pushkin Press).

See also...
- *Spotting talent*, page 1
- *Who do children's authors write for?*, page 99

Writing magic into fiction

Kiran Millwood Hargrave recommends the techniques she uses to feed and inspire her magical stories, and guides us through each stage of the process that allows a writer's fantastical ideas to come to fruition.

All fiction is a kind of magic: a conjuring. From your imagination, you are building whole people, whole worlds, making them so vivid and tangible your reader will be able to touch them, see them, wish they lived in your stories – but how do you layer magic upon magic and introduce a fantastical strand to your story? Perhaps you call it fabulism, perhaps magical realism, perhaps fantasy. They are all branches of the same enchanted tree, and here are my experiences of reading – and rooting my own stories in – magic.

Roots

My earliest love was the *His Dark Materials* trilogy by Philip Pullman. Read first when I was ten, much of it admittedly flew over my head, but I didn't mind because *how* it flew! Like witches on yew twigs, like swan daemons swirling, like angels stirring the clouds. I believe we all have 'books of power', as I term them, often discovered when we are young, that are keystones for the sort of stories we wish to write.

When I look at my own 'books of power', they largely fall into what I used to call magical realism. This was incorrect, as I've recently learned magical realism refers to those writing in the South American tradition, which addresses issues of colonialism. The better term is fabulism. Alongside Pullman's epic trilogy are: *Skellig* by David Almond, the *Chrestomanci* books by Diana Wynne Jones, *The Wolves of Willoughby Chase* by Joan Aiken, *Journey to the River Sea* by Eva Ibbotson and the ubiquitous *Harry Potter* series by J.K. Rowling. All hold very different, varying systems and approaches to 'magic', and often my first task when writing a novel is to decide where I want my book to sit within that spectrum. My debut, *The Girl of Ink & Stars* (Chicken House 2016), plunges into fully-fledged fantasy; my second novel, *The Island at the End of Everything* (2017) finds magic in nature, and my third, *The Way Past Winter* (2018), is folkloric in its telling and so sits on the border of fabulism.

My first challenge to you is to ask: what are your 'books of power'? Do they tell you about the sort of books you love, and give you an insight, as I believe, into the sort of books you should probably be writing? Some of you will be fantasy fans, while others may prefer that world to be recognisable but knocked slightly ajar to let some magic in. I like to keep my 'books of power' on my desk throughout my current writing project (the books change from project to project). It's an excellent procrastination exercise, but also an inspiring one.

Shoots

Your books of power are on your desk; perhaps you're listening to a film soundtrack (Enya is my writing jam); maybe you have a scented candle wafting snatches of 'Mystical Forest' towards you – and now you're ready to write. It's all possibility … like new shoots of green life emerging in spring. Some of you will plunge straight in, others will plan your narrative to within an inch of its life, but as a self-confessed 'pantser' (as in by-the-seat-of-your-pants vs 'planner') I wholly condone the former. There is nothing more exciting to me than plunging into the adventure alongside your characters and, as they take on more life, letting them make the decisions.

That said, I started my writing life as a poet; a bit of structure has always helped me and I give this to myself in the form of a map. This piece of advice is probably most useful to those of you writing a quest narrative – something where the characters travel through landscape – but I've also worked on maps of houses, or schools or streets. As soon as the perimeters of the places your characters will inhabit are solid, your imagination can run wild. Often these places also help to define the sort of magic you'll encounter in your world: if it's rife with mountains and dragons, you're probably reaching for an alternate universe, the rules of which you get to decide; if it's a secret door in an otherwise ordinary garden, you've got a beautiful set-up for fabulism. But my main advice at this stage is not to worry about labelling *what* sort of magic you're choosing. Let your story tell you what will work.

When I say 'draw a map', it does not need to be a work of art. My map for *The Girl of Ink & Stars* was a clumsily drawn circle with childish landmarks, with the routes of my characters plotted through the landscape in different colours for each. The plan for *The Way Past Winter* was even more basic: a house, some trees, some mountains, the sea and an arrow pointing 'North'. Think of it as storyboarding, as they do for films. You have your whole story on one piece of paper – and you can always rip it up and start again.

Rings

I can only speak to describe my own experience of writing – and everyone is different – but I like to charge through my first draft, full pelt towards the conclusion. This results in very short, fast-paced first drafts, but it means that the fear of the blank page is conquered. Something is easier to improve than nothing, so I would encourage you to write your first draft quickly, too. Then, the real work begins.

A tree grows rings as it ages, and so too will your story. These next drafts are for firming up its core, and finding the confidence to set down more firmly what you perhaps only gestured at in first drafts. I would argue this is not the time for brutal editing. Rather, luxuriate in bringing your story more fully into being. If you've written a fantasy, full of mermaids and talking animals, give them their back stories. If you've written in magical objects that transport your character into parallel worlds, think about how they feel, smell, look, where they came from. Put in all those details you would want as a reader: colour your world in. Check that your characters' names suit them and the world they inhabit. Research any asides that observant readers will appreciate and think how clever you are. Enjoy playing around, giving credence to ideas that may not quite be working, but that you think *could* – with just one more draft (or three).

This stage takes the longest for me, but it is also the most fun. It's when I experiment and learn the most about myself as a writer, and about what I want this story to do, and what I want a reader to take from it.

Branches

This next stage may appear to be misleadingly titled, as it implies growth when actually it's very likely that your manuscript will shrink – but editing really *is* like growing branches; it's also a little bit about hacking off the weaker ones.

As a reformed poet, editing holds a special place in my heart. I love it, because finally I know what my story is, and editing will help me get it there. But I know not everyone shares my enthusiasm for hacking at sentences or scenes that took weeks/months/years to write. So my advice to you is this: look at it as *giving* your story something, not taking something away. Only by editing can you find the sub-plots worth growing, and those that need pruning. Only by editing can you find the heart of your story, and make it sing.

Buds

Now you're ready to submit (I hugely dislike this word: when I was on 'submission' to agents I made a spreadsheet to keep track of where/when/who and my husband changed all the headings to things like 'date soul delivered' to denote when I sent out the manuscript, and 'poop or not poop?' to indicate whether I got a full request or a meeting/rejection ... humour helps!). Speaking from experience, the waiting is possibly the worst bit of all. Even when you're waiting to hear from, and often being rejected by, publishers, at least you and your agent are in it together. So hang in there, and give yourself the best possible chance of success by taking special care when choosing which agents you send to.

I made a list from the *Children's Writers' & Artists' Yearbook* and thoroughly researched this shortlist, breaking it into a top-tier I wanted to send to first, and then a second to help me get straight back on the horse if those initial queries bore no fruit. Look at those who represent the writers of your 'books of power', and pop them on the list too. Aim high. I did, and I ended up with my first choice of agent. But there was something I did not do right, and that I would urge you to do – that is to classify what exactly I had written.

I've mentioned that one of my 'books of power' was *His Dark Materials* by Philip Pullman, but another was *One Hundred Years of Solitude* by Gabriel Garcia Marquez and a third was *The Border Trilogy* by Cormac McCarthy. If that sounds like a confused list, it was, and it made for a confused manuscript. Fraught with long descriptions of landscape, and far too much pathetic fallacy, I wasn't sure what I had written. This showed in my query letter, which announced *The Girl of Ink & Stars* (then *The Cartographer's Daughter*) as a 'magical-realist YA/crossover adventure story'... Yes, I really did write all that down, and press 'send'. Luckily, my wonderful agent saw past it, but you can help yourself enormously by really pinning down what sort of book you've written. This is the only point at which this really matters, I would argue. Until you send your book to agents, just follow your instincts and write in whatever way your story needs you to write it. Once you have an agent, they can help you nail down what exactly you've written. We sent *The Girl of Ink & Stars* out as an adventure story and let the fantasy element come as a surprise.

That's why I've called this section 'buds' – it's about making your story look as appealing as possible, making it impossible for them *not* to want to represent you, and showing that you really know what you're talking about and are taking this seriously. So, finesse what you call your book. Perhaps it's a 'YA coming-of-age story with magic', like Harry Potter, or a 'fast-paced action adventure story' like Percy Jackson. Comparisons to other successful books on the market are always a good idea, but you should highlight how your book differentiates itself too.

Know that you are not alone in your fear and trepidation ... or your big dreams. I look forward to reading your no-doubt magical stories.

Kiran Millwood Hargrave is an award-winning writer and poet. Her children's books include *The Girl of Ink & Stars* (2016), winner of the British Book Awards Children's Book of the Year and the Waterstones Children's Book Prize 2017, Costa and Blue Peter Book shortlisted *The Island at the End of Everything* (2017), *The Way Past Winter* (2018), winner of Blackwell's Children's Book of the Year 2018, and *A Secret of Birds & Bone* (2020), which was a Waterstones, *Guardian*, and Big Issue Book of the Year (all published by Chicken House). YA Book Prize shortlisted and Carnegie longlisted *The Deathless Girls* (Hachette Children's 2019) was her debut for YA readers. For adults, she has written the *Sunday Times* bestselling *The Mercies* (Picador 2020). For more information see www.kiranmillwoodhargrave.co.uk. Follow her on Twitter @Kiran_MH.

Reinventing old stories for new readers

Deirdre Sullivan shares her fascination for retellings of fairy tales and the possibilities that arise from looking with fresh eyes at these stories, reworking their age-old power to inspire, influence and connect with young adult readers.

I think we all remember the first stories that spoke to us – however we encountered them, from the mouths of teachers or caregivers or by ourselves. Different voices speak to different readers, and Hans Christian Andersen's *The Little Mermaid* and Oscar Wilde's *The Nightingale and the Rose* spoke to me. I had learned to expect a 'happily ever after', in the way we all do, so these melancholy stories defied my expectations and lodged themselves in my heart, like a shard of the Devil's mirror.

In college I was introduced to the work of Jack Zipes and his anthology, *Don't Bet On The Prince* (Gower 1987) by a friend (to whom the book is dedicated), and I became acquainted with a greater breadth of fairy-tale retellings, in female voices. I had encountered feminist fairy tales before (a small Irish publisher, Attic Press, had published a children's series of these that I used to hunt for in libraries and secondhand bookshops), but revisiting them at the tail end of my adolescence was as potent as a poisoned comb to the skull. Fairy tales have always had what Marina Warner calls a 'suspect whiff of femininity', but I had been raised on stories told by men. Soon I was discovering Madame Leprince de Beaumont and Dortchen Wild. Female tellers had been there all along, it seemed, if you only took the care to look more closely. From then on, fairy-tale motifs wound themselves through my writing, both subtly and explicitly. I became hungry for more fairy-tale retellings, and devoured stories by the likes of Emma Donoghue, Robin McKinley, Neil Gaiman, Aimee Bender, Francesca Lia Block, Isabel Allende and Margaret Atwood.

In the summer of 2015 my publisher, Little Island, approached me about publishing a collection of my fairy-tale retellings. I was instantly excited about it. It felt right. I dusted off some old stories and began work on some new ones. As the collection progressed, though, I ended up writing 12 brand-new retellings, to ensure the themes and voice felt uniform. It wasn't a hardship. When I write, I feel like I am in conversation with myself and with the stories I have been told about the world around me. I run my hands over their edges, and I try to notice new details I am drawn to. I write what I know, but also what I fear and what I love.

Tangleweed and Brine (Little Island 2017) is a book that centres the female experience of the world within the fairy-tale realm. I wanted to write about bodies, and how terrifying and messy they can be. I wanted to talk about being a woman in a society built by and for men. I wanted to talk about fear, but also anger. I wanted to write about the lessons that the world teaches girls, drip by drip or all at once. I was 12 when the last Magdalene laundry closed, and until 2018, I had lived my whole life in the shadow of the eighth amendment. My country was structured in a way that let me know, that let us all know – over and over again – how little women's lives mattered. That casts a shadow, and when I began to piece together the stories for the collection it was largely women in the shadows I was drawn to

– women with bodies that didn't fit societal expectations, women used as pawns for political gain, women who try to find the right thing in a wrong world. It is a sad book, and an angry book, but there are moments of freedom there as well.

… Because there is a witchcraft to being female. From the whisper networks to tampons slipped underneath a cubicle by some kind hand, we find support in each other. There's a shared struggle that binds us. And no one knows that more than a teenage girl. Adolescence can be a very dangerous and lonely place, but there is a power in it, too, an alchemy: changing bodies, fluctuating emotions, the dawning realisations; it's a heady time, and an intense one. It's that mixture of dependence and independence, of forging your own path and being guided along the one envisioned for you. It is a time in my life I remember sharply, and a time that will continue to inspire me. I facilitate creative writing workshops for teenagers, and they are incisive and passionate readers who can enjoy books while recognising their faults. Recently someone asked me when I would write a book 'for adults'; this happens every now and then and is generally framed as a compliment. I brush it off quietly, saying things like 'Oh, you never know', but I'm fairly sure I do know. I write for young adults because I want to, and for the same reason that I tell the stories I do – because they inspire me.

I'm aware that *Tangleweed and Brine* came out at an opportune moment. There was something of a fairy-tale zeitgeist in the air, as well as increased discussion of feminism with the #MeToo movement started by Tarana Burke gaining traction in 2017, when the book had just been published. People, and young people in particular, were becoming increasingly comfortable confronting and unpacking previously unspoken things, looking at the way the world worked and articulating why that wasn't good enough. Whispers were becoming shouts. And my book was not alone – around that time Melissa Albert, Sarah Henning, Louise O' Neill and Daniel Lavery also had books out that reworked or built on old stories and turned them into something of their own. There was something in the air that made writers look at the tales they had been told and hold them up to the light with fresh eyes. And each of us saw something different and built something that was our own from that. There may be a lot of talk about trends in YA but we are all living in the same world; we experience a lot of similar things, consume a lot of the same media, hear the same news headlines. The same inspiration can take two people on very different journeys … I love that.

My advice for someone who wants to rewrite fairy tales would be to be aware of what is out there – to read and reread to give you a sense of what can be done and has been done. Then to listen to yourself. In tarot readings, there are the prescribed meanings of the cards, but sometimes a reader will find themselves drawn to a detail or a symbol; they may not know why, but something about it calls to them. That sense of moving away from what a story is supposed to be towards what it could become for you in this moment – that little, precious space is inspiration. And it's worth worrying at those details like a dog, until you've chewed it into something that's yours alone. With old stories, the more familiar people are with them, the more of a shorthand you can use; a shoe, a wolf, an apple becomes symbolic. Whatever world you put it into, the old story will be humming underneath like a familiar tune. The reader will sense it pulling at them, making them remember when it first spoke to them and all the ways it has spoken to them since. When you retell a fairy tale, you are invoking something very old and very powerful; there's a responsibility to get it right, but a satisfaction when something clicks.

I had two big 'clicks' of this kind when writing *Tangleweed and Brine*. One of them came from years of trying and the other came to me in a dream. The second way was far easier, but I think the first was more satisfying. I had put a lot of 'Little Mermaids' into the collection at first, as it's a story I'm drawn to time and time again. As someone who feels like they spend a lot of time on the outside wondering how people work, I found the mermaid character spoke to me. I grew up beside the ocean, and the tang of salt air was never far away when I was small. The story of *The Little Mermaid* brought me my first sad ending and my first Disney princess, and both of those left small dents on my heart. I had to cull a fair few mermaids as I drafted *Tangleweed and Brine*, but I remember sitting in a café thinking that I could just have my mermaid kill the prince and return to the ocean, and feeling so happy for her. I'm not normally in favour of murder, but I wanted that little tongueless girl – who'd walked on glass for love – to choose herself. And so, in my story, I asked her to do that – and she did. The child I was when I first encountered that story wouldn't have been fond of it ending in a stabbing, but it made sense for me to follow the path not taken in the Andersen story … and to send my mermaid home. The second magic click came with *Bluebeard*. I didn't know what to do; I'd written what was turning into a tender little love story, but the fairy tale demanded a roomful of murdered wives and I just didn't think the *Bluebeard* I had written would do that (#notallbluebeards). I worried and wondered about it for ages, tweaking other stories while I did (one of my favourite things to do when I get blocked on a project is to start something else, even a ridiculous thing; it provides the distance you need to stand back and see what must be done to set things right). It took a dream to point me in the right direction. I woke up with an image seared into my brain: a room full of dead men. And that gave me the key I needed to unlock my version of the story, where the secret is not the things that Bluebeard has done, but who he is and what he has survived.

I care a lot about these old stories. I have tried to inhabit them respectfully, but my experience is only one experience, and that's not enough for such an intricate world. The stories we tell matter. They can and should change. Your voices matter. I look forward to the next retelling and the next one – the same old story, through a different lens, a different heart.

Deirdre Sullivan is the award-winning author of the Primrose Leary trilogy: *Prim Improper* (2010), *Improper Order* (2013) and *Primperfect* (2014), the YA novel *Needlework* (2016) and three books in the *Nightmare Club* series under the name Annie Graves; all published by Little Island. her collection of fairy-tale retellings are, *Tangleweed and Brine* (Little Island 2018), *Perfectly Preventable Deaths* (Hot Key Books 2019) and *Savage Her Reply* (Hot Keys Books 2020). Her short story collection for adults, *I Want To Know That I Will Be Okay* was published by Banshee Press in 2021. Follow her on Twitter @propermiss.

Plotting: how to keep your YA readers reading

Sarah Mussi spells out the function and importance of plot in driving your story along to a gripping climax, and provides a sure-fire plotting route-map you can follow to ensure your readers stay reading.

When I was a child I loved playing chess. I loved the feel of the pieces and the way each one had its own character. My brother, four years my senior, used to challenge me to a daily best of three. I loved obscure openings and mad middles – all those heads that rolled! I adored setting the board up and the names of the pieces – rook and pawn, bishop and knight – but I hardly ever lasted long enough to experience endings. My brother wiped the board with me. At last, one day, he took pity on poor, beaten, eight-year-old me: he said, 'Thing is, sis, chess is a game of strategy – you've got to plot out your moves and, unless you learn how to do that, you're never ever going to win.'

I got a lot better at chess very quickly. I woke up from the dream of touch and name. Part of the magic was gone and I never really enjoyed the game in the same way. But now I won as often as I lost and, in time, the calculations of strategy brought their own pleasures.

Plotting a novel is much the same. In the good old days, I'd start at the beginning and meander through the story at whim, following errant characters and getting so excited about their lives. Somewhere around the middle, just as in those early games of chess, I'd come a cropper and do all I could to salvage the story. Then I'd send it out and cross my fingers ... and get nowhere.

Now I plot. I plot to keep my YA readers thrilled, to keep my publishers coming back, and to succeed at the important craft of storytelling.

So what is a plot?

I think of plot as a journey, and very specific to the story I am setting out to tell. As for any successful journey, there are some basics I need to know, such as where I'm going, and the route; above all I need to know *why* I'm going at all. If the plot, then, is the journey, the structure is the *way* I tell you about it. Blow by blow, or after the event? Or perhaps framed by me sitting up in a hospital bed, in a way designed to raise your curiosity about how I ended up there? How I tell you about my journey is key to engaging your interest, manipulating your emotions, helping you and my teen readers relive the fun and feel the despair.

I believe every story is an emotional journey, and plot is therefore soul food, catharsis and relief from the seemingly random ravages of life. That is the true function of plot, and why it's so important to work hard at delivering it.

Setting the route

When considering any journey, it's a good idea to see who has made that journey before and whether they left a map. Luckily, since ancient Greek times, writers of story have charted many maps, among them the ubiquitous five-act structure of Shakespearean drama and Greek tragedy (six for comedy), which later inspired the three-act structure of modern storytelling and film. All share important features, but the key to delivering the story is in capturing causality. Without causality, the structure of the story starts to descend into happenstance, with random events taking over – a bit like in real life. One thing I have learned is: never let real life get in the way of a good story!

The key to causality lies in setting up a *character-driven plot*. The action can be driven by either the protagonist or the antagonist. The only difference is that in the former, a protagonist-driven narrative, the protagonist acts from his/her own desire to achieve a goal whereas in the latter, an antagonist-driven narrative, the protagonist reacts often in order to survive. The narrative equation I like to establish, in either case, before embarking on my story journey is:

character + goal (*desire/survival*) – obstacles + solutions = climax and catharsis

Therefore the key, in tying character and events together to form a balanced plot, is in *character motivation*. This drives the action and creates cause and effect. So one key question I ask both my protagonist and my antagonist is: what is motivating you?

Setting out on the journey

When I finally put fingers to keyboard, I want to know how the opening of my story will draw the reader in. The initial setting out (I prefer this term to 'setting', which risks being static) of the story must reveal the everyday life of my hero and establish reader identification with them. I check to make sure my hero is indeed heroic. I'd hate to go on a long car journey with a miserable moaning teenager – and I feel the same is true in story. I have to be selective about what to include about their backgrounds. Exposition is always clunky, so I work on a strictly need-to-know basis. If the reader doesn't need to know any bit of information, I don't tell them.

Being guided by the principal that every character needs a *purpose* (and a purpose in a story forms the foundations of plot), I try to always have my characters wanting something, even if it's just a glass of water. Then I make sure they don't get the water easily. Being mean to my characters is paramount.

The most useful story goal is one that is dramatic, for example your character receiving a gold medal as opposed to wanting to win. If I find my protagonist being driven to act by too much internalised feeling I stop and ask myself what would that look like? And jot the answer down under the section entitled: Planning the climax.

However, journeying towards a destination is not going to be momentous unless something is at stake. If the mission fails, there needs to be some consequence. Any journey could soon be aborted if nothing would be lost by doing so. I like to think of the stakes as the negative goals. Many a hero might have said, 'Oh heck to this, I'm going home,' when presented with the first obstacle – unless there was no home to go back to. The higher the stakes the better, too. If I can fix it so that the existence of the universe hinges on the achievement of the quest, then I know I've got a page-turner.

Understanding why the hero sets out to achieve their goal at all is key. Very early on I like to introduce the inciting incident – maybe even on the first page – sometimes even before that. I present my hero with an irresistible opportunity to start them on their journey.

I like to try and fill in a through line, just to be sure I'm staying on track, for example:

_____(*story title*)_____ is about _____ (*character/characters*) _____who set(s) out to _____ (*the goal*) _____because _____ , but all does not go smoothly because _____ (*the problem and stakes*) _____so he/she/they end(s) up _____ (*the solution*).

Story beginnings are hard to get right. I personally like to be tutored by the ancients. I like to begin, as they did, *in medias res* (in the middle of things). Sometimes, of course, you have to work up to that and, like slicing the crust off a loaf to get to the yummy bit, you have to slice off your first few chapters. I console myself that my initial opening work will not be lost: after the story gets going and I head towards my first set piece, I can cut the characters enough slack to drip-feed in those key bits of background I had worked on initially.

Setting up the set piece

I consider a set piece to be a big scene and describe it as a set piece because it needs setting up. So, after 'setting out' comes 'setting up': I start by mentioning the event, then foreshadowing it. I remind the reader that 'something is coming'.

The set piece, like all set pieces when it arrives (Oh, that moment when Lucy and her siblings actually go through the wardrobe together ...), should deliver a twist or a turning point. It should reverse the fortunes of the protagonist.

When it comes to a turning point, I love the word 'volte-face'. It reminds me to make sure my character comes out of the scene drastically changed by that experience. For example in *Snow White*, after the inciting incident (that unwelcome message from the mirror) the huntsman takes Snow White into the woods to be slaughtered. The fact that he spares her doesn't change the volte-face. She goes from being rich to penniless, from a princess to a beggar, from being alive to dead (in the reported sense).

So how do I deliver this? Well, I think it should be dramatic (i.e. a big scene) and pose a dilemma. It should leave the protagonist in a situation that is directly at odds with the one they were in when they entered the scene. The dilemma posed by the set piece needs to force the protagonist to act in a way that they had probably never considered before.

Middle or muddle?

Now the story has got punch. Each event can trigger the next and so on, upping the stakes as they occur, until the point of no return is reached.

And then what does your character do? Well, hopefully they make things a lot worse. Why so? Because no story is gripping without tension. So your character during Act Two must struggle onwards and fail, until nearly overcome by the challenges. For as Oscar Wilde said: 'The suspense is terrible, let's hope it will last.'

The setting (or the antagonist) can provide the challenges, as can the inner demons of the protagonist themselves. Like God testing Job on his rubbish tip, our job as gods in our narratives is to test our heroes by making things truly appalling.

But how do we deliver this? Well, plotting a downhill path for the hero means remembering that for every challenge the protagonist needs to formulate a solution. Each solution should not solve the problem, but instead *cause* the next problem. Inside every solution should be that built-in flaw. Each flawed solution might tap into the protagonist's main tragic flaw.

Using conflict in this way, I build until we reach the most serious volte-face, which reverses the fortunes for my hero so drastically that the darkest hour – the well of despond or last straw – is reached.

As the protagonist sits on his rubbish tip (à la Job) or feels despair in his cave (Robert the Bruce) or lies slaughtered upon the stone table (Aslan), it is worth considering the position of the antagonist and refreshing the readers' memory as to what the antagonist's motivations are, and especially what is their Achilles' heel. Think Smaug's loose scale or the White Witch's failure to study the Deep Magic. For therein lies the moment of truth, when the hero can search inside themselves and act from their inner essence to exploit their antagonist's vulnerability and reverse their own fortunes for the last time. Then they can go into the final set piece, the Act Three volte-face, the obligatory scene, the ordeal, the shoot-out at OK Corral, the climax of the plot, *and win*.

Setting the question

Several things must occur at the climax of the story: firstly, the hero must face their biggest obstacle or it will be an anticlimax. They must determine their own fate and the story goal must be resolved once and for all.

Hopefully during the climactic scene, as in a good pantomime, all of my key characters will appear. Hopefully I will have foreshadowed the setting, and visited it already early in the story, as this will avoid me engaging in any distracting description. I might have paired the scene with an earlier one as well, to mirror the action; I can't help thinking of Steinbeck when I plot out my climaxes – his so superbly plotted *Of Mice and Men* is a master class in how to deliver climaxes.

All that remains now is to enable my protagonist to: stay on a collision course with the antagonist; win by losing (to be kept heroic); undergo a 'seeming' death only to be reborn (without it all getting too B-movie). At the very end, I like to narrow things down to one simple action (the pull of a trigger as in *Of Mice and Men*; the dropping of a ring in *Lord of the Rings*); this focuses me and gives an elegance to the ending.

However, no story ends precisely with the resolution of the hero's objective. Readers want to know what happens afterwards; they want to know everyone gets their just deserts. I usually try to keep this as short as possible. Whilst readers do want to know, they don't want to know much. After a penalty shoot-out everyone wants to head home. So I keep it short and head home myself.

Writing a novel does indeed mean plotting out your moves. But I'll leave the last word on that to Wilkie Collins, a far greater master of it than myself:

> '*Make 'em laugh. Make 'em cry. Above all, make 'em wait.*'

Sarah Mussi's first novel *The Lion Skin Rug* was shortlisted for the BBC Worldwide Children's Talent Fiction Award and her second novel, *The Door of No Return* (Hodder Children's 2007) won the Glen Dimplex & Irish Writers' Children's Book of the Year Award and was shortlisted for the Branford Boase Award. Other books include *The Last of the Warrior Kings* (Hodder 2009), *Angel Dust* (Hot Key Books 2012), *Siege* (Hodder 2013), *Breakdown* (Hot Key Books 2014), *Riot* (which won the Lancashire Book Award 2014) and *Bomb* (2014) both published by Hodder Children's; Sarah's Snowdonia Chronicles trilogy: *Here Be Dragons*, *Here Be Witches* and *Here Be Wizards* (Vertebrate Publishing 2015 & Shrine Bell Publishing 2017 and 2020) and *Room Empty* (published by Oneworld 2017). Her most recent YA title, *You Can't Hide*, was published by Hodder Children's Books in 2019. See her website www.sarahmussi.com.

Writing historical novels

Michelle Paver shares her thoughts on how to approach writing historical novels for children and the importance of focusing on the story.

Books about how to get published sometimes advise new writers to research the market thoroughly. Read the competition, see what sells – that sort of thing. If that appeals to you, fine, but I've never liked the idea and have never done it. In my view it isn't necessary, or even a good thing. You might just find it confusing and intimidating, and it could put you off what you really want to write.

I think it's better to concentrate on the story *you* want to write. The characters. The premise. The historical setting. You may not even know *why* you want to write it. But you do, and that's the main thing.

The period

Before you make a start, though, it's worth asking yourself why you want to set the story in your chosen historical period. Are you especially attracted to it? Did you daydream about it as a child; maybe you still do? Or does it simply have a vague appeal, perhaps based on having seen a few films or read some novels set in that time?

There's no harm in being drawn to a particular period for tenuous reasons. But if that is the case, I'd suggest that you become a little more familiar with it before deciding whether to use that time for your story. You'll need to know your chosen period pretty thoroughly; and if you decide halfway through writing your novel that it isn't quite as fascinating as you'd thought, then the chances are that the reader will think so too, and your story probably won't work. In short, you must be prepared to live and breathe it for months or even years.

The story is king

This would seem to be the logical point to talk about research, but I'm going to leave that for later because I don't think it's the most important thing. The most important thing is the story. Always. And particularly for children. In general, children don't read a book because it got a great review in *The Times*, or because they want to look impressive reading it on the train. They read it because they want to know what's going to happen next.

That might seem trite, but it's amazing how easy it is to forget, especially when you've done a ton of research on a particular period, and there are so many terrific things about it that you just can't wait to share with everybody else.

So it's worth reminding yourself that the basics of any good story need to be firmly in place: characters about whom you care passionately; a protagonist who wants or needs something desperately; perhaps a powerful villain or opposing force which poses a significant threat. Big emotions: anger, envy, pride, hate, loyalty, love, grief. And just because the book will be read by children, don't shy away from the bad stuff (although obviously, you'll need to handle it responsibly). Death, violence, neglect, loneliness. Children want to know. They're curious about everything.

The beginning

Everyone knows that the first page of a story is critical, but this is especially so for children. In fact, the first paragraph is even more critical. And the first sentence is the most critical of all.

This poses a special challenge if you're writing a historical novel. How do you root the story in the past without getting bogged down in clunky exposition?

There's no magic formula, but the idea of 'show, don't tell' is a good place to start. Perhaps you could begin with a situation that's specifically of that period, like a witch-burning. Or, as part of the story, weave in an object of the period, like a flint knife.

You might be tempted to write a 'prologue', like the ones they used to have at the beginning of old movies ('London, England. The Cavaliers and Roundheads are at war …'). By all means write one of these. I did, for the first draft of *Wolf Brother*. But you may well ditch it before you finish the final draft. You may find that by then it has done its work by helping to anchor you, the writer, in the period. If you leave it in, it might have a distancing effect for the reader, diminishing the immediacy of the story.

Telling the story

What I said about the beginning of the story goes for the rest of it, too. The challenge for the writer of historical novels is to make the reader 'live' the story along with the characters. Somehow you've got to make them see, feel, touch, taste that period – without resorting to wodges of boring description that might slow things down, or overdone 'period' dialogue which is tiring to read and may distance the reader.

Again, there's no formula, but a good guiding principle is to make the essential exposition an integral part of the story. Make this a story that couldn't really have happened at any other time in history – even though the emotions involved are universals with which the reader can readily identify.

If you do this, then it'll become fairly clear what needs to stay in and what should come out. And there will probably be a lot of cutting. Pare down the exposition to what's essential. For instance, you may not need to explain the background to the entire war; just the particular skirmish in which your heroine has been caught up.

And for the essential exposition, it can help to introduce it in a highly charged emotional way: perhaps an argument or a fight. 'Exposition as ammunition' was a favourite motto of the film-maker Ingmar Bergman and it's one that can serve you well. But don't get so hung up on explaining things that you lose sight of the emotional focus of the scene.

The same goes for 'period atmosphere'. I would think long and hard before including anything for this reason alone. Try to make your period details part of the story. Then cut them back, then cut them back some more. What you need is a swift, vivid, unforgettable image with *just* enough detail to bring it alive – but no more.

Research

Which brings me (finally) to research. Some novelists don't do any. If that works for them, that's great. But if you're setting your story in the past, I don't think you can get by without doing at least some. And probably rather a lot. You need to know, intimately, what it was like to live back then. It's the little everyday details which interest readers, particularly children. What did people eat, wear, live in? How did they fight, travel, work, entertain themselves? What did they *think*? How were they similar to us? How were they different? And the more you can actually experience some of this for yourself the better – for example, by location research, trying out the food of the period – because it will give you all sorts of intriguing ideas and insights that you couldn't have got in a library.

Bear in mind, too, that research isn't just a matter of getting the details right. It'll probably spark ideas for the story itself: incidents, twists, particular scenes. These are gold dust. Use them. (Provided, of course, that they work in the context of the story as a whole.)

Perhaps the hardest thing about research is that the vast bulk of what you've lovingly unearthed isn't going to make it into the final draft. Be ruthless about keeping *only* those details that you really need: either to move the story along, or to develop character or to set the scene. And shun any whiff of teaching; this is a story, not a history lesson.

This means that you'll probably go through a rather painful process of cutting over the course of your first, second, and successive drafts. But don't grieve too deeply for your lost treasures. *You* know all that background, and your in-depth knowledge will give your writing an assurance that it wouldn't otherwise have.

Language and style

This can be especially tricky: a kind of balancing act between keeping the story and the characters accessible, while leaving the language with just enough special vocabulary or dialogue to remind us that we're in another time. All this without distancing us too much, or (just as bad) without obvious anachronisms.

I'm often asked if I write differently when I'm writing for children, as opposed to when I'm writing for adults. The answer is, no, not at all. For me, it's the nature of the story that dictates the language and the style. If you're writing a story set in a middle-class Victorian home, your vocabulary and style will be utterly different from that which you'd use if you were writing about a forest of the Stone Age.

Having said that, if children are going to be among your readers, one important thing to bear in mind is that lengthy flashbacks can weaken the force of a story by reducing its immediacy. Because children read to know what's going to happen next, it helps too, to have unexpected twists, surprises, action, high emotion, flashes of humour and lots of dialogue, as well as the odd cliffhanger chapter ending. You've got to give them a reason to turn the page and to keep turning the pages, all the way to the end.

Who are you writing for?

'What age group are you "aiming" at?' is a frequently asked question. For myself, the answer is: none. Apart from a general idea that I'm not writing a picture book for six-year olds, I prefer to leave age groups to editors and publishers, and concentrate on the story.

Besides, once you start thinking in terms of 'aiming' a story at a particular group of people, where does it end? For instance, say you're 'aiming' a story at 9–12 year-olds. Well, what kind of 9–12 year-olds? They're not a homogeneous mass. Boys or girls, or both? And what kind? Middle-class or underprivileged? Immigrant or home-grown? Gifted, average or special needs? If you start thinking like that, you run the risk of killing your story.

The same thing goes for the publisher's Holy Grail of the 'crossover' novel that's read by both adults and children. If you have this at the forefront of your mind when you're writing, it's unlikely that you'll do justice to the story. It may well end up being a mess which *nobody* will want to read.

Although this may sound a bit uncompromising, I have the same view when it comes to trying out your story on your own children – if you have them – or on others. In my view, this is risky and I prefer not to do it. (Well, in my case, I couldn't, because I don't have children, and don't know any very well.) In fact, quite a few children's writers don't have children of their own, but what many do have is a strong memory of what it was like to be a child and an ability to write from a child's perspective. That's what you need. Not market research.

Being true to your story, knowing your chosen period inside out but only including the most telling of details … Of course, none of this is going to guarantee success. But with luck, it'll improve your chances on the slush pile. *And* you'll have a lot more fun than if you'd been slavishly studying the market!

Michelle Paver is the author of the bestselling *Wolf Brother* series, which has been published in 37 languages and the film rights sold to Sir Ridley Scott. The seventh book in the series, *Viper's Daughter*, was published by Zephyr in 2020 and the eighth book, *Skin Taker*, was published in April 2021. The series has also been recorded as audiobooks read by Sir Ian McKellen. Her first ghost story, *Dark Matter*, became an immediate bestseller and drew critical comparisons to the great M.R. James. Her second ghost story, *Thin Air*, was published in 2016 by Orion. Her most recent book for adults is *Wakenhyrst* (Head of Zeus 2019), which was selected by the Radio Two Bookclub, and was a *Times* Book of the Month. Her website is www.michellepaver.com.

See also...
- *Who do children's authors write for?*, page 99
- *Writing ghostly stories*, page 133

Books

Writing for teenagers

Holly Smale discovered the importance and freedom of writing *for herself*, rather than for any imagined readership. She suggests that there are no limits and no rules to teen fiction but that, above all, in those exciting, terrifying teenage years, readers appreciate a story told with honesty, humour and empathy.

I never wanted to write for teenagers. Frankly, I didn't even know what they wanted when I *was* one. The vast majority of my adolescence was spent studying my peers, observing what they liked and did not like – which words they used, what brand of trainers they wore – and then getting it consistently wrong, with humiliating consequences.

By the age of 14, in fact, I hated teenagers so much I decided to skip being one entirely. Overnight, I replaced my beloved children's books with Hardy, Austen and Dickens; I studied obsessively and avoided social situations that might harbour lurking adolescents; I put my hair up like a grown-up Anne Shirley, with a kitchen sponge tucked underneath for volume. And I committed myself to a lifetime of writing *adult* books. That, I had already decided at the precocious age of five, was where my future lay. I adored words and stories, and I was going to write big, important novels for big, important people so that everyone would know that I, too, was big and important. There would be money, fame and awards, and grown-ups would flick with misty eyes through my hardback works and declare they had never seen such wisdom in anyone so young (or – I liked to think – with such lovely, puffy hair).

So I diligently set to work. With the *Writers' & Artists' Yearbook* by my side like a trusty steed I couldn't quite ride yet, I ploughed on, picturing exactly who would be reading my writing and what they would think of it, and of me. Until finally – in my early twenties – I started the Book That Would Change My Life. It was very long and very serious, it was for adults, it was about death and there were entire chapters about muffins and jam (unexplored metaphors about the transience of life, obviously). It took two solid years, then I packed it up optimistically and sent it off to agents as instructed: double-spaced, one-sided, Times New Roman. And I waited. I waited. I waited a little bit longer...

Finally (after about two days) I got bored of waiting. I grabbed my computer, and I started telling another story. Or, more specifically, the story started telling *me*. Because this time it was different. This time I didn't care about it being Big and Important, because my Real Book was on submission and nobody would want this one anyway. It was 2009, and there were no vampires; it was (I was told at various stages) 'niche', 'unfashionable' and 'unsellable' – which also freed me from hopes of money, success, awards, even any imagined *readers*.

This time it was just me and a 15 year-old girl, Harriet Manners: awkward, lonely, unpopular, insecure, trying to fit in at any cost. This time it was just me and a story I needed to tell, and I was going to unpack into this totally free therapy every raw emotion I could remember from my teenage years. As honestly as I could, I was going to tell the very story I had spent my entire life avoiding, about the very people I had gotten as far away from as possible.

And I was going to make it fiction, because otherwise it was no fun; and I was going to make it funny, because I was tired of writing about death and muffins; and I was going to enjoy it, because I was sick to the back teeth of jumping through imaginary hoops, trying to impress an audience I couldn't see. In short, I wrote the story for *me*.

Geek Girl (HarperCollins Children's 2013) became the biggest-selling teen book in the UK the year it came out. Nine books, a few awards and nearly a million sales in 30 different countries later, it has been kindly credited with 'changing the face of teen comedy'. The other book? It's still in a drawer, unpublished and unwanted. But *both* books changed my life, because they both taught me what I needed to finally be 'A Writer'.

The first and most important reader is yourself. You cannot write *for* anyone else; not for other adults, not for commissioning editors, and certainly not for teenagers. Those mystical approving or disapproving readers in your head don't exist, and even when they do exist, every single one of them will be different, have different interests and passions, and want something else from you. So stop worrying about them. Find the voice inside you that needs out, and let it out. Discover the story you really *want* to tell, and tell it.

And if that story just so happens to be about a teenager – even though you don't understand teenagers and you've avoided them your whole life and the story is about a teenager who doesn't understand other teenagers – go for it. The story will determine who you write for, not the other way around.

Teenagers haven't changed. That's what I've realised and had confirmed, over and over again – at schools, in festivals, over lunches, in workshops. They're the same now as they were when I was one. They don't *want* you to copy them. They don't want you to work out what's 'hot' and what's 'now', and to try and follow suit. They don't want to be patronised or talked-down to; they don't want to be second-guessed; and they *definitely* don't want you to attempt to keep up with them, because – and here's the secret – you never will.

The harder you chase your reader – the tighter you hold on, the more you try to impress them – the faster they will put your book down and sit as far away as possible. Readers (but especially teenage readers) don't want to read a story written *for them* – just as they didn't want my Green Flash trainers worn *for them* either. Take one glance at the bookshelf of a teenager and you'll find it stuffed with brilliant YA novels of every genre, every narrative style, every possible topic: comedy, horror, romance, dystopian, historical, tragedy, poetry. Told sensitively and with respect, there are no limits and there are no rules to teen fiction. You can forge your own path, and your readers will love you all the more for it. All a teenager wants is honesty – to read a good story, told with the story put first.

As for me, I came full circle. In accidentally writing about a teen, I finally realised what I should have realised at school: that being a teenager is the most glorious, raw and candid time in our lives, and that we are *all* just trying to find our way. In those few precious years, we blaze an exhilarating path between the safety of childhood and the freedom of adulthood, teetering and fumbling and flying as we go. Everything is new. Everything is fresh. Everything is exciting and terrifying, in equal measure. Channel that, and there are no boundaries to what you can write about, or how.

The truth I finally understood is this: there are no more 'important' books than those written about teenagers. Because if they can chart that heady journey truthfully, with empathy and understanding, teen novels have the power to change the lives of their readers; to help them work out who they are, what they want, how they see the world and other people, and who they want to be. They have the power to comfort, to inspire, to challenge, to provide escape, to amuse, encourage and support. Written honestly, these are the books we treasure even when our teenage years are over. *These* are the books that matter.

So here's my advice: find your inner teenager, tell your story and let your readers find you. Never, ever the other way round.

Holly Smale is the author of *Geek Girl*, the No. 1 bestselling young adult fiction title in the UK in 2013, which won the 2014 Waterstones Children's Book Prize and was shortlisted for the Roald Dahl Funny Prize. The *Geek Girl* series has now sold over 3.4 million copies in 32 languages worldwide. Holly's latest book is *Love Me Not* (2021), the final book in the critically acclaimed series, *The Valentines*, published by HarperCollins Children's Books. Holly has a BA in English Literature from Bristol University, as well as an MA in Shakespeare. Follow her on Twitter @HolSmale.

See also...
- *Writing thrillers for teenagers,* page 163
- *Plotting: how to keep your YA readers reading,* page 142

Plotting and pace in your middle-grade adventure

Christopher Edge understands the highs and lows, twists and turns that are needed to hold the attention of middle-grade fiction readers with a thirst for adventure. Here he shares valuable advice on how to structure a plot and drive forward an emotionally engaging storyline that has all the essential elements.

'Adventure is just bad planning.' So said the great Norwegian explorer, Roald Amundsen, who was the first man to reach both the North and South poles but who, as far as I know, never wrote a single word of children's fiction – so I really wouldn't go listening to him when it comes to planning your middle-grade adventure.

But what is a 'middle-grade adventure'? Well, the first part is easy to define, as middle-grade is the term the publishing industry uses to describe novels for children aged 9–12. Now, I'm a subscriber to C.S. Lewis's dictum that the best children's books which can be enjoyed at the age of ten are equally worth reading at the age of 50 and beyond, so when we talk about middle-grade we're definitely not talking about fiction that is any way middle-of-the-road or second-rate. These are the stories that can shape young readers' lives, opening doors into new realities, allowing them to escape into other lives, and inspiring them to step boldly forward to mark their own place in the world. And as for adventure, I'd argue it's not so much a genre but more an attitude that's woven into the fabric of children's fiction. Whether it's fantasy, mystery, historical, contemporary, science fiction or even comedy, from Lewis Carroll's *Alice's Adventures in Wonderland* (Macmillan 1865) to *Rowley Jefferson's Awesome Friendly Adventure* by Jeff Kinney (Penguin Random House 2020), the drumbeat of adventure can always be heard as we turn the pages of the novels we find on the bookshelves labelled 'Fiction 9–12'.

This is certainly true of my own fiction. I find it difficult to pin the stories I write down to a single genre, but adventure is an 'ever-present'; from *The Many Worlds of Albie Bright* (Nosy Crow 2016) where Albie climbs inside a cardboard box to travel to parallel universes in search of his mum, to *The Infinite Lives of Maisie Day* (Nosy Crow 2018) where Maisie's adventures are contained within the four walls of her home after the universe outside her front door disappears. In children's fiction there are no hard-and-fast rules about where adventure can be found and, in stories such as *The Longest Night of Charlie Noon* (Nosy Crow 2019) which begins, 'Once upon a time, three kids got lost in the woods', I've enjoyed twisting familiar tropes into unexpected new shapes. But why do readers of middle-grade fiction have such a thirst for adventure? In surveys about children's reading habits, such as Scholastic's biennial *Kids & Family Reading Report*, children aged 9–12 respond that they want books that have characters that look like them; this reaffirms the need for all readers to find themselves represented in the fiction they read, but also that they want characters they wish they could be like because they're smart or strong or brave. So this thirst for adventure could be viewed as a form of wish fulfilment, as young readers seek out stories in which they can see idealised reflections of themselves, placed in exciting and dangerous situations. For these readers, reading can be role-play, their identification with the heroes and heroines of middle-grade fiction offering them a vicarious agency they might not be able to find in their everyday lives.

I think another reason why such a rich thread of adventure runs through middle-grade fiction can be found in the world-view of its readers. Still shaping their understanding of the world around them, these are curious readers who read with fearless eyes. Their tastes aren't fixed in the same way that an adult readers often are. This isn't a jaded audience, but it is an audience with high expectations who will only keep turning the pages of a story if it delivers on its promise of adventure. So how can you craft a middle-grade adventure that will keep these readers turning the pages? The first thing to consider is plot. Now plot is just another name for story – it's the sequence of events that take place in a narrative. And the plotting stage is where you decide exactly what these events will be and the best way to structure them. This is a stage of writing that I love. For me, stories rarely land in my brain fully formed. The initial spark of inspiration might arrive in the form of a character, a situation, or a setting. For *The Infinite Lives of Maisie Day*, I had an image of a girl opening her front door to find an infinite darkness outside. Like any spark of inspiration, this image initially existed in what Russell T. Davies dubs 'the quantum state of Maybe' – with seemingly infinite possibilities it could spawn in terms of the story sparking in and out of existence inside my mind. Through a process of asking questions, researching ideas, and making connections, I started to shape these possibilities into a definitive storyline.

But how could I be sure that the plot I was building was taking the right shape? Lots of theories about story structure come from the world of film. From the three-act structure of set-up, confrontation and resolution, with key scenes that tip the story from one act to the next, to mythic structures such as the 'Hero's Journey' where a protagonist heeds a call to adventure, faces tests, trials and challenges before seizing their reward, screenwriting formulas seemingly offer a short cut to crafting the perfect plot. However, I must admit I don't consciously hold any theories like these in the front of my mind when plotting my adventures. For me, the plot always grows from character or, more accurately, plot and character grow together.

Stories are about change and change is driven by character. Examining your protagonist's motives can help you to build your plot, as you consider the actions they might pursue as they try to attain their goal. In *The Many Worlds of Albie Bright*, the motive that spurs Albie to set out on his adventure is his desire to see his mum again, with this goal fuelling his creation of the Quantum Banana Theory – the invention that enables him to travel into parallel worlds. Handily, this universe-hopping device also gave me a skeleton structure for the story, as Albie journeys through these alternate universes in search of the one where his mum is still alive. Now if your protagonist achieves their primary goal straight away, there's not much of a story – so you need to think about what's going to stand in their way. This could be an antagonist whose own motives and goals place them in conflict with your protagonist. In every adventure there needs to be obstacles, complications and confrontations which your protagonist has to navigate to get closer to their goal. Some scenes might shine brightest in your mind at this point, but thinking about the cause-and-effect of these key moments can trigger ideas for other scenes and help you start to sequence these into a coherent plot. I sometimes draw a flow chart to plot the action of the story – this helps me to visualise the links between different events and keep track of how characters develop.

Every scene should have a purpose that drives the plot forward; deciding what this is can help you to focus on the details that matter when you start writing. Begin each scene as far into the action as possible and as soon as the purpose is achieved that should be your signal to end the scene. Each scene should contain the seeds of the next and, as the story moves forward, you want to keep raising the stakes – but you also need to vary the rhythm of the story so that it doesn't become predictable for the reader. Think about the rhythm you want to create, perhaps balancing action-packed scenes with quieter moments of description and dialogue that slow the narrative pace and give the reader a chance to catch their breath.

Now every adventure must come to an end. Some authors only discover the ending of a story through the act of writing it, but I usually find mine before I even write the very first line. At the outset I have a clear picture in my mind of the opening scene and also the climax of the story, with these two moments tracing the emotional arc of my protagonist's adventure. In *The Many Worlds of Albie Bright*, Albie's journeys through different parallel worlds show him the alternative lives he could have lived, and these experiences change Albie and help him to come to an understanding of what he's really searching for as the story reaches its climax. An adventure isn't just an action-packed sequence of events but an emotional journey too, as characters make discoveries, find out things about themselves, and are changed by their experiences.

Writing itself can be an adventure, so don't be afraid to follow your own path. There will be trials and challenges along the way, and you may even feel lost at times as you hack through the thickets of a first draft – but always try to take pleasure in the journey. And when you make it to the end, the reward you find can be greater than any treasure hoard: it's the sight of a young reader turning the pages of your story, their eyes shining with excitement as they escape into a world of adventure.

Christopher Edge is an award-winning author whose novels for children include *Twelve Minutes to Midnight* (2012), *The Black Crow Conspiracy* (2014), *The Many Worlds of Albie Bright* (2016), *The Jamie Drake Equation* (2017), *The Infinitive Lives of Maisie Day* (2018) and *The Longest Night of Charlie Noon* (2019), all published by Nosy Crow. His latest novel is *Space Oddity* (Chicken House 2021). He also is an experienced teacher, the author of guides to creative writing for children and teenagers, *How to Write Your Best Story Ever!* (OUP 2015) and *How to be a Young #Writer* (OUP 2017), and a freelance publisher and education consultant. For more information see his website www.christopheredge.co.uk. Follow him on Twitter @edgechristopher.

See also...

- *Plotting: how to keep your YA readers reading*, page 142
- *Writing mystery and adventure stories*, page 156

Writing mystery and adventure stories

H.L. Dennis shares her own imaginative method of creating and refining a story, and bringing adventures and emotions fully to the page, using the structure and inspiration of a film-maker's craft.

I'm going to tell you a secret. I'm not a writer at all … actually, I'm the Chief Executive of my very own Imagination Headquarters. It's a game I play, and it makes writing such an adventure that I'm going to let you in on the mystery of how it works. Not everyone will like this method, but you just might ... so I hope you'll enjoy it too.

I've never been to film school – but being the Ceo of Imagination HQ is like being an entire studio working on a film. After all, a good book plays like a film inside our heads. We watch as characters experience triumph and despair, happiness and pain. And, if the story is a good one, we feel those emotions too. That's my aim: to generate emotion in the reader, to make them laugh, gasp or cry. I want readers to feel, to believe, to remember. I hope they'll adventure with me, racing through the pages of my story as the mystery unfolds.

So now let me show you how it works – in Imagination HQ – as I try to achieve this.

Time for popcorn ...

It begins with the 'popcorn stage'. This is a time that fuels my spirit – when I'm reminded of the power of good stories. I watch film and TV avidly, re-watching sections, trying to understand the storyteller's craft. I analyse moments when I'm on the edge of my seat, and I break down scenes where I'm sobbing or screaming at the screen. I try to establish exactly how the lighting, music and camera angles make me feel. Then I use exactly the same close analysis on my favourite books; I reread extracts over and over, in precisely the same analytical way. I immerse myself in adventures and mysteries well told. Only then am I ready to start work myself.

Stage One: Development

1. Find the theme – First of all, your story needs to get the 'green light'. You must know why this story needs telling and why it's you who needs to tell it. The theme is the light that guides all the decisions later. It's why the story is emotionally significant. Your job isn't to preach, but to explore a theme that matters to you

My series *Secret Breakers* (Hodder Children's 2012-) was about children's hidden potential. Working as a teacher at the time, I was concerned about how education rated some skills more highly than others. You, too, need to find an area that fascinates, angers, worries or intrigues you. Find something that makes you *feel*; this will become the 'why' that lights your way.

2. Choose your story world – In *Secret Breakers* I wanted to celebrate the abilities of children to do more than adults thought possible. The world of code-cracking was a perfect fit. You might choose to explore the theme of fairness, for example, through the world of sport or science, theatre or space travel. So find a world where you can explore your theme. Ground your adventure in this particular, chosen world.

3. Prepare the trailer – Film trailers pare back films to their basic elements. Trailers give us a sense of the story's 'palette'. They prepare us for high octane, thrilling action or quiet, sinister mystery. We know what to expect because trailers sell us emotions the film promises to deliver. Your adventure could be created in a range of different tones, so establish the emotional impact you want by analysing film trailers. Then attempt to write a basic summary of a story, noting what you want the reader to feel as they read.

Stage Two: Pre-production

1. Select your locations – If you can set your story anywhere – real or imagined – be purposeful and selective about every single location you use. In my *River of Ink* series (Hodder Children's 2017-) I explored the theme of what makes a life worth living. I chose the world of alchemy to do this and, as the elixir of life was central to this theme, I focused on river locations for my adventure. You need to make every location work to support the story. Choose contrasting locations, intriguing locations, locations that will provoke emotion! Work as a 'location scout', visiting places you can't visit in reality – via guidebooks or the internet.

2. Cast the characters – We care about stories because we care about characters. Make sure you rigorously audition every member of your cast, to be certain they're worthy of screen time. The hero of an adventure becomes such after she is tested and because of the difficult choices she makes. We must feel for the characters – even the villains. Make us cheer on an underdog, empathise with the lost soul, root for the character who is scared just like us.

You need characters who give elements of contrast to your theme. In *River of Ink*, a girl with a life ruled by schedules would learn the value of spontaneity. Characters must change as a result of their adventures, so think about how you'd like your character to be in the final stage of your story, then work backwards to create your character at the beginning. Audition a cast of contrasting characters and show us what they're truly like, through their actions and interactions, decision-making and discoveries.

*I like to set up Pinterest boards at this stage – with pictures of locations, sketches of characters and quotes that support my theme. This helps create a sense of tone and sets me up for the more technical stages ahead.

Stage Three: Production

1. Prepare the shooting schedule – You can now begin to sketch out the major arc of an adventure. Think about: an inciting incident; times of crisis when all hope seems lost; then the ultimate life-changing climax. Why is the mystery your characters are trying to solve so important? What obstacles are in the way? What is there to gain or lose? Just as you didn't settle for mediocre locations or cast, make sure the stakes are as big as possible, as meaningful as they can be and the most likely to provoke emotion. We need our characters to be scared about losing everything in order for the adventure to mean everything to us.

2. Compose the storyboard – By this I don't mean a drawn storyboard (although this might be just your thing); take the schedule and break it into scenes. It's important, particularly in mysteries, to work out what needs to be revealed when and in what order. You might also have an idea about some key set pieces, and indeed the finale which you're working towards. I envisioned one particular scene, at the end of *Secret Breakers* Book Six, before I ever wrote the words 'Book One: Chapter One'. I was always striving towards this culmination of the adventure – a point when the characters were at their most desperate, and the risk of making the wrong decision the most intense. I could see the weather in the scene, and even hear the musical soundtrack in my head. Here my characters' emotions were at their most raw (and hopefully the reader's would be too!).

The big reveal of the mystery must be worth the pay-off, so give the finale a massive amount of your time, energy and thought. Your ending must deliver all the emotional punch you planned from the trailer stage. Be sure to build anticipation as your storyboard develops; keep the adventure moving, the characters changing, and the stakes increasing.

3. Rehearse the scenes – Now I've worked out the gist of what will happen in each scene and, finally, I get to rehearse. A film director might shoot the same scene many times – you can too.

Don't offer your reader your first thoughts about how to show that scene. Try lots of different ways of 'staging' it. For this, I find the 'record card' system really satisfying: on record cards, jot down how variations of each scene could look. Experiment by changing camera angles and focusing on one character more than others or elevating one emotion over another. Try different ways of revealing character through dialogue and actions. The aim of these rehearsals is to choose a version of the scene that will best generate the suspense, worry, fear or elation in the reader you hoped for. Don't settle. Be the director who demands the ultimate take.

4. Make a rough cut – By this stage I've worked through all the angst of how best to show something; I've built up tension by heightening anticipation; I've put characters through the very worst situations they (or I) could imagine. So now I cut together the ultimate version of each scene and begin to type them out in a document labelled 'My Book'. This is my Director's Cut – and now it's ready for editing.

Stage Four: Post-production

1. Add effects – Every single scene must be worthy of the reader's time. So I cut, I tighten, I search for the most powerful phrase, the truest character reaction, the most poignant beat to build emotion. You can speed up shots or change the lighting to get closer to the characters and show their emotions more clearly. It's fun to scrutinise every page, every paragraph and every sentence, to make sure it's the best it can be.

2. Check continuity – Now I ask whether the whole thing hangs together as one seamless piece. Does the internal logic of the whole adventure make sense? Does the mystery unfold without stuttering or confusing? It's time to ask if you've done everything you promised the reader you would. The record cards are packed away and it's time to focus on the whole story you've created, splicing together the joins so no-one can see the technicalities of your craft!

Stage Five: Distribution

Release – This is it. You've created a story. You've written an adventure full of emotion, twists, turns and cliffhangers, which all build to the solution of your mystery and the emotional punch you guaranteed! Now, at last, it's time to grab your copy of the *Children's Writers' & Artists Yearbook* and – if you have any of those record cards left – use them to jot down a list of agents to approach. It's time to send your story out into the world to find its audience.

Time for popcorn again

And now you wait ...

Remember though – some people might dislike my suggestions about how to create a story; some fear that such a technical approach might clutter the magic of creation. There's also a chance your story might not resonate with all who read it, but that is part of the adventure – the mystery of the power of words. I personally believe magic *can* come from design, emotion from knowing direction and a powerful story through purposeful attention to detail.

So, if at every stage of the operation of Imagination HQ you've worked hard and refused to settle for mediocre, then you need to relax now and trust in your process. You *will* find an audience. The right reader is waiting. Just enjoy another bowl of popcorn, while your story makes its way out into the world to find them.

Helen Dennis is the award-winning author of the *Secret Breakers* six-book series and the *River of Ink* quartet, both published by Hodder Children's Books. *Secret Breakers: The Knights of Neustria* (2013) was nominated for the Carnegie Medal and the series has been optioned for a live action TV series. *River of Ink: Genesis* was selected as a BookBuzz book by BookTrust 2016 and included in their Deaf Awareness Week Recommendation List 2019. Helen worked for 20 years as a junior school teacher before becoming a full-time writer. She has an MA in Creative Writing Education and the Arts from Sussex University. For more information see www.helendennisbooks.com and www.hldennis.com. Follow her on Twitter @HLDennisauthor.

Books

Books

World-building in your fantasy fiction

L.D. Lapinski explores the creative art of world-building, with its imaginative potential and hidden depths, and has advice on how writers can bring their fantasy worlds, and the characters that navigate through them, to life in a way that engages and absorbs young readers.

World-building is such a strange and magical thing: using just your mind, you are bringing entire populations, places and universes almost to life. Creating a new reality that can feel as precious and vulnerable and enticing as the one we live and breathe in is a fantastic exercise, and one that – given how little we have been able to travel recently due to the global pandemic – seems increasingly tempting. The world you build is not an empty set; it can have as much character as your hero, or as much menace as your villain. The world you create takes your reader on a journey which can be as close to home or as far flung as you desire.

I have always created imaginary places and worlds. Reading and writing have been my creative escape for as long as I can remember (and possibly even further back than that), and I have very fond memories of spending a rainy holiday in a caravan hunched over, drawing a detailed map and plotting a vast history for 'The World of Bunny Rabbits'. The real world wasn't appealing right then, so I made my own. And I'm still doing it. My first novel for children 9+, *The Strangeworlds Travel Agency* (Orion Children's 2020), arrived in bookshops at the start of the pandemic and, though it was a very unexpected baptism, I hope it offered an escape to young readers looking for ways to get away from our world and into others.

However, simply hurling a new world at a reader does not a story make. Novels are, at their very heart, entertainment. The story needs to seize us by the wrist and drag us along a journey, not simply abandon us, mapless, in a new place with no sense of direction. Any world you create is there to work with and for your characters – it is a backdrop that you can change to fit and make the most impact in your story and, although your characters may navigate it with ease, the world they explore and tell the reader about still needs to be strong and 'real' enough to support their narrative journey. And this support is quite a literal concept when it comes to fantasy worlds!

Picture a penguin. Add the David Attenborough narration, if you like, as the camera pans back to reveal that the tiny penguin has hitched a ride on the top of an iceberg, and the iceberg drops deep into the depths below, far more of it below the waterline than above it. This iceberg, and the penguin, is your world-building. As you might expect, there is always so much more going on below the surface when writing fantasy books, but in this analogy what's really important for you to focus on isn't the iceberg at all. It's the penguin. As the writer, that tiny wee penguin is the amount of world-building you're actually going to have the space and words to include in your children's book. The iceberg above the surface is the amount and detail that you, your editor, and your agent will know. And, sadly, that huge mass below the surface is everything that not one other person will ever, ever, see. You might not even write it down.

Then surely we can get rid of it? Well, you could do. Take the iceberg away and the penguin would be able to swim for a bit. But it wouldn't be able to keep it up forever, and eventually it would get eaten by a sea leopard. The iceberg, even the unseen and unwritten part, protects and supports the penguin on its journey. In the same way, your characters and their journey could not carry on for very long without the supporting detail and facts of your world-building.

Tell me again how a world should feel

In *The Strangeworlds Travel Agency* series so far, Flick and Jonathan have travelled to 14 different worlds in the space of two books. Hardly a great feat for them, given that there are 743 magical suitcase-portals in the travel agency, but certainly a challenge for me to keep a handle on when writing. Such a plethora of worlds could rapidly have felt over-whelming and difficult to keep track of, but – rather than begin an encyclopaedic collection of notes – I consciously crafted the worlds so that each one would appear distinct, without having to deep-dive into the history of each one, particularly since some of the characters' visits are rather fleeting.

I designed each individual world to evoke a specific emotional reaction from both the characters and the reader, and in such a way that each reaction would not be deliberately repeated. I created one world written to be deliberately frightening, another to be inno-cently joyful, one to be calm and soothing, and so on. In doing so, I was able both to show off the vast potential of *The Strangeworlds Travel Agency*'s magical suitcases, and to ensure that each of the worlds visited by the reader would be memorable. Even if the name of the place was forgotten, a younger reader might remember that one world was 'the scary one' and another 'the funny one', because they will relate to the world in the same way that Flick and Jonathan do. The characters' emotional reaction would be tied to the setting and what happened there, and will be mirrored by the reader, who wants to find out more and find out what will happen next.

Fantasy rules! Okay...?

Who runs the world? Well, you do! The great thing about fantasy world rules is you get to make them up. And they can be as 'normal' or as outlandish as you like. They don't even have to serve a purpose beyond being entertaining! If everyone has to stand on their chair and shout 'WAHOOEY!' after eating, you can make that a rule. Perhaps this is never explained – and that's completely fine too. But how many of those rules you want to include is dependent on several factors: firstly and most importantly, your readers (and probably your characters) are children. Whether they are visiting this world for a brief visit like in *Strangeworlds*, or they live there full time, they are only going to focus on the aspects of their world that are the most pressing and interesting to them – the parts of their world that are driving their story, and their journey, forward. And if this element is shouting WAHOOEY, your characters might not bother mentioning the complex political systems of their world. Thinking again of the penguin atop the iceberg of world-building and how aware it may be about what's going on below it, remember that, however much you might know your fantasy world inside and out, your reader wants your characters to navigate the world you have built, not to read a travel guide about it.

Secondly, the amount of description you have space to include will always be restricted by the word count. There's nothing wrong with having enough world-building potential to fill a 500,000-word book, but editors and agents generally prefer shorter books (and it helps to keep printing costs down!). Tell readers what they need to know straight away, and use the rest of your imagined rules as iceberg-style unseen support for the story. It's still important, it's just out of sight.

Think fast!

Anyone familiar with video games will know that at the start of a game there is often a video, less than three minutes long, in which the world of gameplay is introduced – a few minutes of speedy world-building for games that can take dozens of hours to complete. I checked a few of these out, and on average an introductory video accounts for about 0.1% of total gameplay time. That's like doing all your introductory world-building in the space of a paragraph that takes up about one third of a page. That sounds pretty extreme, doesn't it?

Actually, no. A decent chunky paragraph at the start of a book can work extremely hard, just as the intro to a video game might. That initial chunk of world-building description introduces what sort of world this is, whether there's anything readers can recognise and relate to, whether there's magic or not, and it sets the scene for other, smaller bits of world-building which can be 'confettied' through the rest of the story. A first world-building paragraph has to be enticing; it may be the deciding factor as to whether someone carries on reading your book or not, having picked it up in a shop to browse through. The first impressions the reader of your fantasy world receives need to be rich, engaging … and brief. Readers should want, nay *need*, to know how your characters are going to navigate this wonderful or terrifying new place. They may even have an initial idea about the sort of problems they may encounter or the fun they might have. That early paragraph of world-building is advertising the journey your characters are about to go on; show off the best bits, and leave the details for later. And if, as in *The Strangeworlds Travel Agency*, the concept of your world is what you want to showcase rather than a description of a place, remember to hint at the richness of its potential but leave the reader hungry for more. Your character's journey is to get from A to B (whether this is physically or emotionally), but your reader's journey is to find out the details and to get thoroughly lost in your new world of fantasy and magic.

To be able to build a world for young readers to explore is a wonderful thing. Whether or not we can ever throw open the doors to our fantasy worlds completely, by writing them down at all we are inviting readers to wander within, to make up their own minds about the potential dangers or excitements – and inspiring them to create escapes of their own.

L.D. Lapinski is the author of *The Strangeworlds Travel Agency* (2020) and *The Edge of the Ocean* (2021), published by Orion Children's Books; the third book of the trilogy, *The Secrets of the Stormforest*, will be published in April 2022. They have worked as a primary school teacher and have an MA in Creative Writing from Nottingham Trent University. For more information see www.ldlapinski.com. Follow them on Twitter @ldlapinski.

See also...
• *Writing magic into fiction*, page 136

Writing thrillers for teenagers

Sophie McKenzie considers the ingredients for writing a successful thriller for teenagers.

When people ask me what sort of books I write, I tend to reply that I write thrillers for teenagers and, more recently, for adults as well. But actually, I do no such thing – at least not deliberately … I just write the kind of stories I like to read, involving characters I care passionately about. And I write to please myself – not for a specific audience. So here's the only rule I'm going to suggest you stick to – always write what matters to you … not what you think other people want, need or expect. Everything else (i.e. the rest of this article) is just my opinion – a few thoughts and suggestions that helped me and might be useful to you.

A strong story

This is definitely my number one requirement in a top thriller – whatever the age of the audience. Remember that a story is *not* simply an interesting situation, though it may start with one. In a story, stuff happens. A good way to check if you have a really interesting story is to look at whether the scenario you've created gives your main character something they really want or need – *and* a big fat problem that gets in the way of that ambition. In my book, *Girl, Missing,* for instance, Lauren *really* wants to find out who her birth mother is and whether she was stolen from her original home as a toddler. Her main problem, at the start of the story, is that her parents refuse to talk about her adoption. This also means that Lauren can't look to her parents to sort out her problem, thus ensuring the story follows one of the basic principles of children's fiction and gets the adults out of the way as fast as possible! It also deepens the problem, as Lauren starts to suspect that her adoptive parents may have been the ones who stole her from her birth mother.

High stakes

Your character's needs and problems must be important to them. If they care and you care, chances are you'll get your reader to care too.

There are millions of things your character might want or need to find fulfilment and/or salvation. And a top story will certainly need an original twist. But there are a few fundamental ambitions that almost everyone relates to. Most thrillers and adventure stories revolve around one or more of the following, though there are others:

• Coming home. This is a common desire, especially in children's stories – I'm talking here about characters who are trying to find their way back home – like Dorothy in *The Wizard of Oz* – and about characters trying to find a new home – like Harry in Robert Westall's marvellous *The Kingdom by the Sea.*

• Working out or accepting who you really are and/or finding your place in the world. This is another huge need shared by characters in identity/rites of passage stories as varied as *Being* by Kevin Brooks (YA) and Tamsin Winter's excellent *Jemima Small Versus The Universe* (Middle Grade). This 'goal' is particularly common in fiction for younger teens – identity issues seem to resonate strongly with adolescents (or those approaching puberty) aware they are no longer fully children but not yet sure how to be adults.

• Then there's love. Will the boy get the girl; will the child be reunited with the parents?

• And, of course, there's survival. Whether your character's goal is to save his own life, the lives of those he loves or the entire planet, survival stories usually involve plenty of action and interesting villains. In fact, baddies often provide stories with the best problems: imagine the Harry Potter books without Voldemort or *101 Dalmatians* without Cruella de Vil.

Not worrying about taboo subjects

Personally I don't think there's any subject that can't be tackled. What counts is how you treat the material. Teenagers, like the rest of us, want to read about subjects that matter to them. Families, friendships, loss, guilt, identity, ambitions in work and in love – are all relevant. Sometimes I think teens get a raw deal. Just because young people are aware of difficult topics doesn't necessarily mean they want to read about them in a heavy duty way. Beware of turning your thriller into an 'issues' book in which the main character only 'angsts' and 'never acts'. If you want to write a thriller around a challenging topic, that's great. Just make sure there's a strong story holding the whole thing together. In *Blood Ties,* I wanted to write about how it might feel to discover, aged 15, you'd been cloned as a replacement for your dead sister. That could easily have been the starting point for a much less pacy book than the one I ended up writing, which attempts to weave its thought-provoking subject material in and out of a fast-moving action story.

A central character to care about and identify with

A good story *has* to involve individuals we care about. And a teenage novel will usually feature one or more teenage protagonists. If memory (I was a teen), personality (I act like a teen) and research (I talk to teens) don't help you imagine yourself into the head of an adolescent, then you may struggle to write teenage books.

The stories I like best often incorporate a relationship drama that bubbles under the main action. From a writing point of view, focusing on the development of a romantic relationship – as well as a high-octane thriller plot – helps make your characters more interesting and your story more meaningful. *The Set-Up* is the first book in my *Medusa Project* series about a group of teens with psychic abilities. It begins with Nico, who narrates the story, discovering he has the gift of telekinesis. He uses this developing power on missions as well as trying to impress the girl he likes, Ketty. By the second book of the series, *The Hostage*, Nico and the other teens have been brought together to form a crime-fighting force. Much action and danger ensues from this, yet the story – this time narrated by Ketty herself – also focuses on what she really thinks about Nico.

Will boys read stories that contain an element of romance? Well, many won't, but I'm also certain that it's a complete myth to say that boys don't care about romantic relationships at all – they just don't want you to spend pages analysing them!

A clear sense of the point of view you're writing from

Whose story are you telling? Make sure you know, right from the start. Then try and keep that character at the centre of the action, moving the story along. In his commentary on the film adaptation of *The Lord of the Rings,* director Peter Jackson talks about the importance of turning the camera on the film's heroes at least every third shot. A useful tip – which translates in novel terms as follows: don't stray too far from what your main character can think, feel, see, touch, smell and hear. Writing from an omnipotent, narrator perspective is a perfectly valid choice but it does tend to distance the reader from the main character's mind. Almost all children love to identify with their heroes. And thrillers definitely benefit from the immediacy of a strong viewpoint. I wrote each book in the *Medusa Project* series from a different character's point of view to explore each character's particular psychic power and personality.

Planning and plotting before you write

Some writers plan. Some don't. Personally, I like to plan the foundations – the outline of the story showing where the characters are going – before I start. But I save the fun stuff – showing how the characters are going to get there – for while I'm writing.

I came to the conclusion that planning was helpful after starting no fewer than 17 books in my first year of serious writing. Some of these had some merit – an interesting character here, an exciting scene there – but almost all of them fell apart by chapter five or so because the plots simply didn't pan out. Planning can feel like an overwhelming task. But unless you try and work through your story in advance, it's all too easy for the whole thing to crumble in your hands. This is, of course, particularly true for thrillers, which require suspenseful twists and turns in order to deliver their thrills.

Managing a plot is a bit like driving a chariot pulled by several huge, powerful horses. You have to concentrate on what you're doing – and be as fit and strong as possible – in order to hold together the reins and make sure that the various strands of the story you're weaving don't career down separate paths and send your chariot tumbling to the ground.

If you want to write thrillers, study thriller writers

I spent a lot of time studying other people's plots, working out how various authors whose plotting skills I admire handled that aspect of their writing. For instance, I read the first three books in Anthony Horowitz's *Alex Rider* series and wrote down everything that happened (literally, just the actions) that moved the story on.

That experience taught me many things – not least the value of breaking my plots into manageable amounts. When planning *The Set-Up*, I knew halfway through the story that Nico, the main character, would discover the man he had trusted up to that point was actually plotting to betray him. This enabled me to break the story down into two halves, making it less daunting to plan each one.

Have a laugh along the way

Just because you're writing a thriller doesn't mean your story can't have its lighter moments. An ironic narrative voice, a character with a great sense of humour or a funny situation do more than make the reader laugh – they provide a release for tension, allowing the next plunge into suspense to be even more powerful.

Creating suspense – hooks and hangers

The most important chapter is the first – get that right, drawing your reader in with a dramatic 'inciting incident' (as Robert McKee puts it in *Story*) and you will, hopefully, have set up your story in an interesting way and hooked the reader in. Some sort of conflict is usually necessary here, as exemplified by one of the best kids' thriller first chapters I've ever read – *Thief* by Malorie Blackman. And never forget the power of D.R.A.T. – that's the Desperate Race Against Time, guaranteed to inject a shot of excitement into any story!

Cliffhangers are great too – whenever I'm coming to the end of a scene, I try and work out what I need to write to give the reader a pay-off for sitting through that chapter – and what I can leave unexplained, as a hook to make them want to turn the next page.

And finally...

Here are my top three tips for producing a thrilling story: (1) Get into the story as fast as possible; (2) Make sure that every plot twist is unexpected but convincing; (3) Don't be indulgent … if what you've written doesn't move the story on, cut it.

In the end, if all else fails, remember that so long as you're trying to write the best book you're capable of writing, nothing else really matters. So don't give up.

Sophie McKenzie is the award-winning author of *Girl, Missing, Blood Ties* and *Split Second*, all of which won the Red House Children's Book Award. Her latest book is the mystery adventure: *Hide and Secrets* (2021). Other publications include sequels to the *Missing, Blood Ties* and *Split Second* series, plus the six-book *The Medusa Project* series, the suspenseful *All My Secrets*, psychological drama *SweetFreak* (2017), which was nominated for the CrimeFest - Best Crime Novel for Young Adults Award 2018 and *Becoming Jo* (2019), a modern-day re-imagining of the children's classic *Little Women*. Sophie has also written two teen romance series - the *Luke & Eve* stories and the *Falling Fast* books and four psychological thrillers for adults, *Close My Eyes* (2013), *Trust in Me* (2014), *Here We Lie* (2015) and *The Black Sheep* (2017). Sophie's website is www.sophiemckenziebooks.com and she can be found on Twitter @sophiemckenzie_.

See also...

- *Writing for the teenage market,* page 295
- *Plotting: how to keep your YA readers reading,* page 142

Dealing with tough issues in YA fiction

Holly Bourne shares advice for YA authors on how to deal with sensitive and difficult issues through fiction in a responsible, truthful and supportive way that provides 'a safe space for teenagers to explore the dark'.

The YA author has an undeniable influence on their readers, which is why it is vital that they write sensitively and responsibly. I believe that the right book given to a teenager at the right time can change – maybe even save – their life.

Puberty is a pretty ruthless stage in life; it is when weird things happen to your body, a time of first love and first heartache, of first-time sex, and maybe when bullying, loneliness, exam stress or mental illness cast a shadow over your life (75% of people who develop mental illness in their lifetime do so before the age of 18). In short, it is a period when you are grappling with your sense of identity, trying to figure out *who you are*. Being a teenager can be exhausting, exhilarating and terrifying, and I believe fiction can offer both refuge and respite during this time. The best stories don't only provide a gripping plot but also help young readers to make sense of their lives or to feel less alone.

As a YA writer, you must convey essential truths about the teen experience for your stories to have any hope of connecting with your readership. Teenagers are not naive about the hardships of their existence. I travel to schools all over the country to talk about books and mental health and I'm always blown away by how sensitive teenagers are to emerging social issues. There's not much darkness they're not already hugely aware of or personally wrestling with. They're hugely grateful to have books that shed light on the concerns that preoccupy them. Remember that teenagers are legally children and therefore, as a YA writer, you have a responsibility to tell the truth *safely*; you must ensure your story is truthful but not harmful. This delicate balancing act is something it can be tricky to get right.

Before I became a full-time author, I spent five years working as an advisor for young people at a charity called The Mix. This experience gave me a concrete understanding of teen issues and how to engage with young people about their problems within a rigorous safeguarding framework. This has provided me with an invaluable background to my fiction career, in which I feel able to tackle the darkest subject matter in a way I know is as safe for readers as possible. In my novels I've tackled suicide, self-harm, abusive relationships, rape and sexual assault, obsessive compulsive disorder, alcoholic and neglectful parents and many other 'tough issues'. If you research your topics intensively and remember any safeguarding training you have had and expert advice at all times, there are no limits to how dark you can go in your fiction. In fact, teenagers may be grateful that you have.

This safeguarding underpinning must be there at all times. Never let your writerly ego, or the thrill of writing the more dramatic bits on the page, seduce you away from your responsibility to provide a safe space for teenagers to explore the dark. Whatever issues you decide to tackle, you'll need to research them more vigorously than simply reading

Books

this article, but I hope the following guidelines will be a useful starting point. Now, where's the torch?

Writing suicide safely

I'm starting at the very darkest of where the dark can go. That's because it's a hugely common theme running through YA books and one that can have literally fatal consequences if tackled insensitively. Unfortunately, many YA books that have handled this topic dangerously have gone on to achieve huge publishing success. Rather than making it a free-for-all, we need to learn lessons from this – educating ourselves and trying to do better. Any author who wants to explore this issue should research its copycat nature and how getting it wrong can cost someone's life. For instance, Google searches for 'how to commit suicide' rose by 26% after Netflix released the first season of *13 Reasons Why*.

Strong starting-points for research include the Samaritans guidance for covering suicide, as well as the World Health Organization's media guidelines for preventing suicide. Here are some of the most important guidelines:

• Try not to include any detailed suicide methodology

Leave out any technical details about how a character may take their own life, such as how many pills to take, and never discuss the 'success rate' of any method. Never imply there's any quick or painless way of completing suicide.

• Never show suicide as a solution to a problem

I once heard suicide described as 'a very permanent solution to a temporary problem.' Even if that is what's going on in a character's head, avoid glamorising the fatal notion that suicide is an 'answer' to life's hardships. Instead perhaps strive to show a character who overcomes this suicide idealisation, gets help and goes on to enjoy happiness. This is something I did in my novel *Are We All Lemmings and Snowflakes?* (Usborne Publishing 2018) which opened with my protagonist Olive in a suicidal state, but ended with her in a much better place. I was also careful to focus mostly on Olive's suicidal 'feelings' rather than showing her detailed thoughts.

• Avoid giving characters who have completed suicide 'notoriety'

The element of notoriety that may result when someone takes their own life is something that can glamorise it and cause copycat behaviours, which young people are particularly susceptible to.

• Suicide is never triggered by just one thing

It's is a hugely complicated behaviour, with no a + b = c formula behind it, so it's important not to give a reason 'why' a character was triggered to take their own life.

The right book can save someone's life. Suicide is certainly not a subject to avoid; just ensure you take the time and consideration to write about it safely – there can be catastrophic consequences if you don't.

What is 'triggering'? And how to avoid it

Triggering is a word with a huge amount of misunderstanding and stigma attached to it. Currently we're seeing a backlash against so-called 'sensitive snowflakes' who demand 'trigger warnings' in art. To some extent it is true that you cannot produce any art that doesn't trigger someone, somewhere, somehow, but the term 'triggering' does actually relate to known psychological responses to trauma which it is important to write about safely. No, you can't keep every reader safe from being triggered, but the following guidelines will certainly minimise any unintentional harm in your writing:

• Self-harm
This is a behaviour that, like suicide, can have a copycat element to it, and reading descriptions of it can 'trigger' people to self-harm. Try to keep any description of self-harm off the page, focusing instead on the *feelings* rather than the behaviour itself. Certainly never describe the method a character uses to harm themselves, and avoid graphic descriptions of bleeding.

• Disorder eating
When writing about someone who overeats or under-eats, never actually state that character's specific weight or dress size. This can cause the reader to compare themselves with that character, triggering shame and further disordered eating. The same goes for calories consumed and calories burned by a character's exercise regime – giving these specifics can be very unhelpful, especially as they're so easily avoided.

• PTSD
The phenomenon most commonly associated with the word 'trigger' is when something triggers a devastating flashback in somebody suffering with Post Traumatic Stress Disorder. A memory of trauma is not stored in the brain in the same way as other memories and therefore, for a PTSD sufferer, reading something similar to what they've been through can cause a flashback. A flashback is when the victim essentially feels like they're reliving their trauma in the present moment, which is obviously hugely upsetting. Although people may be triggered by many different things, I feel it's wise at least to try and minimise graphic descriptions of violence, and especially sexual violence, in your writing. Sadly, many young people are living with trauma and sexual trauma – one in thirteen young people have PTSD by the age of 18 – so keep that in mind when writing about these subjects. You don't need to explicitly 'go there' in order for your story to be powerful. If you get published, do flag the parts of the book you're worried about with your editor. They can then hire a sensitivity reader to check the manuscript, as well as putting a trigger warning on the cover. This is something we've decided to do in my book *The Places I've Cried in Public* (Usborne 2019) which has an off-page rape in it. My publisher hired a psychologist specialising in sexual violence triggers to go through the manuscript and the tweaks she suggested didn't impact the narrative in any way.

Remember mental illness does not exist in a vacuum
Recently there's been a welcome shift away from a simplistic biological explanation for mental illness. The World Health Organization has stated that it is inexplicably linked to human rights issues, and leading experts are campaigning for us to ask people 'What happened to you?' rather than 'What's wrong with you?'. The causes of mental illness might be environmental, socioeconomic or biological, so make sure your character's illness makes sense in the context of the wider world they live in. This is what I tried to explore in *Am I Normal Yet?* (Usborne 2015) about a girl called Evie who has OCD. The book explored both mental illness and gender inequality, making links between the two. I was careful to make sure Evie was never just characterised by her mental illness but was depicted as a fully rounded character who happened to have a mental illness.

An issue isn't a story

Just as a character is not merely representative of a single attribute or one defining feature, a single 'issue' is never a good substitute for an engaging, well-structured plot. It's completely natural that, when writing for and about teenagers, you should want to include tough issues, simply a realistic interpretation of a teenager's life, but the fundamentals of successful storytelling must not be lost.

Always offer hope

I feel a responsibility as a children's writer to ensure my novels have a hopeful tinge, especially when dealing with the tougher stuff. Though I'm careful never to perpetuate unhelpful fantasies such as *Love can cure mental illness*, I do want teen readers who see aspects of themselves in my characters to believe that light can emerge from the darkness. Whether that's through caring parents, the power of good friendships or showing positive experiences of teenagers using mental health services, I believe a YA writer should always offer hope, and that your book should be a light that guides them towards it.

Holly Bourne is a bestselling author whose YA books, all published by Usborne Publishing, include the award-winning *Spinster Club* series: *Am I Normal Yet?* (2015), *How Hard Can Love Be?* (2016), *What's a Girl Gotta Do?* (2016) and *And a Happy New Year?* (2016). Her other books include *Soulmates* (2013), *It Only Happens in the Movies* (2017), *Are We All Lemmings & Snowflakes?* (2018) and *The Places I've Cried in Public* (2019). Her latest YA book is *The Yearbook* (Usborne 2021). Holly has worked as a news journalist, an editor, relationship advisor and 'agony aunt' for The Mix, a youth charity which helps young people with their relationships and mental health. Follow her on Twitter @Holly_BourneYA.

See also...
- *Writing about love and loss for children*, page 171
- *Writing for teenagers*, page 150

Writing about love and loss for children

Natasha Farrant considers the responsibility shouldered by authors who write about love and loss for children and teenagers and how such novels can be a valuable opportunity for young readers to explore challenging emotions and life experiences.

Years ago, when I started out working in children's publishing and before I was published myself, I went to a lecture given by Anne Fine. A member of the audience asked her what the difference was between writing for children and writing for adults. She replied that you could write about all the same subjects, whatever the age of your readers, but that you would tell the story differently. It was all a question, she said, of the angle at which you shone the light. I want to explore that question here in relation to writing about loss and love, because these are subjects I have returned to again and again in my own books.

Even as I write this, I read in *The Bookseller* that authors John Boyne, Malorie Blackman and Sam Copeland, presenting their titles at the Penguin Random House Children's Showcase, 'spoke of transgender issues, experiences of psychosis and how to cope with anxiety as a small child'. And this focus on difficult themes is by no means new to children's literature. From *The Railway Children* to *The Secret Garden*, *Matilda* to *Journey to the River Sea* and *Harry Potter*, authors have dealt with parental imprisonment, poverty, bereavement, loneliness, persecution, child neglect – all huge issues; all, one way or another, connected with loss.

'Struggle and hardship are the essential ingredients of narrative', writes Trisha Lee, theatre director and founder of MakeBelieve Arts, in *Princesses, Dragons and Helicopter Stories* (Routledge 2015). She goes on to quote Kieran Egan in *Teaching as Storytelling* (University of Chicago Press 1989) who believes that it is our desire to explore global concerns with binary opposites – good and evil, fair and unfair, cruel and kind – that engages us with fiction. This is true whatever age the reader. It's up to us, the reader, to make that exploration as engaging, accessible and, dare I say it, as age-appropriate as possible.

My first book for young people, *The Things We Did For Love* (Faber 2012), is a Second World War love story based on the massacre which took place at Oradour-sur-Glane, near Limoges in South West France, in 1944. Years later, a friend still hasn't got over my writing this: 'A children's book! About a massacre!' Well, it wasn't a children's book, as was made clear by the cover. I have no desire to give it to a child – frankly, there are gentler ways for them to learn about man's brutality to man. But teenagers are a different matter. The novel deals with subjects most teens I know are familiar with: sex and desire, jealousy, shame, the awareness that although they long to do the right thing they often feel coerced by social pressure to do the opposite. Most teenagers, by dint of the online world we live in, do know about war. My book offers them a chance to reflect further on what it means.

What, though, makes it a book for teens, and not for adults? It's a tricky question. A book for young people doesn't mean adults can't enjoy it too. It doesn't mean it can't have adult characters. It doesn't mean, for example, that the characters can't have sex. Sex! How often have I heard book pitches along the lines of 'It's a love story, but don't worry, it's for teens so it doesn't have sex in it' – as if teenagers didn't have sex! In *The Things We Did For Love* my teenage protagonists Arianne and Luc have sex. In fact, Arianne uses sex, rather naively thinking that if she sleeps with Luc, he won't join the Resistance and leave her. I don't show them having sex. I show rose petals leading up to a door (corny, but I couldn't resist), and I show that door closing. But we know perfectly well what is happening, and it's the sort of device that's used in plenty of grown-up fiction.

So again, if I can show torture and I can (sort of) show sex, what makes this a book for teens rather than adults? How have I shone the light? Well, there's the characters, I guess – three of the main protagonists are teenagers; one is a child (and one is a fully-grown man, but we'll put that to one side). They have teen and childhood preoccupations, like falling in love and doing homework. Arianne is trying to fill the gap left by her dead mother and her imprisoned father. She believes she may have found her answer in Luc. She believes she can use her love for him to keep him from harm. And the unnamed teenage narrator, after the massacre, writes that the lovers will be together forever. As adults, we suspect that this is unlikely. As teenagers, it's important (I think) to believe that it is true. Maybe that is the key – that belief in the redemptive power of love.

One of my golden rules, when writing for young people, is this: do not leave the reader without hope. Do not destroy that belief that the world can do better. It's difficult, if you're writing about certain subjects. Climate change is a classic example. But I would suggest that if you see no future for humanity yourself, then perhaps writing for young people is not for you. There are various forms of redemption to be found in *The Things We Did For Love*. They were hard to find, in the bleakness of that event, but the focus of the book (and indeed its inspiration) is the small acts of heroism I discovered in the course of my research and which give the book its title. Because writing for children comes with a certain responsibility.

Scientific research has shown that 'when we connect with a story, parts of our brain related to a particular emotion or action light up, and our neurons start firing as if we were engaged in the activity ourselves' (Kieran Egan; *Princesses, Dragons and Helicopter Stories*). And what is true for us as adults is even more true for a child, during the plastic years of brain formation. Philip Pullman writes about his experiences of playing at Davy Crockett in the suburbs of Adelaide when he was growing up: 'When we children play at being characters we admire, doing things we value, we discover areas and depths of feeling it would be hard to reach otherwise. Exhilaration, heroism, despair, resolution, triumph, noble renunciation, sacrifice: in acting these out we experience them in miniature or, as it were, in safety' (*Daemon Voices: Essays on Storytelling*, David Fickling Books 2017). He goes on to write that, through play, he was 'building patterns of behaviour and expectation into my moral understanding'.

As children play, so they read. They *live* the books they love, and these books offer tremendous opportunity to learn about love and loss and everything in between. They will shape their young readers and make them who they are. And yet, remember this. When you are writing for children, know that you are writing for some of the toughest, most critical readers there are, who will not suffer unnecessary babble. Know that that babble includes you pontificating on love and loss, on how sad your heroine is, or how hard she is crying, or how slowly time is passing. Never forget that other golden rule: 'Show don't tell.' *Show* the loss. *Show* the emotion. *Show* the redemptive love. Use every writing trick at your disposal – metaphor, imagery, leitmotiv – to make them come to life. They're never going to live your book if they're bored.

My middle-grade book *The Children of Castle Rock* (Faber 2018) traces the grief of the main protagonist, Alice, as she mourns the death of her mother. The book opens as she prepares to leave her family home forever. Rather than linger on Alice's emotions, I choose to focus on her refusal to leave without taking her mother's commemorative rosebush, which is dug up and squished into the car. The rosebush then reappears periodically – on a balcony, as a watercolour and eventually in a new garden – in a way which shows the reader without spelling it out that Alice, without forgetting, is nevertheless learning to move on.

As I wrote the story, I asked myself these questions: What has Alice lost? What does she want? What does she need? These are the questions which drive the plot. Alice has lost her mum, her dad is completely unreliable and her home is sold. She needs to rebuild a sense of family, she wants her dad to do this for her but she needs to understand that he never will. These are the questions which give the novel emotional depth and a sense of purpose. They are not what make it an exciting read, though. The excitement comes from the fact that, in her pursuit of these needs, Alice runs away from boarding school, camps on a Scottish beach, almost drowns, breaks into a house and gets chased onto a stack of rocks by a bunch of Italian gangsters, where she gets cut off by the tide … and in the end conquers both her fear of losing her dad and her fear of heights by abseiling down a cliff.

Even as I write this, I'm aware how complex this question of responsibility is. It is absolutely not about watering down difficult subjects, but it's about rendering them in such a way that a child can explore them – as Pullman writes in the quote I cited earlier – in safety. Children, like all readers, will take what they can and what they need from a story. A child who has experienced severe loss will be alive to Alice's grief. A child with less experience of loss may simply enjoy the adventure. The story may lead to greater understanding; it may simply entertain. All forms of reading are valid.

In *The Children of Castle Rock*, as in all my other books, I have tried to acknowledge that bad things do happen, that the people you love are not always reliable, but that there are others who love you if you can open your eyes and heart to them. I have also tried to fulfil my other responsibility as a writer, which is to make my story as cohesive, exciting and as good as I possibly can. But there my task as a writer is finished. Alice's story is in the world, to be completed in as many ways as there are readers. Which is just as it should be.

Natasha Farrant is a writer and literary scout. Her books include *The Children of Castle Rock* (Faber 2018) and *Eight Princesses and a Magic Mirror* (Zephyr 2019) as well as *The Things We Did for Love* (2012) and four titles in her popular children's series *The Diaries of Bluebell Gadsby*: *After Iris* (2013), *Flora in Love* (2014), *All About Pumpkin* (2015) and *Time for Jas* (2016), all published by Faber & Faber. Her latest book is *Voyage of the Sparrowhawk* (Faber 2020) which won the Costa Children's Book Award, and was *The Times* Children's Book of the Year. For more information visit www.natashafarrant.com, and follow her on Twitter @NatashaFarrant1.

Including LGBT+ characters in children's fiction

Lauren James makes diversity the bedrock of her writing. She knows the importance of enabling children to grow up reading about and relating to LGBT+ characters, and has good advice for writers on how to promote inclusivity and avoid prejudices and stereotyping across all genres in fiction.

Looking back, the first and only character I can remember reading about as a child who was LGBT+ (Lesbian, Gay, Bisexual, Transgender or another queer identity) was Albus Dumbledore in *Harry Potter*. And even he barely counts – his character isn't explicitly written as gay. When I started writing, I realised that I wasn't the only one who'd grown up without LGBT+ role models. I decided that this dearth of LGBT+ representation in fiction was something I wanted to address in my work. I make no apologies for being a writer with an avowed agenda: telling stories that can change attitudes.

Children's and Young Adult writers have the ears of a whole generation; that comes with a huge responsibility beyond simply providing entertainment. Children read books to learn how the world works, and we have to make sure that the world they read about is as varied and diverse and representative as real life.

Before I was even sure whether I was going to be published, I had decided that the main character in my second novel, *The Last Beginning* (Walker Books 2016), would be gay. It would be clear from the very start that Clove was a lesbian, but the story would be about more than her sexual orientation. She would have clearly defined character traits – with flaws and positive qualities – and, like any well-drawn character, she would navigate her way through an enticing plot (and she'd 'get the girl' along the way too).

I knew that I might face negative consequences for this decision from the publishing industry; even today, publishers reject stories about LGBT+ characters, and give reduced exposure and publicity to those they do publish. Books are bought based on sales estimates, and in the case of LGBT+ titles it's only recently that there have been children's bestsellers, such as *Simon vs the Homo Sapiens Agenda* by Becky Albertalli (Penguin 2015) and *The Raven Cycle* series by Maggie Stiefvater (Scholastic), to prove that there is a huge market of readers searching for diverse titles.

Feedback from other authors in the YA online community who have written LGBT+-focused stories suggests a subdued reaction to LGBT+ fiction from bloggers and readers as well as from publishers. This is particularly true when a novel is female-focused and doesn't include a male main character, as in a novel with lesbian protagonists. In fact, when I started researching existing LGBT+ novels while writing my own, I was surprised by how many there *were* – but how few of them I had seen in bookshops or press reviews.

Librarians also tend to categorise children's fiction containing LGBT+ romances in a more mature or explicit category than they would with a novel containing a straight romance with the same substance. There is also the chance of reviewer criticism for getting it wrong, such as *My Brother's Name is Jessica* by John Boyne (Puffin 2019), which faced backlash for misgendering a trans female character in the title, and not properly researching the reality of being trans.[1]

1. www.pinknews.co.uk/2019/04/16/my-brothers-name-is-jessica-john-boyne-criticised/

I knew that I ran the risk of not finding an agent – or not selling the novel at all. Despite this, I decided to write the book. I thought that if it was good enough, it would stand up on its own merits and find the audience it deserved. As I was writing, I kept thinking about the teenagers who would read the book – the ones who knew they were gay, the ones who had gay friends, the ones who hadn't yet realised they might be a member of the LGBT+ community. It has been proven that people who read have more empathy and social skills,[2] so for children to grow up reading about and relating to LGBT+ characters can only help to reduce prejudice.

Even though I was braced for rejection, my agent, editors and publisher didn't miss a beat when I told them I was writing a story with an LGBT+ protagonist. I had only just secured a book deal for my debut novel *The Next Together* (Walker Books 2015), so I didn't have a track record to prove that the book would sell regardless of content – but it may have helped that *The Last Beginning* was the sequel to a heterosexual romance in *The Next Together*. This was an intentional decision on my part, as I wanted to get the LGBT+ book in the hands of readers who might not otherwise pick it up. This will have guaranteed the book an audience that a standalone LGBT+ novel from a debut author might not have found.

My publisher was happy to comply when I specifically requested that the cover and blurb clearly indicate that the novel contained an LGBT+ romance. This is not always the case, as often publishers will conceal diverse elements in the marketing information, to ensure that the book is not seen as a heavy-hitting 'issues' book. I wanted the story to have a chance of getting to its audience of teenagers, especially those who were too afraid or confused to search out LGBT+ books for themselves. The publisher also made sure I was pitched for LGBT+-focused panels, festivals and articles. I wrote and released a bonus short story, *Another Beginning*, about my LGBT+ characters which was published free on Amazon Kindle for publicity. It was promoted at major YA conventions like YALC (Young Adult Literature Convention, www.londonfilmandcomiccon.com/index. php/zones/yalc) and Summer in the City (www.sitc-event.co.uk). A campaign which ran on Twitter in 2018 under the hashtag #PrideMonthReads served to promote even more books with LGBT+ characters.

Recommended reads

Lesbian

Top Marks for Murder by Robin Stevens (Puffin 2019);

The Deepest Breath by Meg Grehan (Little Island 2019)

Gay

Alex in Wonderland by Simon James Green (Scholastic 2019);

The Black Flamingo by Dean Atta (Hodder Children's Books 2019)

Bisexual

Grasshopper Jungle by Andrew Smith (Electric Monkey 2014);

The Pearl Thief by Elizabeth Wein (Bloomsbury Children's 2017)

Transgender

Birthday by Meredith Russo (Usborne 2019);

George by Alex Gino (Scholastic 2015)

Queer

The Prince and the Dressmaker by Jen Wang (First Second 2018);

Wain: LGBT reimaginings of Scottish folktales by Rachel Plummer (The Emma Press 2019)

Asexual

Radio Silence by Alice Oseman (HarperCollins 2016);

Clariel by Garth Nix (Hot Key Books 2015)

The Lady's Guide to Petticoats and Piracy by Mackenzi Lee (Katherine Tegen Books 2018)

Books

2. Kidd, D., & Castano, E. (2017). *Different stories: How levels of familiarity with literary and genre fiction relate to mentalizing.* Psychology of Aesthetics, Creativity, and the Arts, 11(4), 474-486. http://psycnet.apa.org/record/2016-37488-001

We're lucky enough that there are now enough LGBT+ books to keep a teenager very well supplied with reading matter – and the number is increasing every year.[3]

I'm still learning about how to write diversely and I'm sure I've made mistakes in the past. With that in mind, here are some of the most important things I've learnt about writing LGBT+ characters into my work:

1. Don't write books about the experience of being LGBT+ unless you are LGBT+ yourself

This doesn't mean that you should avoid writing stories containing LGBT+ characters, only that their identity should not be the main focus of the novel. For example, trans authors are best placed to write an authentic book about what it is like to transition genders.

2. Do your research

Make sure that you read books written by people with the identities you want to include in your fiction (these books are known as 'own voices' fiction) and talk to anyone you know personally about their experiences; also reach out to people on social media or hire a sensitivity reader to check your manuscript for accuracy. You can find databases online of freelance editors who offer sensitivity services to help make sure that your writing isn't harmful to any readers; search for 'We Need Diverse Books' or 'Write in the Margins'. Some publishers will help with the costs of hiring sensitivity readers.

3. Avoid stereotypes

Not all gay men are fashionable, lesbians aren't always butch and LGBT+ people don't all love Pride parades and nightclubs. There is no universal gay experience, just as there's no single straight experience. Even a 'nice' stereotype is harmful, because believing that traits are genetic or biological reinforces a belief in negative stereotypes too. An easy way to avoid unintentional stereotyping is to make sure that your character's sexuality is not their only character trait. Avoid a sassy 'gay best friend' who has no real character development or plot involvement, or an LGBT+ antagonist whose terrible deeds are driven by their sexuality. Villains in children's media are often queer-coded (think of Hades, Ursula and Jafar in Disney films) and this can send the subliminal message that being LGBT+ is a negative trait.

Be intersectional with your characters too – don't be afraid to write disabled or BAME (Black, Asian and Minority Ethnic) LGBT+ characters. LGBT+ people are multi-faceted, just like anyone else.

4. Include LGBT+ characters in all genres

LGBT+ characters deserve complicated adventures where they get to save the world too. It is important to show teenagers that life continues beyond coming out, by giving them books to read in addition to contemporary coming-of-age novels. If you write historical fiction, remember that LGBT+ people have existed throughout all of history, even if at the time they weren't visible or their culture didn't have the words to describe them. If you are writing science fiction and fantasy, remember that the social prejudices you choose to include in your fictional world say more about you than anything else; there's no real reason for homophobia in a world of magic and dragons, and a futuristic novel with no diverse characters is more of a dystopia than anything else.

3. www.malindalo.com/blog/2017/10/12/lgbtq-ya-by-the-numbers-2015-16

5. Don't bury your gays

It's so common for media featuring LGBT+ characters to end with their deaths that it even has a trope name – 'Bury Your Gays'. This trope began in the 1950s, when traditional publishers only agreed to publish books about LGBT+ characters if they had an unhappy ending. Don't let this terrible pattern continue - try to flip convention and let your gay characters live at the end of your story. Remember that your young LGBT+ readers might not know about the historical or social context of prejudice against LGBT+ communities; all they will see is people like themselves being the focus of hate crimes. You're writing fiction, so feel free to take some liberty with the details. Show your readers that it's possible for them to have a happily ever after.

It can be difficult and traumatic to write about your own life experiences, so be kind to yourself as well as your characters if you are writing about difficult issues surrounding an LGBT+ identity.

6. Write LGBT+ characters of all ages

Including only teenage LGBT+ characters sends the unintentional message that LGBT+ people have no future. Sexuality is a spectrum, and people can discover they are LGBT+ at any age. You could include a newly transgender grandparent, a divorced dad in a relationship with a man for the first time or a happily single bisexual aunt. Remember that children can realise they aren't straight very young too, often before puberty.

7. Don't be afraid of terminology

Demisexual, cisgender, aromantic – these all might sound like scary textbook terms that have no place in a children's book. However, think of a child reading your book and coming across the exact word they need to google to explain all the feelings they've never understood about themselves. It also gives parents of LGBT+ children a way to learn more about their child's identity. Make your character's identity explicit by putting the word on the page. It's worth remembering that terminology is an ever-evolving science (consider the changing implications of 'transvestite' and 'queer' over the last few decades), so make sure that the words you choose to use are up to date and not considered a slur. Some words can only be used by members of the community themselves, and not by allies.

8. Don't shy away from representing physical intimacy

There's nothing more explicitly sexual about two boys kissing than a snogging boy and girl, and yet only occasionally is the former casually represented in children's fiction. At a time when sex education in schools around the world still fails to teach teenagers accurately about LGBT+ sexual health, books are often the only place where a confused teenager can find the information they need in a safe and reliable format.

9. Don't just have a token LGBT+ character

It is exceptionally rare for one LGBT+ person to be found alone in a group of straight friends. Having an isolated LGBT+ character sends the message to young LGBT+ readers that they will grow up to be the only person they know with their identity. To accurately reflect the real world, include multiple people of different LGBT+ identities in the same friendship group. LGBT+ people have deeply important platonic relationships with each other as well as romantic ones; not all gay characters exist to be shipped together. If you have LGBT+ side characters, make sure they have their own lives beyond the plot, with goals and personalities. Their identity shouldn't be the only interesting thing about them.

10. Make sure you have real, human representation

Often authors will use an alien, robot or sentient animal as a metaphor for a diverse identity. It's a way of including a different, unusual type of character in a story without needing to do research into real minorities. A sexless robot isn't a replacement for an asexual character, and a 'transhuman' character who wants to leave their human body to live on the internet isn't a substitute for a transgender person. Try to include real representation alongside your fantastical creatures.

11. Discuss LGBT+ issues

It isn't a sign of forward-thinking acceptance if LGBT+ characters never discuss their identity with anyone. Not all LGBT+ people are obvious (a trans man in a relationship with a woman will be straight-passing, for example), but if your characters never mention their sexuality, like Albus Dumbledore, it's an indication that they might not feel comfortable enough to discuss it, and are censoring themselves. This is not the sign of a progressive social environment.

Including diversity of all kinds is now one of the first things I think about when starting a story. Since *The Last Beginning* was published in 2016, I've written *The Quiet at the End of the World* (Walker Books 2019), which contains bisexual and trans representation; *The Deep Sea Duke* (Barrington Stoke 2020), a gay romance; and *The Reckless Afterlife of Harriet Stoker* (Walker Books 2020), which has gay, pansexual and bisexual representation. I believe it's an essential foundation for writing a novel in the 21st century. Novels provide a 'mirror' to reflect our own experiences back to us, or a 'window' to offer a view of other people's lives. Deciding to write about LGBT+ protagonists may have been a risk, but it has opened so many doors for me – from speaking on LGBT+-focused panels at festivals and schools to writing for publications about sexuality. But nothing matches the time a young girl attending a signing with her mum told me that she had just come out, and my book was the first she'd ever read about a lesbian like her. Providing a role model for even one teenager made the whole thing worthwhile.

Lauren James is the twice Carnegie-nominated author of young adult science fiction published by Walker Books, including *The Next Together* (2015), *The Last Beginning* (2016) and *The Loneliest Girl in the Universe* (2017). She has also written the YA Book Prize shortlisted *The Quiet at the End of the World* (2019) and *The Reckless Afterlife of Harriet Stoker* (2020), as well as two dyslexia-friendly novellas for Barrington Stoke, *The Starlight Watchmaker* (2019) and *The Deep Sea Duke* (2020). *The Last Beginning* was named one of the best LGBT-inclusive works for kids and young adults by the *Independent*. Lauren is an Arts Council grant recipient and wrote the foreword to *The Bi-ble: An Anthology of Personal Narratives and Essays about Bisexuality* (Monstrous Regiment 2017). She teaches Creative Writing, including workshops on writing diversely, for the University of Coventry, WriteMentor and Writing West Midlands. She is the founder of The Climate Fiction Writers League; her climate-change thriller *Green Rising* (Walker Books) is published in September 2021. Her website is www.laurenejames.co.uk.

Series fiction: writing as part of a team

Writer Lucy Courtenay spills the beans on the profitable world of series fiction: its fictional authors, the publishers and packagers, and the skilled teams of editors and writers that create and produce it.

Once upon a time, a group of editors sat around a table, brainstorming ideas for a new children's series for girls aged 6–9. It needed to be collectable with a strong series identity. One editor put up her hand. 'I had an idea for a series when I was seven years old,' she said. 'It was about seven fairies. One for each colour of the rainbow.'

The series, *Rainbow Magic* by Daisy Meadows, has since spawned over 200 titles. There are mini-series of four or seven interconnected titles within the overarching series which share common themes: the rainbow, the weather, the ocean, popstars and parties and animals, to give a few examples. Sales of the series currently stand at over ten million copies worldwide.

You might assume, on those statistics, that *Rainbow Magic* has made its author rich. It has, but not in the way you might imagine. If you remember, it was an editor's idea. Daisy Meadows herself doesn't exist. She is an amalgam of dozens of different writers and editors, all of whom have taken a share of her profits. She is successful because she is the product of professional, dedicated teams who know how to produce books that children love. The same is true of Lucy Daniels – whose *Animal Ark* series could be said to have started the whole series fiction phenomenon in the 1990s – and Adam Blade, more recently of the *Beast Quest* series. There are plenty of other examples, but these are perhaps the best known. When people first learn this, they are often surprised and baffled. What is the point? they want to know. Why do publishers produce books in this way? Shouldn't they be supporting original talent, promoting original authors?

A fictional author has no rights over a series, which makes that series more flexible and profitable for a publisher or a packager. A fictional author can also write six or more books at the same time, which does wonders for a publisher's production line and (you've guessed it) profits. A fictional author can be designed to fit a niche in the market. They can be given an alphabetically appropriate name to meet a browser's eye level or queue-barge on to the shelf ahead of the direct competition. They can be designed to fit as many commercial platforms as possible, should opportunity present: clothing, online games, stationery. They can also enjoy lives far more exotic than those of real authors. Adam Blade's biography charmingly gives him a pet capuchin monkey called Omar, while Lucy Daniels apparently lives in Yorkshire with Russian Blue cats.

If this seems hard-nosed and commercial, it is. Publishing is a business, and it has to think like a business in the current climate where books fight to be heard above the clamour of YouTube. And, as if the competition weren't tough enough, publishing is an industry with very low margins. A book is cheap compared to a games console; it's cheap compared to a pair of decent socks. In order to turn a profit these days, publishers need to sell a lot of books. A title ideally needs to shift around 10,000 copies a year. More if it's an expensive full-colour book.

Adam Blade, Daisy Meadows and friends sell in these quantities. Their success bankrolls the quieter titles, the books that publishers love but which won't set a financial spreadsheet alight: the standalones, the ones with sad endings and quirky illustrations and unusual production values, the literary prizewinners and the poetry, and all the things which keep a publishing list energised and wide-ranging.

There are dozens of well-known authors now established in their own right who have written packaged series fiction at some point in their careers. Advances aren't high, but the steady stream of royalties and the great and glorious mysteries of PLR income (see *Public Lending Right*, page 417) often mean that the projects are worthwhile. It is a dependable source of income in an unreliable industry. Or 'gas-bill money', as literary agent Lesley Hadcroft once put it.

Publishers are wise to the series-fiction juggernaut and regularly design their own series, commissioning authors and illustrators. But series fiction also originates with packagers. Packagers are an intermediary business. They produce ideas and source writers. But they still have to pitch those ideas to publishers for publication and distribution. In that respect, they are in the same boat as the author rapping on doors to get a commissioning editor's attention. However, publishers take packagers with good track records more seriously than they might a first-time author. Working Partners, for example, has produced some of the biggest series in recent years, including *Rainbow Magic* and *Beast Quest*.

Packagers employ teams of highly experienced editors who have regular meetings to exchange ideas for series, like the meeting described in my opening paragraph. When an idea has been agreed, they will either find a publisher to take it on the strength of the idea (a rare Holy Grail) or, more often, they will ask writers to produce some sample material to fit the concept before presenting it to publishers. The writer is given character names, scenes and complete chapter breakdowns by the packager, with express instructions to fill out the characters and develop the scenes as energetically as possible. There is no fee for sample material, but writers are usually happy to oblige in the knowledge that a little free work can sometimes net a paid project. In terms of cold hard cash, there is usually a small advance if the project is accepted, with around one-third of the royalty charged by the packagers going to the writers.

And here's the good news. Commercial fiction packagers don't need established names to write for them. They simply need writers who can write, and who are able and happy to follow a detailed brief. What's more, they actively recruit them. Go to the website for Working Partners (www.workingpartnersltd.co.uk) and it's hard to miss the great big button shouting APPLY NOW! There are forms to fill in regarding experience and interests, and you are asked to submit some sample writing. Not everyone will make the cut, but if you can turn a phrase and hold a story together, you have as good a chance as anyone else.

It's important to note that packagers are not interested in your magnificent idea about a talking wombat. They are only interested in the mechanics of your writing. In the world of team fiction, it is up to them to produce the ideas. Your job is to fill in the gaps as fluently and excitingly as you can. As such, writing as part of a series team can be a humbling exercise. You might produce your best joke or most moving sentiment in years, but if it doesn't fit the flavour of the series you are writing for, it will be binned as swiftly and unthinkingly as old yoghurt. A successful team writer is the person who can produce writing that fits seamlessly into the whole, not the person with the individual edge.

If your ego can take it, writing series fiction is an incomparable crash course in how to write. I learned a vast amount at the coalface as Lucy Daniels/Adam Blade (yes, I'm both) about pacing, plotting, cliffhangers, world-building, character development and all those other building blocks of successful storytelling. You work closely – often line by line – with expert industry editors, whose practical advice and guidance can feel like a creative writing course without the fee. Instead, miraculously, you are the one who gets paid. There's even a published book to show for your efforts at the end of it all. Writing in this way can be a valuable apprenticeship for the big bad world of author-led fiction that all writers hope lies in their future. Bring an open mind and a flexible pen to the process, and you will find that the craft of writing will lose several of its many mysterious layers.

You will note that producing series fiction in this way is about the writer, not the illustrator. Illustration and design for this type of series fiction lies strictly with the publisher who buys the concept. If you are an illustrator or author-illustrator, the series-fiction route probably isn't for you. If you are a writer: Hello, opportunity!

Lucy Courtenay has been writing children's fiction for 20 years, working as a team writer on series such as *Animal Ark* and *Beast Quest*. She has several series under her own name, most recently *Mermaid School* (2020) for Andersen Press with illustrator Sheena Dempsey, and has also written contemporary teen romances for Hodder Children's. She is the Managing Editor for Fiction at Egmont, a freelance editor of children's fiction for Cornerstones Literary Consultancy and Curtis Brown Creative, and the author of *Get Started in Writing an Illustrated Children's Book* for the *Teach Yourself* series (John Murray 2016). She tweets @LucyCourtenay1.

The long and winding road to publication

Paul Stewart tells how he achieved his childhood dream of becoming a writer, championing illustrated books for children, and shares his experience of the submission process, rejection and success, and finding the ideal collaboration.

When I was at school, other boys in my class wanted to be footballers or train drivers. One wanted to be an astronomer. Me, I didn't have a clue. Possibly a singer in a band. Then, when I was eight, I was given a prize by a music teacher. Her husband worked for Collins and the prize was a book: *The Phantom Tollbooth* by Norton Juster, with illustrations by Jules Feiffer (Collins 1962). She apologized that it was an uncorrected proof, but thought I would love it. She was right. The novel took me to somewhere wonderful and, from that moment on, I knew I wanted to be a writer.

I started work on my own children's novel – as well as drawing the pictures to accompany it. I soon discovered two things: writing was more difficult than I'd thought, while illustrating was beyond me. I abandoned the project, but I never lost that new-found enthusiasm for my future career.

At university I studied English, choosing Lancaster because they offered a unit in Creative Writing. Then I applied for a (then almost unknown) writing MA at UEA, run by Malcolm Bradbury and Angela Carter. By the end of the course I had a folder of 20 short stories and an idea for a novel. One of those stories – a reimagining of Andersen's *The Snow Queen*, called *Ice* – was published in a literary magazine, *Bananas*. I still remember the thrill of reading their letter of acceptance: '… we'd like to use it in the next issue due out at the end of this month.' It was my first short story in print. I'd arrived.

I hadn't, of course. The other 19 stories – separately and as a collection – were not published, and the novel remained an idea. I decided that if it was indeed true that you should write about what you know, then I needed to know more. It was time to go travelling.

This was back before computers. Up until then I had been writing on an olive-green Olympia SM3 – allegedly a portable typewriter, but Charles Atlas would probably have had problems lugging it about. So I bought a lightweight Olivetti Lettera 32 and, following Malcolm's parting comment – 'I don't have the address but it is, like all the other addresses, in the *Writers' & Artists' Yearbook*' – got hold of a copy. Then I set off.

I lived in Greece, Germany and Sri Lanka; I travelled through Europe, India, parts of the Far East, Australia, the US, Kenya. I had numerous jobs – factory packer, security guard, fork-lift truck driver, bank operative, translator, EFL teacher, you name it – and I wrote something every day. The typewriter went everywhere I went, and each time I completed a piece of writing, I would search through the *Yearbook* for an appropriate publication. A growing number of magazines and publishers in the UK received examples of my work.

Most, to their credit, were kind in their rejections. Many offered advice. I always tried to match the manuscript to the publication, though not always successfully. A leading women's magazine responded to one story with the comment: 'The idea was ingenious but … we do try to keep death out of our stories.'

I also discovered that I was receiving letters from people I'd actually heard of: Robert McCrum, Bill Buford, Paul Samwell-Smith (ah, yes … still nurturing dreams of singing in a band, I'd also submitted a cassette of songs for appraisal). The thrill of communicating with famous people was tempered by the fact that they were sending me rejection letters – one after the other they arrived, enough to paper my walls, and I was feeling increasingly disheartened, though unable to stop writing.

It was this optimistic response from Tom Maschler of Jonathan Cape that set me back on track: 'The above said [i.e. the inevitable rejection], I don't like to lose sight of you because frankly I am convinced that you will make it as a serious writer, and think it likely that we would want to publish you in the future if we had the opportunity.'

I was in Sri Lanka in the '80s when civil war broke out. The school I'd been teaching in was closed, and I returned to England to find that the adult novel I'd almost completed over there suddenly seemed flippant and superficial. So I went back to the children's book I'd been musing over for more than two decades and, three months later, *The Thought Domain* was finished. Published by Viking in 1988, it was my first children's novel in print. For a second time, I'd arrived.

Largely on the strength of that published book, I was taken on by a literary agent. This took a lot of the hard work – and inevitable heartache – out of the process of trying to find a home for my scribblings. I now had someone to do it for me. Three years later, a deal was secured for a book I'd been researching. Based on a true story I'd stumbled upon in Kenya, it was accepted by – yes – Jonathan Cape. In 1991, my first adult book, *Trek*, was duly published. I'd *arrived* …

Apart from that one book (and even *Trek* itself reads like a *Boy's Own* tale of gung-ho misadventure), it was children's literature that I pursued. I liked the discipline of writing for a younger audience, as well as the rigour, clarity and sincerity it demands. My early books were our-world-but-with-a-twist fantasies, often starting with a simple What if…? premise. What if there was a dimension where our thoughts were stored? What if a child was born able to communicate with animals? What if a video machine could record our nightmares?

After the publication of *The Thought Domain*, I submitted fresh proposals in the form of the first three chapters of the new work, a rough outline of the entire novel and a working title, in order to gauge whether my primary editor thought it had legs. If he didn't, my agent would send it to other publishers. I had, by this time, given up teaching EFL to devote myself to writing full time. I did not intend to return to the classroom. Not only did I generate my own stories, but I also started taking on commissions – writing to order, following briefs. I wrote football stories, puzzle adventures books, graded readers, horror and fantasy novels; I had short stories published in themed anthologies.

All these pieces of work, even the ones for older children, were illustrated. I considered this a good thing; I still do. There is, I believe, something perverse about using pictures to lure children into the world of books and then, when they've cracked reading, to remove them. It feels almost like a punishment. If I'd been able to I would have illustrated my own texts but, since I wasn't good enough, the next best thing was to find an illustrator I could work closely with.

Books

This proved far from easy. Publishers often keep authors and illustrators apart. An American editor once explained that this was company policy, as authors 'tend to bully illustrators'. A likely story! Had there been closer cooperation between me and my various illustrators, however, maybe a scene I'd written about a boy on a bike being attacked by a slavering dog wouldn't have been depicted by an old bicycle leaning up against a wall. I mentioned my disappointment to my editor and was given a new illustrator – based in Tasmania ...

It was at a publisher's party in London that I first got talking to Chris Riddell. Beforehand, we had seen each other at the nursery our two sons went to, but we'd never spoken. On our train journey home that evening we talked about working together and, after a couple of false starts, produced a picture book about a rabbit and a hedgehog: *A Little Bit of Winter* (Andersen Press). It was my first picture book and my first collaboration.

The year was 1998, and that wasn't the only work we had published ... Working together on *Rabbit and Hedgehog*, we'd both realized how much we enjoyed the collaborative process. Chris drew me a fantasy map entitled The Edge: 'Here's the world,' he said. 'What happens in it?'. It was at this stage that we tested our ability to work together to the max. This wasn't a 12-page spread picture book; it would be a long novel for 11-year-olds, illustrated throughout. There were times when we both wondered whether it would ever be completed, but finally, 15 months later, *Beyond the Deepwoods* (Doubleday 1998) – the first of what would become a 13-part fantasy series, *The Edge Chronicles* – was on the shelves. I'd arrived. Again!

Oddly, the series nearly didn't happen. I'd spoken to my editor at the time about the idea. She thought pictures would make the fantasy look too young. 'Not Chris's pictures', I assured her and, though unconvinced, she suggested I send in the proposal. In the usual way, I printed up the three chapters we'd completed, plus a rough synopsis of the book and outline of the world, and included a wad of Chris's pictures. The envelope came back return of post. Being a writer with a string of rejections under his belt, I naturally assumed they'd dismissed it out of hand as a rubbish idea. It was two days later when a tentative phone enquiry revealed that a youngster on a Youth Opportunities scheme had decided to tidy up the office and sent back all the manuscripts that were lying around – ours included. I've often fantasized about other novels that might have been rejected in the same batch ...

Chris and I have written and illustrated more than 40 books together to date. One of us will come up with a very general idea, then we talk, talk, talk. If that initial idea starts to fly, we set about building a self-contained world – with maps, characters, names, back histories – for the two of us to immerse ourselves in; a place where we discover the stories that will turn into books. A flying box containing an ominous warning became the first *Far-Flung Adventure* – *Fergus Crane* (Doubleday 2004); a Victorian delivery lad with an insight into the supernatural became the *Barnaby Grimes* novels; a trio of aliens on a spurious mission to Earth became *The Blobheads*; humans versus killer robots – *Scavenger*; cowboys and dragons – *Wyrmeweald*.

Since Chris and I come to a piece of work from different perspectives, the text itself goes through many revisions. Although it is immensely enjoyable working with someone else – the writing, the events, the festivals, plus the fact that 'writer's block' is impossible if two of you are working together on a piece – collaboration is never easy. If we had tried working together when we'd first left college, it might not have worked. By the time we did start, I think we were both old enough to realize that the finished item was of far more importance than our individual egos. And certainly, none of the books we produced together could have been done by either of us alone.

Looking back on my writing career, it seems to have been so arbitrary. I kept thinking I'd arrived, only to discover that it was not my final destination – that there was always somewhere else to go to. All I know is that, ever since first realizing that 'I wanted to be a writer', everything has been geared towards making that a possibility. Publishing is currently changing. It is interesting to see that in the latest *Children's Writers' & Artists' Yearbook* there is a section on 'self-publishing'. I wonder where I will arrive at next ...

Paul Stewart is the bestselling author of children's and adult books, co-creator (with Chris Riddell) of the *Edge Chronicles* series, the *Far-Flung Adventures* series including *Fergus Crane* (Gold Smarties Prize winner), *Corby Flood* and *Hugo Pepper* (both Silver Nestlé Prize winners), as well as the *Barnaby Grimes* series (published by Penguin Random House), and the *Free Lance*, *Wyrmeweald* and *Scavenger* trilogies. His other books include two *Muddle Earth* adventures and the *Blobheads* series (for younger readers), published by Macmillan Children's, and the *Rabbit and Hedgehog* picture books (Andersen Press). *Brian the Brave* (Otter-Barry Books 2019), the second picture book he has worked on with illustrator Jane Porter, won the 2020 Derby Children's Book Award. Barrington Stoke has re-issued both the *Free Lance* trilogy and his *Football Mad* series. Paul has written six titles for OUP's *Hero Academy* series and a biography of footballer Alex Oxlade-Chamberlain (Scholastic 2021). For more information see www.edgechronicles.co.uk.

Murderous inventions

Robin Stevens reveals how her murder mystery books, written for her 12-year-old self, have tapped into children's fascination for the nasty parts of life. When so much of a writer's career depends on chance, she stresses the value of following your instinct and of finding exactly the right agent and editor to share one's vision and passion.

It's probably not surprising that I'm an author. I grew up in a family that believed in books, and there's never been a moment of my life that I haven't told stories. I have always known with absolute determination that I wanted to have those stories published – but as a child I also wanted to own a zoo, be a wizard and live inside an Eva Ibbotson novel, and all of those ambitions seemed about as likely as each other. So no, it's not surprising that I'm an author – but all the same, I still wake up delighted every single morning by my bewildering good fortune, because *Murder Most Unladylike* (Corgi 2014) was not supposed to be the book that got me published.

I wrote the first draft of it in 2010, during NaNoWriMo (National Novel Writing Month). I really want to stress that I did not have even the smallest insight into the children's book market at the time. The simple fact was that there was no story that made more sense to me. I had discovered Agatha Christie's murder mysteries aged 12 and was then sent to Cheltenham Ladies' College aged 13. Detective stories and boarding schools are in my blood, and so deciding to write a murder mystery set at a boarding school was as obvious as falling in love – a feeling of: ... *Oh, of course it's you.*

Murder Most Unladylike let me work through all my confused memories of a boarding-school life that was neither as good nor as bad as Enid Blyton had promised it would be. The structure of its detective story felt like a reassuring arm around my shoulders in an adult world which was turning out to be far less organised that I had been expecting. I knew no one else would want this story, but I realised that I really needed it.

That sounds like a fairy tale, but of course the truth of writing an actual book is not a fairy tale at all. I wrote the first 50,000 words in a wild rush unlike anything I'd done before. I had a full-time job at the time, and so I had to hammer out my word count during lunch breaks, early in the morning and late at night. Daisy and Hazel were the only characters who had names, and they spent long scenes just chatting emptily to each other because I didn't know what was supposed to happen next. I wrote that first draft in 30 days, but I spent two years heavily working and reworking my text before I felt confident enough to actually send the book out to agents.

Once I'd decided to do that, though, I truly realised that I had no idea how to go about it. How did people find agents for their books? And, for that matter, what was my book? It was about children who solved a murder – so did that make it for children, or for adults? The only thing I did know was that when I thought about my favourite authors, they wrote for children. So off I marched to a bookshop, bought a copy of the *Writers & Artists' Yearbook 2012* (I still own it) and began to randomly pick children's agents from its pages.

I know now that this was a terrible idea. I should not have just been looking for an agent who works on children's books. I should have looked for children's agents who had specific experience in the type of book I had written. I *should* have been seeking out agents with a specialty in adventurous crime stories that centre on female characters. Hindsight is obviously a wonderful thing, but I wish I could take my younger self by the hand and gently explain to her that genres are important, that picture books are not the same as children's fiction which is not the same as YA fiction, that there are differences between commercial books and prize winners.

Of course, I got a lot of rejections – partly because what I was pitching was a murder mystery for kids, but mostly because I was approaching the wrong people. I have learned since that this is really the cause of almost every 'No' you'll ever get: the people rejecting you are not stupid, or cruel, or wicked – they are simply not obsessed with what you have written. An agent doesn't just need to *like* your book, they need to *love* it with every fibre of their being. They need to be able to spend five, or ten, or twenty years of their lives so wild about it that they will collar random strangers at parties to tell them how brilliant it is. As an author, you shouldn't want an agent that isn't perfect for you – and I was lucky enough (it really was the most incredible luck) to find the perfect agent in Gemma Cooper.

One day I stumbled on a blog post Gemma had written about how much she loved shows like *Murder She Wrote* and *Poirot*, and how she'd love to find a book like that for children – and I suddenly realised where I'd been going wrong. I sent my manuscript to her, not as a random children's agent but as a lover of murder mysteries who understood the children's book market. And it worked. Gemma met me and bowled me over with her enthusiasm for my book and her keen business sense. I signed with her a week later and she helped me trim my flabby and chaotic 80,000-word manuscript (this word count makes me wince to remember it) into a 60,000-word crime novel squarely aimed at children. We sent the book out to UK publishers in the spring of 2013.

Again, we got a lot of rejections. I want to stress that if any author tells you no one ever rejected them, they are either lying or the luckiest human on the planet. *Everyone gets rejected.* J.K. Rowling got rejected *repeatedly*, and the publishers who rejected J.K. Rowling were not idiots. They were just *not the right publishers* for J.K. Rowling. If one of them had bought *Harry Potter*, they would not have cared about it with enough passion to propel it higher into the bestseller charts with every title. It would not have become the global phenomenon that it is, and other authors would not have to spend so much time explaining to their friends and family why they are not as rich as J.K. Rowling.

Only Random House offered for *Murder Most Unladylike*, because only my editor Natalie Doherty was right for my book. She was besotted with it eight years ago, and she's still wild about it today, which is how I know this is true. She believed so passionately that a children's book about murder would sell that she convinced her publicity team and sales team, and they convinced booksellers, and then … the book sold.

I need to be very honest here and say that I was not expecting *Murder Most Unladylike* to do this well. By the time it came out, in June 2014, I was working in children's publishing myself. I knew the size of the market, and I was realistic about a debut author's chances. Most books – and aspiring authors should prepare themselves for this – sell about 1,000 copies. If you are selling more than 100 books a week you are doing very well indeed. If you sell more than 300 copies a week your publishers will have a small party at their desks in your honour. There are a lot of books on the market, and most of them get lost in the noise. And that was what I was prepared for. I'm still pinching myself that this is not what happened.

I was helped by a lot of things that I had nothing to do with: I had a great cover; I got a few nice reviews; my second book was chosen as the Waterstones Children's Book of the

Month in February 2015; and then I won the Waterstones Prize for Younger Fiction in March. I could not have influenced those events, but I'm not sure I would have been able to write a nine-book series today if even one of them had not occurred. A lot of what happens to an author happens outside their orbit – all you can do is react as calmly as possible to the news in your inbox every morning. This lack of control is slightly horrific, and it's a lot to take on board. In fact, what I have realised is that there is only one aspect of my writing career that is within my control – as it is in the control of every writer in the world: the books I write. And I think the content of those books certainly helped me, because the truth is that children *love* thinking about murder.

As adults (or at least, as the good sort of adults), we work very hard to keep children safe. The world is a horrible, stressful place that we struggle to deal with ourselves, and so we put a lot of effort into making sure children do not realise how awful it is until they are grown up and it is too late. Children, on the other hand, spend pretty much every waking hour trying to work out everything they can about the nastiest parts of life. Children are *desperate* to know what adults do to each other, why they behave the way they do, why bad things happen and what those bad things look like.

When you write for children, you have to stop being an adult and remember what it's like to be a child. Children want to understand and explore the darkest places in the universe, and as authors we can let them do that. (We always make sure that we leave behind invisible safety trails, of course, but they're more for us than for our audience). And children also want to be shown that sometimes small is powerful; that kids can be strong and brave and save the day, even when they feel weak and scared; that sometimes adults are good, and sometimes adults are bad; and that it's possible to work out the difference.

I didn't consciously know I was doing all of this when I wrote *Murder Most Unladylike*, of course I didn't. I'm not that clever. But watching how children respond to my series, I've realised this is the key to its success, and to the success of every good children's book ever written. I thought I didn't know who I was writing for, but of course I was lying to myself. I wrote for that 12-year-old Robin who was very grown up but also not grown up at all, who wanted life to be okay and worried that it wasn't, who cared very deeply about crime and justice. This is the only key to success as a children's author that I can pass on to you. *So* much is down to chance and circumstance. You can't hope to give the market what it wants. All you can do is write the book that would have set your younger self's world on fire, and trust that we're all very similar underneath.

Robin Stevens is the author of the *Murder Most Unladylike* mystery series. These include *Murder Most Unladylike* (2014), *First Class Murder* (2016) and most recently *Death Sets Sail* (2020), all published by Puffin, and five *Wells and Wong Mysteries*, reissued by Simon & Schuster. She is also the author of *The Guggenheim Mystery* (Puffin 2017), from an idea and characters by Siobhan Dowd. Her latest books are a collection of *Murder Most Unladylike* short stories, *Once Upon a Crime* (Puffin 2021), and the first book in a new series *The Ministry of Unladylike Activity* (Puffin 2022). Born in California, Robin came to live in England at the age of three. She worked as an editor in children's publishing before becoming a full-time writer. For more information see https://robin-stevens.co.uk, and follow her on Twitter @redbreastedbird.

See also...
● *Writing thrillers for teenagers,* page 163

Self-publishing

Books

From self-publishing to contract

Janey Louise Jones shares her tale of how she successfully self-published her first *Princess Poppy* book, which led to a contract with Random House and huge sales.

My journey to self-publishing

For some children, a bookshop has more delicious flavours than a sweetshop. I was one of those children. When I was a little girl, I wanted to be a writer *and* a princess. So, with my *Princess Poppy* books now selling in their millions around the world, I find myself reflecting on the life experiences which have led to me realising my childhood dreams.

People often say that the story of Princess Poppy, going from a childhood notion, to kitchen table, to self-published success, then on to a Random House contract, is a fairy tale in itself. Perhaps so, but even fairy tales are laced with problems and trials, and self-publishing has been a very challenging experience. I highly recommend starting alone as a way of presenting a vision, proving strong sales and learning the full craft of producing a book – but it is not an easy process.

As a child, I saw witches at my window, and fairies in the moonlight. I loved ballet and the flower fairies, and made petal perfume. I was idealistic and romantic and although I was very loved, I never felt special enough. So I developed a perfectionist streak – always driven to do my very best. I began to express my feelings and identity through words. Like so many book lovers, I loved the physical look and texture of a book as much as what it said to me.

Growing up in the 1970s, it wasn't fashionable to be gender specific for children. Being ultra-feminine was frowned upon as frothy in a way that it isn't now. Did any other girls of the 1970s have a dark brown, checked, floor-length party dress, or was I especially unlucky? I felt a conflict between wanting to be educated, well read and serious on the one hand, and wanting to be a pretty fairy princess, on the other. Could I possibly be 'Fairy Blue Stocking'?

My favourite childhood books included *The Secret Garden*, *Little House on the Prairie*, *Little Women*, *The Children of the New Forest* and *The Diary of Anne Frank*. Later on, at Edinburgh University in the late 1980s, I became intrigued with the concept of 'the novel' and through my love of Victorian and early 20th century authors, I was asked to contribute to *Chambers Dictionary of Literary Characters*. This was my first formal writing experience, which taught me the valuable lesson that when it comes to writing, effort and remuneration are not always commensurate.

Somehow, during my degree course, the wistful child within me resurfaced and I produced a storyboard for a magical, mythical character – Princess Poppy. People often ask me: 'Is she your child, your daughter?' (I have three boys). But no, she isn't my child, she is *me* as a child. I found it difficult to enter adulthood and Poppy beckoned me back to my childish dreams. So, the cliché that one's first and best work is autobiographical is certainly true for me.

Back at this early stage, I lacked confidence and direction, my ideas blowing in the wind – all too easily blown away. (It is so important to hold with your vision at this stage.) In fact, I was convinced by someone that there was no chance of such a character coming to life and so I actually put Poppy to one side for many years. I also heard the well-rehearsed adages that you can't write well until you're at an age when you've experienced life, and also that if you're a proper writer, it will just happen. There might be a bit of truth in these notions.

I became an English teacher, in an Edinburgh girls' school akin to that of Miss Jean Brodie. Then like any self-respecting princess in an ivory tower, I needed to be rescued by a dashing knight. Or, to put it another way, teaching wasn't much fun, and domesticity seemed more appealing. Conveniently, I fell in love with a Royal Marine Commando. This fitted neatly into my script. After a fairy tale wedding, I settled into the real 'grown-up' world of motherhood.

My main writing outlet in this period was a mother's answer to *Bridget Jones's Diary* – Jane Jones's Dairy – a kitchen sink drama of the daily intrigues of the 'stay-at-home-mum' with three infants under four years of age. My years of 'extreme mothering' definitely prepared me for the world of publishing and made my writing much more real and touching.

Curiously, Poppy re-emerged with great vibrancy when my grandmother died in 2000. I wrote about my wonderful granny, Emma Brown, in a eulogy entitled *Pale Pink, Lace and Pearls*. This piece of writing was so well received in my family, that I felt a burst of confidence, which is very elusive when little children take over your world. I finally left behind my own childishness and began to write as an adult, looking into childhood.

I found that Poppy was becoming an 'every girl' princess, instead of a traditional or mythical princess as she had been before. The theme of my Poppy stories is that through family love, every girl is a true princess. I don't like the idea of so-called 'alpha females' – lucky girls who are richer, prettier or smarter – every child has a right to feel equally special. Poppy is innocent, but not old-fashioned. Although I am nostalgic in some ways in my writing, I often think there is something rather brutal about girl stories of the 1950s, as if children were somehow less cherished then, so my books do not hark back. I prefer to reach the children who are growing up, right now, in the 21st century. Childhood is so precious and I want to prolong it, as most mothers do, so I attempt to evoke a world which is both contemporary and yet aspires towards a sweeter way of life.

Self-publishing Princess Poppy

As the Poppy book idea gathered energy, the story became quite focused. The decision to focus on one clear plot was a breakthrough after months of endless bright ideas. I plumped for a birthday party to introduce the heroine, her world and the cast of additional characters. The biggest challenge was with the visual, illustration side of my first book. I collected a roomful of reference materials: wild flowers, books, cards, magazines, fairies, photographs, butterflies, bridesmaids, princesses, tiaras and ballerinas. Slowly and almost imperceptibly, my own sketches became good enough for the trial book. Asking artists to sketch Poppy was potentially tricky. What if the publisher liked the pictures, but not the words, or vice versa? Arrangements between authors and illustrators at pitching stage have to be very clear cut.

I decided to self-publish when I became frustrated with the slow ways of the publishing world. I had sent off a few versions of Poppy, as well as some other ideas, and I'd had one helpful phone call from a publisher and some other words of encouragement – but no deal was in sight. I was in the Lake District when I realised that Beatrix Potter had self-published, along with many other stars such as Virginia Woolf, John Grisham and James

Joyce. I decided there and then to speed up my career by producing the book as I imagined it. I had every confidence of it selling well. I dismissed the idea of using a firm specialising in self-publishing, even though some are perfectly respectable because I believed, and still do, that you can project manage it yourself and use your budget on strong production values instead of a middle-person.

There is something about making the financial investment which proves one's serious intentions: you can produce your book with plenty of trial copies for the cost of a holiday. I broke the self-publishing process down into the following ten-point battle plan:

1. Write a good, fast-paced story of the right length for your audience. (Ask for a few objective opinions. If there is not one common criticism, ignore all negative comments.) Remember: theme, character, plot and dialogue are the building blocks of any story.

2. Edit it objectively. (Ask a friend if necessary.) Know when to let go of words. Ask yourself if it is truly original. Innovate, don't imitate.

3. Illustrate it if it's a picture book. (Ask an artist to do this, either for a fee or as part of the pitch.)

4. Think of a wonderful jacket design, explore fonts, imagery and message.

5. Design and lay out the pages. (Use a professional designer who will also advise on a printer.)

6. Have it printed in sensible quantities. Use a printer who has produced 'perfect bound' books before, i.e. *not* those stapled down the spine, which would look amateurish. Test the market with a few hundred copies.

7. Hand-sell it to bookshops, both chains and independents.

8. Have it distributed. Ensure that the distributor has relationships with all the national chains.

9. Promote it to get it noticed (radio, television, articles).

10. Offer to do events and festivals to ensure ongoing sales.

After self-publishing: getting the deal and beyond

The first Princess Poppy book sold 40,000 copies in six months, which meant that the concept was noticed in the trade. All the main bookseller chains, as well as independents, were incredibly supportive. I was invited to visit headquarters of booksellers and soon the chains were distributing the book to their branches. All of this relied on good distribution, which is hard to find with only one title, but persistence is the key.

I paid for professional public relations which helped a lot, but is not essential. I began to be invited to book parties across Edinburgh and found that the publishing reps from large publishing houses were very willing to help. They took news of my book to London offices and soon I was being invited to these for meetings. At this point, I produced a second book, and a doll, which showed the series potential of the Princess Poppy concept. But it was all getting too much for one person. I was running a business now, with printers to liaise with as well as the press, the distributors and events co-ordinators. When two offers for Poppy came in on my newly set up email, I didn't have to think twice about accepting.

I have been lucky enough to have a great relationship with my editor and publisher. Working with a major publisher requires the right amount of compromise, without losing personal direction and control. I believe in professional standards and feel that being part of an arts-based work cycle is no excuse for being chaotic. I always deliver texts on time and try not to be needlessly awkward or diva-ish. The author is simply a bit-part player in the successful production of a book. If you are incredibly hung up on ownership of rights, trademarks and the like, then self-publishing really might be best for you. Ironically, once you are published by a traditional publisher, you have to let all of that go.

I wouldn't change the way I did it, as I understand the whole world of publishing much more than I would have done otherwise. And I may never have got the deal at all, without self-publishing first. For those who say it is vain to self-publish, I would say, yes it is, as is the whole idea of wanting others to pay for your written words. But when one's main pleasure in life is reading, it makes perfect sense to create stories for others to enjoy. I can think of no better career, and when fan letters drop through the door, the whole process is complete.

Janey Louise Jones continues to write the *Princess Poppy* series, the latest title is *Princess Poppy: Adore our Animals!* (Eden Copper 2021). Her latest title for tweens is *Anushka* (Eden Copper 2021). Her *Superfairies* series was published in the USA (Capstone Books) and in the UK. Follow Janey on Twitter @janeyjones23.

See also...

Books

An indie's journey to award-winning success

Setting aside the idea of her novel being published traditionally, Griselda Heppel found the high standards and professionalism of a self-publishing company gave her the best of both worlds.

It used to be so simple. Aspiring writers had two options: to land a contract with a traditional publishing house or, failing that, pay for publication themselves, thus earning the undying scorn of the literary world for anyone resorting to the so-called 'vanity press'. A book not published in the usual way must, the argument went, by definition be badly written, poorly edited and have no appeal to anyone but the writer and their own loyal family.

Well, if that was true once it isn't anymore. In today's competitive publishing world it is extremely hard for unknown authors to be taken on by traditional firms. Where once an editor might have had time to nurture a new talent, now financial realities demand strong projected sales that makes such slow-burn methods increasingly unlikely. The new book and the new author have to be winners from the word go and that is a big ask, especially if your book does something no one has ever tried before.

Like creating a children's version of Dante's *Inferno*, for instance.

I've always loved stories that draw on great myths and epics: *The Iliad* and *The Odyssey*, Greek and Roman legends, Norse sagas, King Arthur and Robin Hood. Classical works provide rich narrative material and form the basis for many of the best books ever written for children. Yet the *Inferno*, in which Dante imagines himself descending into ever darker circles of Hades, having to deal with Cerberus, Harpies, Minotaur, Furies – a gold mine of fantasy and adventure if ever there was one – seems to have been neglected in this respect, and I was determined to put that right. Dante became 12-year-old Ante (Antonia) who finds herself plunged on this hellish journey, accompanied by her arch enemy, Florence, and a mysterious 13-year-old boy called Gil (Virgil – a reference to the Roman poet who is Dante's guide).

When I sent the completed manuscript to publishers and agents, it attracted some interest but ultimately no offers. Some of the rejection letters contained useful feedback, for which I was grateful. Others told me my story was too complicated for children; they'd be confused by the combined themes of Hell, mythical creatures and the First World War (an important element in *Ante's Inferno*). I knew they were wrong about this. My book had already been read by 40 or so children, aged 9–16 years, not one of whom had any difficulty in understanding it, and the fact that young people's abilities can still be so underestimated frankly puzzled me.

It struck me that however much I rewrote *Ante's Inferno*, as an unknown author I'd never get past this conservative view from mainstream publishing companies. I realised that if I wanted to see my book in print, I'd have to get on with it myself. I knew it would be hard but there were advantages: how and when the book was published would be up to me, I could commission my own cover illustration and I'd have the final say on design, print and production. I'd be in control.

The rapid growth in recent years of ways in which to self-publish has opened up a number of choices to authors. I was determined that *Ante's Inferno* should be a top-quality book, well-designed with high production values. There'd be an ebook version, of course, but for children the act of holding, feeling, smelling a book is a vital part of their enjoyment (actually, it is for me too); *Ante's Inferno* should be a pleasure to pick up in bookshops, where it wouldn't look out of place among all the traditionally published titles, and retailers should be able to order it from their wholesalers in the usual way. In short, what I needed was an established publishing company that would do a professional job.

Google 'self-publishing' and you'll come up with a bewildering array of companies offering services. Some of these are very basic and very cheap and, not surprisingly, their books look it. But there are others whose high standards mean their products can compete with the best of any published books. I settled on Matador, which, as an imprint of trade publishing company Troubador, offers partnership services to authors supported by professional expertise in copy-editing, design, production, marketing and distribution fields. 'For authors whose work we are happy to publish,' says Matador on its home page, 'we will undertake as much or as little of the publishing process as required.'

And there you have it: the gulf between self-publishing and the low quality control associated with the vanity press. Submitting your manuscript to Matador does not guarantee publication. Matador may offer partnerships in which authors take on financial risk, but they will only do so if they consider the books to be of a high enough standard. If not, an author will be advised to rework the manuscript, perhaps after undergoing a critical assessment from a literary consultancy or a professional editor. A significant proportion of all books offered to Matador are rejected in this way.

This brings me to the heart of getting your book published by whatever method, traditional or independent: the quality of the book itself. I rewrote *Ante's Inferno* many times, responding to feedback from literary agents, editors and writing mentors, before sending it to Cornerstones Literary Consultancy for a critique. Their editorial report was tough and hard-hitting. It was difficult criticism to take on board but it proved invaluable, enabling me to resolve structural issues and tighten up the writing. By the time I submitted *Ante's Inferno* to Matador, it had already gone through a rigorous editorial process and was a much better book as a result.

Once taken on by Matador, I could have left it all to them but I didn't want to. For the cover, I commissioned Hilary Paynter, a top wood engraver, to create a dark and menacing image of the path down to Hell, reminiscent of the haunting illustrations of Dante's *Inferno* by Gustave Doré. Designer Pete Lawrence used the wood engraving to create an atmospheric, eye-catching cover. With my publisher, I had input, too, the page design and typeface used but was glad for them to take charge of production, printing, distribution and marketing. I had no illusions that bookshops throughout the UK would instantly stock *Ante's Inferno* – the thousands of new children's titles that appear every year are all fighting for the same space, after all – but Matador would present them with every opportunity to do so.

Next came the hard bit: promotion. Unless you have the full weight – and budget – of a large firm's publicity department, it is extremely difficult to get your book noticed by the media. Even authors signed by traditional publishing companies can be disappointed to find the funds allocated to publicising their book are relatively small. Increasingly they are expected to promote themselves, in a way not demanded before (and often contrary to their nature – not all authors are confident extroverts!). It's not enough just to write books, it seems; you need to establish an online presence by blogging, tweeting and updating Facebook and website pages with amusing snippets (not just sales pitches) to charm and entertain potential readers. All this can be fun, but it's also time-consuming, not to mention stressful (am I tweeting/blogging/facebooking enough?).

I entered this world of social media with some trepidation but found it a great way of connecting with other writers, readers, agents and editors and making new friends, as well as spreading the word about *Ante's Inferno* and garnering a good number of reviews. In addition, my publishers ran a publicity campaign which achieved a decent amount of press coverage – local, mainly, but also some on a national level – on radio programmes, in newspapers and magazines. Eager to share my interest in Dante with children, I put together an illustrated talk about the themes that inspired *Ante's Inferno*. This goes down extremely well in schools (Years 5–8) and I fit in a few school visits every term.

It was a wonderful feeling when *Ante's Inferno* won a Silver in the Wishing Shelf Awards (www.thewsa.co.uk), swiftly followed by – even more exciting – the Children's category of the People's Book Prize (www.peoplesbookprize.com). Both competitions are judged exclusively by readers: the Wishing Shelf Awards by schoolchildren alone, and the People's Book Prize by any member of the public, either online or through their local library. For me it was a solid endorsement, not just of *Ante's Inferno*, but of the independent publishing method I'd gone for.

There are downsides, however. Partnership publishing has been a terrific experience but there's no disguising the amount of time and effort it takes up, arguably leaving less of both for the writing itself. A well-known, mainstream firm can inevitably give a book wider exposure than *Ante's Inferno* has achieved (though selling out its first 1,000 copy print run in eight months isn't bad).

Still, I have a tried and trusted model that I know works. With my next book, *The Tragickall History of Henry Fowst* (Matador 2015) I engaged the same dream team of Hilary Paynter and Pete Lawrence to come up with a brilliantly spooky cover for this tale of a 13-year-old boy who – somewhat unwisely – makes a pact with a demon. Hilary Paynter and Pete Lawrence have created the jacket for *The Fall of a Sparrow* (Matador, 2021), its warm, summery atmosphere deftly hinting at a dark mystery lurking just below the surface.

With each new title, the thrill of seeing my vision for the book translated into reality remains as strong as ever. So strong in fact that, while as a writer I'll always be open to the possibility of mainstream publishing, it would take a very good offer to tempt me.

Perhaps even a Faustian pact.

Hm, now there's an idea …

Griselda Heppel read English at Cambridge and worked in publishing before moving to Oxford with her husband to bring up their four children. Her first book, *Ante's Inferno* (Matador 2012) won the People's Book Prize and a Silver Wishing Shelf Award. In 2017 it underwent a special reprint for the Passchendaele Centenary 1917– 2017. Her other novels include *The Tragickall History of Henry Fowst* (2015) and *The Fall of a Sparrow* (2021), both published by Matador. Find out more at www.griseldaheppel.com.

See also...
- *From self-publishing to contract*, page 190
- *What do self-publishing providers offer?*, page 197
- *Editorial services and self-publishing providers*, page 208

What do self-publishing providers offer?

Jeremy Thompson presents the options for engaging an author services company.

Now that self-publishing is widely accepted and it is easier to do it than ever before, authors are presented with a broader range of opportunities to deliver their book or ebook to readers. This brings with it a greater responsibility to you, the author and publisher, to make the right choices for your publishing project. The various options for self-publishing may seem bewildering at first, and each has their pros and cons. But some relatively simple research will prove invaluable in ensuring you make the right choices for your book.

Motivation influences method

There are many reasons why authors choose to self-publish, and contrary to popular belief, the decision to do so is not always motivated by the aspiration to be a bestselling novelist. That is only one reason; others include the wish to impart knowledge to a wider audience; the desire to publish a specialist book with a relatively small target audience; the fulfilment of a hobby; publishing as part of a business or charity; and yes, vanity (a wish to see one's name on a book cover is fine, as long as you have realistic expectations of your work).

Understanding why you are self-publishing is important, as the reasons for doing so can help point to the best way in which to go about it. For example, if you are publishing simply for pleasure, and have few expectations that your book will 'set the world alight', then you'd be wise not to invest in a large number of copies; using 'print on demand' (POD) or producing an ebook could be a good way forward. If you have a book that you're publishing to give away or sell as part of your business to a relatively captive audience, then a short print run of a few hundred copies might be wise. If you want your novel to reach as many readers as possible and to sell it widely, you'll need to have physical copies to get into the retail supply chain and in front of potential readers, so opt for a longer print run of perhaps 500 or more. The more copies you print, the greater the economies of scale.

Decisions on how to self-publish are often influenced by the money you are prepared to invest in (and risk on) your project. Making a decision on what self-publishing route to take based on financial grounds alone is fine, as long as you understand the implications of that decision. For example, as the name implies, print-on-demand (POD) books are only printed when someone actually places an order for a copy; there are no physical copies available to sell. As POD books are largely sold on a 'firm sale' basis, bookshops will rarely stock them, so most POD sales will be made through online retailers. This is particularly the case when authors publish with Amazon KDP…bookshops are very reluctant to source books from Amazon! In addition, as the POD unit print cost is higher than if a quantity of books are printed in one go, the retail price of a book is likely to be fairly high to cover the print cost and retailer's discount, and make you some profit. Authors often assume that POD is some miracle form of low-cost book publishing, but if that were so, why don't major commercial publishers distribute all of their books in this way? The disadvantages of POD include limited retail distribution and high print cost; these can work for many types of book, like specialist non-fiction titles or academic books that command high cover prices, but it can be difficult to make it cost-effective for fiction or children's books.

At the other end of the scale, printing 3,000 copies of a novel will only pay off if you can get that book onto the retailers' shelves and in front of potential readers, or if you have some other form of 'captive' readership that you can reach with your marketing. Distribution to retailers works largely on the 'sale or return' model, using distribution companies and sales teams to sell new books to bookshops (and bookshops are still the largest sellers of books in the UK). If you can't get your book into the bookshop distribution chain, you are limiting the prospect of selling your 3,000 copies, and money tied up in unsaleable stock is money wasted.

Publishing an ebook is an increasingly popular method of self-publishing, but it too has its pros and cons. On the up side, it can be done very cheaply and quickly; the flip side is that, as hundreds of new ebooks are published each day, how do you get yours noticed? Authors who publish an ebook alone need to spend a lot of time and effort on getting noticed, and sadly most will rarely sell a great number of copies.

As a self-publisher, you need to make sure you understand the limitations of each form of publishing method before you decide on the best route for your book. It can make the difference between success or failure for your book before it's even produced.

Choosing an author services company

In its truest sense, self-publishing means that you as author undertake all the processes undertaken by a commercial publisher to bring a book to market: editing, design, production, marketing, promotion and distribution. If you're multi-talented and have a lot of spare time, then you may want to do all of these things yourself, but for most authors it's a question of contracting an author services company to carry out some or all of the tasks required. From the start it should be understood that most author services companies make their money by selling their services to you as the author; very few have a lot of market knowledge and even fewer offer any real form of active marketing or have bookshop distribution. Choosing the right company to work with is crucial in ensuring that your self-publishing expectations stand a chance of being met. Author services companies come in various guises, but they can broadly be broken into three categories:

• **DIY POD services.** You upload your manuscript and cover design, and your book (or ebook) is simply published 'as is'. It's relatively cheap, and great if you are not too concerned about the design quality and POD or electronic distribution is what you want.

• **Assisted services companies.** These companies offer typesetting and cover design, and perhaps some limited distribution and marketing options. If you're looking for a better product and some basic help in selling your book then this could be right for you.

• **Full service companies.** These suppliers tend to work at the better quality end of the self-publishing market, offering authoritative advice, bespoke design, active trade and media marketing and, in a couple of cases, real bookshop distribution options.

In addition, there is a plethora of companies and individuals offering component parts of the book production and marketing process, such as copy-editing, proofreading, cover design, public relations, etc.

The key for any self-publisher in choosing a company to work with is research. Having decided why you are self-publishing and set your expectations from doing so, the next step is to see who offers what, and at what cost, and to match the right company with what you are seeking. A search on the internet for 'self-publishing' will present you with many choices, so explore the company websites, compare what is being offered, and generally get a feel for what each says they do. Are they just selling services to authors, or are they selling their authors' books? Do they offer active marketing or just 'marketing advice'? Don't take their word for it, though: seek independent advice from other authors or independent industry commentators – there are three sources of reliable, independent information on self-publishing service providers: this *Yearbook* and associated website (www.writersandartists.co.uk); ALLi (see page 355); and the Independent Publishing Magazine (www.theindependentpublishingmagazine.com), which gives authoritative reviews of self-publishing companies and an annual ranking of the best (and worst) based upon author feedback.

Having identified some companies that look as if they will help you meet your publishing expectations, you need to establish how much it will cost. Get detailed quotations from companies and compare like-for-like. Ask questions of those companies if anything is in doubt: ask to see a contract; ask for a sample of their product (many companies still produce terrible quality books!). Time spent at this stage will ensure that you get a good feel for the company you're considering working with, and that can be the difference between a happy self-publishing experience and a disastrous one.

Marketing and distribution

Authors often concentrate on producing a book or ebook and ignore the part of the equation that actually sells the book. Examine carefully what author services companies offer. Distribution includes all the processes involved in getting a book or ebook in front of potential readers, but many companies offer simply a limited, online-only service. Marketing is the process of alerting both the media (whether in print, on air or online) and potential readers that a book is available. Similarly, very few companies spend much effort to actively market their authors' work. The right choice of marketing and distribution service can make or break a book even before production has started.

As the author and self-publisher, you must decide how the world will find out about your book, and how to get it into the hands of readers. You will need to make decisions on whether POD distribution or wider retail distribution is required; whether the marketing services offered by an author services company are enough for your book; or if a public relations company might be the way forward. Remember, this is 'self'-publishing, so it is up to you to make the right choices for yourself.

A brave new world

Self-publishing offers authors a host of opportunities to make their work available to readers. Making the right decisions to meet your expectations for your book or ebook in the early stages of the publishing process will pay dividends. Understand your motivations; research the production options well; understand distribution choices; give marketing the importance it requires; and above all, enjoy your self-publishing experience.

Jeremy Thompson FRSA founded Troubador Publishing (www.troubador.co.uk) in 1996 and started the Matador (www.troubador.co.uk/matador) self-publishing imprint in 1999, which has since helped over 10,000 authors to self-publish. Troubador also runs the annual Self-Publishing Conference and holds a 'Self-Publishing Experience' Day at its offices near Leicester. Troubador also runs Indie-Go (www.indie-go.co.uk), offering component author services, and in 2015 it acquired The Book Guild Ltd, an independent partnership publisher. Jeremy was elected as a Fellow of the Royal Academy of Arts in 2019 in recognition of his work in independent publishing.

How to hire a freelance editor

Jenny Bowman has helpful advice for the self-publishing author on how to set about hiring the ideal editor. She clarifies what is involved in the editorial process, what to look for in an editor and why their role is essential in ensuring your book is perfectly polished and ready for publication.

Self-publishing has become a widely accepted avenue for publishing children's books, from picture books to young adult novels. In contrast to the traditional way of publishing a book, self-published authors can bypass the need for an agent, as well as maintain complete creative control of their manuscript from start to finish. Self-publishing can be particularly attractive to picture book authors who prefer to select and collaborate with their illustrators.

There are many reasons an author might decide to self-publish their book: maybe they have researched the traditional route and decided it's just not the path they want to take; they might be writing to fill a need for a specific audience; or they may plan to write just one book. Being clear on motivation for self-publishing is important and will guide you through every step of the process. Since self-published books forgo the rigorous editing performed when a book is acquired by a publisher, hiring a freelance editor is a must. It's important to understand the different types of editorial services available to authors, and the order in which they are typically employed.

Types of editing

1. Developmental editing

Developmental editing is the first editing step; it is a comprehensive process that reviews the major backbone of a manuscript while also looking at the details, and then at how it all works together. Developmental editors will evaluate your manuscript as a whole and will offer relevant writing advice, constructive criticism and – if they're good – words of encouragement. Developmental editors typically evaluate:

• the book's core intentions and goals;
• the underlying premise and the story;
• character development and dialogue;
• narrative voice;
• the book's overall pacing, style and language;
• the age of the readership in relationship to themes and category.

Look for someone who is willing to offer a fluid working relationship and who will communicate openly on major changes. Out of all the editors you may hire, you will do the most rigorous revisions while working with your developmental editor.

2. Copy-editing

A copy-editor will check your manuscript making sure the syntax is smooth and the writing adheres to the conventions of grammar. They will spot minor inconsistencies in plot and story or character development, and comment on readability. They will bring your manuscript to a professional level before you format your book in preparation for a proofread and print. Copy-editors typically evaluate:

• overall readability;
• grammatical conventions and punctuation;
• consistency in content layout, such as chapters or sections, and content delivery;

• syntax and sentence structure;
• overall style and tone of the manuscript.

3. Proofreading

A proofreader is the detail-oriented, 'fan-of-the-red-pen' person whose job it is to make sure your book is error-free. Both you and your editor will know your manuscript inside and out; this means that errors such as simple grammar, formatting and spelling mistakes might easily be overlooked. Hiring a proofreader is an absolute must for authors wishing to self-publish. Many self-published authors even hire two proofreaders before going to print. Proofreaders typically:
• evaluate and correct grammar, typos and punctuation;
• ensure the document is error-free and consistent in style;
• review formatting and ensure that the book is ready for print.

Hiring an editor

There are hundreds of children's book editors available, and the range of editorial services is wide. With so many editors available, how do you know which one to choose? To start, select an editor who specialises in writing for children. You want someone who understands the complex category systems within the umbrella of children's books. This is especially important when you are at the developmental stage, or if you are unsure which category your children's book falls within. Are you writing a picture book, chapter book or easy reader? Is your book for middle-grade readers or young adults? How many words should your book have in order to be age-appropriate? What themes or topics are typically relevant? These are some of the more generalised questions your developmental editor can answer for you.

Where to start

A Google search for a children's book editor is the best place to start. Look for an editor who is specialised, or who has edited books similar to your own. An easy way to do this is to open a few of your favourites in tabs and check out each editor's website and 'About me' section. Take a look at their testimonials; see if any stand out to you.

Another resource to check out are the acknowledgements in your favourite children's book. For example, if you're writing a middle-grade novel, hop to the back of your most recent read and see who the author thanked. Even traditionally published authors hire freelance editors, and they often return to these same editors time and again. This is a fantastic way to narrow your search down stylistically.

Check out the Editorial Freelancers Association (EFA) – a vetted, members-only organisation. The EFA website (www.the-efa.org) has a user-friendly search tool for narrowing down your selections, and provides information such as years worked in editing and editor bios, all in one place. The UK equivalent is the Chartered Institute of Editing and Proofreading (CIEP), which includes a Directory of contacts, www.ciep.uk/directory. Use the *Children's Writers' & Artists' Yearbook*, or *The Book* from the Society of Children's Book Writers and Illustrators (SCBWI; see page 356). Both publications have listings for editorial services.

What to look for in an editor

Once you have a list of prospective editors, study their websites to narrow down your choices. Some qualifications you might look for are:
• How long have they been editing?

• Have they edited books similar to your own?
• What do their testimonials say?
• What are their rates, if published online?
• Besides a list of services, does their website offer helpful resources for new and emerging authors?
• Is there helpful information about self-publishing children's books?

When to contact an editor

Once you have narrowed down your options to a few editors, get in touch with them. If they have a contact form on their website, use it to submit the information they need to offer a quote on services, rates and timeline. If not, send your core questions via email. You might ask the following:
• What editing services will you provide?
• Do you have experience of editing books in my category and/or genre?
• What are your rates?
• What is your turnaround time and when are you available to start?
• Do you offer an opportunity for a follow-up call?

Communicating via email is often enough to get your questions answered. If not, find out if the editor is willing to talk with you about your project before being hired. Most editors will include the opportunity to chat at some point during the process. Be mindful of the time you are requesting; if you have a 500-word manuscript that needs a copy-edit, it's unrealistic to ask a freelance editor to attend an hour-long interview before getting hired.

Key points to remember
Budget

Be up-front about your budget. Most freelance editors publish their fees online, so you can get a sense of what you'll be spending. If you find that your dream editor, and their rates, are out of reach, think twice before asking for a discount, as this may come across as devaluing the freelancer's qualifications and expertise. Rather, be proactive. Ask if the editor will consider a payment plan, or look for another editor who fits your budget.

Timing

Plan ahead. Many freelance editors are booked well in advance. If you have a tight deadline, or you have prearranged other services such as illustrations, or have a launch date goal in mind, be sure to get your editor booked. Expect to wait a month or more once you find your editor.

About sample edits

The editor's web presence, testimonials and credentials should be enough to qualify them for hire. It's unrealistic to ask for a sample edit. Sample edits are not reflective of the multiple manuscript reviews, suggested rewrites, inline edits and comments that are part of a full edit. It's equally unrealistic to ask an editor to send a sample of something they've previously edited, since most editors work under an agreement of confidentiality with their authors.

What to expect after hire

Typically, editors will outline the process – from hire to project completion – by email. After you initiate hire, you should receive a comprehensive contract that outlines the entire process. Most editors do line edits using 'track changes' in MS Word. Certainly with a developmental edit, and sometimes with a copy-edit and proofread, you will receive an editorial assessment of the document as well; this will review any problem areas, with steps to tackle revisions, and will also point out the areas that are really strong and working well. While editing your manuscript, editors will reach out if any pressing questions come up. When editing is complete, they will provide an in-depth review of their recommendations and answer any questions you may have.

Special considerations for picture book writers

• Picture books take a surprising amount of work – every word matters. The overall structure of the book, as well as specific placement of each word or sentence, each refrain, really matters. You will want to hire an editor who has unique experience in editing picture books.

• Is your book in rhyme? If so, hire an editor who is an old hand with poetry. Your rhyme and metre will need to be deliberately crafted with purpose. Today's market is choosy when it comes to rhyming picture books; there is definitely an art to writing a successful one.

• Hire your editor *before* you commission illustrations. Quality illustrations are pricey. How heartbreaking it is when an author completes illustrations, only to realise during the editing process that major changes are needed to their book which make those illustrations obsolete. Hire your illustrator when all editing, apart from the final proofread, is complete.

Finding an editor to collaborate with is an essential step in producing a polished and complete book for publication. It can also be a rewarding learning experience, especially at the developmental stage, when it comes to the craft of writing for kids. Self-publishing your children's book is an exciting path to follow, with one of the most satisfying endings – the joy of holding your first printed book, and then revisiting that feeling every time someone reads your story. Happy writing!

Jenny Bowman is a creative writer and children's book editor with experience editing books on the *New York Times* bestseller list, and books with international acclaim. Having edited over 100 books for children to young adults, Jenny is well-versed in all genres of children's literature. She is an active member of the EFA, the Society for Children's Books Writers and Illustrators, the Children's Literature Association, and participates annually in both the 12x12 Picture Book Challenge and Inked Voices. Her website is www.jennybowman.com.

The hybrid author: you can do it all – your way!

Shelli R. Johannes explains what it is to be a hybrid author, explores the pros and cons of traditional publishing and self-publishing, and describes how an author can enjoy the best of both worlds.

My journey

When I was a little girl, I never believed there was only one way of doing things. So I grew up trying to accomplish things in a different way. As you can imagine, my parents weren't always thrilled about me 'thinking outside the box'. Years later, nothing has changed. I feel the same way about publishing. As a writer, I was always told there was a right way and a wrong way to break down walls in the secret society of publishing. Like many writers, I stood outside the closed doors to publishing, banging my head against invisible barriers. If I couldn't find my way in, I decided I would carve my own passage.

In 2011, when I first decided to self-publish, this was still considered to be 'taboo' in the industry. To many, taking that route meant I was cheating the system – that maybe I wasn't good enough to barge through the front door of traditional publishing. In my heart, I knew that wasn't true. I had an agent who loved my writing. My books had made it to acquisitions at several publishing houses. But as many of you know, writing is like any art – it's subjective and it's competitive. At any given time, there are hundreds of other manuscripts vying for that same opening at a publishing house. So I thought maybe self-publishing was my way.

Eventually, I ended up selling over 200,000 ebooks of my *Nature of Grace* series. I have self-published five books to date and plan to continue. Not only did I sell well, but I also loved the whole process – the control in creating my own covers, the excitement of watching my sales numbers, choosing where and when I wanted to publish. It was like nurturing my own books. However, although I loved it, I still wanted to publish in the traditional way because I wanted the experience of working with a big publisher. Again, I was told I had to choose – it was one way or the other. In addition to self-publishing, so far I have sold twelve children's books to Greenwillow Books, HarperCollins Children's Book and Philomel, an imprint of Penguin.

Self-publishing: pros and cons

PROS
- control over process
- retain rights
- higher royalties
- digital printing options
- fast to market
- timely topics

CONS
- minimal distribution
- stigma
- tough marketing
- publishing expense
- author handles business end-to-end
- hard to find direct readers

Until recently, there wasn't a word or even a title for authors who straddled both sides of the great divide. Now, we call it *hybrid publishing*.

What is a hybrid author?

A hybrid author is someone who publishes through many different media. For example, hybrid authors can self-publish some books while selling other books to a traditional publisher. I realized publishing doesn't have to be one way or the other. For a long time, I wavered between playing them all at once or deciding which one to play first. With so many pros and cons to each channel, everything was exciting and new.

So, what are the pros and cons of being a hybrid author? In general, a hybrid author gets the benefits of the traditional advance, professional editing, distribution and marketing. But they also get the self-publishing benefit of creative control, flexible pricing, and the opportunity to write and publish timely titles for immediate earnings (see boxes: *Self-publishing/Traditional publishing: pros and cons*).

How to be a successful hybrid author

As authors, we have no reason to stay in one lane. We can do it all. But it's important for an author to understand what he or she is getting into and how to do it right. Before you dive into hybrid publishing, it's important to research – do your homework and seek advice. Here are a few points to keep in mind when preparing your action plan:

1. Write an amazing book

Always have a book in your queue. I like to write for my agent first because the traditional path tends to be much slower than the self-publishing channel. Once my book is on submission or in my agent's hands, I work on developing my own novels for self-publishing. This way, I'm always working on something that can move my career forward. It's also critical to 'go for high-quality' in all your writing. Every piece of work should be your absolute best. Being a hybrid author isn't a short cut to writing, it's a short cut to market. So write the best book possible and *then* figure out how to publish it. Bad writing doesn't sell in *any* market or in any channel – no matter how you publish.

2. Be prepared to run a business

To be a successful hybrid author, you have to be prepared to manage your writing as a business. You will have to juggle many different processes at the same time. Traditional publishing will include the basics in editing and marketing; in self-publishing, you have to do those things too, but self-publishing also demands a business acumen and an entrepreneurial spirit to keep everything moving forward. You will be expected to learn about and manage the production of the book (covers, editing, jacket copy, etc), plus the business side of publishing such as inventory, sales, distribution, finances, marketing and much more. Some people don't mind this part – but it can be overwhelming at times. It also takes away from your writing time, so you need to be efficient and organised. Find out what works for you. Being a hybrid author requires a different business mindset from traditional publishing because you have to juggle simultaneous processes across multiple

Traditional publishing: pros and cons
PROS
• advance
• team makes book
• mass print distribution
• validated
• access to TV, film, etc
• access to reviewers
CONS
• sells rights
• little marketing
• lower royalty
• slower to market
• risk averse in type of book published
• decreasing revenue

channels. Don't be scared – it can be done, but it is a tough process. You will have to try new things, not be afraid of failing and take risks. It's all part of the process.

3. Do yourself a favour and get an agent!

If you think you are going to be a hybrid author, I believe you need to get an agent. Agents can help you figure out which books are best for each publishing path. They know the market. They can also help you navigate some of the other tasks, like contract negotiation and managing other rights – foreign, subsidiary, etc. Of course, you need an agent who believes in the hybrid model. You must find the right agent/agency that truly believes there are viable sales on both publishing paths. Make sure they are experienced in digital publishing and open to any and all opportunities that arise. Eight years ago, I was lucky enough

How an agent can help you succeed:
• **Channel management** – Helps decide which path is best for your books.
• **Contract negotiation** – Reviews any issues that might surface.
• **Editorial advice** – Provides manuscript revisions and edits.
• **Market knowledge** – Gives insight into the various markets/channels.
• **Networking** – Has access to a variety of resources.
• **Rights management** – Can facilitate the sale of other rights.
• **Trusted partner** – Offers advice on whole career and portfolio.

to find my agent Lara Perkins at Andrea Brown Literary Agency at a conference; she understood and valued the possibilities of the self-publishing model. You need someone on your side, and someone who has your best interest and career in mind. Trust me, agents are worth their 15%, and then some! (see box *How an agent can help you succeed*).

4. Make a book plan

Decide which books you want to publish traditionally and which ones you want to keep for yourself. My agent helps me choose the best path for each book idea we discuss. Because, let's face it, self-publishing doesn't work for all books, and traditional publishing doesn't work for everything either. For example, my picture books (such as *Ceca Loves Science*) and chapter books on submission are better suited for traditional publishing currently, whereas some of my YA material based on a timely topic (such as *ReWired*) or that may target a leaner audience (such as the *Nature of Grace* wilderness thriller series), may be better geared toward self-publishing. So decide what you want to write and then figure out what the best channel to market may be; consider time, topic and level of control.

5. Always keep writing

The indie world is very fast paced while the traditional model is much slower. Doing both can bog you down in tasks, project management and marketing. But it's important to always keep writing. This is the best way to build a portfolio. When one book is in edits, work on a new idea. When one manuscript is in your agent's or critique partner's hands, outline your next book. Never sit and wait for something to happen. Make something happen. It's all worth it in the end!

I want to continue with my hybrid career because I love both the traditional and self-publishing options for very different reasons. I value the flexibility and control that self-publishing offers. BUT I also enjoy the collaborative process of working with an editor at a publishing house. As I develop as a writer, I want to remain open to ANY writing opportunity or path available. I want to pave my own way in this exciting, frustrating, wonderful and challenging industry. Because at the end of the day, I just want to write great books and reach people across all ages with my words. I'm proud to be a hybrid author – one who publishes my work, my way.

Remember, there is no right way to make this journey, there's only *your* way!

Shelli R. Johannes is the co-author of the nine-part science picture book series, *Loves Science* (Greenwillow/HarperCollins). She is also the author of the forthcoming picture book *Theo Thesaurus* (Putnam/Penguin 2021) and *Unicorn* (HarperCollins Children's 2021). Shelli writes middle grade and YA, and has self-published six books, selling over 200,000 ebooks. After earning a Masters in Marketing and working in corporate America as a Senior Vice President, Shelli traded in her heels and suits for flip-flops and jeans to follow her passion for writing. For more information see www.srjohannes.com and follow her on Twitter or Instagram @srjohannes.

See also...
- *An indie's journey to award-winning success*, page 194
- *Do you have to have an agent to succeed?*, page 245

Books

Editorial services and self-publishing providers

This is a selection of the expanding list of companies that offer editorial, production, marketing and distribution support predominantly for authors who want to self-publish. As with all the organisations mentioned in the *Yearbook*, we recommend that you check carefully what companies offer and what they would charge. Note that in the entries below, 'POD' refers to 'print on demand'.

Amolibros
Loundshay Manor Cottage, Preston Bowyer,
Milverton, Somerset TA4 1QF
tel (01823) 401527
email amolibros@aol.com
website www.amolibros.com
Director Jane Tatam

Offers print and ebook design, production, copy-editing and distribution through online retailers. Sales and marketing services include design and production of adverts, leaflets, author websites, distribution of press releases and direct mail campaigns.

Betterwrite
107A Maas Road, Birmingham B31 2PP
tel 0121 475 5876
email robertmatthews_edit@yahoo.co.uk
website https://betterwrite.com
Contact Rob Matthews

Experienced team of twelve editors, all members of the Chartered Institute of Editing and Proofreading (formerly SfEP), working across all fiction genres: crime/thriller/mystery, adventure/fantasy/romance, sci-fi, historical, children's books, YA fiction and commercial women's fiction. Non-fiction projects also undertaken.

Once authors are matched with the most appropriate editor for their work, the text is prepared for publication or self-publication via a three-stage procedure. First, there is a developmental/structural edit, advising authors of big-picture issues like character, plot and narrative technique. Second, authors can revise their text following the guidance of a development editor, so that they remain in control of their writing. Third, the work undergoes a line and copy-edit, correcting grammar, spelling and punctuation errors and improving the overall flow.

Phone or email for a free sample edit.

Blue Falcon Publishing
The Mill, Pury Hill Business Park, Alderton Road, Towcester, Northants NN12 7LS
tel 07955 002040
email books@bluefalconpublishing.co.uk
website www.bluefalconpublishing.co.uk
Facebook www.facebook.com/bluefalconpublishing
Twitter @bluefalconpub
Instagram @bluefalconpub

Small independent company publishing children's fiction books with a focus on high-quality, personal service. Services include: editing; typesetting; publishing and ebook production. Prices start from £450 for the basic service.

Bookollective
email hello@bookollective.com
website www.bookollective.com
Facebook www.facebook.com/bookollective
Twitter @bookollective
Contacts Esther Harris (editorial), Aimee Coveney (design), Helen McCusker (publicity)

Award-winning team offering a range of publicity, promotion and marketing options, editing services, book-cover design and website creation. Works alongside publishers, industry professionals and direct with writers. Also hosts regular networking events and literary areas within festivals.

BookPrinting UK
Remus House, Coltsfoot Drive, Woodston, Peterborough PE2 9BF
tel (01733) 898102
email info@bookprintinguk.com
website www.bookprintinguk.com
Twitter @BookPrintingUK
Contact Naz Stewart

Offers colour and b&w printing and POD books in a range of bindings. Can provide custom illustration and interior layout options, as well as typesetting. Supplies templates for formatting manuscript files before sending. Can also distribute print books direct to customers. Prints bookmarks, posters and flyers.

Clink Street Publishing
71–75 Shelton Street, London WC2H 9JQ
tel 020-7993 8225
email info@clinkstreetpublishing.com
website www.bookpublishing.co.uk

Boutique self-publishing imprint from Authoright, with an experienced team of editors, project managers, designers and publicists publishing and promoting writers across all genres. Also has links with literary scouts with a view to securing foreign translation rights. Case studies and testimonials available on request.

eBook Versions

27 Old Gloucester Street, London WC1N 3AX
website www.ebookversions.com

Offers ebook, paperback and hardback self-publishing and distribution through online retailers and trade wholesalers including Amazon Kindle Direct Publishing, Apple iBookstores, Kobo Books, Gardners Books, IngramSpark and more than 300 independent high street booksellers. Fees begin at £95 for ebook conversion of a manuscript of up to 100,000 words. POD paperback and hardback pre-press production is available from £295. OCR scanning of hardbacks, paperbacks and typescripts is also offered.

Frank Fahy Publishing Services

5 Barna Village Centre, Barna, Galway, H91 DF24, Republic of Ireland
tel +353 (0)86 2269330
email frank.fahy0@gmail.com
website https://frankfahypublishing.wordpress.com/

Specialises in preparing manuscripts for book production, either as printed books or digital ebooks. This can include, as required, copy-editing and/or proofreading, or preparing presentations for submission to publishers. Estimates are free of charge and authors' individual requirements discussed. Publishing projects of all kinds considered, from individuals, institutions or businesses. Founded 2007.

Grosvenor House Publishing

Link House, 140 The Broadway, Tolworth, Surrey KT6 7HT
tel 020-8339 6060
website www.grosvenorhousepublishing.co.uk
Founder Kim Cross

Publishes across a range of genres including children's and non-fiction in colour, b&w, POD, paperback, hardback and ebook formats. Offers a £795 publishing package which includes typesetting and five free print copies as well as an ISBN, and print and ebook distribution via online retailers. Marketing services include producing posters and postcards, and website set-up from template with two years' hosting. Ebook publishing costs £195 if the print edition of the book has been produced by the company and £495 otherwise. Print costs and royalties depend on book specification. A proofreading service is offered at a rate of £5 per 1,000 words. See website for full list of costs.

Jelly Bean Self-Publishing

Candy Jar Ltd, Mackintosh House,
136 Newport Road, Cardiff CF24 1DJ
tel 029-211 57202

email submissions@jellybeanselfpublishing.co.uk
website www.jellybeanselfpublishing.co.uk
Twitter @Jelly_BeanUK
Director Shaun Russell

Self-publishing imprint of Candy Jar Books. Offers a bespoke service for new and experienced authors at any step of the publishing process, including but not limited to editing and typesetting, illustration, cover design, website design, audiobook production and marketing services. Submissions are welcomed, and meetings are available on request. Founded 2012.

Kindle Direct Publishing

website https://kdp.amazon.com
Facebook www.facebook.com/KindleDirectPublishing
Twitter @AmazonKDP

Ebook self-publishing and distribution platform for Kindle and Kindle Apps. Its business model offers up to a 70% royalty (on certain retail prices between $2.99–$9.99) in many countries and availability in Amazon stores worldwide. POD options are also available. Note that KDP Select makes books exclusive to Amazon (which means they cannot be sold through an author's personal website, for example), but authors can share in the Global Fund amount every time the book is borrowed from the Kindle Owners' Lending Library.

Kobo Writing Life

email writinglife@kobo.com
website www.kobo.com/gb/en/p/aboutkobo
Facebook www.facebook.com/KoboWritingLife
Twitter @kobo

Ebook self-publishing platform where authors can upload manuscripts and cover images. These files are then converted into ebooks before being distributed through the Kobo ebookstore. Authors are able to set pricing and DRM territories, as well as track sales. Royalty rates vary depending on price or territory; enquire directly. Free to join. Owned by Rakuten.

Little Steps

Uncommon, 126 New King's Road, Fulham, London SW6 4LZ
tel 020-3962 4459
email info@littlestepspublishing.co.uk
website www.littlestepspublishing.co.uk
Facebook www.facebook.com/littlestepspublishinguk
Instagram @littlestepspublishinguk

Provides a complete service for the aspiring children's author, including printing, design, marketing, editing, proofreading, public relations, production and distribution. The author financially invests in their own book, entitling them to receive majority royalties. Founded in the UK 2019; has been operating for over 10 years in Australia.

Manuscripts & Mentoring

25 Corinne Road, London N19 5EZ
tel 07973 300276

Books

email manuscriptmentoring@gmail.com
website www.genevievefox.com
Twitter @genevievefox21
Contact Genevieve Fox

Helps both fledgling and experienced writers of fiction, non-fiction and YA fiction get from first draft to finished manuscript. Primary services: editing; one-to-one tutoring; manuscript overviews; advice on structure, plot, themes and characterisation; submission to agents; and self-publishing. Also available: mentoring; writing plans; ghostwriting; media coaching; and creative writing courses. Genevieve Fox is a published author, journalist and creative writing tutor.

Matador

Troubador Publishing Ltd, 9 Priory Business Park, Wistow Road, Kibworth Beauchamp, Leicester LE8 0RX
tel 0116 279 2299
email books@troubador.co.uk
website www.troubador.co.uk/matador
Facebook www.facebook.com/matadorbooks
Twitter @matadorbooks
Managing Director Jeremy Thompson, *Operations Director* Jane Rowland

The self-publishing imprint of Troubador Publishing. Offers POD, short-run digital- and litho-printed books as well as audiobooks and ebook production, with distribution through high-street bookshops and online retailers. Also worldwide ebook distribution. Author services include all book, ebook and audiobook production, trade and retail marketing, plus bookshop distribution via Orca Book Services and Sales Representation by Star Book Sales.

For audiobooks, authors choose from a range of available narrators. Once studio recording has been completed and the finished audiobook approved, the author can choose to distribute themselves or through Matador. Production prices start at £1,450 for a book of up to 40,000 words, and distribution is a one-off fee of £40. Prices include audiobook artwork, and individual support and advice throughout the process. Founded 1999.

MJV Literary Author Services

71–75 Shelton Street, London WC2H 9JQ
email authors@mjvliterary.com
website www.mjvliterary.com
Contact Matt McAvoy

Offers professional proofreading, copy-editing and beta-reading services for authors of all genres, including fiction, non-fiction and children's books, as well as a popular ebook and KDP-ready Kindle-book creation service, at $69.

As part of the company's #ReturnToRealBooks campaign, KDP-formatted print-ready typesetting is offered free with all proofreading and copy-editing instructions. Other services include translation into English with full copy-editing, for non-English language authors.

Editing services start from $6.50 per 1,000 words, and include two editor passes as standard. Clients include self-published and traditionally published authors from all over the world, as well as publishers.

Senior Editor Matt McAvoy also operates a popular book-review blog (www.mattmcavoy.com), and is a member of the Chartered Institute of Editing and Proofreading (CIEP).

Peahen Publishing

tel 0117 427 0126
email info@peahenpublishing.com
website www.peahenpublishing.com
Twitter @peahenbooks
Contact Carly Corlett

Independent publisher specialising in children's books, from storybooks to rhyming books, memoirs and novels to short story collections. Guides authors through the publishing process, from initial manuscript consultation to illustration, from paper and font selection to print. Founded 2015.

PublishNation

Suite 544, Kemp House, 152 City Road, London EC1V 2NX
email david@publishnation.co.uk
website www.publishnation.co.uk
Publisher David Morrison

Offers POD paperback and Kindle format ebooks, available through Amazon. Publication in both print and digital formats costs £250 or £150 for Kindle format. Images may be included from £2.95 each. A range of book sizes is available, as are free template book covers. Enhanced cover design costs £40. Marketing services include creation of a press release, social media accounts and author website. Standard proofreading is £7 per 1,000 words, while an 'express' option from £125 focuses on the beginning of the manuscript. Editorial critique reports range in price from £99 for manuscripts of up to 15,000 words to £219 for manuscripts of up to 120,000 words.

SilverWood Books

14 Small Street, Bristol BS1 1DE
tel 0117 910 5829
email enquiries@silverwoodbooks.co.uk
website www.silverwoodbooks.co.uk
Twitter @SilverWoodBooks
Publishing Director Helen Hart

Offers complete 'done for you'/self-publishing services, including manuscript feedback, editing and proofreading, professional cover and page design, typesetting, ebook hand-formatting and conversion, b&w and colour POD, short-run and lithographic printing, one-to-one support and coaching. Distributes to bookshops via wholesalers and to online retailers including Amazon.

Partner Member of The Alliance of Independent Authors. Lists books in its own SilverWood online bookstore. UK wholesale distribution via Central Books. Nielsen Enhanced Data Listing. Book marketing services and consultations available. VAT at the standard rate added to services but not print. See website for price information.

WRITERSWORLD

2 Bear Close Flats, Bear Close, Woodstock, Oxon OX20 1JX
tel 0800 1214966
email enquiries@writersworld.co.uk
website www.writersworld.co.uk
Founder & Owner Graham Cook

Specialises in self-publishing, POD books and book reprints. Also issues ISBNs on behalf of authors, pays them 90% of the royalties and supplies them with copies of their books at print cost. Worldwide book distribution. Founded 2000.

York Publishing Services

64 Hallfield Road, Layerthorpe, York YO1 7ZQ
tel (01904) 431213
email enqs@yps-publishing.co.uk
website www.yps-publishing.co.uk
Facebook www.facebook.com/YorkPublishingServices/

Offers print and ebook publishing options, as well as distribution to bookshops and online retailers including Amazon. Services include: copy-editing; proofreading; page and cover design; and printing. Provides page proofs and sample bound copy before main print run. Marketing services include: compiling a press pack with press release sent to media; social media set-up (£250 plus VAT); posters; and direct mail campaigns. Book is also listed on the YPS online bookstore. Printing and editing price dependent on specification.

Books

Poetry
Writing poetry for children

Rachel Rooney reflects on how she re-engaged with a childhood passion and sought out valuable educational and competitive opportunities and challenges to sharpen her poetic skills. With advice for new poets, she sees how both serendipity and tenacity played their part on her path to publication and award-winning success.

I fell in love with poetry twice – once as a bookish child and again, much later, as a middle-aged woman. Maybe it was the 27-year hiatus that fuelled my desire to become a poet for young people, an urge to pick up from where I'd left off. With my third son starting school, and while taking a short break in my teaching career, I signed up to a weekly Writing for Children course run by Roger Stevens, the founder of the online children's website The Poetry Zone (https://poetryzone.co.uk). It ran over three terms, with the main focus on fiction writing, but it quickly became clear that my strengths lay in poetry. I rediscovered a pleasure in its rhythms, rhymes and patterning, and found a natural tendency to condense ideas rather than expand on them.

Soon I became hooked and began to experiment with different forms and styles. I read widely for inspiration, from childhood favourites such as Christina Rossetti and Charles Causley through to contemporary poets. Then I sought out the winning collections from the CLPE Poetry Award (now named the CLiPPA Award; see page 388) as well as those from its predecessor, The Signal Poetry Award. While admiring playful, sharp wordplay and well-crafted light verse, I was also drawn to the 'adult poets' such as Matthew Sweeney, Philip Gross and Carol Ann Duffy, those who turned their skills to the writing of subtle, weighted poems for a younger audience. The scope of children's poetry was opening up to me – from early infant lullabies through to teen/adult crossover free-verse, and I was keen to embrace it all.

It was at this time I first had a poem published in an anthology, which had been submitted as part of a challenge organised by the tutor. The early 2000s was a barren era for single-poet collections, but there was a proliferation of anthologies for children and, as an emerging poet trying to get a toehold in the publishing industry, it was perfect timing. My details were soon passed to other anthologists who keep informal lists of poets to contact when calling for submissions. The submission briefs sent out tend to be specific in nature, targeting a particular age-range and dictating the subject matter to be covered. While this can feel a little restrictive at times, it serves well as a homework-type exercise and a handy writing prompt. Assuming that the most obvious angles and poetic forms would be covered, I learned to submit poems from slant, unusual perspectives, increasing the likelihood they'd be chosen. The fee offered is low – for as long as I can recall it has mysteriously remained at an average of £50 per poem. As the saying goes, there's no poetry in money and no money in poetry. But I gained a fairly decent strike rate and soon became an established contributor.

By now I had a notion to publish a collection for children, but this was overshadowed by a desire to learn more about the art itself. I felt driven to explore 'adult' poetry, with all its nuance, variations and complexities. So, while juggling a return to special needs teaching, motherhood and a crumbling marriage, I attended a year-long evening class, followed by a part-time two-year Creative Writing certificate at the University of Sussex, both under the excellent tutorage of the poet and novelist Ros Barber. Her rigorous teaching helped sharpen up my technical skills and deepened my appreciation of the art. Workshopping poems taught me to accept critical feedback and to constructively critique the writing of others. And in the process I developed supportive relationships with those at a similar stage in their writing careers, some of which continue to this day. After completing the certificate, I refocused on children's poetry. I entered the Belmont Prize, which at the time was the only national poetry competition for a single children's poem. Getting shortlisted in this was an early highlight and gave me reassurance that I was on the right path. The Belmont is now sadly defunct, but two other national single-poem competitions have taken its place: the Caterpillar Prize (see page 387), run by the children's magazine *The Caterpillar*, and the YorkMix Poems for Children Competition (https://yorkmix.com/yorkmix-poems-for-children-competition). There may also be other local and regional competitions to be found.

I'd accumulated a healthy number of poems over four years, but had come to a frustrating impasse. While I was confident I had the basis of a decent collection, I was at a loss to know how to proceed. Most publishers weren't willing to accept unsolicited manuscripts and securing an agent as an unknown poet was unlikely, especially as there was little demand for single-poet collections back then. But I was determined to be published – why, I'd even written 'Win CLPE Poetry Award' on my list of Things I Must Do, hadn't I? To keep myself buoyant, I splashed out on an Arvon residential course (see page 225), Writing Poetry for Children, run by Carol Ann Duffy. These courses don't come cheap but spending five full days (and evenings) immersed in all things poetic, free from real-life distractions and with the perfect tutor, was a magical and productive experience.

Despite Carol Ann's encouraging response to my writing, I fell back into a despondent personal place. So I decided to channel this feeling into a rhyming picture book text titled *A Patch of Black* – a night-time lullaby about fear of the dark. I made multiple submissions to publishers I thought might suit; although none were taken up I did receive a few positive-sounding rejections and this spurred me on to source a mentor, the late Gerard Benson, whose poetry I admired. Having contacted him through his publisher Smith-Doorstop, I sent him a selection of my poems to see if we'd be a 'good fit' and he agreed to critique my work for a reasonable fee. Gerard was a perceptive reader and an assured editor. We developed an email correspondence over several months and met up at a few poetry events. At one event – a children's poetry showcase at The Society of Authors – he introduced me to a few industry employees including Suzanne Carnell, then the Editorial Director at Macmillan Children's Books. Gently prompted by Gerald, I mentioned that I'd submitted *A Patch of Black* but hadn't heard anything back. Suzanne gave me her business card and suggested I contacted her directly, which I duly did. Though I wasn't aware at the time, I had just engaged in what some might term 'networking', thanks to Gerard's generous manoeuvres.

Eventually, *A Patch of Black*, illustrated by Deborah Allwright, was taken up by Macmillan and was to be published in 2010. Now, the hunt for an agent was on. I had no idea where to begin, so I rifled though the *Writers' & Artists' Yearbook* and selected several potential agents to contact. I was delighted to eventually be taken up by Caroline Walsh at David Higham and we've worked together happily ever since. I struck lucky here; after all, poets aren't the most lucrative clients to take on. And, again, the timing was good – Janetta Otter-Barry at Frances Lincoln (now Quarto) was setting up a rare single-poet poetry list and was looking to launch new poetry voices. My agent pitched my work, and *The Language of Cat* was published by Frances Lincoln in 2011, along with a wonderful endorsement from Carol Ann Duffy herself. It was longlisted for the Carnegie Medal and also went on to win the CLPE Prize. Two more poetry collections have followed, both shortlisted for the CLiPPA, with one winning the North Somerset Teachers' Award. *Hey, Girl!*, a collection for young teens, will be published by Otter-Barry Books in August 2021 and a picture book, *The Fears You Fear* is currently in production – the last in a set of three rhyming stories based around emotions, illustrated by the wonderful Zehra Hicks.

My publishing journey reads like a dream come true, and in retrospect I think it has been. However, that isn't the whole story – or poem, if you will. There have been real challenges along the way. Many times it has felt like an uphill struggle, a salutary lesson in remaining tenacious. As in the careers of most published writers, there has been an element of serendipity at play, of chance meetings and fortuitous timings. Unfortunately, you can never factor these in when you set out. In recent years, the publishing landscape has altered somewhat. Children's poetry is inhabiting a more central position, and social media platforms such as Twitter and Instagram provide visibility and exposure for newcomers and established writers alike. Online courses and readings are now commonplace and accessible to most. And the children's poetry world is a relatively small and welcoming one, especially when raw talent is spotted.

So, what advice might I give a poet starting out? I remember once meeting an editor who told me she had real difficulty sourcing new poets for her list. When I asked her why, she told me it was because writing children's poetry is deceptively difficult and most people think it an easy thing to do. With this in mind, my foremost advice is to focus on the craft itself; if your poetry is strong enough, it's sure to get noticed eventually. Good luck!

Rachel Rooney is a trained teacher in Primary and Special Education. Her first poetry collection *The Language of Cat* (Frances Lincoln Children's Books 2011) won the CLPE Poetry Award and was longlisted for the Carnegie Medal. Her other collections, *My Life as a Goldfish* and *A Kid in My Class* have both been shortlisted for the CLiPPA Award. She performs at festivals and for The Children's Bookshow. In 2017 she was the Chair of Judges for the CLiPPA and has judged the Betjeman Poetry Prize. Rachel visits schools for workshops and lives in Brighton. See her website www.rachelrooneypoet.com for more information, and follow her on Twitter @RooneyRachel.

See also...

Poetry

Flying the poetry flag

Poet and anthologist John Foster explains the difficulties faced by aspiring children's poets and offers practical advice on writing poetry for children.

Once upon a time, there was a teacher who enjoyed sharing poems with the children she taught. As well as reading them poems from books in the class library, she read some of the poems she had written herself. She was encouraged by their response and decided to see if she could get the poems published. She looked in publishers' catalogues and found that there were numerous anthologies of poetry for children, as well as a number of single author collections.

She chose a publisher and sent them her poems. The publisher liked the poems. But as she was unknown they did not think they could risk a single author collection. However, they thought her poems showed promise, so they forwarded them to one of their anthologists. Although the anthologist liked the poems too, they did not fit into the anthology that he was currently working on. But he added her to the list of contacts to whom he sent details of new anthologies, specifying the subject of the collection and the types of poem he was looking for. When he next did an anthology, she submitted a number of poems for consideration and the anthologist chose three of them to be included.

She managed to track down other anthologists and they sent her details of the anthologies they were compiling. She became a regular contributor to anthologies and an established name in the children's poetry world, and gave up full-time teaching so that she could accept invitations to visit schools to read her poems and run poetry workshops. She struggled to find a publisher to do a single author collection. But eventually she managed to get a collection published and it sold well on her school visits. She didn't make a fortune from writing children's poetry, but her success and the obvious enjoyment children got from her poems was gratifying.

That was how it was in the late 1980s, throughout the 1990s and in the early 2000s, when children's poetry was in fine fettle. How lucky she and the rest of us children's poets were then and how times have changed. Whereas in those days there were plenty of poetry books for children published annually, now there are only a few and new anthologies are a rarity.

Briefly, in 2010/11 it looked as if children's poetry might be making a comeback. Writing in the summer 2011 *Carousel* magazine, Brian Moses heralded what he hoped was a new spring for children's poetry, spearheaded by the launch of a new poetry list by Salt Publishing and a new imprint from Frances Lincoln. However, the Salt Children's Poetry Library has failed to make an impact and, despite the best efforts of Macmillan, A&C Black and Frances Lincoln, children's poetry publishing remains in the doldrums.

What explains the dearth of new children's poetry books? There are a number of factors involved. But it has nothing to do with children's attitudes towards poetry. Children enjoy reading poetry as much as they did in the boom years of the 1990s. Children's poets are as in demand at Book Weeks in schools as they have always been. They perform their poems to rapt audiences, who go on to get their parents to buy whatever poetry books they have managed to get publishers to publish or, in desperation, have self-published.

So why has children's poetry publishing declined? It is partly due to the attitude of booksellers. They argue that poetry books don't sell. Of course they don't, if they don't stock them. Walk into the children's section of a bookshop today and you'll find a handful of poetry books, often hidden away on the bottom shelf, alongside the joke books. In the past, you'd find a shelf full of poetry books at eye-level.

In the eyes of the book buyers, who control what is stocked in bookshops, children's poetry isn't fashionable at present. This has a knock-on effect. The publisher's sales team report back that poetry books don't sell, despite the evidence to the contrary from the travelling poets, who sell hundreds of pounds' worth of their books during their school visits. So the publishers only publish a fraction of the poetry books that they used to. It's a vicious circle.

And the economic climate doesn't help. A full-colour poetry book aimed at younger children is like a picture book in terms of how much it costs to produce. But poetry doesn't translate in the way that stories do, so it isn't possible to sell foreign rights as a way of recouping the costs of production. It can be hard for a commissioning editor to convince the publishing committee to back a poetry project that will not make much money on the first printing.

Nevertheless, while many of the mainstream children's book publishers still shy away from publishing poetry, smaller independent publishers, such as Martin West at Troika and Janetta Otter-Barry at Otter-Barry Books, are producing an increasing number of poetry books. But the number remains very small when compared to the number of children's novels that are published annually.

Consequently, the aspiring children's poet faces a daunting task. There aren't the anthologies that it was possible to contribute to in the past and it is even harder these days to get a single author collection accepted. But if you are determined to write children's poetry, here are a few tips.

Get inspired by children

Starting with the most obvious, get to know children's language. If you are writing about an experience from a child's point of view, you must get the language right. It is, perhaps, not surprising that many of the most successful children's poets are from a teaching background – for example, Tony Mitton, Wes Magee, Judith Nicholls, Paul Cookson and Brian Moses. Teachers not only know what children's interests are, but they also know how children think and how they express themselves. Steep yourself in children's language, not just the language of your children and those of your friends, but of children from all sorts of backgrounds and cultures.

Try to arrange to visit schools in different areas. But always go through the correct channels with a letter to the literacy coordinator, copied to the headteacher, explaining the reasons you would like to visit. Schools these days are, quite rightly, very security-conscious.

If you are visiting a school, you can offer to run a writing workshop. You have the opportunity to try out your poems too. There's nothing like a deafening wall of silence greeting that punchline which you thought they would find so amusing to let you know that, in fact, the poem doesn't work!

Visiting schools is also worthwhile because you can bring yourself up to date with how poetry is being used in the classroom. For example, the new curriculum requires that pupils learn poems by heart. Literacy co-ordinators will therefore be on the lookout for new performance poems. There is an educational as well as a trade market for children's poems and it is worth knowing what the educational publishers might be looking for.

Schools are also a good source of ideas. Many a poem comes from a child's tale or a teacher's comment. In one school, I met a girl called Alison, who told me what had happened when she tried to pull a loose tooth out with a piece of string. So I went home and wrote this poem, 'When Allie Had a Loose Tooth':

> *When Allie had a loose tooth*
> *She did as her dad said.*
> *She went into the kitchen*
> *And found a piece of thread.*
> *She tied it round the tooth.*
> *She tied it to the door.*
> *But when she slammed the door shut,*
> *The knob fell on the floor.*

Appealing to the reader

Visiting schools will also give you an idea of what interests children have and what subjects to write about. Then it's up to you to think of something that will appeal to them. But a word of warning: be careful of being risqué just to appeal to the reader. Avoid being rude for the sake of it, and especially don't be crude. Besides, you could easily get yourself labelled! During a performance in Glasgow, I included two poems which made references to 'bottoms' and 'knickers', getting the usual delighted response from the audience. However, I was taken aback when I asked them to suggest why publishers won't allow me to illustrate my poetry books. Instead of giving me the expected – and correct – answer that my drawings are no good, the first boy that I asked said: 'Because your poems are dirty!'

You want your poems to stand out for some reason, so try to come up with something that is different. One way of making your poem stand out is to write it in a more unusual form. For example, say you are going to write a poem about St George and the dragon, instead of writing it in couplets, you could write it in the form of an encyclopedia entry, as a series of entries in St George's diary or even as a text message. Try experimenting with forms, not just haiku and cinquains but triolets, villanelles and univolics. You can find examples in *The Works – Every shape, style and form of poem that you could ever need for the Literacy Hour* (Macmillan 2009).

Children enjoy the ridiculous and the bizarre, but getting an idea can be hard. If you are stuck for a humorous idea, one way of trying to find one is to look through a book of jokes. I was racking my brains to think of an idea for a new poem to include in a book of magic poems, when I came across this joke: Why are the ghosts of magicians no good at conjuring? Because you can see right through their tricks! This led to:

> *The ghost of the magician said:*
> *'I'm really in a fix.*
> *The trouble is the audience*
> *Sees right through all my tricks!'*

I learned a great deal about how to write children's poetry by being an anthologist. So study the work of established children's poets and learn, for example, about how to play with words by reading Roger McGough's poems and about how to write story-poems as dramatic monologues by reading Michael Rosen's poems. You can get ideas, too, from researching what established poets have written. Two of my nonsense poems, both of which are well received in schools, 'The Land of the Flibbertigibbets' and 'On the Clip, Clop Clap' were inspired by Spike Milligan poems – 'In the Land of the Bumbley Boo' and 'On the Ning Nang Nong'.

If you get the opportunity, go along to a school, library or festival at which a children's poet is performing. In addition to listening to what they have to say, you may be able to talk to them afterwards. But don't expect them necessarily to be prepared to look at your poems and to give you a free tutorial on how to write children's poetry.

It's also worth looking at the websites of established writers. One particularly useful website is The Poetry Zone (http://poetryzone.co.uk), set up by the poet Roger Stevens. It consists of articles about writing children's poetry, as well as reviews and interviews with children's poets. The children's section of the Poetry Archive (https://poetryarchive.org/) is worth visiting too.

Getting into print

So how does the aspiring children's poet get published? As I've explained, it's far harder now than it used to be, in the days when there were lots of anthologies being published. One way is to do it yourself. Self-publishing is not as expensive as it used to be. You can get 500 copies of an A5 booklet printed for around £500 and, if you get onto the school circuit, you can sell them directly yourself and more than cover your costs.

Then, there's the internet. You can post your poems on a website. You won't, of course, make any money from doing so and once the poems are out there, then there's the danger that someone else will copy them and claim to have written them. But at least they'll be there for people to read.

You can also consider publishing your poems as an ebook. But there are so many other books available as ebooks that you probably won't sell many copies.

It's not easy for the aspiring children's poet to get recognised at present and you certainly won't make a fortune. But children's poetry is far from dead, as the enthusiastic audiences that greet visiting poets in schools show. So good luck! Keep writing. Visit schools and fly the poetry flag. Join the campaign for a national poetry month, such as exists in the USA. Children's poetry may not be as fashionable as it once was, but it's far from finished!

John Foster's collected poems *The Poetry Chest* (2007) is published by Oxford University Press. His latest book, *Eggs with Legs*, illustrated by Korky Paul, was published in 2018 by Troika. His anthologies *Fantastic Football Poems*, *Dragon Poems* and *Dinosaur Poems*, also illustrated by Korky Paul, have recently been reissued by Oxford University Press.

See also...
- *An interview with my shadow*, page 220
- *Poetry organisations*, page 222

Poetry

An interview with my shadow

Brian Patten talks about writing poetry.

Who are you?
I'm your shadow.

What's that you're eating?
It's the shadow of an apple.

Surely shadows can't detach themselves from walls and eat shadow-apples?
They can if they are writers' and poets' shadows.

Why do you write for children as well as for adults?
I don't know, it just happened that way. But I really do believe that writing for one is no easier than writing for the other. If somebody tries to write for adults and finds they aren't any good at it, then they will very likely be even worse at writing for children.

Can you really appreciate poetry at seven or even 11 years old?
Of course you can! Adults have no monopoly on feelings. I suspect that many adults never feel as intensely about things as they did when they were younger.

What are the best kinds of things to write about?
You can write about anything you want. Sometimes the weirder the better. At ten you will probably write very different poems than when you're 14 and when you are 40 you'll write different poems again.

How about telling stories through poems?
Very short stories, yes. But not long stories. For long stories children prefer prose, and quite rightly I think. Part of poetry is to do with condensing, not expanding. It is different if you are writing a series of poems about the same character or about a particular situation or unusual creatures or seeing certain themes from different angles. Then snapshots can build up into a story. But there have been very few successful long story-poems written for children.

I thought poets were supposed to be daydreamers. Some people think poetry is a bit soft.
Modern poetry for children is usually anarchic – anything but soft. Having said this, there is an awful lot of bad so-called 'children's poetry' about. Almost as much as bad 'adult poetry'.

How so?
Well, there is more rhyme and word play in contemporary children's poetry than in contemporary adult poetry. People can make things rhyme, but they either don't or can't work on the scansion, and then the whole metrical structure falls apart. People who think they can get away with writing sloppy verse simply because it's for children are deluding themselves. No matter how good an idea, it is the execution of the work that brings it to life.

Did you intend that last sentence to be ironic?

Yes. And it is true. Would-be writers forget it at their peril! Children won't be fobbed off with lazy work.

Why did you begin writing poetry? Did anyone teach you?

No, one day I just started writing things down. You see, as a child I lived in this tiny house with three adults. They were all unhappy people. My mother was young and couldn't afford a place of her own, so we lived with my grandmother. My grandmother wore callipers and she dragged herself round the house by her hands. I remember thinking they were like talons.

What has this got to do with poetry and beginning to write it?

Everybody in that little house was miserable and they didn't talk to each other, and although they knew they were miserable and why they were miserable, they couldn't explain why.

You mean they could not express themselves?

Yes, and because they could not express themselves they kept everything walled up inside them, where it hurt and festered for want of light.

Were you like this as well?

To begin with. I don't know how it happened, or why, but I realised the only way I could express my feelings was by writing them down. I think that is how I started to become a poet. I began writing down what I felt. So really, I began writing poetry before I even began reading it. I needed to express my feelings and writing poetry was like writing a very intense diary.

Would you say you were a 'real' poet at that age? I mean, when you began writing did you think that you would ever become a professional poet?

No. That happened when I began changing words and moving lines around. When you begin to *make* something out of the words is when the professional element comes into play. A good poem is something that carries your feelings and ideas inside it. People remember a good poem because of the way it is written, just as much as because of what it says.

Would you like a bit of my apple?

I'm not sure. What does a shadow-apple taste like?

Brian Patten was born in Liverpool and writes poetry for adults and children. His publications for adults are *Collected Love Poems* (Harper Perennial 2007) and *Selected Poems* (Penguin 2007), and for children, *The Big Snuggle-Up* (2011) and *Can I Come Too?* (2013), both illustrated by Nicola Bayley and published by Andersen Press, and *The Monster Slayer* (Barrington Stoke 2016), with illustrations by Chris Riddell. His most recent book, *The Book of Upside Down Thinking*, is a collection of humorous and thought-provoking verse inspired by traditional folk stories from the Near and Middle East (From You to Me Ltd 2018). A new specially updated version of *Monster Slayer* for older children, *Monster Slayer: A Beowulf Tale* was published by Barrington Stoke in 2020. His website is www.brianpatten.co.uk.

See also...

- *Flying the poetry flag*, page 216
- *Poetry organisations*, page 222

Poetry organisations

Below are some organisations which provide budding poets with opportunities to develop their skills, perform and engage with audiences and other poets.

⚠ Some poetry events will not go ahead in their usual way due to ongoing coronavirus-related restrictions. Please check websites for details.

WHERE TO GET INVOLVED

A range of organisations – from local groups to larger professional bodies – exists at which emerging and established poets can access support or learn more about others' work. A concise selection appears below.

Literature Wales
Glyn Jones Centre, Wales Millennium Centre, Bute Place, Cardiff CF10 5AL
tel 029-2047 2266
email post@literaturewales.org
website www.literaturewales.org

National company for the development of literature in Wales. Working to inspire communities, develop writers and celebrate Wales' literary culture. Activities include the Wales Book of the Year Award, the Children's Laureate Wales and Bardd Plant Cymru schemes, creative writing courses at Tŷ Newydd Writing Centre, writer's bursaries and mentoring, and the National Poet of Wales initiative. The organisation is a member of the Arts Council of Wales' Arts Portfolio Wales.

The Poetry Book Society
Milburn House, Dean Street, Newcastle Upon Tyne NE1 1LF
tel 0191 230 8100
email enquiries@poetrybooksociety.co.uk
website www.poetrybooks.co.uk
Facebook www.facebook.com/poetrybooksoc
Twitter @poetrybooksoc

Book club for readers of poetry founded in 1953 by T.S. Eliot. Every quarter, expert poet selectors choose one outstanding publication (the PBS Choice), and recommend four other titles; these are sent to members, who are also offered discounts on other poetry books. The PBS also produces the quarterly membership magazine, the *Bulletin* (available to all members), which contains the poet selectors' reviews of the Choice and Recommendations, interviews with international poets, reviews and listings. Also offers a range of educational memberships for secondary school libraries with expert teaching tips and posters to inspire students with a love of poetry.

The Poetry Business
Campo House, 54 Campo Lane, Sheffield S1 2EG
tel 0114 438 4074
email office@poetrybusiness.co.uk
website www.poetrybusiness.co.uk

Publishes pamphlets by young poets between the ages of 17 and 24 under The New Poets List imprint; runs the literary magazine, *The North*. Also organises a national pamphlet competition for young poets between the ages of 17 and 24, writing days, and residential courses.

Poetry Ireland
11 Parnell Square East, Dublin D01 ND60, Republic of Ireland
tel +353 (0)1 6789815
email info@poetryireland.ie
website www.poetryireland.ie

Organisation committed to achieving excellence in the reading, writing and performance of poetry throughout the island of Ireland. Poetry Ireland receives support from The Arts Council / An Chomhairle Ealaíon and The Arts Council of Northern Ireland and enjoys partnerships with arts centres, festivals, schools, colleges and bookshops at home and abroad. Its commitment to creating performance and publication opportunities for poets at all stages of their careers helps ensure that the best work is made available to the widest possible audience. Poetry Ireland publishes the well-regarded journal, *Poetry Ireland Review*.

The Poetry Society
22 Betterton Street, London WC2H 9BX
tel 020-7420 9880
email info@poetrysociety.org.uk
website www.poetrysociety.org.uk

The Poetry Society is Britain's leading voice for poets and poetry. Founded in 1909 to promote a more general recognition and appreciation of poetry, the Society has nearly 4,000 members. With innovative education, commissioning and publishing programmes, and a packed calendar of performances, readings and competitions, the Society champions poetry in its many forms.

The Society also publishes education resources for teachers and educators; organises high-profile events including an Annual Lecture and National Poetry Day celebrations; runs Poetry Prescription, a critical appraisal service; and provides an education advisory service, INSET packages for schools and networks of schools, a poets in schools service, school membership, youth membership and a website.

Competitions run by the Society include the annual National Poetry Competition, with a first prize of £5,000, and the Foyle Young Poets of the Year Award.

Tower Poetry
Christ Church, Oxford OX1 1DP
tel (01865) 286591
email tower.poetry@chch.ox.ac.uk
website www.chch.ox.ac.uk/towerpoetry
Facebook www.facebook.com/towerpoetry/
Twitter @towerpoetry

Exists to encourage and challenge everyone who reads or writes poetry. Funded by a generous bequest to Christ Church, Oxford, by the late Christopher Tower, the aims of Tower Poetry are to stimulate an enjoyment and critical appreciation of poetry, particularly among young people in education, and to challenge people to write their own poetry.

WHERE TO GET INFORMATION

Your local library is a good first port of call, and should have information about the poetry scene in the area. Many libraries are actively involved in spreading the word about poetry as well as having modern poetry available for loan.

Alliance of Literary Societies (ALS)
email allianceoflitsocs@gmail.com
website www.allianceofliterarysocieties.org.uk
Acting Hon Treasurer and Membership Secretary Linda J. Curry

Umbrella organisation for literary societies and groups in the UK. It provides support and advice on a variety of literary subjects, as well as promoting cooperation between member societies. Its publications include a twice-yearly members' newsletter, *Not Only But...*, and an annual journal, *ALSo*. ALS holds an AGM weekend which is hosted by a different member society each year, moving around the UK, or online. Founded 1973.

Arts Council England
tel 0161 934 4317
email enquiries@artscouncil.org.uk
website www.artscouncil.org.uk

National development agency for the arts in England, providing funding for a range of arts and cultural activities. It supports creative writing including poetry, fiction, storytelling, spoken word, digital work, writing for children and literary translation. It funds a range of publishers and magazines as well as providing grants to individual writers. Contact the enquiries team for more information on funding support and advice.

Arts Council of Wales
Bute Place, Cardiff CF10 5AL
tel 0845 8734 900
email information@arts.wales
website www.arts.wales

Independent charity, established by Royal Charter in 1994. It has three regional offices and its principal sponsor is the Welsh Government. It is the country's funding and development agency for the arts, supporting and developing high-quality arts activities. Its funding schemes offer opportunities for arts organisations and individuals in Wales to apply, through a competitive process, for funding towards a clearly defined arts-related project.

Manchester Poetry Library
Manchester Metropolitan University, Oxford Road, Manchester M15 6BR
email poetrylibrary@mmu.ac.uk
website www.mmu.ac.uk/poetrylibrary
Twitter @McrPoetryLib
Director Becky Swain

New public poetry library, due to open in 2021. Sets out to expand access to poetry and to encourage the writing of it at all levels, from primary school to professional standard. Its core collection will include 19th- to 21st-century poetry in English from around the world, as well as poetry in translation. Audio and print versions will be available. Will run events for children and adults, celebrating the role of local communities and languages in the process.

National Association of Writers' Groups
Old Vicarage, Scammonden, Huddersfield HD3 3FT
email info@nawg.co.uk
website www.nawg.co.uk

Aims to bring cohesion and fellowship to isolated writers' groups and individuals, promoting the study and art of writing in all its aspects. There are many affiliated groups and associate (individual) members across the UK.

National Poetry Library (Children's Collection)
Level 5, Royal Festival Hall, Southbank Centre, London SE1 8XX
tel 020-7921 0943
email info@poetrylibrary.org.uk
website www.nationalpoetrylibrary.org.uk
Facebook www.facebook.com/NationalPoetryLibrary
Twitter @natpoetrylib
Instagram @nationalpoetrylibrary

Comprises thousands of items for young poets of all ages, including poetry on CD and DVD. The library has an education service for teachers and writing groups, with a separate collection of books and materials for teachers and poets who work with children in schools. Group visits can be organised, allowing children to interact with the collection in various ways, from taking a Poetry Word Trail across

Southbank Centre, to exploring how the worlds of science and poetry interact, engaging with war poetry via the Letters Home booklet, or becoming a Poetry Library Poetry Explorer. Nursery schools can also book a Rug Rhymes session for under-5s. Children of all ages can join for free and borrow books and other materials. A special membership scheme is available for teachers to borrow books for the classroom. Contact the library for membership and opening time details.

Northern Poetry Library

The Chantry, Bridge Street, Morpeth, Northumberland NE61 1PD
tel (01670) 620391
email mylibrary@northumberland.gov.uk
website www.northernpoetrylibrary.org.uk
Twitter @nplpoetry

Largest collection of contemporary poetry outside London, housing over 15,000 titles and magazines covering poetry published since 1945. Founded 1968.

Scottish Poetry Library

5 Crichton's Close, Canongate, Edinburgh EH8 8DT
tel 0131 557 2876
email reception@spl.org.uk
website www.scottishpoetrylibrary.org.uk

Houses over 45,000 items: books, magazines, pamphlets, recordings and the Edwin Morgan Archive (featuring rare works by Morgan). The core of the collection is contemporary and classic poetry written in Scotland, in Scots, Gaelic and English, but classic Scottish poetry as well as contemporary works from almost every part of the world are also available. All resources, advice and information are readily accessible, free of charge. The SPL holds regular poetry events, including reading and writing groups, details of which are available on the library website. Closed Saturday and Sunday. Founded 1984.

ONLINE RESOURCES

There is a wealth of information available for poets at the click of a mouse: the suggestions below are a good starting point.

The Children's Poetry Archive

website https://childrenspoetryarchive.org

World's premier online collection of recordings of children's poets reading their work. Visitors to the website may listen, free of charge, to the voices of contemporary English-language poets and of poets from the past. Featured poets include Allan Ahlberg, Michael Rosen and Valerie Bloom, but the Archive is added to regularly. The recently updated website has a range of search options, so that users can search by theme, poet name, lyric, and so on.

LoveReading4Kids.co.uk

website www.lovereading4kids.co.uk/

Independent literature recommendation site designed to inspire and inform parents about the best new reads in children's publishing from toddlers to YA, including poetry. Features include: categories broken down by age range and theme; downloadable opening extracts of featured books; like-for-like recommendations for discovering new authors; exclusive online book reviews by children's books experts including Julia Eccleshare, Andrea Reece and Joanne Owen; and authentic reader reviews from children across all relevant age groups. Includes book price comparison linked to a wide range of affiliates and Bookshop.org. A wide variety of content produced every month, making it easy to find a child's next favourite book and encourage reading for pleasure. Also offers The Book Box by LoveReading4Kids – a gift and book subscription service for children.

LoveReading4Schools.co.uk

website www.lovereading4schools.co.uk/

Independent literature recommendation site designed to support teachers, school librarians and parents to inspire and inform about the best new reads in children's publishing from toddlers to YA, including poetry. Features include: categories broken down by Key Stage, year group and theme; downloadable opening extracts of featured books; like-for-like recommendations for discovering new authors; exclusive online book reviews by children's books experts including Julia Eccleshare, Andrea Reece and Joanne Owen; and authentic reader reviews from children across all relevant age groups.

Also included are updated reading lists for every year group which are refreshed for the beginning of each academic year. Experts also curate other reading lists to map many key curriculum areas like The Stone Age, Mythology and Ancient Greece, The Victorians, The Great Fire of London, Awesome Earth and many others.

The site enables schools to sign up for free as members, curate their own reading lists and share these lists with their parental communities to encourage reading for pleasure at home and school. It also enables its members to order books directly from the site from its exclusive supplier, Browns Books.

The Poetry Kit

email info@poetrykit.org
website www.poetrykit.org

Collates a wide variety of poetry-related information, including events, competitions, courses and more for an international readership.

Poetry Space

email susan@poetryspace.co.uk
website www.poetryspace.co.uk

Specialist publisher of poetry and short stories, as well as news and features, edited by Susan Jane Sims. Operates as a social enterprise with all profits being used to publish online and in print, and to hold events to widen participation in poetry. Submissions of poems, stories, novel extracts, photographs and artwork accepted all year for Young Writers' and Artists' Space (18s and under; work by under 16s particularly welcomed).

Seven Stories – National Centre for Children's Books

email info@sevenstories.org.uk
website www.sevenstories.org.uk
Twitter @7Stories
Chief Executive Mairi Kidd

Seven Stories is the only place in the United Kingdom dedicated to the art of children's books. Its website features a blog and online catalogue that may be of use to researchers and authors.

Teachit: English Teaching Resources

Queen Anne House, 11 Charlotte Street,
Bath BA1 2NE
website www.teachitenglish.co.uk
Twitter @TeachitEnglish

Resource website for teachers, with over 20,000 pages of classroom worksheets, PowerPoint presentations and activities that have been written and edited by experienced English teachers. The website offers free pdfs as well as teaching packs, classroom posters and books designed for Key Stages 3, 4 and 5.

WHERE TO CELEBRATE POETRY

Festival information should be available from Arts Council England offices (see page 366). See also *Children's literature festivals and trade fairs* on page 398.

The British Council

British Council Customer Service UK,
Bridgewater House, 58 Whitworth Street,
Manchester M1 6BB
tel 0161 957 7755
email uk-literature@britishcouncil.org
website https://literature.britishcouncil.org
Twitter @litbritish

Visit the website for information on events, authors and projects.

Imagine: Writers and Writing for Children

Southbank Centre, London SE1 8XX
tel 020-7960 4200
website www.southbankcentre.co.uk/whats-on/festivals-series/imagine-childrens-festival
Twitter @southbankcentre

Takes place February

An annual festival celebrating writing for children featuring a selection of poets, storytellers and illustrators.

Ledbury Poetry Festival

The Master's House, St Katherine's, Bye Street,
Ledbury HR8 1EA
tel (01531) 636232
email manager@poetry-festival.co.uk
website www.poetry-festival.co.uk
Festival Director Chloe Garner, *Festival Manager* Phillippa Slinger
Takes place July and throughout the year

The UK's biggest celebration of poetry and spoken word, attended by poets from all over the world. Established and upcoming talents take part in a wide variety of events, from masterclasses, walks, talks and films through to breakfasts, music, exhibitions and bike rides. International Poetry Competition launches every February.

WHERE TO WRITE POETRY

Arvon

Lumb Bank – The Ted Hughes Arvon Centre,
Heptonstall, Hebden Bridge,
West Yorkshire HX7 6DF
tel (01422) 843714
email lumbbank@arvon.org
Totleigh Barton, Sheepwash, Beaworthy, Devon EX21 5NS
tel (01409) 231338
email totleighbarton@arvon.org
The Hurst – The John Osborne Arvon Centre,
Clunton, Craven Arms, Shrops. SY7 0JA
tel (01588) 640658
email thehurst@arvon.org
website www.arvon.org

Arvon's three centres run five-day residential courses throughout the year for anyone over the age of 16, providing the opportunity to live and work with professional writers. Writing genres explored include poetry, narrative, drama, writing for children, songwriting and the performing arts. Bursaries are available to those receiving benefits. Arvon also runs online courses and events throughout the year. Founded 1968.

City Lit

1–10 Keeley Street, London WC2B 4BA
tel 020-7831 7831
email advice@citylit.ac.uk
website www.citylit.ac.uk
Twitter @citylit

Offers classes and courses (currently online only, but check website for updates) on poetry appreciation, as well as a wide range of other topics.

Poetry

The Poetry School

1 Dock Offices, Surrey Quays Road, Canada Water,
London SE16 2XU
tel 020-7582 1679
website www.poetryschool.com

Teaches the art and craft of writing poetry, with
courses in London and around the UK, ranging from
evening classes, small seminars and individual
tutorials, to one-day workshops, year-long courses
and an accredited MA. Activities for beginners to
advanced writers, with classes happening face-to-face
and online. Three termly programmes a year, plus
professional skills development projects and
CAMPUS, a social network for poets.

Tŷ Newydd Writing Centre

Llanystumdwy, Cricieth, Gwynedd LL52 0LW
tel (01766) 522811
email tynewydd@literaturewales.org
website www.tynewydd.wales

Tŷ Newydd, the former home of Prime Minister
David Lloyd George, has hosted residential creative
writing courses for writers of all abilities for over 30
years. Open to everyone over the age of 16. Courses
cover everything from poetry and popular fiction to
writing for the theatre, developing a novel for young
adults. No qualifications are necessary. Staff can
advise on the suitability of courses, and further details
about each individual course can be obtained by
visiting the website, or contacting the team by phone
or email. Tŷ Newydd also offers courses for schools,
corporate courses and away days for companies. Tŷ
Newydd is also home to Nant, the writers' retreat
cottage located on site. Tŷ Newydd Writing Centre is
run by Literature Wales, the national company for
the development of literature in Wales.

HELP FOR YOUNG POETS AND TEACHERS

National Association of Writers in Education (NAWE)

Tower House, Mill Lane, off Askham Fields Lane,
Askham Bryan, York YO23 3FS
tel 0330 3335 909
email admin@nawe.co.uk
website www.nawe.co.uk

National membership organisation which aims to
further knowledge, understanding and enjoyment of
creative writing and to support good practice in its
teaching and learning at all levels. NAWE promotes
creative writing as both a distinct discipline and an
essential element in education generally. Its
membership includes those working in Higher
Education, the many freelance writers working in
schools and community contexts, and the teachers
and other professionals who work with them. It runs

a national database of writers, produces a weekly
opportunities bulletin, publishes two journals –
Writing in Education and *Writing in Practice* – and
holds a national conference. Professional
membership includes public liability insurance cover.

Poetry Society Education

The Poetry Society, 22 Betterton Street,
London WC2H 9BX
tel 020-7420 9880
email educationadmin@poetrysociety.org.uk
website www.poetrysociety.org.uk

An arm of The Poetry Society aiming to facilitate
exciting and innovative education work. For over 30
years it has been introducing poets into classrooms,
providing comprehensive teachers' resources and
producing accessible publications for pupils. It
develops projects and schemes to keep poetry
flourishing in schools, libraries and workplaces,
giving work to hundreds of poets and allowing
thousands of children and adults to experience poetry
for themselves.

Through projects such as the Foyle Young Poets of
the Year Award and Young Poets Network, The
Poetry Society gives valuable encouragement and
exposure to young writers and performers.

Schools membership offers a range of benefits,
including quarterly Poetry Society publications,
books and posters, and free access to the Poets in
Schools placement service. Youth membership is also
available (for ages 11–18; from £20 p.a.) and offers
discounts, publications, poetry books and posters.

Young Poets Network

email educationadmin@poetrysociety.org.uk
website https://ypn.poetrysociety.org.uk
Facebook www.facebook.com/YoungPoetsNetwork
Twitter @youngpoetsnet

Online resource from The Poetry Society comprising
features about reading, writing and performing
poetry, plus new work by young poets and regular
writing challenges. Open to anyone under the age of
25.

YOUNG POETRY COMPETITIONS

Children's competitions are included in the
competition list provided by the Poetry Library: this
is free online at www.nationalpoetrylibrary.org.uk/
write-publish/competitions. Further information on
literary prizes can be found on the BookTrust website
(www.booktrust.org.uk/what-we-do/awards-and-
prizes/).

Foyle Young Poets of the Year Award

The Poetry Society, 22 Betterton Street,
London WC2H 9BX
tel 020-7420 9880

email fyp@poetrysociety.org.uk
website www.foyleyoungpoets.org
Facebook www.facebook.com/thepoetrysociety
Twitter @PoetrySociety

Annual competition for writers aged 11–17. Prizes include publication, mentoring and a residential writing course. Deadline 31 July. Free to enter. Founded 2001.

Christopher Tower Poetry Prize
Christ Church, Oxford OX1 1DP
tel (01865) 286591
email tower.poetry@chch.ox.ac.uk

website www.chch.ox.ac.uk/towerpoetry
Twitter @TowerPoetry

Annual poetry competition (open from November to March) from Christ Church, Oxford, aimed at students aged between 16 and 18 in UK schools and colleges. The poems should be no longer than 48 lines, on a different chosen theme each year. Prizes: £3,000 (1st), £1,000 (2nd), £500 (3rd). Every winner also receives a prize for his or her school.

See also...
- *Flying the poetry flag,* page 216
- *Interview with my shadow,* page 220

Further reading

Addonizio, Kim, *Ordinary Genius: A Guide for the Poet Within* (W.W. Norton and Co. 2012)

Bell, Jo, and Jane Commane, *How to Be a Poet: A 21st Century Guide to Writing Well* (Nine Arches Press 2017)

Bell, Jo, and guests: *52: Write a Poem a Week – Start Now, Keep Going* (Nine Arches Press 2015)

Chisholm, Alison, *A Practical Guide to Poetry Forms* (Compass Books 2014)

Fairfax, John, and John Moat, *The Way to Write* (Penguin Books, 2nd edn revised 1998)

Greene, Roland, *et al., Princeton Encyclopedia of Poetry and Poetics* (Princeton University Press, 4th edn 2012)

Hamilton, Ian, and Jeremy Noel-Tod, *The Oxford Companion to Modern Poetry in English* (Oxford University Press, 2nd edn 2014)

Kowit, Steve, *In the Palm of Your Hand: A Poet's Portable Workshop* (Tilbury House, 2nd edn 2017)

Maxwell, Glyn, *On Poetry* (Oberon Books 2017)

Oliver, Mary, *Rules for the Dance: Handbook for Writing and Reading Metrical Verse* (Houghton Mifflin 1998)

Padel, Ruth, *52 Ways of Looking at a Poem: A Poem for Every Week of the Year* (Vintage 2004)

Padel, Ruth, *The Poem and the Journey: 60 Poems for the Journey of Life* (Vintage 2008)

Roberts, Philip Davies, *How Poetry Works* (Penguin Books, 2nd edn 2000)

Sampson, Fiona, *Poetry Writing: The Expert Guide* (Robert Hale 2009)

Sansom, Peter, *Writing Poems* (Bloodaxe 1993, repr. 1997)

Whitworth, John, *Writing Poetry* (A&C Black, 2nd edn 2006)

Literary agents
What do agents *do* for their commission?

Generally, literary agents take 15% of their clients' earnings as their commission. Julia Churchill explains what she does in her role of literary agent in return for that percentage.

My role as a literary agent is to help my authors have successful careers. I endeavour to make money in as many rights streams as possible (with an eye on the long term), and enable an easier professional life for my clients so that they can focus on writing. My job involves spotting talent, helping to develop it and selling it.

Some of my clients came to me as established authors wanting to take their careers up a gear, but most have come via my slush pile, as debut writers. I get well over 100 submissions a week, and I may take on a new writer every few months (if I'm lucky). Spotting talent is often where my job starts. I think I have good taste, and I know that my taste isn't unique. If I love a book, it is likely that there are others who will love it too.

I tend not to follow trends, but I am aware of them. There are two markets to consider, and a good agent will have a clear understanding of both. The first is what I focus on when I sell books to publishers. The editor is the buyer and I need to think about their enthusiasms and needs for their list. Then there's the real market, which is reflected in what people are buying from booksellers right now. Both these markets change constantly and part of my job is to keep up to date with trends, and the preferences of individual editors. This knowledge feeds into my decision-making when considering new authors and guidance for my existing clients, although there are also many opportunities outside of obvious trends. To some extent I'm looking for what's fashionable, but more than anything I'm looking for what may be evergreen.

What I am looking for

When I read a manuscript, I'm looking to connect with a voice, a concept, a character and a story, a book with something to say. I'm looking for clarity and intent in the storytelling, and to be taken somewhere new.

Most debut manuscripts that arrive in my office are not yet ready to sell to a publisher, and I may work with the author to focus on what's best about the character(s) and story. Every edit is different. We may sit down together with a cup of tea and talk through the book, exploring such questions as: What does the writer do best? Where does the story lose focus? How can we keep raising the stakes? Why does this section not work? Is it needed? Is the story pulling in too many directions? What is the book about, in the small ways and the big ways?

Before I offer to represent an author, I'll talk them through the work that I think their manuscript needs. I want to be sure, for the author's sake as well as my own, that we're pointed in the same direction and in sync with our ambitions. It's my job to help the author bring out what is best in the manuscript. Sometimes these conversations are about the architecture of the book, and at other times just the interior design. I do what's necessary to maximise the chance of achieving a book deal and the value of that deal.

When I'm satisfied that the book is ready, I submit it to editors. On occasion, I may approach just one editor, and one publishing house, if there is a very specific reason why this would be the best possible outcome for the author. This is matchmaking. More often, I send out the manuscript widely in order to find the publisher with the most passion for the book and the best plan for it.

Selling the book

My favourite aspect of being a literary agent is seeing talent before the rest of the world does. The publishing business relies on having champions for books and an agent is the first professional champion. The agent shares their passion about a book with editors, who in turn pass it on to sales and marketing experts, publicists, reviewers, bloggers, librarians, booksellers and then finally readers.

Sometimes it takes just a few days to sell a book and for other books it can take months – on occasion it has taken years. An auction is lively, but more than anything it's a logistical challenge and requires being organised and systematic. Auctions provide an opportunity for the agent and author to see each publisher's vision, and they give maximum leverage for the best possible deal. Although the idea of an auction may sound exciting, I probably get as much professional satisfaction from humbly selling a book that's been very tough to place as I do from an eight-publisher auction that takes days to tie up.

Looking at contracts

Being a literary agent is not all about passionate pitches, editorial chats over cups of tea and champagne celebrations. There is some glamour to our business, but in many ways an agent's job is quite mundane and is taken up with working on contracts between publishers and authors. A contract has a long life and it requires rigour and experience to convert a publisher-friendly contract into one that is author-friendly. Negotiating contracts is not confined to increasing the advance and pushing for the best royalty and high discount rates, although that is where an agent is likely to show the most immediate value. It's also about ensuring that the author gets their rights back if the book stops selling above a certain level, that the pay-out is staggered in a way that favours the author, that certain sub-rights revert if they are unexploited, that the delivery and acceptance terms are favourable, that in a multi-book deal the books are accounted separately, that the split of sub-rights are as good as they possibly can be, that there is total clarity on what electronic rights the publisher has and that they don't cut across the author's reserved rights. The list of considerations is long: there is a lot to cover in a contract.

An agency will often sell translation rights, and television and film rights. Some of my clients make more money in Brazil or Norway than they do in the USA or UK. And while some markets shrink, others thrive, so for books with reach, it's important to have a strong international team and relationships with film scouts and production companies.

As in any career, a writer is faced with opportunities and decisions to make. Some are small and possibly of little consequence, and some are big and important to get right. Every now and then, there are huge forks in the road which require bravery, clear-minded counsel and an ally. The role of an agent is to be informed and to guide each of their authors to make the best decisions. On behalf of the author, an agent is responsible for talking through grievances, ensuring that publishers deliver what has been promised, feeding into conversations about strategy regarding their work, saying 'no' when it's appropriate, finding work and pushing back.

While everyone concerned in the publishing process wants a book to succeed, my interests as an agent are the same as those of my client. Publishers' interests obviously dovetail with those of the author, but they aren't identical. This is why we generally find ourselves harmonious and in accord with the process, but occasionally in conflict with it. It's my job to have the necessary conversations to look after my authors, to do everything I can to ensure they have the career they want. We are in it together.

Julia Churchill is the Children's Agent at A.M. Heath Ltd. She is always on the lookout for new writing talent and considers the slush pile to be the greatest place on earth. She is looking for debut and established authors with storytelling magic, from picture book texts through to young adult fiction. Follow her on Twitter @JuliaChurchill.

See also...
- *Choosing the right agent*, page 236
- *Do you have to have an agent to succeed?*, page 245
- *Children's literary agents UK and Ireland*, page 249
- *Children's literary agents overseas*, page 261
- *Society of Authors*, page 349

Literary agents

Submission to a literary agent (the when, what and how...)

Hannah Sheppard offers practical advice on the process of submitting your finished work to a literary agent and provides top tips and inside knowledge on how to find the representation that might be right for you.

Congratulations! You've finished your novel. This is a huge achievement – not everyone manages to see the task through to completion (I know this from experience ... twice). But, what should you do next?

At the risk of being a complete bore – unless you've already done this, now you need to *get back to work and start editing.*

Honing your final manuscript

The first rule of submitting to literary agents is: ***don't* submit your first draft**. It's time to read your work objectively. Where does the pace drop? Where do the characters do things that don't fit with their motivations? Remember that section you really love but know, if you're honest, isn't moving the plot forward? Cut it.

Find a critique partner (Twitter and local writers' groups can be a good place to start); read and give feedback on their novel in return for feedback on your own. You'll learn as much from exercising your inner editor on someone else's work as you will from the feedback they give you.

Go back and re-write. Do it again. Do it until, hand on heart, you cannot see another thing that might need changing. Then print your freshly edited story in a font you haven't seen it in before (alternatively stick the manuscript on your e-reader or phone, or read it aloud to yourself); this will help you see the words with fresh eyes and make it easier to spot any lingering typos, word repetitions or slightly awkward sentences, so you can fix those. Only now are you ready to start thinking about submitting to a literary agent, and first, you'll need to decide who to submit to.

Making your agent list

The second rule of submitting to literary agents is: ***don't* send your work to everyone**. Agents have different tastes and specialisms and there's enough information out there to help you narrow down a list of those who might be suitable for your manuscript. The amount of time authors spend waiting for a response to submissions would be a lot shorter if everyone stuck to this rule!

Luckily, you currently have in your hand the fount of all knowledge when it comes to literary agents – well done. Make your way through the *Children's Writers' & Artists' Yearbook* (but not yet, finish reading this first) looking for agents who represent your genre, and make yourself a longlist. Then look these agents up online – nearly all will have a website, many will also have Twitter accounts, and if you keep hunting you might find articles they've written and also their manuscript wish lists. All of this will give you some clues as to whether each agent might be right for you and your work.

It's also worth thinking about what's important to you when it comes to this relationship. Do you want someone who is a cut-throat dealmaker who is all about the business side of publishing, or someone a little more approachable? (If I'm honest, they're all pretty lovely – I haven't met many of the first kind.) Do you want someone who will be hands-on editorially or do you feel like you've got that covered? My top piece of advice is to find someone you can ask basic questions to without feeling stupid ... because there are going to be a lot of those. Quite honestly, there's no reason you *should* know all about how this industry works. Publishing can be flummoxing at times – even for someone who's been working in it for over 15 years.

After researching everyone on your longlist, put them into some sort of order – from those who feel like the closest fit in terms of their list and who you think you might gel with personally, down to those who could be a bit of wild card but are not completely beyond the realms of possibility. But if an agent says they don't represent your genre, it's unlikely they're going to start doing so just because of *your* book; this is about their publishing contacts as much as anything – and you want an agent who knows the right editors to sell your work.

Putting together a submission package

After selecting the agents to approach, you'll need to prepare your submission package, and the third rule of submitting to literary agents is: **always follow their guidelines**. As well as your *manuscript* (usually the first three chapters or 10,000 words, and always from the beginning of your manuscript), the submission package should generally include a *synopsis* and a *cover letter*. But it's important to check exactly what each agent wants and how they want it sent. These may be different for every agent on your list. Yes, that may be tiresome, but the guidelines are there to enable your chosen agent to get through their inbox as fast as possible (they've worked out a system that works for them) and get an answer to you. And if an author appears to think they're above following the guidelines, I ask myself – why would I want to work with someone who doesn't respect me? Could I feel confident promoting them to editors I have good working relationships with? The harsh truth is, I don't even need to read the material in these cases.

There's a lot of great advice online about writing a synopsis (see for example, www.writersandartists.co.uk/advice/synopsis) but, in short, this should be one page of A4, size 12 font (typically Times New Roman or something similarly readable), single-spaced. Don't play with the margins or shrink the font; think about the person who has to read it – if it's tiny, densely packed text, you've probably lost them. White space on the page is always good.

A synopsis should be a very functional overview of your protagonist's emotional journey. This isn't about trying to wow an agent with your style (but be sure to proofread – try using the different font trick mentioned above). You don't need to include every plot point or introduce every character, but agents do need to know the cause-and-effect structure of your plot – all of it. We *want* the spoilers here please. An agent needs to know that the mechanics of your story work; from this they can see where there might be structural issues to address.

For your cover letter, it's good to strike a professional yet personable tone. This isn't a casual approach, but an agent does want to see some of your personality, to judge whether you're someone they might work well with. Overleaf is the kind of letter I like to see – the focus is very much on the character and story, rather than themes or why the author wrote it.

(1) Dear Hannah/Ms Sheppard

(2) I'm writing to submit *Romeo and Juliet*, a tragic love story for YA readers, complete at 75,000 words.

(3) When Romeo Montague and Juliet Capulet fall in love, it enrages their feuding families. Can they find a way to be together before Juliet is married off to someone else?

(4) Juliet can't even remember what started the argument between her family and the Montagues, it's been going on so long, and as a result she hasn't seen her childhood friend Romeo for years. But when fate brings them together at a school dance which Romeo and his friends have gate-crashed, the connection is immediate. They are meant to be together. Surely their families will see that? But they don't. And in an effort to keep Romeo and Juliet apart, Juliet's family arrange a marriage between Juliet and a friend of her father. Horrified, Romeo and Juliet hatch a plan to escape together, but a series of mixed messages and missed connections lead to disaster.

(5) *Romeo and Juliet* will appeal to readers of *Othello* and *Antony and Cleopatra* and fans of Christopher Marlowe.

(6) I am a debut writer who has …

(7) I am submitting to you because …

(8) Yours sincerely/Regards …

(1) I'm happy with either style. Some agents prefer more formality … but, above all, spell it correctly.

(2) Clearly state your title, target market and word count.

(3) This is your short elevator pitch – it's great to have something like this prepared for chance encounters with an agent, but also for post-publication when you're at promotional events in front of an audience and you're asked to introduce your book. A useful structure is: When A (inciting incident) happens, B (protagonist) must do C (action) otherwise/ before D (stakes) happen.

(4) This gives you a chance to expand a little on the story. You want to focus on the main story line and the emotional journey of your protagonist, making sure that the stakes are clear – knowing what the character stands to lose is important for emotionally engaging your reader. Think of this paragraph a little like the blurb on the back of a book; you want to make me care about the character and intrigue me. The synopsis is where you give the full story.

(5) This is your chance to position your work within the market and demonstrate that you understand the area you're writing into. Try not to include only the mega-sellers, as that suggests you don't read widely in the market – and it's important that you do.

(6) We don't need a huge amount of information about you at this point, but try to include anything pertinent, e.g. have you joined SCBWI; are you part of a writers' group; have you completed a writing course or won a writing competition? None of this is essential, but anything you have done will show how seriously you're taking your writing. My top tip here is **keep it positive**. So, for example, if you haven't won any writing competitions, just don't mention them.

(7) Show that you've done your research and understand a little about the particular agency and agent you're submitting to. Have you read an article in which I talked about my love for the type of story you've written? Does it fit with something my agency has mentioned on its manuscript wish list? Are you a huge fan of one of our existing clients and feel your mutual fandom of that body of work suggests we might like yours too?

(8) Polite sign off … Use your actual name, not just initials or a pseudonym, even if that's what you want to write under. The agent is going to have a working relationship with you.

A few final top tips:

• Use your own, professional email address – almost all submissions are via email now. My agency, DHH Literary, no longer accepts hard copy submissions, and many agencies have the same policy. Don't use an email address you share with your partner or one that was funny when you were a student. Email accounts are easy and free to set up, so have a separate one for your work.

• Make attachment file names as useful as possible... 'synopsis for Hannah' is not very helpful (I receive hundreds with a similar description). Instead include your name and the title of your book.

• Try testing the water by contacting four or five agents initially, to see what response you get. That will give you the chance to tweak your submission. Maybe start midway down the list you drew up of those to contact. If you start getting positive reactions, you can always quickly send the submission to the agents at the top of the list too.

• Brace yourself for a long wait. Agents don't do this to torture you; we're very busy and we use our office time working for our existing clients. This means reading submissions happens in the evenings and at weekends. I typically receive ten submissions a day.

• Start writing your next book, so that you're not focused solely on the fate of the first one you send out. This should ideally be something new rather than a sequel, just in case your first submission doesn't work out.

• Usually a gentle nudge is fine if you haven't heard back within the time stated on the agent's website, but always stay polite. Definitely update an agent if you've had a full manuscript request elsewhere or have been offered representation, and withdraw the submission if you accept that representation.

• If you get feedback, take it seriously. I'm so busy that I rarely give personalised feedback and only when I think there's something easy to fix which would make a significant difference to an author's chances.

• Remember that rejections are part of the process. They don't always mean your book or your writing is bad; they can simply mean that yours wasn't the right book for that agent at that time. There's a lot of luck and serendipity involved here too.

• If all you are getting are standard rejections, take some time out to think about whether you need to do more work. Perhaps you should get a professional assessment on your manuscript? Or maybe it's time to begin a different project (luckily you followed my earlier tip and have already started one, right?).

• Keep an open mind, the right agent for you might not be the person you initially put at the top of your wish list. How you get on at a personal level when you chat with an agent will be important.

So that's it ... you're ready to start submitting. Good luck, hold your nerve and keep trying.

Literary agent and development editor **Hannah Sheppard** worked as an in-house editor with Macmillan Children's Books and Headline Publishing Group before joining the DHH Literary Agency in 2013. She represents authors from across children's fiction (middle grade, teen and YA) and adult fiction (crime/thriller and women's fiction). For more information see www.dhhliteraryagency.com/hannah-sheppard.html. Follow Hannah on Twitter @YA_Books.

Literary agents

Choosing the right agent

Literary agent Gill McLay describes some of the differences between big and small agencies, and identifies some of the ways you can discover which might be the right one for you to approach and to sign up with if you are offered representation.

After completing my marketing and publishing degree I moved to London and went straight into my first publishing job. Over 25 years later I am still in publishing. I have worked for small, independent publishers and large global publishers, always on the publicity, marketing and sales side of the business. Then, about 15 years ago, I decided I wanted to work for myself. One of the many things I did was to set up the Bath Festival of Children's Literature, the largest festival in Europe devoted exclusively to books, authors, illustrators and readers of children's books – from picture books right up to YA. I knew it had to start big if it was to compete in the already vibrant and well-developed literary festivals calendar. After our success with the festival, we have evolved again to establish, Events of Wonder (www.eventsofwonder.com) which stages events for children in Bath, Bristol and beyond. Creating these magical moments for children and families remains very close to my heart and having a wider range of partners has meant we can now reach so many more people. It has also allowed us to stage art exhibitions, other festivals and develop clubs that ensure we work at a truly grassroots level.

It was while I was working more closely with authors, through the festival, that I started to be asked for publishing advice. I would frequently recommend agents that fledging writers could approach and was repeatedly asked why I didn't offer an agent service myself. Being an agent is an all-encompassing job and I knew it would need me to be full-time, so I decided that when my son started school I would do it!

At the time, I was running media training courses for authors and was always surprised by the questions they asked (or hadn't dared or thought to ask). I decided that if I was to be an agent, I would manage careers rather than projects and I would allow authors to become a fully engaged part of my agency. For me, part of surviving in this tough and competitive business is to help my clients be prepared, and to share my knowledge of why decisions are made and how. As well as showing respect for my authors' writing and other creative work, I set out to establish working relationships based on mutual respect, understanding and gratitude for the respective skills of both author and agent; from such close links, greater successes emerge. *Teams* of people create books, and I wanted to put this team spirit right at the heart of my agency.

The Bath Literary Agency is a relatively small company that offers a very hands-on style of management for writers and illustrators of children's books. We are one of many small literary agencies based outside London, the main publishing metropolis, and we like to think that we offer authors something different to what a larger agency provides. The agency is now ten years old and continues to go from strength to strength, due to my clients who work incredibly hard to deliver saleable books. Together we are always working on our next project.

How can *you* find the right agent?

I believe that having an agent is essential. Once you are lucky enough to find your publishing home, it makes a big difference if you can focus on the creative side and let your agent focus on the business aspects of your writing.

This doesn't mean you don't get involved. You *must* be involved. It does, however, mean that you can talk through things with your agent and ask all the questions you like without fear of asking the wrong thing – which might not be the case if you were talking directly to a publisher. It also gives you a greater understanding of which things to challenge and which to accept, both contractually and creatively. There is a huge difference between writing for yourself and writing to be published; an agent can help you navigate this fine line.

What are the differences between small and large agencies?

Bigger agencies, London-based agencies, multimedia agencies and small boutique agencies (with only one or two agents, say) all offer different things. They each have their strengths and weaknesses; the most important thing for you, as a new author, is to get the right agent for *your* books and *your* needs.

The size of the agency is actually irrelevant in many ways, because everything comes down to the relationship you have with one person: your own agent.

That relationship should be symbiotic, with writer and agent coming together to make the strongest possible offering to a publisher, and thus ultimately to your readership or market. Your respective strengths and weaknesses should complement each other.

This is why you need to know your agent's experience. Agents come from all

> **In a nutshell**
>
> **Know what you want:**
> • Do you want to be a big fish in a small pond?
> • Do you write across several genres; if so, does the agent represent them all?
> • Do you want an agent with editorial skills to help shape your writing?
> • Do you want personal support or purely business/commercial help?

sorts of different backgrounds, which can make a huge difference to their individual approach. Many have been editors, some move over from selling rights in publishing houses to agenting and others have come from the sales and book-buying side of publishing. Each set of skills and experience has its own strengths.

My background is in sales and marketing. As a result, I approach things from a very commercial angle and spend almost as much time scouting for new opportunities as I do creating them. When I advise my clients, we talk about long-term objectives and career progression. The individual books are important, but I am always keen to find out what else an author can do and where they want to be.

An agent with an editorial background, however, may focus more on the individual manuscript. For some authors this is essential and they need this support, but others may already have confidence and feel secure in their writing, but they may need help to understand the market and publishing process and to pitch their story to the right audience and gatekeepers (i.e. publishers).

Part of this writer-development process, fostering authors of tomorrow, comes from the other professional hats I wear. Media training for authors, Events of Wonder and the festival I have run has given me a real insight into the life of a successful author today. Gone are the days of being able to write, send your script to an agent, sell your book and then start writing again. An author needs to promote and reach their audience. The first book you sell to a publisher will be the last before you add the role of juggler to your CV, as you tackle the balancing act of writing *and* promoting!

Literary agents

A larger agency will often have staff who specialise in rights, contract, legal, accounts and admin support. A smaller agency is more likely to have only a couple of these specialists, and sometimes they will have none; the agent may coordinate all aspects of the process. Which you prefer and works best for you is completely personal. Do you want to work with one person who answers everything, or do you wish to work with a team? Larger agencies may also be able to offer you other focused advice. For example, if you wish to write for adults, write plays or film scripts, they may have people on hand to advise or represent you beyond, for example, your initial work in YA fiction. Smaller agencies can sometimes do this too, but tend to be more specialised.

Ideally, you should meet agents from both large and smaller agencies – that's if you are lucky enough to be offered representation by more than one agency. This will help you make an informed decision. It is in no one's interest for you to be with the wrong agent. Choosing the right agent is a balance of gut instinct and information; do your research before you contact them with your initial submission, and then again when they have shown interest in representing you.

One thing that everyone needs is an agent who is nice to work with, but also one who is an effective and strong dealmaker. When selecting your agent, there are some **key things to consider**:

1. How many clients do they have and who are they? If you feel that you will need and want a lot of hands-on support with your writing, a large agency may not be for you. If you are a confident writer and want someone who has big agency presence, then maybe the children's agent in a bigger agency would suit you.

2. Do they have clients that write in the same genre as you? This is a great indicator that they have strong contacts with the right commissioning editors and can sell this genre. But if they have lots of authors in this field, will you be competing with other clients within their agency? The balance needs to be right. So do look at their client list.

3. Where are they based? These days this seems to matter less and less but, if they are not near you, how often could you and they travel to a mutually sensible location (e.g. London)?

4. What sort of agent are they? Do you want an editor or commercial management? Do you have one book that you need an agent to sell, or do you have multiple ideas that you want someone to help you develop?

5. Can you relax and feel comfortable with them? You need to be able to communicate well with your agent. Is this someone you can work with? The relationship will become really important as you set off on the rollercoaster ride of getting published; you need to be yourself and have complete trust in your agent.

Always trust your gut instinct. If this is the agency and person you can imagine working with, then take the next step and sign up. Getting published is a long process, success doesn't come overnight, so who you share your journey with is important. Big agency or small agency, it's all about best fit and only you can decide which is right for you.

Gill McLay runs the Bath Literary Agency (www.bathliteraryagency.com) which specialises in children's books. She is co-founder of the annual Bath Festival of Children's Literature. She runs Events of Wonder (www.eventsofwonder.com) with her husband John McLay.

A message for under-represented writers: We Want You

Davinia Andrew-Lynch knows that, as well as a good story, agents and editors are also on the lookout for talented writers from groups and communities currently under-represented in the world of children's publishing. She has advice for marginalised writers on how to find the representation, confidence and support they need.

Despite the increasing number of children's books published each year, many budding authors find the world of publishing daunting. And, for those of you from under-represented groups (including, but not limited to, minority ethnic/religious, LGBTQ+ and working-class communities), this London-centric industry can seem wholly unwelcoming.

Things are changing, however. The vital importance of youngsters seeing themselves reflected in the books they read has become an issue more frequently recognised by 'gate-keepers' across the industry. The inclusion of these different narratives is not only good for society; it is also good for the health of our business. So, let's get practical. Whilst this book contains a plethora of information to get you on your way, the advice offered highlights how you, as an under-represented writer, can kick-start your career and get noticed.

When submitting to agents, always *do your research*. Does the agent you're looking at represent picture books, middle grade, YA or all of these? What genres do they favour? Are they newer agents actively on the hunt for talent? Studying an agent's existing list will answer many of your questions, but Twitter can also provide you with extra up-to-date information. You never know, an agent's simple #MSWL (Manuscript Wish List) alert may just equate to the very book you've written. And check out #DVPit (strapline 'A Twitter Pitching Event for Marginalized Voices'); it's a great *free* opportunity.

At the same time, do not be deterred from approaching an agent whose list *doesn't* seem obviously inclusive. Time and time again I have met authors who have not submitted work to an agency because they didn't feel that they were reflected by an agent's existing clientele. And, do you know what? Often agents will say that they're just not hearing from marginalised writers, and that they don't understand *why*. Clearly there's a bit of a catch-22 situation going on here, because I for one know that you exist. Remember that agents are essentially looking for a good story and, granted, it is their job to look for talent in (and from) all forms and places; by not submitting your work, you are limiting your chance of discovery. If your story has the elements of a potential success, then the right agent will give you that chance of representation. So, if you like the look of an agent and think your work may appeal, type that email and hit Send!

If you are not yet ready to submit your manuscript, an extensive satellite industry of advice and support has developed to provide authors with the tools to navigate the world of publishing. And, now more than ever, many of these programmes are actively looking to reach out to those who may not have previously believed or found publishing to be a welcoming space. Often you will find events giving you access to many of the individuals on the 'inside', and these insiders (including agents and editors) want to hear from *you*. Understand, these gatekeepers are not wanting to pay lip service to a fad; they are driven by the satisfaction of finding and supporting genuine talent.

Literary agents

Writers' conferences and festivals can often be a good place to start. Yes, they can be an expense, but they can also be a worthwhile investment. Not only are they a vast source of information but, by giving you a couple of days to immerse yourself in a space which celebrates and encourages your writing, they can be the perfect boost for your confidence. You will have the opportunity to attend specific workshops, panel events, hear keynote speeches and often you can book a one-to-one appointment with an agent or editor. For many authors, these one-to-ones can be particularly valuable, and in fact I met one of my current clients at the Winchester Writers' Festival in this way. One of the most prominent such events, focusing on children's content, is hosted by SCBWI, a worldwide members network (see page 356). Their conference offers all of the above, but it also gives you access to a community of like-minded authors, and this can be a particular draw and comfort.

Do check the conference listings in this *Yearbook* (which start on page 403). As you will see, there are a number of them taking place around the country, at different times of the year and sometimes focusing on a specific area of publishing. But do understand, it is not about attending as many as possible. Assess your situation; consider what it is that you want to know about the industry and then do your research. If you are making the choice to spend your money in this way, then you should ensure that it is cash well spent – you want to leave that conference feeling better equipped to deal with what will, hopefully, be a future career. If the idea of a conference feels too much, then consider the many evening salons, day workshops and afternoon panel sessions offering more tailored advice. There really are events aplenty, and sometimes these are more affordable financially and timewise.

How do you find out about these events? Check out your local regional literary organisations, for instance, New Writing North/South, Writing West/East Midlands and Spread the Word (London) are a few of the most prominent (see *Societies, associations and organisations* section, starting on page 366). Each of these bodies work tirelessly to support new writers – and particularly those who may have to overcome varying barriers due to a, frankly, institutional bias (however unintentional). Not only do these organisations host their own events but they will often highlight and promote worthwhile external opportunities. A good example of this is the Free Reads Scheme organised by The Literary Consultancy (one of the largest editorial services companies in the country). In conjunction with the Arts Council, the scheme works with local literary organisations to find authors who may require and appreciate a subsidised manuscript assessment service. It is a brilliant opportunity which acknowledges that the choice to write is not necessarily an affordable one – a fact which in itself makes publishing seem as though it should only be for the privileged few. And, on the issue of expense, you may find that some of these services will offer bursaries for specific groups of people. They are there to help, not isolate. Do not hesitate to get in touch with those who are organising such events and ask whether there is anything you can apply for.

Do also keep an eye out for upcoming competitions; industry magazine *The Bookseller* often announces the most notable of these. While many are open to all writers, it is also worth investigating the increasing number which specifically target under-represented groups. These competitions may not land you with the hallowed publishing deal or representation but, depending on the scheme, they may offer the opportunity for you to get a foot in the door. For instance (and please excuse the personal plug here, ahem ahem ...): the FAB Prize (see page 388) was set up by Faber Children's and Andlyn, looking specifically for un-agented and un-published BAME writing/illustrating talent. The individual category winners are awarded with mentoring, and an anthology of their work and the work of the runners-up is circulated around children's literary agents. Since the Prize's inception, a number of entrants have gone on to gain representation and get published. The prize was a *platform*, but these writers reached their goal off the back of their own merit. Be sure to use these opportunities – that is what they are there for.

I would be remiss not to mention the Arts Council (see page 366) in this context. Easily forgotten, but open to all, it has a number of grant schemes which provide writers with the time and space to focus on their writing. It has to be said that, particularly within children's publishing, the body is incredibly keen to help address the imbalance of marginalised voices. As mentioned, the financial implications of wanting to be a writer stretch far and wide; if this applies to you, see whether there is a grant for which you may qualify.

Having dealt with the practical side of pursuing your writing career, here's my take on how our identities can enrich the stories we tell. Children's publishing has always been synonymous with the idea that its stories and literature can teach children about the society in which they live. Yet statistics (most recently those led by BookTrust and CLPE – the Centre for Literacy in Primary Education – on multicultural diversity) show that there is a serious dearth of stories featuring characters from under-represented backgrounds. In my conversations with authors, the word 'diversity' seems to have inadvertently given way to the suggestion and/or impression that diverse stories should be 'issue'-led, that they should highlight the barriers or difficulties of 'other' lives. And, because there are so few novels in the market featuring minority groups and/or marginalised characters within a British context, it has become all too easy to associate particular kinds of stories with the different under-represented groups.

This means that, to some extent, an element of stereotyping has come in to play. But why? We can learn about each other within the framework of a simply entertaining and *mainstream* story. Your idea, *not* your identity, should be your USP. Remember you want (and deserve) to be measured on the same scale as any other author and, with that, there should be a freedom to write any kind of story. If you want to create an epic 'through the wardrobe'-style adventure, a YA rom-com, or a rather left-of-centre comedy, then you must. Saying that, if you want to write a gritty issue-led tale, feel free to do that too! For those working within the industry, your ability to produce an excellent narrative is the attraction, but when your stories reflect you, your community, your *rarely seen world* – that is refreshing, and frankly a bonus.

There are many individuals within children's publishing who actively want to change the landscape so that its output is more inclusive. It cannot be denied, however, that our intentions are often left rattling around an echo chamber and that this message of inclusivity isn't necessarily being received on the 'outside'. So I am saying this very clearly now: as an industry we need your stories but, more importantly, we want you ... *all of you, not just your demographic.* We look forward to hearing from you soon!

Davinia Andrew-Lynch founded the literary agency Andlyn in 2015, and specialises in children's and YA fiction and content. She previously worked as an associate agent at the Dench Arnold Agency, a film/TV agency, and as a freelance children's fiction editor and reader. For more information see www.andlyn.co.uk. Follow Davinia on Twitter @nocturnalreader.

See also...
● *Opportunities for under-represented writers*, page 396

Literary agents

The life and works of a literary scout

Sophie Clarke explains just what a literary scout's role and life entails, with its varied and challenging workload and often all-consuming pace, the buzz of staying well-informed and well-connected, and the satisfaction that comes from matching the right book to the right client.

Entitling this article 'the life and works of a literary scout' seems unusually apt because, as with many jobs in publishing, trying to separate the personal from the professional in the career of literary scout is nigh on impossible. It is a job that relies on forming, maintaining and nurturing connections, assessing the industry with a finely-honed eye to see which way the winds are blowing, and on reading accurately and critically at speed. Your role is to deliver professional judgement with a personal touch to your clients, who need guidance or advice to help them find the books which will work best for them. You are, in effect, a literary matchmaker. The clients of a literary scout are foreign publishers seeking to buy titles originally published in one language in order to translate them into their own, for publication and sale in their territory or market. Scouts can work across a range of languages, for example all literature from the Scandinavian countries, or in one language, such as just the UK or USA.

The information game

Literary scouts, unlike agents and editors, do not work directly with authors. They trade in information, gossip, industry buzz and foreign-market knowledge. A good scout has their finger on the pulse of the market they are scouting. They know which books are out on submission from agents to editors and, of those, which are making noise and going up for auction or being pre-empted. They are aware of which editors are moving between publishing houses, going on parental leave or sabbatical, or looking to acquire specific types of titles. They stay up-to-date on which new authors an agent might be representing; announcements on Twitter are particularly helpful for this. Before titles go on submission (the process where agents send manuscripts to editors for them to sign-up or 'buy' for publication), scouts actively check in with agents about any titles which sound particularly interesting, or any which might be particularly suited to specific clients of theirs.

In order to gather this information, at least half of the scout's role is to talk – and to as many people as possible. Scouts are in contact day-to-day with primary agents (representing authors), rights agents (selling titles internationally) and publishing editors (acquiring titles and working with authors) via email and WhatsApp, as well as via video, phone and in-person meetings. These conversations allow scouts to build up a picture of what is currently going on in UK publishing. The wider and warmer a scout's network of contacts, the better the overall picture they can provide, and the better informed their clients will be – ideally ahead of competitors – and thus able to make decisions faster. A scout's network is more than a directory of contacts. Most become friends or – at the very least – valued acquaintances. It's almost impossible not to build up a close relationship; a scout may talk to a client once a day in peak season to check in on a title that's moving quickly and being acquired widely. Over the course of many meetings and emails, both parties get to know each other well. But of course, the core aspect of the relationship requires that, however kindly one might think of a contact personally, each has professional duties to the other.

Reading ... with a difference

The other half of a scout's role is to read, and to read quickly, professionally and widely in the area they scout in. Some scouts cover all genres; some specialise, for example in children's and YA, like me. Reading and reporting on titles – providing a brief summary of the plot, information on the author and any notable facts or sales for the title – must be prioritised. Often, it must be done at speed. When titles are submitted for acquisition and begin to gather buzz domestically and/or internationally, translation sales begin to fall like dominoes in the right territories. A scout's reading does not always take place in the office or within office hours; with their clients in a variety of different time zones and territories, scouts must always be prepared to support and respond at any time of the day or night. As titles begin to move, auctions (multiple publishing houses bidding and offering on a title) and pre-empts (making an offer so convincing that the title is bought quickly and exclusively without the hassle of an auction) can happen overnight or even within a matter of hours from submission. This means that speed of reading, responding and reporting to clients is of the essence. You may be reading several manuscripts at one time, especially if you cover a broad range of titles. It's not uncommon for an individual scout to read between seven and ten titles a week – sometimes even more, around the busy book-fair seasons. You read with several different hats on, as there are many considerations: Will this title work in the UK market? Will it work in any of my client markets? Will any of the client's editors like it, even if it might not seem to be something for their market? Is it, objectively, any good? Do you, personally, like it – and would you be willing to recommend it, based on your own tastes, despite any other minor flaws to it? Addressing such questions, while reading to tight deadlines before reporting back to clients on a title, turns a seemingly simple task into one filled with nuance that requires a scout's expertise and professional knowledge.

Networking nous

Networking, as with the reading, isn't entirely limited within office hours either. Scouts are a regular fixture at parties, book launches and other publishing industry events – in fact anywhere where it's possible to hobnob and mix with the widest possible number of people and have the most wide-ranging conversations, gleaning titbits of gossip and information. Breakfasts, lunches, coffees, dinners and drinks meetings all feature regularly in scout life as well – meaning that we're extremely well-fed, as well as well-informed! As a scout, you quickly become very comfortable with walking into events where you might only know a few people, and leaving having befriended at least a few more. This skill comes in particularly useful at the international trade book fairs. These happen throughout the year, but the main ones are in Frankfurt in the autumn, London and Bologna in the spring. Bologna is specifically focused on children's and young adult titles. Editors, agents and rights agents from a multitude of countries gather to buy, sell and discuss titles. Scouts are at the heart of it – talking to their clients, meeting with editors and rights agents from outside their home territory and attending as many events as possible so as to meet the maximum number of people. Rights fairs are key for rights sales and for getting material, authors and passion in front of editors' noses. A scout's enthusiasm for a particular title, and their awareness of information ahead of it being public knowledge, can create excitement and help their publisher clients strike deals.

Author's friend

Indirectly, a scout is helping an author, even though they'll probably never meet and an author may be unaware of a scout's role across the publishing process. Across the course of many weeks, months or years, a scout may constantly re-flag an author's work or a specific title to their clients, demonstrating the momentum that a book or author is gathering both in their home territory and across other territories too. Sometimes, a book moves very quickly and there are swift acquisitions in the UK, the USA and a host of international territories – that's the dream scenario. But often books and authors take time to garner success and recognition and, as each building block of that process is achieved (e.g. sales figures, prize-shortlisting or -winning, accrued rights sales), a scout can be instrumental in reminding their clients of a title, seeing whose publishing list or taste might have changed enough to acquire it now, even if they passed over it previously.

To be a successful scout involves a high level of networking and reading, but of course there is far more to it than that. It also involves a huge volume of email traffic, lots of administration to stay on top of contacts – their changing roles and keeping up-to-date on correct territory contacts at each publisher and agency, organising meeting schedules for the book fairs, and reporting regularly to clients. All of this builds up to an ever-changing and shifting role – which is precisely what makes it one of the most exciting jobs in publishing. Scouts come from a variety of different backgrounds: some have started as interns at scouting agencies and worked their way up; others have previously worked at a publisher in rights or in editorial; others have come from a literary agency and are able to employ their already keen understanding of the industry. Most have some knowledge of a foreign language and culture, although almost all communication between scout and client is in English, and all reading is done in English too. Regardless of how they entered the industry, the key element a scout must have is a passion for, and deep knowledge of, the area of literature they are working in – no matter how broad or narrow that patch. Also helpful are the enthusiasm and energy to work more than occasional long hours, a curiosity about foreign markets, a desire to be well-informed about as much as possible, and the ability to read and network and manage emails beyond the office. And you need to be prepared – at peak book-fair season, when the pace becomes frenetic and the pressure to remain ahead of competitors becomes high – to be almost consumed by the job!

Reading back through this, I'm afraid I may have made scouting sound far too serious, when actually it's the most fun job I've ever had. There's a lot of stress, to be sure, but there also is a lot of laughter and camaraderie in the team as everyone works so closely together to deliver a great service to their clients. It's nigh on impossible to complain (and I certainly wouldn't now, amidst the pandemic) about drinks events and book launches and parties and trips to the book fairs, even if they are outside office hours. You read books months and even years before the general public sees them. It's fair to say that scouting, in both little and big ways, shapes your life because it dictates the structure of your social and professional weeks, months and seasons; but it also shapes the lives of authors. For a scout, when a client acquires a title that you loved – one that has the potential to be successful for them and you also know the deal will be wonderful for the author – it really is the best feeling. Literary match … made.

Sophie Clarke is a scout for children's books at Daniela Schlingmann Literary Scouting (https://schlingmann.co.uk). She has previously worked at the publisher Penguin Random House Children's and at the Literary agencies Curtis Brown and Bell Lomax Moreton.

Do you *have* to have an agent to succeed?

Bestselling children's author Philip Ardagh has over 100 titles to his credit but chooses not to have a literary agent to represent him. In this article he tells us why.

There are a lot of people out there who think that they're children's writers ('I was a child myself once, you know') and who send unsolicited manuscripts directly to publishers in their hundreds – possibly thousands – every year. These manuscripts usually end up on what is called the 'slush pile'. Some publishers won't even read them. Some do but, usually, only after a very long time. Many manuscripts are very badly written or very badly presented. Some are perfectly good but a little too much like something already out there in the bookshops, or they lack that indefinable something that makes them stand out from the crowd. Others are perfectly good but are sent to completely the wrong publisher. The best children's fantasy novel ever isn't going to appeal to a publisher specialising in adult DIY manuals, is it? Getting an agent cuts through this process.

Having an agent

Firstly, if an agent submits a manuscript it will go to the publisher they think that it's best suited to, and probably to the most suitable editor within that company – more often than not someone they know or have had dealings with in the past. So your manuscript is being seen by the right people at the right place. It's also neatly bypassed the slush pile. It will actually get read. Hurrah! The agent has acted as a filter. The publisher knows that, if you've been taken on by a reputable agent, your words are probably *worth* reading. You're ahead of the game.

An agent knows the ins and outs of advances, royalties, escalators, foreign rights and a million and one other things that make the humble writer's head spin. Agents know the 'going rates' and will get you the very best deal they can if a publisher wants to publish your work. And, should there be problems further down the line, your agent can play the bad guy on your behalf – renegotiating contracts and doing the number crunching – whilst you only deal with the nice fluffy creative side with your editor.

That's the theory, of course, and much of it is true. They take their 10–15% share but they're not a charity and, if they're on a percentage of your earnings, it's generally in their interest to make you as much money as possible, isn't it?

The question is: is it possible to be a successful children's author without an agent? Of course it is. Anything's possible. I'm an agentless author and I'm doing fine, but not without help, advice, common sense, good luck and, as time has passed, experience.

So what are the disadvantages of having an agent? If you've got the right agent, the answer is probably very few, if any. Sure, you're not earning the full advance or royalty because you're giving them a percentage but your manuscript may never have become a book (or the advance and royalty may have been much lower) if they didn't represent you in the first place. If you have an agent you don't get directly involved in every aspect of negotiation and discussion with your publisher because you've handed that role over. And if you like the on-hands approach (for that read 'are a control freak'), you may miss out on that but, overall, the pros seem to outweigh the cons.

If you're *not* happy with your agent, though, it can be a very different story. You're not your agent's only client and you may feel – rightly or wrongly – that they're not giving you enough attention. Many is the writer and illustrator I know who has said, 'I find more work for myself than my agent does', or who isn't happy with the advance they've received and said, 'I'm not sure why my agent was so keen for me to agree to this deal.' Another familiar lament is, 'She seemed so enthusiastic when I first signed up, but now she's gone really quiet.' Your filter has become a barrier.

There may also be jobs which your agent is reluctant for you to take. In children's non-fiction, many authors are still paid flat fees, and small ones at that. Many agents will tell you not to touch them with a barge pole but – if you are at the beginning of your career – who knows what that little job might lead to? I once wrote the text to a book that owed its subsequent international success not to the beauty of my prose but to the illustrations and brilliant paper engineering. My fee was peanuts and, in immediate financial terms, it made no difference if the book sold three copies or 300,000. But it did my writing career the power of good. My name was associated with a successful title, I got known by various people within that particular publishing house, I went on to write many more books for them *with* royalties and added to my reputation, generating interest from other publishers.

Going it alone

I enjoy that getting-to-know aspect of developing a relationship with publishers and, when it comes to contracts, I have a very useful not-so-secret secret weapon. I may not have an agent but I can call on the contracts experts at the Society of Authors (see page 349). As a member of the Society, they'll go through a contract line by line for me, free and for nothing, offering comments, suggestions and advice. They also publish excellent easy-to-understand pamphlets on various aspects of publishing. If you're not already a member, rush out and join immediately! If you don't understand something, don't be afraid to ask.

Remember, whatever impression a publisher might give, there is very rarely such a thing as a standard contract, written in stone, that can't be altered; sometimes significantly. Be prepared to concede some minor points, maybe, in return for sticking to your guns over a point which may really matter to you. (Different things matter to different writers.)

My big break came by luck, but luck borne out of developing contacts and making real friendships in the course of my agentless foray into the children's publishing world. The bulk of my 100 or so titles are non-fiction, but the bulk of my income and 95% of my recognition comes from my fiction, but one grew from the other. Because I was involved and enthusiastic, I was invited to promote one of my non-fiction titles at a sales conference. As a result of how I ad-libbed at the conference, following a mighty cock-up, I was asked if I wrote fiction. *Awful End* (my first Eddie Dickens book) was pulled out of the drawer and a deal was done. One thing had, indeed, led to another. Eddie's adventures are in over 30 languages and read around the world, and have picked up a few literary awards along the way.

Your rights

Publishers love to have world rights to books. Agents love to sell the rights separately. You can see why. An agent will argue that they can get more for you (and therefore more for them) by selling foreign rights separately to foreign publishers – perhaps creating a US auction for your fabulous book, for example – rather than your signing everything over to your UK publisher in one fell swoop. If, however, you sell the world rights to the publisher, and you have a good relationship with them, they're in effect acting as your agent on foreign deals and can still negotiate some excellent ones *in consultation with you*. And, having your world rights, they can share in your international success when it comes, so may be more keen to nurture you (and your money-generating, recognition-building world rights) in the future than, possibly, another writer whom they only publish in the UK.

And remember, an advance is an advance of royalties. If the advance is small and the book is a success, it simply means that the advance is earned out sooner and the cheques start rolling in. My advance for *Awful End* was just a four figure sum, but the money I've earned from additional royalties has been very-nice-thank-you-very-much. And my advances for the later Eddie Dickens books and other fiction were significantly larger.

Making the right decision

I know from friends and colleagues that, when you're starting out, you can find it as hard to get an agent as a publisher, which is why some people choose to go straight for the publishing houses. My advice – and this may surprise some of you – is to stick at trying to get an agent. If I was starting out now, I'd do that. Having an agent from the beginning makes sense.

If you're dead against the idea, feeling convinced that you can do a great job or are exhausted trying, there are a few obvious things you can do. Even now, I sometimes ask myself 'Am I getting the very best deal?' and 'Could an agent do better for me?' Financially, the answers to these are probably 'Maybe not' and 'Yes', but are these the right questions? Surely what I need to ask is: 'Am I happy with this deal?' and 'Is it a reasonable sum reflecting what I think I'm worth and showing the commitment and understanding of the publisher?' And the answer to that is, more often than not, 'Yes'. And remember, money ain't the be-all and end-all. A good working relationship with an editor and publisher who understand you, consult with you, nurture you and your writing and promote and market you in a way you're happy with is beyond price.

Approaching a publisher

But let's not get ahead of ourselves. One of the most important, important, *important* – it's important, get it? – things you need to be sure of before sending a manuscript to an agent *or* a publisher is that it's ready to be seen. Some unpublished writers are so keen to show their work to others in the hope of getting it published as soon as possible that it's still in a very raw state. They're not doing themselves any favours. In fact, they could be ruining their chances. Sure, there is such a thing as overworking a piece, but you really need to be confident that it's about as good as it's going to get, especially if you're bypassing the agent route and going direct to the publisher. With no agent 'filter', you've got to be sure that you're representing yourself, through your work, in the very best possible light.

Look in bookshops to find out who publishes what. Once you've chosen a publisher, look them up in this *Yearbook*, find out their submissions procedure and ring them up. Ask the receptionist the name of the person you should send your manuscript or sample chapters to. This way you can address and write a letter to a particular person, rather than taking the 'Dear Sir/Madam' approach.

Literary agents

The covering letter you should write to the publisher is almost identical to the one for writing to a prospective agent (see *Submission to a literary agent (the when, what and how ...)* on page 232) except, of course, that you should also include the reason why you think they'd be the right people to publish your work.

Finally, do treat the business side of selling yourself as a business. It's not simply that 'the writing's the important bit' and that it'll 'sell itself'. Network, send in invoices on time, get in touch when you say you'll get in touch and be contactable (there's no excuse for dropping off the radar in this age of emails and mobile phones). If you're shy or don't like parties, still go to the ones you're invited to by your publisher. You never know what that chance meeting with that rather scruffy bloke by the chilli dips might lead to. He could end up turning your book into a 24-part television series.

Oh, and one last thing: never admit that, secretly, you enjoy writing so much that you'd happily be published for nothing. Oops. Me and my big mouth!

Agented or agentless, good luck.

Philip Ardagh is an award-winning children's author, reviewer and commentator, whose prizes include the Roald Dahl Funny Prize and the prestigious Deutscher Jugendliteraturpreis. He is an ambassador for the Stratford Literary Festival and for the Northern Children's Book Festival, as well as being Lifetime Ambassador for the School Libraries Group of CILIP, the library and information association. Philip became International Children's Literary Consultant for Listowel Writers' Week, in Ireland, in its 50th year. He has collaborated with illustrators such as Axel Scheffler and David Roberts, with whom he celebrated 20 years of Eddie Dickens's adventures in 2020. He also collaborated with Sir Paul McCartney on the children's book, *High in the Clouds*, currently being developed as a feature film by Netflix and Gaumont. He is currently working with Rob Biddulph on *The Nine Lives of Furry Purry Beancat* (Simon & Schuster), having recently collaborated with illustrator Jamie Littler on the *Secret Diary* series for the National Trust (Nosy Crow), in which 'only the facts are true'. A lifelong Moomin fan, he wrote *The World of Moominvalley*, the definitive guide to Tove Jansson's Moomins. His books have been translated into over 40 languages. Follow Philip on Facebook, or on Twitter @PhilipArdagh.

See also...
● *What do agents do for their commission?*, page 229
● *The Society of Authors*, page 349

Children's literary agents UK and Ireland

The *Children's Writers' & Artists' Yearbook*, along with the Association of Authors' Agents and the Society of Authors, takes a dim view of any literary agent who asks potential clients for a fee prior to a manuscript being placed with a publisher. We advise you to treat any such request with caution and to let us know if that agent appears in the listings below. Agents may charge additional costs later in the process but these should only arise once a book has been accepted by a publisher and the author is earning an income. Authors should also check agents' websites before making an enquiry and should familiarise themselves with submission guidelines.

*Member of the Association of Authors' Agents
sae = self-addressed envelope

The Agency (London) Ltd*
24 Pottery Lane, London W11 4LZ
tel 020-7727 1346
email childrensbooksubmissions@theagency.co.uk
website https://theagency.co.uk/childrens-books/childrens-home/
Twitter @TALLChildrens
Children's Book Agents Hilary Delamere and Jessica Hare

Works in conjunction with overseas agents. The Agency also represents screenwriters, directors, playwrights and composers. Represents picture books, including novelty books, fiction for all ages including teenage fiction and series fiction. *Commission* Home 15%, overseas 20%. Submission guidelines on website. *Founded* 1995.

Aitken Alexander Associates Ltd*
291 Gray's Inn Road, London WC1X 8QJ
tel 020-7373 8672
email reception@aitkenalexander.co.uk
website www.aitkenalexander.co.uk
Twitter @AitkenAlexander
Instagram AitkenAlexander
Agent Amy St Johnston

Children's and young adult fiction. Handles fiction for 9+ to young adult. *Commission* Home 15%, overseas 20%. Email preliminary letter with half-page synopsis and first 30 pages of sample material via agency website or to submissions@aitkenalexander.co.uk. No picture books.

For a full list of clients, see the website. *Founded* 1977.

Darley Anderson Children's Book Agency Ltd*
Suite LG4, New Kings House,
136–144 New Kings Road, London SW6 4LZ

tel 020-7385 6652
email childrens@darleyanderson.com
website www.darleyandersonchildrens.com
Twitter @DA_Childrens
Instagram da_childrens
Contacts Darley Anderson (Managing Director), Camilla Bolton (Director), Clare Wallace (Senior Agent), Lydia Silver (Agent), Sheila David (TV and Film Rights), Chloe Davis (Junior Agent/Assistant to Clare Wallace)

Children's fiction and non-fiction (for all ages from picture book to middle grade through to young adult and crossover). For illustrators, please refer to the Darley Anderson Illustration Agency. *Commission* Home 15%, USA/translation 20%, film/TV/radio 20%. Send covering letter, short synopsis and first three chapters by email. No scripts or screenplays.

Clients include Cathy Cassidy, John Connolly, Caroline Crowe, Martyn Ford, Stewart Foster, Lindsay Galvin, A.M. Howell, Polly Ho-Yen, Rachel Ip, Rachel Morrisroe, Beth Reekles, Dave Rudden, Nick Sheridan, Rashmi Sirdeshpande, Deirdre Sullivan. *Founded* 1988.

ANDLYN
tel 020-3290 5638
email submissions@andlyn.co.uk
website www.andlyn.co.uk
Twitter @andlynlit
Founder and Agent Davinia Andrew-Lynch

Represents authors of picture books, middle grade, young adult and crossover fiction – all genres. Also represents adult fiction and non-fiction. *Commission* Home and audio 15%, USA, foreign/translation, film/TV, multi-platform and online media rights 20%. See website for submission guidelines.

Clients include Malcolm Duffy, Bex Hogan, Julie Middleton, Annabelle Sami. *Founded* 2015.

Bath Literary Agency*
5 Gloucester Road, Bath BA1 7BH
tel (01225) 317894

email submissions@bathliteraryagency.com
website www.bathliteraryagency.com
Twitter @BathLitAgency
Instagram bathlitagency
Contact Gill McLay

Specialist in fiction for children and young adults. Also accepts submissions in picture books, non-fiction and author illustrators. *Commission* UK 15%, overseas 20%, film/TV 20%. For full submission details, refer to the website.

   Clients include Lou Abercrombie, Fox Benwell, Conor Busuttil, Philippa Forrester, Dr Jess French, Tweedy, Joe Haddow, Demelsa Haughton, Harry Heape, Laura James, Pippa Pixley, Dr Shini Somara, Tessa Strickland, Anna Terreros Martin, Chris Wakling. *Founded* 2011.

The Bell Lomax Moreton Agency*

Suite C, Victory House, 131 Queensway, Petts Wood, Kent BR5 1DG
tel 020-7930 4447
email agency@bell-lomax.co.uk
website www.belllomaxmoreton.co.uk
Twitter @BLM_Agency
Executives Paul Moreton, Lauren Gardner, Jo Bell, Katie Fulford, Justine Smith, John Baker, Lorna Hemingway, Rory Jeffers, Sarah McDonnell

Will consider most fiction, non-fiction and children's (including picture books, middle grade and young adult) book proposals. Submission guidelines on website. Physical submissions should be accompanied by an sae for return and an email address for correspondence. Does not represent poetry, short stories or novellas, education textbooks, film scripts or stage plays. *Founded* 2000.

The Bent Agency*

17 Kelsall Mews, Richmond TW9 4BP
email info@thebentagency.com
website www.thebentagency.com
Agents Molly Ker Hawn, Nicola Barr, Gemma Cooper, Sarah Hornsley, Zoe Plant (UK); Jenny Bent, Claire Draper, Louise Fury, James Mustelier, John Silbersack, Laurel Symonds, Desiree Wilson (USA)

Full-service literary agency with offices in the UK and USA. Represents authors of fiction and non-fiction for adults, children and teenagers. Unsolicited submissions welcome by email only: query and first ten pages pasted into body of email. See complete guidelines on the website.

   Clients include Faridah Abike-Iyimide, Sophie Anderson, P.G. Bell, Dhonielle Clayton, Stephanie Garber, Alwyn Hamilton, Matt Killeen, Hilary McKay, Mo O'Hara, Sibeal Pounder, Robin Stevens, Jessica Townsend. *Founded* 2009.

The Blair Partnership*

PO Box 7828, London W1A 4GE
tel 020-7504 2520

email info@theblairpartnership.com
email submissions@theblairpartnership.com
website www.theblairpartnership.com
Twitter @TBP_agency
Founding Partner Neil Blair, *Agency Director* Rory Scarfe, *Agent* Josephine Hayes

Represents a range of people internationally from debut and established writers to broader talent across business, politics, sport and lifestyle. Range of work spans fiction, non-fiction, digital, TV and film production. Considers all genres of fiction and non-fiction for adults, young readers and children. Will consider unsolicited MSS. Fiction: email a covering letter, a one-page synopsis and the first three chapters. Non-fiction: email a proposal document and writing sample. Not currently accepting screenplays, short stories or poetry.

   Clients include Bana Alabed, Claire Barker, Michael Byrne, Dawn Coulter-Cruttenden, Helena Duggan, Emma Farrarons, Sir Chris Hoy, Inbali Iserles, Frank Lampard, Virginia Clay, Kieran Larwood, Zoom Rockman, J.K. Rowling and Nicki Thornton. *Founded* 2011.

The Bravo Blue Agency*

email charlotte@bravoblue.co.uk
website www.bravoblue.co.uk
Contact Charlotte Colwill

Boutique literary agency. Literary fiction and narrative non-fiction, category fiction, lifestyle, health, history, children's fiction and non-fiction, picture books. Send first five pages, synopsis and covering letter via email.

   Authors include Bill Swiggs, Megan Vickers, Cecily Blench, Brian Schofield, Gianni Washington, Jacob Avila. *Founded* 2018.

The Bright Agency*

103–105 St John's Hill, London SW11 1SY
tel 020-7326 9140
50 West Street, C12, New York, NY 10006
tel +1 646-578-6542
website https://thebrightagency.com/uk
Contacts UK Vicki Willden-Lebrecht (Founder), Arabella Stein (MD), Nicky Lander (Head of Illustration), *Agents* Helen Biles, Amy Capelin, Freddie Dawson, Amy Fitzgerald, Lucie Luddington, Anne Moore, Robyn Newton, Susan Penny, *Associate agents* Georgia Tournay-Godfrey, Ilaria Vigilante, *Agent assistants* Edward Palmer, Emmajane Turner

A collective of specialist agents representing the best in global talent across all areas of children's publishing, art licensing, illustration, theatre, film and TV. Picture books, children's fiction and non-fiction, activity books, novels, pre-school, illustration, art licensing and educational. See website for full submission requirements. No submissions by post.

   Authors include Benji Davies, David Litchfield, Jarvis, Yasmeen Ismail, Fiona Woodcock, Laura

Hughes, Galia Bernstein, Mechal Roe, Maddie Frost, Zoe Perisco, Aura Lewis, Karl James Mountford. *Founded* 2003.

Jenny Brown Associates*

31 Marchmont Road, Edinburgh EH9 1HU
tel 0131 229 5334
email childrens@jennybrownassociates.com
website www.jennybrownassociates.com
Contact Lucy Juckes

Writing and illustration for children, fiction and non-fiction. Has a preference for working with writers or illustrators based in Scotland. *Commission* Home 12.5%, overseas/translation 20%. A small agency which only reads submissions at certain points in the year; always check website before sending work.

Clients include Christopher Edge, Keith Gray, Helen Kellock, Emily MacKenzie, Jonathan Meres, Alison Murray. *Founded* 2002.

Felicity Bryan Associates*

2A North Parade, Banbury Road, Oxford OX2 6LX
tel (01865) 513816
email agency@felicitybryan.com
website www.felicitybryan.com

Translation rights handled by Andrew Nurnberg Associates; works in conjunction with US agents. Fiction for children aged 8–14 and young adult, and adult fiction and general non-fiction. *Commission* Home 15%, overseas 20%. All submissions and queries through website. No science fiction, fantasy, horror, erotica, romance, self-help, graphic novels, scripts or poetry.

Children's authors include David Almond, Katya Balen, Matt Burton, Jenny Downham, Sally Gardner, Natasha Farrant, Clare Furniss, Liz Kessler, Annabel Pitcher, Meg Rosoff, Alom Shaha, Lauren St John, Chris Vick, Lisa Williamson, Lucy Worsley. *Founded* 1988.

C&W Agency*

(previously Conville & Walsh)
Haymarket House, 28–29 Haymarket, London SW1Y 4SP
tel 020-7393 4200
website www.cwagency.co.uk
Twitter @CWAgencyUK
A boutique and very select list of fiction for 5–8 and 9–12 year-olds, teenage fiction, series fiction and film/TV tie-ins. Also handles adult literary and commercial fiction and non-fiction. *Commission* Home 15%, overseas 20%. Submissions welcome: first three chapters, cover letter, synopsis by email. Part of the Curtis Brown Group of Companies; simultaneous submission accepted. Not taking on picture books.

Children's authors include Kate Cann, Katie Davies, Connie Glynn, Matt Haig, Rebecca James, P.J. Lynch, Joshua Mowll, Paula Rawsthorne, Niamh Sharkey, Nicky Singer, Piers Torday, Steve Voake, Savannah

Brown and the estates of John Burningham and Astrid Lindgren. *Founded* 2000.

Georgina Capel Associates Ltd*

29 Wardour Street, London W1D 6PS
tel 020-7734 2414
email firstname@georginacapel.com
website www.georginacapel.com
Agents Georgina Capel, Rachel Conway

Literary and commercial fiction, history, biography; film and TV; also writers for children and young adults. *Commission* Home/overseas 15%. Postal submissions preferred, but do accept email. Include a covering letter, synopsis of work and first three chapters of your work. Film & TV scripts for established clients only. *Founded* 1999.

The Catchpole Agency

53 Cranham Street, Oxford OX2 6DD
tel 07789 588070
email james@thecatchpoleagency.co.uk
website www.thecatchpoleagency.co.uk
Proprietor James Catchpole

Agents for authors and illustrators of children's books from picture books through to young adult novels, with a specialism in editorial work. See website for contact and submissions details.

Authors include Polly Dunbar, SF Said, Michelle Robinson, Emer Stamp, Sean Taylor. *Founded* 1996.

Anne Clark Literary Agency*

email submissions@anneclarkliteraryagency.co.uk
website www.anneclarkliteraryagency.co.uk
Facebook www.facebook.com/anneclarkliterary
Twitter @AnneClarkLit
Contact Anne Clark

Specialist in fiction, picture books and non-fiction for children and young adults. *Commission* Home 15%, overseas 20%. Submissions by email only. See website for submission guidelines.

Clients include Mike Barfield, Anne Booth, Moira Butterfield, Lou Carter, Patricia Forde, Pippa Goodhart, Miriam Halahmy, Cath Howe, Penny Joelson, Rebecca Patterson, Lucy Rowland. *Founded* 2012.

Coombs Moylett Maclean Literary Agency

120 New Kings Road, London SW6 4LZ
tel 020-8740 0454
website www.cmm.agency
Contacts Lisa Moylett, Jamie Maclean, Zoe Apostolides

Looking for outstanding voices and for writing that is fresh, original and effective. Will accept the following submissions: young adult books only. *Commission* Home 15%, overseas 20%, film/TV 20%. Works with foreign agents. Please note that whole books and manuscript submissions via post and/or email will not be accepted. Check the website for details on how to submit. Does not handle poetry, plays or scripts for film and TV.

Authors include Sam Haysom. *Founded* 1997.

Creative Authors Ltd

11A Woodlawn Street, Whitstable, Kent CT5 1HQ
email write@creativeauthors.co.uk
website www.creativeauthors.co.uk
Twitter @creativeauthors
Instagram creativeauthors
Director Isabel Atherton

Fiction, women's fiction, literary fiction, non-fiction, humour, history, science, autobiography, biography, business, memoir, health, cookery, arts and crafts, crime, children's fiction, picture books, young adult, graphic novels and illustrators. *Commission* Home 15%, overseas 20%. Only accepts email submissions.
  Authors and illustrators include Guojing, Ged Adamson, Coll Muir, Bethany Straker, Lucy Scott, Colleen Kosinski, Jules Miller, Grace Sandford, Megan Tadden, Cassie Liversidge. *Founded* 2008.

Rupert Crew Ltd*

Southgate, 7 Linden Avenue, Dorchester DT1 1EJ
tel (01305) 260335
email info@rupertcrew.co.uk
website www.rupertcrew.co.uk
Managing Director Caroline Montgomery

International representation, handling accessible literary and commercial fiction and non-fiction for adult and children's (8+) markets. *Commission* Home 15%, overseas, TV/film and radio 20%. No unsolicited MSS: see website for current submission guidelines. No picture books, plays, screenplays, poetry, journalism, science fiction, fantasy or short stories. *Founded* 1927.

Curtis Brown*

Haymarket House, 28–29 Haymarket,
London SW1Y 4SP
tel 020-7393 4400
email cb@curtisbrown.co.uk
website www.curtisbrown.co.uk
website www.curtisbrowncreative.co.uk
Twitter @CBGBooks
Twitter @cbcreative
Children's Agents Stephanie Thwaites, Isobel Gahan (Associate)

Children's fiction ranges from picture books to young adult novels across all genres. Represents prominent writers, from debut authors to established prize winners and bestsellers. Actively seeking talented new writers, particularly for books aimed at 8–12 year olds, adventure, fantasy, gothic stories and humour. Curtis Brown manages the international careers of authors with strong relationships in translation and US markets.

Clients include fiction and non-fiction debuts and established brands, and a number of well-known thinkers and personalities. *Founded* 1899.

DHH Literary Agency*

23–27 Cecil Court, London WC2N 4EZ
tel 020-7836 7376
email enquiries@dhhliteraryagency.com
website www.dhhliteraryagency.com
Facebook www.facebook.com/dhhliteraryagency
Twitter @dhhlitagency
Agents David H. Headley, Broo Doherty, Hannah Sheppard, Harry Illingworth, Emily Glenister

Children's fiction and young adult fiction. Also adult fiction, women's commercial fiction, crime, literary fiction, science fiction and fantasy; and non-fiction including history, cookery and humour. *Commission* UK 15%, overseas 20%. Send informative preliminary email with first three chapters and synopsis. New authors welcome. No picture books, plays or scripts, poetry or short stories.
  Authors include Matthew Crow, Phyllida Shrimpton, James Goodhand, Abi Elphinstone, Keris Stainton, Gabrielle Kent, Kate Mallinder, Darren Charlton, Amy Beashel. *Founded* 2008.

Diamond Kahn & Woods Literary Agency*

Top Floor, 66 Onslow Gardens, London N10 3JX
tel 020-3514 6544
email info@dkwlitagency.co.uk
email submissions.ella@dkwlitagency.co.uk
email submissions.bryony@dkwlitagency.co.uk
website www.dkwlitagency.co.uk
Twitter @DKWLitAgency
Agents Ella Diamond Kahn, Bryony Woods

Children's, young adult and crossover fiction; literary and commercial fiction (including all major genres) and non-fiction. Interested in new writers. *Commission* Home 15%, USA/translation 20%. Email submissions only. Send three chapters and synopsis to one agent only. See website for further details on agents, their areas of interest and submission guidelines.
  Clients include Virginia Macgregor, Nicole Burstein, David Owen, Sharon Gosling, Sylvia Bishop, Sarah Baker, Katherine Orton, Dan Smith, Jamie Russell, Tom Huddleston, Caroline O'Donoghue, Daisy May Johnson. *Founded* 2012.

Eddison Pearson Ltd*

West Hill House, 6 Swains Lane, London N6 6QS
tel 020-7700 7763
email enquiries@eddisonpearson.com
website www.eddisonpearson.com
Contact Clare Pearson

Small, personally run agency. Children's and young adult books, fiction and non-fiction, poetry. *Commission* Home 10–15%, overseas 15–20%.

Enquiries and submissions by email only; email for up-to-date submission guidelines by return. May suggest revision where appropriate.

Authors include Valerie Bloom, Sue Heap, Caroline Lawrence, Robert Muchamore, Mary Murphy, Megan Rix. *Founded* 1997.

Fraser Ross Associates
6 Wellington Place, Edinburgh EH6 7EQ
tel 0131 553 2759 / 0131 657 4412
email agentlmfraser@gmail.com
email kjross@tiscali.co.uk
website www.fraserross.co.uk
Facebook www.facebook.com/fraserrossassociates
Twitter @FraserRossLA
Instagram fraserrossassociates
Partners Lindsey Fraser, Kathryn Ross

Represents writers and illustrators. See website for submission guidelines.

See website for a complete list of writers and artists represented. *Founded* 2002.

The Good Literary Agency*
email info@thegoodliteraryagency.org
website www.thegoodliteraryagency.org
Twitter @thegoodagencyuk
Instagram thegoodagencyuk

Represents authors from backgrounds under-represented in UK publishing including writers of colour, working class, disability, LGBTQ+ and anyone who feels that they or their stories are under-represented. Non-fiction (including history, science, economics, politics, self-help, lifestyle, pop culture and memoir); fiction (all genres, in particular crime and thriller, contemporary love stories, family sagas, science fiction and fantasy and historical); children's and young adult. For detailed submission guidelines, visit the website.

Authors include Saima Mir, Hafsa Zayyan, Musa Okwonga, Irfan Master, Lizzie Huxley-Jones, Paula Akpan, Elijah Lawal, Eva Verde, Jon Ransom, Nicole Crentsil, Sharan Dhaliwal, Nicola Garrard, Penny Pepper and Clare Weze. *Founded* 2018.

Annette Green Authors' Agency
5 Henwoods Mount, Pembury,
Tunbridge Wells TN2 4BH
tel (01892) 263252
email annette@annettegreenagency.com
website www.annettegreenagency.co.uk
Partners Annette Green, David Smith

Fiction: Literary, general and teenage fiction. Non-fiction: popular culture, history and science. *Commission* Full-length MSS: home 15%, overseas 20–25%. Preliminary letter, synopsis, sample chapter and sae essential. No picture books, dramatic scripts, poetry, science fiction or fantasy. *Founded* 1998.

The Greenhouse Literary Agency
tel 020-7841 3958
email info@greenhouseliterary.com
website www.greenhouseliterary.com
Twitter @sarahgreenhouse
Twitter @chelseberly
Director Sarah Davies, *Agent* Chelsea Eberly

Specialist children's book agency with a reputation for impressive transatlantic deals. Represents picture book author-illustrators through to writers for teens/young adults. Select children's/teen non-fiction and women's fiction by referral. Represents UK, Irish and North American authors. *Commission* USA/UK 15%, elsewhere 25%. No postal submissions. All submissions by e-query via Query Manager. Strict submission criteria (see website for details). No pre-school or novelty material. No picture book texts unless also illustrated by author.

Authors include Julie Bertagna, Sarwat Chadda/Joshua Khan, Tae Keller, Dawn Kurtagich, Cori McCarthy, Megan Miranda, Ali Standish, Brenna Yovanoff. *Founded* 2008.

Marianne Gunn O'Connor Literary, Film/TV Agency
Morrison Chambers, Suites 52 & 53,
32 Nassau Street, Dublin D02 RX59,
Republic of Ireland
email submissions@mariannegunnoconnor.com
Contact Marianne Gunn O'Connor

Literary fiction, upmarket fiction including book club and psychological suspense. Also handles children's books, middle grade, young adult, new adult and crossover fiction, as well as exciting new non-fiction authors with a focus on narrative non-fiction, health, some memoir and biography. No screenplays. *Founded* 1996.

Hardman & Swainson*
S86 Somerset House, London WC2R 1LA
tel 020-3701 7449
email submissions@hardmanswainson.com
website www.hardmanswainson.com
Twitter @hardmanswainson
Directors Caroline Hardman, Joanna Swainson

Literary and commercial fiction, crime and thriller, women's, accessible literary, young adult and middle-grade children's fiction. Non-fiction, including memoir, biography, popular science, history, philosophy. *Commission* Home 15%, USA/translation/film/TV 20%. Submissions by email only; check the website for details. Will work editorially with the author where appropriate. No poetry, screenplays or picture books.

Clients include Alex Bell, Justin Davies, Fiona Sandiford, Maria Kuzniar. *Founded* 2012.

Antony Harwood Ltd
103 Walton Street, Oxford OX2 6EB
tel (01865) 559615

email mail@antonyharwood.com
website www.antonyharwood.com
Contacts Antony Harwood, James Macdonald, Jo
Williamson (children's)

General and genre fiction; general non-fiction.
Commission Home 15%, overseas 20%. Will suggest
revision.
  Children's authors include Tamsyn Murray, Jennifer
Gray, Peter Bunzl. *Founded* 2000.

A.M. Heath & Co. Ltd*

6 Warwick Court, London WC1R 5DJ
tel 020-7242 2811
email enquiries@amheath.com
website www.amheath.com
Twitter @amheathltd
Contact Julia Churchill

Children's fiction and non-fiction from picture books
to young adult. Also handles adult literary and
commercial fiction and non-fiction. *Commission* Full-
length MSS: home 15%, USA/translation 20%. Film/
TV 15–20% by agreement. Digital submission via
website. No screenplays, poetry or short stories except
for collections.
  Children's authors include Nicholas Allan, Sam
Copeland, Sarah Crossan, Conn Iggulden, Pip Jones,
Michelle Harrison, Sarah Lean, Jenny McLachlan,
Joanna Nadin, Amy Sparkes, Patricia Toht, Holly
Webb and the estates of Noel Streatfield, Joan Aiken
and Christianna Brand. *Founded* 1919.

Sophie Hicks Agency*

email info@sophiehicksagency.com
website www.sophiehicksagency.com
Twitter @SophieHicksAg
Agents Sophie Hicks, Sarah Williams

Fiction for 9+. Also handles adult fiction and non-
fiction. *Commission* UK/USA 15%, translation 20%.
Email submissions only, see website for guidelines.
No poetry or scripts.
  Children's authors include: Herbie Brennan, Anne
Cassidy, Lucy Coats, Eoin Colfer, Andrew Donkin,
Kathryn Evans, Emerald Fennell, Padraig Kenny,
Sarah Mussi, Siobhan Parkinson, Alexander Gordon
Smith, Kate Thompson, Shamim Sarif, Sif
Sigmarsdóttir. *Founded* 2014.

David Higham Associates Ltd*

6th Floor, Waverley House, 7–12 Noel Street,
London W1F 8GQ
tel 020-7434 5900
email dha@davidhigham.co.uk
website www.davidhigham.co.uk
Managing Director Anthony Goff, *Books* Veronique
Baxter, Anthony Goff, Caroline Walsh, *Foreign Rights*
Allison Cole, *Film/TV/Theatre* Nicky Lund, Georgina
Ruffhead, Clare Israel, Penelope Killick

Children's fiction, picture books and non-fiction.
35% of the agency's list is for the children's market.

Represented in all foreign markets. Also represents
illustrators for children's book publishing (home
15%). Submit colour copies of artwork by post or via
email. Include samples that show children 'in action'
and animals. Handles novelty books, picture books,
fiction for 5–8 and 9–12 year-olds, teenage and young
adult fiction, series fiction, poetry, plays, film/TV tie-
ins, non-fiction and audio. Also handles adult fiction,
general non-fiction, plays, film and TV scripts.
Commission Home 15%, USA/translation 20%,
scripts 10%. See website for submissions policy.
  Clients include Martin Brown, Emma Chichester
Clark, Cressida Cowell, Nicola Davies, Anna Kemp,
Geraldine McCaughrean, Tom McLaughlin, Michael
Morpurgo, Kate O'Hearn, Liz Pichon, Catherine
Rayner, Nick Sharratt, Jonathan Stroud, Jenny
Valentine and Jacqueline Wilson. *Founded* 1935.

Johnson & Alcock Ltd*

Bloomsbury House, 74–77 Great Russell Street,
London WC1B 3DA
tel 020-7251 0125
website www.johnsonandalcock.co.uk
Contact Anna Power, Ed Wilson, Liz Dennis

All types of children's fiction and non-fiction (ages
9+), young adult and teenage fiction. *Commission*
Home 15%, USA/translation/film 20%. Send first
three chapters (or 50 pages), full synopsis and brief
covering letter with details of writing experience. For
submission guidelines see website. Return postage
essential. No short stories, poetry or board/picture
books. *Founded* 1956.

Kane Literary Agency*

2 Dukes Avenue, London N10 2PT
tel 020-8351 9680
website www.kaneliteraryagency.com
Twitter @YasminKane3
Director Yasmin Kane

Interested in discovering new writers and launching
the careers of first-time writers. Also handles literary
and commercial fiction for adults. Children's fiction –
middle grade and up, all young adult, no picture
books. *Commission* Home 15%, overseas 20%. Send
submissions by email only; no submissions by post.
Send first three chapters and synopsis (one side of
A4) with a covering letter, all double-line spaced. No
picture books.
  Authors include Sarah Harris, Andrew Murray.
Founded 2004.

Lambs to Lions Literary Agency

Centurion House, Leyland Business Park,
Centurion Way, Farington, Leyland PR25 3GR
tel 07546 415403
email info@lambstolions.co.uk
website https://lambstolions.co.uk
Managing Director Anthony Sergeant, *Ceo* Jake
Pilkington

Literary agents for talented children's authors. Supporting them right through from original manuscript, to polished, published and promoted novels. Children's fiction, middle grade, picture books, adventure, speculative fiction and non-fiction. Email in first instance using the form on the website regarding submission.

LBA Books*

91 Great Russell Street, London WC1B 3PS
tel 020-7637 1234
email info@lbabooks.com
website www.lbabooks.com
Twitter @LBA_Agency
Agents Luigi Bonomi, Amanda Preston, Louise Lamont, Hannah Schofield

Fiction and non-fiction. Keen to find new authors and help them develop their careers. Works with foreign agencies and has links with film and TV production companies. Fiction: young adult and children's, commercial and literary fiction, thrillers, crime, psychological suspense, women's fiction, fantasy. Non-fiction: history, science, memoir, parenting, lifestyle, cookery, TV tie-in. *Commission* Home 15%, overseas 20%. Send preliminary letter, synopsis and first three chapters. No postal submissions. No poetry, short stories or screenplays.
  Authors include Virginia Bergin, Anna Carey, Rebecca Cobb, Julia Gray, Helen Hancocks, Rachael Lucas, Julie Mayhew, Anne Miller, Ben Miller, S.A. Patrick, Lucy Strange, Tamsin Winter, Laura Wood, Katherine Woodfine, Emma Yarlett. *Founded* 2005.

Lindsay Literary Agency*

East Worldham House, Alton, Hants GU34 3AT
tel (01420) 831430
email info@lindsayliteraryagency.co.uk
website www.lindsayliteraryagency.co.uk
Twitter @LindsayLit
Director Becky Bagnell

Specialists in children's fiction and non-fiction, teen/ young adult, middle grade, picture books. *Commission* Home 15%, translation 20%. Send first three chapters, synopsis and covering letter by email. No submissions by post. Will suggest revision.
  Authors include Pamela Butchart, Christina Collins, Donna David, Sam Gayton, Ruth Hatfield, Larry Hayes, J.M. Joseph, Giles Paley-Phillips, Sharon Tregenza, Rachel Valentine, Sue Wallman, Joe Wilson. *Founded* 2008.

Luithlen Agency

88 Holmfield Road, Leicester LE2 1SB
tel 0116 273 8863
email penny@luithlenagency.com
website www.luithlenagency.com
Agents Jennifer Luithlen, Penny Luithlen

Children's fiction, all ages to young adult. *Commission* Home 15%, overseas 20%, performance rights 15%. See website for submission information. *Founded* 1986.

Eunice McMullen Ltd

Low Ibbotsholme Cottage, Off Bridge Lane, Troutbeck Bridge, Windermere, Cumbria LA23 1HU
tel (01539) 448551
email eunice@eunicemcmullen.co.uk
website www.eunicemcmullen.co.uk
Director Eunice McMullen

Specialises exclusively in children's books, especially picture books and older fiction. Handles novelty books, picture books, fiction for all ages including teenage, series fiction and audio. *Commission* Home 15%, overseas 15%. No unsolicited scripts. Telephone or email enquiries only.
  Authors include Ross Collins, Emma Dodd, Alison Friend, Charles Fuge, Cally Johnson Isaacs, Sarah Massini, James Mayhew, David Melling, Angela McAllister, Angie Sage. *Founded* 1992.

Andrew Mann Ltd*

6 Quernmore Road, London N4 4QU
tel 020-7609 6218
email tina@andrewmann.co.uk
website www.andrewmann.co.uk
Twitter @AML_Literary
Contacts Tina Betts

Currently closed to new submissions. *Founded* 1975.

Marjacq Scripts Ltd*

The Space, 235 High Holborn, London WC1V 7LE
tel 020-7935 9499
website www.marjacq.com
Twitter @MarjacqScripts
Contact Catherine Pellegrino (children's and YA); Sandra Sawicka (YA only)

Handles all rights. In-house legal, foreign rights and book-to-film support. All genres represented. *Commission* Home 15%, overseas/film 20%. See website for submission guidelines.
  Clients include James Campbell, Rose Edwards, Roopa Farooki, Steve Feasey, Gemma Fowler, Nick Garlick, Finbar Hawkins, T.C. Shelley, Claire Waller, Harriet Whitehorn. *Founded* 1973.

MBA Literary and Script Agents Ltd*

62 Grafton Way, London W1T 5DW
tel 020-7387 2076
website www.mbalit.co.uk
Twitter @mbaagents
Children's book agent Sophie Gorell Barnes, *Film & TV agent* Diana Tyler

Fiction and non-fiction, children's books. Foreign rights handled by Louisa Pritchard Associates. *Commission* Home 15%, overseas 20%, TV/theatre/ radio 10%, films 15%. See website for submission guidelines.
  Clients include Sita Brahmachari, Christopher William Hill, Mark Wheeller. *Founded* 1971.

Madeleine Milburn Literary, TV & Film Agency*

The Factory, 1 Park Hill, Clapham, London SW4 9NS
tel 020-7499 7550
email childrens@madeleinemilburn.com
website www.madeleinemilburn.co.uk
Facebook www.facebook.com/
MadeleineMilburnLiteraryAgency
Twitter @MMLitAgency
Contacts Madeleine Milburn, Giles Milburn
(Directors), Liane-Louise Smith (Rights Director),
Georgina Simmonds (Rights Agent), Emma Dawson
(Operations), Hannah Ladds (Dramatic Rights
Agent), Chloe Seager (Children's & YA Agent)

Special interest in launching the careers of debut
authors and illustrators. Represents a dynamic and
prize-winning range of children's and young adult
fiction and non-fiction. Award-winning and popular
fiction including fantasy, real life/contemporary,
young adult thrillers, mystery, action, historical,
science fiction, romance, coming of age and film/TV
tie-ins.

Represents British, American, Canadian and
international authors. Handles all rights in the UK,
US and foreign markets including film/TV/theatre/
radio (for clients with book deal in place only) and
digital. Areas include picture books, 6–8 years, 9–12
years, 12+, teen, young adult, new adult and books
appealing to both children and adults. *Commission*
Home 15%, USA/translation/film 20%. No
submissions by post. See submission guidelines and
agency news on website. Works editorially with all
clients.

Authors include Holly Bourne, Anna Fargher,
Kathryn Foxfield, Kate Weston, Lara Williamson, Ben
Oliver, Damaris Young, Danielle Jawando, Benjamin
Dean, Katie Kirby, Jen Carney, Helen Rutter.
Founded 2012.

Miles Stott Children's Literary Agency Ltd*

East Hook Farm, Lower Quay Road, Hook,
Haverfordwest, Pembrokeshire SA62 4LR
tel 07855 252043
email nancy@milesstottagency.co.uk
email mandy@milesstottagency.co.uk
email victoria@milesstottagency.co.uk
website www.milesstottagency.co.uk
Twitter @milesstott
Instagram milesstott
Director Nancy Miles, *Associate Agents* Victoria
Birkett, Mandy Suhr

Specialist in children's novelty books, picture books,
fiction for 6–9 and 10–12 year-olds, young adult
fiction and series fiction. *Commission* Home 15%,
film, TV & overseas 20%. Fiction submissions by
email only to fictionsubs@milesstottagency.co.uk
including covering letter, brief synopsis and first three
chapters. Picture book submissions by email only to
picturebooksubs@milesstottagency.co.uk including

covering letter, complete text and/or pdfs of sample
artwork.

Authors include Kirsty Applebaum, Atinuke, Rachel
Bright, Stacy Gregg, Frances Hardinge, Caryl Hart,
Gill Lewis, Tom Percival, Tom Pollock and Mark
Sperring. *Founded* 2003.

Morgan Green Creatives Ltd

157 Ribblesdale Road, London SW16 6SP
email kirsty@morgangreencreatives.com
website www.morgangreencreatives.com
Founder Kirsty McLachlan

Actively looking for fresh talent and want to be
challenged with new ideas, inspired and moved by
great writing, and to find unique and distinct voices
with compelling stories to tell. Represents fiction and
non-fiction, children's book writers, poets,
scriptwriters, and illustrators. Submission by email
which includes a covering letter within the body of
the email, plus 30 pages of your work attached.
See website for full client list. *Founded* 2020.

Northbank Talent Management*

email info@northbanktalent.com
email childrens@northbanktalent.com
website www.northbanktalent.com
Twitter @northbanktalent

Commercial fiction, non-fiction and children's
books. Fiction: young adult, young teen, middle
grade, children's. Non-fiction: science, nature,
history, biography, motivational. *Commission* Home
15%, overseas and rights in other media 20%. Send
cover letter, synopsis and first three chapters as Word
or Open Document attachments. Aims to give initial
response within two weeks. No poetry, academic
books, plays, scripts or short stories.

Authors include Sheila Kanani, Liam Hackett,
Rachel Wells, Shelina Janmohamed, Michelle
Kenney, Alexandra Fryer, Amy Forbes-Robertson.
Founded 2006.

Paper Lion Ltd

13 Grayham Road, New Malden, Surrey KT3 5HR
tel 07748 786199 / (01276) 61322
email katyloffman@paperlionltd.com
email lesleypollinger@paperlionltd.com
website www.paperlionltd.com
Agents Katy Loffman, Lesley Pollinger

A cross-media literary agency which brings together
the digital publishing expertise of Katy Loffman and
Lesley Pollinger's extensive experience as a literary
agent. The client list includes award-winning authors,
literary estates and publishers. Has a strong focus on
the exploration of digital opportunities and expertise
in solving complex copyright, dramatic rights and
literary issues from the present and past.

Clients include Max Allen, Michael Coleman, Vince
Cross, Cordelia Feldman, Fiction Express, Catherine
Fisher, Dave Gatward, Bruce Hobson, Saviour Pirotta

and the estates of authors including Gene Kemp and Gwynedd Rae. *Founded* 2017.

Joey Quincey Literary Agency

17 Carlton House Terrace, St James's, London, SW1Y 5AH
tel 07396 344505
email joey@jq-agency.co.uk
website www.jq-agency.co.uk
Director Joey Quincey

Actively looking for authors from BAME backgrounds who explore identity, cultural duality and diaspora, particularly in urban, inner-city areas. The Agency represents Children's middle-grade, young adult and fantasy fiction; commercial literary fiction and lifestyle non-fiction. Email in first instance with a summary of the book plus an author biography. *Founded* 2019.

Redhammer Management Ltd

website www.redhammer.info
Vice President Peter Cox

A boutique literary agency providing in-depth management for a restricted number of clients. Specialises in works with international book, film and television potential. Submissions must follow the guidelines given on the website. Do not send unsolicited MSS by post. No radio or theatre scripts.

Rogers, Coleridge & White Ltd*

20 Powis Mews, London W11 1JN
tel 020-7221 3717
email info@rcwlitagency.com
website www.rcwlitagency.com
Twitter @RCWLitAgency
Instagram rcwliteraryagency
Managing Director Peter Straus, *Directors* Sam Copeland, Stephen Edwards, Natasha Fairweather, Georgia Garrett, Laurence Laluyaux, Zoë Waldie, Claire Wilson, *Agents* Cara Jones, Jon Wood

International representation for all genres of fiction, non-fiction, children's and young adult. *Commission* Home 15%, USA 20%, translation 20%. See website for submissions information.
  Clients include David Baddiel, Frank Cottrell Boyce, Cerrie Burnell, Catherine Doyle, Lissa Evans, Anna James, Femi Fadugba, Alice Oseman, Katherine Rundell, Katie and Kevin Tsang. *Founded* 1967 as Deborah Rogers Ltd, 1989 as Rogers, Coleridge and White Ltd.

Steph Roundsmith Literary Agent

7 Stubbs Close, Billingham,
Stockton-on-Tees TS23 3GH
email submissions@stephroundsmith.co.uk
website https://stephroundsmith.co.uk
Facebook www.facebook.com/stephroundsmith
Contact Steph Roundsmith

Specialises exclusively in fiction for children. Accepts picture books and fiction to age 12. Send synopsis

and first three chapters for longer works, and the full MS for picture books. Email submissions only. Include a short biography. Submissions currently closed.

Elizabeth Roy Literary Agency

White Cottage, Greatford, Nr Stamford, Lincs. PE9 4PR
tel (01778) 560672
website www.elizabethroy.co.uk

Children's fiction, picture books and non-fiction – writers and illustrators. *Commission* Home 15%, overseas 20%. Send preliminary letter, synopsis and sample chapters with names of publishers and agents previously contacted. Return postage essential. *Founded* 1990.

Caroline Sheldon Literary Agency Ltd*

71 Hillgate Place, London W8 7SS
tel 020-7727 9102
email info@carolinesheldon.co.uk
website www.carolinesheldon.co.uk
Twitter @CarolineAgent
Twitter @FelicityTrew
Contacts Caroline Sheldon, Felicity Trew

Represents in all areas of children's fiction, whether picture book, middle grade or young adult. Looks for strong concepts, wonderful characterisation and excellent story-telling and compelling non-fiction. Also represents leading illustrators of children's books. All genres of children's writing including fantasy, humour, contemporary life, thriller, stories set in schools and non-fiction. *Commission* Home 15%, USA/translation 20%, film/TV 20%. Authors – send an introductory email addressed to either Caroline or Felicity with the first three chapters or equivalent length attached. In the subject line write 'Proposal' and title of the work. At head of the email include a three-line synopsis of the work and give further full information in the email about the work and about yourself. Illustrators – send an introductory email addressed to either Caroline or Felicity with work attached or a link to your work. In the subject line write 'Proposal from Illustrator', and include information about yourself and your work in the email.
  Represents prominent, award-winning and bestselling clients in all fields including books, audio, digital and theatre. Works closely with a media agent on film, TV and other opportunities. *Founded* 1985.

Dorie Simmonds Agency Ltd*

tel 020-7736 0002
email info@doriesimmonds.com
website https://doriesimmonds.com/
Twitter @Dorie_Simmonds
Contact Dorie Simmonds

Children's fiction, general non-fiction and commercial fiction. *Commission* Home 15%, USA

15%, translation 20%. Send a short synopsis, two to three sample chapters and a CV with writing/publishing background; sae required. Does not represent poetry or screenplays. *Founded* 1997.

Skylark Literary Limited
19 Parkway, Weybridge, Surrey KT13 9HD
tel 020-8144 7440
email info@skylark-literary.com
email submissions@skylark-literary.com
website www.skylark-literary.com
Facebook www.facebook.com/SkylarkLiteraryLtd
Twitter @skylarklit
Directors Joanna Moult, Amber Caraveo

Specialists in children's and young adult fiction. All genres considered. *Commission* Home 15%, overseas 20%. Keen to support new and established authors. Will consider unsolicited submissions. Agents have editorial backgrounds and will work closely with clients on their manuscripts to increase chances of publication. Submissions by email only. Will suggest revision where appropriate. No adult fiction/non-fiction.

Clients include Amy Wilson, Simon James Green, Alyssa Hollingsworth, Rachel Burge, Nizrana Farook. *Founded* 2014.

The Soho Agency Ltd*
(previously LAW/Lucas Alexander Whitley Ltd)
16–17 Wardour Mews, 2nd Floor, London W1F 8AT
tel 020-7471 7900
email admin@thesohoagency.co.uk
website www.thesohoagency.co.uk
Twitter @TheSohoAgencyUK
Agent Philippa Milnes-Smith

Novelty books, picture books, fiction for 5–8 and 9–12 year olds including series, young adult, film/TV and non-fiction. Special interests: projects with cross-media potential, diverse voices, visual storytelling, innovative non-fiction. *Commission* Home 15%, overseas 20%. Representation in all markets. Unsolicited and debut work considered. See website for further information about the clients and genres represented and essential information on submissions. No postal submissions.

Clients include Lauren Child, Steve Cole, Linda Chapman, Gillian Cross, Emily Gravett, Chris Judge, Sophie Kinsella, Philip Reeve, Chris Riddell, Niamh Sharkey, Sarah Webb. *Founded* 1996.

SP Literary Agency
email info@sp-agency.co.uk
website https://sp-agency.co.uk/
Facebook www.facebook.com/sp.literary.agency
Agents Philippa Perry, Abigail Sparrow

Represents authors and illustrators across children's, young adult and adult fiction and non-fiction. Email submissions are preferred; attach a synopsis and the first three chapters to a covering email. Children's or young adult submissions should also be clearly marked in the subject line.

See website for client list.

Abner Stein*
Southbank House, Suite 137, Black Prince Road, London SE1 7SJ
tel 020-7373 0456
email info@abnerstein.co.uk
website www.abnerstein.co.uk
Contacts Caspian Dennis, Sandy Violette

Fiction, general non-fiction and children's. *Commission* Home 15%, overseas 20%. Not taking on any new clients at present.

Rochelle Stevens & Co
2 Terretts Place, Upper Street, London N1 1QZ
tel 020-7359 3900
email info@rochellestevens.com
website www.rochellestevens.com
Twitter @TerrettsPlace
Directors Rochelle Stevens, Frances Arnold

Scripts for TV, theatre and radio. *Commission* 10%. Send preliminary letter, CV, short synopsis and opening ten pages of a drama script by post (sae essential for return of material). See website for full submission guidelines. *Founded* 1984.

Sarah Such Literary Agency
81 Arabella Drive, London SW15 5LL
tel 020-8876 4228
email info@sarah-such.com
website https://sarahsuchliteraryagency.tumblr.com
Twitter @sarahsuch
Director Sarah Such

High-quality literary and commercial non-fiction and fiction for adults and children. Always looking for original children's and young adult writers and projects. Translation representation by The Buckman Agency. Film/TV representation by Lesley Thorne, Aitken Alexander Associates Ltd. Particular focus on debut young adult novels, topical middle-grade non-fiction, children's fiction series, picture books and graphic novels. *Commission* Home 15%, TV/film 20%, overseas 20%. Will suggest revision. Submit synopsis and three sample chapters (as a Word attachment by email) plus author biography. No postal submissions unless requested. No unsolicited MSS or telephone enquiries. TV/film scripts for established clients only. No radio or theatre scripts, poetry, fantasy, self-help or short stories (unless full collections).

Authors include Matthew De Abaitua, Jeffrey Boakye, Kit Caless, Maxim Jakubowski, Antony Johnston, Amy Lankester-Owen, Louisa Leaman, Vesna Maric, Heather Martin, Benjamin J. Myers QC, Rachel Pashley, John Rowley, Caroline Sanderson, Nikhil Singh, Sara Starbuck. *Founded* 2007.

Two Piers Literary Agency

email hello@twopiersagency.com
website https://twopiersagency.com/
Facebook www.facebook.com/TwoPiersAgency
Twitter @TwoPiersAgency
Instagram twopiersagency
Agent Rufus Purdy

Represents fiction and non-fiction including children's (from 7+) and memoir. Submissions through form on website. For fiction, submit the first three chapters and synopsis; while for non-fiction send three chapters and proposal. Submissions must include a covering letter. *Founded* 2021.

Tyild's Agency

email tyildsagency@gmail.com
website www.tyildsagency.co.uk
Twitter @tyilds
Agents Kate Scarborough, Frances McKay

A children's literary agency, set up particularly for teachers who write. Represents authors of picture books, young readers and middle-grade fiction, as well as non-fiction. Actively looking for new voices - wonderful storytellers with an innate understanding of children. *Commission* Home 15%, overseas 20%. See website for more details on how to send in submissions. *Founded* 2020.

United Agents LLP*

12–26 Lexington Street, London W1F 0LE
tel 020-3214 0800
email info@unitedagents.co.uk
website www.unitedagents.co.uk
Agents Jodie Hodges (children's/young adult writers and illustrators), Emily Talbot (children's/young adult writers and illustrators). Other agents also represent children's writers. See website for individual lists.

Fiction and non-fiction. *Commission* Home 15%, USA/translation 20%. See website for submission details. *Founded* 2008.

Jo Unwin Literary Agency*

West Wing, Somerset House, London WC2R 1LA
email submissions@jounwin.co.uk
website www.jounwin.co.uk
Twitter @jounwin
Twitter @rachelphilippa
Agents Jo Unwin, Rachel Mann

Represents authors of literary fiction, commercial women's fiction, non-fiction, cookery, young adult fiction and fiction for children aged 5+ (picture books only accepted if written by established clients).
  Authors include Wibke Brueggemann, Jack Meggitt-Phillips, Sarah Moore Fitzgerald, Hayley Scott, Nadia Shireen, Emma-Jane Smith-Barton, Lucy Cuthew, Bethany Rutter. *Founded* 2016.

Watson, Little Ltd*

Suite 315, ScreenWorks, 22 Highbury Grove, London N5 2ER
tel 020-7388 7529
email office@watsonlittle.com
email submissions@watsonlittle.com
website www.watsonlittle.com
Twitter @watsonlittle
Contacts James Wills (Managing Director), Laetitia Rutherford (Agent), Megan Carroll (Agent), Rachel Richardson (Rights Director)

Film and TV Associates: Ki Agency and The Sharland Agency; US Associates: Howard Morhaim Literary Agency and The Gersh Agency. Young adult and middle-grade fiction, picture books and children's non-fiction in all genres. *Commission* Home 15%, USA/translation 20%. Send informative preliminary letter, synopsis and sample chapters by email only. No poetry, TV, play or film scripts.
  Authors include Tom Clempson, Rebecca Elliott, Tim Hall, Richard Joyce, Lynne Reid Banks, Margaret Mahy. *Founded* 1970.

Whispering Buffalo Literary Agency Ltd

97 Chesson Road, London W14 9QS
tel 020-7565 4737
email info@whisperingbuffalo.com
website www.whisperingbuffalo.com
Director Mariam Keen

Commercial/literary fiction and non-fiction, children's and young adult fiction. Special interest in book-to-screen adaptations; TV and film rights in novels and non-fiction handled in-house. *Commission* Home 15%, overseas 20%. Only accepts submissions by email. Will suggest revision. *Founded* 2008.

Eve White Literary Agency Limited*

15 Alderney Street, London SW1V 4ES
tel 020-7630 1155
email eve@evewhite.co.uk
email ludo@evewhite.co.uk
website www.evewhite.co.uk
Twitter @EveWhiteAgency
Contact Eve White, Ludo Cinelli

Boutique agency representing young, middle grade, teenage and young adult fiction, picture books and film/TV tie-ins. Also handles adult commercial and literary fiction and non-fiction; 35% of the list is for the children's market. *Commission* Home 15%, overseas 20%. Will suggest revision where appropriate. See website for up-to-date submission requirements. No submissions by post.
  Children's clients include Andy Stanton, Rae Earl, Tracey Corderoy, Abie Longstaff, Elli Woollard, Sarah Naughton, Iona Rangeley-Wilson, Alex Barclay, James Bishop, Sarah Coyle, Ivan Brett. *Founded* 2003.

Alice Williams Literary*

tel 020-7385 2118
email submissions@alicewilliamsliterary.co.uk
website www.alicewilliamsliterary.co.uk
Twitter @alicelovesbooks
Contact Alice Williams

Specialist literary agency representing writers and illustrators of picture books, children's fiction and teen/young adult fiction. Also children's non-fiction. *Commission* Home 15%, USA/translation/film/TV 20%. Open to submissions, by email only. Attach full typescript and synopsis, two or three picture book texts, or illustration portfolio. See website for further guidelines.

 Clients include Zoe Armstrong, Lauren Beard, Jo Clarke, Rachel Delahaye, Lucy Freegard, Rebecca Harry, Lara Hawthorne, Natelle Quek, Rose Robbins, Fabi Santiago, Suzy Senior, Ciara Smyth, Cat Weldon, Clare Helen Welsh, Pete Williamson. *Founded* 2018.

Susan Yearwood Agency*

2 Knebworth House, Londesborough Road, London N16 8RL
tel 020-7503 0954
email submissions@susanyearwoodagency.com
website www.susanyearwoodagency.com
Twitter @sya_susan
Contact Susan Yearwood

Children's fiction 9+ and young adult. *Commission* Home 15%, overseas 20%. Send submission with covering letter and brief synopsis via email. Submissions not accepted by hand or post. Tends not to read science fiction/fantasy in adult fiction, short stories or poetry. *Founded* 2007.

Children's literary agents overseas

This list includes only a selection of agents across the English-speaking world. Before submitting material, writers are advised to visit agents' websites for detailed submission guidelines and to ascertain terms.

AUSTRALIA

ALM: Australian Literary Management
tel +61 (02) 9818 8557
email alphaalm8@gmail.com
website www.austlit.com

For full details of genres represented and submission guidelines, see website. Does not consider TV or film scripts of any kind, poetry, science fiction, self-help, fantasy or books for children by unpublished authors. Does not accept self-published work or previously published works including ebooks or writing by non-Australian authors.

The Authors' Agent
PO Box 577, Terrigal, NSW 2260
email briancook@theauthorsagent.com.au
website www.theauthorsagent.com.au

Specialises in adult fiction, narrative non-fiction and children's books. Accepts submissions by email. For detailed guidelines, see website.

Golvan Arts Management
website www.golvanarts.com.au
Facebook www.facebook.com/Golvan-Arts-Management-153871021304383/

Represents a wide range of writers including writers of both adult and children's fiction and non-fiction, poetry, screenwriters and writers of plays. Also represents visual artists and composers. See the General Information section on the website before making contact via online form.

Margaret Kennedy Agency
PO Box 1433, Toowong, Brisbane, QLD 4066
tel +61 (0)7 3870 9996
email hannah@margaretkennedyagency.com
website www.margaretkennedyagency.com
Twitter @mkliterary
Agent Hannah Douglas, *Consultant* Margaret Kennedy

A full-service literary agency representing general non-fiction, a limited range of fiction and high-quality children's literature. Areas of special interest in non-fiction include biography, current affairs and social issues, language, philosophy, religion, science, history, food and wine and Australia and the Pacific. Does not accept fantasy, science fiction, chick lit, chook lit, horror and erotica. Children's picture books, chapter books and teen and young adult literature, including non-fiction, are welcomed from established writers. For fiction, send a brief query letter with the first 50 pages by email. For non-fiction, send a brief query letter with a proposal by email. *Founded* 1996.

Mayfair Literary Agency
PO Box 3247, Warner QLD 4500
email admin@mayfairliteraryagency.com.au
website www.mayfairliteraryagency.com.au
Contact Justine Barker

Dedicated exclusively to children's and young adult fiction. Areas of interest include: picture books, humour, Australian historical, contemporary, drama, friendship, action, comedy, dystopian, mystery, fairy tale retellings, fantasy, science fiction, myth, sport and magical realism. All submissions by e-query. The agency's vision is to discover exceptional authors and cultivate bestselling, long-term writing careers. See the submissions page of the website for full guidelines. Does not accept paper submissions.

Sarah McKenzie Literary Management
email submissions@smlm.com.au
website www.smlm.com.au

Provides advice, advocacy and representation for Australian authors, helping them to shape and polish their writing projects, negotiate the best possible terms in their contracts and identify and create opportunities to build a writing career. Actively seeks established and emerging authors of fiction, non-fiction and children's fiction. Does not represent works that have been previously self-published in any form. For detailed submission guidelines and for a full list of genres accepted, see the website.

CANADA

CookeMcDermid
email admin@cookemcdermid.com
website https://cookemcdermid.com
Agents Dean Cooke, Sally Harding, Martha Webb, Suzanne Brandreth, Ron Eckel, Rachel Letofsky, Stephanie Sinclair, Paige Sisley

CMD represents authors of literary, commercial and science/fantasy fiction; a broad range of narrative non-fiction; health and wellness resources; and middle grade and young adult books. See https://cookemcdermid.com/submissions for submissions guidelines and form. Sells Canadian and American rights directly. Cooke International represents UK and translation rights, in conjunction with a network of co-agents around the world. CMD also sells film and TV rights directly, in addition to working with associates in New York and LA. *Founded* 2017.

Carolyn Swayze Literary Agency Ltd

7360-137th Street, Suite 319, Surrey, BC V3W 1A3
email reception@swayzeagency.com
website www.swayzeagency.com
Proprietor Carolyn Swayze

Fiction and non-fiction for teens and middle-grade readers. No science fiction, poetry, screenplays or children's picture books. Eager to discover strong voices writing contemporary, historical or supernatural stories if the metaphor reflects relevant themes. No telephone calls: make contact by email. Provide résumé, publication credits, writing awards, education and experience relevant to the book project. Allow six weeks for a reply. *Founded* 1994.

Transatlantic Agency

2 Bloor Street East, Suite 3500, Toronto, ON M4W 1A8
tel +1 416-488-9214
website www.transatlanticagency.com
Facebook www.facebook.com/TransLitAgency
Twitter @TransLitAgency

Represents more than 700 American, Canadian and internationally bestselling and award-winning clients, with a team of 14 experienced agents based in cities across North America, offering a full spectrum of career representation to authors (adult, children's and young adult, and illustrators) and storytellers (speakers, industry leaders and influencers) across all genres and formats for book, content development, speaking and TV & film. *Founded* 1993.

NEW ZEALAND

Delaney Worner International

email info@delaneyworner.com
website www.delaneyworner.com
Contacts Joseph Delaney, Linda Worner, Joanne Delaney

Specialises in children's, teen and young adult books but will consider all types of fiction. While the agency does not seek non-fiction or poetry submissions, it welcomes picture books which use rhyme as the text narrative. *Founded* 2016.

Frances Plumpton Literary Agency

PO Box 15061, New Lynn, Auckland 0640
tel +64 (0)9 827 6785
email submissions@francesplumpton.com
website www.francesplumpton.com
Facebook www.facebook.com/Frances-Plumpton-Literary-Agency-685680644791804/

Represents picture books, junior and young adult fiction and children's non-fiction by New Zealand writers and/or illustrators. No poetry or short stories. Submissions should be sent as an attachment (Word or pdf) with the manuscript title in the subject line. See website for submission guidelines. *Founded* 2012.

TFS Literary Agency

PO Box 6292, Dunedin North, Dunedin 9059
email tfs@elseware.co.nz
website www.elseware.co.nz

General fiction, non-fiction, children's books. No poetry, individual short stories or articles. Enquiries from New Zealand authors only. Email queries but no attachments. Hard copy preferred. Also offers assessment reports, mentoring and courses. *Founded* 1988.

USA

*Member of the Association of American Literary Agents

Adams Literary*

7845 Colony Road, C4 Suite 215, Charlotte, NC 28226
tel +1 (704) 542-1440
email info@adamsliterary.com
website www.adamsliterary.com
Facebook www.facebook.com/adamsliterary
Twitter @adamsliterary
Agents Tracey Adams, Josh Adams

Exclusively children's from picture books to teenage novels. *Commission* Home 15%, overseas 25%. Submissions through website. See website for guidelines. Temporarily closed for submissions. *Founded* 2004.

Bradford Literary Agency*

5694 Mission Center Road, Suite 347, San Diego, CA 92108
email queries@bradfordlit.com
website www.bradfordlit.com

Currently looking for picture books, chapter books, middle grade, young adult in both fiction and non-fiction categories. Query by email only. For detailed submission guidelines, see website.

Andrea Brown Literary Agency*

email andrea@andreabrownlit.com
website www.andreabrownlit.com
President Andrea Brown, *Agents* Laura Rennert, Caryn Wiseman, Jennifer Laughran, Jennifer Rofe, Kelly Sonnack, Jamie Weiss Chilton, Jennifer Mattson, Kathleen Rushall, Lara Perkins, Jennifer March Soloway

Exclusively all kinds of children's books. Represents both authors and illustrators. Email and form submissions only. See website for guidelines. *Founded* 1981.

Maria Carvainis Agency Inc.*

Rockefeller Center, 1270 Avenue of the Americas, Suite 2915, New York, NY 10020
tel +1 212-245-6365
email mca@mariacarvainisagency.com
website www.mariacarvainisagency.com
President and Literary Agent Maria Carvainis

Young adult fiction (home 15%, overseas 20%). Also handles adult fiction and non-fiction. Send a query letter, a synopsis of the work, first 5–10 pages and a note of any writing credentials. See website for full submission guidelines. *Founded* 1977.

The Chudney Agency

72 North State Road, Suite 501, Briarcliff Manor, NY 10510
tel +1 914-465-5560
email steven@thechudneyagency.com
website https://thechudneyagency.com
Contact Steven Chudney

Represents authors of children's books and adult fiction. Does not accept science fiction, non-fiction, plays, screenplays or film scripts. See website for full guidelines for queries and submissions, and for details of genres represented. *Founded* 2002.

Curtis Brown Ltd*

228 East 45th Street, New York, NY 10017
tel +1 212-473-5400
email info@cbltd.com
website www.curtisbrown.com
Twitter @CurtisBrownLtd
Instagram curtisbrown.ltd
Ceo Timothy Knowlton, *President* Peter Ginsberg, *Contacts* Ginger Clark (*Vice President*), Katherine Fausset, Sarah Gerton, Elizabeth Harding (*Vice President*), Ginger Knowlton (*Executive Vice President*), Jonathan Lyons, Steven Salpeter, Laura Blake Peterson (*Vice President*), *Film and TV Rights* Holly Frederick, *Translation rights* Sarah Perillo

Fiction and non-fiction, juvenile (see Agent page on website as not all agents handle juvenile), film and TV rights. No unsolicited MSS. See individual agent's entry on the Agents page of the website for specific query and submission information. *Founded* 1914.

Liza Dawson Associates*

121 West 27th Street, Suite 1201, New York, NY 10001
email lwu@lizadawson.com
website www.lizadawsonassociates.com
Twitter @LizaDawsonAssoc
Ceo Liza Dawson

A full-service agency which draws on expertise as former publishers. Young adult, middle grade: thrillers, mysteries, romance, historical fiction,

science fiction and fantasy, contemporary. See website for submission guidelines and email contacts. *Founded* 1996.

Sandra Dijkstra & Associates*

PMB 515, 1155 Camino Del Mar, Del Mar, CA 92014
tel +1 858-755-3115
website www.dijkstraagency.com
Contacts Sandra Dijkstra, Elise Capron, Jill Marr, Thao Le, Andrea Cavallaro, Jessica Watterson, Suzy Evans, Jennifer Kim

Young adult science fiction, fantasy and contemporary, middle-grade fiction and non-fiction and picture books by author/illustrators only (home 15%, overseas 20%). Works in conjunction with foreign and film agents. Email submissions only. Please see website for the most up-to-date guidelines. *Founded* 1981.

Dunham Literary Inc.*

email dunhamlit@gmail.com
website www.dunhamlit.com
Contact Jennie Dunham, Leslie Zampetti

Children's books (home 15%, overseas 20%). Handles picture books, fiction for 5–8 and 9–12 year-olds and teenage fiction. Also handles adult literary fiction and non-fiction; 50% of list is for the children's market. Send query by email to query@dunhamlit.com with first five pages of your manuscript. Submission guidelines on website. Do not send full MS. *Founded* 2000.

Dystel, Goderich & Bourret LLC*

1 Union Square West, New York, NY 10003
tel +1 212-627-9100
website www.dystel.com
Facebook www.facebook.com/DGandB/
Twitter @DGandBTweets
Contacts Michael Bourret, Jim McCarthy, Stacey Glick, John Rudolph, Lauren Abramo, Michaela Whatnall

Children's fiction (home 15%, overseas 19%). Handles picture books, fiction for 5–8 and 9–12 year-olds, teenage fiction and series fiction. Looking for quality young adult fiction. Also handles adult fiction and non-fiction. See website for submission guidelines. *Founded* 1994.

The Ethan Ellenberg Literary Agency*

155 Suffolk Street, Suite 2R, New York, NY 10002
tel +1 212-431-4554
email agent@ethanellenberg.com
website www.ethanellenberg.com
President and Agent Ethan Ellenberg, *Senior Agent* Evan Gregory, *Associate Agent* Bibi Lewis

Fiction and non-fiction. Interested in all types of children's fiction: new adult, young adult, middle grade, chapter books, picture books. Will consider all genres: literary, mystery, romance, fantasy, science fiction, humorous. Will consider other illustrated works. *Commission* Home 15%, overseas 20%. No scholarly works, poetry, short stories or screenplays.

Accepts unsolicited MSS and seriously considers all submissions, including first-time writers. For fiction, submit synopsis and first three chapters. For shorter children's works, send complete MS. Illustrators should send a representative selection of colour copies (no original artwork). Unable to return any material from overseas. See website for full submission guidelines. *Founded* 1983.

Flannery Literary
email jennifer@flanneryliterary.com
website www.flanneryliterary.com
Contact Jennifer Flannery

Specialises in children's and young adult, juvenile fiction and non-fiction (home 15%, overseas 20%). *Founded* 1992.

Folio Literary Management*
The Film Center Building, 630 9th Avenue, Suite 1101, New York, NY 10036
website www.foliolit.com
Twitter @FolioLiterary

Represents both first-time and established authors. Seeks upmarket adult fiction, literary fiction, commercial fiction that features fresh voices and/or memorable characters, and narrative non-fiction. Folio Jr is devoted exclusively to representing children's book authors and artists. Consult agents' submission guidelines on the website before making contact.

Barry Goldblatt Literary LLC*
594 Dean Street, Brooklyn, NY 11238
website https://bgliterary.com
Contact Barry Goldblatt

Represents young adult and middle-grade fiction, as well as adult science fiction and fantasy. No non-fiction. Has a preference for quirky, offbeat work. Query only. See website for full submission guidelines. *Founded* 2000.

The Greenhouse Literary Agency*
4114 Legato Road, 5th Floor, Fairfax, VA 22033
tel +1 571-758-5615
website www.greenhouseliterary.com
Director Sarah Davies, *Agent* Chelsea Eberly

Children's fiction from picture book authors/illustrators through to teen/young adult (USA/UK 15%, elsewhere 25%). Occasional non-fiction projects and women's fiction will also be considered. Represents both US and UK authors. No poetry or film scripts. Will suggest revision. See website for submission guidelines.

Authors include Andrea Contos, Tami Lewis Brown, Sarwat Chadda, Elle Cosimano, Alexandra Diaz, Bill Doyle, Ashley Elston, Tae Keller, Dawn Kurtagich, Cori McCarthy, Joanna Meyer, Megan Miranda, Mae Respicio, Ali Standish, Kat Yeh, Allen Zadoff, Brenna Yovanoff. *Founded* 2008.

John Hawkins & Associates Inc.*
80 Maiden Lane, Suite 1503, New York, NY 10038
tel +1 212-807-7040
email jha@jhalit.com
website www.jhalit.com
Agents Moses Cardona (President), Warren Frazier, Anne Hawkins

Fiction, non-fiction, young adult. *Founded* 1893.

kt literary*
9249 S. Broadway 200–543, Highlands Ranch, CO 80129
tel +1 720-344-4728
email contact@ktliterary.com
website https://ktliterary.com
Twitter @ktliterary
Agents Kate Testerman, Sara Megibow, Hannah Fergesen, Renee Nyen, Hilary Harwell, Kelly Van Sant, Jas Perry, Chelsea Hensley, Aida Z. Lilly

Primarily middle-grade and young adult fiction. No picture books. Some select narrative non-fiction for children. Email a query letter and the first three pages of manuscript in the body of the email (no attachments) as per website instructions. No postal submissions.

Clients include Maureen Johnson, Stephanie Perkins, Matthew Cody, Ellen Booraem, Trish Doller, Amy Spalding, Jaleigh Johnson, Stefan Bachmann. *Founded* 2008.

Gina Maccoby Literary Agency*
PO Box 60, Chappaqua, NY 10514
tel +1 914-238-5630
email query@maccobylit.com
website www.publishersmarketplace.com/members/GinaMaccoby/
Contact Gina Maccoby

Looking for high-quality upmarket fiction and non-fiction for adults and children. An engaging narrative voice and strong premise are most important; across all forms the agency is looking for compelling stories and fresh perspectives. Children's, young adult, middle grade, picture books of writers/illustrators only. Non-fiction areas of interest include history, biography, popular science and narrative journalism. No unsolicited submissions. Query first: query@maccobylit.com. Due to the volume of submissions received, will only reply if interested. *Founded* 1986.

McIntosh & Otis Inc.*
207 E. 37th Street, Suite BG, New York, NY 10016
tel +1 212-687-7400
email info@mcintoshandotis.com
website www.mcintoshandotis.com
Head of Children's Department Christa Heschke

Board books, picture books (fiction and non-fiction), fiction for 5–8 and 9–12 year-olds, teenage fiction, series fiction, poetry and non-fiction for children. No unsolicited MSS for novels; query first via email, see website for instructions. *Founded* 1928.

Erin Murphy Literary Agency

824 Roosevelt Trail, Suite 290, Windham, ME 04062
tel +1 928-525-2056
website https://emliterary.com
President Erin Murphy, *Senior Agent* Ammi-Joan Paquette, *Agents* Tricia Lawrence, Kevin Lewis, *Associate Agents* Tara Gonzalez, Miranda Paul

Children's books: fiction, non-fiction, picture books, middle grade, young adult (home 15%, overseas 20–30%). No unsolicited queries or submissions; considers material only by referral or through personal contact such as at conferences or online pitch event requests. *Founded* 1999.

Olswanger Literary LLC*

email anna@olswangerliterary.com
website www.olswanger.com
Contact Anna Olswanger

Specialises in representing author-illustrators of picture books and graphic novels. Clients have won the Newbery Medal, Asian Pacific American Award for Literature, Flora Stieglitz Strauss Award for Non-fiction, Orbis Pictus, PEN/Steven Kroll Award for Picture Book Writing, Parents Choice Gold Award, Bank Street College of Education Best Children's Book, Sibert Award and the Ezra Jack Keats Book Award, and have been on the *New York Times* bestseller list.

Alison Picard, Literary Agent

PO Box 2000, Cotuit, MA 02635
tel +1 508-477-7192
email ajpicard@aol.com

Adult fiction and non-fiction, children's and young adult (15%). No short stories, poetry, plays, screenplays or science fiction/fantasy. Please send query via email (no attachments). *Founded* 1985.

Pippin Properties Inc.

110 West 40th Street, Suite 1704, New York, NY 10018
tel +1 212-338-9310
email info@pippinproperties.com
website www.pippinproperties.com
Facebook www.facebook.com/pippinproperties
Twitter @LovethePippins
Contact Holly McGhee, Elena Giovinazzo, Sara Crowe, Cameron Chase, Ashley Valentine, Rakeem Nelson

Focuses on children's book authors and artists, from picture books to middle grade, graphic novels and young adult novels, and adult trade books on occasion. *Commission* Home 15%, overseas 25%. Query by email. *Founded* 1998.

Rodeen Literary Management

email submissions@rodeenliterary.com
website www.rodeenliterary.com
Facebook www.facebook.com/RodeenLiterary/
Twitter @RodeenLiterary

Open to submissions from writers and illustrators of all genres of children's literature including picture books, early readers, middle-grade fiction and non-fiction, graphic novels, as well as young adult fiction and non-fiction. Whether you are an aspiring writer, illustrator or experienced author, review the submission guidelines online and send your work via email. *Founded* 2008.

Susan Schulman Literary Agency LLC*

454 West 44th Street, New York, NY 10036
tel +1 212-713-1633
email susan@schulmanagency.com
Twitter @SSchulman

Agents for negotiation in all markets (with co-agents) of fiction, general non-fiction, for picture books, middle-grade and young adult markets, and associated subsidiary rights including plays, TV adaptation and film. *Commission* Home 15%, UK 7.5%, overseas 20%. Return postage required. Email enquiries to queries@schulmanagency.com.

Stimola Literary Studio, Inc.*

308 Livingston Court, Edgewater, NJ 07020
tel +1 201-945-9353
website www.stimolaliterarystudio.com
President and Founder Rosemary B. Stimola, *Vice President and Agent for Graphic Novels* Peter K Ryan, *Senior Agent* Erica Rand Silverman, *Agents* Adriana Stimola, Allison Hellegers, *Associate Agent* Allison Remcheck

Children's fiction and non-fiction, from preschool to young adult; adult fiction, non-fiction, cookbooks and lifestyle (home 15%, overseas 20%). Most clients come via referral. *Founded* 1997.

WME

11 Madison Avenue, 18th Floor, New York, NY 10010
tel +1 212-586-5100
website www.wmeentertainment.com

Represents bestselling authors, critically acclaimed literary writers, award-winning thought leaders and up-and-coming talent.

Writers House LLC*

21 West 26th Street, New York, NY 10010
tel +1 212-685-2400
website www.writershouse.com

Fiction and non-fiction, including all rights; film and TV rights. See website for submission guidelines and contact details for agents. *Founded* 1973.

Illustration
Notes from a successful children's author and illustrator

Lauren Child describes how *Clarice Bean, That's Me* came to be published and shares her experiences of taking advice from publishers and editors.

My first attempt at writing a children's book was when I was 18 – my friend Bridget and I had an idea. Everything seemed simple – we were going to write a book, get it published and get on with something else. Almost immediately, and by sheer fluke, we had an interested publisher. We were invited along for a 'working lunch' to discuss the story development. The editor made some suggestions for improvement which we were quite happy about – we really had no objection to rewriting; we were happier still with the business lunch and were fuelled by the confidence of youth that life would always be this easy. We did nothing, of course, and the whole thing fell through which, with hindsight, was a relief – I think we would both be squirming now. It was a number of years later before I even thought to write anything else.

Please yourself

The next time I learnt the hard way, by trekking around uninterested publishers with my portfolio – something it would be almost impossible to do now, as no one wants to see unsolicited work. I used any contacts I had, however distant. I forced myself to phone complete strangers in order to get appointments and advice, which I hated doing. When I met with publishers they seemed to have very set views on what a children's book should be. I listened to their advice and always tried to write the book they wanted me to write. But, whenever I went back to them with my work, there was always something missing – I could never write the book they had in mind.

So, unable to interest publishers, no matter how hard I tried to give them what they said they wanted, I forgot about the whole project and got on with other things. One day, having reached a rather low point in my life, and having looked at every possible career path, a friend suggested that I leave my portfolio of designs, drawings and ideas with her so she could show it to her business manager who had created and managed various successful companies. When I met with this woman, I mentioned I had an interest in film and animation and also designing products for children. Although I had no relevant training, she suggested that I try to write a children's book because, hopefully, it would prove I could create characters and invent a world for them. I think that I was just at a point where I was ready to listen – perhaps because she was very successful, perhaps because it made sense, perhaps because she was a complete stranger.

I started to write the odd sentence, then draw a character, then write a bit more … there was no order to it, no plot structure. I wasn't even sure what I was writing, all I knew was that I was interested when I hadn't been before. I think it helped enormously that I wasn't fixated on creating the perfect children's book – it was merely a means to an end, a way to get into something else. I stopped being self-conscious about what I was doing and stopped trying to please everyone else. When I took this book – *Clarice Bean, That's Me* – to publishers, the difference was very obvious – they were all interested! However, no one was willing to take it on – they all thought it was unpublishable and told me so. But I had written something that had at least got their attention.

Listening to publishers

Nearly every publisher made suggestions of what I should change in order for this book to be published, some of them quite fundamental. I was told to drop the illustrations and simplify the text. I was told that varying fonts and integrating text and pictures was too complicated, that it would confuse young readers. I listened to them all; I considered what they had to say, but I knew they were all wrong – I knew they were wrong because I knew I wouldn't be happy with the end result. Because I had written something which felt right to me, it seemed better not to be published at all than to publish a book that wasn't really mine. After four or so long years, I eventually found a publisher who was willing to take the book on pretty much as it was.

And I think this is one of the most important things to know – how far will you go, how far *should* you go to be published? When it comes to this you have to follow your gut instinct. Despite my experience, I do think it is important to listen to what publishers have to say – it is always wise to listen, but it is not always right to take it on board. In the end, they can give you the benefit of their experience, but they cannot write the book for you, and you cannot write the book for them. As the writer, the book has to come from you. Of course, if more than one or two people pick up on the same thing then it may be worth following that advice, but for me it is never worth making a change when, after much consideration, it still feels wrong.

Know who you are writing for

When it comes to the question of writing for the 6–9 year-old market, I would say there is no formula. I don't write for 6–9 year-olds, I write for myself. My books are for anyone who wants to read them. For me, writing young fiction is less about writing for a particular audience or age group and more about telling a story that interests me. I have never thought 'Is this a book for 6–9 year-olds?' or 'Is this a book for 8–12 year-olds?'. I feel the same when writing picture books; they are there to be enjoyed by both adults *and* children because while the child looks at the pictures, it is the adult who usually reads the story.

How does a writer come up with the interesting ideas in the first place? As an adult writing a children's book, is it helpful – even necessary – to have children of your own? My own view is that it is simply irrelevant. First, we have all been children and anyone who wants to write for children must have strong feelings from his or her own childhood to draw upon. But more importantly, good fiction writing is not about imitation – it is about imagination. Just as having children does not mean you have anything to say to them in book form, so not having children is no bar to writing in a manner to which they will respond. Writing for anyone is about having something to say – a point of view. Writing for children is no different. When it comes to writing fiction, I think that any good writer will see children as people first, and as children second. Of course the context of childhood experiences is different from those of adults, but there is no emotion experienced as a child which is not felt equally in adult life.

At the more practical level, I do not believe that there are any fixed rules. I know that many writers plot a book out before they start, and I had always been told that I needed to plot my books and understand where they were going if I was to write successfully. But I never begin writing a book knowing how it is going to end. I never normally know how it is going to start either. I generally just begin with a sentence taken at random. For me, it is all about an idea taking hold, and the writing tends to be more about a feeling than anything. *Clarice Bean, Don't Look Now* began as a book about love and ended up being a book more about loss than anything else. I wrote a few sentences about Clarice's inability to sleep and from that the whole mood of the book was determined. I started to write about insomnia and then wondered why Clarice might experience this, which led to thinking about her worries, which in turn led to the idea that she might be feeling very insecure and start questioning things around her. So, in a way, a few sentences shaped the whole plot because they reflected something that I felt personally at the time. I didn't try to force a story that I wasn't interested in writing; instead it became a book about Clarice's anxieties, her inability to explain the world to herself and some recognition on her part that not only is life something which cannot be controlled, but it's also something which can only be imperfectly understood.

I write a lot of material and read it over and over, until I see what themes are emerging and then I look for a way to hang it all together. Once it has a solid plot, I start to cut. Writing picture books is a very good discipline for writing novels because with just 800 or so words to play with, you have to decide what is important and what isn't: what exactly is this book *about*? Writing picture books makes you much less frightened of editing out the bits that you love. You really can't be indulgent, and have to pare your writing down to the essence of what that story is about. Although, of course, a novel gives you much more freedom – *Don't Look Now* was 42,000 words – I still consciously try to make sure that every chapter is pushing the story forward and has something to say.

A good editor

That brings me on to another important part – your editor. I really have to trust who I am working with. I rely so much on my editor because of the patchwork way I work. A good editor will let you debate back and forth until you've finally reached a point where you know that you can't make something any better. You do have to trust them because it is so easy to lose your perspective about your own work. You may think it's great and not listen to criticism, but more often than not you will get doubtful and think it's all rubbish, and that's where an editor can keep you believing in your work.

If there's a single piece of advice I could offer for writing fiction, it would be to write from the heart. When I wrote *Clarice Bean, That's Me*, I became passionate about what I was writing and found it exciting. If you're bored when you're writing, you will write a boring book. And no matter how hard you find the early stages, keep going. You just need to write and write until you've written the imitation stuff out of you. It is hard but it is very rewarding too. Writing is one of the best things in the world – a licence to discuss ideas – even if it's just with yourself.

Lauren Child's picture books have won many awards, including the Kate Greenaway Medal in 2000 for *I Will Not Ever Never Eat a Tomato* (2000); the Smarties Gold Award in 2002 for *That Pesky Rat* (2002); and the Smarties Bronze Award for *Clarice Bean, That's Me* (1999); *Beware of the Storybook Wolves* (2000); and *What Planet Are You From, Clarice Bean?* (2001). In 2002 she published *Utterly Me, Clarice Bean*, the first of three

Clarice Bean novels. Three animated TV series of *Charlie & Lola* have been shown on CBBC and on channels around the world, and the series has won four BAFTAs. From 2011–16 she wrote the *Ruby Redfort* novels, a six book adventure series for young teens and illustrated new editions of Astrid Lindgren's *Pippi Longstocking* series as well as P.L. Travis' *Mary Poppins*. Her latest books are *The Goody* (Orchard Books 2020) and *Clarice Bean Think Like An Elf* (HarperCollins 2021). Lauren has written and/or illustrated over 50 books. She was Children's Laureate 2017–19 and is a Fellow of the Foundling Museum and a trustee of the House of Illustration. Her websites are www.milkmonitor.com and www.staringintospace.me.

See also...

- *Who do children's authors write for?*, page 99
- *Writing books to read aloud*, page 104

The craft of the illustrator

Salvatore Rubbino describes how he finds inspiration by looking at the world around him with curiosity and wonder, and explains the exciting creative and collaborative process by which sketches and ideas are woven together into finished picture books.

Looking is a wonderful thing

As a picture book illustrator, I spend my day drawing and thinking about stories. I love words – the music they make and the taste they leave behind in my mouth – but above all I think in pictures. My task is to shape a tangible graphic world where story events and characters can thrive, a world that the reader can believe in. Pictures are a perfect story-telling tool and stories help to give a context to experience and our lives. We simply can't live without them!

Looking at the world around me is where my ideas come from. Drawing roots me to the spot and turns an initial glance into a long hard stare. It connects me to my surroundings and reminds me how interesting and varied life can be. Looking and drawing is a process of discovery; it helps me to notice the 'overlooked' and feeds my imagination.

We live a good deal of our lives in the humdrum (punctuated every now and then, perhaps, with something extraordinary) but I find the 'everyday' and the tiniest events inspiring and full of poetry. I carry a notebook with me wherever I go, ready to capture those special moments; I have little books for drawing on crowded trains should I see a compelling face, and larger paper that I might lay out on the pavement for more sustained work. I like to collect characters – we are all interesting and everyone comes with a story, and I have certain themes that I often return to. Musicians give the city a rhythm; they perform to be noticed and I have pages full of expressive players, particularly accordionists, so I hope one day to weave my musical drawings into a tale.

I've overheard some astonishing phone conversations whilst out walking – albeit only one half of the exchange (if you're an illustrator you're allowed to be nosey!). We continue to be expressive, pulling faces and gesturing vigorously, even when we can't see the other person on the line, and this gives me the chance to record some wonderfully animated behaviour. I can never pass a group of gossiping ladies without straining to hear what they're talking about and capture them in a picture. To be an illustrator, it's also necessary to cultivate a sense of wonder. This starts with a willingness to look with curiosity and to train the eye to find meaning in everything around you. I'm still learning.

From observation to imagination

City life has always inspired me – almost any street corner will do, although the busier the better, a spot where I can watch little everyday dramas unfold. My first picture book was set in New York (*A Walk in New York*; Candlewick Press 2009) and describes a walk over the course of a day. It follows a real route that a family might attempt (importantly no more than 3km), with stops for lunch and cheesecake – and no doubt the loo, too. It was quite a rigorous process to join up landmarks and beautiful views to form a satisfying sequence. When I was thinking about the characters, I asked myself, 'Well, who do you know?'. In the end I decided to have a dad based on me (more dapper and taller, why not? – after all, anything is possible in a story) and the boy who was a version of my son. At the time my son was only six months old, but I imagined him as a boy aged about seven, in a striped T-shirt and occasionally dragging his tired feet, even though in real life he had not yet learned to walk. I showed both of us craning our necks to look up at the skyscrapers, just as I did on my visit to the Big Apple when collecting ingredients for the book.

As a Londoner, I was excited when asked to make my next walk and subsequent book, *A Walk in London* (Candlewick Press 2011), about 'my' city. When you've lived somewhere all your life it's easy to feel you know it, the challenge was to see the city with fresh eyes. So, I bought a very large sketchbook and set out to audition locations and landmarks for a role in the book. One of my favourite places is Trafalgar Square. There's something quite joyful about a spurting fountain, especially on a hot day when you can put your hand in the water to cool down. I can't think of many national landmarks that you're allowed to climb, but, as long as you're careful, no one actually tells you off if you decide to sit on one of the lions guarding Nelson's column at the heart of the Square.

I am a little embarrassed to admit that I had never seen the Changing of the Guard ceremony in front of Buckingham Palace until I chose to include it in my story. It's a spectacle of synchronised walking accompanied by an orchestra and a cheerful tune. It begins with military precision at 11.27 a.m., and I made sure I had a place in front of the palace in good time, as I knew it would get crowded. And then it happened – an elegant lady wearing a wide-brimmed hat walked out of a side door, accompanied by her entourage; she got into her car and drove away – it was, of course, the Queen! I was astonished, but the encounter triggered an idea. I introduced a 'spot the royals' game, with the royal car weaving its way through the book; it's not mentioned explicitly, but the characters (a girl and her mother this time) receive a royal wave on the last page. I doubt if I would have thought of the idea without this experience of 'meeting the Queen'.

My early visual thinking for all pages in the London book was a flat plan. It records a conversation I had with my publisher when we made decisions about what to include, what to say about London and how to organize everything into a coherent whole. There are crossing outs and several blank pages, so it is still a work in progress. Your publisher or editor may have different opinions, and – whilst it's important to have an honest discussion – it's worth remembering that they want to find the best treatment for the story too. Trust your creative instinct, but also be prepared to listen.

Marshalling your creativity

The text for a story arrives, via the publisher rather than directly from an author, in a compact form – usually a couple of sides of A4, accompanied by a few notes from the publisher ending with 'Please let me know if you're interested' (I'm always very interested!). By the time it reaches me the text has already undergone a rigorous process of rewriting, and has a well-crafted plot and clear point of view. Being invited to illustrate someone else's words is like collaborating with someone else's imagination – it's extremely exciting. I may sometimes meet the author and discuss the project, but our paths don't cross very often. Our relationship is via the publisher, who realises that I need to respond to the text in my own way.

I tend to start with a slow read-through of the story and then I reread it whilst busily scribbling first impressions all over the manuscript. These notes might be about mood, a sense of place, character or anything that's particularly vivid. I don't start work straight away. Instead I let the story sink in over the next few days. I will try to visit places or find aspects of the story that I can see and draw. I don't want to illustrate the text word for word (like a list) but instead I slide up to the story ... sideways. I'm trying to find a way into the heart of the story. I'm looking for interesting things to describe, dramatic moments full of visual friction with the potential for mark-making or moments that might allow me to draw the things that I like and a chance to celebrate beauty.

My first drawing attempts for a book are usually quite unrefined. There is no process or formula an illustrator has to follow, or indeed that I follow, for each new project. In every case, I'm meeting the book's characters for the first time, getting to know them and the world they inhabit. I might simply respond to one line or phrase to begin with, until eventually I feel confident enough to start mapping a composition on the page. A book takes time.

I tend to approach a new book rather like a method actor learning a role. *A Book of Feelings* (Walker Books 2015) allowed me to be expressive and play with character in a way I had not tried before. I purchased a mirror so that I could practice a grimace or gesture, in order to draw myself and understand the way in which the child characters in the story might feel and behave and look – even doing a range of voices to help inhabit each emotional state I was depicting. The face has over 40 muscles, which makes it a fantastically elastic communication tool. I try to think about situations in my own life that relate to those described in a story, to provide me with creative inspiration.

What else can illustrators do?

If you are a commissioning editor reading this, I'd like to remind you that illustrators are resourceful people and good problem-solvers. Support them and help to celebrate images together. If you're an author, it's worth adding that illustrators make keen collaborators and will relish the chance to draw your story. And if you're an illustrator, why not consider sharing your appetite for creating pictures? Illustration can be a solitary business, but talking about pictures, running workshops or teaching can be very rewarding, as well as another way to support yourself financially. I'm often invited to take part in festivals and events and I like to cultivate this (time permitting). I also teach, as a visiting tutor, and regularly deliver activities at schools and museums.

I always find watching other people draw or demonstrate a technique quite magical. From humble beginnings something takes shape until it becomes more substantial, to form a face, an animal or a landscape full of life. We all seek to express ourselves, and drawing and creating is a perfect vehicle. People are keen to know 'how it's done' and as an illustrator you can take them on a behind-the-scenes tour.

The picture books I make often have a family at the heart of the story, doing things together; there's friction sometimes, but a good deal of understanding too. Running family activities allows me to observe how children and adults collaborate and eventually find a solution by working together, feeling proud of their achievements by the end of the task. One child might be busy cutting whilst their dad holds the card; another sibling is gluing, untroubled about sticky fingers, and at the same time mum or a grandparent may be helping to colour in. Explaining to others what I do, and thinking about pictures with others, makes me deeply aware of my own creative practice; at the same time it exposes me to lots of refreshingly different points of view – and so, whilst sharing, you never stop learning.

Salvatore Rubbino graduated from the Royal College of Art in 2005. His first picture book, *A Walk in New York*, was published in 2009 by Candlewick Press, followed by *A Walk in London* in 2011. His other books, all published by Walker Books, include *Just Ducks!* (2012) written by Nicola Davies, *A Walk in Paris* (2014), *A Book of Feelings* (2015), *Our Very Own Dog* (2016) written by Amanda McCardie and *Harry Miller's Run* (2015) by David Almond. His latest book is *Ride the Wind* written by Nicola Davies (Walker Books 2020). He received a Booktrust Best New Illustrators Award in 2011.

See also...

- *Finding your voice and point of view*, page 70
- *How to write a picture book*, page 126

Being an illustrator *and* a writer

Writer and illustrator of children's books, Liz Pichon, tells how persistence and hard work – and following the urge to create the kind of books *you* would have enjoyed as a child – can bring successful and very enjoyable results.

Illustration

I always loved drawing and writing stories, but it wasn't something I ever thought I could do for a living. I was a bit hopeless at spelling (and still am). My route to becoming an author came through being asked to work on other people's stories as an illustrator. I found it too stressful sitting around waiting for someone else to give me a job, so I had a go at writing my own picture book ideas to illustrate as well. I already had an agent for my illustration work in books (Caroline Walsh at David Higham Associates), who was very encouraging (and has stuck by me for over 16 years).

My first picture book, *Square Eyed Pat*, was published in 2004. This was followed by *My Big Brother, Boris*, which won the Smarties Book Prize Silver Award (0–5 Years) and gave me more confidence to keep writing and drawing.

This year is the 10th anniversary of my *Tom Gates* series and I have just published the 18th book. The series started life as a picture book idea. Publishers said they liked the format but didn't think there was sufficient story. So eventually, after rewriting it in different formats, I sat down and wrote afresh the first pages in a school exercise book. I imagined Tom writing about a rotten camping holiday he'd had with his family which included his teacher's comments as well as lots of drawings and doodles.

This was about the third (or fourth) go I'd had at it. But when Caroline sent out this version we got seven offers from seven different publishers within two weeks – which of course had NEVER happened to me before.

Here's my advice to anyone who wants to write or illustrate children's books:
• Be persistent. I know lots of people who have had their first efforts turned down or ideas rejected. But if the comments from publishers are positive, keep going and don't give up. Take feedback on board, especially if you're being told the same thing from different publishers. (However, some of my best ideas have lingered around for a while.)
• Think about what kind of books YOU really enjoyed reading when you were a child. I was crazy about a series about a bear called Mary Plain. Looking at them now, I realise that the main stories didn't really engage me, but Mary used to write letters with lots of drawings and doodles as part of them. I loved these bits so much that I would skip through the whole book to devour her letters. This is exactly why the *Tom Gates* books have so many doodles and drawings in them: I wanted to write a book that I would have enjoyed as a child.

The *Children's Writers' & Artists' Yearbook* is a fantastic source of information, STUFFED full of useful FACTS to help you get writing (and drawing). So be sure to make good use of it. And if you're lucky enough to get a book published – ENJOY it! Put together an event and do anything you can to help it along the way. I love going to schools and doing events now, although I found it tricky at first. It's really fantastic to be invited to talk about your books and meet the children and other people who are reading them. I often get ideas from going out and about.

As I look back on ten years of *Tom Gates* and am working on the next book in the series, I can honestly say I've never worked so hard on anything or enjoyed myself so much. So keep going and don't give up!

Here's my feet   not touching the ground

– because that's what has happened to me since *The Brilliant World of Tom Gates* was published in April 2011.

Liz Pichon is a writer and illustrator of children's books, including *A Tale of Two Kitties, Bored Bill, My Big Brother, Boris* (winner of the Smarties Book Prize Silver Award in 2004), *The Very Ugly Bug, Spinderella, Square Eyed Pat, Penguins, My Little Sister, Doris* and *The Three Horrid Pigs and the Big Friendly Wolf.* Her first standalone middle-grade title is *Shoe Wars* (Scholastic 2020). 2021 is the 10th anniversary of the *Tom Gates* series; it has sold over 11 million copies, has been a multiple No. 1 children's bestseller and has been translated into 45 languages. Liz has launched a podcast, *Tremendous Tales,* to celebrate this milestone. The latest title in the series is *Tom Gates: Ten Tremendous Tales* (Scholastic 2021). *The Brilliant World of Tom Gates* won the 2011 Roald Dahl Funny Prize (7–14 Years), the 2012 Red House Children's Book Award (Younger Readers) and the 2012 Waterstones Children's Book Prize (Best Fiction for 5–12s); and *Tom Gates – Genius Ideas (Mostly)* won the 2013 Blue Peter Book Awards (Best Story). Liz co-wrote the script for *Tom Gates Live,* which toured around the UK and Ireland in 2019, and co-writes and presents the DRAW IT section of the Sky Kids TV animated/magazine-style adaptation of *The Brilliant World of Tom Gates.* Find out more on her website http://lizpichon.com/ and follow her on Twitter @LizPichon.

See also...
● *Notes from a successful children's author and illustrator,* page 267

Matador® Serious Self-Publishing

Reliable and realistic advice on self-publishing from the UK's most widely recommended author services company

Whether it be writers' services like Jericho Writers, high street or online retailers, literary agents, other publishers – not to mention the *Writers' & Artists' Yearbook*... time and again Matador is recommended to authors wishing to self-publish a book, ebook or audiobook for pleasure or profit.

"A new breed of self-publishing companies offer authors a kind of halfway house between conventional self-publishing and the commercial kind. Of these, the company that has gone the furthest is Matador..." Writers' & Artists' Yearbook Guide to Getting Published

We produce books for authors to their specifications at a realistic price, as print on demand, or as a short or longer print run book. As well as a high quality of production, we insist on a high quality of content, and place great emphasis on the marketing and distribution of our books to high street retailers. We also offer great customer service.

Matador is ranked as the best self-publishing services supplier in the world by *The Independent Publishing Magazine* (Nov 2018 & Nov 2019)

But publishing a book is the easy part... getting it into the shops is harder. We offer a full sales representation and distribution service through our distributor and dedicated sales team. We also offer a full ebook and/or audiobook creation and distribution option to our authors, distributing ebooks and audiobooks worldwide.

"We've always liked Matador because they have the best values in their industry. Apart from anything else, they actually try to sell books. It sounds crazy, but most of their rivals don't. They print 'em, but don't care about selling 'em. Matador do." Jericho Writers

Ask for a free copy of our guide to self-publishing, or download a copy from our website. Or call us if you want to speak to a human being!

www.troubador.co.uk/matador

Matador, Troubador Publishing Ltd,
9 Priory Business Park, Kibworth, Leics LE8 0RX

Tel: 0116 279 2299
Email: matador@troubador.co.uk

Matador
exhibiting at
the 2019
London
Book Fair

Golden Egg

Courses for writers of children's fiction

'I want to see everything Golden Egg recommends.'

Barry Cunningham, Publisher, The Chicken House
Discoverer of J K Rowling

We nurture writers through their writing journey.

Over 75 published and agented authors since 2014.

We are *the* trusted academy for writers of children's books.

www.goldeneggacademy.co.uk

faber
academy

Manuscript
Assessment

Just finished a new draft? Getting ready to submit to agents? Or looking for an honest, professional steer on your work-in-progress? Our experienced readers provide constructive, comprehensive reports to help your manuscript stand out from the crowd.

the novelry

The online creative writing course that takes you to the literary agent's desk

BESTSELLING TUTORS

A team of supportive, and energetic tutors at your side while you write to keep you on track. From children's fiction and YA to romance, historical murder, mystery, and psychological thrillers...

INSPIRING COURSES

Voted 'The best course to write your novel' by The Bookfox. With five star reviews. Original and exciting daily guidance to complete your novel step-by-step in style.

WHERE WRITERS BECOME AUTHORS

Guest tutors: Val McDermid, Adele Parks, Kathy Lette, Meg Rosoff. Guest sessions with our literary agency partners.

A warm welcome to writers at all stages of their writing.

Do judge a book by its cover

Thomas Taylor explains how a good cover can tell you, at a glance, just how it feels to read the book, and he describes the key, defining, attention-grabbing elements that, thanks to the skills of designer, publisher and marketing team, combine to sell your book to the reader.

Not its contents, of course – I would never suggest that the quality of someone's writing or their ability to tell a story can be fairly assessed by how the book appears; but do judge the book as an object – by how it looks on the shelf or feels in your hand – because a lot of effort went into making it that way.

When my middle-grade novel *Malamander* (Walker Books 2019) was being prepared for publication, I was eager to do the cover art myself. I am, after all, an illustrator, and my first published piece of illustration – straight out of art school – was the cover art for *Harry Potter and the Philosopher's Stone* (Bloomsbury 1997) by J.K. Rowling. Editor Barry Cunningham contacted me, after seeing some sample drawings I left at the offices of Bloomsbury, and invited me to make a painting for the cover of a debut book by an unknown author. The brief was simple: paint Harry beside the Hogwarts Express, on Platform Nine and Three Quarters, and then paint a wizard ('any wizard will do') for the back cover. After some to-ing and fro-ing with rough sketches, I produced the paintings, which were then whisked into book cover shape by a designer. At the time I had little inkling what this 'whisking' entailed.

Given this experience – and the years of working on picture books that followed – it seemed only natural that I would do the cover art for my own middle-grade novel too, and not just the incidental interior drawings and the map. Indeed, I'd doodled and sketched right through the process of writing *Malamander*, so I was ready to go. But that's not what happened.

One of the questions I get asked most by up-and-coming writers looking to break into traditional publishing and asking for guidance is: 'Do I need to find an illustrator before I submit to publishers?'. This comes up especially frequently with picture book writers, who correctly sense the importance images will have as a vehicle for their storytelling, but don't always know how to handle it if they're not doing the art themselves. Well, there's some good news. The answer to this is: you *never* need to find an illustrator. Not if you are following the traditional publishing route.

Selecting the right visual match for your writing and storytelling is a complex business, and one the publishers will definitely want to be in control of. Art directors bring enormous expertise to this process, as well as the contact details of some of the best cover artists and designers in the industry. Actually, be *glad* that they'll handle all this for you; querying an agent or prospective publisher as a double act will make you much harder to deal with anyway, and will throw up unnecessary complications that no editor wants to deal with.

When you have a publishing contract, you may get some say in the look of the book – probably further down the line, once the work has essentially been done. But this is likely to be a polite request for comment, rather than an invitation to send the designers back to the storyboard. Well-established writers may be able to exert more influence on the process, perhaps thanks to a clause they (or more likely their agent) were able to insert into the contract. Whether they *should* or not is a point for debate, though; an author may have strong feelings about how the book should look, but their preferences may not marry up with current trends or other marketing factors that could be crucial to a book's success in a highly competitive market.

Sometimes it can be hard when an author sees their cover for the first time and it is nothing like they imagined it would or should be. The publishing process can often appear mysterious and veiled, especially for new writers, who may feel that they are on the receiving end of arcane decisions made in secret conclave. But it's important to trust that the publishers know the market and how to position your book successfully in it, and to remember that they are on your side and have every interest in seeing your book succeed. This isn't to say you shouldn't use your chance to comment on the cover design, or that you should be shy of sharing your ideas. Just be aware that your voice is only one of many.

The first thing I noticed when the cover art for *Malamander* was being discussed was just how many people had input or a say in the process – from publishing and sales directors, through marketing and PR reps, to representatives of export sales, special sales, book club sales, etc. Oh, and designers of course. And that's before factoring in key account (bookshop chains, for example) managers and buyers who will have to actually sell the book, and who may well have strong views on what does or doesn't work on the shop floor. And yes, these views are sometimes strong enough to get a book cover design changed, in order to secure a substantial order.

This process has become more intense since my own experience of producing the cover art for *Harry Potter* back in 1996, due not only to ever-increasing competition in children's fiction but also to the rise of digital platforms. For example, the question of how a cover will display as a thumbnail is more important than ever, because that tiny postage-stamp-sized image that scrolls down an iPhone screen in a second may be the book's only chance to connect with potential readers. If the actual physical book benefits from a foil finish, or sprayed edges or embossed lettering, it still has to look good at just 107 pixels wide by 160 high (standard thumbnail dimensions), where all these flourishes will be invisible. Delicate typography might vanish altogether at that resolution, and subtle artwork become little more than a blob.

For similar reasons, the spine of a book – so often overlooked – might be the only side of your work a browsing reader sees as they scan the shelves. But a good designer can tell them the author's name, the title, the publisher and something of the flavour of the story – all in the narrow strip of paper that holds the book together. And in a way that catches the eye too.

Series recognition and author branding often rests entirely on how that author's books appear. Get this right from the beginning and you can create a graphic language that tells us, at a glance, that the new book by X is out. Often this is achieved simply by choosing (and sticking with) a distinctive font for the author's name and making this the dominating graphic element of the cover. Think Rankin, Ellroy and Le Carré, and now you know where the term 'Big Name author' comes from.

They say a good cover tells you how it will *feel* to read the book. So alongside the practical considerations of text hierarchy – the relative graphic importance of the title, author's name, and straplines and quotes – there are other, less literal design components at play. Photography, painted or decorative elements that conjure a sense of the story for the reader and entice them in, are complex considerations and easy to overdo. Clever font choice can straddle both of these fields, clearly communicating key information, whilst also hinting at the regional or temporal flavour of the story or summing up that elusive 'feel'.

There's only so much 'room' on a book cover. Doing a lot with font, for example, means you can't also add complex imagery without potentially overloading the design and creating a mess that the eye struggles to read at a glance. And when it comes to selling books by cover alone, a glance might be all you get.

What is or is not a good design is not entirely subjective. There are certain key elements that are usually combined to create a harmonious whole: what the book is called and who wrote it; how reading the story will make you feel; how the book can grab attention on displays; how the book cover fares when miniaturised to a thumbnail or glimpsed from across the street in a bookshop window. I now have a far greater appreciation for what designers do than I did when I painted those *Harry Potter* cover pictures way back at the start of my career.

I had my own lesson in the importance of the content of book cover art too, when the wizard I painted for the back cover of *Harry Potter* (the 'any wizard will do' wizard I mentioned at the start) became the subject of much fan speculation, and even consternation. With the rise of Pottermania, the identity of the wizard I originally painted there became the subject of debate – even some conspiracy theories. I was accused by some of having secret advance information about the then unwritten books, and of deliberately leaving clues and toying with readers. Nobody wanted to hear that the character I painted was just a generic wizard based on my own dad! Bloomsbury asked me, some years later, to paint a replacement picture – the image of Albus Dumbledore that most fans seemed to expect – and my father's brief career as an infamous magician came to an end.

In the ever-narrowing bricks-and-mortar retail space, and across the expanding and fiercely visual digital landscape, the appearance of your book has probably never been more important. So while it's still true that a good cover should tell you how it feels to read the book, these days it can't hurt if it also looks stunning on a coffee table, turns heads from across the street or launches a viral 'This was totally a cover buy, but …' Instagram wave.

I didn't do the cover art for *Malamander* in the end. I quickly became overwhelmed by how complex the process was, and how much editing and writing time it would take away. It was genuinely a relief to pass the task over to George Ermos, whose gorgeous art adorns the cover now – subtly suggesting the tone of the story within and how it will feel to read it, whilst also making a splash in a bookshop window. And yes, thanks to George, it also looks fabulous in an Instagram post.

Thomas Taylor is an author and illustrator. He has illustrated and contributed to dozens of books, and has also written and illustrated four of his own picture books, including *The Loudest Roar* (2003) and *The Biggest Splash* (2005), both published by OUP. His most recent books, in the *Legends of Eerie-on-Sea* series published by Walker Books for middle-grade readers, are *Malamander* (2019), *Gargantis* (2020) and *Shadowghast* (2021). For more information see www.thomastaylor-author.com; follow him on Twitter @ThomasHTaylor.

See also...
• *Being an illustrator* and *a writer*, page 275

How to create a graphic novel

Isabel Greenberg has valuable advice for the would-be graphic novelist, provides tried-and-tested practical rules and tips for visual storytellers, and shares her knowledge of this creative and engaging medium.

Contrary to how they are often presented, graphic novels (or comics) are not a genre – like science fiction or fantasy or crime or historical fiction, but a medium – like film, poetry, interpretative dance or prose novels. They are a way of telling stories. I can introduce you to some of the conventions or 'un-conventional' aspects of this medium and talk you through my own process, but to instruct you in how to create a graphic novel in one short article is as impossible a task as instructing someone on how to write a novel or make a film. That said, what I can do is tell you how I make *my* graphic novels. I'll present you with some tips, pointers and thoughts that I think might be useful for anyone embarking on this creative route … for it is a mammoth undertaking.

Definitions

Whether you choose to call it a graphic novel or a comic book, or just a story told in pictures, is entirely up to you. For me, if it's the length of a novel, I call it a graphic novel. This doesn't mean its content is necessarily more 'highbrow' than your average comic; for me it simply denotes the length of the book. A short episodic periodical or a zine, regardless of its content, I would refer to as a comic. But hot debate surrounds this issue, with many comic fans feeling that the term 'graphic novel' has been used to make the medium more palatable to audiences who might balk at reading 'comic books'. I tend to feel that whether this is true or not doesn't matter, so long as it means more readers are willing to access this wonderful medium.

Where to start?

With your story of course – and how you begin to find this is up to you. For some writers, a character might be their catalyst; for others it's a plot or premise. This is a visual medium, however, so that is something worth thinking about. Much as a film-maker might struggle to make an arresting film that takes place entirely in a pitch-black room, so you, as a visual storyteller, might also (that being said, you may be up for a challenge!).

As with standard novels, graphic novels encompass a vast array of genres. You can read a graphic novel adventure, a thriller, horror, biography or history. And yes, there are graphic novels that feature superheroes! Autobiography is extremely popular too; the most well-known examples of the medium are *Persepolis* by Marjane Satrapi (Jonathan Cape 2003) and *Maus* by Art Speigelman (Pantheon Books 1991), to name two of the most seminal.

Many graphic novelists write and draw their own books. I am one of these. But if you are an aspiring writer who would like to team up with an artist, that is also possible. Some publishers may be willing to help facilitate this but, with such a visual medium, it is hard to pitch the project on words alone, and you might want to consider approaching an artist to work on the pitch with you. A note here: do not ask an artist to illustrate your graphic novel pitch free of charge, unless you are equally invested artistic partners in the project.

If you need someone to facilitate your vision, you must pay for this service. Illustrating a graphic novel is an extremely complex and time-consuming task.

For me, everything starts with the story. I would not even begin to sketch or imagine characters or setting until I had the bare bones of a premise to work upon. Even my first book, which was set in an imaginary world called Early Earth, started with a creation story, rather than the building of the world itself. Many people like to start by building the world, but this aspect can be addictive, and your world can swiftly become too huge to handle. Remember that you are sculpting a narrative; the richer your world, the better. Of course, you can and should know all the back stories and places that go on off the page – but keep your focus on the story you want to tell in your book.

My most recent graphic novel, *Glass House* (Jonathan Cape 2020), began with research, as it is part biography, part fantastical interpretation of the Bronte siblings' childhood world-building. Many graphic novelists write their words like a film script. I do this to some extent, but I often play with writing as prose, and I'll frequently break off from the script to draw little moments or scenes so I can see how they might play out.

Rules to break or keep

I won't tell you how many panels should be on a page, or how many words should be in a speech bubble. Some of my favourite graphic novels are totally silent, such as *The Arrival* by Shaun Tan (Hachette Children's 2007) and *Bad Island* by Stanley Donwood (Hamish Hamilton 2020), and some have so many words it's almost a challenge to separate them from the images, so of course these rules and conventions are there to be broken. But there are a few important maxims I do try to stick to:

• One action per panel

You cannot direct a character to cross a room and open a window in a single panel (writers who have written for film are often the worst culprits in this area). You are working with still images. A character may be pictured mid-stride, crossing a room in the first panel, and opening a window in the next.

• Communication is paramount

Test your story out on a reader at every point. If they do not understand what is happening, if your images are too oblique or you have too much going on, then you will need to adapt. I particularly like to test my work out on readers who are not familiar with, or do not read a lot of, this medium. If a reader does not understand what you want them to, then you need to rethink how you are telling the story. Writers who work with artists can sometimes assume that the images can clear up confusing motives or explain things they do not want to say in words. Sometimes this is the case, but remember that – unlike with film – you cannot control how long your reader lingers on a moment or panel, or puzzles over the expression and emotion of a character. If there is something important you want them to know, you must endeavour to communicate it. Above all, remember that if your reader doesn't understand something, this is not their fault; the responsibility is on you, as the creator, to convey your own message adequately.

• If a moment is important, make them stay

I just said above that you cannot control how long a reader lingers on a panel. This is quite true, but you can certainly try. If a moment is important, emotionally or as a crux to your story, let your reader know this. You could signify it with a full bleed spread for example (this is a single image that runs the entire width and height of your double page). It can create impact if not used too frequently in your story. This might be a point of emotional significance, or perhaps a scene-setting moment – to introduce a character's arrival in a certain setting, or to show a moment of excitement or action.

• The page-turn is powerful

Don't show a big reveal as the last panel on a spread or page. Your reader will first see the page as one image before their eye adjusts and they read it as panels. This means you cannot stop spoilers if you show them on the same page. If you have a surprise, let the reader discover it as they turn the page.

• If your picture is saying something, your words don't need to

If your images are showing or saying something, then there is no need for you to say it in words too. If your image shows a character looking into a beautiful sunrise, you do not need to say '[XX] looked at the beautiful sunrise'. But you might use your words to say something your image cannot convey, or to add another layer to the narrative: '[XX] had not seen a sunrise for nearly a year'. Or you may choose to let the image breathe, and speak for itself, letting your reader decide what your character is feeling at this moment of sunrise contemplation.

I tend to use narration in my work, rather than leaving the story to be told purely through dialogue and action. But this is a stylistic choice, and many writers and artists will try to avoid narration; it can seem like unnecessary, or obvious, exposition. I do use such exposition to capitalise on the humour of having an omniscient narrative voice.

• Consider keeping your text on a separate layer

Whether you are hand lettering or using a font, this is worth considering. In all likelihood, your editor may come back to you with tweaks or spelling and grammatical corrections. I found early on that if I kept my text on a separate layer to my artwork, this made shuffling and changing much easier. Furthermore, it meant that when the works went into foreign translation, I was able to easily provide my font (which I made from my own handwriting) when appropriate, and when it needed to be re-lettered (for different alphabets) my text was easy to remove.

Pitching

Most publishers will require a full synopsis and plot breakdown, as well as at least six to ten example spreads, showing your words and artwork together. Some will require even more of a completed script. When choosing your example spreads, pick a variety that can show your range. Perhaps you want some quiet, some dialogue-heavy spreads, and some action or full-page images, if your story will call for these, so that they can see the full visual scope of the story.

You may choose to approach an agent to represent you before approaching a publisher. Choose who you approach prudently. Not all publishers or agents will be right for your work. Pick a selection of graphic novels by writers or artists whose work you feel has a parallel with your own stylistically, and see who publishes or represents them. Remember you have to appeal to a publisher both visually and in terms of your story; one is no good without the other. Consider both of these things when deciding who to approach. Look through a publishers' back catalogue and see if they have a house 'style'. Don't attempt to change your work to fit that style, but do bear it in mind if you get a rejection – they just may not be the right place for you. An agent can advise you on this, and will guide you through the process of pitching, should you choose to get one.

Making graphic novels your profession

Be aware that even the most generous advance from a publisher is unlikely to be enough for you to live on entirely whilst you make your book. The market is neither as large, nor as lucrative, as regular fiction, and the advances publishers offer will sadly reflect this. Most graphic novelists and comic artists will have several strings to their bow. Some may also do children's books, freelance writing, commercial illustration, hire themselves out to be the artist on another writers' work or have another day job completely.

And finally ...

Good luck! Graphic novels are a mammoth undertaking. But they are also a unique medium in that you have the power to do absolutely everything: you are in charge of set design, lighting, script, costume and location. You are the director of your own world, and it can be created without having to source a million-dollar budget and deal with a staff of hundreds. This is a wonderful thing, so enjoy it.

Illustrator and writer **Isabel Greenberg** studied Illustration at the University of Brighton and completed an MA at the Royal College of Art in experimental animation. Her bestselling graphic novels, all published by Jonathan Cape in the UK, are *The Encyclopaedia of Early Earth* (2013), winner of the Best Book category at the British Comic Awards, *The One Hundred Nights of Hero* (2016), a *New York Times* Graphic Books Bestseller and *Glass Town* (2020). Her work also includes comics and illustration, animation and children's books. See www.isabelgreenberg.co.uk for more information, and follow her on Twitter @isabelgreenberg and @isabel_greenberg on instagram.

Illustration

Notes from the first Children's Laureate

Quentin Blake was the first Children's Laureate (1999–2001).

I started life – my life as someone who does pictures to appear in print, that is – by doing illustrations and cartoons for magazines. It wasn't so long, however, before I got the idea that I would like to be on my own between two covers; or at least on my own with an author. There were various reasons. One was that I wanted to organise a sequence of images that would follow a narrative; another was to get into a wider range of subject matter, a wider range of mood and atmosphere than was supplied by humorous commentary on current everyday life. I had been trained as a teacher, and I thought it was possible that, as the humour I had to offer was mainly visual, children might appreciate it as much as adults. The prospect of children's books was an attractive one, but I had no idea at all about how to begin. In the event I asked a friend, John Yeoman, if he would write something for me to illustrate. He could read Russian and it was a sample Russian folk-tale that he offered to me, which I illustrated, and which we submitted to Faber and Faber. We fell on our feet. I think perhaps we had hoped for a picture book, but Faber said that if we could find another handful of stories they would publish them – and in due course they became a book called *A Drink of Water*.

So we were very lucky. We were spared the frustrating (and generally unavoidable) round of submissions, and we had something printed. And there is nothing, I suspect, so reassuring to a prospective commissioning editor as seeing drawings actually in print.

Now (50 years later), holding the *Children's Writers' & Artists' Yearbook* in my hand, it's clear to me that, if we hadn't been as lucky as we were, how useful such a volume as this would have been. It has two great virtues. One, of course, is the wealth of information it contains. From their listing in 'Children's book publishers UK and Ireland', for example, we discover that Faber and Faber won't look at unsolicited manuscripts – so we wouldn't have got far with them nowadays.

The other is an impressive raft of notes, comments and advice from practitioners in every aspect of the business. It's as good as a correspondence course in the creation of children's books. As well as the sage advice of such examples as Raymond Briggs and Tony Ross, there are more recent personal reactions. I was fascinated to read accounts of self-discovery from Lauren Child and David Lucas. The great advantage of such a personal approach is that the advice you find there is not merely prescriptive. In fact, though there is useful advice to be had, nothing is certain. Conventional wisdom would no doubt say that a readership of eight- and nine-year-olds wouldn't want to be given a heroine years younger than themselves, nor would that age group want to read about a middle-aged bachelor trying to persuade a middle-aged woman to marry him. But Matilda is a huge success, and Esio Trot does pretty well too. The book that you now hold in your hand is a wonderful guidebook, but it's still nice to think that none of us know quite where we may be going.

This piece was written for the seventh edition of the *Children's Writers' & Artists' Yearbook*, published in 2010.

Quentin Blake CBE has always made his living as an illustrator, as well as teaching for over 20 years at the Royal College of Art where he was Head of Illustration 1978–86. His first drawings were published in *Punch* when he was 16 and he continued to draw for *Punch*, the *Spectator* and other magazines over many years. He entered the world of children's books with *A Drink of Water* by John Yeoman in 1960 and has since collaborated with other writers such as Russell Hoban, Joan Aiken, Michael Rosen and, most famously, Roald Dahl. He has also illustrated classics such as *Don Quixote* and *Candide*, and created much-loved characters of his own, including Mister Magnolia and Mrs Armitage. Since the 1990s Quentin Blake has curated shows in, among other places, the National Gallery, the British Library and the Musée du Petit Palais in Paris. His work can be seen in the wards and public spaces of several London hospitals and mental health units in England and France. He has been very involved in setting up the House of Illustration, which will relaunch as the Quentin Blake Centre for Illustration in 2022. His books have won numerous major prizes and awards. In 1999 he was appointed the first ever Children's Laureate. In 2012 he won the Prince Philip Designers Prize. He was knighted in 2013 and in 2014 was appointed a Chevalier of the Légion d'Honneur. Between 2019 and 2020, he published a series of 20 large-format books of drawings, entitled *The QB Papers*. He illustrated Michael Rosen's poetry collection about migration, *On The Move* (Walker Books 2020).

See also...

- *Notes from a Children's Laureate*, page 73
- *How to create a graphic novel*, page 280
- *Eight great tips to get your picture book published*, page 286

Illustration

Eight great tips to get your picture book published

Tony Ross gives some sound advice for illustrators and writers of children's picture books.

I have always had the uncomfortable feeling that if I can get published, anyone can. A belief that being published is something that only happens to other people, holds some very good writers and illustrators back.

Assuming you have drawings – or a story – to offer, there are several ways to go about it. Probably the best way is to have a publishing house in the family! Failing that, all is not lost.

Work can be sent directly to a publisher's office. Most editors receive a good amount of unsolicited work, so be patient with them for a reply. A stamped addressed envelope for the return of postal submissions is always appreciated, bearing in mind that the majority of work submitted is refused. At the beginning of a career, refusal is quite normal and a great deal about yourself and your talent can be gleaned from this experience. Sometimes, advice gained at this stage can change your future.

Starting on a drawing career is an exciting time and I think it's a good idea to get yourself in perspective. Visit the library and some bookshops to look at all the styles that are around. Get a sense for what's out there: you don't want to regurgitate it, but to get a feel for the parameters. You can learn a lot, maybe more than you learned at art school, from looking at great artists such as Edward Ardizzone, E.H. Shepard, Maurice Sendak and Chris Van Allsburg.

Great Tip No. 1: Use black and white

There is great appeal in working in full colour but it's good to remember black and white. Sometimes a publisher may have a black and white project waiting for an illustrator, while all of the big interest is going into the colour picture book list. Some of the greatest children's books are illustrated in black and white – A.A. Milne and E.H. Shepard made one of the greatest partnerships with those tiny black ink drawings contributing so much to a great classic. Not a bad place to start, eh?

Ink drawing is simple in the hands of a master but not easy. That unforgiving fluid! Wonder at the uncomplicated, straightforwardness of the Pooh drawings. Consider Toad in *The Wind in the Willows*. When he applied to do the illustrations, Kenneth Graham said to Shepard: 'I have seen many artists who can draw better than you, but you make the animals live.' Can you learn anything from that? Look at Ardizzone's ability to draw mood. He can show both a summer afternoon and a cold November morning simply by using black ink. There is so much to look at, so much to learn from.

Try to include black and white work in your folder. Also include a series of perhaps 30 drawings, such as a fully illustrated story, where you show your ability to be consistent with the characters and the style, without repetition or irrelevance (like the radio programme *Just a Minute*).

It is a duty of an illustrator to be able to read, i.e. to try and understand the writer's aims, and to help them rather than to inflict a totally different angle onto the book (again, think of the Milne and Shepard partnership). Much of this comes down to being sensitive enough to recognise the tone of the writing, and skilful enough to draw in the same tone. So the importance of really taking an interest in the story cannot be overstressed. In the text, there will be either clues or blatant instructions to help the drawings gel. Be very aware.

Great Tip No. 2: Experiment

I have known illustrators who convinced themselves that they couldn't use black ink. Mostly this was because they were using the wrong ink, the wrong pen and/or the wrong paper. Types of black ink vary: waterproof behaves differently from water soluble. Fine nibs and broad nibs each give a totally different result, as does an old fountain pen or a sharpened stick. Try ten different inks, 50 different nibs, odd sticks and all the papers you can find: tracing, layout, calendered, five different cartridges, smooth and rough water-colour, handmade, wrapping paper, anything at all. It's a case of finding the combination that suits your hand and your intention. Your own genius, unrecognised at art school, could surprise you.

Many of the points I've made about black and white work also apply to colour. The marriage of image to text will be in your hands, but it must work.

Great Tip No. 3: Choose the right words

I am hesitant to give advice to writers. After all, there are few rules, and the next J.K. Rowling may read this. My own view is really quite simple, and rather obvious. I write mainly for under eight year-olds, so my stories are as short as I can make them. I feel that it is good to have a magnetic first sentence, and an ending that EXPLODES WITH SURPRISE. I think that the ending is the most important part of the story. The bit in the middle should waft the reader along, remembering that the *sound* of words and sentences can be a useful tool.

I like stories to be either funny or scary. *Very* funny, or *very* scary. To be dull is the worst thing in the world! That sounds so obvious, but it gets overlooked. If you are not excited with your work, maybe nobody else will be either.

A picture book has about 23 pages of text (but this can be flexible). I think those pages should have fewer than 2,000 words; 1,000–1,500 is good. One word per page would be great, if the one word was brilliant. As brilliant as the story. Don't be frightened of editing out surplus words. One brilliant one will work better than a dozen mundane ones.

Don't fall into the mindset that writing for children is easy. It has all the disciplines of writing for adults, with the added problem of understanding a child's mind and world. The great writers have a passport to a child's world – think of Roald Dahl. I have seen many brilliant ideas, with less than brilliant pictures, make wonderful books. I have seen a bad idea saved by wonderful illustrations. So, writing style apart, be your own concept's greatest critic. It is quite natural to be protective of your baby, of your story. But try to remember that there are a lot of good editors out there and it will be in your own interest to consider their advice. So don't be a young fogey: be flexible, listen, understand experienced points of view. This can be a good time to change for the better, and to start a relationship with one publishing house that may serve you for a lifetime.

Great Tip No. 4: Choose what you draw

Don't plan huge drawing problems into your submitted roughs. They may be accepted, and the editor will expect the final art to be better than the roughs.

I illustrate my own writing. This appeals to me for all sorts of reasons, few of them noble. Firstly, I get all of the available fee and/or royalty because I don't have to let half or more go to a writer. Secondly, if there is something I don't like to draw, I don't write about it. For instance, most of my stories take place in the summer, because I prefer to handle trees with their leaves on.

Illustrations being worked on to be published is not the place to practise your drawing. *Practise, change, experiment* all the time, but not in a publishing project. Your finished illustrations must be as good as you can make them. I know an illustrator who won't draw feet, always hiding the ends of legs in grass, water, behind rocks, etc. This is okay if the text will allow; a well-drawn puddle is better than a badly drawn foot any day. It is better to think around a drawing problem, than just to go along with it.

Great Tip No. 5: Experiment with your main character

Before you start, try drawing your main character (the most important visual element of the story) in all sorts of ways. A day spent doing this can be so valuable. Getting the main character right can indicate ways to proceed with the whole book.

Great Tip No. 6: Think global

Remember that editors react well to stories with wide appeal, rather than niche interests. Foreign sales are in everyone's interest, so try to allow your work to travel. Rhyme is sometimes difficult to translate, as are unusual plays on words.

Great Tip No. 7: Plan the whole book

Do little mock-up books for yourself to plan what text goes on which page. This helps to get the story right throughout the book. A 32-page children's book (the most common extent for a picture book) includes covers, end papers, title and half-title pages. This leaves you 23–25 pages to play with. These little mock-ups are for your own use, not to be presented as roughs, so they can be quite workaday.

By working out what text goes on which page you will get some sort of an idea of which illustrations go where. Just as the drawings are creative, so is their use on the page. If you use a full double-page spread, another can be expected to follow it. But imagine the effect if the next page explodes with huge typography and tiny pictures? I am not suggesting you do this, only reminding you that pages of a book are there to be turned, and the turning can be unpredictable and adventurous. Book design is important, along with everything else.

Great Tip No. 8: Persevere

So much to do, so much to remember. The main thing is, every children's illustrator and writer I know who has kept trying has got there in the end and been published. But I've also seen great talents give up far too early. Remember that rejection is normal: it's only someone's point of view. Some great books have had long hunts for a publisher. Be open to change and always bear in mind that editors have the experience that you may lack and an editor's advice is meant to help you, not choke you off. However, not all of their advice may apply in your case, so try to recognise what applies to you. When I worked in advertising, I had an art director who said: 'Half of what I say is rubbish. Trouble is, I don't know which half.'

And a reminder

Don't waste time by sending work to publishers who don't publish material like yours. Libraries and bookshops are worth exploring to familiarise yourself with which publishing houses favour what types of work. Research of this kind is time well spent.

Try to show your work in person so that you get a chance to talk, and learn. Do not, however, just drop in. Make an appointment first and hope that these busy people have some time available.

There are also agents prepared to represent new talent (see *Illustrators' agents* on page 290). Of course, an agent will take a percentage of the fee for work sold, but as my dad used to say, '75% of something is better than 100% of nothing.'

I am troubled by giving advice. I can't help thinking of the young composer who approached the slightly older Mozart and asked, 'Maestro, how should I compose a concerto?' to which Mozart replied, 'You are very young, perhaps you should start with a simple tune'.

The young composer frowned and argued: 'But, Maestro, *you* composed a concerto when you were still a child!'

'Ah yes,' said Mozart, 'but I didn't have to ask how'.

Tony Ross is a renowned illustrator of international repute and the creator of such classics as *The Little Princess* and *I Want My Potty*. His first book was published in 1976 and since then he has illustrated around 3,000 books including titles by David Walliams, Astrid Lindgren, Francesca Simon, Roald Dahl and Jeanne Willis. His most recent books are *I Want a Bunny!* and *I Don't Want to Wash My Hands!* both published by Andersen Press in 2020.

See also...

- *Notes from a successful children's author and illustrator*, page 267
- *How to create a graphic novel*, page 280

Illustration

Illustrators' agents

Before submitting work, artists are advised to make preliminary enquiries and to ascertain terms of work. Commission varies but averages 25–30%. The Association of Illustrators (see page 368) provides a valuable service for illustrators, agents and clients.

*Member of the Society of Artists Agents
†Member of the Association of Illustrators

Advocate Art Ltd

Suite 7, The Sanctuary, 23 Oakhill Grove, Surbiton, Surrey KT6 6DU
tel 020-8390 6293
email mail@advocate-art.com
website www.advocate-art.com
Director Edward Burns

Has seven agents representing 300 artists and illustrators. Bespoke illustration for children's books, greeting cards and fine art publishers, gift and ceramic manufacturers. For illustrators' submission guidelines see website. New: animation, design and original content represented through LaB – Writers and Artists colLaBorate. Also original art gallery, stock library and website in German, Spanish and French. Founded 1996.

Allied Artists/Artistic License

tel 07971 111256
email info@allied-artists.net
website www.alliedartists-illustration.com
Contact Gary Mills

Represents over 90 illustrators ranging in styles from realistic through stylised to cute for all types of publishing but particularly children's illustration. Commission: 35%. Founded 1983.

Arena Illustration Ltd*†

Arena Illustration Ltd, 31 Eleanor Road,
London E15 4AB
tel 020-8555 9827
website www.arenaillustration.com
Contact Tamlyn Francis

Represents 27 artists illustrating mostly book covers, children's books and design groups. Average commission: 25%. Founded 1970.

The Art Agency

21 Morris Street, Sheringham, Norfolk NR26 8JY
tel (01263) 823424
email artagency@me.com
website www.the-art-agency.co.uk
Facebook www.facebook.com/illustrationagency

Provides non-fiction, reference and children's book illustration. Specialises in non-fiction illustrations across a wide variety of subjects and age groups.

Submit by email up to six samples along with a link to your website. Founded 1990.

The Artworks†

14 Cranbourne Avenue, London E11 2BQ
email submissions@theartworksinc.com
website www.theartworksinc.com
Contacts Stephanie Alexander-Jinks, Alex Hadlow, Lucy Scherer

Represents 35 illustrators for design and advertising work as well as for non-fiction children's books, book jackets, illustrated gift books and children's picture books. Commission: 25% advances, 15% royalties, 25% book jackets. Founded 1983.

Astound US Inc

Suite 143, 61 Victoria Road, Surbiton KT6 4JX
tel 07465 772271
email contact@astound.us
website https://astound.us/publishing
Director Vince Verma

A new kind of artist representation business based in New York City and London. Offers contemporary children's book illustration, and both licensing and commercial art from around the world.

Beehive Illustration

42A Cricklade Street, Cirencester, Glos. GL7 1JH
tel (01285) 644001
email enquiries@beehiveillustration.co.uk
website www.beehiveillustration.co.uk
Contact Paul Beebee

Represents 200 artists specialising in ELT, education and general children's publishing illustration. Commission: 25%. Founded 1989.

The Big Red Illustration Agency

tel 0808 120 0996
email enquiries@bigredillustrationagency.com
website www.bigredillustrationagency.com
Director Adam Rushton

Offers a high standard of talented, professional and dedicated illustrators. Over the years has developed strong relationships with a wide range of clients including children's book publishers, design agencies, greeting card companies and toy manufacturers. Founded 2012.

The Bright Agency

103–105 St John's Hill, London SW11 1SY
tel 020-7326 9140
US Office 50 West Street, C12, New York, NY 10006
tel +1 646-604-0992
email mail@thebrightagency.com
website www.thebrightagency.com
Contacts UK: Vicki Willden-Lebrecht (founder),
Arabella Stein (director), Lucie Luddington (senior
agent, educational illustration), Nicky Lander (senior
agent, children's & fiction), Amy Fitzgerald (agent,
art licensing), Helen Biles (senior agent, illustration);
US: James Burns (managing agent), Anne Moore
Armstrong (managing agent); China: Lucie
Luddington (senior agent)

A collective of specialist agents representing the best
in global talent across all areas of illustration,
children's publishing, art licensing, literary, theatre,
film and TV. Genres include picture books, children's
fiction and non-fiction, activity books, novels, preschool, advertising, editorial, animation, branding,
packaging, digital, art-licensing and educational. For
submissions guidelines see website. No submissions
by post. Clients include: Benji Davies, David
Litchfield, Yasmeen Ismail, Chris Chatterton, Diane
Ewen, Fiona Woodcock, Laura Hughes, Galia
Bernstein, Mechal Roe, Zoe Perisco, Aura Lewis,
Beatrice Blue, Karl James Mountford. Founded 2002.

Jenny Brown Associates – see page 251

The Catchpole Agency

53 Cranham Street, Oxford OX2 6DD
tel 07789 588070
email james@thecatchpoleagency.co.uk
email celia@thecatchpoleagency.co.uk
website www.thecatchpoleagency.co.uk
Proprietors James Catchpole, Celia Catchpole

Agents for authors and illustrators of children's books
from picture books through to young adult novels,
with a specialism in editorial work. See website for
contact and submissions details. See also page 251.
Founded 1996.

The Copyrights Group Ltd

3 Pancras Square, London N1C 4AG
tel 020-3880 0134
email info@copyrights.co.uk
website www.copyrights.co.uk
SVP UK Licensing & Retail Rachel Clarke, *SVP Brand
and International Licensing* Polly Emery, *VP Creative
Services* Demi Patel

A Vivendi company, a full-service international
brand licensing company offering strategic worldwide
brand development, licensing and retail expertise.
Focuses on the long-term development of IPS and
quality merchandise programmes around the world.
Properties include *Paddington Bear, Mush-Mush and
the Mushables, The Country Diary of an Edwardian*

Lady, Father Christmas, Fungus The Bogeyman and
Greenwich Polo Club. Founded 1984.

Darley Anderson Illustration Agency

Suite LG4, New Kings House,
136–144 New Kings Road, London SW6 4LZ
tel 020-7385 6652
email clare@darleyanderson.com
website www.darleyandersonillustration.com
Twitter @Illustration_da
Managing Director Clare Wallace, *Directors* Darley
Anderson, Rosanna Bellingham, *Agent* Lydia Silver,
Agent's Assistant Chloe Davis

Represents bestselling and award-winning illustrators.
Works across all areas of publishing, from picture
books to gift titles to graphic novels, across fiction
and non-fiction, collaborating with both adult and
children's publishers worldwide. Actively looking for
new talent, especially illustrators from under-
represented backgrounds. Commission: 20%.
Submission guidelines: send an email with portfolio
attached as a pdf or in the body of the email, along
with information about yourself and links to social
media channels used to display your work. Author-
illustrators should send texts as pdf or Word
attachments, along with a brief synopsis and
illustration samples. Submissions should be made
directly to the agent of choice. Founded 1988.

David Lewis Agency

3 Somali Road, London NW2 3RN
tel 020-7435 7762 / 07931 824674
email david@davidlewisillustration.com
Director David Lewis

All kinds of material for all areas of children's
publishing, including educational, merchandising and
toys. Represents approx. 25 artists, half of whom
produce children's material. Also considers complete
picture books with text. Send A4 colour or b&w
copies of samples with return postage. Commission:
30%. Founded 1974.

Good Illustration Ltd

71–75 Shelton Street, Covent Garden,
London WC2H 9JQ
tel 020-8123 0243 (UK) / +1 347-627-0243 (US)
email draw@goodillustration.com
website www.goodillustration.com
Directors Doreen Thorogood, Kate Webber, Tom
Thorogood

Represents 50+ artists for advertising, design,
publishing and animation. Send return postage and
samples. Commission: 25% publishing, 30%
advertising. Founded 1977.

Graham-Cameron Illustration

59 Hertford Road, Brighton BN1 7GG
tel (01273) 385890

email enquiry@gciforillustration.com
Alternative address The Art House, Uplands Park,
Sheringham, Norfolk NR26 8NE
tel (01263) 821333
website www.gciforillustration.com
Partners Helen Graham-Cameron, Duncan
Graham-Cameron

Represents 37+ artists and undertakes illustration for
publishing and communications. Specialises in
educational, children's and information books. Phone
before sending A4 samples with sae or email samples
or link to a website. No MSS. Founded 1985.

David Higham Associates Ltd – see
page 254

IllustrationX*†

2 Salamanca Place, Albert Embankment,
London SE1 7HB
tel 020-7720 5202
email hello@illustrationx.com
website www.illustrationx.com
Facebook www.facebook.com/weareillustrationx
Twitter @_illustrationx

Welcomes submissions from illustrators and
animators whose work is distinctive and innovative.
Only accepts applications from artists through
submissions page: www.illustrationx.com/
applications. Founded 1929.

Inky Illustration

Kemp House, 152–160 City Road,
London EC1V 2NX
tel (0121) 330 1312
email info@inkyillustration.com
website https://inkyillustration.com/
Facebook www.facebook.com/inkyillustration
Twitter @inkyillo

Showcases the work of talented artists from across the
globe. The range of illustrators have experience
working with clients, on international advertising
campaigns, publications and editorials, as well as
commissions for smaller companies. Always happy to
receive new work. New artists should fill out the
application form on the website or email to:
submissions@inkyillustration.com. Hard copies of
work are accepted with a sae if the work is to be
returned.

B.L. Kearley Art & Antiques

Glebe House, Bakers Wood, Denham,
Bucks. UB9 4LG
tel (01875) 832145
email christine.kearley@kearley.co.uk
website www.kearley.co.uk
Agent C.R. Kearley

Represents over 30 artists and has been supplying
top-quality illustrations for over 70 years. Mainly
specialises in children's book and educational

illustration for the domestic market and overseas.
Known for realistic figurative work. Specialises in the
sale of original book illustration artwork.
Commission: 25%. Founded 1948.

Kids Corner

The Old Candlemakers, West Street, Lewes BN7 2NZ
tel 020-7593 0506
email claire@meiklejohn.co.uk
website www.kidscornerillustration.co.uk
Managing Director Claire Meiklejohn

Represents illustrators, from award-winning to
emerging artists for children's publishing. Styles
include fun, cute, stylised, picture book, young
fiction, reference, graphic, traditional, painterly and
digital. Founded 2015.

Lemonade Illustration Agency

Hill House, Suite 231, 210 Upper Richmond Road,
London SW15 6NP
tel 07891 390750
email gary@lemonadeillustration.com
US office 347 Fifth Ave, Suite 1402, New York, NY
10016
website www.lemonadeillustration.com

Represents 150+ illustrators and character designers
for all kinds of media from TV to children's books.
Offices in London, New York, Austin, Sydney and
Wakefield. Works with leading children's book,
kidslit, ELT and educational publishers in the
industry. Any submissions from illustrators by email
must contain a website link (no attachments) or hard
copies of samples can be sent by post with a sae to the
London office. The company cannot reply to all
emails because so many artist submissions are
received.

Frances McKay Illustration

17 Church Road, West Mersea, Essex CO5 8QH
tel (01206) 383286
email frances@francesmckay.com
website www.francesmckay.com
Proprietor Frances McKay

Represents 15–20 artists for illustration mainly for
children's books. For information on submissions
please look at website. Submit email with low-res
scans or colour copies of recent work; sae essential for
return of all unsolicited samples sent by post.
Commission: 25%. Founded 1999.

The Monkey Feet Illustration Agency

email enquiries@monkeyfeetillustration.com
website www.monkeyfeetillustration.com

Presents portfolios for artists creating work for
children's book publishers, design agencies, greeting
cards and toy companies. Founded 2012.

NB Illustration*

Home Farm, East Horrington, Somerset BA5 3EA
tel 07720 827328

email info@nbillustration.co.uk
website www.nbillustration.co.uk
Directors Joe Najman, Charlotte Dowson

Represents over 50 artists, 40% of whom produce children's material for picture books and educational publishing. For submission details see website. Submissions by email only. Commission: 30%. Founded 2000.

Plum Pudding Illustration

Chapel House, St. Lawrences Way, Reigate, Surrey RH2 7AF
tel (01737) 244095
email letterbox@plumpuddingillustration.com
website www.plumpuddingillustration.com
Director Hannah Whitty

Represents 100+ artists, producing illustrations for children's publishing, advertising, editorial, greeting cards and packaging. See website for submission procedure. Commission: 30%. Founded 2006.

Sylvie Poggio Artists Agency

36 Haslemere Road, London N8 9RB
tel 020-8341 2722
email sylviepoggio@blueyonder.co.uk
website www.sylviepoggio.com
Directors Sylvie Poggio, Bruno Caurat

Represents 40 artists producing illustrations for publishing and advertising. Founded 1996.

Elizabeth Roy Literary Agency

White Cottage, Greatford, Nr Stamford, Lincs. PE9 4PR
tel (01778) 560672
website http://elizabethroy.co.uk

Handles illustrations for children's books. Only interested in exceptional material. Illustrators should research the children's book market before sending samples, which must include figure work. Send by post with return postage; no CD, disk or email submissions. See also page 257. Founded 1990.

Caroline Sheldon Literary Agency Ltd

71 Hillgate Place, London W8 7SS
tel 020-727 9102
email info@carolinesheldon.co.uk
website www.carolinesheldon.co.uk
Twitter @CarolineAgent
Twitter @FelicityTrew
Contacts Caroline Sheldon, Felicity Trew

Represents leading illustrators working in a broad range of styles, selling their work throughout the world and in all media. All genres of illustration. Commission: UK 15%, USA/translation 20%, film/TV 20%. Submission guidelines: Send an introductory email with work attached or a link to your work. In the subject line write 'Proposal from Illustrator', and include information about yourself and your work in the email. Clients: represents prominent, award-winning and bestselling clients in all fields including books, illustration, audio, digital and theatre. Works closely with a media agent on Film, TV and other opportunities. Exclusions: None. See also page 257. Founded 1985.

The Soho Agency Ltd

16–17 Wardour Mews, 2nd Floor, London W1F 8AT
tel 020-7471 7900
website www.thesohoagency.co.uk
Contacts Philippa Milnes-Smith

Previously LAW/Lucas Alexander Whitley Ltd. Illustrators for children's publishing for children 0–16 years. See website for submission requirements. Special interests: authors/artists creating their own projects, projects with cross media potential, illustrators from diverse backgrounds, original talent. Clients include Lauren Child, Emily Gravett, Chris Judge, Steve McCarthy, Jane Porter, Chris Riddell and Niamh Sharkey. Commission: 15% (20% overseas). See also page 258. Founded 1996.

Tallbean

tel (01728) 454921
email heather@tallbean.co.uk
website www.tallbean.co.uk
Founder Heather Richards

Provides a single source of specialist illustrators offering a range of styles. The team of well-established and creative illustrators is kept relatively small to ensure a close working relationship. Founded 1996.

Vicki Thomas Associates

195 Tollgate Road, London E6 5JY
tel 020-7511 5767
email vickithomasassociates@yahoo.co.uk
website www.vickithomasassociates.com
Twitter @VickiThomasA
Instagram @VickiThomasA
Consultant Vicki Thomas

Represents approx. 30 artists, 75% of whom produce children's material for all ages. Specialises in gift products and considers images for publishing, toys, stationery, clothing, decorative accessories. Email sample images, covering letter and CV. Commission: 30%. Founded 1985.

United Agents LLP

12–26 Lexington Street, London W1F 0LE
tel 020-3214 0800
email info@unitedagents.co.uk
website www.unitedagents.co.uk
Agents Jodie Hodges, Emily Talbot

Representing illustrators of children's books for all ages (home 15%, USA/translation 20%). See website for submission details. Founded 2008.

Magazines and newspapers
Writing for the teenage market

How can a writer try to please today's teenage audience, who have so many added distractions, demands and pressures on their time? Michelle Garnett sets out some important guidelines, advising you to jettison any preconceptions and to respect the individuality, intelligence and concerns of this complex and fascinating age group.

There's no denying that the reading habits of teenagers have changed dramatically in recent years. Rewind to the 1990s and most likely your average adolescent reader would be sitting quietly, turning the pages of a book or a magazine. Fast forward to the present day and they're scouring their iPhone on the move, or devouring information on their tablet or laptop in bite-sized chunks. It's not surprising, considering of 12–15 year-olds, 91% own smartphones and 59% own a tablet (Ofcom – *Children and Parents: Media Use and Attitudes Report* 2020/21).

But enough of the stats. Times might be a-changing, but teenagers are still the same complex – and fascinating – individuals they always were. Adolescence is an intense time. Just starting out in the world, teens are attempting to navigate the transition from childhood to adulthood, walking the fine line between feeling invincible and feeling totally lost, while ticking off a rapid succession of firsts: first love, first car, first job, first holiday with their mates ... the list goes on.

They're breaking away from their parents and making their own decisions – and consequently notching up a fair few mistakes along the way. They're also starting to look outward, finding their place in the world and figuring out how their actions affect others. And under the influence of the continuously expanding internet and evolving social media they're having to grow up faster than ever, with so many distractions and demands on their time.

So with all this in mind, how does a writer even begin to try to please these (demanding, streetwise and fickle) customers?

1. Get to know your readers
If you're going to write for a teen audience you've got to get into their mindset and suss out what makes them tick. Young people are too often made to feel inconsequential and their views are commonly ignored. Talk to them, ask their opinion, find out what their priorities are, what fires their passions, what dreams and ambitions they have. They'll appreciate your interest – and, given the chance to talk, they'll be searingly honest.

You also need to discover how much they already know about your proposed subject, whether you're likely to be challenging any prejudices and what kind of questions your feature might prompt. By painting a clear picture of your reader in your mind you'll find it so much easier to define your motive. They'll only care how much you know when you show how much you care – and that means showing that you're aware of who they are and what they're about.

2. Lay off the teen slang
If you're talking to teens, you need to use their lingo, right? Wrong. Forget about any attempts to sound cool. Put down that 'yoof' dictionary. You'll struggle to keep up with

their ever-evolving language and your efforts will reek of 'trying too hard' – a trait that's a total no-no when it comes to appealing to young people.

'*When adults use text talk or slang it's annoying and embarrassing*', confirms Emily (16). '*Teenagers don't actually say LOL when they're talking.*'

Instead, be direct and informative. Adopt an authoritative tone, but keep it chatty.

3. Offer reassurance

Puberty is a confusing, and sometimes lonely, time. Reach out to your readers by talking about their worries and insecurities. Sure, not all of them are necking vodka in their school lunch break, risking unprotected sex or having panic attacks over their exams, but for many, it's their reality. Whether it's online bullying, unwanted pregnancy, peer pressure, drugs, abusive relationships or an uncertain future, it's happening out there all around them and even if your readers aren't directly experiencing these issues, you can bet a classmate, a teen neighbour or a 'friend of a friend' will be.

Teen magazines historically adopted the guiding tone of an older sister. It's a good starting point. Build trust by being frank with your facts and crystal clear with your message. And be sure to let your readers know that they're not alone.

4. Celebrate individuality

The teen years are full of contradictions. Most young people yearn to belong and be part of a community while also testing out their emerging individual attributes and attitudes, and pinpointing what makes them unique. Big up that uniqueness. Let them know it's good to be different.

And avoid making assumptions about what motivates them. They don't all aspire to being permatanned, WAG-wannabes or football fanatics with chiselled six-packs. Goth girl, tech geek, eco-warrior, skater boy ... they're all guises teens adopt as they seek out their true identities.

Jack (14) points out that teens' interests are as far-reaching and diverse as those of adults: '*We don't all listen to R&B, you know. One of my friends listens to opera music!*'

Carla (16) agrees: '*I can't bear it when all teens get tarred with the same brush. Adults assume we're all the same, but very few teenagers are 'yobs', hanging around in parks causing trouble, and we're not all 100% obsessed with social media. We have other interests too.*'

And get this: some teens are well-rounded, untroubled, rational individuals who, contrary to the navel-gazing, introspective stereotype, are (gasp!) capable of showing interest in and empathy for others.

5. Don't underestimate teens ... ever

Today's teens are far savvier than previous generations. They have the world with all its gritty realism at the swipe of a finger. What's more, having come to the realisation that their parents don't actually know as much as they initially made out, they have a tendency to mistrust 'adults telling them how it is'.

So don't lecture them or come across as 'preachy' and condescending. Most teens have a finely tuned, built-in radar that hones in on an author who believes themselves to be superior simply because of their more advanced years. After all, the majority of young people soak up the same TV programmes and websites as adults, and those nearing the end of their teen years are only a short amble from adulthood itself.

As 16 year-old Sam points out, '*I don't think there always needs to be much deviation when writing for teens from how you would write for adults. I'm obviously not speaking for all of teen-kind, but there's so many mind-numbing reality shows and celebrity magazines out there, I actually enjoy having my intellect challenged now and then.*'

Respect their intelligence and integrity.

6. Find your inner teen

You were an adolescent yourself once upon a time (maybe not that long ago in fact), so dredge the deep recesses of your mind for memories of your youth. One word of caution: beware when making references to popular teen culture. Raving on about the finer points of NSYNC's first album or discussing the complex love triangles on *Dawson's Creek* will blow your cover. Remember, most of your readers were still in nappies when Busted bounced onto the pop scene. Gulp …

7. Consider the where and when

Think about where and when your teen readers are likely to be reading your copy. Will you have their full concentration or will they be interacting with other media at the same time (listening to music on their phone, watching TV, scrolling through Instagram)?

Keep the flow of your writing fast-paced. Use shorter, to-the-point sentences and split up long copy with frequent paragraph breaks. Your article will appear less daunting and your readers will have more opportunity to dip in and out as desired. With so many distractions threatening to steal their attention, there's an even greater need than normal to write a punchy opener, use bullet points, lists, sub-heads and box features to create an easily digestible format and create a clear, logical structure.

'*It's easier to read features when they're broken up into chunks. Then you can just choose the bits that are more interesting or apply to you,*' says Clara (16). But as Jack (14) rightly points out, '*It's important to get the correct balance. You want some detail in there so the feature is useful, but if it's too long, it just becomes plain dull.*'

8. Think about your tone

The success of books like *The Hunger Games*, with its themes of warfare, betrayal and sacrifice, and the *Twilight* series, which explores vampire romance and the old standby of Good versus Evil, is proof of teenagers' craving to read about the deeper, darker side of reality.

What attracts them? Well, adult and teen brains work differently. Adults think with the rational area of their noggins, while teens use the emotional part and they're hungry for gritty, thought-provoking material.

They also have a thirst for humour. With exams, emotional upheavals and friendship issues to contend with, life can be tense. '*Even when I'm reading about a serious subject, I don't want it to be written in a long-winded, serious way,*' says Jack (14).

Entertain them. Make them laugh. Play up to their love of sarcasm and dry wit.

9. Relax the rules of grammar

I'm not suggesting you take an anarchic approach to grammar, dropping punctuation and scrimping on your syntax with every tap of your keyboard, but remember: this is one audience who might appreciate you being a little more informal with your writing. Feel free to allow sentences to end abruptly and prematurely or to double back on themselves.

As long as you put your point across clearly, a casual regard of the rules will give your text a more youthful, friendlier feel.

10. Give them what they want

Avoid topics that your audience have had more than enough of from teachers, parents and other scholarly types. *'I like reading things that we don't learn in school – advice that's useful to my age group, like how to travel safely alone,'* says Emily (16).

Put simply, yet another 'How To' guide to studying will provoke immediate boredom. Sure there's already a plethora of features online exploring drugs, self-harm, sexism, eating disorders – but that's why it's your challenge to take on an old issue that affects your audience directly, and to find a new angle to tackle it from. Reading about other teens' lives is also a winner, nine times out of ten, but the stories don't have to be overwhelmingly traumatic and depressing. Choose ones that show the wonderful variety amongst the young individuals out there.

To sum up

Shake off those preconceptions of the stereotypical teen; recognise the demands being placed on their rapidly eroding free time; give young people the respect they deserve – and the credit to handle weighty issues with intelligence and empathy, and offer them reading matter that doesn't just dish out the same old lazy messages, but ignites their enthusiasm, seeks to reassure them and empowers them to greater thoughts and actions.

Michelle Garnett is an ex-teen magazine editor who now divides her time between copywriting and subbing for various B2B publications, and writing, interviewing and editing at weekly celebrity titles including *OK!* magazine. Her website is www.michellegarnett.co.uk.

See also...
● *Writing for teenagers*, page 150
● *Writing thrillers for teenagers*, page 163

Creating a children's comic

Tom Fickling shares his passion and enthusiasm for the weekly comic, no longer a thing of the past but an exciting, cutting-edge technology with the ability to inspire a love of reading. He describes the reader-focused philosophy which drives the creativity of his team at *The Phoenix*.

Just as my deadline for this article was looming we found out that our printer had gone into administration. Not a nice thing to hear when you have the relentless *Phoenix* schedule perched on your shoulder, but also not an enormous surprise. The print business is a tough one, with ridiculously tight margins and expensive machinery that takes years to earn out.

But though it wasn't much of a shock, it was panic stations at *Phoenix* HQ. Because when you make a comic that comes out every week of the year, usually on the same day (it's called 'Phoenix Friday'), not having a printer can really throw a spanner in the works!

Everyone in the team shared the same immediate thought: 'We have to ensure the readers get their comic next week!'. It doesn't matter what you make – be it book or comic or something else – the reader should come first. That is perhaps brought into starker relief with a weekly publication because you have to make a lot of decisions on a very tight timescale, with the impact of those decisions being felt only a few days later. But it's true across the board.

We often get asked why we started *The Phoenix*, and of course there are lots of reasons, but ultimately the answer is: for the readers. But what does that really mean? And why do these readers (or in this case, children) need a weekly comic? After all, common sense tells us that weekly comics are a thing of the past and that's where they should stay.

People say we need to move forward, that we need new and exciting things. You know, tablets and gadgets and VR headsets and the like. (Alright, we definitely need the headsets). Comics may have been around for a while but I want to tell you that, far from being outdated, comics are a *cutting-edge technology*. A cutting-edge *reading* technology.

That's the thing about *common sense* – it never really leads anywhere interesting. And while *The Phoenix* may be a weekly comic, we prefer to think of it as a medium that has been honed and crafted over the years until it has become the most incredible story-delivery device known to adult or child. And it's one that goes right to the homes of children across the country. Wham! What a delight! What a wonder! It's a story-jack that feeds straight into the brains of children every week.

Our aim at *The Phoenix* is simple: to delight, to inspire, to fill minds with awe and wonder. Above all *The Phoenix* is *for* its readers. We want to make them go 'wow' when they tear open that envelope. We want their hearts pounding with excitement. We want them hooked on the story, totally mesmerised by fascinating non-fiction and their minds blown to smithereens by awesome puzzles.

We try desperately hard to inhabit the minds of those reading the comic. We don't always get it right, of course. But this celebration of the reader was instilled in me by my father. He's a publisher and he's published some stone-cold classics. In fact, of the 2016 World Book Day top 10 list of future children's book classics, he had published three of them. And commissioned a fourth that was on the list. So on these matters I take his advice quite seriously.

Magazines and newspapers

That cherishing of the reader and how they feel has been drummed into me. It is one of the most valuable pieces of advice I have ever received. And it applies to writers and artists as much as it does to publishers. It goes right to the heart of what I believe to be one of the key skills of a great storyteller. And I use the term 'storyteller' to mean anyone who is trying to convey a story via some creative medium. It's not just about writing – which seems a frequent misconception. That great skill is the ability to hold what *you* want as the creator side by side with what you think the *reader* wants: being able to satisfy your own creative urges while not disappointing the person consuming your story. It's hard. It means holding doubt and confidence hand in hand, both of which can be damaging in their own way.

At *The Phoenix* this means publishing things we know for a fact that children will love, alongside things that we *think* they will love. Because often the reader doesn't *know* what they want. And asking them what they want rarely produces the right answer. As Henry Ford said, if he'd asked people what they wanted before he mass-produced the first car they'd have just asked for a faster horse. It's the same with books. It took J.K. Rowling, not a focus group, to introduce us to Harry Potter. Philip Pullman conjured *His Dark Materials* from a lifetime of thinking and the words of Milton, not from a feedback form.

All this focus on the reader is not entirely altruistic. The thinking goes like this: make an awesome comic that a child and their family will love. Not *like*, but *love*. And love so much they want to tell people about it. The more they love it, the more people they will tell and the more readers we will have. We do think of them first, not what they can do for us (though, of course, we think of that too).

So back to the question; why start *The Phoenix*? Well, a weekly comic is a great way to inspire love. Love of stories and, importantly, love of reading. Think about it – has a better hook for reading been invented? Regular exciting stories, the anticipation of its arrival, the cliffhanger, the enormous array of content and lots more. There are other magazines for children that care about things like this. *Okido*, *Anorak*, *Aquila* and so on. But these are all independent companies, just like *The Phoenix*. Most other publications for children seem to spend little on storytelling and much more on marketing, plastic cover mounted toys and promotion. That's why *The Phoenix* is a subscription-focused comic that relies on word of mouth to really drive it. And word of mouth comes from love and passion and trust in something – which all originates from the reader.

But to inspire love you need amazing content. We are tremendously lucky to work with some incredible story creators at *The Phoenix*. Some are writers, some artists, many are both. Some are novelists, some are practised comic creators and some complete novices. All are welcome. Of course, working with such a varied group presents us with an editorial problem of tone, but our approach to that is again rooted in the experience of the reader. *The Phoenix* readership is aged roughly 6–12 years. That's a much broader range than most book publishers have to consider for specific titles.

We want excitement and adventure and scares and all the rest of it, but we also want six and seven year-olds to love it. There are plenty of examples of stories that can be enjoyed by all ages. Anyone heard of *Star Wars*? That's the kind of cross-generation appeal we ultimately aim for. It's a great target audience. Some might say it means dumbing things down, but I think that actually it means cutting straight to the heart of what a story is about. You can't hide behind gratuitous violence or gore or other salacious details. You just have to nail the story. It's tough, and rarely done, of course, but amazing when someone hits it out of the park and grandparents can enjoy it side by side with their grandkids.

So all you storytellers out there, no matter what medium you choose to tell your stories in, remember the reader. Or the watcher or the puzzler or whatever else they might be. And perhaps you might consider comics. It is a gloriously visceral medium to work in. For you writers it's a true joy to send off a script and have it returned beautifully illustrated by an amazing artist. And I know many brilliant illustrators who really enjoy bringing a writer's ideas to life. And for you publishers, consider the comic. And by comic we mean anything that is of the comic art form. There is no real difference between a graphic novel and a comic beyond the format. The methods of storytelling are essentially the same. Because kids love comics; they love them all over the world and it's time we recognised that again in the UK.

People are always talking about the need to raise literacy levels, to encourage 'reading for pleasure'. Comics are immediate and accessible and exciting. Children like reading comics because they like reading them. Not because someone told them to. I like the way Art Spiegelman put it (have you read *Maus* by the way? If not, you should!): 'Comics are the gateway drug to reading.' What an appropriately inappropriate way of putting it. And that fits comics perfectly.

P.S. If you've got a great idea for a comic story or non-fiction series, send it in to us! Apologies in advance if we are slow to respond. We're a tiny team. You can check out our submission guidelines at www.thephoenixcomic.co.uk/Page/Index/Submissions. To find out what sort of thing we are looking for, the best thing to do is to grab a copy of *The Phoenix*. Or even better, find a child you know and stick one in their hand to see what items they respond to best. But don't discount your own view because remember – it's all about the reader. And that means you too.

Tom Fickling was part of the core team that published *The DFC*, the precursor to *The Phoenix*. He joined *The Phoenix* full time in 2012 and was appointed Editor in May 2015 and managing director in 2016. In 2019, Tom was appointed managing director of David Fickling Books.

See also...
- *Magazines and newspapers for children*, page 302
- *How to create a graphic novel*, page 280

Magazines and newspapers

Magazines and newspapers for children

Listings of magazines about children's literature and education start on page 307.

AdventureBox
Bayard, PO Box 61269, London N17 1DF
tel 0800 055 6686
email contact@bayard-magazines.co.uk
website www.bayard-magazines.co.uk
Facebook www.facebook.com/
BayardPresseBoxMagazines
Twitter @BayardKidsMags
10 p.a. From £67 p.a.

Aimed at 6–9 year-old children starting to read on their own. Each issue contains a 44pp illustrated story plus games, a nature/science feature and comic strips. Specially commissions most material. Founded 1996.

Animals and You
D.C. Thomson & Co. Ltd, 2 Albert Square, Dundee DD1 1DD
tel (01382) 575863
email animalsandyou@dcthomson.co.uk
website www.animalsandyou.co.uk
Twitter @animalsandyou
Every 4 weeks £4.99

Features, stories and posters for readers who love animals. Founded 1998.

Anorak
3rd Floor, 86–90 Paul Street, London EC2A 4NE
email anorakmagazine@gmail.com
website www.anorakmagazine.com
Twitter @AnorakMagazine
Editor Cathy Olmedillas
4 p.a. £7.50

Aimed at children aged 6+, and designed to encourage creativity. Founded 2006.

Aquila
Studio 2, 67A Willowfield Road, Eastbourne, East Sussex BN22 8AP
tel (01323) 431313
email submissions@aquila.co.uk
email illustrators@aquila.co.uk
website www.aquila.co.uk
Facebook www.facebook.com/
AquilaChildrensMagazine
Twitter @AquilaMag
Instagram @aquila.magazine
Editorial Director Freya Hardy
Monthly £60 p.a.

Dedicated to encouraging children aged 8–13 to reason and create, and to develop a caring nature. Short stories and serials of up to three parts. Occasional features commissioned from writers with specialist knowledge. Approach in writing with ideas and sample of writing style, along with sae. Length: 700–800 words (features), 1,000–1,100 words (stories or per episode of a serial). Payment: by arrangement. Founded 1993.

The Astonishing Spider-Man
Panini UK, Brockbourne House, 77 Mount Ephraim, Tunbridge Wells TN4 8AR
tel (01892) 500100
email astonspid@panini.co.uk
website https://comics.panini.co.uk
Facebook www.facebook.com/
MarvelCollectorsEditions
Editor Brady Webb
Every 2 weeks £4.50

52pp of comic strips, including both contemporary and classic stories.

BBC Doctor Who Magazine
Panini UK, Brockbourne House, 77 Mount Ephraim, Tunbridge Wells TN4 8AR
tel (01892) 500100
email dwa@panini.co.uk
website https://doctorwhomagazine.com/
Twitter @DWMtweets
Editor Marcus Hearn
Monthly £5.99

Magazine for 6–12 year-old fans of *Doctor Who*. Readers are immersed into the world of the Doctor, taking them on an adventure into time and space, with monsters and creatures, excitement, action, adventure and humour. Founded 2006.

Beano
D.C. Thomson & Co. Ltd, 2 Albert Square, Dundee DD1 1DD
email beano@dcthomson.co.uk
website www.beano.com
Facebook www.facebook.com/BeanoOfficial
Twitter @BeanoOfficial
50 p.a. £2.75

Comic strips for children aged 6–12. Series, 8–20 pictures. Artwork and scripts. Payment: on acceptance.

The Caterpillar

Ardan Grange, Milltown, Belturbet, Co. Cavan, Republic of Ireland
tel +353 (0) 87 2657251
email editor@thecaterpillarmagazine.com
website www.thecaterpillarmagazine.com
Facebook www.facebook.com/thecaterpillarmagazine
Founders Rebecca O'Connor and Will Govan, *Editor* Rebecca O'Connor
Quarterly €7, €28 p.a. (UK and Republic of Ireland), €32 p.a. (RoW), including postage

Features original poetry and short stories written by adults for children aged 7–11, alongside full-colour artwork. Submissions from adults welcome, but contributors should familiarise themselves with magazine content first. Send no more than six poems or two short stories (max. 1,500 words) by email or post (sae). Also publishes *The Moth* and runs The Caterpillar Poetry Prize (€1,000 for best poem written for children by an adult). Founded 2013.

CBeebies Art

Immediate Media Co. Ltd, Vineyard House, 44 Brook Green, London W6 7BT
tel 020-7150 5021
email hello@cbeebiesart.com
Twitter @CBArtmag
Senior Editor Stephanie Cooper
Every 4 weeks £4.99

Aimed at young children who like art. Linked to popular CBeebies art brands including Mister Maker and Get Squiggling.

CBeebies Magazine

Immediate Media Co. Ltd, Vineyard House, 44 Brook Green, London W6 7BT
tel 020-7150 5119
email hello@cbeebiesweekly.com
website www.bbc.co.uk/cbeebies
Twitter @cbeebiesmag
Editor Stephanie Cooper
Weekly £3.50

Preschool magazine with educational content targeted at 3½-year-olds. Actively promotes learning through play. Showcases new characters, presenters and programmes as they appear on the CBeebies channel. Founded 2006.

Cocoa Boy

Studio 210, 134–146 Curtain Road, London EC2A 3AR
website https://cocoaboy.com/
website www.cocoagirl.com/submissions
Instagram @cocoaboymag
Publisher and Creative Director Serlina Boyd
6 p.a. £3.99

The first UK magazine aimed specifically at young Black boys. Includes empowering content aimed at teaching children about Black culture and celebrating

role models. Actively encourages submissions from children aged 7 to 11. Founded 2020.

Cocoa Girl

Studio 210, 134–146 Curtain Road, London EC2A 3AR
website www.cocoagirl.com/submissions
Instagram @cocoagirlmag
Publisher Serlina Boyd, *Editor* Faith Boyd
6 p.a. £3.99

The first UK magazine aimed specifically at young Black girls. Includes empowering content aimed at teaching children about Black culture and celebrating role models. Actively encourages submissions from children aged 7 to 11. Winner of Launch of the Year at the British Society of Magazine Editors' 2020 Awards. Founded 2020.

Commando

185 Fleet Street, London EC4A 2HS
email generalenquiries@commandomag.com
website www.commandocomics.com
Facebook www.facebook.com/pages/Commando-Comics/168688426504994
Twitter @CommandoComic
8 per month (four new, four reprints) £2.25

Fictional stories set in time of war told in pictures. Scripts: about 135 pictures. Synopsis required as an opener. Submissions information can be found at www.commandocomics.com/submissions. Payment: on acceptance. Founded 1961.

DiscoveryBox

Bayard, PO Box 61269, London N17 1DF
tel (0800) 055 6686
email contact@bayard-magazines.co.uk
website www.bayard-magazines.co.uk
Facebook www.facebook.com/BayardPresseBoxMagazines
Twitter @BayardKidsMags
10 p.a. From £67

Voyage of discovery through nature, science and history for children aged 9–12. Every issue contains: animal topics, information about important historical events, articles about the world, DIY activities, comic strips, games and more. Founded 1996.

DOT

3rd Floor, 86–90 Paul Street, London EC2A 4NE
email anorakmagazine@gmail.com
website www.anorakmagazine.com/dot
Editor Cathy Olmedillas
4 p.a. £6

Ad-free magazine aimed at encouraging creativity and learning in the under-5s.

Eco Kids Planet

Eco Kids Planet, 41 Claremont Road, Barnet EN4 0HR

tel 0800 639 1365
email hello@ecokidsplanet.co.uk
website www.ecokidsplanet.co.uk
Twitter @EcoKidsPlanet
Editor Anya Dimelow
11 p.a. £3.99

Aimed at 7–11 year-old children. Each issue is dedicated to a different ecosystem and contains facts, photographs, puzzles and projects. The magazine uses fun, fictional characters in a story format to convey facts about nature and the environment. It also provides children with real-world examples of how they can make a difference on the planet. Length: 500–1,200 words (themed articles). Requirements: well-researched, up-to-date, informative articles, creative approach, interesting language. Specially commissions most material. Payment: by arrangement. Founded 2014.

FirstNews

7 Playhouse Court, 62 Southwark Bridge Road, London SE1 0AT
tel 020-3195 2000
email info@firstnews.co.uk
website www.firstnews.co.uk
Twitter @First_News
Editor Nicky Cox
Weekly Fri £2.25

Covers news and events in the UK and internationally for children aged 8–14. Founded 2006.

Girl Talk

Immediate Media Co. Ltd, Vineyard House, 44 Brook Green, London W6 7BT
tel 020-7150 5000
email hello@girltalkmagazine.com
Twitter @girltalkmags
Editor Kelly Wilks
Fortnightly £2.99

Magazine for children aged 7–12. Contains pop, TV and film celebrity features, personality features, quizzes, fashion, competitions, stories. Length: 500 words (fiction). Payment: £75. All material is specially commissioned. Founded 1997.

Headliners

49–51 East Road, London N1 6AH
tel 020-7749 9360
email enquiries@headliners.org
website www.headliners.org
Twitter @HeadlinersUK
Chief Executive Ali Talbot

Award-winning journalism and multi-media charity, offering young people aged 8–18 the opportunity to write on issues of importance to them, for newspapers, radio and TV. Founded 1995.

KiCK!

Kennedy Publishing, Greenway Farm, Bath Road, Wick, Bristol BS30 5RL

tel 0117 937300
email info@kennedypublishing.co.uk
Twitter @KiCKmagazine
Editor Ash Rose
13 p.a. £3.99

Football magazine for boys and girls aged 7–14. Reports on leading players and teams from a variety of divisions, including the Premier League; also includes puzzles, competitions and interviews.

Kids Alive! (The Young Soldier)

The Salvation Army, 101 Newington Causeway, London SE1 6BN
tel 020-7367 4911
email kidsalive@salvationarmy.org.uk
website www.salvationarmy.org.uk/kidsalive
Editor Justin Reeves, *Deputy Editor* Cara Mott
Weekly £52 p.a.

Children's magazine: scripts and artwork for cartoon strips, puzzles, etc; Christian-based articles with emphasis on education and lifestyle issues. Illustrations: half-tone, line and four-colour line, cartoons. Payment: by arrangement. Founded 1881.

Kookie

Missprint Media, PO Box 2410, LL11 0NY
email hello@kookiemagazine.com
website www.kookiemagazine.co.uk
Twitter @kookiemagazine
Instagram @kookiemagazine
Editor Vivien Jones
4 p.a. £6.50

Award-winning, ad-free magazine for girls aged 7–12+. Features interviews with inspiring women and girls, original fiction, information on key science, sports and IT topics as well as craft, book reviews and a problem page. Founded 2017.

Marvel Legends

Panini UK, Brockbourne House, 77 Mount Ephraim, Tunbridge Wells TN4 8AR
tel (01892) 500100
email astonspid@panini.co.uk
website www.paninicomics.co.uk
Facebook www.facebook.com/
MarvelCollectorsEditions
Editor Brady Webb
Every 4 weeks £4.50

52pp of comic strips, including both contemporary and classic stories.

Match!

Kelsey Media, The Granary, Downs Court, Yalding Hill, Yalding, Kent ME18 6AL
email match.magazine@kelsey.co.uk
website www.matchfootball.co.uk
Twitter @matchmagazine
Editor Stephen Fishlock
Monthly £2.40

Aimed at teenage football fans. News, statistics and information on leading Premier League, Football League and Scottish Premier League teams.

Match of the Day

Immediate Media Co. Ltd, Vineyard House, 44 Brook Green, London W6 7BT
tel 020-7150 5111
email shout@motdmag.com
website www.motdmag.com
Deputy Editor Lee Stobbs
Weekly £2.75

Aims to bring football-crazy youngsters closer to their sporting-heroes with interviews, facts & stats, the latest transfer gossip and results, posters and quizzes, as well as comic strips and funnies.

National Geographic Kids

12–14 Berry Street, London EC1V 0AU
email kids@ngkids.co.uk
website www.ngkids.co.uk
Facebook www.facebook.com/ngkids
Twitter @ngkidsuk
Editor Tim Herbert
Monthly From £39 p.a.

Facts and figures about the environment, different cultures, animals and history for children aged 8–12.

The Official Jacqueline Wilson Mag

D.C. Thomson & Co. Ltd, 2 Albert Square, Dundee DD1 1DD
tel (01382) 223131
email contact@jw-mag.com
website www.jw-mag.com
Every 3 weeks £3.99

Based on the books and characters of award-winning author, Dame Jacqueline Wilson. Aimed at readers aged 7–12, content is tailored to encourage literacy and creativity across a range of reading abilities. Contains interactive features, art and writing projects, recipes and crafts; for less confident readers, educational benefits are presented in a fun and interesting format – e.g. story-starter games and writing prompts, design challenges and word puzzles. Dame Jacqueline contributes photos, stories and writing tips and her illustrator, Nick Sharratt, supplies drawings and art secrets.

Okido

1–5 Vyner Street, London E2 9DG
email info@okido.co.uk
website www.okido.com
Twitter @okidomagazine
Monthly £5

48pp arts and science magazine for KS1 children aged 3–7 and their families. Designed to engage young children in the scientific world around them in the most creative manner. Contains stories, characters, games, experiments, doodles, recipes, poems and a fan page. Produced in-house and with regular guest artists; fully illustrated on heavyweight FSC paper using biodegradable vegetable inks. Advertisement-free. Founded 2007.

The Phoenix

29 Beaumont Street, Oxford OX1 2NP
email theeditor@thephoenixcomic.co.uk
website www.thephoenixcomic.co.uk
Twitter @phoenixcomicuk
Editor Tom Fickling
Weekly £3.25

32pp weekly anthology comic for boys and girls aged 7–14. Features serialised stories and one-off stories as well as non-fiction. Encourages reading for pleasure and children's critical thinking, creative writing and drawing skills. Contributors include Jamie Smart and Neill Cameron. Founded 2011.

PONY Magazine

Olive Studio, The Timber Yard, Grange Road, Tilford, Farnham, Surrey GU10 2DQ
tel (01428) 601020
email pony@djmurphy.co.uk
website www.ponymag.com
Twitter @PONY_mag
Editor-in-Chief Louise Kittle
13 p.a. from £3.99

Lively articles and short stories with a horsey theme aimed at readers aged 8–16. Technical accuracy and young, fresh writing essential. Length: up to 800 words. Payment: by arrangement. Illustrations: drawings (commissioned), photos, cartoons. Founded 1949.

Scoop

email hello@scoopthemag.co.uk
email illustration@scoopthemag.co.uk
website www.scoopthemag.co.uk
Twitter @scoop_the_mag
Founder Clementine Macmillan-Scott, *Editor* Sarah Odedina
Bi-monthly £6.50

64pp magazine for boys and girls aged 7–12. Features fiction, non-fiction, illustration, comics and competitions, and invites readers to think for themselves through many different types of story-telling. Contributors include Raymond Briggs, Laura Dockrill and Chris Riddell. Founded 2016.

Shout

D.C. Thomson & Co. Ltd, 2 Albert Square, Dundee DD1 1DD
tel (01382) 223131
email contact@shoutmag.co.uk
website www.shoutmag.co.uk
Facebook www.facebook.com/shoutmag
Twitter @shoutmag
Monthly £3.99

Magazine for 10–13 year-old girls. Includes fashion and beauty; celebrity gossip and interviews; TV and pop content; real-life stories; emotional and advice features with a teen focus. Length of article accepted: up to 1,000 words. Illustrations: links to online portfolios or websites welcome, but illustrations are commissioned on a feature-by-feature basis only. Payment: on acceptance. Founded 1993.

Storybox

Bayard, PO Box 61269, London N17 1DF
tel (0800) 055 6686
email contact@bayard-magazines.co.uk
website www.bayard-magazines.co.uk
Facebook www.facebook.com/
BayardPresseBoxMagazines
10 p.a. From £67

Aimed at 3–6 year-old children. Each issue presents a new, full-colour, 24pp story created by teams of writers and illustrators for laptime reading. A non-fiction section linked to a theme in the story follows, together with pages of games and craft ideas. Also includes games, an animal feature, science and a cartoon. Length: 500–1,000 words (stories). Requirements: rhyme, repetition, interesting language. Specially commissions most material. Payment: by arrangement. Founded 1996.

Storytime

61 Bridge Street, Kington HR5 3DJ
email hello@storytimemagazine.com
website www.storytimemagazine.com
website www.storytimeforschools.com
Facebook www.facebook.com/StorytimeMag
Twitter @StorytimeMag
Monthly From £36.99 p.a.

Illustrated bedtime story magazine for children aged 3–8. Accepting submissions from illustrators: see website for full submission guidelines. Calls for submissions from short-story writers also occur periodically; check online for details.

Teen Breathe

GMC Publications, 86 High Street, Lewes BN7 1XN
tel (01273) 477374
email hello@breathemagazine.com
website www.teenbreathe.co.uk
Publisher Jonathan Grogan
Bi-monthly £4.50

Tips, exercises and ideas on how to make mindfulness part of teenagers' lives so that they can stay positive and improve their wellbeing. Submissions welcomed from experienced or new writers, and from illustrators. See www.teenbreathe.co.uk/submissions for specific requirements for each type of potential contributor.

Top of the Pops

Immediate Media Co. Ltd, Vineyard House, 44 Brook Green, London W6 7BT
tel 020-7150 5123
email totpmag@totpmag.com
Editor Peter Hart
Monthly £3.99

Celebrity gossip and news, primarily aimed at girls aged 10–14. Founded 1995.

Toxic Magazine

Egmont UK Ltd, 2 Minster Court, London EC3R 7BB
email mpratt@euk.egmont.com
website www.toxicmag.co.uk
Twitter @ToxicMagUK
Editor Matthew Pratt
Every 3 weeks Price varies

Topical lifestyle magazine for 8–12 year-old boys. Includes competitions, pull-out posters, reviews and jokes. Covers boys' entertainment, sports, video games, films, TV, music, fashion and toys. Slapstick humour. Showcases latest products, events and trends. Payment: by arrangement. Founded 2002.

2000 AD

Rebellion Publishing, Riverside House, Osney Mead, Oxford OX2 0ES
website www.2000adonline.com
Twitter @2000AD
Weekly £3.10

Cult science fiction and fantasy comic. Submissions accepted by post only. Founded 1977.

The Week Junior

Dennis Publishing Ltd, 31–32 Alfred Place, London WC1E 7DP
tel 020-3890 3890
email hello@theweekjunior.co.uk
website https://theweekjunior.co.uk
Twitter @theweekjunior
Editorial Director Anna Bassi, *Editor* Felicity Capon
Weekly £2.99

Covers news and events in the UK and internationally for children aged 8–14.

Wolverine and Deadpool

Panini UK, Brockbourne House, 77 Mount Ephraim, Tunbridge Wells TN4 8AR
tel (01892) 500100
email paninicomics@panini.co.uk
website https://comics.panini.co.uk
Every 4 weeks £4.99

76pp comic based around the exploits of the eponymous Marvel heroes.

Magazines about children's literature and education

Listings of magazines and newspapers for children start on page 302.

Armadillo

Louise Ellis-Barrett, 32 Cannon Court Road,
Maidenhead SL6 7QN
tel (01628) 914516
email armadilloeditor@gmail.com
website www.armadillomagazine.co.uk
Facebook www.facebook.com/Armadillomag
Twitter @Armadillomag
Instagram @ArmadilloMagazine
YouTube www.youtube.com/channel/
UC2DiXYfS3zKHWZkZuX88gDQ
Editor Louise Ellis-Barrett
4 p.a. Free

Online children's book review magazine including
reviews, interviews, features, competitions, profiles
and downloadable activities. Weekly newsletter for
subscribers. Weekly blog; daily social media posts;
issues posted March, June, September and December.
New reviewers and writers always welcome.
Founded 1999.

Books for Keeps

30 Winton Avenue, London N11 2AT
tel 020-8889 1292
email andrea@booksforkeeps.co.uk
website www.booksforkeeps.co.uk
Twitter @booksforkeeps
Editor Andrea Reece
Bi-monthly Free

Features, reviews and news on children's books.
Readership is both professionals and parents.
Founded 1980.

The Bookseller

Floor 10, Westminster Tower,
3 Albert Embankment, London SE1 7SP
tel 020-3358 0369
email katie.mansfield@thebookseller.com
website www.thebookseller.com
Twitter @thebookseller
Editor Philip Jones
Weekly £5.95

Journal of the UK publishing and bookselling trades.
The *Children's Bookseller* supplement is published
regularly and there is news on the children's book
business in the main magazine. Produces the
Children's Buyer's Guide, which previews children's
books to be published in the following six months.
The website features news on children's books,
comment on the children's sector, author interviews
and children's bestseller charts. Founded 1858.

Children's Bookshelf

Publishers Weekly, 71 West 23 Street, Suite 1608,
New York, NY 10010, USA
tel +1 212-377-5500
email childrensbooks@publishersweekly.com
website www.publishersweekly.com
Facebook www.facebook.com/pubweekly
Twitter @PWKidsBookshelf
Children's Books Editor Diane Roback
Semi-weekly Free

E-newsletter about children's and young adult books.
Published under the auspices of *Publishers Weekly*,
which was founded in 1872. Children's book news,
feature story ideas, new trends and pitches for author
or illustrator interviews should be sent to the Editor.
Visit website for PW's submission guidelines.

Educate

National Education Union, Hamilton House,
Mabledon Place, London WC1H 9BD
tel 020-7380 4708
email educate@neu.org.uk
website https://neu.org.uk/educate
Editor Max Watson
6 p.a. Free to NEU members

Articles, features and news of interest to all those
involved in the education sector. Email outline in the
first instance. Length: 500 words (single page), 1,000
(double page). Payment: NUJ rates to NUJ members.

Inis – The Children's Books Ireland Magazine

Children's Books Ireland,
17 North Great George Street, Dublin D01 R2F1,
Republic of Ireland
tel +353 (0)1 8727475
email jenny@childrensbooksireland.ie
website www.childrensbooksireland.ie
Editor and Deputy CEO Jenny Murray
3 p.a. €5

Wide variety of children's literature articles and
features, as well as in-depth reviews of new titles for
young people of all ages, from babies to teenagers.
Published by Children's Books Ireland.
Founded 1989.

Literacy

UK Literacy Association, Room 9 c/o VAL,
9 Newarke Street, Leicester LE1 5SN
tel 0116 254 4116
website https://ukla.org/
Editors Diane R. Collier, Natalia Kucirkova
3 p.a. (subscription only)

Official journal of the United Kingdom Literacy
Association (see page 382), aimed at those interested
in the study and development of literacy. Readership
comprises practitioners, teachers, educators,
researchers, undergraduate and graduate students. It
offers educators a forum for debate through
scrutinising research evidence, reflecting on analysed
accounts of innovative practice and examining recent
policy developments. Length: 2,000–6,000 words
(articles). Illustrations: b&w prints and artwork.
Formerly known as *Reading – Literacy and Language*.
Published by Blackwell Publishing. Founded 1966.

Nursery World

MA Education, St Jude's Church, Dulwich Road,
London SE24 0PB
tel 020-8501 6693
email liz.roberts@markallengroup.com
website www.nurseryworld.co.uk
Editor Liz Roberts
Fortnightly From £119 p.a.

For all grades of primary school, nursery and
childcare staff, nannies, foster parents and all
concerned with the care of expectant mothers, babies
and young children. Authoritative and informative
articles, 800 or 1,300 words, and photos on all aspects
of child welfare and early education, from 0–8 years,
in the UK. Practical ideas, policy news and career
advice. No short stories. Illustrations: by
arrangement. Payment: by arrangement.

Publishers Weekly

71 West 23 Street, Suite 1608, New York, NY 10010,
USA
tel +1 212-377-5500
email childrensbooks@publishersweekly.com
website www.publishersweekly.com
Facebook www.facebook.com/pubweekly
Twitter @PWKidsBookshelf
Children's Books Editor Diane Roback

International news magazine for the book industry.
Covers all segments involved in the creation,
production, marketing and sale of the written word
in book, audio, video and electronic formats. In
addition to reaching publishers worldwide, it
influences all media dealing with the acquisition, sale,
distribution and rights of intellectual and cultural
properties.
Children's books for review published in the U.S.
market, from preschool to young adult, should be

sent to Children's Books Reviews; note that all
reviews are pre-publication. Also send story
suggestions on children's publishing, new trends,
author or illustrator interviews, etc for the semi-
weekly *Children's Bookshelf* e-newsletter.
Founded 1872.

The School Librarian

School Library Association, 1 Pine Court,
Kembrey Park, Swindon SN2 8AD
tel (01793) 530166
email sleditor@sla.org.uk
website www.sla.org.uk
Features Editor Barbara Band, *Reviews Editor* Joy
Court
Quarterly Free to SLA members, £125 p.a. to others

Official journal of the School Library Association.
Articles on school library management, best practice,
use and skills, literacy, publishing, developing
reading, research skills and information literacy.
Reviews of books, websites and other library
resources from preschool to adult. Length:
1,200–1,800 words (articles). Payment: by
arrangement. Founded 1937

TES (The Times Educational Supplement)

26 Red Lion Square, London WC1R 4HQ
tel 020-3194 3000
email newsdesk@tes.com
email features@tes.com
website www.tes.com
Twitter @tes
Editor Jon Severs
Weekly £30 per quarter print and digital; £15 per
quarter digital only

Education magazine and website. Articles on
education written with special knowledge or
experience; news items; features; book reviews.
Outlines of feature ideas should be emailed.
Illustrations: suitable photos and drawings of
educational interest, cartoons. Payment: by
arrangement. Founded 1910.

TESS (The Times Educational Supplement Scotland)

email scoted@tesglobal.com
website www.tes.com
Twitter @TESScotland
Contact Henry Hepburn
Weekly £3.50

Education newspaper. Articles on education,
preferably 800–1,000 words, written with special
knowledge or experience. News items about Scottish
educational affairs. Illustrations: by arrangement.
Payment: by arrangement. Founded 1965.

Screen and audio
Adapting children's books for stage and screen

Emma Reeves offers her experience of the challenges and rewards of adapting other people's literary creations for the television or stage, with practical advice on securing rights and successfully reimagining and reshaping a story you love in a way that works for the new medium.

If you are a working writer for stage, screen or radio, whether you're writing for children, adults or both, it's highly likely that adaptations will form a regular part of your work – and income. Audio drama, film, TV and theatre have a voracious appetite for valuable IP (intellectual property) and the rights to successful books are fought over ruthlessly. TV companies working in children's television are constantly reading and keeping up with the latest events in children's publishing.

CBBC's two biggest home-grown brands are probably *Horrible Histories* (based on the books by Terry Deary) and *The Dumping Ground*, evolved from *Tracy Beaker Returns* (created by Elly Brewer and Ben Ward), an original TV series which continued the story of Jacqueline Wilson's popular protagonist, Tracy Beaker, and introduced a whole new set of characters and problems. Tracy and her world have now been a vital part of the CBBC landscape for nearly 20 years – yet the CBBC development exec who initially championed Tracy's cause admits that it was an uphill struggle to get the powers that be to buy into the realistic story of a brutally neglected child who experiences bed-wetting, meltdowns, rages and attachment issues as an all-too-plausible result of a heartbreaking upbringing. In the end, Tracy's inimitable spirit – and 20 years of fierce audience loyalty – won the day; but it's worth keeping in mind that, when it comes to commissioning, nothing is ever really a 'no-brainer' – and if you truly believe in an idea, it's probably worth fighting for.

Book adaptations have a strong appeal for TV and theatre producers, who like to have a tangible idea of what they're getting before commissioning a new series or play. This can be frustrating for new writers who are desperate to get their own big new idea out there. It does mean, though, that producers are often looking for the 'right' writer to match with a project, which can be a shortcut to a paid commission. And artistically, it can give you the chance to experience the joy, fear and pain of taking control of a group of beloved characters in a rich, well-realised world.

Riding the highs and lows

The highs and lows of adaptation are dizzying. It's certainly not easier than original work. If you do happen to find it easier, I will sincerely try to be happy for you, but I enviously suspect that you're doing it wrong. In my personal experience, it doesn't hurt any less to fail as an adapter than as an originator – in fact, it's worse. You haven't just let yourself down, you've betrayed your original author, your guide, your travelling companion, maybe even your hero.

Of course, when things *do* work and people profess to love the resulting show, the Bad Voices in every writer's head lose no time in pointing out that *everything good is because of the original author ... everything bad is* your *fault*. And if those voices should ever abandon you (unlikely), there's always the internet ...

Which brings me to Rule One of adapting – no, Rule One of everything, ever: Never, *ever* search the internet. Just don't do it.

Rule Two: when you inevitably ignore my advice and search the internet – remember, they're just people, like you; maybe too much like you. As a child, I was an obsessive reader, and I still suffer from very strong 'fannish' tendencies. I know very well that there are certain books and authors of which no adaptation will ever satisfy me. The people who are hardest to please are the most devoted. If someone comes down hard on your adaptation, console yourself by imagining the review you'd give to any adaptation of *your* favourite book of all time.

The real high of adaptation is that you get to play inside someone else's incredible creation. And what could be better than that? As a stage adapter, I've been privileged to reimagine childhood favourites – *Little Women, Carrie's War, Anne of Green Gables, Sherlock Holmes, Cool Hand Luke, Doctor Jekyll and Mr Hyde* – and also to discover the work of a new generation of children's writers. I've written for *The Story of Tracy Beaker, Tracy Beaker Returns* and *The Dumping Ground* – all based on Jacqueline Wilson's work – and also worked on both the stage and TV versions of her *Hetty Feather*.

Every experience is different and brings its own challenges. Even within the same medium, there are different types of show. On TV, for example, at one end of the scale is the straight, closed-ended adaptation, where you are expected to more or less follow the story of the book. At the other end of the spectrum is the open-ended drama which may take nothing more from its source material than a few names and a situation, relying on the ingenuity of the script writers to come up with episodic plots. Most TV shows are somewhere in between – perhaps a novel may provide the protagonist's journey for series one, but then it's up to the writers to come up with new material.

Check out the rights

A lot of my adaptation work has come about through people approaching me. But what if you've fallen in love with an original work and you just have to adapt it or write a sequel? What should you do? Before you type your first words, make sure the rights are available and that you've got a realistic chance of getting them. The only exception is for out-of-copyright material (where the author has been dead for 70 years or more). Otherwise, anything you write without the blessing of the author or their estate is basically fan fiction; you may enjoy it, your friends may enjoy it, but you can never reach a mass audience, and certainly never make any money, unless you want a lawsuit on your hands. So, if you're serious about sharing your vision with the world, check out the rights before doing anything else.

If you have an agent, or an interested production company, they will be able to help you approach the rights-holders. If not, you can search online for the writer's agent or go through the publisher. Bear in mind that the latest hot properties and surprise hits will almost always be optioned already – but options lapse, so it's worth enquiring about the length of the option and trying again at the appropriate time. Read more obscure work in the hope of finding an un-optioned gem.

Despite all this, securing book rights is comparatively easy compared to getting the rights to adapt film or TV shows. This is particularly tricky for lone writers, as TV and film properties tend to have multiple owners and sorting out the various claims requires an army of showbiz lawyers. As a general rule, it's only worth pursuing if you have a major producing force on your side (both to give you credibility and to pay those lawyers' fees!), but there are always exceptions. If you're really passionate about a project and you think you can persuade the rights-holders, go for it. Our business is built on stories of those few lucky people whose tenacity and love for their project enabled them to break all the rules and succeed.

Reimagining the story

What happens next? A producer friend regularly chides me that he doesn't know why my scripts take so long, when all I have to do is copy down the book and cross out the description. Although I generally laugh bitterly at such comments, adaptation is a broad church and there are some gigs which are perhaps better described as abridging – such as when I worked out a three-hander version of *King Lear* and a four-hander version of *The Importance of Being Earnest* for a small touring company. Although you have to be a bit creative in situations like that, you're working within the intended medium and almost exclusively using the author's original text. At the other end of the scale of fidelity to the original work, I once worked on a children's TV show for two years before anyone informed me that it was actually based on a novel!

These two extremes aside, the job of the adapter is usually to reimagine the story in a way which works for the medium. For example, when I worked on the stage version of *Hetty Feather*, we started with Jacqueline's book and created the show in the rehearsal room with six actors. Using the wealth of material in the book, and even more which was generated by the actors, my job was to steer the story into a coherent structure which would fit into two hours' stage time, streamlining plot moments and making some tough calls about which brilliant bits to jettison. When I wrote episodes of the TV show, I had to come up with self-contained plots lasting half an hour. In the first case I had an overabundance of other people's material to deal with; in the second, it was up to me to tell new stories. People asked if I found it confusing but, to me, the worlds of *Hetty* the book, *Hetty* the stage show and *Hetty* the TV show were so different that I never struggled in that way. In some respects, the medium informs the writing experience possibly more than the original material does.

When you start to adapt a book, you are entering somebody else's world, and meeting their characters. In order to feel comfortable in that world, I always try to read as much of the writer's other work as I can. This may seem like obvious advice, but the benefits are so great that it's worth emphasising. If the author writes a lot about a specific time and place, that's useful for research and background colour. If they are preoccupied with certain ideas or social issues, you can get a greater understanding of where they were coming from when they wrote the book. I have actually transposed scenes from (out-of-copyright!) lesser-known works of authors, in order to illuminate important moments which I felt were glossed over somewhat in the work I was adapting. Cheeky perhaps, but it worked for me.

Creating the shape

So, you've got a handle on the world and the characters. Everything may be clearly set out for you, or you may need to fill the gaps – or change certain elements. You may discover what you need to change as you go along. At this stage, you take a step back from the source material (and its potentially seductive prose) and ask the normal questions of dramatic writing: Whose story is it? What do they want? Who is trying to stop them getting it?

A specific problem I have encountered is that many beloved books are episodic in nature: this happens, then that happens, then this happens … In drama, stories tend to need ongoing hooks: this happens, SO that happens, SO that happens … I find I need to work hard to create a sense of building drama and inevitability. Also, coincidence feels much harder to mask in drama than in novels. I find myself investigating plot conveniences – are they really just happenstance? Or did someone plan it? If you can decide that the events are the result of someone's plan, it immediately feels easier to dramatise plausibly.

You have to keep your characters active and keep your hooks dangling. Keep your protagonist pushing through to the end. When you're watching previews, or in the edit, try to resist the temptation to keep a 'good bit' in if your gut is screaming at you that it's slowing down the story and risks letting the audience's interest drop. Sometimes that comedy interlude just sits too awkwardly at a moment when the hero has to make a life-or-death choice and risk everything. Sometimes, it's time to stop piling torture, misery and despair on a character and let the audience know that they're ready to fight back. As an adapter, you need to take responsibility for the work as a whole – the shape is now up to you. And you may have to keep a mediocre bit at the expense of a good bit if, after a lot of consideration (and discussion with the director, editor or whoever), you realise that that's what the shape of the story needs.

Interestingly, not a word of the paragraph above couldn't also be usefully applied to original drama scripts.

So in summary: enjoy the highs, the fun and the privilege; appreciate the work that other people have done so you don't have to; but if something's not working, don't shrug it off as the original author's problem – look at it from all angles until you find a way to make it work for you. It's the very least that the author deserves. After all, it's probably their name that got you the gig.

Emma Reeves is a twice BAFTA-nominated writer whose credits include developing new versions of *The Worst Witch* and *The Demon Headmaster* for television. She also co-created an original science fiction show, *Eve*, for CBBC. Other TV credits include *The Dumping Ground*, *Tracy Beaker Returns*, *Young Dracula*, *Hetty Feather* and *The Story of Tracy Beaker*. West End stage adaptations include *The Worst Witch*, *Carrie's War*, *Little Women*, *Hetty Feather* and *Cool Hand Luke*. *The Worst Witch* won the Olivier Award for Best Family Show, while *Hetty Feather* (the stage show) was nominated for an Olivier Award and won the first ever CAMEO award for best page-to-stage adaptation. She is currently Chair of the Writers' Guild TV Committee. Follow her on Twitter @emmajanereeves.

See also...
- *Adapting books for the stage*, page 337

Children's literature on radio, podcast and audio

The technologies for transmitting the spoken word to children are developing rapidly. Neville Teller describes the fast-changing world of radio, podcasting and audio, and explores what a writer for the microphone needs to know to break into this market.

'Read me a story' – one of childhood's perennial cries. Until radio arrived, parents found little relief from it (palming it off on grandma or auntie was perhaps the best bet). But from its very beginning, radio included in its schedules stories read aloud for children. So, for part of the time at least, the loudspeaker was able to provide a fair substitute for mummy or daddy by providing literature, specially prepared for performance at the microphone, read by professional actors.

Very early on, actors learned that performing at the microphone was a new skill – the techniques were specialised and quite different from those required on the stage. Writers, too, had to acquire a whole range of new skills in preparing material for radio. Two things quickly became apparent. First, the time taken to read a complete book on the air would be far too long to be acceptable, and in consequence most books would need to be abridged. Secondly, literature simply read aloud from the printed page often failed to 'come across' to a listening audience, because material produced to be scanned by the eye is often basically unsuited to the requirements of the microphone.

Today there are two main outlets in this country for aspiring writers for children in the radio/podcasting sphere: online radio/audio and audiobook publishers. How has this market reached its present position?

Radio/podcast

Children's radio in the UK came into existence in December 1922, just a few weeks after the BBC itself was born, and for some 40 years the daily 'Children's Hour' became an established and much-cherished feature of life.

However, in the 1960s the imminent death of radio was a generally accepted prognostication. Starting in 1961, in the belief that television was children's preferred medium, children's radio was slowly but surely strangled.

The demise of children's radio naturally evoked a massive groundswell of protest. In response the BBC of the day did grant some sort of reprieve. *Story Time* – a programme of abridged radio readings – started life in the old Children's Hour slot with a strong bias towards children's literature. It was not long, however, before more general literature began to be selected, and finally, in 1982, that programme too was dropped. For the next 20 years the only regular children's programme left on BBC radio was *Listen with Mother*, the 15-minute slot for the under-fives.

Early in the new millennium, the BBC – moved, doubtless, by mounting evidence of the undiminished popularity of radio – decided to reintroduce a regular programme for children. All they could offer at the time was a 30-minute programme each Sunday evening on Radio 4 called *Go4It*, a magazine-type show which included a ten-minute reading, and I found myself abridging books for it like *The Lion, the Witch and the Wardrobe* by

C.S. Lewis and *The Wolves of Willoughby Chase* by Joan Aiken. Unfortunately, this renaissance was typically short-lived. *Go4It* was axed on 24 May 2009.

But the door had been pushed ajar, and in the autumn of 2002, when the BBC launched its new digital radio channel, BBC7, its schedules included, as a basic ingredient, daily programmes for children incorporating readings from children's literature, both current and classic. I prepared a considerable number of books for these programmes, including not only classical children's literature like *Robinson Crusoe* and *The Prince and the Pauper*, but also more general classics like *20,000 Leagues Under the Sea* and *Oliver Twist*. The programme for older children also featured up-to-the-moment favourites such as Anthony Horowitz's series about his boy secret agent, Alex Rider, the *Artemis Fowl* novels by Eoin Colfer, Terry Pratchett's *A Hat Full of Sky* and *The Amazing Maurice* and Jackie French's *Callisto* series. For younger listeners, I abridged books like the *Whizziwig* series by Malorie Blackman, the *Lily Quench* books by Natalie Jane Prior and Kaye Umansky's *The Silver Spoon of Solomon Snow*.

All seemed set fair, but towards the end of 2006 came news of major changes. The programme for younger listeners was converted into a radio extension of CBeebies, the BBC's digital television channel for the youngest children, while the BBC7 schedule included readings drawn from the programme's extensive archive, including my own abridgements of, among many others, *Bootleg* by Alex Shearer, *Stop the Train* by Geraldine McCaughrean, *Huckleberry Finn* by Mark Twain, *Slaves of the Mastery* and *Firesong* by William Nicholson, *Stig of the Dump* by Clive King, *The BGF* by Roald Dahl, *The Little House on the Prairie* by Laura Ingalls Wilder, *Dream Master* by Theresa Breslin and *Point Blanc* by Anthony Horowitz.

Nothing lasts for ever, and 2011 saw BBC7 transformed into BBC Radio 4 Extra. With the transformation came a new shape to children's radio – almost a return to the Children's Hour concept of yesteryear, *The Four O'Clock Show* always including abridged readings of children's literature. Among the specially commissioned readings I abridged Frank Cottrell Boyce's *Chitty Chitty Bang Bang Flies Again*, *Wonder* by R.J. Palacio and *Maggot Moon* by Sally Gardner.

Sadly, *The Four O'Clock Show* too succumbed to the rapidly changing technological needs of its audience. 30 April 2015 saw its final transmission. By then only around 5,900 children were listening to the programme each week, and the BBC Trust concluded 'few children would be affected' by its closure. The axing of this hour of dedicated children's radio meant that there is no longer any children's programming on Radio 4 Extra, and its service licence has been amended to remove its commitment to the content.

However, the BBC is providing three online streams of children's programmes. CBeebies Radio is a daily web-based radio show for preschool children. They can either listen online on BBC Sounds through the CBeebies Radio Player or download and keep the podcast, choosing when and where is best for them to listen.

Meanwhile BBC Sounds has built up an impressive selection of radio programmes under its genre category 'Children', including readings and drama. Audio productions provided online to be downloaded and retained are now generally known as podcasts. Find BBC Sounds podcasts for children at www.bbc.co.uk/sounds/category/childrens. In addition, the BBC provides a dedicated online service for 3–5 year-olds via its School Radio programme. The range of podcasts available for download can be found at: www.bbc.co.uk/schoolradio/subjects/earlylearning.

In addition to the BBC, there is a national digital radio station dedicated entirely to children aged 6–12. Fun Kids is a nationwide 18-station digital multiplex whose content is also available via its website (www.funkidslive.com). Its podcasts and videos include stories, drama and educational material.

All these outlets require dedicated writers for children, prepared to adapt existing, or provide new, material in audio format specifically for young listeners.

Audiobooks

Audiobooks are literary works of all types, read by actors and available as CDs or as downloads from the internet. For some years, audiobooks had been the fastest growing area of consumer publishing in the UK. The coronavirus pandemic that locked people in their homes and shut down great swathes of the economy resulted in a further boom in audiobook sales. Nielsen prediction for 2020 was for audiobook revenue to increase by some 30%, reaching £115 million unit sales which would be an increase of nearly 16% on 2019, reaching some £164 million.

Audible dominates the audiobook market and its sales are booming, but it faces growing competition from newcomers such as audiobooks.com, Kobo and Bookbeat, as well as Google and Apple. Current estimates put the children's share of the market at 40% of the total.

The BBC's audio output, including the large and flourishing children's backlist, is now marketed through outlets such as Audible and Random House.

Nowadays, it is common for major publishers to launch a fair number of their new books, including books for older children, in printed and audiobook form simultaneously. Publishers of books for younger children often adopt the 'twin pack' concept – packaging book and audiobook together – so that children can read and listen at the same time. Such products are zero-rated for VAT. However VAT at 20% is still being charged on audiobooks; the UK book industry has mounted a campaign to have it removed.

How children listen

The ways in which children listen to the readings intended especially for them are multiplying at what seems an ever-increasing rate. In addition to online radio heard via digital radio sets, computers, smartphones and tablets, primary school teachers download BBC School podcasts and play them back in class.

Downloads are a growing method for children to access audiobooks especially for them. There are a range of online outlets, including Audible and Apple iTunes through its Audiobooks Store. Taken together, these DTO (Download to Own) providers have available an enormous and expanding list of children's books, and stories are proving a popular second-best to music for many children. Subscribers pay either a monthly fee for the right to download a specific number of titles or pay for downloads book by book. However, these days a surprising number of websites are offering free downloads of children's stories. One US website lists no less than 62 online sites from which children can download stories at no cost. The UK also has a fair number of such sites, including those run by the *Independent*, Storynory, Mashable, Oxford University Press and OpenCulture.

Amazon has some 30,000 children's audiobooks available to be purchased and downloaded. Users can start listening within seconds, transfer the audiobook to a Kindle, computer, tablet, iPod or other device, or burn it to a CD. Other specialist providers of audiobooks for children include Children's Storybooks Online (www.magickeys.com/books) and the Story Home (www.thestoryhome.com). All commission new stories for children.

Young people are increasingly accessing not only their social networks via their smartphones, but also audiobooks. Google, Amazon and Audible are providing access to audiobooks via the mobile phone, and other providers are crowding into the marketplace.

Amazon's ebook reader, the Kindle, and its younger brother, Kindle Fire, which offers a colour touch-screen, have been runaway successes. The Kindle can download a book in about 30 seconds, either to be read on its 6-inch wide screen or to be read aloud to you (albeit in a somewhat robot-like voice). However audiobooks can also be downloaded, though the process is easier on the later versions of Kindle.

Kindle's biggest rival as a non-print reading device is Apple's iPad and iPad Mini, and its growing number of tablet competitors, all of which can download audiobooks speedily, and have loudspeaker and headphone facilities.

In-car MP3 playback, via the car radio, now widely available, is becoming increasingly popular as a means of keeping children happy on long journeys. Children's audiobooks are also now part of in-flight entertainment on long-haul flights.

A recent phenomenon is 'podiobooks', or podcast audiobook novels, released on the internet in instalments and for free. They are commonly offered together with a range of stickers, ringtones and wallpapers – all designed to appeal to the younger market. The pioneer is Scott Sigler, whose website (https://scottsigler.com) offers free audio fiction, together with videos, ebooks and blog posts via social media. The whole concept is aimed particularly at teenagers and young people.

The message of all this for writers is that the radio/audio/podcast market is mushrooming, and that burgeoning technological developments and innovations seem designed to appeal particularly to the internet-savvy younger generations. If you are keen to break into the rapidly changing world of children's literature on radio and audio, this seems as favourable and opportune a time to succeed as ever. For contact details for children's radio, see *Children's television and radio* (page 326) or search online for children's audiobook publishers, and offer your services. Do not be discouraged by initial rejection – that is often a writer's early experience. Persevere. As in all professional fields, the tyro is faced with the classic catch-22 situation: radio producers and audio publishers are reluctant to offer commissions to people without a track record, while it is of course impossible to gain a track record without having won a commission or two. The only advice is to keep plugging away, hoping for that elusive lucky break – and the only consolation on offer is that even the most experienced of today's professionals was once a complete novice.

Writing for the microphone

What of the techniques that need to be applied in converting material produced for the printed page into a script that can be performed by an actor with ease at the microphone, and bring real listening pleasure to the child at the other end?

Getting to grips with abridging books for the microphone requires, in the first instance, the application of some simple arithmetic. Take a book of around 70,000 words. CDs can accommodate some 70 minutes of airtime, which translates to about 10,500 words. So a 140-minute abridgement presented in the form of two CDs will allow the abridger about 21,000 words. Where the writer is called on to abridge specifically for download, the audiobook publishers will specify the length either in terms of time or wordage. Remember, an actor can normally get through about 2,200 words in 15 minutes.

What makes a good abridgement? To reproduce the sense of an original in fewer words while, in addition and quite as important, to retain the character of the original writing. That demands the capacity to respond sympathetically to the feel of an author's style and to be able to preserve it, even when large chunks of the original are being cut away.

How much liberty is the abridger allowed in translating the printed to the spoken word, while reducing the wordage? Some audiobook producers ask for the minimum of interference with the published text; some radio producers are content for the abridger to adapt the original freely, so as to enhance the actor's performance at the microphone. The different approaches reflect the fact that, in acquiring radio reading rights, the BBC retains editorial independence over the final product, while the granting of abridged audio rights is often conditional on the original writer's approval of the abridged text. So audio producers, reluctant to run the risk of rejection, sometimes allow the abridger very little freedom.

Nevertheless it is an undoubted fact that the requirements of eye and of ear do not always coincide, and that a message easily absorbed from the printed page can become surprisingly garbled if transmitted unamended at the microphone.

In crafting a radio/audio script, the needs of the listener must be one of the prime considerations. The needs of the actor who will read it at the microphone are another. The writer must keep in the forefront of their mind the fact that the script has to be performed. The words must 'flow trippingly off the tongue'. With audio the listener is in control, and can switch on or off whenever convenient.

Principles, principles – what about practice? Let me offer a modest illustration, assuming I'm abridging for radio or podcast.

'How are you going?' Harriet said, stifling a yawn.

'The Oxford bus,' returned Pam.

Nothing wrong with that – on the printed page. If faced with it, though, the experienced radio abridger would feel it necessary to present it somewhat along the following lines:

Harriet stifled a yawn.

'How are you going?'

'The Oxford bus,' said Pam.

Why? Let's take the points in order.

Harriet said.

If the speaker's name instantly follows a piece of reported speech, and especially a question, a moment of confusion can arise in the listener's mind. In this instance, it could be unclear for a second whether 'Harriet' is included in, or excluded from, the question. It might be: *'How are you going, Harriet…?'*

The meaning is soon resolved, of course, but impediments to understanding are best eliminated.

'Stifling a yawn' is an indication of the way in which the words were said. If the actor is to provide that indication, he or she needs to know ahead of the speech how it is to be delivered. Moreover, taking the original version, if the actor stifles a yawn while saying Harriet's speech, and then reads 'said Harriet, stifling a yawn,' the passage becomes tautologous.

For this reason it is best to cut back to a bare minimum all indications in the text of how speeches are delivered – 'grimly', 'lugubriously', 'chuckling merrily', and so on. It is better to leave it to the actor and the producer to interpret most of them.

There are no apostrophes on the air. By and large, 'said' is the best radio indicator of speech. An alternative is to precede speech by some description of the speaker, and to insert the words spoken with no further indication of who is speaking. Thus:

Harriet stifled a yawn.

'How are you going?'

It is clearly Harriet speaking.

'The Oxford bus,' returned Pamela.

Two points here. Almost all the literary variants of 'said' ring false through the loud-speaker or headphones – 'cried', 'riposted', 'remarked', 'answered', and so on. For reading purposes, most are best replaced with 'said' (or better, wherever possible, omitted altogether) and the speech in question left to the actor to interpret. In this instance, 'returned' is particularly difficult for the listener – again, for no more than a moment – but is 're-turned' part of the speech? *'The Oxford bus returned…?'* It is surely best to eliminate obstacles to understanding.

This peek into the radio/audio abridger's toolbox might leave one thinking that the business is all gimmick and no heart – noses pressed up so hard against tree trunks that there is no time for the wood. It is certainly necessary in this field, as in any other, for basic techniques to be acquired and then absorbed to the point where they become second nature. Only then can they be applied to ensure that the radio and audio media are used to interpret a writer's intentions as fully and as honestly as possible.

It is, though, equally essential that the abridger of children's books reproduces, as far as possible, the plot, atmosphere and character of the original. The aim must be to leave the listener with as complete a feeling of the original book as possible, given the technical limitations of time and wordage. It is, in short, an essential aspect of the radio/audio writer's craft to keep faith with the author.

Neville Teller MBE has been contributing to BBC radio for over 50 years. He has well over 250 abridgements for radio readings to his credit, some 50 radio dramatisations and 300 audiobook abridgements. He has published *5-Minute Bedtime Stories*, based on classic children's tales he wrote for BBC radio. His most recent radio dramatisation was *Ozma of Oz* by Frank Baum, for broadcast across the USA. That script, together with nine others, was included in his new book *Audio Drama: 10 Plays for Radio and Podcast* (2019) published by Troubador. His recent abridgement of *Bulldog Drummond* by Sapper was broadcast on Radio 4 Extra in January, and radio dramatisations of stories by Edgar Allen Poe and Zane Grey are also due this year once Covid-19 restrictions are lifted. He is a past chairman of the Society of Authors' Broadcasting Committee and of the Audiobook Publishing Association's Contributors' Committee. He was made an MBE in 2006 'for services to broadcasting and to drama'.

See also...

- *Children's audio publishers*, page 53
- *Writing to a brief*, page 323
- *Children's television and radio*, page 326

Writing for visual broadcast media

Jayne Kirkham shares her experience of writing for the ever-changing world of children's broadcast media, confident that the writer's role remains essentially unchanged: the writer needs to tell a story with characters and concepts that their audience will remember and love all their lives.

'Writing for kids' telly? Easy! I mean … how hard can it be?'

So says someone who doesn't write for children. For a start, are kids actually watching a telly? If you watch much children's content (and, if you're interested in writing for children, you should) you'll know they are more likely to be watching YouTube on a phone. Depending on what it is, you may beeven more inclined to think 'No, seriously, how hard can it be?'. But what looks so simple has been put through a furnace of development: even a two minute TikTok, if money is involved somehow, will have been shaped, moulded, reshaped, possibly with a good deal of firing, before it is finally hammered into something that perfectly suits a broadcaster's or platform's particular audience. And that audience is very particular; children have all the myriad tastes and genre preferences of adults but with the different stages of a child's personal, social and physical development thrown in. Furthermore, the content has to be fun or, as kids in a 2019 report put it, 'amazing/cool/excellent' (*Social Media, Television and Children Report 2019: University of Sheffield, BBC Children's and Dubit*). Even the serious stuff must engage or children simply won't watch.

When I started writing for children's TV, it was a hugely competitive but fairly straightforward world to navigate, with only a handful of broadcasters and producers that commissioned shows. If you went to the Children's Media Conference (or Showcomotion, as it was called then), you could fit everyone you needed to meet into one room. Nowadays, if you go to the Children's Media Conference (and if you're interested in writing for children, you should), everyone you need to meet will still be there – but that 'everyone' covers not just TV but online, games, books, apps and toys! Changes in children's media policy, and advances in technology, mean that children and young people have never known anything but access to content (what used to be called 'programmes') whenever and wherever they like, and in all sorts of formats. They might watch something on TV while accessing extra information about it on their tablet and simultaneously playing along on their phone; what's more, they are making and broadcasting their own content.

To write professionally, this it looks like a much harder more bewildering world, to get into. But actually, whatever innovations arise and throw the industry into flux, for a writer the basics remain the same: know your audience and know how to tell a story, with characters and concepts that kids will remember and love all their lives. If you know your audience, you will know what they are watching and where. You will understand that they prefer to watch their content on YouTube rather than CBBC, and you will be aware of the growth of Disney+, Sky Kids, smart speakers and whatever new players are on the scene by the time you read this.

For a writer, things haven't changed as much as everyone would have us believe; children still enjoy drama, comedy, animation, game shows, documentaries and news made by professional media companies. Those companies need writers like you and me, but getting in touch with them can take a bit of detective work – and a decent pause button, so that you can read a programme's credits properly. Another source of information is the programme's entry on www.imdb.com (International Movie Database). Once you know the name of the production company, you can do an online search for their website where you can generally find contact details for particular producers and/or development departments. Before you contact anyone about writing for them, however, find out as much as you can about the producers, production companies and their intellectual properties (IP). What have they made in the past? What are they developing now? What do they want to develop? Remember, the show that you have just watched and enjoyed will probably have been written two years before; what are they doing now?

The children's channels or platforms also have websites you can explore. By 'platforms', I'm referring to online providers such as Disney+, Netflix, Amazon, Apple TV, Azoomee and Hopster, as well as the public service broadcasters (BBC, ITV, Channel 4 and Five) and the commercial digital channels (Nickelodeon, Pop, Cartoon Network, Disney, etc). To get beyond the shiny, public pages of games and fan chat, enter words like 'producer guidelines' or 'commissioning' into your search engine; you need to find the broadcasters' business pages which show what they are looking for. Remember, each channel/platform has its own brand identity, catering for a specific audience. Make sure you know the difference between a Nickelodeon and a Netflix show.

An easy way to compare and contrast the different platforms is to attend a trade event, such as the Children's Media Conference held in Sheffield every July (www.thechildrensmediaconference.com). There are other conferences and festivals, but the CMC is the best for UK children's media professionals; all the broadcasters attend and hold commissioning sessions where they explain what they want to produce in the next few years. It's also a great opportunity to meet producers and other professionals you may want to collaborate with or work for, with lots of time in the conference schedule for networking. In 2020 and 2021, the event was online which made it even more accessible for many.

Children's media has been through some very troubled times in recent years but, thanks to some hard-fought campaigning by organisations such as the Children's Media Foundation and the WGGB (Writers' Guild of Great Britain; see page 352), there are many reasons to be cheerful; tax incentives for children's content, along with the pilot BFI Young Audience Content Fund (see www.bfi.org.uk/supporting-uk-film/production-development-funding/young-audiences-content-fund), have done much to boost the production sector. If you've been watching the credits carefully (and if you're interested in writing for children, you should), you will have noticed that very few shows are the product of one producer and one broadcaster. With the multinational streamers and international co-production as the norm, this means the writing has to appeal to an international audience. It can also mean that you are competing not just with British writers but, writers from overseas. Rather than despair, let this open your eyes to other markets and territories. Countries like China, Brazil, India and many others have looked to the UK for writing talent in recent years. Annual international conferences, such as the Children's Media Conference here in the UK mentioned above, Mipcom Junior in Cannes (www.mipjunior.com) and Kidscreen in Miami (http://kidscreen.com), are great places to meet international companies face to face. Attending these can be costly and time-consuming – it's easier and cheaper to subscribe to their regular newsletters for excellent insider information that you can follow up.

Working for an overseas company is one of the few reasons why a screenwriter might need an agent. I know a good number of non-agented writers working in the UK on existing shows; the contracts are generally straightforward and many follow WGGB guidelines. But when I have had overseas commissions, I've been grateful to have an agent used to dealing with other territories – not least getting the exchange rate and tax implications right.

It surely must be the dream of every screenwriter to get their own show produced. When the traditional broadcasters were the only players in town, new shows were generally commissioned from writers who had already proven themselves on other series. To get their ideas on screen, writers were dependent on the broadcaster's own producers or independent production companies and they often lost much creative control. The internet has created many more routes by which entrepreneurial writers can now reach their intended audience, for example, *Night Zookeeper* – now available on Sky Kids – started as a web-based teaching aid to encourage children to start writing their own stories.

However, no matter how you intend to get your idea in front of your audience, it needs to go through the same rigorous development process: interrogating the concept and the characters to make sure that it is age-appropriate and will engage the audience utterly, not just in its main format but also in different 'transmedia' guises (as an app, books, in social media, video game). And don't forget to consider toys and other merchandising, as appropriate. Different genres will, of course, have different opportunities and limitations. A drama like *The Dumping Ground* is unlikely to sell as many lunchboxes as, say, preschool animation *Paw Patrol*, but that doesn't mean it shouldn't get made. Just remember to allow the potential revenue returns to determine the budget. Rather confusingly, industry people tend to bandy the term 'genre' in their own special way, using it to describe animation, drama, preschool or comedy. If you watch enough kids' content, you will know that nearly all dramas have a lot of comedy, that animation covers everything from wacky shorts to sitcom to intense re-enactments for documentaries, and that preschool covers everything but in a way that's appropriate for the under-sixes. As I've mentioned, the specific requirements for each broadcaster/platform brand should be available on their websites.

Once you have sufficiently developed your idea – and in that development I would include writing some sample scripts to fully prove whether your idea works or not – and have researched the market, it is time to get it out there. Does your intended recipient give guidelines on submitting your intellectual property (IP)? They may ask you to use an online submission portal. If there are no guidelines, write a brief email introducing yourself and your project as succinctly as possible. Can you pitch it in one sentence? Can you explain the series on a single sheet of A4 paper? Do you have a decent sample script to show off your writing talents? Some producers are wary of unsolicited attachments, so you may want to start with just the email and then follow up when they have responded. Again, be led by their specific guidelines.

If you have the opportunity to pitch in person, practise! These are very busy people, so clarity and passion are essential for you and your idea to stand out. Show that you know your audience and any business or creative constraints: how easy would it be to animate your idea? Would young actors be able to deliver your stunts? The first time I pitched in person, I was a quivering jelly and just about as coherent. But – you know what? – I wasn't eaten, and the world didn't end. It sounds silly, but producers and commissioners are people and, in this industry, they're usually lovely people at that.

Screen and audio

Being realistic, it is unlikely that your first project will get picked up. The thing to remember is that this is a business and your intellectual property is a commodity and your skills are a service for hire so don't take rejection personally. There is a lot to learn, so learn it; take feedback when it is offered and get better. It can feel galling to take what feels like a barrage of criticism from a 12 year-old 'executive', but that '12 year-old' will know better than you do what works on their platform. And they may well be in a position to offer you work on another show. It happens. There can be many reasons why an executive doesn't like your project, but that doesn't mean they don't like you or your style of writing. They may not get back to you. But then again, I was once called out of the blue by a producer who had rejected an idea of mine several years before; I ended up writing an animation series and a feature film (and, while the feature is in interminable 'pre-production', I still enjoy the residual fees from the international sales of the TV series).

The best advice I was ever given as a new writer was that you only fail when you give up. So keep on writing; keep on submitting; keep on keeping on.

Jayne Kirkham is a screenwriter and a script and development consultant. With over 30 years' experience working with and writing for children and young people, Jayne has worked on a wide range of theatre, film, TV, radio and online scripts, ranging in size from small conservation films in Africa to international feature films. Jayne taught at the Northern Film School for 14 years, and is a member of the board of directors of the Children's Media Foundation. See her website https://jaynekirkham.com for more information.

See also...
• *Children's literature on radio and audio*, page 313

Writing to a brief

In the exacting process of writing to a brief, the writer has to produce work to satisfy others as opposed to exploring their own project ideas. The writer may work with others as part of a team when script writing or collaborate with an artistic director when adapting a play. Di Redmond looks at three aspects of writing to a brief for children.

Writing to a brief is enormously varied. I never know what's going to land on my desk – it could be an animation, a series of books, a live action drama script or a stage play. When writing to a brief, you need to have the ability to absorb material very quickly and be disciplined enough to put your own ideas on the back burner. If you twist the commissioner's brief in order to accommodate what you want to write you'll very soon be out of a job!

Animation
The writing team
An animation series is usually commissioned in blocks of 26 or 52 ten-minute episodes. US companies like to have commissioning meetings with large numbers of writers brainstorming for two or three days. UK companies generally prefer smaller groups of writers brainstorming for a day at most. You might be invited to meetings through your agent or through your own personal contact with the animation house or broadcaster. At the initial meeting you will be told the content of the show, after which you'll pitch ideas – or 'thumbnails' as they are often called. If they are approved, you will become one of the writing team.

On a financial note, every stage of the writing process should be covered in your writer's contract, from the writers' meeting where you should receive a full day's fee plus travelling expenses, to separate payments for the Treatment, Draft 1, Draft 2 and the Final Polish Draft. If a contract along these lines isn't offered in advance I'd be extremely wary of attending any meeting.

The writing process
Working from the 'Bible', a document which contains everything the writer needs to know, from character descriptions to locations and props, the writing process begins in earnest. It's a real bonus if the 'Bible' contains a fully executed script as it is the best template to work from: an added bonus would be a promo tape to give you the chance to see the characters and hopefully hear their 'speak'. Hearing Neil Morrissey as Bob the Builder on a promo CD crystalised Bob's character for me and made the writing process so much fun and a lot easier too. Your writing will be hugely affected by the animators' criteria. CGI (computer-generated image) animations like Disney's *Zou* and *Wanda and the Alien* are vastly different from stop frame puppetry animation like *Timmy Time* and *Postman Pat*. Discuss the practical problems with the animators at an early stage so you don't waste time writing scripts that are impossible to execute. For example, if your plot line is about bubbles, make sure the studio can do bubbles; if it's about little boats bobbing in a harbour, check that the animators can do different kinds of water – stormy, misty, calm and choppy. There's nothing more frustrating than getting to Draft 1 stage only to discover that one of

the main elements in the story can't be animated. Be bold and ask the practical questions right from the start.

When you finally get the green light to go to Draft 1, remember that behind the dialogue other things are happening simultaneously: action on the set, facial expressions, sound effects and music all have to be written alongside the script.

Storylines

To kick-start a series, storylines might be developed when the writing team meet for the first time. Writers may be invited to choose a storyline that grabs them and develop it into a three- or four-page treatment, which is a detailed scene-by-scene breakdown of a ten-minute episode. The first script is without doubt the hardest because no matter how thorough the 'Bible' is you've still got to familiarise yourself with the characters and their locations, and balance out the A and the B plot. If the script is too long it will be edited down before it's recorded, so make sure that it's the right length before you send it off to the broadcaster. A ten-minute script with opening and closing credits is around 13–15 pages, depending on the font size you use. The commissioners will be looking for scripts that contain humour, warmth, clarity and an understanding of the target audience. If the show is about a builder then a building job will be essential to every plot line; if it's about a postman then he has to do his post round. Most scripts, even if they're only ten minutes long, have an A and a B plot, both of which have to be reconciled by the end of the episode. Some commissioners prefer a three-act structure, with three underpinning questions – What's the goal? What's the risk? What does the character learn? It's a challenging writing process which highlights the dramatic peaks in the story.

The script editor

A good script editor coordinates the scripts and makes sure the series has one voice, whether it's a ballerina, an alien, a runaway train or a sailing boat. Writers have different styles, which is why they've been chosen to do the job. The script editor with her overall view of the show has the sensitive task of liaising with the commissioner and the producer on the writers' behalf. Sometimes you *don't* want to see the notes the producer has made: they may be too abrupt or confusing. A good script editor will work on the notes before handing them on to the writing team; they'll also be rigorous about timing.

Stage plays

As well as writing my own stage plays, I've also adapted stage plays from the classics such as *Hard Times* by Charles Dickens and Homer's *The Odyssey*. *Hard Times* was commissioned for the Edinburgh Festival with a cast of 30, whilst *The Odyssey* was staged at the Polka Theatre in London with a cast of six. Writers should listen hard to the artistic director's requirements and take on board the limitations of the theatre's budget. If too much is spent on props and costumes it may be at the cost of funding an actor, so be prepared to adapt and compromise.

Adapting from the classics

The two books I adapted couldn't have been more different although the writing process was exactly the same. I read both books until I knew them backwards, after which I felt confident about dramatising them for a young modern audience.

The brief for *The Odyssey* was to write a 90-minute play with a ten-minute interval for 8–12 year-olds. But *The Odyssey* is full of sex and the language of Homer, though hauntingly beautiful, is certainly not pitched at children. The greatest challenge was making the story come alive for a very young audience without destroying the nobility of the original piece. Working closely with the artistic director, I wrote three drafts of the play before I felt I'd got it right, by which time I felt like the gods and heroes of Ancient Greece were part of my extended family! It's a knowledge I've never lost and have since written four books based on classical Greek heroes. That's another great thing about writing: you can transpose a story from one art form to another.

Book series

A book series may be commissioned as a result of a writer pitching an idea to a publisher, or a publisher may have spotted a gap in the market that a writer has been invited to fill. The books vary in length – 2,000–40,000 words – depending on the age range.

I've written series on football, show jumping, theatre school, a veterinary practice, a drama queen and a dog. No matter what target age group you're writing for, you have to thoroughly research the subject. For my show-jumping series I virtually lived at the livery yard, trailing the head groom and asking questions. I've been lucky finding professionals who have allowed me into their lives and let me watch them at work, though I have had a few nasty shocks in the process. Once I found myself masked and gloved in an equine operating theatre watching a Newmarket racehorse under the scalpel. You *really* do have to know your subject when you're writing this kind of specialist book. The readers will be highly critical of any inaccuracies, so be careful what you write otherwise you'll get letters of complaint.

Di Redmond is a prolific writer for children's television. She has worked for Disney, Aardman, CBBC, CITV, HIT Entertainment NYC, Milkshake Channel 5, Nickelodeon and Nick Jr. Her credits include *Zou*, *Timmy Time*, *Duckport*, *Wanda and the Alien*, *Elias*, *Bob the Builder*, *Postman Pat*, *Roary the Racing Car*, *Tweenies*, *Fifi Forget-me-Not* and *Angelina Ballerina*. She also writes for screen, stage and radio and as a ghostwriter and has published over 100 books. Di also writes under the pen name Daisy Styles.

See also...

- *Children's literature on radio and audio*, page 313
- *Writing for children's theatre*, page 331
- *Adapting books for the stage*, page 337

Children's television and radio

The information in this section has been compiled as a general guide for writers, artists, agents and publishers to the major companies and key contacts operating within the children's broadcasting industry. As personnel, corporate structures and commissioning guidelines can change frequently, please check the relevant websites for the most up-to-date information.

REGULATION

Advertising Standards Authority

Castle House, 37–45 Paul Street, London EC2A 4LS
tel 020-7492 2222
website www.asa.org.uk
Facebook www.facebook.com/adauthority
Twitter @ASA_UK
Chief Executive Guy Parker

The UK's independent regulator of advertising across all media. Its work includes acting on complaints and taking action against misleading, harmful or offensive advertisements.

Ofcom

Riverside House, 2A Southwark Bridge Road, London SE1 9HA
tel 020-7981 3000, 0300 123 3000
website www.ofcom.org.uk
Facebook www.facebook.com/ofcom
Twitter @Ofcom
Chief Executive Melanie Dawes

Accountable to parliament and exists to further the interests of consumers by balancing choice and competition with the duty to encourage plurality, protect viewers and listeners, promote diversity in the media and ensure full and fair competition between communications providers.

TELEVISION

BabyTV

Baby Network Ltd, 10 Hammersmith Grove, London W6 7AP
email info@babytvchannel.com
website www.babytv.com
Facebook www.facebook.com/BabyTVChannel
Twitter @BabyTVChannel

The world's leading baby and toddler network, for children under five and their parents, airing 24 hours a day and completely ad-free. BabyTV features top-quality shows created by child development experts, designed for child and parent to enjoy together.

The BBC

BBC Broadcasting House, Portland Place, London W1A 1AA
website www.bbc.co.uk
Director, Children's Patricia Hidalgo Reina

The world's largest broadcasting organisation, with a remit to provide programmes that inform, educate and entertain. Established by Royal Charter, the BBC is a public service broadcaster funded by a licence fee. The Director, Children's is responsible for the overall direction and management of all of the BBC's services for children, including CBeebies and CBBC channels and their websites.

Commissioning

CBeebies and CBBC are self-commissioning and self-scheduling, and proposals may be submitted at any time throughout the year. All submissions for TV and online should be made via Pitch. For further details and commissioning guidelines visit:
www.bbc.co.uk/commissioning/tv/childrens
www.bbc.co.uk/commissioning/childrens/0-6
www.bbc.co.uk/commissioning/childrens/6-16
www.bbc.co.uk/commissioning/tv/articles/pitch

CBeebies

website www.bbc.co.uk/cbeebies
Twitter @CBeebiesHQ
Head of Content, BBC Children's Cheryl Taylor, *Commissioning* Michael Towner, Julia Bond (Scotland and Northern Ireland)

CBeebies offers mixed genre output for TV, online and radio and is specifically produced for a young audience using a variety of formats including live action and animation. Content covers drama, comedy, entertainment and factual, and the target audience is children aged 0–6 years. CBeebies is on air daily from 6am–7pm.

CBBC

website www.bbc.co.uk/cbbc
Twitter @cbbc
Commissioning Melissa Hardinge (Comedy), Kez Margrie, Hugh Lawton (Entertainment and Factual), Amy Buscombe (Drama and Comedy), Julia Bond (Scotland and Northern Irealnd)

Offers mixed genre output for TV and online. Content covers drama, factual, comedy, entertainment, animation and news, and the target audience is children aged 6–12 years. CBBC plans to include more content for teenagers aged 13–16 via the iPlayer service. CBBC is on air daily from 7am–9pm.

BBC Writersroom

website www.bbc.co.uk/writersroom
Facebook www.facebook.com/BBCWriters
Twitter @bbcwritersroom

BBC Writersroom is a cross-genre department for scripted content, working with drama, comedy, CBeebies, CBBC, radio, online and others. It is the first port of call at the BBC for unsolicited scripts and new writers. Visit the website to discover:

- how and when to submit a script;
- new opportunities for writers;
- writing tips and success stories;
- interviews and top tips from writers;
- competitions and events.

The BBC Writersroom blog provides a wealth of behind-the-scenes commentary from writers and producers who have worked on BBC TV and radio programmes: www.bbc.co.uk/blogs/writersroom.

Channel 4

124–126 Horseferry Road, London SW1P 2TX
tel 020-7396 4444
website www.channel4.com
Facebook www.facebook.com/Channel4/
Twitter @Channel4
Chief Executive Alex Mahon
Director of Programmes Ian Katz

A publicly owned, commercially funded, not-for-profit public service broadcaster with a remit to be innovative, experimental and distinctive. Its public ownership and not-for-profit status ensure all profit generated by its commercial activity is directly reinvested back into the delivery of its public service remit. As a publisher-broadcaster, Channel 4 is also required to commission UK content from the independent production sector and currently works with over 400 creative companies across the UK every year. In addition to the main Channel 4 service, its portfolio includes: E4, More4, Film4, 4Music, 4seven, channel4.com and a digital service, All 4, which presents all of C4's on-demand content, digital innovations and live linear channel streams in one place online for the first time.

4Talent supports people to build their careers in the media industry across a range of disciplines. Visit https://careers.channel4.com/4talent.

Commissioning

Information about commissioning and related processes and guidelines can be found at www.channel4.com/info/commissioning. Email addresses for most individuals named below can be found on the relevant parts of the website under 4Producers.

Channel 5

17–29 Hawley Crescent, Camden Town, London NW1 8TT
tel 020-3580 3600
website www.channel5.com
Facebook www.facebook.com/channel5uk/
Twitter @channel5_tv
Director of Programming Ben Frow

Channel 5 brands include Channel 5, 5Star, 5USA and 5Select, and an on-demand service, My5. Channel 5 broadcasts over 24 hours of children's programmes every week under the Milkshake brand, which is aimed at children aged 2–5 years and airs daily from 6–9.15am (10am at weekends). Channel 5 commissions, co-produces and acquires preschool programming through a wide range of deals and arrangements.

Commissioning

website www.channel5.com/commissions
website www.channel5.com/childrens-programming

CITV

2 Waterhouse Square, 138–142 Holborn, London EC1N 2AE
website www.itv.com/citv
Facebook www.facebook.com/childrensitv/
Twitter @ChildrensITV
Chief Executive Carolyn McCall

ITV is the UK's largest commercial TV network. In addition to TV broadcasting services, ITV also delivers programming via a number of platforms, including ITV Player. The ITV network is responsible for the commissioning, scheduling and marketing of network programmes on ITV1 and its digital channel portfolio including ITV2, ITV3, ITV4, ITVBe, ITV Encore and CITV, the commercial free-to-air children's channel. CITV commissions and acquires a variety of programmes aimed at children up to age 12 years.

Commissioning

website www.itv.com/commissioning/articles/citv-nbdhkx05-ckc52cce

See website for information about commissioning and how to submit an idea.

Disney Channel UK

3 Queen Caroline Street, London W6 9PE
email help@disney.co.uk
website https://tv.disney.co.uk
Facebook www.facebook.com/DisneyChannel/
Twitter @DisneyChannel

Channels run by the Walt Disney Company specialising in programming for children from preschoolers to teens. There are three channels: Disney Channel, Disney Junior and Disney XD. They are available through the Disney + subscription streaming service.

Nickelodeon UK

17–29 Hawley Crescent, London NW1 8TT
email letterbox@nick.co.uk
website www.nick.co.uk
Facebook www.facebook.com/NickelodeonUK
Twitter @NickelodeonUK

Nickelodeon UK comprises three channels with a target audience spanning children aged approximately 2–12 years: Nickelodeon, NickToons (www.nicktoons.co.uk) aimed at children aged 6–9 years and NickJr (www.nickjr.co.uk) aimed at children aged 2–5 years.

POP

Columbia Pictures Corporation Ltd, 12th Floor, Brunel Building, 2 Canalside Walk, London W2 1DG
email info@popfun.co.uk
website www.popfun.co.uk

Cartoons and live action series for boys and girls aged 4–9 years with two sister channels:

Tiny Pop

website www.tinypop.com
Twitter @TinyPopTV

Cartoons and live action series for children aged 3–7 years.

Pop Max

website www.popmax.co.uk

Animated and live action series aimed at boys aged 7–12 years.

RTÉ

Donnybrook, Dublin 4, Republic of Ireland
email info@rte.ie
website www.rte.ie
Facebook www.facebook.com/RTEjr
Twitter @RTEjr

RTÉ offers a comprehensive range of programmes for children and young people. RTÉjr is aimed at children under 7 years and delivers a mix of original and acquired live action and animated content. TRTÉ is aimed at children aged 8–12 and airs on RTÉ2 in the afternoon, Monday to Friday.

Commissioning

website https://about.rte.ie/commissioning/commissioning-briefs/rte-young-peoples/

See website for information about commissioning and submitting proposals for children and young people.

S4C

Canolfan S4C Yr Egin, Carmarthen, SA31 3EQ
tel 0370 600 4141
website www.s4c.cymru/en
Facebook www.facebook.com/S4C
Twitter @S4C

S4C is the world's only Welsh language TV channel, broadcasting programmes on sport, drama, music, factual, entertainment and culture. S4C also provides services for children including: Cyw for younger viewers and Stwnsh for older children and teenagers. See website for full details of commissioning and production guidelines and personnel.

ORGANISATIONS CONNECTED TO TELEVISION BROADCASTING

BARB

20 Orange Street, London WC2H 7EF
tel 020-7024 8100
email enquiries@barb.co.uk
website www.barb.co.uk
Twitter @BARBtelevision
Chief Executive Justin Sampson

The Broadcasters Audience Research Board is the official source of viewing figures in the UK.

Ipsos MORI

3 Thomas More Square, London E1W 1YW
tel 020-3059 5000
website www.ipsos.com
Twitter @IpsosMORI
Ceo Ben Page

One of the UK's leading research companies and conducts surveys for a wide range of major organisations (such as BARB and RAJAR) as well as for other market research agencies.

Pact (Producers Alliance for Cinema and Television)

3rd Floor, Fitzrovia House, 153–157 Cleveland Street, London W1T 6QW
tel 020-7380 8230
website www.pact.co.uk
Twitter @PactUK
Ceo John McVay

The trade association representing the commercial interests of UK independent TV, film, digital, children's and animation media companies. For details of children's independent TV and film production companies, see the website.

Public Media Alliance

Arts 1.80, DEV, University of East Anglia, Norwich NR4 7TJ
tel (01603) 592335
email info@publicmediaalliance.org
website www.publicmediaalliance.org
Twitter @PublicMediaPMA

World's largest association of public broadcasters. Provides advocacy, support, knowledge exchange, research and training opportunities for public media worldwide.

Royal Television Society

3 Dorset Rise, London EC4Y 8EN
tel 020-7822 2810
email info@rts.org.uk
website www.rts.org.uk
Facebook www.facebook.com/RoyalTelevisionSociety
Twitter @RTS_media

An educational charity promoting the art and science of television and is the leading forum for discussion and debate on all aspects of the TV community.

RADIO

BBC School Radio
website www.bbc.co.uk/schoolradio

BBC School Radio provides audio resources for primary schools including podcasts, downloads, audio and video clips, learning resources and teachers' notes that are curriculum-linked to Key Stages 1, 2, 3 and 4. Some Early Years Foundation Stage (EYFS) resources are also available.

CBeebies Radio
website www.bbc.co.uk/cbeebies/radio

CBeebies Radio is aimed at encouraging preschool children to develop their listening skills. In addition to radio output, the website contains games, songs, make & colour and story-time activities.

Fun Kids
website www.funkidslive.com

A British children's digital radio station (not national) providing programming to entertain children aged 7–12 years with a mixture of songs, stories, competitions and news. Available to listen via the website or on DAB Digital Radio across London and south east England.

ORGANISATIONS CONNECTED TO RADIO BROADCASTING

Media.info
website https://media.info/uk

This website provides detailed listings of UK radio stations plus information about TV, newspapers, magazines and media ownership in the UK.

The Radio Academy
GO8 The Pillbox, 115 Coventry Road, London E2 6GG
email info@radioacademy.org
website www.radioacademy.org
Facebook www.facebook.com/radioacademy/
Twitter @radioacademy

The Radio Academy is a registered charity dedicated to the promotion of excellence in UK radio broadcasting and production. For over 30 years the Radio Academy has run the annual Audio and Radio Industry Awards (ARIAS), which celebrate content and creativity in the industry.

Radiocentre
6th Floor, 55 New Oxford Street, London WC1A 1BS
tel 020-7010 0600
website www.radiocentre.org
Facebook www.facebook.com/RadiocentreUK
Twitter @Radiocentre
Chief Executive Ian Moss

Radiocentre is the voice of UK commercial radio and works with government, policy makers and regulators, and provides a forum for industry-wide debate and discussion.

RAJAR
6th Floor, 55 New Oxford Street, London WC1A 1BS
tel 020-7395 0630
website www.rajar.co.uk
Twitter @RAJARLtd
Chief Executive Jerry Hill

RAJAR – Radio Joint Audience Research – is the official body in charge of measuring radio audiences in the UK. It is jointly owned by the BBC and the RadioCentre on behalf of the commercial sector.

Theatre
Writing for children's theatre

Writing plays for children is not a soft option. David Wood considers children to be the most difficult audience to write for and shares his thoughts here about this challenge.

'Would you write the Christmas play?' These six words, uttered by John Hole, Director of the Swan Theatre, Worcester, unwittingly changed my life, setting me off on a trail I'm still treading over 40 years later. It wasn't a totally mad question, even though I was then cutting my teeth as an 'adult' actor/director – and indeed I have managed to continue these so-called mainstream activities to a limited degree ever since. No, it had already struck me that children's audiences were important and, by doing magic at birthday parties since my teens, I had already developed an aptitude for and delight in entertaining children.

At Worcester I had organised Saturday morning children's theatre, inveigling my fellow repertory actors into helping me tell stories, lead participation songs and perform crazy sketches. And I was still haunted by the memory of seeing, a couple of years earlier, a big commercial panto in which the star comedian cracked an off-colour joke to a matinee house virtually full of children, got an appreciative cackle

Further information

TYA/PYA (Theatre and Performances for Young Audiences)
website www.tya-uk.org

TYA/PYA is the UK Centre of ASSITEJ (International Association of Theatre for Children and Young People). The website lists most of the companies currently in production. In association with Aurora Metro, it publishes *Theatre for Children and Young People* (see 'Further reading'), a comprehensive collection of articles about the development of children's theatre and theatre-in-education in the UK over the last 50 years.

National Theatre Bookshop
National Theatre, South Bank, London SE1 9PX
tel 020-7452 3456
email bookshop@nationaltheatre.org.uk
website www.nationaltheatre.org.uk/your-visit/bookshop

Samuel French
Samuel French Bookshop, Royal Court Theatre, Sloane Square, London SW1W 8AS
tel 020-7387 9373
website https://royalcourttheatre.com/your-visit/bookshop/

A shop for playscripts and books about theatre, details of licensing and performance rights for plays and musicals, and publisher of new plays.

from a small party of ladies in the stalls, then advanced to the footlights and said, 'Let's get the kids out of here, then we can get started!'. In the dark I blushed and my hackles rose. How dare this man show such disdain for the young audience whose parents' hard-earned cash had contributed towards his doubtless considerable salary? It set me thinking about how few proper plays were then written and performed for children. There were traditional favourites like *Peter Pan* in London, the occasional *Wizard of Oz*, *Toad of Toad Hall* and *Alice in Wonderland* in the regions, but that was about it. Nothing new. Later I discovered my assessment had been too sweeping. There were several pioneers out there presenting proper plays for children, including Brian Way (Theatre Centre), Caryl Jenner (Unicorn), John Allen (Glyndebourne Children's Theatre) and John English (Midlands Arts Centre), but their work was not then widely recognised. Their contribution to the development of children's theatre in the UK cannot be overestimated. Also, in 1965, the Belgrade Theatre, Coventry, had created the first theatre-in-education company, touring innovative work into schools; and early in 1967, I had acted in the first production of the TIE Company at the Palace Theatre, Watford.

So writing *The Tinder Box* for Christmas 1967 seemed a natural opportunity and, although I don't think it was very good, it paved the way for me to write around 75 (so far) plays that try to trigger the imagination, make children laugh, cry and think, and hopefully lead them towards a love of theatre. The journey hasn't always been easy. It is frustrating that children's theatre is still often perceived as third division theatre; funding for it is less than for its adult counterpart, even though it often costs as much, sometimes more, to put on, and always commands a lower seat price; critics generally ignore it; and most theatre folk seem to think it is only for beginners or failures, a ridiculous belief, since children are the most difficult and honest audience of all – and yet the most rewarding when we get it right.

Let's pause briefly to talk terminology. The phrase 'children's theatre' means different things to different people. Whereas 'youth theatre' clearly implies that young people are taking part in the play, 'children's theatre' can mean not only children performing but also (more correctly, in my view) theatre produced by adults for children to watch. And, although I have occasionally, and enjoyably, written plays for children to perform (*Lady Lollipop*, from Dick King-Smith's book) or for children to take part in alongside adults (*The Lighthouse Keeper's Lunch*, from Ronda and David Armitage's book and *Dinosaurs and All That Rubbish*, from Michael Foreman's book), the vast majority of my plays have been written for professional actors to perform for children. Don't get me wrong. Participation by children is hugely beneficial and worthwhile, but I like to feel my plays might provide the inspiration to encourage them to want to do it themselves. I believe that children respond to exciting examples that inspire them. I also believe that children are more likely to, say, want to learn to play a musical instrument if they see and hear the best professional musicians playing in a concert. They are more likely to want to excel at football if they see – live or on television – the best professional teams displaying dazzling skills.

So any advice I can offer about children's theatre is mainly aimed towards writers who would like to create plays for grown-ups to perform for children. Having said that, it has always surprised me that several of my professionally performed plays have been subsequently put on by schools and youth groups who cope, showing tremendous flair and imagination, with tricky technical demands. I sometimes wish I could write more plays specifically for schools and youth groups, but I think I might be tempted to oversimplify (which would be patronising) or to try to write enough roles for a very large cast, which might dilute the content and fail to provide a satisfying structure.

Encouragingly, the professional children's theatre scene today is much healthier than when I started. There are many more touring companies (see page 344) large and small, producing high-quality work for all ages. There has been an exciting explosion in the amount of work for under-fives. And at last, we have three full-time children's theatre buildings – Unicorn, Polka and Hullabaloo – who put on their own plays as well as receive other companies' work. Unicorn and Polka are both in London, and Hullabaloo recently opened in Darlington. Hopefully there will in the future be many more such beacons in other cities and towns. Children are entitled to their own theatre, and creating theatre buildings especially for them, run by committed professionals, is the best way to improve the quantity, quality and status of the work. Alongside that, our major theatres, including the National and the Royal Shakespeare Company, should be setting an example by making children's theatre an integral part of their programming, rather than occasionally mounting a children's play as an optional extra. And this means more than coming up with an annual Christmas show.

Study the market

Go to see shows. Which companies are doing what? How many cast members can they afford? Are they looking for original plays as well as adaptations of successful books with big titles and box office appeal? Try to meet the artistic directors, to discuss what they might be looking for. What size spaces are the companies playing in? Studios? Large theatres? Do they have facilities for scene changes? Is there flying? Incidentally, restrictions on cast size and staging possibilities are not necessarily a bad thing. Well-defined parameters within which to work can be a help not a hindrance. I was asked to write a play for the Towngate, Basildon, a theatre that had no flying, not much stage depth and virtually no wing space. And I was allowed a cast of only six. At first I despaired but then managed to think positively and wrote *The Gingerbread Man*, which ended up paying the rent for 30 years! The play is set on a giant Welsh dresser. No props or scenery come on or off stage during the show – the basic set is self-contained. And the six characters are joined by the off-stage voices (recorded) of the 'Big Ones', the human owners of the dresser.

It may be putting the cart before the horse to worry about where and how your play might be performed – before you've written it! But it really is foolish to start before finding out what might be practical and realistic. Quite frankly, a cast of 20, or even a dozen, is going to be out of the question for most professional companies, so if your idea demands such numbers, maybe you should approach a school, a youth drama group or an amateur dramatic society instead.

Rather than rely on others, might you be in a position to create your own openings? Many children's theatre practitioners, including myself, have had to start by 'doing it themselves'. I, like Richard Gill, Vicky Ireland and Annie Wood (former artistic directors of the Polka Theatre) not only write but also direct. And Richard Gill, Tim Webb (Oily Cart), Guy Holland (Quicksilver) and I (Whirligig), went as far as to create companies to produce our own work, because we knew we were unlikely to get other companies to put it on. The TYA (Theatre for Young Audiences) website (see box) lists most of the companies currently in production, and is a useful first port of call to see the scope of the work.

What 'works' for children?

A good, satisfying story makes a helpful start, told with theatrical flair. By that I mean that we should use theatrical techniques to spark the imagination of the audience – scenery, costume, sound, lighting, puppetry, magic, circus skills, masks, mime, dancing and music. The physical as well as the verbal can help to retain the attention and interest of children. Page after page of two characters sitting talking are likely to prove a turn-off. It's better to see them do something rather than just talk about it. I try to introduce lots of 'suddenlies' to help keep the audience riveted to their seats, wanting to know what happens next. I've often said that my life's work has been dedicated to stopping children going to the lavatory. Suddenlies – a new character appearing, a sound effect, a lighting change, a surprise twist, a musical sting – can be a huge help. Compare it to the page-turning appeal of a successful children's book.

Play ideas can be found in fairy tales, myths and legends, traditional rhymes and popular stories. Be careful, however, not to waste time adapting books in copyright, unless you have got the necessary permission – no public performances, paid or unpaid, can be given without this. Approach the publisher or the author's agent to discover if the stage rights are available and, if they are, how much it might cost to acquire them for a year or two. Or you might use an incident from history, a pertinent modern social issue, such as conservation, or the real life of an inspirational or controversial person. Or you could explore a social problem especially relevant to children, like single-parent families or bullying.

In my book *Theatre for Children: A Guide to Writing, Adapting, Directing and Acting*, I identify useful ingredients for children's plays. They are really fairly obvious – things that we know children respond to. They include animals, toys, fantasy, a quest, goodies and baddies, humour, scale (small characters in large environments and vice versa), a child at the centre of the story. And justice – think *Cinderella*. Children, like adults, have a strong sense of fairness and will root for the underdog. Roald Dahl's stories, eight of which I have been lucky enough to adapt, all use this. Sophie (in *The BFG*), James (in *James and the Giant Peach*) and Boy (in *The Witches*) are all disadvantaged orphans whose strength of character leads them through immense difficulties to eventual triumph. They are empowered to succeed in an adult-dominated world, and children identify with them.

The use of audience participation is an option much argued about by children's theatre practitioners. Many hate it. For some plays, it would, indeed, be totally inappropriate. But for others it can be exciting and fun. I'm not talking about basic panto participation – 'he's behind you!' – though even this can be used on occasion with integrity. I'm talking about what I call 'positive participation', in which the audience contribute to the action by helping or hindering, by having ideas or by taking part in a 'set piece'. In *The Selfish Shellfish* they create a storm to fool an oil slick. In *The Meg and Mog Show* (for very small children), they make springtime noises and movements to encourage Meg's garden to grow. In *The See-Saw Tree* they vote on whether to save an ancient oak or allow it to be cut down to make way for a children's playground. In *The Gingerbread Man* they help catch the scavenging Sleek the Mouse under an upturned mug. Their contribution is crucial to the development and resolution of the plot. In *The Twits* the audience fools Mr and Mrs Twit by making them think that they, the audience, are upside down. They all remove their shoes, put them on their hands and stretch their arms up while lowering their heads! The sight of a thousand children all doing this, with joy and not a shred of cynicism, is pure magic to me.

I don't believe that a children's play has to have a moral, a self-improving message for the audience. But I do believe a children's play should *be* moral, presenting a positive attitude and an uplifting, hopeful conclusion. And I resent the notion that children's plays should always be written to tie in with the National Curriculum. Many do, but the educationalists shouldn't dictate our agenda – the tail shouldn't wag the dog.

Before you start

I strongly recommend that you create a synopsis, outlining the events in story order. This leads to clarity of storytelling, to the disciplined pursuit of a through-line, with not too many subplots that could end up as time-wasting, irrelevant cul-de-sacs. For myself, it would be foolish to think I had the brilliance to start a play with only an initial idea and just let my imagination lead me through uncharted waters. I find it far better to let the juices flow during the synopsis stage and, when it comes to writing the play, to conscientiously follow through my original instincts with not too many diversions.

Good luck with getting your first play produced. Getting it published may need determination. It was a very special day for me when Samuel French accepted (after initial rejections) *The Owl and the Pussycat Went to See…*, my second play, co-written with Sheila Ruskin. After its first production at Worcester, I beavered away to get it on stage in London and, thanks to several friends helping financially, managed to produce it at the Jeannetta Cochrane Theatre. To save money I directed it myself. We were lucky enough to get two rave reviews. I approached Samuel French again. They came to see it and, hallelujah, offered to publish it. Since then their loyalty has been more than gratifying – they still publish most of my efforts. There are now several specialist children's play publishers, many of whom also act as licensees of amateur performances. The National Theatre Bookshop and French's Theatre Bookshop stock a fair number of plays and, when searching for a publisher, it is worth checking out their shelves. The internet can help too. Tap in the names of successful children's playwrights, like Mike Kenny, Charles Way, Brendan Murray or the late Adrian Mitchell and see what comes up.

I find that the challenge of writing a play for children never gets easier, however many times I go through the process. It certainly isn't a soft option, i.e. easier than writing a play for adults. And it carries, I believe, a big responsibility. I always worry that I haven't the right to fail: the last thing I want to do is write something that might put children off theatre for life. I'm aware that many in the audience will be first-time theatre-goers, some of whom never asked to come! It's so important to get it right, to enthuse them so much they can't wait to return. And this is where the passion comes in. Most children's theatre practitioners are passionate about what they do, with an almost missionary zeal to stimulate and delight their audience. Also, we all know that, unlike adult audiences who tend to sit quietly and clap at the end, even if they've hated the play, our children's audiences won't be (and shouldn't be) so polite. It is palpably obvious when we 'lose' them. We are dedicated to using our experience and instinct to 'hold' them, to help them enjoy the communal experience of a theatre visit and willingly enter the spirit of the performance. The buzz I get from being in an auditorium of children overtly having a great time – listening hard, watching intently, reacting, feeling, letting the play take them on a special, magical, unique journey – is a buzz I constantly strive for. I suppose that's really why I do it.

Further reading

Bennett, Stuart (ed.), *Theatre for Children and Young People: 50 Years of Professional Theatre in the UK* (Aurora Metro 2005)

Maguire, Tom and Karian Schuitema (eds) with foreword by David Wood, *Theatre for Young Audiences: A Critical Handbook* (Institute of Education Press 2012)

Wood, David, with Janet Grant, *Theatre for Children: A Guide to Writing, Adapting, Directing and Acting* (Faber and Faber 1997)

Ireland, Vicky and Paul Harman (eds), *50 Best Plays for Young Audiences* (Aurora Metro 2016)

David Wood OBE has been dubbed 'the national children's dramatist' by *The Times*. His plays are performed regularly on tour, in the West End and all over the world. In 2006, for the Queen's 80th birthday party celebrations, he wrote *The Queen's Handbag*, which was broadcast live from Buckingham Palace Gardens and watched by eight million viewers on BBC1. Since 2008, his adaptation of Judith Kerr's *The Tiger Who Came to Tea* has toured the UK and abroad and played six West End seasons. The production was nominated for an Olivier Award in 2012. David's grown-up musical, *The Go-Between* (co-written with Richard Taylor, adapted from L.P. Hartley's novel), won Best Musical Production in the Theatre Awards UK 2012 and in 2016 opened in the West End at the Apollo Theatre starring Michael Crawford. His adaptation of Michelle Magorian's novel *Goodnight Mister Tom* won the 2013 Olivier Award for Best Entertainment and Family, following its season at the Phoenix Theatre. It returned to the West End (Duke of York's Theatre) and toured in 2015/16. He has adapted the following Roald Dahl novels for the stage: *The BFG*, *The Witches*, *Fantastic Mr Fox*, *James and the Giant Peach*, *The Twits*, *George's Marvellous Medicine*, *Danny the Champion of the World* and *The Magic Finger*. In 2017 there were tours of David's adaptations of *The Twits*, *Babe*, *The Sheep-Pig* and *The Tiger Who Came to Tea*, which returned to the West End in 2018 and 2019. *The See-Saw Tree* opened at the China National Theatre for Children in Beijing in 2019, and is still in their repertoire. In 2021, Methuen Drama published *David Wood Plays for 5-12 year olds*. His website is www.davidwood.org.uk.

See also...

• *Adapting books for the stage*, page 337

Adapting books for the stage
Stephen Briggs ponders the challenges and rewards of dramatising other people's novels.

Why me?

Stephen Briggs? Stephen Briggs? Who on earth is Stephen Briggs to write about adapting novels for the stage?

Well, many years ago I wrote a stage version of *A Christmas Carol* for my amdram group … no, stick with me on this…. *Then*, a few years later I adapted two Tom Sharpe novels (these were for one-off productions and the scripts are now long gone). *However*, my overwhelming – and more recent – experience has been with dramatising the novels of the late Sir Terry Pratchett. I've now adapted 22 of Terry's books – four for Transworld/Doubleday, three for Samuel French (now part of Concord Theatricals), three for Oxford University Press, six for Methuen Drama and three for Oberon Books (both now part of Bloomsbury), with three more being scheduled for publication as I type. These have been staged by amateur groups in over 20 countries from Zimbabwe to Antarctica (yes, really, Antarctica) and by professional groups in France and the Czech Republic. I also co-scripted the mini-dramatisations used by Sky One to promote their big budget television films of Terry's *Hogfather* and *Colour of Magic*.

I have been involved in amateur theatre since I left school. Not just acting, but also directing, choreography, set design/construction, costume design/construction – even brewing mulled wine for the audiences in our chilly medieval theatre. None of this makes me an expert, not by any interpretation of the word, but I was the one who had to make my scripts work on stage since I also directed them. I was also able to get useful and honest feedback from the original author. Hopefully I've learned a few lessons along the way, which I'm happy to pass on.

Dialogue

When you watch a film, a lot of screen time is taken up by fancy stuff – Imperial star cruisers roaring through space, ill-fated liners ploughing the waves, swooping pan shots over raddled pirate ships. In a play, you don't get any of that stuff. The dialogue has to drive the action.

The methods used to adapt a novel for the stage are as varied as the authors you try to adapt. Terry Pratchett, like Charles Dickens, wrote very good dialogue and the scenes already leap from the page. Other authors make greater use of narrative which the adapter has to weave into the play as well, if they are to keep to the spirit of the original work. Terry was well known for his use of footnotes and, for some of the plays, I even included the Footnote as a 'character' – a Brechtian alienation device, for those who want a more literary justification.

Keep it simple

Terry Pratchett wrote 'filmically' – his scenes cross-cut and swoop like a screenplay. On the silver screen, you can set a scene visually in a second. On the stage it can take longer, and you have to give the audience a chance to realise where they are if they are to have any possibility of keeping up with the – often quite complex – plot.

Theatre

It's important to remember that a theatre audience doesn't have the luxury of being able to reread a page, or skip back to check a plot point – they (usually) get to see the play only once. It's vital, therefore, to ensure that important plot points are not lost along the way while one is tempted to keep in other favoured scenes from the much longer novel.

Keep it moving

Novelists are not constrained by budget – they can destroy cities, have characters who are 60-foot long dragons, write vital scenes involving time travel and other difficult concepts. These can initially appear to be a challenge for anyone without the budget of Industrial Light and Magic (www.ilm.com).

When I write, I have the good fortune to be writing for a theatre which has very limited space – on and off stage – and virtually no capacity for scenic effects. This makes staging the plays a nightma…, ahem… a challenge, but the benefit is that my adaptations can be staged virtually anywhere. I don't write them with essential big effects or big set changes. Of course, drama groups with huge budgets can go wild with all that – but the plays can work without it.

Plays which demand massive set changes or pose huge scenic problems are likely to put off many directors working to a tight budget. It's different if you're Alan Ayckbourn, of course … onstage swimming pool, floating river cruiser … no problem.

People say that radio has the best scenery. Allowing the audience to fill in the gaps can not only save on costly wood and canvas, but on occasions, can even be more effective than an expensive but stagey scenic effect. After all, Shakespeare's *Antony and Cleopatra* includes a sea battle between two great navies – all reported by two blokes standing on a hill.

The plays – like the books – have to keep moving. Scenes need to flow fairly seamlessly into one another. Set changes slow things down. I get to see large numbers of productions of my plays and the general rule is that the ones with frequent set-changes are the ones which plod.

Writing for schools

Three of my plays were written specifically for classroom use. I had to bear in mind that the plays were as likely to be used for reading in a classroom as for production on a stage. So I tried to keep the number of stage directions to a minimum because I know all too well from reading plays with my own amateur drama group that the need to read through huge chunks of explanatory stuff in italics, interspersed with snippets of uninformative dialogue, is very tedious. Here is an example (not, I hasten to add, an extract from a real play):

> (*As Smithers looks out of the window, Bert rushes downstairs, carrying an aspidistra in a brass bowl. He passes, but fails to notice, the gorilla. He trips and falls, dropping the plant and pot on Smithers' head*)
>
> SMITHERS: Oof!
>
> (*Smithers picks up a broom from the floor and chases after Bert. They run into the kitchen and out again, up the stairs and across the landing. Bert takes a wad of banknotes out of his pocket and throws them at Smithers*)
>
> BERT: Take that!

It was also important to avoid characters with just 'one line and a cough'. Nothing is worse in a read-through than to be given the role of 'King of France' only to find that the character speaks one line on page one and then is silent for the rest of the play. Except, perhaps, being allocated a role which contains dialogue that will invite ridicule from the rest of the class: 'Oh la, I am the prettiest person in the world; I do love to wander around wearing frilly pink underwear'.

I also try to ensure that whatever special effects are mentioned should be either easily achievable or not essential and, again, that the plays can be performed with the minimum amount of scenery.

Two of the three plays I wrote for OUP I would not be staging myself. It was really fascinating (and quite gratifying) to see the plays staged by schools and to find that they *worked*.

How do I start?

• **I read the book.** Then I read the book again. I then put it down, leave it for a week and write down all the main plot points I can recall, and a rough list of scenes. That should give me a rough shape for the play. Anything I've forgotten to include can probably go high up on the list of potential material to cut.

• **I write it.** I sit down and write the script. At this stage I don't try to keep to a specific length; I just adapt the book, making mental notes of any scenes that show potential for trimming, cutting or pasting into another as I go along. My overall plan is to keep the play to around two hours. If, when I get to the end, the play is too long, I then go back and look again at each scene and character to ensure they can justify their place in the script.

• **I dump it.** Reducing a 95,000-word novel into a 20,000-word play means that there will have to be an element of trimming. The trick, I suppose, is to ensure that the cuts will not be too glaring to the paying audience ('I reckon if we cut out the Prince of Denmark, we can get *Hamlet* down to an hour and a half, no problem'). Hopefully, there will be subplots, not vital to the main story, which can be excised to keep it all flowing. But even so, occasionally tough decisions have to be made once all the fat's been removed and one is forced to cut into muscle and bone (as it were). It's important to let stuff go – even if it's a favourite scene in the book, or a favourite character.

• **I share it.** It's good then to let someone else read it. It's all too easy to get so far into the wood that you can no longer see the trees. Being challenged on the decisions you made in adapting the book is a very good thing. I'd certainly recommend anyone adapting a book to have the script read by someone who knows the book well, and who can point out any important plot omissions. It is also good to have your script read by someone who does *not* know the book and who can ask the 'what on earth does that mean?' questions.

It's useful for me that many of my drama club are not *Discworld* 'fans'. Their outsider's view of the script is extremely useful. I also then have the luxury of amending the script in rehearsal to tidy up scenes, add in bits and take bits out. This means that the script which is submitted to the publisher is then fully tried and tested.

Some golden rules

It's difficult to be hard and fast about 'rules' for adapting books, but here are a few useful guidelines that I try to stick to:

• **Don't change the principle plot** – there's no point in calling a play *Bram Stoker's Dracula* if you're then going to have Dracula surviving at the end and starting up a flourishing law firm in Whitby.

• **Never sacrifice 'real' scenes in order to add in some of your own** – after all, you've chosen to adapt the author's work because, presumably, you admire their writing. If you think you can improve on their humour/drama/characterisation you should really be writing your own plots and not torturing theirs.

• **Use the author's dialogue whenever possible** – same as the above, really. Also try to attribute it to the right character whenever practicable.

• **Don't add characters** – stick to the ones the author has given you.

• **Don't be afraid to cut material** – after all, you're trying to squeeze a 300-page novel into a two-hour play; you just can't fit everything in, so don't try. Anything which does not advance the main plot should be on your list for potential dumping if your play overruns.

• **If it doesn't *need* changing – don't change it.**

As well as the 22 plays he mentions in his article, **Stephen Briggs** is the co-author, with Terry Pratchett, and illustrator of *Turtle Recall: The Discworld Companion*, *The Streets of Ankh-Morpork*, *The Wit & Wisdom of Discworld* and a small raft of other publications emanating from Terry Pratchett's *Discworld* books. He read the unabridged audio versions of Terry's books for Isis, HarperCollins and for Random House (in the USA). In 2005 he won an Audie Award (Audio Publishers Association, USA) for his reading of Terry's *Monstrous Regiment* and in 2013 was nominated for his reading of *Dodger*. He also won the Audible Audio Download Book of the Year 2008 for *Good Omens* and in 2009 received an Odyssey Award for his recording of Terry's *Nation* for Harper Audio. In 2010 he won two awards from *AudioFile* magazine for his recording of *Unseen Academicals*, and in 2014 he won two more for *Raising Steam* and for *The Science of Discworld*. In 2020, he wrote a new Discworld-based show *Terry Pratchett: Murder in Ankh-Morpork* for staging in 2021, and in 2021 his adaptations of three more Pratchett books *Hogfather*, *Lords and Ladies* and *The Shakespeare Codex* were published (Bloomsbury).

See also...

• *Writing to a brief*, page 323
• *Writing for children's theatre*, page 331
• *Theatre for children*, page 341
• *Adapting children's books for stage and screen*, page 309

Theatre for children

London and regional theatres are listed below; listings of touring companies start on page 344.

⚠ Theatrical performances may not go ahead in their usual way due to coronavirus restrictions. Please check websites for details.

LONDON

Chickenshed Theatre
Chase Side, Southgate, London N14 4PE
tel 020-8292 9222
email info@chickenshed.org.uk
website www.chickenshed.org.uk
Twitter @CHICKENSHED_UK
Artistic Director Lou Stein

Produces theatre for all ages as well as running successful education courses, outreach projects and membership programmes.

Colour House Theatre
Merton Abbey Mills, Watermill Way,
London SW19 2RD
tel 020-7542 5511
email info@colourhousetheatre.co.uk
website www.colourhousetheatre.co.uk
Facebook www.facebook.com/The ColourHouseTheatre
Twitter @ColourHouseThtr
Founder and Chief Executive Peter Wallder, *Resident Artistic Director* Charlie Shakespeare

Grade II-listed building in the riverside setting of Merton Abbey Millls, seating 50–70 people. The resident children's theatre has staged over 100 original musical adaptations of famous fairy tales during the past 25 years. The Children's Theatre achieved charitable status in 2008. The one-hour shows run at the weekends and school holiday days (except July and August) The Theatre also has evening shows, music and comedy nights and is available to hire for events and private parties.

Polka Theatre
240 The Broadway, London SW19 1SB
tel 020-8543 8320
email lynette@polkatheatre.com
website www.polkatheatre.com
Twitter @polkatheatre
Artistic Director Peter Glanville

Theatre of new work, with targeted commissions. Temporarily closed for extensive redevelopment; due to reopen during 2021. Founded 1967.

The Questors Theatre
12 Mattock Lane, London W5 5BQ
email enquiries@questors.org.uk
website www.questors.org.uk
Twitter @questorstheatre
Executive Director Andrea Bath

Largest independent community theatre in Europe. Produces 15–20 shows a year, specialising in modern and classical world drama. Visiting productions hosted too. No unsolicited scripts. Also runs a youth theatre for young people aged between 6–18, as well as summer workshops.

Theatre-Rites
Unit 206, E1 Studios, 7 Whitechapel Road,
London E1 1DU
tel 020-7164 6196
email info@theatre-rites.co.uk
website www.theatre-rites.co.uk
Facebook www.facebook.com/TheatreRites
Twitter @TheatreRites
Artistic Director Sue Buckmaster, *Executive Producer* Claire Templeton

Creates devised theatre for family audiences and young people using a mix of performance, installation, puppetry, dance and sound. Working within the UK and internationally, the company creates site-specific and touring productions. Founded 1995.

Unicorn Theatre
147 Tooley Street, London SE1 2HZ
tel 020-7645 0560
email hello@unicorntheatre.com
website www.unicorntheatre.com
Facebook www.facebook.com/unicorntheatre
Twitter @unicorn_theatre
Artistic Director Justin Audibert, *Executive Director* Bailey Lock

Produces a year-round programme of theatre for children and young people under 21. In-house productions of full-length plays with professional casts are staged across two auditoria, alongside visiting companies and education work. Unicorn rarely commissions plays from writers who are new to it, but it is keen to hear from writers who are interested in working with the theatre in the future.

Do not send unsolicited MSS, but rather a short statement describing why you would like to write for Unicorn along with a CV or a summary of your relevant experience.

A Younger Theatre
website www.ayoungertheatre.com
Facebook www.facebook.com/AYoungerTheatre
Twitter @ayoungertheatre
Instagram @ayoungertheatre_
Managing Director Samuel Sims

Online theatre publication reviewing theatre both in London and across the UK, with features on high-profile industry names and discussions on issues facing young and marginalised people. Writers do so for free in return for seeing a show or in order to build a portfolio of work or promote their own performance work. Content is generally aimed at those aged 35 and under.

REGIONAL

Chichester Festival Theatre

Oaklands Park, Chichester, West Sussex PO19 6AP
tel (01243) 784437
website www.cft.org.uk
Twitter @chichesterFT
Artistic Director Daniel Evans

Stages annual Summer Festival Season April–Oct in Festival and Minerva Theatres together with a year-round education programme, winter touring programme and youth theatre Christmas show. See website for unsolicited scripts policy.

Contact Theatre Company

Oxford Road, Manchester M15 6JA
tel 0161 274 0600
website https://contactmcr.com/
Twitter @ContactMcr
Artistic Director Matt Fenton, *Head of Creative Development* Suzie Henderson

Multidisciplinary arts organisation focused on working with and for young people aged 13 and above.

Creation Theatre Company

tel (01865) 766266
email boxoffice@creationtheatre.co.uk
website www.creationtheatre.co.uk
Facebook https://en-gb.facebook.com/CreationTheatre/
Twitter @creationtheatre
Instagram @creationtheatre
Chief Executive Lucy Askew, *General Manager* Charlie Morley

Stages classic stories in special locations. Commended as leaders in innovative digital theatre and for award-winning digital interactive productions. Creators of a range of holiday and term-time online theatre workshops for ages 5 to 19. No unsolicited manuscripts.

The Dukes

Moor Lane, Lancaster LA1 1QE
tel (01524) 598505
email info@dukes-lancaster.org
website https://dukes-lancaster.org/
Twitter @TheDukesTheatre
Chief Executive Karen O'Neill

Producing theatre and cultural centre. Its Young Writers scheme was launched in January 2017. See website for up-to-date information about the theatre's productions and programming approach.

The Edge Theatre and Arts Centre

Manchester Road, Chorlton, Manchester M21 9JG
tel 0161 282 9776
email info@edgetheatre.co.uk
website www.edgetheatre.co.uk
Twitter @TheEdgeMcr
Artistic Director and Chief Executive Janine Waters, *Musical Director* Simon Waters

Produces and presents theatre for all ages, including families and children. Musical and children's theatre specialities. 70-seat flexible theatre space and studio spaces. Also runs classes, courses and workshops in theatre, dance, music, writing and other creative genres, including: Theatre Club for ages 6–8; Edge Youth Theatre for ages 9–12; Aspire for young people with learning difficulties aged between 13–17; and Edge Youth Dance. Founded 2011.

The Egg

Sawclose, Bath BA1 1ET
tel (01225) 823409 (reception and administration)
email egg.reception@theatreroyal.org.uk
website www.theatreroyal.org.uk/the-egg
Twitter @theeggbath

Part of the Theatre Royal Bath. Purpose-built theatre for young people and their families. Hosts and produces shows for children and young people alongside a year-round participation and outreach programme for people aged 0–21. Opened 2005.

Everyman Theatre Cheltenham

7 Regent Street, Cheltenham, Glos. GL50 1HQ
tel (01242) 512515
email admin@everymantheatre.org.uk
website www.everymantheatre.org.uk
Twitter @Everymanchelt
Creative Director Paul Milton

Regional presenting and producing theatre promoting a wide range of plays. Small-scale experimental, youth and educational work encouraged in The Studio Theatre. Contact the Creative Director before submitting material.

Leeds Children's Theatre

c/o The Carriageworks Theatre, The Electric Press, 3 Millennium Square, Leeds LS2 3AD
email enquiry@leeds-childrens-theatre.co.uk
website www.leeds-childrens-theatre.co.uk
Twitter @LeedsCT

Oldest established Children's Theatre society in the UK. Its members (both adults and children) bring live theatre to young people, often for the very first time. Many of the plays produced are based on well-known children's literature. Stages two productions each year at the purpose-built Carriageworks Theatre, typically in spring (March/April) and late autumn (November). Welcomes school groups as well as families and friends. Founded 1935.

Leeds Playhouse

Playhouse Square, Quarry Hill, Leeds LS2 7UP
tel 0113 213 7700
website https://leedsplayhouse.org.uk
Twitter @LeedsPlayhouse
Artistic Director James Brining, *Executive Director* Robin Hawkes

Leeds Playhouse has been welcoming audiences for 50 years. As a registered charity (No. 255460), the theatre seeks out the best companies and artists to create inspirational theatre in the heart of Yorkshire. A dedicated collaborator, Leeds Playhouse works with distinctive, original voices from across the UK.

Its Artistic Development programme, Furnace, discovers, nurtures and supports new voices, while developing work with established practitioners. It provides a creative space for writers, directors, companies and individual theatre-makers to refine their practice at all stages of their career. The sector-leading Creative Engagement team works with more than 12,000 people aged 0–95 every year reaching out to refugee communities, young people, students, older people and people with learning disabilities. The Playhouse pioneered Relaxed Performances ten years ago.

Norwich Puppet Theatre

St James, Whitefriars, Norwich NR3 1TN
tel (01603) 629921 (box office), (01603) 615564 (admin.)
email info@puppettheatre.co.uk
website www.puppettheatre.co.uk
Facebook www.facebook.com/NorwichPuppetTheatre
Twitter @norwich_puppet
Instagram norwichpuppettheatre

Norwich Puppet Theatre is the base for a professional company which creates and presents its own productions at the theatre, as well as touring to schools and venues throughout the UK and to international venues and festivals. The Theatre also presents the work of other touring theatre companies and has a large outreach programme of workshops.

Nottingham Playhouse

Nottingham Playhouse Trust Ltd, Wellington Circus, Nottingham NG1 5AF
tel 0115 941 9419
website www.nottinghamplayhouse.co.uk
Twitter @NottmPlayhouse
Artistic Director Adam Penford, *Chief Executive* Stephanie Sirr

Seeks to nurture new writers from the East Midlands primarily through its Artist Development programme, Amplify. There are two official Ideas

Submission windows per year, one in the Spring and one in the Autumn. The Playhouse will select the best material and look at bespoke ways of developing these projects. See the website for full information and dates.

The Playhouse offers a range of groups and youth theatres for young people aged two and above. See www.nottinghamplayhouse.co.uk/participation/younger-people for more details.

Queen's Theatre, Hornchurch

(Havering Theatre Trust Ltd)
Billet Lane, Hornchurch, Essex RM11 1QT
tel (01708) 443333
email info@queens-theatre.co.uk
website www.queens-theatre.co.uk
Twitter @QueensTheatreH
Artistic Director Douglas Rintoul, *Executive Director* Mathew Russell

Regional theatre with a rich heritage, working in Outer East London, Essex and beyond, which celebrated its 65th birthday in 2018. Each annual programme includes home-grown theatre, visiting live entertainment and inspiring learning and participation projects.

The Queen's Youth Theatre Programme (QYouth) provides the opportunity for young people aged 6–18 to develop creativity, confidence and teamwork, as well as offering valuable opportunities to perform on the Queen's Theatre stage and elsewhere. Younger members start their journey with the QSteps Programme whilst older members graduate into the Young Company Programme, which offers performance, technical and dance opportunities for those who wish to develop further a range of theatre skills. See the 'Get Involved' section of the website for further details.

Royal Shakespeare Company

The Royal Shakespeare Theatre, Waterside, Stratford-upon-Avon, Warks. CV37 6BB
tel (01789) 296655
email literary@rsc.org.uk
website www.rsc.org.uk
Facebook www.facebook.com/thersc
Twitter @TheRSC
Artistic Director Gregory Doran, *Deputy Artistic Director* Erica Whyman, *Head of Literary* Pippa Hill

On its two main stages in Stratford-upon-Avon, the RST and the Swan Theatre, the Company produces a core repertoire of Shakespeare alongside new plays and the work of Shakespeare's contemporaries. In addition, its studio theatre, The Other Place, produces festivals of cutting-edge new work. For all its stages, the Company commissions new plays, new translations and new adaptations that illuminate the themes and concerns of Shakespeare and his contemporaries for a modern audience. The Literary department does not accept unsolicited work but rather seeks out writers it wishes to work with or

Theatre

commission, and monitors the work of writers in production in the UK and internationally. Writers are welcome to invite the Literary department to readings, showcases or productions by emailing the address above.

Sherman Theatre

Senghennydd Road, Cardiff CF24 4YE
tel 029-2064 6900
website www.shermantheatre.co.uk
Twitter @shermantheatre
Executive Director Julia Barry, *Artistic Director* Joe Murphy

Produces two Christmas productions (for ages 3–6 in English and Welsh and an actor/musician-led production for ages 7+) and actively seeks high-quality work for children and young people as part of its programming. Participatory work with youth theatres for those aged from 5 to 25. Founded 2007.

Theatr Clwyd

Mold, Flintshire CH7 1YA
tel (01352) 344101
email together@theatrclwyd.com
website www.theatrclwyd.com
Twitter @clwydtweets
Artistic Director Tamara Harvey, *Executive Director* Liam Evans-Ford, *Director of Creative Engagement* Gwennan Mair Jones

Aims to be a leading force in developing projects, nurturing writers, offering compelling revivals and the best new writing. The Creative Engagement team produces work for children, young people and their communities.

Visible Fictions

Suite 325/327, 4th Floor, 11 Bothwell Street, Glasgow G2 6LY
email office@visiblefictions.co.uk
website https://visiblefictions.co.uk
Twitter @visiblefictions
Artistic Director Dougie Irvine, *Producer* Laura Penny

Accessible theatre for young people and adults. Also works in creative learning settings – community, educational, institutional and professional – to create bespoke and immersive projects.

TOURING COMPANIES

Arad Goch

Stryd y Baddon, Aberystwyth, Ceredigion SY23 2NN
tel (01970) 617998
email post@aradgoch.org
website www.aradgoch.cymru
Twitter @AradGoch
Artistic Director Jeremy Turner

Performs in Welsh and English and tours nationally throughout Wales, and occasionally abroad. The company is particularly interested in enabling children and young people to recognise and appreciate their own unique cultural identity through theatre. Some of the company's work is based on traditional material and children's literature, but it also commissions new work from experienced dramatists and new writers. Arad Goch performs in theatres and other locations, including schools, and also offers seminars/workshops for students and teachers. The company has its own production house in Aberystwyth which is used by other arts and community organisations and where it programmes a variety of participatory activities for young people. It organises the biennial 'Agor Drysau–Opening Doors' Wales International Festival of Performing Arts for Young Audiences (www.agordrysau.cymru). Founded 1989.

Booster Cushion Theatre

75 How Wood, Park Street, St Albans, Herts. AL2 2RW
tel (01727) 873874
email admin@booster-cushion.co.uk
website www.booster-cushion.co.uk
Facebook www.facebook.com/boostercushiontheatre
Twitter @BoosterCushion
Director Philip Sherman

Comical theatre company formed especially to re-tell traditional tales to primary-school pupils and their families using surprising Big Books. BCT has performed to over 500,000 people in schools, libraries, museums and theatres across the UK using pop-up books up to 3m tall and concertina books over 5m wide.

All productions are solo performing shows using mime, voice and some sign language. They involve a high level of audience participation. Each show is completely portable and can be performed inside or outside; technical requirements are minimal. Founded 1989.

Boundless Theatre

B2–B4 Galleywall Road, Bermondsey, London SE16 3PB
tel 020-7928 2811
email hello@boundlesstheatre.org.uk
website www.boundlesstheatre.org.uk
Instagram @boundlessabound
Artistic Director and CEO Rob Drummer

Creates new plays with and for audiences aged 15 to 25. Tours the UK and internationally. Also runs a variety of projects to help young people develop their creativity; these focus on performance, writing and digital innovation. Founded 2001 (as Company of Angels).

Cahoots NI

109–113 Royal Avenue, Belfast BT1 1FF
tel 028-9043 4349

email info@cahootsni.com
website www.cahootsni.com
Facebook www.facebook.com/Cahoots NI
Twitter @CahootsNI
Artistic Director Paul McEneaney, *Company Administrator* Matthew Bradley, *Creative Engagement Manager* Emma Wilson

Professional children's touring theatre company which concentrates on the visual potential of theatre and capitalises upon the age-old popularity of magic and illusion as an essential ingredient in the art of entertaining. It aims to provide inspiring theatrical experiences for children and to encourage appreciation of the arts in young audiences from all sections of society via outreach work. The company has performed in Ireland, the UK, the US and Asia in theatres, schools and healthcare settings. Founded 2001.

Catherine Wheels Theatre Company
Brunton Theatre, Ladywell Way,
Musselburgh EH21 6AF
tel 0131 653 5255
email admin@catherinewheels.co.uk
website www.catherinewheels.co.uk
Facebook www.facebook.com/
CatherineWheelsCompany
Twitter @cwheelstheatre
Artistic Director Gill Robertson

Producing company that tours the UK and internationally, performing for children and young people. One of the founders of the Theatre in Schools Scotland initiative.

Fevered Sleep
15A Old Ford Road, London E2 9PJ
tel 020-3815 6430
email admin@feveredsleep.co.uk
website www.feveredsleep.co.uk
Artistic Directors Sam Butler, David Harradine

Creates performances, installations and digital art for children and adults that the company describes as 'collaborative, participatory, research-led art'. Founded 1996.

Kazzum Arts
Oxford House, Derbyshire Street, London E2 6HG
tel 020-7749 1123
email hello@kazzum.org
website www.kazzum.org
Twitter @KazzumArts
Artistic Director Alex Evans

Provides opportunities for children and young people to explore their creativity at times in their lives when they are most in need of support. Kazzum facilitates innovative, playful and multi-disciplinary projects which encourage social and reflective skills, enabling young people to foster positive relationships and experience an increased sense of wellbeing. Founded 1989.

Konflux Theatre in Education
4100 Park Approach, Thorpe Park, Leeds LS15 8GB
tel (01937) 832740
email info@konfluxtheatre.com
website www.konfluxtheatre.com
Twitter @KonfluxTheatre
Artistic Director Anthony Koncsol

Theatre in Education company, accredited Gifted & Talented provider and Arts Award Supporter. Works with approx. 700 schools each year, building close working relationships with teachers and other education professionals and ensuring its programmes and their delivery are tailored to the needs of the organisation. Konflux offers over 70 curriculum-based Play in a Day® workshops designed to build confidence and promote team work. They give pupils the opportunity to learn through drama, increase their acting skills and present a performance back to peers and parents. Founded 1998.

Little Angel Theatre
14 Dagmar Passage, London N1 2DN
tel 020-7226 1787
email info@littleangeltheatre.com
website www.littleangeltheatre.com
Twitter @LittleATheatre
Artistic Director Samantha Lane

Committed to working with children and families through schools, the local community and the wider community through its extensive touring programme. Little Angel Theatre develops innovative projects, implements improved access to their creative work, increases opportunities for participation and provides stimulating learning and creativity for all using puppetry. Termly activities are run for children, families and schools, including INSET training for teachers. Regular introductory and professional development courses are held throughout the year for teenagers and adults.

Productions last approximately an hour and many are toured to theatres, arts centres and festivals around the UK. Little Angel Theatre is committed to its education programme and continues to work with schools, youth groups and education authorities.

The London Bubble
(Bubble Theatre Company)
5 Elephant Lane, London SE16 4JD
tel 020-7237 4434
email admin@londonbubble.org.uk
website www.londonbubble.org.uk
Twitter @LBubble

Aims to provide the artistic direction, skills, environment and resources to create inspirational, inclusive and involving theatre for the local community and beyond. Also runs a number of groups for children and young people as well as an adult drama group, a Creative Elders group and the Rotherhithe Shed initiative.

Theatre

M6 Theatre Company
Studio Theatre, Hamer C.P. School,
Albert Royds Street, Rochdale, Lancs. OL16 2SU
tel (01706) 355898
email admin@m6theatre.co.uk
website www.m6theatre.co.uk
Twitter @M6Theatre
Artistic Director Gilly Baskeyfield

Touring theatre company specialising in creating and
delivering innovative theatre for young audiences.

Oily Cart
Smallwood School Annexe, Smallwood Road,
London SW17 0TW
tel 020-8672 6329
email oilies@oilycart.org.uk
website www.oilycart.org.uk
Twitter @oilycart
Artistic Director Ellie Griffiths, *Executive Director* Zoë
Lally

Touring company staging interactive, sensory shows
across the UK and internationally. The company
reimagines theatre for young audiences to make it
more inclusive, and all productions are created for
and with children and young people, regardless of age
or perceived ability. Considers scripts from new
writers, but at present all work is generated from
within the company. Founded 1981.

The Pied Piper Theatre Company
1 Lilian Place, Coxcombe Lane, Chiddingfold,
Surrey GU8 4QA
tel (01428) 684022
email info@piedpipertheatre.co.uk
website www.piedpipertheatre.co.uk
Twitter @PiedPiperLive
Artistic Director Tina Williams

Specialises in bringing new writing for children to the
stage. Typically tours one show a year in the UK,
sometimes two, and occasionally tours in Europe and
Asia. Pied Piper is an ethical ITC member.
Founded 1984.

Prime Theatre
(formerly Sixth Sense Theatre for Young People)
c/o The Wyvern Theatre, Theatre Square,
Swindon SN1 1QN
tel (01793) 614864
email info@primetheatre.co.uk
website www.primetheatre.co.uk
Twitter @PrimeTheatreUK
Artistic Director Mark Powell

Professional theatre company prioritising work with
young people. Prime Theatre produces both issue-
based and creative theatre productions and performs
in schools, theatres and arts centres in the South-
West region and beyond. These productions are
supported by additional young people-led work,
workshops, training sessions and other projects.

Proteus Theatre Company
Proteus Creation Space, Council Road, Basingstoke,
Hants RG21 3DH
tel (01256) 354541
email info@proteustheatre.com
website www.proteustheatre.com
Twitter @proteustheatre
Artistic Director and Chief Executive Mary Swan

Small-scale touring company particularly committed
to new writing and new work, education and
community collaborations. Produces up to three
touring shows per year plus community projects.
Founded 1981.

Replay Theatre Company
East Belfast Network Centre,
55 Templemore Avenue, Belfast BT5 4FP
tel 028-9045 4562
email info@replaytheatre.co.uk
website www.replaytheatre.co.uk
Twitter @ReplayTheatreCo
Artistic Director Janice Kernoghan-Reid, *Chief
Executive Officer* Brian Mullan, *Finance and
Operations Manager* Hayley McBride, *Lead Artist
Inclusion* Andrew Stanford

Innovative, high-quality work for audiences under
the age of 19, including school groups, disabled
children and young people, and families. Each show
is shaped through creative consultation with its
intended audience, and those who live and work with
them. Tours locally, nationally and internationally.
Founded 1988.

Rhubarb Theatre
7 Queensway, Leadenham, Lincoln LN5 0PF
tel (01400) 275133
email info@rhubarbtheatre.co.uk
website www.rhubarbtheatre.co.uk
Artistic Directors Kirsty Mead, Philip Mead

Professional indoor theatre and street theatre
predominantly aimed at family audiences (age 5+).
Productions are newly created stories that include
original music and lots of theatrical devices, i.e.
masks, puppetry, dance, song, movement and mime.
Most of Rhubarb's street shows are wordless and
suitable for booking overseas. Tours nationally and
performs in a host of different small to middle-scale
venues, including theatres, arts centres, village halls,
rural touring schemes and schools, undertaking
approx. 200 performances a year. Other activities
include walkabout, interactive storytelling, workshops
and teaching. Founded 2004.

Spectacle Theatre Ltd
c/o The Factory, Jenkin Street, Porth CF39 9PP
tel (01443) 681024
email steve.spectacletheatre@gmail.com
website www.spectacletheatre.co.uk
Facebook www.facebook.com/Theatr-Spectacle-
Theatre
Twitter @SpectacleTheat1
Manager/Creative Director Steve Davis

Community theatre company. Bilingual performance, workshops, training and mentoring.

Tell Tale Hearts
c/o 4 Oxspring Road, Penistone, Sheffield S36 8AB
email info@telltalehearts.co.uk
website www.telltalehearts.co.uk
Twitter @TellTaleHeart
Artistic Director Natasha Holmes

Produces participatory theatre for primary-school pupils and younger years in a range of settings, from theatres to schools and other community venues. Also runs workshops, INSET training and offers other consultancy services. Note that the Tell Tale Hearts rarely produces theatre from written work; it is a devising company and actively seeks out collaborations with contributing artists. Occasionally works with a writer as part of its collaborative team, but this is to produce new work. Contact the Artistic Director before sending any work in order to gauge interest. Founded 2003.

The Theatre Company Blah Blah Blah
Interplay Theatre, Armley Bridge Road,
North Lane House, North Lane, Leeds LS6 3HG
tel 0113 426 1394
email info@blahs.co.uk
website www.blahs.co.uk
Twitter @theatreblahs
Artistic Director Deborah Pakkar-Hull

Theatre in Education company which specialises in touring theatre for children and young people and residency work in schools. Founded 1985.

Theatr Iolo
Chapter, Market Road, Canton, Cardiff CF14 3HS
tel 029-2061 3782
email hello@theatriolo.com
website www.theatriolo.com
Twitter @theatriolo
Artistic Director Lee Lyford

Theatre company for children and young people. Aims to create high-quality experiences that are stimulating, surprising and meaningful for children and their adults.

Theatre Centre
The Albany, Douglas Way, Deptford,
London SE8 4AG
tel 020-7729 3066
email admin@theatre-centre.co.uk
website www.theatre-centre.co.uk
Facebook www.facebook.com/TheatreCentreUK
Twitter @TClive
Artistic Director (Interim) Rob Watt

Young people's theatre company producing plays and workshops which tour nationally across the UK. Productions are staged in primary and secondary schools, arts centres and other venues. Keen to nurture new and established talent, encouraging all writers to consider writing for young audiences. Also

runs creative projects and manages writing awards: see website for details. Founded 1953.

Theatre Hullabaloo
The Hullabaloo, Borough Road, Darlington DL1 1SG
tel (01325) 405681
email info@theatrehullabaloo.org.uk
website www.theatrehullabaloo.org.uk
Twitter @hullabalootweet
Artistic Producer Miranda Thain

Specialist theatre company that creates, promotes and tours work for young audiences, with a particular emphasis on early years. Promotes greater awareness of the value of theatre to children and young people by working with academic researchers, teachers and others through courses, events and publications. Tours professional theatre productions to schools and venues across the North East and nationally. Dedicated children's theatre and family venue, The Hullabaloo, offers theatre for children, creative play installations and more.

Travelling Light Theatre Company
Barton Hill Settlement, 43 Ducie Road,
Lawrence Hill, Bristol BS5 0AX
tel 0117 377 3166
email info@travellinglighttheatre.org.uk
website www.travellinglighttheatre.org.uk
Facebook www.facebook.com/travellinglighttheatre
Twitter @tl_theatre
Artistic Producer Heidi Vaughan, *Executive Director* Dienka Hines

Professional theatre company producing work for young audiences. Collaborates with many different arts organisations to create original, cross-artform productions that inspire and engage young people. Tours to theatres and festivals throughout the UK and abroad as well as to local schools. Also runs an extensive participation programme engaging with 0–25 year-olds through youth theatre groups, holiday and school projects, work experience, placements and mentoring. Founded 1984.

Tutti Frutti Productions
Shine, Harehills Road, Harehills, Leeds LS8 5DR
tel 0113 388 0027
email emma@tutti-frutti.org.uk
website www.tutti-frutti.org.uk
Twitter @tuttifruttiprod
Artistic Director Wendy Harris

Professional theatre aimed specifically at family audiences (age 3+ and families/carers). Productions are adaptations of children's books and stories or specially commissioned new shows, and include original music together with different art forms, i.e. puppetry, dance, movement. Tours nationally and internationally and performs in a host of different small- and middle-scale venues, including theatres, arts centres, village halls, rural touring schemes and schools, undertaking approx. 250 performances a year. Founded 1991.

Societies, prizes and festivals

Society of Authors

The SoA is the UK trade union for all types of writers, illustrators and literary translators at every stage of their careers.

Founded in 1884, the Society of Authors now has over 10,000 members. Members receive unlimited free advice on all aspects of the profession, including confidential clause-by-clause contract vetting, and a wide range of exclusive offers. It campaigns and lobbies on the issues that affect authors, and holds a wide range of events across the UK, offering opportunities for authors to network and learn from each other. It manages more than 50 literary estates, the income from which helps to fund their work. It also administers a range of literary grants and prizes, awarding more than £400,000 to authors annually.

Members

SoA members include household names, such as J.K. Rowling, Philip Pullman and Joanne Harris, but they also include authors right at the start of their careers. Amongst the SoA membership are academic writers, biographers, broadcasters, children's writers, crime writers, dramatists, educational writers, ELT writers, health writers, ghostwriters, graphic novelists, historians, illustrators, journalists, medical writers, non-fiction writers, novelists, poets, playwrights, radio writers, scriptwriters, short story writers, translators, spoken word artists, YA writers and more.

The benefits available to all SoA members include:

Membership

The Society of Authors
24 Bedford Row, London WC1R 4EH
tel 020-7373 6642
email info@societyofauthors.org
website www.societyofauthors.org
Chief Executive Nicola Solomon
President Philip Pullman

There are two membership bands: Full and Associate membership.

Full membership is available to professional writers, poets, translators and illustrators working in any genre or medium. This includes those who have: had a full-length work traditionally published, broadcast or performed commercially; self-published or been published on a print-on-demand or ebook-only basis and who meet sales criteria; published or had broadcast or performed an equivalent body of professional work; or administrators of a deceased author's estate.

Authors at the start of their careers are invited to join as Associates.

Associate membership is available to anyone actively working to launch a career as an author. This includes: authors who are starting out in self-publishing but who are not yet making a profit; authors who have been offered a contract for publication or agent representation but who are not yet published; students engaged on a course of at least one academic year's duration that will help them develop a career as an author, as well as other activities that mark the early stages of an author's career. Associate members enjoy all the same services and benefits as Full members.

Membership is subject to election and payment of subscription fees.

The subscription fee (tax deductible) starts at £27 per quarter, or £19 for those aged 35 or under. From the second year of subscription there are concessionary rates for over 65s who are no longer earning a significant amount of income from writing.

• assistance with contracts, from negotiation and assessment of terms to clause-by-clause, confidential vetting;

• unlimited advice on queries, covering any aspect of the business of authorship;

• taking up complaints on behalf of members on any issue concerned with the business of authorship;

• pursuing legal actions for breach of contract, copyright infringement and the non-payment of royalties and fees, when the risk and cost preclude individual action by a member and issues of general concern to the profession are at stake;

• conferences, seminars, meetings and other opportunities to network and learn from other authors;

• regular communications and a comprehensive range of publications, including the SoA's quarterly journal, the Author;

• discounts on books, exclusive rates on specialist insurance, special offers on products and services and free membership of the Authors' Licensing and Collecting Society (ALCS; see page 431);

• Academic and Medical Writers Groups – investigating and highlighting the issues faced by these authors, including confusion and concern around Open Access requirements and Creative Commons licensing.

> 'It does no harm to repeat, as often as you can, "Without me the literary industry would not exist: the publishers, the agents, the sub-agents, the accountants, the libel lawyers, the departments of literature, the professors, the theses, the books of criticism, the reviewers, the book pages – all this vast and proliferating edifice is because of this small, patronised, put-down and underpaid person."' – *Doris Lessing*

• Broadcasting Group – representing members working in radio, TV and film;

• Children's Writers and Illustrators Group – a professional community of writers and illustrators who create content for the children's publishing market;

• Educational Writers Group – protecting the interests of educational authors in professional matters, especially contracts, rates of pay, digitalisation and copyright;

• Poetry and Spoken Word Group – a new, increasingly active group to which all new member poets are subscribed on joining SoA;

• Society of Authors in Scotland – organises a varied and busy calendar of activities in Scotland through a committee of volunteers;

• Translators Association – a source of expert advice for individual literary translators and a collective voice representing the profession;

• Writers as Carers Group – a new group designed to help keep writers writing when they take on caring responsibilities for someone with an illness or disability.

The SoA also facilitates many local groups across the UK.

Campaigning and lobbying

The SoA is a voice for authors and works at a national and international level to improve terms and treatment of authors, negotiating with all parties including publishers, broadcasters, agents and governments. Current areas of campaigning include contract terms, copyright, freedom of expression, tax and benefits arrangements and Public Lending Right (PLR; see page 417) – which the SoA played a key role in establishing. It also campaigns on wider matters which affect authors, such as libraries, literacy and a fair playing field for publishing.

In the UK the SoA lobbies parliament, ministers and departments and makes submissions on relevant issues, working closely with the Department for Culture, Media and Sport and the All Party Parliamentary Writers Group. The SoA is a member of the British Copyright Council and was instrumental in setting up ALCS. It is recognised by the BBC in the negotiation of rates for authors' contributions to radio drama, as well as for the broadcasting of published material.

The SoA is highly active and influential at a European level and is a member of the European Writers' Council and applies pressure globally, working with sister organisations as part of the international Authors' Foundation.

The SoA also works closely with other professional bodies, including the Association of Authors' Agents, the Booksellers Association, the Publishers Association, the Independent Publishers Guild, the British Council, the National Union of Journalists and the Writers' Guild of Great Britain.

Awards and grants

The SoA supports authors through a wide range of awards and grants. Over £100,000 is given in prizes each year and more than £230,000 is distributed in grants.

The SoA administers:

• the Authors' Foundation and K Blundell Trust, which give grants to assist authors working on their next book;
• the Francis Head Bequest and the Authors' Contingency Fund, which assist authors who, through physical mishap, are temporarily unable to maintain themselves or their families;
• the Women's Prize for Fiction;
• the *Sunday Times*/University of Warwick Young Writer of the Year Award;
• the *Sunday Times* EFG Short Story Award;
• Travelling Scholarships, which give honorary awards;
• three prizes for first novels: the Betty Trask Awards, the McKitterick Prize and inaugural Paul Torday Memorial Prize;
• the Somerset Maugham Awards for a full-length published work;
• two poetry awards: the Eric Gregory Awards and the Cholmondeley Awards;
• the ALCS Tom-Gallon Award for short story writers;
• two audio drama prizes: the Imison Award for a writer new to radio drama and the Tinniswood Award;
• awards for translations from Arabic, Dutch/Flemish, French, German, Greek, Italian, Spanish and Swedish into English;
• the ALCS Educational Writers' Awards.

WGGB (Writers' Guild of Great Britain)

The WGGB is the TUC-affiliated trade union for writers.

WGGB represents writers working in film, television, radio, theatre, books, poetry, animation, comedy and videogames. Formed in 1959 as the Screenwriters' Guild, the union gradually extended into all areas of freelance writing activity and copyright protection. It comprises professional writers in all media, united in common concern for one another and regulating the conditions under which they work.

Apart from necessary dealings with Government and policies on legislative matters affecting writers, the WGGB is, by constitution, non-political, has no involvement with any political party and members pay no political levy.

WGGB employs a permanent general secretary and other permanent staff and is administered by an Executive Council of around 20 members.

WGGB agreements

WGGB's core function is to negotiate minimum terms in those areas in which its members work. Those agreements form the basis of the individual contracts signed by members. It also gives individual advice to its members on contracts and other matters and maintains a benevolent fund to help writers in financial trouble.

Television

WGGB negotiates minimum terms agreements with the BBC, ITV, Pact (Producers' Alliance for Cinema and Television) and TAC (representing Welsh-language television producers).

WGGB TV agreements regulate minimum fees, residuals and royalties, copyright, credits and general conditions for television plays, series and serials, dramatisations and adaptations, soaps, sitcoms and sketch shows. One of the WGGB's most important achievements has been the establishment of pension rights for members. The BBC, ITV

Membership

The Writers' Guild of Great Britain
First Floor, 134 Tooley Street, London SE1 2TU
tel 020-7833 0777
email admin@writersguild.org.uk
website www.writersguild.org.uk
Facebook www.facebook.com/thewritersguild
Twitter @The WritersGuild
General Secretary Ellie Peers

Full membership: Members pay approximately 1.2% of earnings from professional writing using a banding system (min. £198, max. £2,000 p.a.).

Candidate membership: £108 p.a. restricted to writers who have not had work published or produced at WGGB-approved rates.

Student membership: £30 p.a. for student writers aged 18 or over, studying at BA level or below.

Affiliate membership: £300 p.a. for people who work professionally with writers, e.g. agents, technical advisers.

Members receive a weekly email newsletter. The WGGB website contains full details of collective agreements and WGGB activities, plus a 'Find a Writer' service and a dedicated Members' area; information is also made available on Twitter and Facebook. Other benefits include: legal advice and contract vetting; free training; member events, discounts and special offers (subject to membership tier).

and independent producers pay a pension contribution on top of the standard writer's fee on the understanding that the WGGB member also pays a contribution.

The switch to digital television, video-on-demand and download-to-own services, mobile phone technology and the expansion of the BBC's commercial arm have seen WGGB in constant negotiation over the past decade. WGGB now has agreements for all of the BBC's digital channels and for its joint venture channels. In May 2012 it signed new agreements with the BBC extending minimum terms over online services such as iPlayer. From April 2015 the first payments under the Writers Digital Payments scheme (a not-for-profit company) were paid out to writers whose work had been broadcast on BBC iPlayer and ITV Player. In 2016 WGGB negotiated a 75% fee increase for writers working under its 2003 Pact agreement, and also started work on rewriting the agreement. In 2017 it negotiated a new script agreement for television and online with the BBC.

Film

In 1985 an agreement was signed with the two producer organisations: the British Film and Television Producers' Association and the Independent Programme Producers' Association (now known as Pact). Since then there has been an industrial agreement covering UK film productions and pension fund contributions have been negotiated for WGGB members. The Agreement was renegotiated in February 1992 and consultations on an updated arrangement are in progress.

Radio

WGGB has a standard agreement for Radio Drama with the BBC, establishing a fee structure that is reviewed annually. It was comprehensively renegotiated in 2005 resulting in an agreement covering digital radio. In 1985 the BBC agreed to extend the pension scheme already established for television writers to include radio writers. WGGB has special agreements for Radio 4's *The Archers* and for BBC iPlayer. A separate agreement covers the reuse of old comedy and drama material on digital BBC Radio 4 Extra. It has also negotiated rates for podcasts.

Books

WGGB fought for the loans-based Public Lending Right (PLR, see page 417) to reimburse authors for books lent in libraries. The scheme is now administered by the British Library; WGGB is represented on its advisory committee. WGGB has a Books Committee, which works on behalf of book writers and poets. Issues affecting members include authors' earnings, self-publishing, print-on-demand services and ebooks.

Theatre

In 1979 WGGB, together with the Theatre Writers' Union, negotiated the first industrial agreement for theatre writers. The Theatres National Committee Agreement (TNC) covers the Royal Shakespeare Company, the Royal National Theatre Company and the English Stage Company at the Royal Court. When their agreement was renegotiated in 2007, WGGB achieved a long-standing ambition of a minimum fee of £10,000 for a new play; this has since risen to £12,997.

In June 1986, a new agreement was signed with the Theatrical Management Association (now UK Theatre), which covers 95 provincial theatres. In 1993, this agreement was comprehensively revised and included a provision for a year-on-year increase in fees in line with the Retail Price Index. The agreement was renegotiated in 2015.

After many years of negotiation, an agreement was concluded in 1991 between WGGB and the Independent Theatre Council (ITC), which represents 200 of the smaller and fringe theatres as well as educational and touring companies. This agreement was revised in 2002 and the minimum fees are reviewed annually. WGGB is currently talking to the ITC about updating the agreement. The WGGB Theatre Committee holds an annual forum for Literary Managers and runs the Olwen Wymark Theatre Encouragement Award scheme.

Videogames

WGGB counts games writers amongst its members and holds regular networking events for them, as well as celebrating their achievements at the annual Writers' Guild Awards. The union publishes guidelines for games writers and those who work with them, outlining best practice in this growing area.

Other activities

WGGB is in touch with Government and national institutions wherever and whenever the interests of writers are in question or are being discussed, for example, submitting evidence to a Parliamentary Inquiry on the lack of working-class writers. It holds cross-party Parliamentary lobbies with Equity and the Musicians' Union to ensure that the various artforms they represent are properly cared for, and writers' voices are heard during, for example, the Brexit transition and the Covid-19 pandemic. Working with the Federation of Entertainment Unions, WGGB makes its views known to bodies, such as Arts Council England, the BBC Trust and Ofcom on a broader basis.

WGGB is an active affiliate of the British Copyright Council, Creators' Rights Alliance and other organisations whose activities are relevant to professional writers. An Anti-Censorship Committee has intervened strongly to protect freedom of speech.

Internationally, WGGB plays a leading role in the International Affiliation of Writers Guilds, which includes the American Guilds East and West, the Canadian Guilds (French and English) and the Irish, Mexican, French, Israeli, South African and New Zealand Guilds. When it is possible to make common cause, the Guilds act accordingly. WGGB takes a leading role in the European Writers' Council and the Fédération des Scénaristes d'Europe.

On a day-to-day basis, WGGB gives advice on contracts, and takes up issues that affect the lives of its members as professional writers. Other benefits include access to free and discounted training, exclusive events and discounts and a dedicated online members' area. Full members are entitled to submit a profile for inclusion in the WGGB online *Find A Writer* directory; pay no joining fee for membership to Writers Guild of America East or West; and are eligible for Cannes accreditation. Regular committee meetings are held by specialist WGGB Craft Committees and its active branches across the UK organise panel discussions, talks and social events.

Recent campaigns include Equality Writes, following an independent report commissioned by WGGB and launched in 2018, which revealed the shocking lack of gender equality in the UK screen industries. The union has also campaigned on bullying and harassment in the creative industries.

Each year WGGB presents the Writers' Guild Awards, covering all the areas in which its members work. These are the only cross-media awards in which writers are honoured by their peers.

Alliance of Independent Authors

The ALLi is a professional association of self-publishing writers and advisors.

The Alliance of Independent Authors (ALLi) is a global organisation with a mission of fostering ethics and excellence in self-publishing and advocation for author-publishers globally.

Founded in 2012 at the London Book Fair by author, poet and creative entrepreneur, Orna Ross, ALLi is headquartered in London but with members all over the world. In addition to its member services, the organisation offers outreach education to the self-publishing community through its popular online Self-Publishing Advice Center, which features a blog, podcast, bi-annual online conference and series of guidebooks.

ALLi has an Advisory Board of successful author-publishers, educators and service providers, and an active Watchdog desk which runs a publicly available ratings board of the best and worst self-publishing services. It also publishes an annual Directory of its Partner Members (https:// selfpublishingadvice.org/best-self-publishing-services/): vetted self-publishing services, from large global players like Amazon KDP and Ingram Spark to local freelance editors and designers. Many of these offer discounted services to ALLi author members.

ALLi advocates for the interests of independent, self-publishing authors within and outside the literary, publishing and bookselling industries. 2021 saw the launch of the 'Self-Publishing for All' campaign, where ALLi works with ambassadors, other authors associations, and grassroots organizations to bring self-publishing skills to marginalised voices, those currently denied involvement in mainstream cultural, education or social activity. Other campaigns include 'Open Up To Indie Authors', which urges booksellers, festivals, prize-giving committees, libraries, book clubs and corporate media to include author--publishers in their programmes; and 'Self-Publishing 3.0', which calls on government and creative industry bodies to support authors' digital business development.

Membership

The Alliance of Independent Authors
email info@allianceindependentauthors.org
website www.allianceindependentauthors.org,
https://selfpublishingadvice.org

ALLi offers three grades of membership:

Author membership (£89 p.a.) is open to writers or translators of books for adults who have self-published a full-length title (55,000+ words) or series of shorter books; writers of children's/young adult books who have self-published one or more titles.

Authorpreneur membership (£119 p.a.) is open to full-time self-publishing authors who earn their living from their author business and can show evidence of 50,000 book sales in the last two years; applications are assessed.

Associate membership (£69 p.a.) is open to writing/publishing students with an interest in self-publishing and non-published writers (or translators) preparing a book for self-publication.

Benefits include self-publishing advice, guidance and community; vetted services, service ratings and watchdog desk; legal and contract appraisal; discounts and deals; professional and business development; campaigns and advocacy.

Societies, prizes and festivals

Society of Children's Book Writers & Illustrators

The Society of Children's Book Writers & Illustrators (SCBWI) is the only international professional organisation dedicated to serving people who share a vital interest in children's literature, magazines, film, television and/or multimedia.

Society of Children's Book Writers and Illustrators

Whether you are a professional children's writer or illustrator, or a newcomer to the field, SCBWI has plenty to offer you, from local to national to international events, from advice on getting your first deal to help in navigating your career as a writer or illustrator. Established in 1971, SCBWI now has over 22,000 members in 70 regional chapters worldwide. Membership benefits include professional development and networking opportunities, marketing information, events, publications, online profiles, grants and awards.

What does SCBWI British Isles do?

SCBWI British Isles is a dynamic and friendly chapter of over 1000 members, which aims to support aspiring and published writers and illustrators and provide opportunities for them to network, market their work, hone their craft, make industry connections and develop their careers. Events include an annual two-day conference, a fiction and picture book retreat, an annual Agents' Party, the Industry Insiders series (six talks a year in London aimed at professional development on a variety of topics), the Illustrators' masterclass series (Saturday workshops with a hands-on craft element), sketch and scrawl crawls, author masterclasses, PULSE events (SCBWI PULSE provides professional development opportunities for published members) and an author and illustrator showcase. A network of regional organisers run local critique groups, workshops and social events across the British Isles.

> **Further information**
>
> **Society of Children's Book Writers & Illustrators**
> *website* www.scbwi.org, www.britishisles.scbwi.org
> *Co-Regional Advisors (Co-chairs)* Natascha Biebow and Kathy Evans
> *email* ra@britishscbwi.org
> *email* finance@britishscbwi.org
> *Membership Coordinator* Anita Loughrey
> *email* membership@britishscbwi.org
> *Membership* £75 p.a. and £50 p.a. for students

What SCBWI does for its members

• SCBWI is a professional guild. It speaks as a consolidated global voice for professional children's writers and illustrators. In recent years, SCBWI has successfully lobbied for such issues as new copyright legislation, equitable treatment of authors and artists and fair contract terms.

• It offers a showcase of authors and illustrators' work through the Find a Speaker Directory, Featured Illustrator Showcase and Member Awards, Celebrations & Achievements Showcase (www.scbwishowcase.org).

• It keeps members up to date with industry developments through the SCBWI PULSE series of events, with opportunities to learn more about the 'business' of writing and illustrating, including marketing, school and festival visits, and exclusive networking events with librarians and booksellers.

• It offers members invaluable exposure to editors, art directors and agents through one-to-one manuscript or portfolio reviews at the annual conference and retreats, the members-only Agents' Party, the Slush Pile Challenge and biennial SCBWI Undiscovered Voices (www.undiscoveredvoices.com) competitions.

• It supports professional development for members to hone their craft through the Masterclass series, conference workshops and highly-successful critique groups.

• It gives members increased visibility online with a free profile on its website, which is a point of call for agents, art directors and editors.

• It provides support and a network of like-minded people, helping to answer members' queries through a variety of online resources, including a popular social networking site.

• It facilitates networking opportunities with professionals worldwide.

• Publications include the *Bulletin*, the SCBWI international magazine, *Insight* e-newletter, weekly *Words & Pictures* newsletter blog with weekly content (www.wordsandpics.org) and resources including the annual publications and market guide.

• Website resources include book launch parties, members' bookshop, discussion boards, illustrator gallery, find-a-speaker search facility, webinars and podcasts.

Awards and grants

The SCBWI administers a number of awards and grants:

• The Golden and Crystal Kite Awards are for the most outstanding books published by SCBWI members each year, voted for by SCBWI peers.

• The Sid Fleischman Humour Award is presented to authors whose work exemplifies the excellence of writing in the genre of humour.

• The annual Spark Award recognises excellence in a children's book published through a non-traditional publishing route.

• The Book Launch Award provides authors or illustrators with $2,000 in funds to help the promotion of their newly published work and take the marketing strategy into their own creative hands.

• The Emerging Voices Award fosters the emergence of diverse voices in children's books.

• For Translators: Work-in-Progress Grants to assist children's book writers and illustrators in the completion of a specific project currently not under contract.

• Ann Whitford Paul - Writer's Digest Manuscript Award is an annual award given to the manuscript of the Most Promising Picture Book manuscript.

• SCBWI PJ Library Jewish Stories Award is an award sponsored by the PJ Library to encourage the creation of more high-quality Jewish children's literature.

• Karen Cushman Late Bloomer Award – An award for a work-in-progress from an unpublished author over age 50.

• A. Orr Fantasy Grant – Awarded to young adult and middle grade writers working in the fantasy or science fiction genre.

• BIPOC Scholarship offers an all-expense paid trip to the Winter or Summer Conference for Black, Indigenous, and People of colour.

• Bologna Illustrators Gallery (BIG) is given bi-annually to an illustrator of promise. The winner is announced at the New York Conference, and the winning art is displayed prominently at the SCWBI Bologna Book Fair booth.

• The Multi-Cultural Work-in-Progress Grant assists writers in the completion of a manuscript featuring a voice traditionally underrepresented in children's books.

• The Magazine Merit Awards are presented for outstanding original magazine work for young people.

• The Sue Alexander Most Promising New Work Award is for the best manuscript submitted for individual critique at the LA conference.

• The Martha Weston Grant encourages authors and illustrators to nurture their creativity in a different genre of children's books.

• The Lee Bennett Hopkins Poetry Award recognises and encourages the publication of an excellent book of poetry or anthology for children or young adults (given every three years).

• The Jane Yolen Mid-List Author Grant honours the contribution of mid-list authors.

• Several Work-in-progress Grants are available each year to assist children's book writers and illustrators in the completion of a specific project currently not under contract, in the categories of Picture Book Text, Chapter Books/Early Readers, Middle Grade, Young Adult Fiction, Nonfiction, and Multicultural Fiction or Nonfiction.

• Don Freeman Work-in-Progress Grant is to assist illustrators in the completion of a book dummy or portfolio.

• Narrative Art Award given annually to an illustrator of promise based on a given prompt.

• Tome DePaola Award awards artists with a cash prize of $2,500, in memory of beloved author-illustrator Tome DePaola.

• The Portfolio Award is presented to the best art portfolio on view at the Juried Portfolio Display at the LA conference.

• There are four Student Illustrator Scholarships for full-time graduate and undergraduate students of children's book illustration.

• There are two Student Writer Scholarships to the Summer and Winter conferences for full-time university students in an English or Creative Writing programme.

• There are six Annual Conference Scholarships to attend the annual SCBWI-BI conference.

• A number of scholarship places are awarded at all British Isles region events for under-represented groups in children's publishing, including: SCBWI British Isles members who have financial need; SCBWI British Isles members and non-members who identify as BAME, LGBTQIA+, disabled or working class.

See also...

Seven Stories – The National Centre for Children's Books

At Seven Stories the rich heritage of British children's books is collected, explored and celebrated.

seven stories
National Centre for Children's Books

Once upon a time an idea was born on the banks of the Tyne to create a national home for children's literature – a place where the original work of authors and illustrators could be collected, treasured and celebrated. After ten years of pioneering work by founding directors Elizabeth Hammill and Mary Briggs, that dream became a reality. In August 2005 Seven Stories, the Centre for Children's Books, opened in an award-winning converted seven storey Victorian granary in the Ouseburn Valley, a stone's throw from Newcastle's vibrant quayside. Seven Stories is now officially known as The National Centre for Children's Books, following approval by Arts Council England in 2012. It is the only accredited museum in the UK that specialises in children's books.

The collection

At the heart of Seven Stories is a unique and growing collection of manuscripts, artwork and other pre-publication materials. These treasures record the creative process involved in making a children's book and provide illuminating insights into the working lives of modern authors and illustrators. The collection focuses on work created in modern Britain. It already contains thousands of items by authors such as Peter Dickinson, Michael Morpurgo, Enid Blyton, Berlie Doherty, Jan Mark, Philip Pullman, Michael Rosen, Robert Westall and Ursula Moray Williams; illustrators like Edward Ardizzone, Faith Jaques, Harold Jones, Anthony Maitland, Pat Hutchins, Helen Cooper, Jan Ormerod and Jane Ray; and editors and other practitioners such as Kaye Webb. Many more bodies of work are pledged. A catalogue of the collection is available via the Seven Stories website.

Exhibitions

A celebration of creativity underpins the Seven Stories project: its collection documents the creative act, and its exhibitions and programmes interpret this original material in unconventional but meaningful ways. The aim is to cultivate an appreciation of books and their making, and inspire creativity in its audience.

Seven Stories has been mounting exhibitions since 1998 – first in borrowed venues and now in its own home. Here it provides the only exhibition space in the UK wholly dedicated to showcasing the incomparable legacy of British writing and illustrating for children. With exhibitions changing every year, Seven Stories have showcased the impressive work of children's authors such as Judith Kerr, Michael Morpurgo and David McKee. Their latest exhibition, *Where Stories Come From*, opened in 2020 and explores the idea that every story fits into one of seven basic story plots.

Throughout its seven storeys – from the Studio to the bookshop and café to the Artist's Attic, visitors of all ages are invited to engage in a unique, interactive exploration of creativity, literature and art. In this ever changing literary playground and landscape for the imagination, they can become writers, artists, explorers, designers, storytellers, readers or collectors, in the company of storytellers, authors, illustrators and Seven Stories' own facilitators and learning team.

Seven Stories aims to place children, young people and their books at the heart of the UK's national literary culture. An independent educational charity, it is committed to access for all and has initiated several innovative participation projects. The centre has developed close links with the Newcastle and regional communities, and is working with the Children's Literature Unit in the Department of English Literature, Language and Linguistics at Newcastle University to develop the Seven Stories collection and maximise its potential for research and display.

Seven Stories is dedicated to the celebration of children's literature. It is supported by Arts Council England and Community Foundation Newcastle Culture Investment Fund.

Further information

Seven Stories – The National Centre for Children's Books
30 Lime Street, Ouseburn Valley, Newcastle upon Tyne NE1 2PQ
tel 0300 330 1095
email info@sevenstories.org.uk
website www.sevenstories.org.uk
Public opening hours Tues–Sat 10am–5pm, Sun 10am–4pm, Open daily during school holidays.
Admission charges Adult (17 and over) £7.70; child (4–16)/concession £6.60; toddler (1–3) £2.50; family £23.10; under 12 months free. Annual passes available.

See also...
- *Society of Children's Book Writers & Illustrators*, page 356
- *The Children's Book Circle*, page 361
- *Federation of Children's Book Groups*, page 362

The Children's Book Circle

The Children's Book Circle is open to anyone who has a passion for children's books; the activities of the organisation are introduced here.

Are you passionate about children's books? Since 1962, the Children's Book Circle (CBC) has provided an exciting forum for lively debate on important issues in the children's book world, as well as opportunities to socialise and build a network within the industry. Membership is open to publishers, librarians, authors, illustrators, agents, teachers, booksellers and anyone with an active interest in the field. The CBC caters to both creators and consumers of children's books and holds events throughout the year for aspiring authors and illustrators alongside industry-led panels, talks and meet-ups. It's not a route into getting published, but it will give you opportunities to engage with people from the industry in an informal and enjoyable context.

The CBC meets regularly at venues in central London and frequently invites guest speakers to debate key issues relating to the world of children's books. Previous events have included panel discussions on the importance of diversity and the rise of licensing in children's books, and 'Meet and Critique' evenings for aspiring authors and illustrators to discuss their projects with industry experts. Social drinks and the ever-popular Pub Quiz are fast becoming part of the CBC calendar and are a great chance to catch up with industry contacts and make new ones.

The CBC is also the proud host of the annual **Eleanor Farjeon Award** (sponsored by the estate of Eleanor Farjeon) and the **Patrick Hardy Lecture**. The Eleanor Farjeon Award recognises an outstanding contribution to the world of children's books. Recent winners include The Centre for Literacy in Primary Education (CLPE), Michael Morpurgo, Keats Community Library and Terry Pratchett (posthumously). The Patrick Hardy Lecture is delivered each year at the same event by a distinguished speaker and has previously been presented by Nicola Davies, Lauren St John, Lauren Child, Verna Wilkins (founder of Tamarind Books) and Michael Rosen.

A yearly membership gives you discounted access to all CBC events and keeps you up to date via the newsletter. CBC welcome enthusiasts of children's books from all backgrounds and aims to be as widely representative as possible.

> **Further information**
>
> **The Children's Book Circle**
> *website* www.childrensbookcircle.org.uk
> *Facebook* www.facebook.com/childrensbookcircle/
> *Twitter* @ChildBookCircle
> *Membership* £25 p.a.; students £20 p.a.; corporate membership (up to five staff covered) £100 p.a. Includes free or discounted entry to all events. Non-member tickets can also be purchased for individual events from the website.

See also...

Societies, prizes and festivals

Federation of Children's Book Groups

'The Federation of Children's Book Groups, has, in its own quiet, single-minded way, done more for reading than almost anyone else' – *Anthony Horowitz*

The achievements of the Federation of Children's Book Groups were publicly recognised in 2011 when it was nominated for and subsequently won the Eleanor Farjeon Award (see page 389). Its aim is simple: to bring children and books together, promote children's books and inspire a love of reading through its national and local events. If you are a parent, carer, author, illustrator or professional with a passion for encouraging children to read, the Federation will be of interest to you.

Federation history

The Federation of Children's Book Groups was formed in 1968 by Anne Wood to coordinate the work of the many different children's book groups already in existence across the country and in 2018, it celebrated 50 years of bringing children and books together.

Celebrating its 40th anniversary in 2020, the Children's Book Award, the only national award voted for entirely by children. Throughout the year Federation Testing Groups read and vote on new fiction supplied by publishers. Each year 100,000 votes are cast involving nearly 250 schools and families across the UK. A shortlist (Top Ten) is drawn up with four picture books in the Younger Children category, three shorter novels for Younger Readers and three novels for Older Readers, with children from all over the UK voting in their groups or online. You do not have to be a member to vote in the Top Ten. The Award has a track record of identifying future bestsellers: the first Overall Winner was *Mr Magnolia* by Quentin Blake; other winners include *The Hunger Games*, and the *Harry Potter* and *Percy Jackson* books. For over ten years the Award was supported by Red House, with award ceremonies held at a number of prestigious venues, including the Queen Elizabeth Hall, in London as part of the Imagine Children's Festival (see page 225).

In 1976 National Tell-A-Story-Week was established and it has now grown into National Share-A-Story-Month (NSSM), which takes place each May. It enables groups to focus on the power of story and to hold events which celebrate all forms of storytelling. The theme in 2021 is 'Myths, Magic and Mayhem'. The website hosts the NSSM pack, full of ideas and activities, which is sent to each book group and can also be downloaded by non-members.

In 1977, the first Federation anthology was published, and since then they have compiled booklists covering the whole age range from picture books to the latest teen and young adult novels; these are available on request free of charge via the website. 2019 saw the publication of the *Wordless PictureBooks for All Ages*, which covers a wide age range.

In 2010 the Federation created National Non-Fiction Day to celebrate the quality and variety of information books available for children; this takes place on the first Thursday of each November, with a host of events focused on non-fiction. It has expanded to be

National Non-Fiction November and further details can be found on the website (www.fcbg.org.uk). The theme for 2021 is 'Heroes' and there are always resources to download for free.

Each year the Federation holds a conference: three days of author and illustrator events, panel discussions and seminars enable group and individual members, publishers, authors, illustrators, teachers, librarians and booksellers to meet and exchange ideas. Delegates are inspired by meeting others who share their passion. The 2020 conference was cancelled due to the coronavirus lockdown, however in 2019, Lewes and Oxted hosted the conference, with the theme 'Opening Doors' and a wide range of speakers including Frank Cottrell Boyce, Nick Sharratt, Jane Ray, Francesca Simon, Guy Puzey, Holly Smale and a whole crowd of poets. See http://fcbg.org.uk/conference/ for more details.

The Children's Book Groups

Federation Book Groups exist throughout the UK: from Plymouth to Dundee, from Ipswich to St David's and from Harrogate to Lewes. Their activities are as varied and diverse as the groups themselves, serving their own community's needs, including author and illustrator visits, bonfire par-

Further information

Federation of Children's Book Groups
Wakananai Firs Road, Mardy, Abergavenny,
Wales NP7 6NA
tel 07591 380434
email info@fcbg.org.uk
website http://fcbg.org.uk/

ties, museum and library events, book swaps and parties. But, above all, FCBG are passionate about children's books, bringing together ordinary book-loving families, empowering parents, grandparents, carers and children to become enthusiastic and excited about all kinds of good books. Some book groups are based around schools run by enthusiastic librarians and teachers. You can still be a member of the Federation if there is no book group near you. Individual and professional membership enables everyone to participate in sharing their passion for children's books.

See also...
- *Society of Children's Book Writers & Illustrators*, page 356
- *Seven Stories – The National Centre for Children's Books*, page 359
- *The Children's Book Circle*, page 361

Societies, prizes and festivals

National Literacy Trust

Authors and artists can spark a lifelong love of reading – it just takes one book.

Writers and artists are essential to the National Literacy Trust's mission to raise literacy levels in the UK. We work to improve reading, writing, speaking and listening abilities in the most disadvantaged communities. Creators are not just our natural allies, they are key partners in our campaign to make a difference. It goes without saying that a literacy charity cannot exist without books.

Further information

National Literacy Trust
68 South Lambeth Road, London SW8 1RL
tel 020-7587 1842
email contact@literacytrust.org.uk
website https://literacytrust.org.uk

The literacy challenge in the UK is significant. 27% of children left primary school in England in 2019 unable to read well, rising to 42% for disadvantaged children. This is deeply concerning, not just because it highlights the attainment gap between children from low-income families and their peers. Children need good literacy to succeed at school, to enter the job market as they grow up, and to be able to support their own children's learning as adults. The intergenerational cycle of low-literacy negatively impacts social mobility, meaning a levelled-up society is difficult to achieve.

Authors have the power to transform the way a child engages with books and in doing so unlock a lifetime of benefits. Our research shows that visits from authors to schools have a tangible impact on literacy skills: twice as many children and young people who had a writer visit to their school read above the expected level for their age compared with their peers who didn't have such a visit. What's more, children who have had an author visit to their school also have higher levels of confidence in their reading and enjoy reading and writing more.

We often talk about the magic of school visits. Following a brilliant World Book Day tour from bestselling author and illustrator Rob Biddulph in Manchester, one teacher told us: 'Many of my class ... have very little opportunity to meet an author, never mind visit a library. I was delighted so many were excited by his books – so much so, they have saved up to buy them.' This is just one example of how, by working together, we can do extraordinary things to address the depth of the literacy challenge.

We are grateful when writers ask how they can collaborate with us, and are always looking for support with our campaigning. As a charitable organisation, we are thankful to the people who help us spread the word about our initiatives. Every new like, comment or share is vitally important in helping us reach the people who need our assistance. We launch new research with sharing in mind, so please do visit our website and social pages.

One growing challenge we need writers' and artists' support addressing is the disconnect between creators and the young people who read their work. The lack of diversity is a problem: one in three children and young people do not see themselves reflected in the pages they read. Children from lower socioeconomic backgrounds, in particular minority ethnic communities, are less likely to read for pleasure and more likely to face literacy challenges – and our research shows these are the children who are least likely to see themselves represented in books. We know that books that are representative resonate and can spark a child's lifelong love of reading. What's more, representation will strengthen engagement, supporting more young people from diverse communities to see themselves as readers.

Following the launch of our diversity research, we worked with well-known children's authors and artists to find out when they first saw themselves in a story. Dapo Adeola, award-winning illustrator and designer, told us that a very recent reading of *So Much*, by Trish Cooke and Helen Oxenbury, 'was the first time I felt truly seen in a book.' Author Bali Rai added, 'I always thought books were about other people.'

In the coming year, we will focus on supporting one million children and young people whose literacy and learning has been disproportionately affected by the coronavirus pandemic. We know that the progress made in narrowing the literacy attainment gap over the last decade has been negated due to Covid-19.

Approximately 380,000 (1 in 11) disadvantaged children don't own a book of their own, so we have spent the three national lockdowns distributing nearly 300,000 books to address this issue. We rely on the generosity of authors and their publishers to allow us to do this – and there is so much more to be done.

The unequal impact of school closures highlights the urgent need for our work helping children, young people, families, teachers and communities. Our Arts Council England-funded project 'Connecting Stories' is an excellent example of our response to the pandemic. Publishers large and small are donating books and writers' time to encourage children in 14 areas with low literacy levels to read for pleasure, enjoy their local libraries, and boost their wellbeing. On World Book Day 2021, Cressida Cowell virtually visited hundreds of Connecting Stories schools to increase pupils' access to literacy experiences and books, and shared tips on how they can become authors and illustrators.

As the country recovers from the pandemic and schools and libraries reopen, we hope children will have greater access to books and their brilliant benefits. In the meantime, we will continue our work developing programmes, resources, activities and materials to give children across the country the best chance to develop literacy skills that will help them throughout their lives.

Jonathan Douglas CBE is the Chief Executive of the National Literacy Trust.

See also...
• *Opportunities for under-represented writers,* page 396

Societies, prizes and festivals

Societies, associations and organisations

The societies and associations listed here include appreciation societies devoted to specific authors, professional bodies and national institutions. Some also offer prizes and awards (see page 384).

AccessArt
6 West Street, Comberton, Cambridge CB23 7DS
tel (01223) 262134
website www.accessart.org.uk

A UK Charity which aims to inspire and enable high-quality visual arts teaching, learning and practice. The AccessArt website features over 850 unique resources to inspire practice.

Action for Children's Arts
c/o Mousetrap Theatre Projects,
33 Shaftesbury Avenue, London W1D 7EH
email admin@childrensarts.org.uk
website www.childrensarts.org.uk
Twitter @childrensart
Membership See website for rates or contact membership@childrensarts.org.uk

A membership charity organisation that values children, childhood and the arts. It embraces the UN Convention on the Rights of the Child:

• by campaigning for the right of all children in the UK to experience high-quality arts as an integral part of their childhood;
• by connecting people within and across the cultural and education sectors, across art forms and across the regions and nations of the UK;
• by celebrating achievement, dedication and best practice in artistic activity for and with children.

Louisa May Alcott Memorial Association
Orchard House, PO Box 343, Concord,
MA 01742–0343, USA
email jturnquist@louisamayalcott.org
website www.louisamayalcott.org
Facebook www.facebook.com/
louisamayalcottsorchardhouse/
Twitter @LouisaMayAlcott

A private, not-for-profit association that provides the financial and human resources required to conduct public tours, special programmes, exhibitions and the curatorial work which continues the tradition of the Alcotts, a unique 19th-century family. Founded 1911.

Alliance of Independent Authors – see
page 355

American Booksellers Association
333 Westchester Avenue, Suite S202, White Plains,
NY 10604
tel +1 800-637-0037
email info@bookweb.org
website www.bookweb.org
Twitter @ABAbook

A national non-profit trade organisation that works with booksellers and industry partners to ensure the success and profitability of independently owned book retailers and to assist in expanding the community of the book. Provides education, information dissemination, business products and services, creates relevant awareness programmes and engages in public policy. Founded 1900.

American Society of Composers, Authors and Publishers
website www.ascap.com

An organisation owned and run by its members, it is the leading performance rights organisation representing more than 800,000 songwriters, composers and music publishers.

Arts Council/An Chomhairle Ealaíon
70 Merrion Square, Dublin D02 NY52,
Republic of Ireland
tel +353 (0)1 618 0200
website www.artscouncil.ie/home

The national development agency for the arts in Ireland. Founded 1951.

Arts Council England
tel 0161 934 4317
website www.artscouncil.org.uk
Facebook www.facebook.com/artscouncilofengland
Twitter @ace_national

The national development agency for arts and culture in England, distributing public money from the government and the National Lottery. Between 2018 and 2022, Arts Council England will invest £1.45 billion of public money from government and an estimated £860 million from the National Lottery to deliver its objectives. Through its funding schemes organisations, artists, events and initiatives can receive funding and help achieve the Council's mission of providing art and culture for everyone. There are nine regional offices: Newcastle, Leeds,

Manchester, Nottingham, Birmingham, Cambridge, Brighton, Bristol and London. Visit the website for information on funding support and advice, an online funding finder and funding FAQs.
Founded 1946.

Arts Council of Northern Ireland

Linen Hill House, 23 Linenhall Street,
Lisburn BT28 1FJ
tel 028-9262 3555
email info@artscouncil-ni.org
website www.artscouncil-ni.org
Chief Executive Roisín McDonough

Promotes and encourages the arts throughout Northern Ireland. Artists in drama, dance, music and jazz, literature, the visual arts, traditional arts and community arts can apply for support for specific schemes and projects. The value of the grant will be set according to the aims of the programme. Artists of all disciplines and in all types of working practice, who have made a contribution to artistic activities in Northern Ireland for a minimum period of one year within the last five years, are eligible.

Arts Council of Wales

Bute Place, Cardiff CF10 5AL
tel 03301 242733
website https://arts.wales
Twitter @Arts_Wales_

The official body that funds and develops the arts in Wales. The funding it distributes comes from both the Welsh Government and the National Lottery; most funding goes to artists and art organisations carrying out programmes of work across Wales.
Founded 1994.

North Wales Regional Office
Princes Park II, Princes Drive, Colwyn Bay LL29 8PL

Mid and West Wales Regional Office
The Mount, 18 Queen Street, Carmarthen SA31 1JT

Association for Library Service to Children

American Library Association, 225 N Michigan Ave, Suite 1300 Chicago, IL 60601, USA
tel +1 800-545-2433
email alsc@ala.org
website www.ala.org/alsc
Twitter @wearealsc

Develops and supports the profession of children's librarianship by enabling and encouraging its practitioners to provide the best library service to US children.

Association for Scottish Literary Studies

c/o Dept of Scottish Literature,
University of Glasgow, 7 University Gardens,
Glasgow G12 8QH
tel 0141 330 5309
email office@asls.org.uk
website www.asls.org.uk
President David Goldie, *Secretary* Craig Lamont,
Director Duncan Jones
Membership £60 p.a. individuals; £15 p.a. UK students; £90 p.a. corporate

ASLS promotes the study, teaching and writing of Scottish literature and furthers the study of the languages of Scotland. Publishes annually *New Writing Scotland*, an anthology of new Scottish writing; an edited text of Scottish literature; a series of academic journals; and the eZine *The Bottle Imp*. Also publishes *Scotnotes* (comprehensive study guides to major Scottish writers), literary texts and commentaries designed to assist the classroom teacher, and a series of occasional papers. Organises two conferences a year. Founded 1970.

Association of American Literary Agents

302A West 12th Street, Suite 122, New York, NY 10014
email assistant@aalitagents.org
website aalitagents.org

A professional organisation of over 400 agents who work with book authors and playwrights.
Founded 1991.

Association of American Publishers

455 Massachusetts Avenue, NW Suite 700, Washington DC 20001
tel +1 202-347-3375
email info@publishers.org
website https://publishers.org
Twitter @AmericanPublish

AAP is the largest trade association for US books and journal publishers, providing advocacy and communications on behalf of the industry and its priorities nationally and worldwide. Founded 1970.

The Association of Authors' Agents

c/o Andrew Nurnberg Associates,
3–11 Eyre Street Hill, London EC1R 5ET
tel 020-3327 0400
website www.agentsassoc.co.uk
President Isobel Dixon, *Secretary* Johanna Clarke

The AAA exists to provide a forum which allows member agencies to discuss issues arising in the profession; a collective voice for UK literary agencies in public affairs and the media; and a code of conduct to which all members commit themselves.
Founded 1974.

Association of Canadian Publishers

174 Spadina Avenue, Suite 306, Toronto, Ontario M5T 2C2
tel +1 416-487-6116

email admin@canbook.org
website https://publishers.ca
Executive Director Kate Edwards

Represents approximately 115 Canadian-owned and controlled book publishers from across the country. Founded 1976.

Association of Freelance Editors, Proofreaders and Indexers of Ireland

email info@afepi-ireland.com
website www.afepi-ireland.com
Twitter @AFEPI_Ireland

AFEPI Ireland protects the interests of members and serves as a point of contact between publishers/independent authors and members. Membership is available to experienced professional editors, proofreaders and indexers. For services for publishers and authors, see our online directory of freelance professional editors, proofreaders and indexers based in Ireland and Northern Ireland. Founded 1985.

The Association of Illustrators

Somerset House, Strand, London WC2R 1LA
tel 020-7759 1010
email info@theaoi.com
website www.theaoi.com
Facebook www.facebook.com/theaoi
Twitter @theaoi

Trade association which supports illustrators, promotes illustration and encourages professional standards in the industry. Publishes *Varoom* magazine. Presents an annual programme of events and holds an annual competition, exhibition and tour of the World Illustration Awards in partnership with the *Directory of Illustration* (www.theaoi.com/awards). Founded 1973.

Australia Council

PO Box 576, Pyrmont, NSW 2009
tel +61 (0)2 9215 9000
website www.australiacouncil.gov.au
Ceo Adrian Collette

Provides a broad range of support for the arts in Australia, embracing music, theatre, literature, visual arts and crafts, dance, indigenous arts, community and experimental arts.

Australian Copyright Council

PO Box 1986, Strawberry Hills, NSW 2012
tel +61 (0)2 9101 2377
email info@copyright.org.au
website www.copyright.org.au
Facebook www.facebook.com/AustralianCopyrightCouncil
Twitter @AusCopyright
Chief Executive Officer Eileen Camilleri

Provides easily accessible and affordable practical information, legal advice, education and forums on Australian copyright law for content creators and consumers. It represents the peak bodies for professional artists and content creators working in Australia's creative industries and Australia's major copyright collecting societies, including the Australian Society of Authors, the Australian Writers' Guild and the Australian Publishers Association.

The Council advocates for the contribution of creators to Australia's culture and economy; the importance of copyright for the common good. It works to promote understanding of copyright law and its application, lobby for appropriate law reform and foster collaboration between content creators and consumers. Founded 1968.

Australian Publishers Association

60/89 Jones Street, Ultimo, NSW 2007
tel +61 (0)2 9281 9788
email office@publishers.asn.au
website www.publishers.asn.au
Twitter @AusPublish

The APA is the peak industry body for Australian book, journal and electronic publishers. Founded 1948.

Australian Writers' Guild

Level 4, 70 Pitt Street, Sydney, NSW 2000
tel +61 (0)2 9319 0339
email admin@awg.com.au
website www.awg.com.au

The professional association representing writers for stage, screen, radio and online and has protected and promoted their creative and professional interests for more than 50 years. Founded 1962.

Authors Aloud UK

72 Castle Road, St Albans, Herts. AL1 5DG
tel (01727) 893992
email info@authorsalouduk.co.uk
website www.authorsalouduk.co.uk
Facebook www.facebook.com/Authors-Aloud-UK-497942623573822
Twitter @AuthorsAloudUK
Instagram AuthorsAloudUK
Directors Naomi Cooper, Annie Everall

An author booking agency which brings together authors, illustrators, poets, storytellers and trainers with schools, libraries and festivals in the UK and Internationally, to promote enthusiasm for reading, both for enjoyment and information. Works with children's authors who wish to visit schools and libraries, in person and virtually and who are published by mainstream children's publishers. Also arranges author tours and book related events for publishers and other organisations.

Authors' Licensing and Collecting Society Ltd – see page 431

Enid Blyton Society

email tony@enidblytonsociety.co.uk
website www.enidblytonsociety.co.uk

Provides a focal point for collectors and enthusiasts of Enid Blyton through its magazine *The Enid Blyton Society Journal* (three p.a.) and the website. Founded 1995.

Book Marketing Society

email admin@bookmarketingsociety.co.uk
website www.bookmarketingsociety.co.uk
Twitter @BMSoc

Launched with the objective of becoming the representative body of marketing within the book industry. It provides a forum for sharing best practice, inspiration and creativity across the sector through regular awards and a lively programme of member meetings, development workshops, masterclasses and social events. Anyone who works for a book publisher, book retailer or book wholesaler is eligible for membership, including those working in associated areas of the publishing and book retailing industry.

Books Council of Wales/Cyngor Llyfrau Cymru

Castell Brychan, Aberystwyth, Ceredigion SY23 2JB
tel (01970) 624151
email castellbrychan@books.wales
website https://llyfrau.cymru/en/
website www.gwales.com
Ceo Helgard Krause

A national charity which supports and develops the publishing industry in Wales. It promotes literacy and reading for pleasure through a range of public campaigns, activities and events across Wales, often working in partnership with schools, libraries and other literary organisations. The Council works with publishers to nurture new talent and content in Welsh and English as well as offering specialist editing, design, marketing and distribution services. It administers grants to publishers and independent booksellers. Partly funded by the Welsh Government through Creative Wales and from the commercial operations of its wholesale book distribution centre. Founded 1961.

The Booksellers Association

6 Bell Yard, London WC2A 2JR
tel 020-7421 4640
email mail@booksellers.org.uk
website www.booksellers.org.uk
Twitter @BAbooksellers
Managing Director Meryl Halls

A membership organisation for all booksellers in the UK and Ireland, representing over 95% of bookshops. Key services include National Book Tokens and Batch Payment Services. Founded 1895.

BookTrust

G8 Battersea Studios, 80 Silverthorne Road, London SW8 3HE
tel 020-7801 8800
email query@booktrust.org.uk
website www.booktrust.org.uk
Twitter @Booktrust
Ceo Diana Gerald, *Chair of Trustees* John Coughlan

The UK's largest children's reading charity, dedicated to getting children reading because children who read are happier, healthier, more empathetic and more creative; they also do better at school. BookTrust gets children reading in lots of different ways, but its priority is to get children excited about books and stories.

BookTrust reviews at least one children's book each day and runs the Blue Peter Book Awards, Waterstones Children's Laureate, BookTrust Storytime Prize and BookTrust Lifetime Achievement Award. In 2019, it launched BookTrust Represents, a project to promote authors and illustrators of colour. See website to learn more about BookTrust's work.

BookTrust Represents

BookTrust, G8 Battersea Studios, 80 Silverthorne Road, London SW8 3HE
tel 020-7801 8826
email booktrust.represents@booktrust.org.uk
website www.booktrust.org.uk/booktrustrepresents
Twitter @Booktrust

A project to support and promote authors and illustrators of colour and to reach more readers through school visits, special events and festivals. The project also supports aspiring and new authors and illustrators of colour with training, mentoring, events and an online community. Find out more about the project and the associated research into the ethnicity of authors and illustrators in the UK on the website. Aspiring and established authors and illustrators of colour are encouraged to get in touch and join the group via email at the above address.

The British Council

Bridgewater House, 58 Whitworth Street, Manchester M1 6BB
tel 0161 957 7755
website www.britishcouncil.org
Twitter @BritishCouncil
Interim Chief Executive Kate Ewart-Biggs, *Director of Arts* Skinder Hundal

The UK's international organisation for cultural relations and educational opportunities. It builds connections, understanding and trust between people in the UK and other countries through arts and culture, education and the English language. It finds new ways of connecting with and understanding each other through the arts, to develop stronger creative sectors around the world that are better connected with the UK. Working in close collaboration with book trade associations, the Literature team participates in major international book fairs.

It works with hundreds of writers and literature partners in the UK and collaborates with offices overseas to broker relationships and create activities which link artists and cultural institutions around the world. It works with writers, publishers, producers, translators and other sector professionals across literature, publishing and education. The Visual Arts team shares UK visual arts around the world, connecting professionals internationally through collaborative exhibition programmes, digital networking, training and development and delegations. It manages and develops the British Council Collection and the British Pavilion at the Venice Biennale.

Canadian Authors Association

192 Spadina Avenue, Suite 107, Toronto, Ontario M5T 2C2
tel +1 705-955-0716
website www.canadianauthors.org
Facebook www.facebook.com/ canadianauthorsassociation
Twitter @canauthors
Executive Director Anita Purcell

A membership-based organisation for writers in all areas of the profession. Branches across Canada that provides writers with a wide variety of programmes, services and resources to help them develop their skills in the craft and business of writing. Founded 1921.

The Canadian Children's Book Centre

Suite 200, 425 Adelaide Street West Toronto, Ontario M5V 3C1
tel +1 416-975-0010
email info@bookcentre.ca
website https://bookcentre.ca
Twitter @kidsbookcentre

A national, not-for-profit organisation, that is dedicated to encouraging, promoting and supporting the reading, writing, illustrating and publishing of Canadian books for young readers. CCBC programmes, publications and resources help teachers, librarians, booksellers and parents select the very best for young readers. Founded 1976.

Canadian Publishers' Council

3080 Yonge Street, Toronto, Ontario M4N 3N1
tel +1 647-255-8880
email dswail@pubcouncil.ca
website https://pubcouncil.ca
Twitter @pubcouncil_ca
President David Swail

Represents the interests of Canadian publishing companies that publish books and other media for schools, colleges and universities, professional and reference markets, the retail and library sectors. Founded 1910.

Canadian Society of Children's Authors, Illustrators & Performers

720 Bathurst Street, Suite 503, Toronto, Ontario M5S 2R4
tel +1 416-515-1559
email office@canscaip.org
website www.canscaip.org
Twitter @CANSCAIP
Administrative Director Helena Aalto
Membership $85 p.a. member; $45 p.a. friend

CANSCAIP a membership-based non-profit organisation that supports the professional development of Canada's community of authors, illustrators and performers for children and teens. Founded 1977.

The Lewis Carroll Society

email secretary@lewiscarrollsociety.org.uk
website https://lewiscarrollsociety.org.uk
Facebook www.facebook.com/groups/68678994062
Twitter @LewisCarrollSoc
Membership £25 p.a. UK; £30 p.a. Europe; £35 p.a. elsewhere. Special rates for students and institutions

Promotes interest in the life and works of Lewis Carroll (Revd Charles Lutwidge Dodgson, 1832–98) and to encourage research. Activities include regular meetings, exhibitions and a publishing programme that includes the first annotated, unexpurgated edition of his diaries in nine volumes, the Society's journal *The Carrollian* (two p.a.), a newsletter, *Bandersnatch* (quarterly) and the *Lewis Carroll Review* (occasional). Founded 1969.

Lewis Carroll Society of North America

email secretary@lewiscarroll.org
website www.lewiscarroll.org
Facebook www.facebook.com/LCSNA
Twitter @AliceAmerica
President Linda Cassidy, *Secretary* Sandra Lee Parker
Membership $35 p.a. USA; $50 p.a. elsewhere

An organisation of Carroll admirers of all ages and interests. It is dedicated to furthering Carroll studies, increasing accessibility of research material, and maintaining public awareness of Carroll's contributions to society. The Society has a worldwide membership and meets twice a year. The Society maintains an active publication programme and members receive copies of the Society's magazine *Knight Letter*. An interest in Lewis Carroll, a simple love for Alice (or the Snark for that matter) qualifies for membership. Founded 1974.

The Center for Children's Books

501 East Daniel Street, Champaign, IL 61820, USA
tel +1 217-244-9331
email ccb-asst@illinois.edu
website https://ccb.ischool.illinois.edu
Twitter @iSchoolCCB

CCB houses a non-circulating collection of more than 16,000 recent and historically significant trade books for children, plus review copies of nearly all trade books published in the USA in the current year.

There are over 1,000 professional and reference books on the history and criticism of literature for youth, literature-based library and classroom programming, and storytelling. The collection is available for examination by scholars, teachers, librarians, students and other educators.

Centre for Literacy in Primary Education

Webber Street, London SE1 8QW
tel 020-7401 3382/3
email info@clpe.org.uk
website https://clpe.org.uk
Facebook www.facebook.com/
CentreforLiteracyinPrimaryEducation
Twitter @clpe1

The CLPE is a small independent charity working with all those involved in teaching literacy in primary schools aims to raise the achievement of children by helping schools to teach literacy more effectively and by showing teachers how quality children's literature can be placed at the heart of all learning.

Chartered Institute of Editing and Proofreading

Apsley House, 176 Upper Richmond Road, London SW15 2SH
tel 020-8785 6155
email office@ciep.uk
website www.ciep.uk
Facebook www.facebook.com/EditProof
Twitter @The_CIEP

The CIEP is a non-profit body promoting excellence in English language editing. It sets and demonstrates editorial standards, and is a community, training hub and support network for editorial professionals – the people who work to make text accurate, clear and fit for purpose. The CIEP publishes an online directory of experienced editorial professionals and also runs online courses and workshops in copyediting, proofreading and related skills, for people starting an editorial career and those wishing to broaden their competence.

As well as professional practice, training covers business skills for the self-employed. It also offers in-house training to businesses and organisations on various writing-related skills. The Institute will be instrumental in developing recognised standards of training and accreditation for editors and proofreaders. The CIEP was known as the Society for Editors and Proofreaders before being awarded its Royal Charter in 2019. It has close links with and works alongside other bodies in the publishing sector. Founded 1988.

The Children's Book Circle – see page 361

The Children's Book Council and Every Child A Reader

54 West 39th Street, 14th Floor, New York, NY 10018, USA
email cbc.info@cbcbooks.org
website www.cbcbooks.org
website www.everychildareader.net

The CBC is the non-profit trade association of North American publishers and packagers of trade books and related materials for children and young adults. Every Child a Reader is its charitable component that sponsors Children's Book Week, which celebrated 100 years in May 2019; the Children's & Teen Choice Book Awards; Get Caught Reading; and the National Ambassador of Young People's Literature, in conjunction with the Library of Congress.

The CBC offers children's publishers the opportunity to work together on educational programming, diversity advocacy, and national literacy and public awareness campaigns. The CBC connects member publishers to librarians, teachers, booksellers and caregivers across the country, providing reading lists, student resources and community outreach in coordination with prominent national organisations.

The Children's Book Council of Australia

Level 2 State Library of Queensland, Stanley Place, South Brisbane, QLD 4101
email admin@cbca.org.au
website www.cbca.org.au
Facebook www.facebook.com/theCBCA
Twitter @theCBCA

Aims to foster children's enjoyment of books through managing the Children's Book of the Year Awards; providing information on and encouragement to authors and illustrators; organising exhibitions and activities during Children's Book Week; supporting children's library services; and promoting high standards in book reviewing, along with promoting greater equity of access to reading through community projects.

The Children's Book Guild of Washington DC

website www.childrensbookguild.org
Facebook www.facebook.com/bookguilddc
Twitter @BOOKGUILDDC

A regional association of writers, artists, librarians and other specialists dedicated to the field of children's literature. Its aims are to uphold and stimulate high standards of writing and illustrating for children; to increase knowledge and use of better books for children in the community; and to cooperate with other groups having similar purposes. Founded 1945.

Children's Books Ireland

17 North Great George's Street, Dublin D01 R2F1, Republic of Ireland
tel +353 (0)1 872 7475
email info@childrensbooksireland.com
website www.childrensbooksireland.ie
Ceo Elaina Ryan, *Deputy Ceo* Jenny Murray, *Programme and Events Manager* Aoife Murray

The national children's books resource organisation of Ireland. Its mission is to make books part of every child's life. It champions and celebrates the importance of authors and illustrators and works in partnership with the people and organisations who enhance children's lives through books. Core projects include: the Children's Books Ireland International Annual Conference; the KPMG Children's Books Ireland Awards and its Junior Juries programme for school groups and book clubs; the annual Children's Books Ireland Recommended Reads, a guide to the best books of the year; nationwide Book Clinics; various book gifting initiatives including the Robert Dunbar Memorial Libraries; Bookseed and *Inis* magazine in print and online – a forum for discussion, debate and critique of Irish and international books. CBI administers the Laureate na nÓg project on behalf of the Arts Council and runs live literature events throughout the year. Founded 1996.

Children's Literature Association

3525 Piedmont Road, Building 5, Suite 300, Atlanta, Georgia 30305, USA
tel +1 630-571-4520
email info@childlitassn.org
website https://chla.memberclicks.net
Twitter @chlatweets
Membership $90 p.a. individual membership; $55 p.a. retired; $40 p.a. student; $170 p.a. institutional; $45 p.a. joint

An organisation encouraging high standards of criticism, scholarship, research and teaching in children's literature.

Contact An Author

2 Burns Close, Carshalton SM5 4PY
tel 020-8642 0884
email info@contactanauthor.com
website https://contactanauthor.co.uk
Facebook www.facebook.com/contactanauthor
Twitter @contactanauthor
Instagram contactanauthor

An author-booking agency that connects children with compassionate and creative people to enhance education. Helps schools, libraries, festivals and organisations all over the world to book authors for their events. Its mission is to celebrate books and help to arrange as many author visits as possible. Always happy for authors to join. Founded 2006.

Coram Beanstalk

Coram Campus, 41 Brunswick Square, London WC1N 1AZ
tel 020-7729 4087
website www.beanstalkcharity.org.uk
Facebook www.facebook.com/Beanstalkreads/
Twitter @beanstalkreads
Instagram beanstalkreads

Recruits, trains and supports volunteers to provide consistent, one-to-one reading support to children aged 3–13 who need help. Reading helpers give them the support they need to improve their reading skills, reading ability and confidence. Also provides training to people within the school community who want to help children learn to read for pleasure whilst improving their reading skills.

Creative Industries Federation

22 Endell Street, London WC2H 9AD
tel 020-3771 0350
website www.creativeindustriesfederation.com
Twitter @Creative_Fed

The national organisation for the UK's creative industries, cultural education and arts. Through a unique network of member organisations, influential policy and advocacy work and a UK-wide events programme it brings together the many sectors that comprise the UK's world-leading creative industries. Its membership network includes more than 10,000 individuals from creative organisations, businesses and educational institutions across the UK. Founded 2014.

Creative Scotland

Waverley Gate, 2–4 Waterloo Place, Edinburgh EH1 3EG
tel 0330 333 2000 (switchboard) / 0345 603 6000 (enquiries line)
email enquiries@creativescotland.com
website www.creativescotland.com

The public body that supports the arts, screen and creative industries across all parts of Scotland on behalf of everyone who lives, works or visits there. Through distributing funding from the Scottish Government and the National Lottery, Creative Scotland enables people and organisations to work in and experience the arts, screen and creative industries in Scotland by helping others to develop great ideas and bring them to life. Creative Scotland supports writers and publishers based in Scotland through a range of funds and initiatives.

Cwlwm Cyhoeddwyr Cymru

Elwyn Williams, Bryntirion Villa, Ffordd Penglais, Aberystwyth SY23 2EU
tel 07866 834109
email elwyn_williams@btinternet.com

Represents and promotes Welsh-language publishers. Founded 2002.

Roald Dahl's Marvellous Children's Charity

tel (01494) 890465
email enquiries@roalddahlcharity.org
website www.roalddahl.com/charity
Facebook www.facebook.com/roalddahlcharity
Twitter @RoaldDahlFund

Celebrating its 30th anniversary in 2021, the Charity helps to make life better for seriously ill children in the UK. The Roald Dahl Nurses provide support to children with serious illnesses, and their families. The Charity believes that every child should have the best possible healthcare.

The website is illustrated with the artworks of Quentin Blake, Roald Dahl's principal illustrator and President of the charity, and includes full information about the author, his life and his works.

The Roald Dahl Museum and Story Centre

website www.roalddahl.com/museum
Facebook www.facebook.com/roalddahlmuseum
Twitter @roalddahlmuseum

Houses Roald Dahl's unique archive and is situated in the Buckinghamshire village where Roald Dahl lived and worked for 36 years. The Museum features interactive galleries and the Story Centre provides activities and events to inspire young writers.

Walter de la Mare Society

email info@walterdelamare.co.uk
website www.walterdelamare.co.uk
Membership £10 p.a.

Established to promote the study and deepen the appreciation of the works of Walter de la Mare (1873–1956) through a magazine, talks, discussions and other activities. Founded 1997.

Discover Children's Story Centre

383–387 High Street, Stratford, London E15 4QZ
tel 020-8536 5555
email bookings@discover.org.uk
website https://discover.org.uk
Facebook www.facebook.com/
DiscoverChildrensStoryCentre
Twitter @Discover_Story

The UK's first hands-on creative literacy centre for children aged 0–11 years and their families, carers and teachers. Its mission is to spark children's and adults' imagination, curiosity and creativity in a magical and stimulating environment through creative play. It offers a variety of programmes including schools workshops, family art activities, a literature programme led by children's writers and illustrators, community and education projects, artist residencies in schools and training for professionals that work with children and families. Artists are commissioned to create multisensory installations and exhibitions.

Editors' and Proofreaders' Alliance of Northern Ireland

email info@epani.org.uk
website www.epani.org.uk
Twitter @epa_ni
Coordinator Averill Buchanan

Aims to establish and maintain high professional standards in editorial skills in Northern Ireland. For services for authors, see our directory of freelance professional editors, proofreaders and indexers based in Northern Ireland.

English Association

University of Leicester, University Road,
Leicester LE1 7RH
tel 0116 229 7622
email engassoc@leicester.ac.uk
website www2.le.ac.uk/offices/english-association
Chair Rob Penman

A membership body for individuals and organisations passionate about the English language and its literatures. Membership includes teachers, students, authors, writers and readers, and is made up of people and institutions from around the world. Its aim is to further the knowledge, understanding and enjoyment of English studies, and to foster good practice in their teaching and learning at all levels by:

• encouraging the study of English language, literature and creative writing;
• working towards fuller recognition of English as core to education;
• fostering discussion about methods of teaching English at all levels;
• offering timely conferences and lectures alongside a uniquely diverse and extensive portfolio of publications; and
• responding to national consultations and policy decisions about the subject.

Federation of Children's Book Groups – see page 362

Federation of European Publishers

Chaussee d'Ixelles, 29 box 4-1050, Brussels, Belgium
tel +32 2770 1110
email info@fep-fee.eu
website www.fep-fee.eu
Twitter @FEP_EU

Represents the interests of European publishers on EU affairs; informs members on the development of EU policies which could affect the publishing industry. Founded 1967.

The Gaelic Books Council/Comhairle nan Leabhraichean

32 Mansfield Street, Glasgow G11 5QP
tel 0141 337 6211

email alison@gaelicbooks.org
website www.gaelicbooks.org
Director Alison Lang

Stimulates Scottish Gaelic publishing by awarding publication grants for new books, commissions new works from established and emerging authors and provides editorial advice and guidance to Gaelic writers and publishers. Has a bookshop in Glasgow that stocks all Gaelic and Gaelic-related books in print. All stock is listed on the website.
Founded 1968.

The Greeting Card Association

United House, North Road, London N7 9DP
tel 020-7619 9266
email hello@gca.cards
website www.gca.cards
Facebook www.facebook.com/GreetingCardAssociation
Twitter @GCAUK
Instagram GCA_UK
Chief Executive Amanda Fergusson

The trade association for greeting card publishers. See website for information, including teachers' resources, lesson plans and card-making projects for children of all ages. Official magazine: *Progressive Greetings Worldwide*. Founded 1919.

Guernsey Arts Commission

Candie Museum, Candie Road, St Peter Port, Guernsey GY1 2UG
tel (01481) 709747
email info@arts.gg

The Commission's aim is to help promote, develop and support the arts in Guernsey through exhibitions, a community arts programme and public events.

House of Illustration

2 Granary Square, Kings Cross, London N1C 4BH
email info@houseofillustration.org.uk
website https://houseofillustration.org.uk/
Twitter @illustrationHQ

House of Illustration, soon to evolve in to the Quentin Blake Centre for Illustration, is the UK's centre for illustration. When it reopens at its new central London site in late 2022, it will be the world's largest public arts space dedicated to the art of illustration in all its forms. It will also become a permanent home for the archive of its founder, Sir Quentin Blake, after whom it will be renamed. Until it reopens, House of Illustration's work continues offsite and online through a series of education and events programmes and touring exhibitions.

IBBY

Nonnenweg 12, Postfach CH–4009–Basel, Switzerland
tel +41 61-272 2917

email ibby@ibby.org
website www.ibby.org
Facebook www.facebook.com/ibby.international
Twitter @IBBYINT

IBBY (the International Board on Books for Young People) is a non-profit organisation which represents an international network of people from all over the world who are committed to bringing books and children together. Its aims are:

• to promote international understanding through children's books;
• to give children everywhere the opportunity to have access to books with high literary and artistic standards;
• to encourage the publication and distribution of quality children's books, especially in developing countries;
• to provide support and training for those involved with children and children's literature; and
• to stimulate research and scholarly works in the field of children's literature.

IBBY is composed of National Sections all over the world and represents countries with well-developed book publishing and literacy programmes, and other countries with only a few dedicated professionals who are doing pioneer work in children's book publishing and promotion. Founded 1953.

IBBY UK

71 Addiscombe Court Road, Croydon CR0 6TT
website www.ibby.org.uk
Facebook www.facebook.com/IBBYUK/
Twitter @IBBYUK

IBBY (the International Board on Books for Young People) is a unique international alliance of everyone interested in children's literature including academics, librarians, publishers, booksellers, writers, illustrators, teachers, literacy workers, parents and others.

Imaginate

30B Grindlay Street, Edinburgh EH3 9AX
tel 0131 225 8050
email info@imaginate.org.uk
website www.imaginate.org.uk
Chief Executive Belinda McElhinney, *Festival Director* Noel Jordan

The national organisation in Scotland which promotes, develops and advocates for theatre and dance for children and young people. Works to enable more children in Scotland to experience work that is deeply engaging, innovative and inspiring, and believes that all children deserve the opportunity to develop their creativity, emotional intelligence and reach their true potential. Imaginate's work falls into three strands:

• The Edinburgh International Children's Festival, a celebration of the world's best theatre and dance for

young audiences, attracting 17,000 children, parents, teachers and industry professionals annually.
• A year-round programme for schools. Delivers Theatre in Schools Scotland, the national touring programme of high-quality, affordable performances for schools, in partnership with National Theatre of Scotland. Also delivers focused projects to develop children's and teachers' creativity, including a partnership with six disadvantaged Edinburgh schools.
• A year-round Creative Development Programme for artists who make theatre and dance for children. This includes projects to develop artistic practice and support productions, networking events, mentoring and a Go and See Fund.

Imaginative Book Illustration Society
email ibissec@martinsteenson.co.uk
website www.bookillustration.org
Membership enquiries Martin Steenson

IBIS was established to encourage research into, and to facilitate, the exchange of information on book and periodical illustrations, the artists and their publishers. The Society has a worldwide membership including artists, collectors, bibliographers, writers and general enthusiasts. Whilst IBIS embraces all aspects of illustrative art, the main emphasis is on the illustration of texts in English since the 1830s. Founded 1995.

Independent Publishers Guild
PO Box 12, Llain, Login SA34 0WU
tel (01437) 563335
email info@independentpublishersguild.com
website www.independentpublishersguild.com
Chief Executive Bridget Shine
Membership open to new and established publishers from all sectors and of all sizes, plus suppliers and service providers.

The IPG is the UK's largest network of publishers and has served, supported and represented independents for nearly 60 years. It delivers two popular annual conferences, a range of other events and numerous resources to help members do better business. Coordinates the Independent Publishing Awards, a mentoring scheme, collective stands at book fairs and training via the IPG Skills Hub, and provides members with weekly ebulletins, a business support helpline and special deals on publishing products and services. Due to the impact of the coronavirus outbreak, its 2020 Autumn and 2021 Spring Conferences took place virtually, featuring a wide range of speakers from across publishing and beyond. Founded 1962.

Independent Theatre Council
The Albany, Douglas Way, London SE8 4AG
tel 020-7403 1727
email admin@itc-arts.org
website www.itc-arts.org
Twitter @itc_arts

Enables the creation of high-quality professional performing arts by supporting, representing and developing the people who manage and produce it. It has around 500 members from a wide range of companies, venues and individuals in the fields of drama, dance, opera, musical theatre, puppetry, mixed media, mime, physical theatre and circus. Founded 1974.

International Authors Forum
5th Floor, Shackleton House, 4 Battle Bridge Lane, London SE1 2HX
tel 020-7264 5707
email luke.alcott@internationalauthors.org
website www.internationalauthors.org
Twitter @IntAuthors
Executive Administrator Luke Alcott

Represents authors around the world and has a membership made up of over 70 authors' organisations from every continent. Campaigns for authors' rights at the UN and national levels. Organises events, publications and collaborates with other organisations representing authors to promote the importance of creative work financially, socially and culturally. Keeps members up to date with international developments in copyright law.

International Publishers Association
23 Avenue de France, 1202 Geneva, Switzerland
tel +41 22-704 1820
email info@internationalpublishers.org
website www.internationalpublishers.org
Facebook www.facebook.com/InternationalPublishersAssociation
Twitter @IntPublishers
President Bodour Al Qasimi, *Secretary-General* José Borghino

The IPA is a federation of national, regional and international publishers associations. It promotes and protects publishing worldwide, with a focus on copyright and freedom to publish. Its membership comprises 86 organisations from 71 countries worldwide. Founded 1896.

Irish Writers Centre
19 Parnell Square, Dublin D01 E102, Republic of Ireland
tel +353 (0)1 872 1302
email info@writerscentre.ie
website https://irishwriterscentre.ie
Facebook www.facebook.com/irishwritersctr
Twitter @IrishWritersCtr
Director Valerie Bistany

The national resource centre for Irish writers, the Irish Writers Centre supports and promotes writers at all stages of their development. It runs workshops, seminars and events related to the art of writing which are run by established writers across a range of genres. It hosts professional development seminars

for writers, and provides space for writers, writing groups and other literary organisations.
Founded 1991.

The Kipling Society

Bay Tree House, Doomsday Garden, Horsham,
West Sussex RH13 6LB
tel (07801) 680516
email michaelrkipling@gmail.com
website www.kiplingsociety.co.uk
Chairman Prof. Jan Montefiore
Membership £29 p.a. UK; £31 p.a. Europe; £35 p.a
rest of world; £10 p.a. student (worldwide)

Encourages discussion and study of the work and life
of Rudyard Kipling (1865–1936) by assisting in the
study of his writings, holding discussion meetings,
publishing a quarterly journal and website (with a
Readers' Guide to Kipling's work), maintaining a
Kipling Library at Haileybury School in Hertfordshire
and running an annual story-writing competition for
primary schools.

The C.S. Lewis Society (New York)

84–23 77th Avenue, Glendale, NY 11385–7706, USA
email subscribe@nycslsociety.com
email csarrocco@aol.com
website www.nycslsociety.com
Secretary Clare Sarrocco

The oldest society for the appreciation and discussion
of C.S. Lewis (1898–1963). Founded 1969.

Literature Wales

Glyn Jones Centre, Wales Millennium Centre,
Bute Place, Cardiff CF10 5AL
tel 029-2047 2266
email post@literaturewales.org
website www.literaturewales.org
Facebook www.facebook.com/LlenCymruLitWales
Twitter @LitWales
Chief Executive Lleucu Siencyn

Literature Wales is the national company for the
development of literature in Wales. Working to
inspire communities, develop writers and celebrate
Wales' literary culture, its vision is a Wales where
literature empowers, improves and brightens lives.
Activities include the Wales Book of the Year Award,
the Children's Laureate Wales and Bardd Plant
Cymru schemes, creative writing courses at Tŷ
Newydd Writing Centre, writer's bursaries and
mentoring, the National Poet of Wales initiative, and
more. The organisation is a member of the Arts
Council of Wales' Arts Portfolio Wales.

Little Theatre Guild of Great Britain

tel (01207) 545280
email caroline.chapman1816@gmail.com
website www.littletheatreguild.org
Secretary Caroline Chapman

Promotes closer cooperation amongst the little
theatres constituting its membership, acts as a
coordinating and representative body on behalf of the
little theatres, maintains and advances the highest
standards in the art of theatre, and assists in
encouraging the establishment of other little theatres.

LoveReading4Kids

PTC International Ltd, Turnbridge Mills,
Quay Street, Huddersfield HD1 6QT
tel 020-3004 7204
website www.lovereading4kids.co.uk
Facebook www.facebook.com/lovereading4kids
Twitter @lovereadingkids

A book recommendation site for children's books
ranging from toddlers to teens and ensures that
whatever their age or interest, there is a steady stream
of book recommendations available. Offers a variety
of free services for parents and anyone who is
interested in buying the best books for boys and girls
of all ages. Supports parents, teachers and school
librarians in helping engender a lifelong love of
reading in children. The website features Kids' Zone,
an area designed specifically for children, with
competitions, quizzes and book-related material.
Founded 2005.

LoveReading4Schools

PTC International Ltd, Turnbridge Mills,
Quay Street, Huddersfield HD1 6QT
tel 020-3004 7204
website www.lovereading4schools.co.uk
Facebook www.facebook.com/lovereading4schools
Twitter @lr4schools

A book recommendation website which promotes a
love of books and reading to all by offering the tools,
advice and information needed to help members and
browsers to find their next book, including time-
strapped teachers and librarians in schools to help
engender a lifelong love of reading in their students.
Publishes book lists of relevance to schools including
lists of inspirational books, cultural books, reluctant
readers recommendations and books related to
mental health and wellbeing.

Magazines Canada

Mailbox 201, 555 Richmond Street West, Suite 604,
Toronto, Ontario M5V 3B1
tel +1 416-994-6471
email info@magazinescanada.ca
website www.magazinescanada.ca
Twitter @magscanada
Executive Director Melanie Rutledge

The national trade association representing Canadian
consumer, cultural, speciality, professional and
business media magazines.

The Mythopoeic Society

website www.mythsoc.org

A non-profit international literary and educational
organisation for the study, discussion and enjoyment

of fantastic and mythic literature, especially the works of Tolkien, C.S. Lewis and Charles Williams. 'Mythopoeic' (myth-oh-PAY-ik or myth-oh-PEE-ik) means 'mythmaking' or 'productive of myth' and aptly describes much of the fictional work of the three authors who were also prominent members of an informal Oxford literary circle (1930s–50s) known as the Inklings. Membership is open to all scholars, writers and readers of these literatures. The Society sponsors three periodicals: *Mythprint* (a bulletin of book reviews, articles and events), *Mythlore* (scholarly articles on mythic and fantastic literature), and *Mythic Circle* (a literary annual of original poetry and short stories). Each summer the Society holds an annual conference, Mythcon. Founded 1967.

National Association for the Teaching of English

Office 6, 197–201 Manchester Road, Altrincham, Manchester WA14 5NU
tel 0330 333 5050
email admin@nate.org.uk
website www.nate.org.uk
Twitter @Natefeed

NATE is an educational charity that works to: promote standards of excellence in the teaching of English from early years to university; promote innovative and original ideas that have practical classroom outcomes; support teachers' professional development through access to current research, publications and national and regional conferences; provide an informed national voice on matters concerning the teaching of English and its related subjects; and encourage sharing and collaboration between teachers and learners of English and its related subjects. Founded 1963.

National Association of Writers' Groups

Old Vicarage, Scammonden, Huddersfield HD3 3FT
email info@nawg.co.uk
website www.nawg.co.uk
Facebook www.facebook.com/NAWGNews
Twitter @NAWGnews
Secretary Chris Huck
Membership £50 p.a. per group; £25 p.a. individuals

NAWG aims to advance the education of the general public throughout the UK, including the Channel Islands, by promoting the study and art of writing in all its aspects. Publishes *LNK*, a bi-monthly magazine. Festival of Writing held annually in August/ September. New members always welcome. Founded 1995.

National Association of Writers in Education

Tower House, Mill Lane, off Askham Fields Lane, Askham Bryan, York YO23 3FS
tel 0330 333 5909
email admin@nawe.co.uk
website www.nawe.co.uk
Twitter @NaweWriters

National membership organisation which aims to further knowledge, understanding and enjoyment of creative writing and to support good practice in its teaching and learning at all levels. NAWE promotes creative writing as both a distinct discipline and an essential element in education generally. Its membership includes those working in Higher Education, the many freelance writers working in schools and community contexts, and the teachers and other professionals who work with them. It runs a national database of writers, produces a weekly opportunities bulletin, publishes two journals – *Writing in Education* and *Writing in Practice* – and holds a national conference. Professional membership includes public liability insurance cover.

National Centre for Research in Children's Literature

website www.roehampton.ac.uk/research-centres/ national-centre-for-research-in-childrens-literature
website https://ncrcl.wordpress.com/
Twitter @NCRCL

NCRCL members work on a range of projects related to children's literature and the culture of childhood, publishing in such diverse areas as: ethics and metaphysics; adolescent fiction; memories of childhood reading; the Robinsonade; Romantic childhood; print culture; graphic novels; and the literature of food. News of regular conferences and events hosted by the NCRCL can be found on the NCRCL Blog. Founded 1995.

National Centre for Writing

Dragon Hall, 115–123 King Street, Norwich NR1 1QE
email info@nationalcentreforwriting.org.uk
website https://nationalcentreforwriting.org.uk
Facebook www.facebook.com/ NationalCentreforWriting
Twitter @WritersCentre

Celebrates and explores the artistic and social power of creative writing and literary translation. An ongoing programme of innovative collaborations engages writers, literary translators and readers in projects that support new voices and new stories and respond to the rapidly changing world of writing. Based at the historic Dragon Hall in Norwich, where workshops and mentoring are regularly available for writers at all levels, both face-to-face and online. Projects range from major international partnerships to vibrant festivals such as the Noirwich Crime Writing Festival and the Norfolk & Norwich Festival. Founded 2018.

National Literacy Trust – see page 364

National Society for Education in Art and Design

3 Masons Wharf, Potley Lane, Corsham, Wilts. SN13 9FY
tel (01225) 810134
email info@nsead.org
website www.nsead.org
Twitter @NSEAD1
General Secretary Michele Gregson

The leading national authority concerned with art, craft and design across all phases of education in the UK. Offers the benefits of membership of a professional association, a learned society and a trade union. Has representatives on national and regional committees concerned with art and design education. Publishes *International Journal of Art and Design Education* online (three p.a.; Wiley Blackwell) and *AD* magazine for teachers. Founded 1888.

The Edith Nesbit Society

21 Churchfields, West Malling, Kent ME19 6RJ
email edithnesbit@gmail.com
website www.edithnesbit.co.uk
Membership £10 p.a. individual; £12 p.a. joint; £15 p.a. organisations

Promotes an interest in the life and works of Edith Nesbit (1858–1924) by means of talks, a regular newsletter and other publications, and visits to places associated with her. Founded 1996.

New Writing North

3 Ellison Terrace, Ellison Place, Newcastle upon Tyne NE1 8ST
email office@newwritingnorth.com
website https://newwritingnorth.com
Facebook www.facebook.com/newwritingnorth
Twitter @NewWritingNorth

Supports writing and reading in the North of England. Commissions new work, creates development opportunities and nurtures talent. Founded 1996.

New Zealand Association of Literary Agents

PO Box 6292, Dunedin North 9059
email tfs@elseware.co.nz
website www.elseware.co.nz/NZALA/Index.htm

Set up to establish standards and guidelines for literary agents operating in New Zealand. All members subscribe to a code of ethics which includes working on commission and not charging upfront fees for promotion or manuscript reading.

Newcastle University Library

Philip Robinson Library, Jesmond Road West, Newcastle upon Tyne NE2 4HQ
tel 0191 208 7662
email libraryhelp@ncl.ac.uk
website www.ncl.ac.uk/library
Facebook www.facebook.com/NULibraries
Twitter @nclroblib

A modern academic library with multi-disciplinary collections, including historical children's books. The Library's Special Collections hold many unique archives and rare books. These materials provide great scope for original research for many subject areas and the potential to complement teaching and learning at the university. There are a number of collections and archives dedicated to children's literature. See website for details.

The Office for Standards in Education, Children's Services and Skills

Piccadilly Gate, Store Street, Manchester M1 2WD
tel 0300 123 1231
email enquiries@ofsted.gov.uk
website www.gov.uk/ofsted

Ofsted is a non-ministerial government department. It regulates and inspects to achieve excellence in the care of children and young people, and in education and skills for learners of all ages. It regulates and inspects childcare and children's social care, and inspects the Children and Family Court Advisory and Support Service (Cafcass), schools, colleges, initial teacher training, further education and skills, adult and community learning, and education and training in prisons and other secure establishments. It assesses council children's services, and inspects services for looked after children, safeguarding and child protection.

Owned Voices

website https://ownedvoices.com/
Facebook www.facebook.com/OwnedVoices
Twitter @OwnedVoices
Instagram ownedvoices

Creative writing workshop created specifically for writers from backgrounds traditionally underrepresented in publishing including BAME, working class, LGBTQ+ writers, or writers with disabilities.

Paper Nations

email writers@papernations.org
website https://papernations.org/
Facebook www.facebook.com/papernationsuk
Twitter @PaperNationsUK

A creative writing incubator nurturing communities and creating partnerships to build an inclusive literary ecology. They commission writers in the South West of England to create new work, with particular focus on establishing creative writing opportunities for children and young people, and have recently launched 'Writing for All' programme, for writers of all ages and backgrounds. Founded 2016.

Pathways Into Children's Publishing

Pop Up Projects, 5 City Garden Row,
London N1 8DW
email pathways@pop-up.org.uk
website https://pathways-org.com
Facebook www.facebook.com/PathwaysINTO
Twitter @PathwaysINTO

A ground-breaking two-year illustration programme
for a diverse group of talented and ambitious artists
who want to be the next generation of children's
illustrators. The programme is designed and
organised by Pop Up Projects and House of
Illustration, with support from over 20 publishers
and UK university affiliates. To find out more about
Pathways, contact Ibrahim at the email address
above.

Pen to Print

tel 020-8227 2267
email pentoprint@lbbd.gov.uk
website https://pentoprint.org/
Facebook www.facebook.com/OfficialPentoPrint
Twitter @Pen_to_Print
Instagram officialpentoprint

A free writer development programme based in
libraries. As an Arts Council-funded programme, it
provides a safe, collaborative environment to develop
writers' authentic voices. Aspiring writers are
encouraged to reach communities with their stories
reflecting not just their own journeys but also
inspiring potential in others. Free activities include:

• classes and workshops;
• competitions including The Book Challenge;
• author talks;
• ReadFest literary festival;
• *Write On!* magazine

PICSEL (Picture Industry Collecting Society for Effective Licensing)

112 Western Road, Brighton, East Sussex BN1 2AB
tel (01273) 746564
email info@picsel.org.uk
website www.picsel.org.uk

A not-for-profit collecting society that ensures that all
visual artists, creators and representative rights
holders of images receive fair payment for various
secondary uses of their works. It works to ensure that
all licence fees collected are distributed equitably,
efficiently and in a transparent manner.
Founded 2016.

The Poetry Book Society – see page 222

The Poetry Society – see page 222

Poetry Society Education – see page 226

Pop Up Projects

5 Paper Mill Buildings, City Garden Row,
London N1 8DW

email info@pop-up.org.uk
website www.pop-up.org.uk
Facebook www.facebook.com/popupfestival
Twitter @PopUpFestival

A not-for-profit community interest company which
works with educational, literary and cultural
organisations on projects and literature programmes
that enable children, empower teachers and engage
families from all walks of life to read more widely,
write more creatively and develop visual storytelling
skills. To find out more about the Pop Up Festival,
bespoke projects for schools or professional
development opportunities, contact education@pop-
up.org.uk. Founded 2011.

The Beatrix Potter Society

email info@beatrixpottersociety.org.uk
website www.beatrixpottersociety.org.uk

Promotes the study and appreciation of the life and
works of Beatrix Potter (1866–1943) as author, artist,
diarist, farmer and conservationist. Regular lecture
meetings, conferences and events in the UK and USA.
Quarterly newsletter. Small publishing programme.
Founded 1980.

The Publishers Association

First Floor, 50 Southwark Street, London SE1 1UN
tel 020-7378 0504
email mail@publishers.org.uk
website www.publishers.org.uk
Twitter @PublishersAssoc
President David Shelley, *Ceo* Stephen Lotinga

A member organisation for UK publishing,
representing companies of all sizes and specialisms –
including children's books. Their members produce
digital and print books, research journals and
educational resources across genres and subjects. The
Publishers Association exists to champion publishing
to the wider world and to provide their members
with everything they need to thrive. They have helped
change laws, improved business conditions and
inspired people to become publishers. Founded 1896.

Publishers Association of New Zealand

Level 6, 19 Como Street, Takapuna, Auckland 0622
tel +64 (0)9 280 3213
email admin@publishers.org.nz
website www.publishers.org.nz
Twitter @Publishers_NZ

PANZ represents book, educational and digital
publishers in New Zealand. Members include both
the largest international publishers and companies in
the independent publishing community.

Publishing Ireland/Foilsiú Éireann

63 Patrick Street, Dun Laoghaire, Dublin A96 WF25,
Republic of Ireland
tel +353 (0)1 639 4868

email info@publishingireland.com
website www.publishingireland.com
Facebook www.facebook.com/PublishingIreland
Twitter @PublishingIRL
General Manager Orla McLoughlin

Publishing Ireland enables publishers to share expertise and resources in order to benefit from opportunities and solve problems that are of common concern to all. It comprises most of the major publishing houses in Ireland with a mixture of trade, general and academic publishers as members. Founded 1970.

Publishing Scotland

Scott House, 10 South St Andrew Street, Edinburgh EH2 2AZ
tel 0131 228 6866
email enquiries@publishingscotland.org
website www.publishingscotland.org
Chief Executive Marion Sinclair

A network for trade, training and development in the Scottish publishing industry. Founded 1973.

The Arthur Ransome Society Ltd

Abbot Hall Art Gallery & Lakeland Museum, Kendal, Cumbria LA9 5AL
website www.arthur-ransome.org

Exists to celebrate the life, promote the works and diffuse the ideas of Arthur Ransome (1884–1967), author of the world-famous *Swallows and Amazons* series of books for children. The Society seeks in particular to encourage children and others to engage, with due regard to safety, in adventurous pursuits; educate the public generally about Ransome and his work; sponsor research in relevant areas; be a communications link for those interested in any aspect of Arthur Ransome's life and works. Founded 1990.

Read for Good

26 Nailsworth Mills, Avening Road, Nailsworth, Glos. GL6 0BS
tel (01453) 839005
email reading@readforgood.org
website www.readforgood.org
Facebook www.facebook.com/readforgood
Twitter @ReadforGoodUK

The organisation aims for all children in the UK to be given the opportunity, space and motivation to develop their own love of reading, benefiting them throughout their lives. Many studies show that reading changes lives: from educational outcomes and social mobility to emotional wellbeing. Runs a readathon programme in 3,000 schools and a hospital programme, which focuses on the supply of books and storyteller visits to brighten up the days of 150,000 children in the UK's main children's hospitals.

The Reading Agency

email info@readingagency.org.uk
website www.readingagency.org.uk
Twitter @readingagency

A charity whose mission is to tackle life's big challenges through the proven power of reading. Works closely with public libraries, publishers, health partners and volunteers to bring reading programmes to children across the UK. Funded by Arts Council England, The Reading Agency supports a wide range of reading initiatives for children including the Summer Reading Challenge, run in partnership with libraries, which helps get around three-quarters of a million children into libraries each year; and Chatterbooks reading clubs, which help children build a lifelong reading habit.

RNIB National Library Service

tel 0303 123 9999
website www.rniblibrary.com
website https://readingservices.rnib.org.uk

The largest specialist library for readers with sight loss in the UK. It offers a comprehensive range of books and accessible information for children and adults in braille and Talking Books. Books are also available for download in audio and braille from RNIB Reading Services.

The Malcolm Saville Society

11 Minster Court, Windsor Close, Taunton TA1 4LW
email mystery@witchend.com
website www.witchend.com
Facebook www.facebook.com/MalcolmSaville
Twitter @MSavilleSociety
Membership £15 p.a. UK; £17.50 p.a. Europe; £21 p.a. elsewhere

Promotes interest in the work of children's author Malcolm Saville (1901–82). Regular social activities, library, contact directory and magazine (four p.a.). Founded 1994.

Scattered Authors' Society

email scatteredauthorssociety@gmail.com
website www.scatteredauthors.org

Provides a forum for informal discussion, contact and support for professional writers in children's fiction. Founded 1998.

School Library Association

1 Pine Court, Kembrey Park, Swindon SN2 8AD
tel (01793) 530166
email info@sla.org.uk
website www.sla.org.uk
Facebook www.facebook.com/schoollibraryassociation
Twitter @uksla

The SLA is a UK-focused charity which supports everyone involved in school libraries. It believes that every pupil is entitled to effective school library provision and the educational, emotional and developmental benefits that come with it. Provides training, networking and an information service, publishes guidelines for school library and resource centres, book lists and a quarterly journal which includes current book and digital resources for all school-age children.

Scottish Book Trust

Sandeman House, Trunk's Close, 55 High Street, Edinburgh EH1 1SR
tel 0131 524 0160
email info@scottishbooktrust.com
website www.scottishbooktrust.com
Facebook www.facebook.com/scottishbktrust
Twitter @ScottishBkTrust

Scotland's national agency for the promotion of reading, writing and literature. Programmes include: Bookbug, a free universal book-gifting programme which encourages families to read with their children from birth; an ambitious schools programme including national tours, the virtual events programme Authors Live and the Bookbug Picture Book Prize; the Scottish Teenage Book Prize; the Live Literature funding programme, a national initiative enabling Scottish citizens to engage with authors, playwrights, poets, storytellers and illustrators; a writer development programme, offering mentoring and professional development for emerging and established writers; and a readership development programme featuring a national writing campaign, as well as Book Week Scotland, during the last week in November. Founded 1998.

Scottish Storytelling Forum

Scottish Storytelling Centre, 43–45 High Street, Edinburgh EH1 1SR
tel 0131 556 9579
email reception@scottishstorytellingcentre.com
website www.scottishstorytellingcentre.com
website www.storytellingforum.co.uk
Facebook www.facebook.com/ScotStoryForum
Twitter @ScotStoryCentre, @scotstoryforum

Scotland's national charity for oral storytelling, established to encourage and support the telling and sharing of stories across all ages and sectors of society, in particular those who, for reasons of poverty or disability, are sometimes excluded from artistic experiences. The Scottish Storytelling Centre is the Forum's resource and training centre which presents a year-round programme of storytelling and traditional arts events, workshops and the Scottish International Storytelling Festival in the autumn. The Storytelling Network has over 150 professional storytellers across Scotland. Founded 1992.

Seven Stories – The National Centre for Children's Books – see page 359

Society for Storytelling (SfS)

c/o Paul Jackson, 43 Britannia Road, Norwich NR1 4HP
tel 07775 068886
email membership@sfs.org.uk
website www.sfs.org.uk
Facebook www.facebook.com/societyforstorytelling/
Twitter @sfs_uk

SfS provides information on oral storytelling, events, storytellers and traditional stories. Its volunteers have specialist knowledge of storytelling in education, health, therapy and business settings. To increase public awareness of the art of storytelling it promotes National Storytelling Week. The SfS provides a network for anyone interested in the art of oral storytelling whether they are full-time storytellers, use storytelling in their work, tell stories for the love of it or just want to listen. It holds an annual conference and produces a quarterly newsletter. Founded 1993.

Society of Artists Agents

website https://saahub.com
Twitter @SaaAgents

Formed to promote professionalism in the illustration industry and to forge closer links between clients and artists through an agreed set of guidelines. The Society believes in an ethical approach through proper terms and conditions, thereby protecting the interests of the artists and clients. Founded 1992.

The Society of Authors – see page 349

Society of Children's Book Writers and Illustrators (SCBWI) – see page 356

Society of Editors

University Centre, Granta Place, Mill Lane, Cambridge CB2 1RU
tel (01223) 304080
email office@societyofeditors.org
website www.societyofeditors.org
President Alison Gow
Membership up to £230 p.a. depending on category

Formed from the merger of the Guild of Editors and the Association of British Editors, the Society of Editors has members in national, regional and local newspapers, magazines, broadcasting and digital media, journalism education and media law. It campaigns for media freedom, self regulation, the public's right to know and the maintenance of standards in journalism.

Society of Young Publishers

c/o The Publishers Association, First Floor, 50 Southwark Street, London SE1 1UN
email sypchair@thesyp.org.uk
website www.thesyp.org.uk
Twitter @SYP_UK

Twitter @SYPIreland, @SYP_LDN, @SYPNorth, @Oxford_SYP, @SYPScotland, @SYP_SouthWest
Membership £30 p.a. employed standard; £24 p.a. student/unemployed; £18 p.a. digital membership

Supports those of any age looking to get into publishing, or those within the first ten years of their career who are looking to get ahead. The SYP is made up of six regional committees (Ireland, London, North, Oxford, Scotland and South West), and a UK team responsible for the organisation's oversight. These committees organise mentorship schemes for current and aspiring publishers based in the UK and Ireland. Two annual conferences are held, as well as numerous in-person and digital events each month – including socials, career panels, and more. The website is routinely updated with articles and guides on how to progress in the publishing industry. Founded 1949.

Speaking of Books

44 Blackheath Park, London SE3 9SJ
tel 07931 929325
email jan@speakingofbooks.co.uk
website www.speakingofbooks.co.uk
Twitter @speakingofbks

Arranges school visits by writers, illustrators, poets and storytellers, plus other high-quality speakers and workshop facilitators. Also Inset days relating to literacy and the arts.

Spread the Word

The Albany, Douglas Way, London SE8 4AG
tel 020-8692 0231 ext. 249
email hello@spreadtheword.org.uk
website www.spreadtheword.org.uk
Facebook www.facebook.com/spreadthewordwriters
Twitter @STWevents
Instagram spreadthewordwriters

London's writer development agency, helping writers make their mark on the page, the screen and in the world. Kick-starts the careers of London's best new writers, and energetically campaigns to ensure mainstream publishing truly reflects the diversity of the city. Supports the creative and professional development of talent, by engaging those already interested in literature and those who will be, and by advocating on behalf of both.

The Robert Louis Stevenson Club

website https://robert-louis-stevenson.org/rls-club/

Aims to foster interest in Robert Louis Stevenson's life (1850–94) and works through various events and its newsletter. Founded 1920.

The Story Museum

42 Pembroke Street, Oxford OX1 1BP
tel (01865) 807600
email hello@storymuseum.org.uk
website www.storymuseum.org.uk
Facebook www.facebook.com/TheStoryMuseum
Twitter @TheStoryMuseum

The Story Museum celebrates story in all forms and explores their enduring power to teach and delight. It aims to inspire present and future generations by providing great ways of engaging with great stories. Also runs an active education and outreach programme alongside exhibition and events. The Museum fully reopened in October 2020 following a £6m major redevelopment project with nine new story-themed gallery and activity spaces including a flexible performance space.

Story Therapy CIC

1 Sugworth Lane, Radley, Abingdon-on-Thames, Oxon OX14 2HZ
email admin@storytherapyresources.co.uk
website www.storytherapyresources.co.uk
Facebook www.facebook.com/storytherapy
Twitter @StoryTherapy
Contact Hilary Hawkes

A non-profit social enterprise creating resources, especially story-themed resources, that support children's emotional health and mental wellbeing. Founded 2016.

The Swedish Institute for Children's Books

email info@barnboksinstitutet.se
website www.barnboksinstitutet.se

Svenska barnboksinstitutet is a research and information centre for children's and young adult literature with a special library open to the public. Founded 1965.

The Tolkien Society

website www.tolkiensociety.org
Facebook www.facebook.com/TolkienSociety
Twitter @TolkienSociety
YouTube The Tolkien Society
Membership £30 p.a. online or £10 p.a. students; Postal: £30 p.a. UK; £35 p.a. EU; £45 p.a. rest of world; for family membership, add £15 p.a.

An educational charity and literary society devoted to the study and promotion of the life and works of J.R.R. Tolkien.

United Kingdom Literacy Association

Room 9 c/o VAL, 9 Newarke Street, Leicester LE1 5SN
tel 0116 254 4116
website www.ukla.org
Twitter @The_UKLA

UKLA is a registered charity, which has as its sole object the advancement of education in literacy. It is committed to promoting good practice nationally and internationally in literacy and language teaching and research. Founded in 1963.

V&A Museum of Childhood

Cambridge Heath Road, London E2 9PA
tel 020-8983 5200

email moc@vam.ac.uk
website www.vam.ac.uk/info/transforming-the-va-museum-of-childhood
Facebook www.facebook.com/museumchildhood
Twitter @MuseumChildhood

Holds one of the largest and oldest collections of toys and childhood artefacts in the world. As well as its permanent displays, the museum has temporary exhibitions, workshops and activities for all. Closed until 2022 for refurbishment.

Voice of the Listener & Viewer

The Old Rectory Business Centre, Springhead Road, Northfleet DA11 8HN
tel (01474) 338716
email info@vlv.org.uk
website www.vlv.org.uk
Facebook www.facebook.com/VLVUK
Twitter @vlvuk
Administrator Sarah Stapylton-Smith
Membership From £30 p.a. Academic, corporate and student rates available

VLV's mission is to campaign for accountability, diversity and excellence in UK broadcasting, seeking to sustain and strengthen public service broadcasting to the benefit of civil society and democracy in the UK. It holds regular conferences and seminars and publishes a bulletin and an e-newsletter. Founded 1983.

Writers Advice Centre for Children's Books

Shakespeare House, 168 Lavender Hill, London SW11 5TG
tel 020-7801 6300
email info@writersadvice.co.uk
website www.writersadvice.co.uk
Facebook www.facebook.com/writersadvice
Twitter @writersadvice
Managing Editor Louise Jordan

Dedicated to helping new and published children's writers by offering both editorial advice and tips on how to get published. The Centre also runs

workshops, an online children's writing correspondence course and publishes a small list of its own under the name of Wacky Bee Books (www.wackybeebooks.com). Founded 1994.

WGGB (Writers' Guild of Great Britain) – see page 352

Young at Art

Cotton Court, 30–42 Waring Street, Belfast BT1 2ED
tel 028-9023 0660
website www.youngatart.co.uk
Twitter @Young_at_Art

Coordinates the annual Belfast Children's Festival as well as a wide variety of projects that encourage children and young people to enjoy the arts, develop awareness of its impact on their lives, and have a say in what their arts provision should be. These include engagement programmes, workshop programmes, commissions, seminars, training, research and online resources. Founded 2000.

Youth Libraries Group

CILIP, 7 Ridgmount Street, London WC1E 7AE
email secretary.YLG@cilip.org.uk
website www.cilip.org.uk/ylg
Twitter @youthlibraries
Secretary Sue Polchow

YLG is open to all members of the Chartered Institute for Library and Information Professionals (CILIP) who are interested in children's work. At a national level its aims are:

• to influence the provision of library services for children and the provision of quality literature;
• to inspire and support all librarians working with children and young people;
• to liaise with other national professional organisations in pursuit of such aims.

At a local level, the YLG organises regular training courses, supports professional development and provides opportunities to meet colleagues. It holds an annual conference and judges the CILIP Carnegie and Kate Greenaway Awards (see page 387).

Societies, prizes and festivals

Children's book and illustration prizes and awards

This list provides details of prizes, competitions and awards relevant to children's writers and artists.

⚠ Awards presentations and ceremonies may not go ahead in their usual way due to coronavirus restrictions.

Academy of British Cover Design: Annual Cover Design Competition

website https://abcoverd.co.uk
Twitter @ABCoverD

This annual competition awards covers produced for any book published between 1 January and 31 December each year, by any designer in the UK, for a UK or overseas publisher. Ebooks are eligible. Designers may enter their own work or the work of other designers. There are ten categories: children's, young adult, science fiction/fantasy, mass market, literary fiction, crime/thriller, non-fiction, series design, classic/reissue and women's fiction. A cover can only be submitted in one category unless it is entered as an individual cover and again as part of a series design. Entry is free.

ALCS Educational Writers' Award

The Society of Authors, 24 Bedford Row, London WC1R 4EH
tel 020-7373 6642
email prizes@societyofauthors.org
website www.societyofauthors.org/ALCS-award

This is an annual award alternating each year between books in the 5–11 and 11–18 age groups. It is given to an outstanding example of traditionally published non-fiction (with or without illustrations) that stimulates and enhances learning. The work must have been first published in the UK, in the English language, within the previous two calendar years.

The Alligator's Mouth Award for Illustrated Early Fiction

2A Church Court, Richmond, Surrey TW9 1JL
tel 020-8948 6775
email award@thealligatorsmouth.co.uk
website www.thealligatorsmouth.co.uk/award

Celebrating its third year in 2021, this award celebrates highly illustrated early fiction. The award is open to books published in the UK in English from the last year for readers aged 6–8, which have illustrations on the majority of the internal spreads. To enter the awards, publishers are invited to submit highly illustrated children's books which have been published between 1 October and 30 September each year. Longlist announced in March. Entry form, submissions criteria and entry rules can be downloaded from the website. The winner of the prize receives The Alligator's Mouth Award trophy. 2020 winner: Adam Stower for *King Coo: The Curse of the Mummy's Gold* (David Fickling Books).

The Hans Christian Andersen Awards

International Board on Books for Young People, Nonnenweg 12, Postfach CH–4009 Basel, Switzerland
tel +41 61 272 2917
email ibby@ibby.org
website www.ibby.org
Facebook www.facebook.com/ibby.international
Twitter @IBBYINT

This Award is the highest international recognition given to an author and an illustrator of children's books. Given every other year by IBBY, the awards recognise lifelong achievement and are presented to an author and an illustrator whose complete works have made an important, lasting contribution to children's literature. The selection criteria include the aesthetic and literary qualities of writing and illustrating, as well as the ability to see things from the child's point of view and the ability to stretch the child's curiosity and imagination. The complete works of the author and of the illustrator are taken into consideration. The Author's Award has been given since 1956 and the Illustrator's Award since 1966.

Association for Library Service to Children Awards

American Library Association, 225 N Michigan Ave, Suite 1300, Chicago, IL 60601, USA
tel +1 800-545-2433 ext. 2163
email alsc@ala.org
website www.ala.org/alsc/awardsgrants/bookmedia
Facebook www.facebook.com/Associationforlibraryservicetochildren
Twitter @wearealsc

The following awards are administered by ALSC:

• The Caldecott Medal (named in honour of the 19th-century English illustrator Randolph Caldecott) is awarded annually to the artist of the most distinguished US picture book for children.
• The Newbery Medal (named after the 18th-century British bookseller John Newbery) is awarded annually

to the author of the most distinguished contribution to US literature for children.

• The Geisel Medal (named after the world-renowned children's author a.k.a. Dr Seuss) is given annually to the author(s) and illustrator(s) of the most distinguished contribution to the body of children's literature known as beginning reader books published in the USA during the preceding year.

• The Robert F. Sibert Informational Book Medal is given annually to the author of the most distinguished informational book published in English during the preceding year.

• The Children's Literature Legacy Award honours authors and illustrators published in the US whose books have made a substantial and lasting contribution to literature for children.

• The Excellence in Early Learning Digital Media Award is given to a digital media producer that has created distinguished digital media for an early learning audience.

• The Batchelder Award is awarded annually to an outstanding children's book translated from a language other than English and originally published in a country other than the United States.

• The Belpré Awards are presented annually to a Latino/Latina writer and illustrator whose work best portrays, affirms and celebrates the Latino cultural experience.

• The Odyssey Award is given for the best audio book produced for children and/or young adults. Co-administered with YALSA and Booklist.

Bardd Plant Cymru (Welsh-Language Children's Poet Laureate)

Books Council of Wales, Castell Brychan, Aberystwyth, Ceredigion SY23 2JB
tel (01970) 624151
email castellbrychan@books.wales
website https://llyfrau.cymru/en/

Aims to raise the profile of poetry amongst children and to encourage them to compose and enjoy poetry. During his/her term of office the bard will visit schools as well as help children to create poetry through electronic workshops. The scheme's partner organisations are: S4C, the Welsh Government, the Books Council of Wales, Urdd Gobaith Cymru and Literature Wales.

J.M. Barrie Award

email admin@childrensarts.org.uk
website www.childrensarts.org.uk/celebrate
Twitter @childrensarts

The Action for Children's Arts J.M. Barrie Award is given annually to a children's arts practitioner or organisation for a lifetime's achievement in delighting children whose work, in the view of the trustees, will stand the test of time. 2020 winner: Anna Home OBE.

The Bath Children's Novel Award

PO Box 5223, Bath BA1 0UR
email info@bathnovelaward.co.uk
website www.bathnovelaward.co.uk
Twitter @bathnovelaward

This annual international prize is for unpublished or independently published writers of novels for children or young adults. Submissions: first 5,000 words plus one-page synopsis. Entries open June until November. Entry fee: £28 per novel with sponsored places available for low-income writers. Children and teenagers vote for the shortlist, with the winner chosen by a literary agent. Prize: £3,000 plus introductions to literary agents.

BBC Young Writers' Award

website www.bbc.co.uk/ywa

With Cambridge University, this award seeks out writers between 14–18 who submit a story of no more than 1,000 words on any topic they choose. The winner will have their story broadcast on the BBC and published in an anthology, and will receive a personalised mentoring session with an author. Entry is by online form.

The James Berry Poetry Prize

Newcastle Centre for the Literary Arts, Percy Building, Newcastle University, Newcastle upon Tyne NE1 7RU
tel 0191 208 7787
email jamesberrypoetryprize@gmail.com
website www.ncl.ac.uk/ncla/james-berry/#theprize

Newcastle University's Centre for Literary Arts (NCLA) and Bloodaxe Books are working in partnership to award three equal winners a £1,000 cash prize, with mentoring and a debut collection published by Bloodaxe. Open to poets of colour who have not published a book-length collection, with special consideration given to LGBTQ+/disabled poets and poets from disadvantaged socio-economic backgrounds. See website for entry criteria. Founded 2021.

Blue Peter Book Awards

BookTrust, G8 Battersea Studios, 80 Silverthorne Road, London SW8 3HE
tel 020-7801 8843
email bluepeter@booktrust.org.uk
website www.booktrust.org.uk/books/awards-and-prizes

Awarded annually, winners are shortlisted by a panel of expert adult judges, then a group of young *Blue Peter* viewers judge the two categories, which are: the Best Story and the Best Book with Facts. Winning books are announced on *Blue Peter* in March. Founded 2000.

International Award for Illustration Bologna Children's Book Fair – Fundación SM

email illustratori@bolognafiere.it
website www.bolognachildrensbookfair.com

The aim of the award is to support the illustration work of young artists, the special quality of whose work has yet to be acknowledged. This annual award is granted to one of the young illustrators selected each year from the Bologna Children's Book Fair Illustrators Exhibition. Founded 2009.

BolognaRagazzi Award

Piazza Costituzione 6, 40128 Bologna, Italy
tel +39 051-282111
email bolognaragazziaward@bolognafiere.it
website www.bolognachildrensbookfair.com/
highlights/premi/bolognaragazzi-award
Facebook www.facebook.com/
BolognaChildrensBookFair
Twitter @BoChildrensBook

One of the world's most highly regarded international prizes in the sector of children's publishing, it celebrates the finest illustrated children's books and honours the best productions in terms of their graphic and editorial qualities, providing an international launch pad for authors and illustrators thanks to the high profile recognition that the winners receive during the fair. There are four main award categories: Fiction, Non-fiction, Opera Prima (for unpublished authors and illustrators) and, from 2020, the new permanent category, Comics, divided into three sections: Early Reader, Middle Grade and Young Adult. A special New Horizons award is made to a particularly innovative book. Founded 1966.

Bookbug Picture Book Prize

Scottish Book Trust, Sandeman House,
Trunk's Close, 55 High Street, Edinburgh EH1 1SR
tel 0131 524 0160
email info@scottishbooktrust.com
website www.scottishbooktrust.com/reading-and-stories/bookbug-picture-book-prize

Scotland's national picture book prize which recognises the favourite picture book of children in Scotland by writers and illustrators resident in Scotland. Visit the Scottish Book Trust website for more details.

Books Are My Bag Readers Awards

website www.nationalbooktokens.com/vote

Curated by bookshops and chosen by readers, categories include Fiction, Non-Fiction, Poetry, Young adult Fiction, Children's fiction, Breakthrough author and Readers' choice. Reader's choice is nominated exclusively by readers.

BookTrust Storytime Prize

BookTrust, G8 Battersea Studios,
80 Silverthorne Road, London SW8 3HE
tel 020-7801 8826
email StoryTimePrize@booktrust.org.uk
website www.booktrust.org.uk/prizes

An annual prize to celebrate the best books for sharing with young children aged 0–5 with a particular focus on books that have a wide appeal to parents and carers across our diverse nation, and for stories which can be read and enjoyed over and over again. The prize is run in collaboration with Youth Library Group (YLG) and the shortlisted titles are shared with families by public librarians across the UK to find the best book. Publishers are invited to enter up to five books per imprint. See website for further details and timings.

The Branford Boase Award

8 Bolderwood Close, Bishopstoke, Eastleigh,
Hants SO50 8PG
tel 023-8060 0439
email anne.marley@tiscali.co.uk
website www.branfordboaseaward.org.uk

An annual award of £1,000 is made to a first-time writer of a full-length children's novel (age 7+) published in the preceding year; the editor is also recognised. Its aim is to encourage new writers for children and to recognise the role of perceptive editors in developing new talent. The Award was set up in memory of the outstanding children's writer Henrietta Branford and the gifted editor and publisher Wendy Boase who both died in 1999. Closing date for nominations: end of December.

Caledonia Novel Award

email enquiries@thecaledonianovelaward.com
website https://thecaledonianovelaward.com/

Award for unpublished and self-published novelists. Novels can be of any genre for adult or young adult fiction. The award is open to writers of any nationality who are over 18+. Entries cost £25, with the winner receiving £1,500. The Award provides a number of sponsored places to eligible, low-income writers who are unable to afford the fee. For more information, see the competition rules on the website.

The Carmelite Prize

c/o Hachette Children's Group, Carmelite House,
50 Victoria Embankment, London EC4Y 0DZ
email carmeliteprize@hachettechildrens.co.uk
website www.hachettechildrens.co.uk/imprint/
hcgdivision/page/the-carmelite-prize-2020/
Twitter @HachetteKids

An annual award run by Hachette Children's Group which recognises excellence in children's book illustration, with the aim of encouraging and inspiring the next generation of illustrators for children's stories. The competition is open to all students aged 18 and over who are studying illustration and design in the UK in further or higher education. Only one entry per person. Entries will not be accepted from agents, third parties or in bulk. The winner and two runners-up will be chosen from the top five entries: first prize £1,000, first runner-up £500, second runner-up £250. See website for full terms and conditions.

Carnegie Medal – see The CILIP Carnegie and Kate Greenaway Children's Book Awards

The Caterpillar Poetry Prize

Ardan Grange, Milltown, Belturbet,
Co. Cavan H14 K768, Republic of Ireland
tel + 353 (0)87 2657251
email enquiries@thecaterpillarmagazine.com
website www.thecaterpillarmagazine.com

The Caterpillar Poetry Prize is for a single unpublished poem written by an adult for children. The writer of the winning poem receives €1,000 and has their poem published in *The Caterpillar*. The prize is open to anyone over the age of 16. The entry fee is €14 and writers can submit as many poems as they like. Closing date 31 March. For full entry details and guidelines, see the website.

The Caterpillar Story for Children Prize

Ardan Grange, Milltown, Belturbet,
Co. Cavan H14 K768, Republic of Ireland
tel + 353 (0)87 2657251
email enquiries@thecaterpillarmagazine.com
website www.thecaterpillarmagazine.com

An annual prize for a single story written by an adult for children. The writer receives €1,000 and has their story published in *The Caterpillar*. The prize is open to anyone over the age of 16. The entry fee is €14 and writers can submit as many stories as they like. Closing date 30 September. For full entry details and guidelines, see the website.

Cheltenham Illustration Awards

email eevans@glos.ac.uk
website www.cheltenham-illustration-awards.com

Exhibition and Annual submissions are invited and can be freely interpreted in a narrative context. Submissions of work are free and open to all students, emerging and established illustrators and graphic novelists. A selection panel will assess entries. The selected work will be showcased in an exhibition and published in the *Cheltenham Illustration Awards Annual*, which will be distributed to education institutions and publishers. Deadline for submissions: June.

The Children's Book Award

email childrensbookaward@fcbg.org.uk
website https://childrensbookaward.org.uk/
Twitter @CBACoordinator

Awarded annually to authors and illustrators of children's fiction published in the UK. Children participate in the judging of the award. Awards are made in the following categories: Books for Younger Children, Books for Younger Readers and Books for Older Readers. Founded 1980.

The KPMG Children's Books Ireland Awards

Children's Books Ireland,
17 North Great George's Street, Dublin 1 D01 R2F1,
Republic of Ireland
tel +353 (0)1 872 7475
email info@childrensbooksireland.ie
website www.childrensbooksireland.ie

Leading annual children's book awards in Ireland. The awards are: the Book of the Year, the Eilís Dillon Award (for a first children's book), the Honour Award for Fiction, the Honour Award for Illustration, the Judges' Special Award and the Junior Juries Award. Schools and reading groups nationwide take part in the Junior Juries programme: participating groups make their own selection of suitable titles from the books shortlisted for the awards in March, using a specially devised activity pack to guide them in their reading; each group then votes for their favourite book Closing date: December for work published between 1 January and 31 December of an awards year. Shortlist announced in March; winners announced in May. Founded 1990.

The Children's Laureate

BookTrust, Studio G8, Battersea Studios,
80 Silverthorne Road, London SW8 3HE
tel 020-7801 8800
email childrenslaureate@booktrust.org.uk
website www.childrenslaureate.org.uk
Contact Charlotte Copping

The idea for the Children's Laureate originated from a conversation between (the then) Poet Laureate Ted Hughes and children's writer Michael Morpurgo. The post was established to celebrate exceptional children's authors and illustrators and to acknowledge their importance in creating the readers of tomorrow. Quentin Blake was the first Children's Laureate (1999–2001), followed by Anne Fine (2001–2003), Michael Morpurgo (2003–2005), Jacqueline Wilson (2005–2007), Michael Rosen (2007–2009), Anthony Browne (2009–2011), Julia Donaldson (2011–2013), Malorie Blackman (2013–2015), Chris Riddell (2015–2017), Lauren Child (2017–2019) and Cressida Cowell (2019–2022). Founded 1999.

The CILIP Carnegie and Kate Greenaway Children's Book Awards

CILIP, 7 Ridgmount Street, London WC1E 7AE
tel 020-7255 0650
email ckg@cilip.org.uk
website www.ckg.org.uk

Nominations for the following two awards are invited from members of CILIP (the library and information association), who are asked to submit one title per Medal, accompanied by an explanation of how the book they have selected meets the Medal criteria. The awards are selected by librarian judges from the Youth Libraries Group of CILIP. One title from each shortlist will receive a prize awarded by children who take part in the Awards shadowing scheme who vote for their favourites.

Carnegie Medal

Awarded annually for an outstanding book for children (fiction or non-fiction) written in English and first published in the UK during the preceding year or co-published elsewhere within a three-month time lapse. The Carnegie Medal winner is awarded £5,000 prize money from the Colin Mears Award annually.

Kate Greenaway Medal

Awarded annually for an outstanding illustrated book for children first published in the UK during the preceding year or co-published elsewhere within a three-month time lapse. Books intended for older as well as younger children are included, and reproduction will be taken into account. The Colin Mears Award (£5,000) is awarded annually to the winner of the Kate Greenaway Medal.

CLiPPA (Centre for Literacy in Primary Poetry Award)

CLPE, 44 Webber Street, London SE1 8QW
tel 020-7401 3382/3
email info@clpe.org.uk
website https://clpe.org.uk/poetryline/clippa
Facebook www.facebook.com/CentreforLiteracyinPrimaryEducation
Twitter @clpe1

CLiPPA is an award that honours excellence in children's poetry. Organised by the Centre for Literacy in Primary Education (CLPE), it is presented annually for a book of poetry published in the preceding year. The book can be a single-poet collection or an anthology. Submissions deadline: end of January. Founded 2003.

Copy*right* Essay Prize

The Copyright Licensing Agency Ltd, 5th Floor, Shackleton House, 4 Battle Bridge Lane, London SE1 2HX
email CLAessayprize@cla.co.uk
website https://cla.co.uk/essayprize

The annual competition is open to 16–19 year olds based in UK schools and colleges to write a 1,500 word essay around subjects concerning copyright and intellectual property. The overall winner will receive a £300 cash prize. Each year the CLA will set a specific essay question that the students must respond to. See website for more details. Founded 2020.

Costa Book Awards

The Booksellers Association, 6 Bell Yard, London WC2A 2JR
tel 020-7421 4640

email costabookawards@booksellers.org.uk
website www.costa.co.uk/costa-book-awards
Contact Naomi Gane

The awards celebrate and promote the most enjoyable contemporary British writing. There are five categories: Novel, First Novel, Biography, Poetry and Children's, plus one overall winner. Each category is judged by a panel of judges and the winner in each category receives £5,000. Judges then choose the Costa Book of the Year from the five category winners. The overall winner receives £30,000. There is also a seventh award, the Short Story Award, given for a single short story. Total prize money for the Costa Book Awards is £60,000. Submissions must be received from publishers. Shortlist announced: November. Closing date: end of June. For full eligibility and submission guidelines, see the website. Founded 1971.

English Association English 4–11 Children's Book Awards

The English Association, University of Leicester, Leicester LE1 7RH
tel 0116 229 7622
email engassoc@leicester.ac.uk
website www2.le.ac.uk/offices/english-association/primary/english-4-11-book-awards

Awarded to the best children's picture books of the year. Categories are Fiction and Non-fiction in the age ranges 4–7 years and 7–11 years. The winning books are chosen by the editorial board of *English 4–11*, the journal for primary teachers published by the English Association and the United Kingdom Literacy Association from a shortlist selected by a panel of teachers and primary education specialists. Founded 1995.

Etisalat Award for Arabic Children's Literature

email info@uaebby.org.ae
website www.etisalataward.ae
Facebook www.facebook.com/EtisalatAward
Twitter @EtisalatAward

The prize of one million UAE dirhams is open only to children's literature written in the Arabic language; translated content is not eligible. The Award has widened its scope since its inception, adding new categories in order to highlight the individual achievements of writers, illustrators and publishers. The value of the Award is distributed between six categories: best text, best illustration, best production, children's book of the year, young adult book of the year and Warsha-Etisalat Workshops for Children's Books, an initiative aimed at nurturing a new generation of Arab authors, illustrators and publishers of Arabic children's books.

FAB Prize for Undiscovered Talent

email prize@fabfaber.co.uk
website www.fabprize.org
Twitter @FaberChildrens

Set up by Faber Children's and Andlyn Literary Agency, this is an annual competition for unagented and unpublished writers and illustrators from Black, Asian and/or non-white minority ethnic backgrounds. Now with the additional backing of BookTrust and the Association of Illustrators, the competition winners and runners up are not only offered mentoring, but also exposure to literary agents and editors alongside access to training and shadowing schemes. The prize offers a unique opportunity to kick start a writing or illustrating career and get a foot in the door. Entries must be text or artwork for children aged 1–18 years. First prize of £500 for text and £500 for illustration. Founded 2017.

The Eleanor Farjeon Award
website www.childrensbookcircle.org.uk

An annual award which may be given to an individual or an organisation. Librarians, authors, publishers, teachers, reviewers and others who have given exceptional service to the children's book industry are eligible for nomination. It was instituted in 1965 by the Children's Book Circle (page 361) for distinguished services to children's books and named after the much-loved children's writer Eleanor Farjeon.

500 Words
email contact@500words.me
website https://500words.me/
Twitter @500WordsMe

The UK's most successful short story-writing competition for children between the ages of 5 and 13. It seeks to get children excited about reading and writing, no matter what their ability, experience or background. Entrants must write an original story, on any subject, of no more than 500 words in length and submit it online. Stories are judged anonymously, without regard to grammar, punctuation or spelling. The final is broadcast live on Virgin Radio. A full list of FAQs regarding entries and submissions can be found on the website. Founded 2011.

The Klaus Flugge Prize
website www.klausfluggeprize.co.uk
Twitter @KlausFluggePr

This prize is awarded to the most promising and exciting newcomer to children's book illustration. It honours the work of publisher Klaus Flugge in the field of illustration and children's picture books, and the winning debut illustrator receives £5,000.

Foyle Young Poets of the Year Award – see page 226

Grampian Children's Book Award
website https://gcbookaward.wixsite.com/gcba
Twitter @GrampBookAward

This award is for the best fiction book, judged solely by pupils in participating schools in Aberdeen City,

Aberdeenshire and Moray. Anyone in Grampian who is aged 15 and under can vote.

Kate Greenaway Medal – see The CILIP Carnegie and Kate Greenaway Children's Book Awards

Indie Book Awards
6 Bell Yard, London WC2A 2JR
tel 020-7421 4656
email emma.bradshaw@booksellers.org.uk
website www.indiebookshopweek.org.uk
Twitter @booksaremybag
Instagram booksaremybag

Awards are given in four categories: fiction, non-fiction, children's fiction and picture book. For entry guidelines and shortlist details see the website.

Invisible Prize for Illustrators
email info@picturehooks.org.uk
website www.picturehooks.org.uk/the-invisible-prize/

A biennial award which acknowledges the quiet reach and huge influence of the illustrator. Founded 2020.

Jhalak Children's & YA Prize
email info@jhalakprize.com
website www.jhalakprize.com/childrens-ya
Twitter @jhalakprize

Awarded annually, this prize seeks out the best books by British or British resident BAME writers and awards one winner £1,000. Entries can be for fiction, non-fiction, short story, graphic novel, poetry, picture books and all other genres intended for children and young adult readers. Started by authors Sunny Singh and Nikesh Shukla and Media Diversified, with support from The Authors' Club and a prize donated by an anonymous benefactor, the prize exists to celebrate the achievements of writers of colour. For submission guidelines and details of key dates see the website. Founded 2020.

The Kelpies Prizes for Writing and Illustration
Floris Books, Canal Court, 40 Craiglockhart Avenue, Edinburgh EH14 1LT
tel 0131 337 2372
email kelpiesprize@florisbooks.co.uk
website https://discoverkelpies.co.uk/kelpies-prizes/

Annual awards for emerging writers and illustrators who are committed to developing their skills and creating quality books for children. The Kelpies Prizes are open to anyone who lives or works in Scotland. The winners will receive £1,000 cash, a year of mentoring with an experienced editorial or design team, and the possibility of a publishing contract with Floris Books. Submit writing or illustration samples and entry form online; see website for full details. Closing date: end February.

Kindle Storyteller Award
website www.amazon.co.uk/
b?ie=UTF8&node=12061299031

Open to submissions of new English-language books in any genre. Titles must be previously unpublished and be available as an ebook and in print via Kindle Direct Publishing. The winning author will receive £20,000. Competition entry period runs from 1 May to 31 August.

Lancashire Book of the Year Award
tel 0300 123 6703
email ReadingAndLearningDevelopmentTeam@
lancashire.gov.uk
website www.lancashire.gov.uk

This annual prize is awarded to the best work of fiction for children in the 12–14 year group, published in the UK. It is the longest-running regional book award in the country and the award is voted for by Year 9 students in high schools around the county of Lancashire. Winner announced in September.

Laxfield Literary Launch Prize
website https://laxfieldliterary.com/new-anglia-manuscript-prize/

Debut novel prize of any genre is open to all unpublished writers. Winners receive £500 and representation from Laxfield Literary Agency. There is no fee to enter, submissions open in early October and close in early December. See website for submission guidelines. Founded 2020.

The Astrid Lindgren Memorial Award
Swedish Arts Council, PO Box 27215,
SE–102 53 Stockholm, Sweden
tel +46 8-51926400
email literatureaward@alma.se
website https://alma.se/en/

An award to honour the memory of Astrid Lindgren, Sweden's favourite author, and to promote children's and youth literature around the world. The award is five million Swedish kronas, the world's largest for children's and youth literature, and the second-largest literature prize in the world. It is awarded annually to one or more recipients, regardless of language or nationality.

Authors, illustrators, storytellers and promoters of reading are eligible. The award is for life-long work or artistry rather than for individual pieces. The prize can only be awarded to living people. The winner is selected by a jury based on nominations for outstanding achievement from selected nominating bodies around the world. Administered by the Swedish Arts Council. Founded 2002.

Little Rebels Children's Book Award
email info@letterboxlibrary.com
website https://littlerebels.org/
Twitter @littlerebsprize

Recognises children's fiction for readers aged 0–12 years which promotes social justice or social equality, challenges stereotypes or is informed by anti-discriminatory concerns. The award is given by the Alliance of Radical Booksellers. Winning prize: £2,000. See website for submission guidelines. Founded 2010.

The Macmillan Prize for Illustration
Macmillan Children's Books, The Smithson,
6 Briset Street, London EC1M 5NR
email macmillanprize@macmillan.co.uk
website www.panmacmillan.com/macmillanprize

Three prizes are awarded annually for unpublished children's book illustrations by art students in higher education institutions in the UK. Prizes: 1st: £1,000, 2nd: £500 and 3rd: £250. Founded 1985.

The Mythopoeic Fantasy Award for Children's Literature
email awards@mythsoc.org
website www.mythsoc.org

This award honours books for younger readers (from young adults to picture books for beginning readers), in the tradition of *The Hobbit* or *The Chronicles of Narnia*. The Mythopoeic Awards are chosen from books nominated by individual members of the Mythopoeic Society and selected by a committee of Society members. Authors, publishers and their representatives may not nominate their own books for any of the awards, nor are books published by the Mythopoeic Press eligible for the awards. The Mythopoeic Society does not accept or review unsolicited manuscripts.

New Anglia Manuscript Prize
website https://laxfieldliterary.com/new-anglia-manuscript-prize/

Sponsored by the National Centre for Writing in Norwich, this debut novel prize is open to unpublished writers from Suffolk and Norfolk. There is no fee to enter and submissions open in early October and close in early December. See website for submission guidelines. Founded 2020.

New Zealand Book Awards for Children and Young Adults
c/o NZ Book Awards Trust, Te Wharepōuri Street,
Wellington 6023
tel +64 (0)27 773 9855
email childrensawards@nzbookawards.org.nz
website www.nzbookawards.nz/new-zealand-book-awards-for-children-and-young-adults

Annual awards to celebrate excellence in, and provide recognition for, the best children's books published in New Zealand. Awards are presented in six categories: Picture Book, Junior Fiction (the Wright Family Foundation Esther Glen Award), Young Adult

Fiction, Non-Fiction (the Elsie Locke Award), Illustration (the Russell Clark Award) and te reo Māori (the Wright Family Foundation Te Kura Pounamu Award). Each of these awards carries prize money of $7,500. The overall prize, the Margaret Mahy Book of the Year award, carries a further prize of $7,500. A Best First Book prize of $2,000 is also awarded to a previously unpublished author or illustrator. Eligible books must have been published in New Zealand between April and March in the period preceding the awards' August ceremony date.

North East Book Award

Cramlington Learning Village, Cramlington, Northumberland NE23 6BN
tel (01670) 712311
email earmstrong@cramlingtonlv.co.uk
website https://northeastbookaward.wordpress.com
Contact Eileen Armstrong

Awarded to a book written by a UK/Ireland resident author and first published in paperback the previous year. The shortlist is selected by school librarians, teachers and the previous year's student judges. The final winner is decided entirely by the student judges (Year 7/8) and is announced in June.

North East Teen Book Award

Cramlington Learning Village, Cramlington, Northumberland NE23 6BN
tel (01670) 712311
email earmstrong@cramlingtonlv.co.uk
website https://northeastteenagebookaward.
wordpress.com
Contact Eileen Armstrong

Awarded to a book written by a UK/Ireland resident author and first published in paperback during the previous year. The shortlist is selected by school librarians, teachers and the previous year's student judges. The final winner is decided entirely by the student judges (Year 9+) and is announced in March.

Nottingham Children's Book Awards

Nottingham Library Service, Culture and Libraries, Aspey Library, Nottingham NG8 5DD
tel 0115 915 2844
email charlotte.blount@nottinghamcity.gov.uk
website www.nottinghamcity.gov.uk/ncba
Facebook www.facebook.com/NottinghamLibraries
Twitter @readingnottm
Contact Charlotte Blount

Nottingham children aged 2–4 years choose their favourite picture books from books published the previous year. The shortlist of titles is drawn up by the end of July with the help of local schools and nurseries. In the autumn, library staff visit settings to read the three books to pre-school children asking them to vote for their favourite. Families can also vote in libraries and via the website. The winner is announced at the beginning of December.
Founded 1999.

Oscar's Book Prize

Lower Ground Floor, 111 Charterhouse Street, London EC1M 6AW
email info@oscarsbookprize.co.uk
website www.oscarsbookprize.co.uk

This £10,000 prize supported by Amazon and The National Literacy Trust, in partnership with the *Evening Standard*, is awarded to the preschool book published in the UK the previous year that the judges consider to be the best.
Publishers may enter up to five books per imprint. Collections and anthologies are not eligible. Previously published, self-published books and ebooks are not eligible. Full terms and conditions and a digital entry form are available on the website. Previous winners include Rachel Bright and Jim Field, Gemma Merino, John Dougherty and Laura Hughes and Steve Antony. Founded 2013.

The People's Book Prize

email thepeoplesbkpr@aol.com
website www.peoplesbookprize.com
Facebook www.facebook.com/pages/The-Peoples-Book-Prize/200637717319384
Twitter @PeoplesBkPrize
Founder and Prize Administrator Tatiana Wilson, *Patron Emeritus* Frederick Forsyth, *Founding Patron* Dame Beryl Bainbridge

Awards are given in six categories: fiction, non-fiction, children's, first-time author (the Beryl Bainbridge First Time Author Award), TPBP Best Achievement Award and TPBP Best Publisher Award. Titles must be submitted by publishers, with a limit of three titles per category, per collection. Winners are announced at an awards ceremony in May at the Worshipful Company of Stationers and Newspaper Makers, Stationers' Hall, London.

Phoenix Award

Children's Literature Association,
3525 Piedmont Road, Building 5, Suite 300, Atlanta, GA 30305, USA
tel +1 630-571-4520
email info@childlitassn.org
website www.childlitassn.org

This Award is presented by the Children's Literature Association (ChLA) for the most outstanding book for children originally published in the English language 20 years earlier which did not receive a major award at the time of publication. It is intended to recognise books of high literary merit.
Founded 1985.

The Queen's Knickers Award

The Society of Authors, 24 Bedford Row, London WC1R 4EH
tel 020-7373 6642
email prizes@societyofauthors.org
website www.societyofauthors.org/Prizes/Society-of-Authors-Awards/The-Queens-Knickers-Award
Twitter @Soc_of_Authors

An annual prize, generously funded by the author of *The Queen's Knickers*, Nicholas Allan, for outstanding children's illustrated books for ages 0–7. The prize recognises books that strike a quirky, new note, in any combination of words and/or pictures and in any physical format including pop-ups, flap books and board books. Submissions must be made by the print publisher. The winner receives £5,000 as well as a golden Queen's Knickers badge, and the runner-up receives £1,000 and a silvered badge. The prize will be shared between the author and illustrator if applicable. Closing Date: 30 November.

The Royal Society Young People's Book Prize

The Royal Society, 6–9 Carlton House Terrace, London SW1Y 5AG
tel 020-7451 2500
email sciencebooks@royalsociety.org
website https://royalsociety.org/grants-schemes-awards/book-prizes/young-peoples-book-prize/
Facebook www.facebook.com/theroyalsociety
Twitter @royalsociety

This prize is open to books for under-14s that have science as a substantial part of their content, narrative or theme. An expert adult panel choose the shortlist, but the winner is chosen by groups of young people in judging panels across the UK. The winning entry receives £10,000 and shortlisted entries receive £2,500. Entries open in December each year. Pure reference works including encyclopedias, educational textbooks and descriptive books are not eligible. The Prize is offered thanks to the generosity of an anonymous donor. Founded 1988.

RSPCA Young Photographer Awards

Brand Marketing and Content Department, RSPCA, Wilberforce Way, Southwater, Horsham, West Sussex RH13 9RS
email ypa@rspca.org.uk
website https://young.rspca.org.uk/ypa/home

Annual awards open to anyone aged 18 or under. The aim of the competition is to encourage young people's interest in photography and to show their appreciation and understanding of the animals around them. See website for a full list of categories and submission guidelines. Founded 1990.

Rubery Book Award

PO Box 15821, Birmingham B31 9EA
email enquiries@ruberybookaward.com
website www.ruberybookaward.com

An annual award for published books on any subject, including children's books, with prizes totalling £2,000 (Book of the Year receives £1,500 and category winners £150 each). Books published by independent presses and self-published books are eligible. See website for entry fees and submission guidelines.

Scholastic Laugh Out Loud Book Awards

email laughoutloud@scholastic.co.uk
website https://shop.scholastic.co.uk/lollies
Twitter @lolbookawards

Known as The Lollies, the Laugh Out Loud Book Awards are awarded to books in three categories: Best Picture Book, Best Book for 6–8-year-olds and Best Book for 9–13-year-olds. A judging panel selects four books to make up a shortlist for each category, but winners are decided entirely by children's votes, with voting taking place via the website and promoted through Scholastic Book Clubs and Book Fairs. See website for full entry and submission guidelines.

Sheffield Children's Book Award

Schools & Young People's Library Service, Stadia Technology Park, 60 Shirland Lane, Sheffield S9 3SP
tel 0114 250 6844
email jennifer.wilson@sheffield.gov.uk
website www.sheffield.gov.uk/home/libraries-archives/book-awards

Presented annually in November to the book chosen as the most enjoyable by the children of Sheffield. Categories include: Baby Book Award, Toddler Books, Picture Book, Emerging Reads, Shorter Novel, Longer Novel and Young Adult.

Wilbur Smith Adventure Writing Prize

The Wilbur & Niso Smith Foundation, Unit 9, 5–7 Wells Terrace, London N4 3JU
email submissions@wilbur-niso-smithfoundation.org
website www.wilbur-niso-smithfoundation.org
Facebook www.facebook.com/WNSmithFoundation
Twitter @Wilbur_Niso_Fdn

An international writing prize that supports and celebrates today's best adventure writing. The Prize is open to writers of any nationality, writing in English. Awards are presented for fiction in three categories: Best Published Novel (prize: £10,000); Best Unpublished Manuscript (prize: a publishing deal with Bonnier Books UK) and Author of Tomorrow (prizes: £150–£1,000 depending on age category, plus book tokens and digital publication). The Author of Tomorrow award seeks to find the adventure writers of the future and is open to young people across the world (in age categories 16–21 years, 12–15 years and age 11 and under) who have completed a short piece of adventure writing in English. Submission guidelines, eligibility criteria, entry fees, shortlist dates and details of the previous winners for each category can be found on the website.

The Stephen Spender Prize

PO Box 1618, Oxford OX4 9LW
email charlotte@stephen-spender.org
website www.stephen-spender.org/spender_prize.html

Annual competition for poetry in translation, with categories for young people (14 and under, 16 and under, and 18 and under) as well as an open category for adults. Translate into English any poem from any language. Overall winner will win a £1,000 cash prize. All entrants must be UK or Irish citizens or residents, or pupils at a British School overseas. Founded 2004.

STEAM Children's Book Prize

UCLan Publishing, c/o Greenbank Hub, Greenbank Building, Preston PR1 2HE
email uclanpublishing@uclan.ac.uk
website https://uclanpublishing.com

The aim of this prize is to highlight the importance of STEAM subjects (science, technology, engineering, art and maths) and praise the publishing industry and authors for championing them. By providing children with engaging, fun and exciting literature, they will hopefully be inspired to take an interest in STEAM further into their education. Now in its second year, this is the first prize to concentrate solely on STEAM in children's books and covers all ages from 0 to young adults, as well as all genres and subject matters. Award categories are Early Years, Middle Grade, Young Adult and Information and there is also an Overall Winner. Submissions open in September, shortlist announced in February and winners announced in June.

The Times/Chicken House Children's Fiction Competition

Chicken House, 2 Palmer Street, Frome, Somerset BA11 1DS
tel (01373) 454488
email competitions@chickenhousebooks.com
website www.chickenhousebooks.com
Twitter @chickenhsebooks
Contact Kesia Lupo

This annual competition is open to unpublished writers of a full-length children's novel (age 7–18). Entrants must be over 18 and novels must not exceed 80,000 words in length. The winner will be announced in *The Times* and will receive a worldwide publishing contract with Chicken House with a royalty advance of £10,000. The winner is selected by a panel of judges which includes children's authors, journalists, publishers, librarians and other key figures from the world of children's literature. For competition opening and closing dates, consult the Chicken House website.

Tir na n-Og Awards

Books Council of Wales, Castell Brychan, Aberystwyth, Ceredigion SY23 2JB
tel (01970) 624151
email wbc.children@books.wales
website https://llyfrau.cymru/en/gwobrau/tir-na-nog
Facebook www.facebook.com/LlyfrDaFabBooks
Twitter @LlyfrDaFabBooks

Established with the intention of promoting and raising the standard of children's and young people's books in Wales. Three awards are presented annually by the Welsh Books Council and are sponsored by the Chartered Institute of Library and Information Professionals Cymru/Wales:

• The best English-language book of the year with an authentic Welsh background. Fiction and factual books originally in English are eligible; translations from Welsh or any other language are not eligible. Prize: £1,000.
• The best original Welsh-language book aimed at the primary school sector. Prize: £1,000.
• The best original Welsh-language book aimed at the secondary school sector. Prize: £1,000. Founded 1976.

Christopher Tower Poetry Prize – see page 227

UKLA Book Awards

tel 0116 254 4116
website www.ukla.org/awards/ukla-book-award

A national, annual award for children's books and is judged by teachers. There are four categories covering the ages 3–16+. Teachers are looking for books which evocatively express ideas and offer layered meanings through the use of language, imaginative expression and rich illustration/graphics. Detailed submission criteria can be found on the website.

The V&A Illustration Awards

Victoria & Albert Museum, London SW7 2RL
email villa@vam.ac.uk
website www.vam.ac.uk/info/va-illustration-awards

These annual awards are open to illustrators living or publishing in the UK and students who have attended a course in the UK over the last two years. Awards are made in the following categories: book illustration, book cover design, illustrated journalism and student illustrator. Founded 1972.

The Warwick Prize for Women in Translation

email womenintranslation@warwick.ac.uk
website https://warwick.ac.uk/fac/cross_fac/womenintranslation
Coordinators Chantal Wright and Holly Langstaff

Awarded annually to the best eligible work of fiction, poetry, literary non-fiction, work of fiction for children or young adults, graphic novel, or play text, written by a woman, translated into English by a translator (or translators) of any gender, and published by a UK or Irish publisher. The £1,000 prize is divided between the writer and her translator/s. Founded 2017.

Waterstones Children's Book Prize

Waterstones, 203–206 Piccadilly, London W1J 9HD
tel 020-7071 6395

email childrensbookprize@waterstones.com
website www.waterstones.com

The aim of the prize is to reward and champion new and emerging children's writers, voted for by booksellers. For the 2022 prize, books must be new during 2021. There are three categories: Illustrated Books, Books for Younger Readers and Books for Older Readers. Submission criteria:

Illustrated Books. Illustrated books authored and illustrated by the same person: The author/illustrator may not have previously published more than two titles of any fiction genre worldwide (educational titles are exempt). Author/illustrator partnerships: Neither the author nor illustrator may have previously solely published more than two titles of any fiction genre (which includes picture books) worldwide (educational titles are exempt). Author/illustrator partnerships may not have previously published more than two titles together.

Books for Younger Readers and *Books for Older Readers.* No more than one previously published title of any fiction genre worldwide (educational titles are exempt). The title must make sense as a standalone novel. If the title is illustrated, and the illustrator matches submission criteria for Illustrated Books, then the illustrator will be considered eligible for this category. Narrative non-fiction is also eligible for submission.

The 2022 shortlist is announced in February 2022. Winners announced March 2022. Publishers to declare any titles written under another name, including series fiction. Writing and concept must be solely the work of the author. Titles must have been published in 2021. There will be one winner in each category. There will be an overall winner from the category winners.

Wildlife Photographer of the Year

The Natural History Museum, Cromwell Road, London SW7 5BD
website www.nhm.ac.uk/visit/wpy/competition.html

This annual award is given to the photographer whose individual image is judged to be the most striking and memorable. There is an adult competition for photographers aged 18 or over and a young competition for photographers aged 17 or under. See website for submission guidelines.

World Illustration Awards

Association of Illustrators, Somerset House, Strand, London WC2R 1LA

tel 020-7759 1010
email awards@theaoi.com
website www.theaoi.com/world-illustration-awards
Facebook www.facebook.com/theaoi
Twitter @theaoi
Instagram WorldIllustrationAwards

Presented in partnership with the *Directory of Illustration*, the awards programme sets out to celebrate contemporary illustration across the globe. A panel of international judges create a 500 strong longlist and shortlists 200 projects, which are celebrated in an online showcase, a printed catalogue and with an online industry events programme. For submission guidelines, categories and prizes, see the website.

YA Book Prize

website www.thebookseller.com/ya-book-prize-2021
Facebook www.facebook.com/YABookPrize
Twitter @yabookprize

First prize to specifically focus on fiction for young adults. Organised by *The Bookseller*, in partnership with the Hay Festival. Open for titles published between 1st January and 31st of the previous year. Author must be living in the UK or Ireland at publication. Winner receives £2,000. Founded 2014.

YouWriteOn.com Book Awards

tel 07948 392634
email edward@youwriteon.com
website www.youwriteon.com

Arts Council-funded site publishing awards for new fiction writers. Random House and Orion, the publishers of authors such as Dan Brown and Terry Pratchett, provide free professional critiques for the highest rated new writers' opening chapters and short stories on YouWriteOn.com each month. The highest rated writers of the year are then published, three in each of the adult and children's categories, through YouWriteOn's free paperback publishing service for writers. The novel publishing awards total £1,000. Writers can enter at any time throughout the year: closing date is 31 December each year. Previous YouWriteOn.com winners have been published by mainstream publishers such as Random House, Orion, Penguin and Hodder, including Channel 4 TV Book Club winner and bestseller *The Legacy* by Katherine Webb. Founded 2005.

Prize winners

This is a selection of high-profile literary prize winners from the last year presented chronologically. Some awards have been postponed due to the coronavirus lockdown, please see individual awards websites for details. Entries for many of these prizes are included in the *Yearbook*, starting on page 384.

April 2020

BolognaRagazzi Award
Meine liebsten Dinge müssen mit by Sepideh Sarihi, illustrated by Julie Völk (Fiction); *Marie Curie. Nel Paese Della Scienza* by Irène Cohen-Janca, illustrated by Claudia Palmarucci (Non-fiction); *Lullaby for Grandmother* by Iwona Chmielewska (New Horizons); *Where is Your Sister* by Puck Koper (Opera Prima)

May

KPMG Book of the Year Award
Nóinín by Máire Zepf

Children's Book Award
D-Day Dog by Tom Palmer (Overall Winner); *The Runaway Pea* by Kjartan Poskitt, illustrated by Alex Willmore (Book for Younger Children); *Mutant Zombies Cursed My School Trip* by Matt Brown, illustrated by Paco Sordo (Book for Younger Readers); *On the Come Up* by Angie Thomas (Book for Older Readers)

Tir na n-Og Awards
Storm Hound by Clare Fayes

Scottish Teenage Book Prize (Scottish Book Trust)
One Shot by Tanya Landman

The V&A Illustration Awards
Eva Eland for *When Sadness Comes to Call* (Book Cover Award); Clive Hicks-Jenkins for *Hansel & Gretel: A Nightmare in Eight Scenes* (Book Illustration); Ann Kiernan for *How Twitter is gagging Arabic users and acting as morality police* (Illustrated Journalism Award and Moira Gemmill Illustrator of the Year); Sally Dune for *Kakuma Refugee Camp* (Student Illustrator of the Year)

YA Book Prize
Meat Market by Juno Dawson

June

The Macmillan Prize for Children's Picture Book Illustration
Can I Read My Books, Please? by Jake Alexander

The CILIP Carnegie Medal
Lark by Anthony McGowan

The CILIP Kate Greenaway Medal
Tales from the Inner City by Shaun Tan

East Sussex Children's Book Awards
I Go Quiet by David Ouimet

July

Lancashire Book of the Year Award
The Year I Didn't Eat by Samuel Pollen

UKLA Book Awards
Mixed by Arree Chung (3–6+ years); *The Eleventh Trade* by Alyssa Hollingsworth, illustrated by Hannah Horn (7–10+ years); *No Fixed Address* by Susan Nielsen (11–14+ years)

CLiPPA (Centre for Literacy in Primary Poetry Award)
Cherry Moon by Zaro Weil

Branford Boase Award
Bearmouth by Liz Hyder (and her editor Sarah Odedina)

August

Mythopoeic Fantasy Award for Children's Literature (USA)
Dragon Pearl by Yoon Ha Lee

The Kelpies Prize for Writing
Jude Reid

The Kelpies Illustration Prize
Leanne Goodall

January 2021

Costa Children's Book of the Year
Voyage of the Sparrowhawk by Natasha Farrant (Costa Children's Book of the Year)

BookBug Picture Book Prize (Scottish Book Trust)
This is a Dog by Ross Collins

February

Scholastic Laugh Out Loud Book Awards
Ten Fat Sausages by Michelle Robinson, illustrated by Tor Freeman (Picture book); *World's Worst Children 3* by David Walliams, illustrated by Tony Ross (Book for 6–8 year-olds); *I Bet I Can Make You Laugh* by Joshua Seigal, illustrated by Tim Wesson (Book for 9–13 year-olds)

March

Blue Peter Book Awards
A Kind of Spark by Elle McNicoll (Best Story); *Rise Up: A Day in the Life of a Poo, a Gnu and You* by Mike Barfield (Best Book with Facts)

Opportunities for under-represented writers

There has been an acknowledgement across the publishing industry that many voices have not found it easy to be heard and promoted amongst the many hundreds and thousands of books published every year. Publishers, agents, authors and prize-awarding organisations have collectively started to actively encourage and nurture a more diverse range of writers who have new stories to tell. There has been an increase in open submissions, prizes, bursaries and other schemes in 2020–21 aimed at previously less represented groups. Some of the more established awards have full entries in this *Yearbook* (as indicated below) and some of the newer ones are listed in full here.

PRIZE AND AWARDS

FAB Prize for Undiscovered Talent
See page 388

Golden Egg Award
See page 403

Jhalak Children's & YA Prize
See page 389

The London Writers' Awards
The Albany Centre, Douglas Way, London SE8 4AG
email bobby@spreadtheword.org.uk
website www.spreadtheword.org.uk/projects/london-writers-awards/

Award programme set up by Spread the Word for London-based prose writers who identify as being from a background currently under-represented in publishing: disabled, LGBTQIA+, working class or writers of colour. The awards are given across four genres: literary fiction, commercial fiction, narrative non-fiction and young adult/children's (including middle-grade and young adult fiction, excludes picture books). *Founded* 2018.

The Times/Chicken House Children's Fiction Competition
See page 393

EVENTS, BURSARIES AND OTHER SCHEMES

The Malorie Blackman Scholarships for Unheard Voices
website www.citylit.ac.uk/malorie-blackman-scholarships

Three annual awards worth up to £1000 each, to fund one year's study within the Creative Writing department at City Lit. Students are welcome from students from under-represented groups, including (but is not exclusive to) those with disabilities, people from minority backgrounds and communities, members of the LGBTQ+ community, individuals from lower socioeconomic backgrounds, and BAME writers.

BookTrust Represents
See page 369

Creative Access
3rd Floor, 2 Waterhouse Square, 140 Holborn, London EC1N 2AE
email info@creativeaccess.org.uk
website www.creativeaccess.org.uk
Facebook www.facebook.com/CreativeAccessUK
Twitter @_Creative Access

A social enterprise and one of the UK's leading diversity organisations helping those from under-represented communities secure paid training opportunities, full-time jobs and leadership roles in the creative industries. It also provides a range of services to support employers create inclusive workplaces, including recruitment of trainees and permanent staff, mentoring programmers and training. Founded 2012.

Curtis Brown Creative
website www.curtisbrowncreative.co.uk/the-breakthrough-writers-programme
email cbccourses@curtisbrown.co.uk

CBC runs the Breakthrough Writers' programme, providing programmes, mentoring and scholarships for under-represented writers. See page 403

Elevate Mentoring Scheme
2 Green Barton, Swyre, Dorchester, Dorset DT2 9DN
tel (01308) 897374
email helen@cornerstones.co.uk
website https://cornerstones.co.uk/elevate-mentoring-scheme/

An Arts Council funded scheme that pairs low-income and/or under-represented writers with specialist editors best suited to help them develop their craft.

Emerging Writers Programme

tel 020-7766 4765
email email emergingwriters@londonlibrary.co.uk
website www.londonlibrary.co.uk/emerging-writers

Open to all writers above the age of 16, the Programme offers writers, in all genres, one year's free membership of The London Library and includes writing development masterclasses, literary networking opportunities, peer support and guidance in use of the Library's resources. The Virago Participation Bursary (funded by Virago Books) is awarded as part of the Programme for black female and black non-binary writers to assist with any financial issues that might prevent them from accessing the full Programme.

Future Bookshelf

website www.thefuturebookshelf.co.uk
Twitter @FutureBookshelf

Part of Hachette UK's 'Changing the Story' programme, this free creative writing resource is for under-represented writers, providing tips and exercies on writing a book and inspiring content from authors, agents and experienced editors.

Inscribe

website www.peepaltreepress.com/inscribe
Twitter @INSCRIBEwriters

Supporting writers of colour in England to professionally advance their creative work and their careers through coaching, mentoring, workshops, residentials, training, newsletters, publications and general advice.

Megaphone Writer Development Scheme

email megaphone.write@gmail.com
website https://megaphonewrite.com/
Twitter @MegaphoneWrite

An Arts Council England funded project which offers a year of one-to-one mentoring and masterclasses for writers of colour based in England who are wrtiting a novel for children or teenagers.

Owned Voices

See page 378

TLC/Arts Council England Free Reads Scheme

East Side, King Cross Station, London NC1 4AX
tel 020-7324-2563
email info@literaryconsultancy.co.uk
website www.literaryconsultancy.co.uk/editorial/ace-free-reads-scheme
Director Aki Schilz

TLC receives funding from Arts Council England to provide bursaries, via its Free Reads Scheme, for professional manuscript assessment to writers from low-income households. Free Reads are selected by a range of literature development bodies from across the UK; for detailed submission guidelines and eligibility information, see the website.

Working Class Writers Festival

Twitter @ClassFestival
Instagram @classfest
Artistic Director Natasha Carthew
Takes place 21–24 October 2021

Run as part of Bristol's Festival of Ideas, the Festival aims to give exposure to working class writers and make the event physically and financially available to all audiences, regardless of income, taking place in both physical and digital spaces.

WriteNow Programme

WriteNow - The Penguin Random House Group, 20 Vauxhall Bridge Road, London SW1V 2SA
email writenow@penguinrandomhouse.co.uk
website www.penguin.co.uk/company/creative-responsibility/writenow.html
Twitter @PenguinUKBooks

A programme by PRH which aims to nurture and publish new, unpublished writers from under-represeneted communities. Its workshops provide the aspiring writer with tools, contacts, information and access to getting published.

Writers & Artists

Bloomsbury Publishing plc, 50 Bedford Square, London WC1B 3DP
tel 020-7631 5985
email AccessWA@bloomsbury.com
website www.writersandartists.co.uk/accessible-to-all
website www.writersandartists.co.uk/bursary-opportunities

Bursary places with a combined total of £4,000 are available to help ensure that everything W&A offers – events, writing courses and editing services – is accessible to all. See the website for more details and eligibility.

Children's literature festivals and trade fairs

Some of the literature festivals in this section are specifically related to children's books and others are general arts festivals which include literature events for children.

⚠ Events may not go ahead in their usual way due to coronavirus restrictions.

Aspects Irish Literature Festival

email arts@ardsandnorthdown.gov.uk
website www.aspectsfestival.com
Twitter @aspectsfestival

An annual celebration of contemporary Irish writing with novelists, poets and playwrights. Includes readings, children's events and exhibitions.

Aye Write! Glasgow's Book Festival

Glasgow Life, Commonwealth House,
38 Albion Street, Glasgow G1 1LH
email ayewrite@glasgowlife.org.uk
Takes place May

Brings together the best undiscovered local talent with a wealth of established writers from the city, and nationwide. A free children's festival runs in tandem with the main festival. Creative writing workshops and masterclasses are on offer at the Festival. Founded 2005.

Baillie Gifford Borders Book Festival

Harmony House, St Mary's Road, Melrose TD6 9LJ
tel (01896) 822644
email info@bordersbookfestival.org
website www.bordersbookfestival.org
Facebook www.facebook.com/bordersbookfestival
Twitter @BordersBookFest
Instagram bordersbookfest
Takes place September 2021

An annual festival with a programme of events featuring high-profile and bestselling writers, including a Family Festival programme. Winner of the Walter Scott Prize for Historical Fiction is announced during the festival. Founded 2004.

Barnes Children's Literature Festival

website www.barneskidslitfest.org
Facebook www.facebook.com/BarnesKidsLitFest
Twitter @kidslitfest
Takes place May/June

The Barnes Children's Literature Festival is London's largest dedicated literature event. The Festivals have starred some of the best-known names in children's literature including Axel Scheffler, Piers Torday, Sally Gardner, Roger McGough, Lauren Child, Jacqueline Wilson, Philip Reeve, Cornelia Funke and Danny Wallace. Offers a full schedule of family-friendly events.

Bath Children's Literature Festival

The Bath Festival, 9–10 Bath Street, Bath BA1 1SN
tel (01225) 614180
email info@bathfestivals.org.uk
website https://bathfestivals.org.uk/childrens-literature/
Twitter @bathkidslitfest

Europe's largest annual dedicated children's literature festival.

Beyond the Border: The Wales International Storytelling Festival

tel (02921) 660501
email info@beyondtheborder.com
website www.beyondtheborder.com

An international festival celebrating oral tradition and bringing together storytellers, poets and musicians from around the world. This is the largest event of its type in the UK and features storytelling, poetry, music, singing, theatre, circus and film.

Bologna Children's Book Fair

Piazza Costituzione 6, 40128 Bologna, Italy
tel +39 051-282111
email bookfair@bolognafiere.it
website www.bolognachildrensbookfair.com
Facebook www.facebook.com/BolognaChildrensBookFair
Twitter @BoChildrensBook
Takes place Spring

Held annually, this is the leading children's publishing event. Publishers, authors and illustrators, literary agents, app developers, e-publishing professionals, licensors and licensees and many other members of the children's content community meet in Bologna to buy and sell copyrights, establish new contacts and strengthen their professional relationships, discover new illustrators, develop new business opportunities, learn about the latest trends and developments and explore children's educational materials, including new media products. Entry is restricted to professionals in children's content.

Cambridge Literary Festival

209 Wellington House, East Road,
Cambridge CB1 1BH

tel (01223) 515335
email hello@cambridgeliteraryfestival.com
website https://cambridgeliteraryfestival.com
Facebook www.facebook.com/CamLitFest
Twitter @camlitfest
Takes place April and November

From poetry to politics, fiction to finance, history to hip-hop and comedy to current affairs, Cambridge Literary Festival brings an eclectic mix of today's best writers, thinkers and speakers to Cambridge all year round. Founded 2003.

Cardiff Children's Lit Fest

County Hall, Cardiff CF10 4UW
email events@cardiff.gov.uk
website www.cardiffkidslitfest.com
Twitter @CDFKidsLitFest
Takes place March/April

The Cardiff Children's Literature Festival is an annual event aimed at young people who appreciate the magic of books and grown-ups who want to write them. The festival includes events with local and national authors and comprises a number of educational sessions for schools.

The Times and *The Sunday Times* Cheltenham Literature Festival

109–111 Bath Road, Cheltenham, Glos. GL53 7LS
tel (01242) 511211
email boxoffice@cheltenhamfestivals.com
website www.cheltenhamfestivals.com/literature
Facebook www.facebook.com/cheltenhamfestivals
Twitter @cheltlitfest
Takes place 8–17 October 2021

This annual festival is one of the oldest literary events in the world. The festival features adult, family and schools programmes for everyone with around 500 events over 10 days. Events for families and schools include presentations from the very best children's authors and illustrators alongside workshops, shows, storytellers, story trails, discussions and free drop-in craft activities. Founded 1949.

Derby Book Festival

13 Lavender Row, Darley Abbey, Derby DE22 1DF
email hello@derbybookfestival.co.uk
website www.derbybookfestival.co.uk
Takes place over 10 days in May/June and a weekend Autumn Edition

Celebrates the joy of books and reading for all ages and interests, with a programme featuring great writers, poets, historians, politicians, illustrators, storytellers and musicians. Each year the festival welcomes internationally celebrated bestselling authors as well as a broad range of local writing talent and includes a children's, families and educational programme. Founded 2015.

Edinburgh International Book Festival

Edinburgh College of Arts, 74 Lauriston Place, Edinburgh EH3 9DF
tel 0131 718 5666
email admin@edbookfest.co.uk
website www.edbookfest.co.uk
Twitter @edbookfest
Takes place 14–30 August 2021

The largest public celebration of the written word in the world. In addition to a unique independent bookselling operation, around 1,000 UK and international writers appear in over 900 events for adults and children. Programme details available in June. Founded 1983.

Edinburgh International Children's Festival

30B Grindlay Street, Edinburgh EH3 9AX
tel 0131 225 8050
email info@imaginate.org.uk
website www.imaginate.org.uk
Takes place May/June

The Edinburgh International Children's Festival presents the world's best theatre and dance for young audiences aged 0–15, with performances that are deeply engaging, innovative and inspiring. With an emphasis on striking visual productions, the international programme continuously goes beyond expectations of children's and young people's work. The shows, aimed at 0–15 year olds, include a mix of theatre and dance and attract an audience of over 17,000 children, families and schools every year. The Festival is also one of the best places for programmers from all over the world to see work of the very highest standard and regularly attracts over 300 industry delegates.

The Hay Festival

The Drill Hall, 25 Lion Street, Hay-on-Wye HR3 5AD
tel (01497) 822620
email admin@hayfestival.org
website www.hayfestival.com
Facebook www.facebook.com/hayfestival
Twitter @hayfestival
Takes place May

This annual festival of literature and the arts in Hay-on-Wye, Wales, brings together writers, musicians, film-makers, historians, politicians, environmentalists and scientists from around the world to communicate challenging ideas. Hundreds of events over ten days. Within the annual festival is a festival for families and children, HAYDAYS, which introduces children, from toddlers to teenagers, to their favourite authors and holds workshops to entertain and educate. Programme published April.

Ilkley Literature Festival

9 The Grove, Ilkley LS29 9LW
tel (01943) 601210

email info@ilkleylitfest.org.uk
website www.ilkleyliteraturefestival.org.uk
Facebook www.facebook.com/ilkleylitfest
Twitter @ilkleylitfest
Director Erica Morris, *Coordinator* Becky Wholley
Takes place 1–17 October 2021

One of the UK's longest-running and widest-ranging literature festivals with over 150 events, from author discussions to workshops, readings, literary walks, children's events and a festival fringe. Founded 1973.

Imagine: Writers and Writing for Children
Southbank Centre, London SE1 8XX
tel 020-7960 4200
website www.southbankcentre.co.uk/whats-on/festivals-series/imagine-childrens-festival
Twitter @southbankcentre
Takes place February

An annual festival celebrating writing for children featuring a selection of poets, storytellers and illustrators.

Independent Bookshop Week
website www.indiebookshopweek.org.uk
Facebook www.facebook.com/booksaremybag
Twitter @booksaremybag
Instagram booksaremybag
Takes place June

An annual celebration of independent bookshops, part of the Books are My Bag campaign to promote all high street bookshops in the UK and Ireland and the idea of shopping locally and sustainably.

Jewish Book Week
ORT House, 126 Albert Street, London NW1 7NE
tel 020-7446 8771
email info@jewishbookweek.com
website https://jewishbookweek.com
Twitter @JewishBookWeek
Festival Director Claudia Rubenstein
Takes place February/March

A 10-day festival of writing, arts and culture, with contributors from around the world and sessions in London and nationwide. Includes events for children and teenagers. Founded 1952.

Laureate na nÓg/Ireland's Children's Laureate
Children's Books Ireland,
17 North Great George's Street, Dublin 1 D01 R2F1, Republic of Ireland
tel +353 (0)18 727475
email info@childrenslaureate.ie
email info@childrensbooksireland.ie
website www.childrenslaureate.ie
Laureate na nÓg Project Manager Aingeala Flannery

This is a project recognising the role and importance of literature for children in Ireland, established to engage young people with high-quality literature and to underline the importance of children's literature in Ireland's cultural and imaginative life. It was awarded for the first time in 2010. The laureate participates in selected events and activities around Ireland and internationally during their newly extended three-year term as of 2020.

The laureate is chosen in recognition of their widely recognised high-quality children's writing or illustration and the positive impact they have had on readers as well as other writers and illustrators. Laureate na nÓg 2010–12, Siobhán Parkinson; 2012–14, Niamh Sharkey; 2014–16, Eoin Colfer; 2016–18, P.J. Lynch; 2018–20, Sarah Crossan; 2020–22, Áine Ní Ghlinn.

London Literature Festival
email customer@southbankcentre.co.uk
website www.southbankcentre.co.uk
Facebook www.facebook.com/southbankcentre
Twitter @southbankcentre
Takes place 21–31 October 2021

The Southbank Centre runs a year-round programme of readings, talks, workshops and debates. The annual London Literature Festival kicks off each year with Poetry International, the Southbank Centre's longest running festival, bringing together a wide range of poets from around the world. Founded 1967.

Manchester Children's Book Festival
Manchester Metropolitan University,
All Saints Building, Manchester M15 6BH
tel 0161-247 2000
email mcbf@mmu.ac.uk
website www.mmu.ac.uk/mcbf
Facebook www.facebook.com/MCBFestival
Twitter @MCBFestival
Instagram mcbfestival

A festival of year-round activities celebrating the very best writing for children, inspiring young people to engage with literature and creativity across the curriculum and offering extended projects and training to ensure the event has an impact and legacy in classrooms. Founded 2009.

May Festival
Festivals and Events Team, University of Aberdeen, King's College, Aberdeen AB24 3FX
tel (01224) 273233
email festival@abdn.ac.uk
website www.abdn.ac.uk/mayfestival
Takes place May

The Festival offers more than 120 events spanning popular themes including literature, music, film, science, visual arts and sport. The University of Aberdeen offers a *Discover* strand of events which gives audiences the opportunity to gain an insight into the research going on at the university. In addition, the Festival features a tours programme and historic exhibitions, and offers a programme of events to celebrate and showcase north east Scotland's unique cultural landscape.

Off the Shelf Festival of Words Sheffield
Cathedral Court, 46 Church Street, Sheffield S1 2GN
tel 0114 222 3895
email offtheshelf@sheffield.ac.uk
website www.offtheshelf.org.uk
Takes place 15–30 October 2021

A lively and diverse festival featuring children's authors and illustrators with activities and events for young people and lots of family events.

Oundle Festival of Literature
email kidlithillfield@live.com
website www.oundlelitfest.org.uk
Facebook www.facebook.com/
OundleFestivalOfLiterature
Twitter @OundleLitFest
Festival Director Helen Shair
Takes place early March

Kid Lit Week includes a writing competition and events for infant and junior school aged children. The Festival also runs a programme of all year round events aimed at exciting, informing, entertaining and educating a wide variety of people through talks, discussions and workshops by award-winning and local authors and poets. The Festival uses a variety of venues in the market town of Oundle, plus online Zoom Webinar events.

FT Weekend Oxford Literary Festival
c/o Critchleys, Beaver House,
23–28 Hythe Bridge Street, Oxford OX1 2EP
email info@oxfordliteraryfestival.org
website https://oxfordliteraryfestival.org
Takes place March/April

An annual festival for both adults and children held in venues across the city and university. Presents topical debates, fiction and non-fiction discussion panels, and adult and children's authors who have recently published books. Topics range from contemporary fiction to discussions on politics, history, science, gardening, food, poetry, philosophy, art and crime fiction.

Richmond upon Thames Lit Fest
Orleans House Gallery, Orleans Road,
Twickenham TW1 3BL
tel 020-8831 6000
email artsinfo@richmondandwandsworth.gov.uk
website www.richmondliterature.com
Twitter @richmondlitfest
Takes place November

An annual literature festival featuring a diverse programme of authors in venues across the borough.

The festival includes an exciting programme of author events for children and families as well as opportunities to explore creativity in literature through workshops and interactive sessions.

Scottish International Storytelling Festival
43–45 High Street, Edinburgh EH1 1SR
tel 0131 556 9579
email reception@scottishstorytellingcentre.com
website www.scottishstorytellingcentre.co.uk
Festival Director Donald Smith
Takes place October

A celebration of Scottish storytelling set in its international context, complemented by music, ballad and song. Takes place at the Scottish Storytelling Centre and partner venues across Edinburgh and Scotland.

The Self-Publishing Conference
tel 0116 279 2299
email books@troubador.co.uk
website www.selfpublishingconference.org.uk
Twitter @Selfpubconf

The UK's only dedicated self-publishing conference. This annual event covers all aspects of self-publishing from production through to marketing and distribution. The conference offers plenty of networking opportunities and access to over 16 presentations. Founded 2013.

Shanghai Children's Book Fair
email ccbf@bfchina.net
website www.ccbookfair.com/en
Facebook www.facebook.com/ccbookfair/
Twitter @ccbookfair
Takes place 19–21 November 2021

The only fair fully dedicated to books and specific contents for children aged from 0–16 in Asia Pacific. Offers unique opportunities for face-to-face interaction with publishers, popular authors, translators and illustrators from the region. Founded 2013.

StAnza: Scotland's International Poetry Festival
tel (01334) 475000 (box office) / (01334) 474610 (programmes)
email stanza@stanzapoetry.org
website www.stanzapoetry.org
Facebook www.facebook.com/stanzapoetry
Twitter @StAnzaPoetry
Instagram stanzapoetry
Festival Director Lucy Burnett
Takes place March

The festival engages with all forms of poetry: read and spoken verse, poetry in exhibition, performance poetry, cross-media collaboration, schools work, book launches and poetry workshops, with numerous UK and international guests and weekend children's events. Founded 1997.

Stratford-upon-Avon Literary Festival

email info@stratfordliteraryfestival.co.uk
website www.stratlitfest.co.uk
Facebook www.facebook.com/stratfordlitfest
Twitter @StratLitFest
Takes place May with events in autumn

The main festival takes place in May plus more events in November. The Festival is a feast of workshops, panel discussions, celebrity and best-selling author events. A charity, the festival also runs a programme of educational events and projects for families and regional schools aimed at entertaining and inspiring children, as well as events in the community and bedtime story writing workshops in prisons.

Stratford-upon-Avon Poetry Festival

website www.shakespeare.org.uk
Facebook www.facebook.com/ShakespeareBT
Twitter @ShakespeareBT
Takes place June

This annual festival celebrates Shakespeare's creative genius. Organised by the Shakespeare Birthplace Trust, the festival presents an exciting line-up of readings, performances and workshops showcasing the talents of inspirational and award-winning artists from all over the world. It also includes a special programme of family-friendly events. For more information and ticket bookings visit the website.

The Summer Festival of Writing

4 Acer Walk, Oxford OX2 6EX
tel 0345 459 9560 , +1 646-974-9060 (US)
email info@jerichowriters.com
website https://jerichowriters.com/events/summer-festival-of-writing/
Takes place June–August 2021

A three-month online festival for all writers providing the opportunity to connect with others from across the world. Writers will have the opportunity to hear from literary agents, publishers, and professional authors. This includes pitching work to literary agents; receiving live feedback from industry professionals; and enter writing competitions.

Wigtown Book Festival

Wigtown Festival Company, 11 North Main Street, Wigtown DG8 9HN
tel (01988) 402036
email mail@wigtownbookfestival.com
website www.wigtownbookfestival.com
Facebook www.facebook.com/WigtownBookFestival
Twitter @WigtownBookFest
Takes place 23 September– 3 October 2021

An annual celebration of literature and the arts in Scotland's National Book Town. Includes author events, theatre, music, film and children's and young people's programmes.

World Book Day

email wbd@education.co.uk
website www.worldbookday.com
Facebook www.facebook.com/worldbookdayuk
Twitter @WorldBookDayUK
Ceo Cassie Chadderton
Takes place First Thursday in March

World Book Day changes lives through a love of books and shared reading. Its mission is to promote reading for pleasure, offering every child and young person the opportunity to have a book of their own. Reading for pleasure is the single biggest indicator of a child's future success – more than their family circumstances, their parents' educational background or their income. They want to see more children, particularly those from disadvantaged backgrounds, form a life-long habit of reading for pleasure and the improved life chances this brings them.

The Writers' Weekend

website https://writersweekend.uk
Facebook www.facebook.com/WritersWkend
Twitter @WritersWkend
Director Sara Gangai
Takes place June/July

A conference for emerging writers, working in all genres and at all levels. Attendees participate in writing workshops, informative talks and one-to-one appointments with top literary agents to pitch their manuscripts. The Weekend is full of opportunities to network with fellow writers, published authors, agents and editors, attend panels, discuss topics of interest in small groups and share writing at open mics to a supportive and friendly crowd. The keynote speakers change every year. Award-winning children's author/illustrator, Chris Riddell, gave a keynote talk in 2021. In addition to the Weekend, four competitions are also held.

YALC (Young Adult Literature Convention)

email yalc@showmastersevents.com
website https://londonfilmandcomiccon.com/yalc
Facebook www.facebook.com/ukYALC
Twitter @yalc_uk
Takes place Annually in July

YALC is a celebration of the best young adult books and authors. It is an interactive event where young adult fiction fans can meet their favourite authors, listen to panel discussions and take part in workshops. YALC is run by Showmasters, which runs the London Film and Comic Con. Lots of opportunities available for promotional activities. Founded 2014.

Children's writing courses and conferences

Contact your local library, college or university for further information about the courses that might be most suited to you and the stage you are at with your writing.

⚠ Face-to-face courses and retreats may not go ahead in their usual way due to coronavirus restrictions.

Blue Elephant Storyshaping
email hello@blueelephantstoryshaping.com
website www.blueelephantstoryshaping.com
Editor, Coach and Mentor Natascha Biebow MBE

Offers one-to-one coaching, individual manuscript reviews and marketing advice to writers of picture books up to middle grade fiction. The Cook Up a Picture Book online course offers coaching and mentoring, and is aimed at picture book writers who wish to fine-tune their work, plus illustrators who would like to write and illustrate. The Small-Group Coaching Course is a six-week course featuring weekly, one-to-one detailed editorial feedback and top tips on key aspects of picture book craft and publishing. The aim is to create at least one marketable picture book. There is the opportunity to submit to an editor or agent at the end of this course. See website for full details of services available.

Budding Writers
8–10 Dutton Street, Manchester M3 1LE
email buddingwritersuk@gmail.com
website www.buddingwriters.co.uk
Facebook www.facebook.com/BuddingWritersUK/
Twitter @buddingwriters1

Budding Writers, an Arts Award Centre, offers an online Bronze Arts Award course for young writers up to the age of 25, writing clubs for school age children, both online and face-to-face, as well as online workshops via Zoom for adults.

Curtis Brown Creative
28–29 Haymarket, London SW1Y 4SP
tel 020-7393 4201
email cbccourses@curtisbrown.co.uk
website www.curtisbrowncreative.co.uk
Facebook www.facebook.com/CurtisBrownCreative
Twitter @cbcreative
Instagram curtisbrowncreative

The writing school led by one of the UK's leading talent agencies, offering writing classes in London and online. With 110+ students going on to get publishing deals so far, alumni include Jessie Burton, Jane Harper, Nicholas Searle and Laura Marshall. As well as offering courses on the novel, Curtis Brown Creative have an expanding roster of online courses,

covering memoirs, short stories, screenwriting, children's picture books and more. They also run the Breakthrough Writers' Programme, which offers fully funded courses, mentoring and scholarships for under-represented writers.

The Federation of Children's Book Groups Conference
email info@fcbg.org.uk
website www.fcbg.org.uk/conference
Twitter @FCBGnews
Takes place April

Held annually, guest speakers include well-known children's authors as well as experts and publishers in the field of children's books. Publishers also exhibit their newest books and resources.

The Golden Egg Academy
The Wool House, 6 Cork Street, Frome, Somerset BA11 1BL
email info@goldeneggacademy.co.uk
website www.goldeneggacademy.co.uk
Twitter @TheGEAcademy
Founder and Managing Director Imogen Cooper

Runs writing courses for authors who want to develop their writing to publication standard. All courses are run online and include: Write Your Successful Children's Novel; Writing for Children and Young Adults; Work on Your Novel and the picture book plan. Selective courses comprise virtual workshops, one-to-one editorial surgeries and regular online group seminars. Students also have the opportunity to meet industry professionals and benefit from presentations by some of the best writers in their field. Fiction writers enjoy an exclusive non-binding 'First Look' deal with Chicken House; picture book writers enjoy an exclusive non-binding 'First Look' deal with Andersen Press and Peters, Fraser and Dunlop. Also runs the Golden Egg Award for BAME, LGBTQ+, disabled and financially disadvantaged groups. Winners are awarded a free place on the twelve-week Write Your Successful Children's Novel course.

IBBY Congress
Nonnenweg 12, Postfach CH-4009-Basel, Switzerland
tel +41 61-272 2917

email ibby@ibby.org
website www.ibbycongress2020.org
Twitter @IBBYINT

IBBY's biennial international congresses bring together IBBY (the International Board on Books for Young People) members and other people involved in children's books and reading development from all over the world. The congresses are excellent occasions to make contacts, exchange ideas and open horizons. Every two years a different National Section hosts the Congress. Several hundred people attend the lectures, panel discussions, seminar sessions and workshops on current congress themes. An IBBY International Congress also serves as a framework not only for the General Assembly and other meetings, but also for the presentation of different exhibitions and celebrations such as the Hans Christian Andersen Awards and the IBBY Honour List. The 37th IBBY will take place in Moscow in September 2021.

Jericho Writers

4 Acer Walk, Oxford OX2 6EX
tel 0345 459 9560 / +1 646-974-9060 (US)
email info@jerichowriters.com
website https://jerichowriters.com
Twitter @JerichoWriters
Instagram JerichoWriters
Founder Harry Bingham

An inclusive online writing organisation that offers editorial services for all genres, tutored courses (including writing for children), and events for all genres. Jericho Writers also offer guidance for self-publishers; masterclasses; AgentMatch (a database of over 1,000 literary agents); a free Community for writers to connect; and expert guides to writing and publishing (Jericho Writers Publishing).

The London School of Journalism

tel 020-7432 8140
email admin@lsjournalism.com
website www.lsj.org/courses/distance-learning/writing-for-children

Part of the School's distance learning programme, this year-long course guides the writer as they work in your chosen genre, including picture books, story books, early readers, teenage fiction, activity books, non-fiction and books for the education market. You'll learn how to construct a story that children will enjoy reading, how to create believable characters and realistic dialogue.

Oxford University Day and Weekend Schools

Oxford University Department of Continuing Education, Rewley House, 1 Wellington Square, Oxford OX1 2JA
tel (01865) 270368
email ppdayweek@conted.ox.ac.uk
website www.conted.ox.ac.uk/about/day-and-weekend
Contact Day School Administrator

Creative writing courses including Writing for Young Adults. Topics vary from year to year. Courses always held on Fridays.

SCBWI-BI Annual Conference and Masterclass Series

email scbwi@scbwi.org
website https://britishisles.scbwi.org/masterclasses/
website www.scbwi.org
Twitter @scbwi
Instagram scbwi_british_isles
Contact Natascha Biebow

The SCBWI-BI (Society of Children's Book Writers and Illustrators – British Isles) annual conference offers a mix of inspiration, networking and fun for writers and illustrators, both published and unpublished. Offers the opportunity for published authors and illustrators to meet librarians and booksellers and market their books. Features a faculty of award-winning authors, illustrators and other industry professionals.

The Masterclass Series offers sessions for authors and illustrators to develop their knowledge and skills in a variety of areas covering a range of topics including fiction, series fiction, picture books, illustration and poetry.

SCBWI-BI Writers' Events

email araevents@britishscbwi.org
website https://britishisles.scbwi.org/events
Twitter @scbwi
Instagram scbwi_british_isles

See website for latest information about retreats and other writing and literary events organised by SCBWI-BI.

Swanwick, The Writers' Summer School

Hayes Conference Centre, Swanwick, Derbyshire DE55 1AU
tel (01290) 552248
email secretary@swanwickwritersschool.org.uk
website www.swanwickwritersschool.org.uk
Facebook www.facebook.com/SwanwickWriters
Twitter @swanwickwriters
Takes place 7–13 August 2021

Operating for over 70 years, Swanwick offers the opportunity to learn new skills and hone existing ones. There is an extensive choice of courses, talks and workshops. Offers several highly subsidised places for writers aged between 18 and 30, and assistance for writers unable to afford the full course fee. Full details of the programme and information on how to apply for the TopWrite Programme and Assisted Places Scheme are available on the website.

Tŷ Newydd Writing Centre

Tŷ Newydd, Llanystumdwy, Criccieth, Gwynedd LL52 0LW

tel (01766) 522811
email tynewydd@literaturewales.org
website www.tynewydd.wales
Twitter @ty_newydd

Tŷ Newydd, the former home of Prime Minister David Lloyd George, has hosted residential creative writing courses for writers of all abilities for over 30 years. Open to everyone over the age of 16. Courses cover everything from poetry and popular fiction to writing for the theatre and developing a novel for young adults. No qualifications are necessary; staff can advise on the suitability of courses. Also offers courses for schools, corporate courses and awaydays for companies. Tŷ Newydd is also home to Nant, the writers' retreat cottage located on site. Run by Literature Wales, the national company for the development of literature in Wales.

Writers & Artists

Bloomsbury Publishing plc, 50 Bedford Square, London WC1B 3DP
tel 020-7631 5985
email writersandartists@bloomsbury.com
website www.writersandartists.co.uk
Facebook www.facebook.com/WritersArtistsYearbook
Twitter @Writers_Artists
Contacts James Rennoldson, Clare Povey

Writers & Artists (W&A) run online and offline masterclasses, conferences and writing courses throughout the year. These are run independently or in collaboration with literary festivals, universities and charities such as Book Aid International, Literature Works and the Open University. An annual How to Write for Children & Young Adults conference is held in February, while writing courses – which cover a variety of genres – take place on weekday evenings. W&A also offers a range of editing services, and works regularly with literary agents to provide guidance on the submission process. The W&A platform is free to join, contains hundreds of writing and publishing advice articles, and offers a lively community area and personalisation features.

UNIVERSITY COURSES

Bath Spa University

Bath Spa University, Newton Park, Newton St Loe, Bath BA2 9BN
tel (01225) 875875
email admissions@bathspa.ac.uk
website www.bathspa.ac.uk/schools/school-of-creative-industries

MA Writing for Young People, PhD in Creative Writing.

University of Bolton

Deane Road Campus, Bolton BL3 5AB
tel (01204) 900600
email enquiries@bolton.ac.uk
website www.bolton.ac.uk/subject-areas/english-and-creative-writing
Facebook www.facebook.com/UniversityofBolton
Twitter @BoltonUni

Creative Writing specialisms.

University of Central Lancashire

School of Art, Design and Fashion, University of Central Lancashire, Preston PR1 2HE
tel (01772) 893364
email swilkin@uclan.ac.uk
website www.uclan.ac.uk

The MA Children's Book Illustration is a taught master's course that was founded in 2005 and which explores the practice of illustration for children's picture and story books. The course is designed to encourage pursuit of a unique and personal line of research into an artist's chosen area of children's book illustration. Many graduates have gone on to careers as published illustrators. The course runs both full and part time.

University of Chichester

Bishop Otter Campus, College Lane, Chichester, West Sussex PO19 6PE
tel (01243) 816000
email h.frey@chi.ac.uk
email h.dunkerley@chi.ac.uk
website www.chi.ac.uk
Contacts Prof. Hugo Frey (Head of Department), Dr Hugh Dunkerley (MA in Creative Writing Programme Coordinator)

BA Creative Writing, MA Creative Writing, PhD Creative Writing. Students work with practising writers. Specialisms include: novels, short stories, creative non-fiction, writing for children, screenwriting and poetry. Hosts regular visits by high-profile writers, editors and agents. Visiting Professors: Kate Mosse and Alison MacLeod. Many students go on to publish and win prizes.

University of Cumbria

tel 0808 291 6578
email enquirycentre@cumbria.ac.uk
website www.cumbria.ac.uk
Facebook www.facebook.com/universityofcumbria
Twitter @CumbriaUni

MA Creative Writing, MA Literature, Romanticism and the English Lake District, MA Graphic Novel and Children's Book Illustration

University of London, Goldsmiths

Goldsmiths, University of London, London SE14 6NW
tel 020-7919 7171
website www.gold.ac.uk
Facebook www.facebook.com/GoldsmithsUoL
Twitter @GoldsmithsUoL
Instagram @goldsmithsuol

Postgraduate courses include Art and Ecology, Artists' Film and Moving Image, Art Psychotherapy, Arts and Learning, Black British Literature, Children's Literature, Children's Illustration, Computational Arts, Computer Games Art and Design, Creative and Life Writing, Creative Writing and Education, Curating, Digital Media, Dramaturgy and Writing for Performance, Film and Screen Studies, Filmmaking, Fine Art, Journalism, Performance Making, Radio, Script Writing, Translation.

The Manchester Writing School at Manchester Metropolitan University

Arts & Humanities Building, Cavendish Street, Manchester M15 6BG
tel 0161 247 1787
email writingschool@mmu.ac.uk
website www.mmu.ac.uk/english/mcr-writing-school
Twitter @McrWritingSchl
Contact (admission and general enquiries) James Draper, Manager

Master of Fine Arts (MFA) and Master of Arts (MA) in Writing for Children & Young Adults, campus-based and international online distance learning, available to study full-time (MA: one year, MFA: two years) or part-time (MA: two years; MFA: three years). September and January enrolment. Scholarships available (including Joyce Nield Fund for non-UK Commonwealth students). Evening taught, with strong industry links. MFA students complete a full-length book. Optional unit in Teaching Creative Writing. PhD in Creative Writing – including PhD by practice and PhD by published work: Children's Writing. Tutors include Catherine Fox, Livi Michael and Alex Wheatle. Visiting Teaching Fellows: Sherry Ashworth, Mandy Coe and Paul Dowswell. Home of the Manchester Children's Book Festival (mcbf.org.uk) and Carol Ann Duffy's national and international education projects, including Mother Tongue Other Tongue (recipient of the Queen's Anniversary Prize).

Nottingham Trent University

School of Arts and Humanities, Clifton Lane, Nottingham NG11 8NS
tel 0115 848 4200
email rory.waterman@ntu.ac.uk
email hum.enquiries@ntu.ac.uk
website www.ntu.ac.uk/course/english-linguistics-creative-writing
Twitter @ntuhum
Contact Dr Rory Waterman, Programme Leader

MA Creative Writing. A practice-based course in Nottingham UNESCO City of Literature, and one of the longest-established and successful programmes of its kind in the UK (currently celebrating 27 years), with close links to the writing industry, an annual anthology, a programme of guest talks and workshops and many highly successful graduate writers. Diverse module options include: Fiction, Poetry, Writing for Stage, Radio and Screen, and Children's and Young Adult Fiction.

Plymouth Marjon University

Derriford Road, Plymouth, PL6 8BH
tel (01752) 636890
email admissions@marjon.ac.uk
website https://www.marjon.ac.uk/courses/ma-literature-for-children/

MA Literature for Children and Young Adults which includes creative writing modules.

University of Roehampton

Grove House, Roehampton Lane, London SW15 5PJ
tel 020-8392 3000
website www.roehampton.ac.uk
Facebook www.facebook.com/roehamptonuni
Twitter @RoehamptonUni
Instagram uni_roehampton

Postgraduate courses include Children's Literature, Journalism, Creative Writing, Screenwriting, Publishing, Film Practices.

University of Southampton

Avenue Campus, Highfield Road, Southampton, Hampshire SO17 1BF
tel 023-8059 5000
email enquiries@southampton.ac.uk
website www.southampton.ac.uk/courses/creative-writing-masters-ma

MA Creative Writing and Publishing which includes a module on Writing for Children and Young People.

University of Suffolk

Waterfront Building, 19 Neptune Quay, Ipswich IP4 1QJ
tel (01473) 338833
website www.uos.ac.uk/courses/pg/ma-creative-and-critical-writing

MA Creative and Critical Writing which includes a module on Children's Literature: Through the Looking Glass.

Publishing practice
Editing your work

If you are publishing, via a traditional publisher or independently, editing your work is an essential part of the process. This article outlines for authors what is involved.

What is editing?

Broadly speaking, editing involves refining your writing ('copy') to make it as readable as possible and thus ready to be published. There are four main editorial stages:

• **Manuscript assessment/critique** is an initial assessment of the strengths and weaknesses of your work, with general suggestions for improvement.

• **Developmental/structural editing** gives more in-depth feedback on aspects of your work such as pace, writing style and appropriate language for your readership, and technical features such as characterisation (fiction) or reference styles (non-fiction).

• **Copy-editing** focuses on the detail, accuracy, completeness and consistency of your text, including grammar, spelling and punctuation.

• **Proofreading** is the final check of the layout and also picks up anything overlooked earlier.

Should I edit my work before submitting it to an agent or publisher?

Most fiction is not submitted direct to a publisher but will find its way to a commissioning or acquisitions editor via a literary agent (see the articles in this *Yearbook* in the *Literary agents* section, which starts on page 249). Some specialist non-fiction can be submitted directly to an appropriate publisher. The listings under *Children's book publishers*, starting on page 11, will indicate if a company accepts unsolicited scripts. In all cases it is important to follow the agent or publisher submission guidelines.

You should always check any submission for basic spelling and grammatical mistakes ('typos') and to ensure that there are no blatant inconsistencies or factual inaccuracies. It is up to you whether you pay a professional editor to do this for you, but you are unlikely to need a full copy-edit of your whole work at this stage. It may help, though, to have an outsider or beta-reader give you feedback.

What if I am self-publishing?

Independent authors do not have to obtain or pay for editorial advice, but if you want to sell a book that looks as good and reads as well as a professionally produced one, you are unlikely to achieve this on your own. There are a host of individuals and companies available to review and edit your work at all stages in the writing process, and to guide you through design and layout to publication and marketing.

When engaging a professional editor, be cautious and read the small print about what services are being offered and what qualifications the provider has to do the job. Decide what type of help you require and employ people with a track record and recommendations. Importantly, agree a fair price for the work. If you seek out the cheapest offering you are unlikely to get the best result. Writers & Artists offer editorial services for authors.

Look also at the advice, rates, and directory of editorial professionals provided by the Chartered Institute of Editing and Proofreading (www.ciep.uk).

What happens during editing?

While processes differ from publisher to publisher, the sequence of events from draft manuscript to published copy is roughly similar. If you are self-publishing and working direct with an editor the sequence of events will be determined by which services you buy. You should not have your manuscript designed or typeset before it has been edited.

• If your work needs structural or developmental editing the publisher or freelance editor will make suggestions and you will need to revise your work accordingly.

• You will then submit the finished work for copy-editing. You should make sure you follow your publisher's style and formatting guidelines or ask your freelance editor to devise a style guide for you. This will save time in the detailed copy-edit because the text will be made consistent in line with this style guide. The editor or publisher may ask you to answer queries that arise during copy-editing.

• When the text is finalised it will be sent for typesetting or layout. If you are publishing independently, unless you are very experienced, you should find a reputable professional to do your interior page layout for print and ebook and commission a professional cover designer.

• You may be sent one or more sets of proofs of the layout, or your publisher may handle this stage. Again, if you are self-publishing then checking the proofs carefully is up to you. See the handy checklist in the **Common mistakes** box.

• Your work is now ready for publication – and the all-important marketing.

What are the differences between copy-editing and proofreading?

Copy-editing and proofreading are crucial stages in the publishing process and, while the two can often be confused or referred to interchangeably, there are important differences. The copy-editing function normally takes place when your work is complete but before typesetting or design, allowing substantial revisions to be made at minimal cost. Proof-reading, on the other hand, typically takes place after your work has been copy-edited and typeset and serves to 'fine-polish' the text to ensure that it is free from editorial and layout inaccuracies.

Copy-editing

This is the essential stage for all writers and should be done after you are happy with the general structure and content of your work. As this is the detailed, line-by-line edit, if you rewrite or add material after this stage your work will need to be edited again. The aim of copy-editing is to ensure that whatever appears in public is accurate, easy to follow, fit for purpose and free of error, omission, inconsistency and repetition. This process picks up embarrassing mistakes, ambiguities and anomalies, alerts you to possible legal problems and marks up your work for the typesetter/designer. Typically, copy-editing involves:

• checking for mistakes in spelling, grammar and punctuation;
• creating a style sheet; applying consistency in spelling, punctuation, capitalisation, etc;
• making sure the text flows well, is logically ordered and is appropriate for your target audience;

- marking up or formatting the structure for the designer – e.g. headings, tables, lists, boxed items, quotes;
- checking any illustrations and figures correspond with what's written in the text;
- checking that any bibliographical references and notes are correctly ordered and styled and that none are missing;
- making sure you have any necessary introductory pages (prelims);
- querying obvious errors of fact, misleading information or parts that are unclear.

How much editing your copy will require (and therefore how long it will take) depends on a number of factors, including:
- the complexity of the subject matter;
- how consistent you have been;
- whether you have correctly followed a publisher's house style (or your own);
- the quality of your writing.

In the past, manuscripts were copy-edited on paper, which was labour-intensive and time-consuming. These days, nearly all copy-editing is carried out electronically, usually using Microsoft Word (or sometimes a bespoke publishing system). Suggested changes are usually made using the Track Changes function; queries for the author or publisher are often

---

Common mistakes to look out for when editing and proofreading

- Punctuation mistakes, especially with direct speech and quotations.
- Inadvertently repeated words, e.g. 'and and . . .'.
- Phrases used inappropriately, e.g. 'should of' instead of 'should have' or 'compare to' instead of 'compare with'.
- Apostrophe misuse, e.g. its/it's and plurals (*not* banana's).
- Words with similar spelling or pronunciation but with different meanings used incorrectly, e.g. their/they're/there and effect/affect.
- Mixed use of past and present tenses.
- Use of plural verbs with single subjects (or vice versa), e.g. 'one in five children *are*...' instead of 'one in five children *is*...' or '[the company] *has* 100 employees and [the company] *provide* free childcare' instead of 'provides' (or 'have' and 'provide').
- Obvious factual errors, e.g. 'the Battle of Hastings in 1766'.
- Inconsistent use of abbreviations and acronyms.
- Abbreviations/acronyms that have not been defined at least once in full.
- Missing bullet points or numbers in a sequenced list.
- Typing errors, e.g. '3' instead of '£'.
- Inconsistent layout of names, addresses, telephone numbers and email/web addresses.
- Incorrect or no use of trademarks, e.g. 'blackberry' instead of 'BlackBerry™'.
- References in the text that do not correspond to footnotes.
- Inaccurate or inadequate cross-referencing.
- Index listings not found on the page given in the index.
- Text inadvertently reordered or cut during the typesetting process.
- Headings wrongly formatted as body text.
- Running heads (at the top of pages) that do not correspond to chapter headings.
- Fonts and font sizes used incorrectly.
- Formatting inconsistencies such as poorly aligned margins or uneven columns.
- Captions/headings omitted from illustrations, photographs or diagrams.
- Illustrations/photographs/diagrams without appropriate copyright references.
- Widows and orphans, i.e. text which runs over page breaks and leaves a word or a line stranded.

inserted using Comments. Copy-editors and publishers work in different ways. You may be asked to work through the changes and comments accepting, rejecting or answering each one; you may be sent a 'clean' edited version to approve; or you may just be sent queries to answer.

Proofreading

As this is the final check for errors and layout problems, you should not make major changes at this stage. These days you will normally receive proofs as pdf documents, which should be marked up using in-built commenting tools. Learn how to use the strikeout, insertion and commenting tools in your preferred pdf program (the free version of Adobe Reader, for example, will be sufficient). Proofs may be marked-up using proof correction marks (see below), but this is now less common – check with your publisher or editor which method you are expected to use. Some publishers still work with hard copy paper proofs, or you may prefer to work this way yourself, in which case it will be useful to learn to use the main proof correction marks.

What are proofreading symbols and why do I need to know them?

Proofreading symbols (proof correction marks) are the 'shorthand' that some copy-editors and proofreaders use for correcting written material and they are set by the British Standards Institution (BSi). Typesetters, designers and printers also sometimes use these as part of correcting page layout, style and format.

If you are sent a set of page proofs using this method it is important that you have at least a basic understanding of the main marks so that you can interpret corrections that have been made or add your own corrections quickly, uniformly and without any ambiguity. The main proof correction marks you need to know are shown in the tables which follow.

Using the marks

• When proofreading, make a mark in the text to show exactly where the correction needs to be made. The marginal mark is used to specify what needs to be done.
• If there is more than one mark in a line, mark from left to right and use both margins if you need to.
• Every marginal mark should be followed by an oblique stroke, unless it is already followed by the insert mark or the amendment is a delete symbol.
• Circle any comments or notes you write in the margins to distinguish them from the corrections.
• For copy-editing, marks are made in the text only.

Handy proofreading tips

Effective proofreading takes time and practice but by following these tips you'll be able to spot mistakes more quickly and accurately:
• Set aside adequate time for proofreading. It requires concentration and should not be rushed.
• Before starting on a proofreading task, make sure you have easy access to a dictionary and thesaurus, and ensure that you have any relevant style guides for spellings, use of capitals and format/design.
• If possible, proofread the document several times and concentrate on different aspects each time, e.g. sense/tone, format, grammar/punctuation/use of language.

Proof-correction marks

These marks conform to BS 5261C: 2005. In the tables below, 'character' means a letter or individual mark in the text; 'matter' means the content and could be text, a table or a picture.

Marks/symbols for general instructions

INSTRUCTIONS	MARGIN	TEXT
Leave the text in its original state and ignore any marks that have been made: *stet* (Latin for 'let it stand')	⊘	_ _ _ _ under the characters to be left as they were
Query for the author/typesetter/printer/publisher	⑦	A circle should be placed around matter to be queried
Remove non-textual marks	✕	A circle should be placed around marks to be removed
End of change	/	None

Marks/symbols for inserting, deleting and replacing text

INSTRUCTIONS	MARGIN	TEXT
Matter to be inserted	New matter, followed by ⋏	⋏
Additional matter supplied separately	⋏ followed by a letter in a diamond which identifies ⟨A⟩ additional matter	⋏
Delete a character (and close up)	℘	/ through the character
Delete text (and close up)	℘	⊢⊣ through text
Character to replace marked character	New character, followed by /	/ through the character
Text to replace marked text	New text, followed by /	⊢⊣ through text

Marks/symbols for grammar and punctuation

INSTRUCTIONS	MARGIN	TEXT
Full stop	⊙	⋏ at insertion point or / through character /
Comma	،	As above
Semi-colon	;	As above
Colon	⊙	As above
Hyphen	⊢—⊣	As above
Single quote marks	⸖ or ⸌	As above
Double quote marks	⸌⸌ or ⸌⸌	As above
Apostrophe	⸌	As above
Ellipses or leader dots	⸛	As above
Insert/replace dash	⑅ Size of dash to be stated between uprights	As above

Marks/symbols for altering the look/style/layout of text

INSTRUCTIONS	MARGIN	TEXT
Put text in italics		___ under text to be changed
Remove italics, replace with roman text		Circle text to be changed
Put text in bold		~~~ under text to be changed
Remove bold		Circle text to be changed
Put text in capitals		≡ under text to be changed
Put text in small capitals		= under text to be changed
Put text in lower case	or	Circle text to be changed
Change character to superscript	under character	│ through character to be changed
Insert a superscript character	under character	at point of insertion
Change character to subscript	above character	│ through character to be changed
Insert a subscript character	above character	at point of insertion
Remove bold and italics		Circle text to be changed
Paragraph break		
Remove paragraph break, run on text		
Indent text		
Remove indent		
Insert or replace space between characters or words		at relevant point of insertion or │ through character
Reduce space between characters or words		│
Insert space between lines or paragraphs	Mark extends into margin	─(or)─
Reduce space between lines or paragraphs	Mark extends into margin	→ or ←
Transpose lines		
Transpose characters or words		
Close space between characters		character ⌒ character
Underline words	(underline)	⊂⊃ circle words
Take over character(s) or word(s) to next line/column/page	Mark extends into margin	
Take back character(s) or word(s) to previous line/column/page	Mark extends into margin	

• Always double-check scientific, mathematical or medical symbols as they can often be corrupted during the typesetting process. Accented characters and currency symbols can also cause problems.

• If possible, have a version of the pre-typeset, copy-edited text to refer to while you proofread – it might help solve minor inaccuracies or inconsistencies more quickly.

Further resources

Butcher, Judith; Drake, Caroline and Leach, Maureen, *Butcher's Copy-editing: The Cambridge Handbook for Editors, Copy-editors and Proofreaders* (Cambridge University Press, 4th edn 2006)

Butterfield, J., *Fowler's Dictionary of Modern English Usage* (Oxford University Press, 4th edn 2015)

Hunter, Margaret, *Proofreading or Copyediting? A Quick Guide to Using Editorial Professionals* (CIEP 2020)

Ritter, R.M., *New Oxford Dictionary for Writers and Editors: The Essential A-Z Guide to the Written Word* (Oxford University Press, 2nd revised edn 2014)

The Chicago Manual of Style: The Essential Guide for Writers, Editors, and Publishers (University of Chicago Press, 17th edn 2017; www.chicagomanualofstyle.org/home.html)

Waddingham, Anne (ed.), *New Hart's Rules: The Oxford Style Guide* (Oxford University Press, 2nd edn 2014)

The Chartered Institute of Editing and Proofreading (CIEP) offers training, mentoring, support and advice for editors and proofreaders and a freely searchable directory of editorial professionals, www.ciep.uk (see page 371)

This article has been written by three professional editors. **Lauren Simpson** (lauren.simpson73@gmail.com) has over 20 years' experience as an editor, writer, publishing consultant and proofreader, both freelance and in-house. She is currently the Managing Editor at Globe Law and Business. **Margaret Hunter** (daisyeditorial.co.uk) offers copy-editing, proofreading and layout services to businesses, organisations and independent authors. She joined the CIEP Council in 2015. **Gerard M-F Hill** (much-better-text.com) served on the CIEP Council from 2007 to 2016 and co-led its successful bid for chartership. He has worked as a copy-editor, indexer, proofreader, consultant and ghostwriter.

ISBNs: what you need to know

The Nielsen ISBN Agency for UK & Ireland receives a large number of enquiries about the ISBN system. The most frequently asked questions are answered here; for more information visit www.nielsenisbnstore.com.

What is an ISBN?

An ISBN is an International Standard Book Number and is 13 digits long.

What is the purpose of an ISBN?

An ISBN is a product number, used by publishers, booksellers and libraries for ordering, listing and stock control purposes. It enables them to identify a particular publisher and allows the publisher to identify a specific edition of a specific title in a specific format within their output.

Contact details

Nielsen ISBN Agency for UK and Ireland
3rd Floor, Midas House, 62 Goldsworth Road, Woking GU21 6LQ
tel (01483) 712215
email isbn.agency@nielseniq.com
website www.nielsenisbnstore.com

Does an ISBN protect copyright?

A widely held belief is that an ISBN protects copyright. It doesn't, it is an identifier, a product code. The copyright belongs to the author. In general, publishers don't tend to buy copyrights for books. They license the copyrights, which the author retains.

What is a publisher?

The publisher is generally the person or organisation taking the financial and other risks in making a product available. For example, if a product goes on sale and sells no copies at all, the publisher loses money. If you get paid anyway, you are likely to be a designer, printer, author or consultant of some kind.

What is the format of an ISBN?

The ISBN is 13 digits long and is divided into five parts separated by spaces or hyphens.
• Prefix element: for the foreseeable future this will be 978 or 979
• Registration group element: identifies a geographic or national grouping. It shows where the publisher is based
• Registrant element: identifies a specific publisher or imprint
• Publication element: identifies a specific edition of a specific title in a specific format
• Check digit: the final digit which mathematically validates the rest of the number
The four parts following the prefix element can be of varying length.
Prior to 1 January 2007 ISBNs were ten digits long; any existing ten-digit ISBNs must be converted by prefixing them with '978' and the check digit must be recalculated using a Modulus 10 system with alternate weights of 1 and 3. The ISBN Agency can help you with this.

Do I *have* to have an ISBN?

There is no legal requirement in the UK and Ireland for an ISBN and it conveys no form of legal or copyright protection. It is simply a product identification number.

Why should I use an ISBN?

If you wish to sell your publication through major bookselling chains, independent book-shops or internet retailers, they will require you to have an ISBN to assist their internal processing and ordering systems.

The ISBN also provides access to bibliographic databases, such as the Nielsen Book Database, which use ISBNs as references. These databases help booksellers and libraries to provide information for customers. Nielsen Book has a range of information, electronic trading and retail sales monitoring services which use ISBNs and are vital for the dissemination, trading and monitoring of books in the supply chain. The ISBN therefore provides access to additional marketing opportunities which could help sales of your product.

Where can I get an ISBN?

ISBNs are assigned to publishers in the country where the publisher's main office is based. This is irrespective of the language of the publication or the intended market for the book.

The ISBN Agency is the national agency for the UK and Republic of Ireland and British Overseas Territories. A publisher based elsewhere will not be able to get numbers from the UK Agency (even if you are a British Citizen) but can contact the Nielsen ISBN Agency for details of the relevant national Agency.

If you are based in the UK and Ireland you can purchase ISBNs online from the Nielsen ISBN Store: www.nielsenisbnstore.com.

How long does it take to get an ISBN?

If you purchase your ISBNs online from the Nielsen ISBN Store you will receive your ISBN allocation within minutes. If you are purchasing ISBNs direct from the ISBN Agency via an off-line application, it can take up to five days. The processing period begins when a correctly completed application is received in the ISBN Agency and payment is received.

How much does it cost to get an ISBN?

Refer to www.nielsenisbnstore.com or email the ISBN Agency: isbn.agency@nielsen.com.

What if I only want one ISBN?

ISBNs can be bought individually or in blocks of ten or more; visit the ISBN Store to find out more.

Who is eligible for ISBNs?

Any individual or organisation who is publishing a qualifying product for general sale or distribution to the market. By publishing we mean making a work available to the public.

Which products do NOT qualify for ISBNs?

Any publication that is without a defined end should not be assigned an ISBN. For example, publications that are regularly updated and intended to continue indefinitely are not eligible for an ISBN.

Some examples of products that do not qualify for an ISBN are:

• Journals, periodicals, serials, newspapers in their entirety (single issues or articles, where these are made available separately, may qualify for ISBN);

• Abstract entities such as textual works and other abstract creations of intellectual or artistic content;

• Ephemeral printed materials such as advertising matter and the like;

• Customised print-on-demand publications (Publications that are available only on a limited basis, such as customised print-on-demand publications with content specifically

Publishing practice

tailored to a user's request shall not be assigned an ISBN. If a customised publication is being made available for wider sale, e.g. as a college course pack available through a college book store, then an ISBN may be assigned);

• Printed music;
• Art prints and art folders without title page and text;
• Personal documents (such as a curriculum vitae or personal profile);
• Greetings cards;
• Music sound recordings;
• Software that is intended for any purpose other than educational or instructional;
• Electronic bulletin boards;
• Emails and other digital correspondence;
• Updating websites;
• Games.

Following a review of the UK market, it is now permissible for ISBNs to be assigned to calendars and diaries, provided that they are not intended for purely time-management purposes and that a substantial proportion of their content is textual or graphic.

What is an ISSN?

An International Standard Serial Number. This is the numbering system for journals, magazines, periodicals, newspapers and newsletters. It is administered by the British Library, *tel* (01937) 546959; *email* issn-uk@bl.uk; *website* www.bl.uk/help/Get-an-ISBN-or-ISSN-for-your-publication#

Where do I put the ISBN?

The ISBN should appear on the reverse of the title page, sometimes called the copyright page or the imprint page, and on the outside back cover of the book. If the book has a dust jacket, the ISBN should also appear on the back of this. If the publication is not a book, the ISBN should appear on the product, and on the packaging or inlay card. If the publication is a map, the ISBN should be visible when the map is folded and should also appear near the publisher statement if this is elsewhere.

I am reprinting a book with no changes – do I need a new ISBN?

No.

I am reprinting a book but adding a new chapter – do I need a new ISBN?

Yes. You are adding a significant amount of additional material, altering the content of the book.

I am reprinting a book with a new cover design – should I change the ISBN?

No. A change of cover design with no changes to the content of the book should not have a new ISBN.

I am changing the binding on the book to paperback rather than hardback. Do I need a new ISBN?

Yes. Changes in binding always require new ISBNs even if there are no changes to the content of the book.

I am changing the price – do I need a new ISBN?

No. Price changes with no other changes do not require new ISBNs and indeed must not change the ISBN.

Public Lending Right

Under the PLR system, payment is made from public funds to authors and other contributors (writers, illustrators/photographers, translators, adapters/retellers, ghostwriters, editors/compilers/abridgers/revisers, narrators and producers) whose books (print, audiobook and ebook) are lent from public libraries. Payment is annual; the amount authors receive is proportionate to the number of times that their books were borrowed during the previous year (July to June).

How the system works

From the applications received, the PLR office compiles a database of authors and books (the PLR Register). A representative sample of book issues is recorded, consisting of all loans from selected public libraries. This is then multiplied in proportion to total library lending to produce, for each book, an estimate of its total annual loans throughout the country. The estimated loans are matched against the database of registered authors and titles to discover how many loans are credited to each registered book for the calculation of PLR payments, using the ISBN printed in the book (see below).

Parliament allocates a sum each year (£6.6 million for 2019/20) for PLR. This fund pays the administrative costs of PLR and reimburses local authorities for recording loans in the sample libraries (see below). The remaining money is divided by the total estimated national loan figure for all registered books in order to work out how much can be paid for each estimated loan of every registered ISBN.

Further information

Public Lending Right
PO Box 751, Boston Spa, Wetherby,
West Yorkshire LS22 9FW
tel (01937) 546030
website www.bl.uk/plr
website www.plrinternational.com
Contact Head of PLR Operations

The UK PLR scheme is administered by the British Library from its offices in Boston Spa. The UK PLR office also provides registration for the Irish PLR scheme on behalf of the Irish Public Lending Remuneration office.

Application forms, information and publications are all obtainable from the PLR Office. See website for further information on eligibility for PLR, loans statistics and forthcoming developments.

British Library Advisory Committee for Public Lending Right

Advises the British Library Board, the PLR Head of Policy and Engagement and Head of PLR Operations on the operation and future development of the PLR scheme.

Limits on payments

If all the registered interests in an author's books score so few loans that they would earn less than £1 in a year, no payment is due. However, if the books of one registered author score so high that the author's PLR earnings for the year would exceed £6,600, then only £6,600 is paid. (No author can earn more than £6,600 in PLR in any one year.) Money that is not paid out because of these limits belongs to the fund and increases the amounts paid that year to other authors.

The sample

Because it would be expensive and impractical to attempt to collect loans data from every library authority in the UK, a statistical sampling method is employed instead. The sample represents only public lending libraries – academic, school, private and commercial libraries are not included. Only books which are loaned from public libraries can earn PLR; consultations of books on library premises are excluded.

Publishing practice

The sample consists of the entire loans records for a year from libraries in more than 30 public library authorities spread through England, Scotland and Wales, and whole data is collected from Northern Ireland. Sample loans represent around 20% of the national total. All the computerised sampling points in an authority contribute loans data ('multi-site' sampling). The aim is to increase the sample without any significant increase in costs. In order to ensure representative sampling, at least seven libraries are replaced every year and a library cannot stay in the sample for more than four years. Loans are totalled every 12 months for the period 1 July–30 June.

An author's entitlement to PLR depends on the loans accrued by his or her books in the sample. This figure is averaged up to produce first regional and then finally national estimated loans.

ISBNs

The PLR system uses ISBNs (International Standard Book Numbers) to identify books lent and correlate loans with entries on the PLR Register so that payments can be made. ISBNs are required for all registrations. Different editions (e.g. 1st, 2nd, hardback, paperback, large print) of the same book have different ISBNs. See *ISBNs: what you need to know* on page 414.

Authorship

In the PLR system the author of a printed book or ebook is any contributor such as the writer, illustrator, translator, compiler, editor or reviser. Authors must be named on the book's title page, or be able to prove authorship by some other means (e.g. receipt of royalties). The ownership of copyright has no bearing on PLR eligibility. Narrators, producers and abridgers are also eligible to apply for PLR shares in audiobooks and e-audiobooks.

Co-authorship/illustrators. In the PLR system the authors of a book are those writers, translators, editors, compilers and illustrators as defined above. Authors must apply for

---

Summary of the 38th year's results

Registration: authors. When registration closed for the 38th year (30 June 2020) there were 66,888 authors and assignees.

Eligible loans. The loans from UK libraries credited to registered books – approximately 33% of all library borrowings – qualify for payment. The remaining loans relate to books that are ineligible for various reasons, to books written by dead or foreign authors, and to books that have simply not been applied for.

Money and payments. PLR's administrative costs are deducted from the fund allocated to the British Library Board annually by Parliament. Total government funding for 2019/20 was £6.6 million. The amount distributed to authors was just over £6 million. The Rate per Loan for 2019/20 was 9.55 pence.

The numbers of authors in various payment categories are as follows:

*299	payments at	£5,000–6,600
356	payments between	£2,500–4,999.99
790	payments between	£1,000–2,499.99
838	payments between	£500–999.99
3,189	payments between	£100–499.99
16,225	payments between	£1–99.99
21,697	TOTAL	

* Includes 200 authors whose book loans reached the maximum threshold

registration before their books can earn PLR and this can be done via the PLR website. There is no restriction on the number of authors who can register shares in any one book as long as they satisfy the eligibility criteria.

Writers and/or illustrators. At least one contributor must be eligible and they must jointly agree what share of PLR each will take based on contribution. This agreement is necessary even if one or two are ineligible or do not wish to register for PLR. The eligible authors will receive the share(s) specified in the application.

Translators. Translators may apply for a 30% fixed share (to be shared equally between joint translators).

Editors and compilers. An editor or compiler may apply to register a 20% share if they have written at least 10% of the book's content or more than ten pages of text in addition to normal editorial work and are named on the title page. Alternatively, editors may register 20% if they have a royalty agreement with the publisher. In the case of joint editors/compilers, the total editor's share should be divided equally.

Audiobooks. PLR shares in audiobooks are fixed by the UK scheme and may not be varied. *Writers* may register a fixed 60% share in an audiobook, providing that it has not been abridged or translated. In cases where the writer has made an additional contribution (e.g. as narrator), she/he may claim both shares. *Narrators* may register a fixed 20% PLR share in an audiobook. *Producers* may register a fixed 20% share in an audiobook. *Abridgers* (in cases where the writer's original text has been abridged prior to recording as an audiobook) qualify for 12% (20% of the writer's share). *Translators* (in cases where the writer's original text has been translated from another language) qualify for 18% (30% of the writer's share). If there is more than one writer, narrator, etc the appropriate shares should be divided equally.

Dead or missing co-authors. Where it is impossible to agree shares with a co-author because that person is dead or untraceable, then the surviving co-author or co-authors may submit an application to register a share which reflects their individual contribution to the book.

Transferring PLR after death. First applications may not be made by the estate of a deceased author. However, if an author registers during their lifetime the PLR in their books can be transferred to a new owner and continues for up to 70 years after the date of their death. The new owner can apply to register new titles if first published one year before, or up to ten years after, the date of the author's death. New editions of existing registered titles can also be registered posthumously.

Residential qualifications. To register for the UK PLR scheme, at the time of application authors must have their only home or principal home in the UK or in any of the other countries within the European Economic Area (i.e. EC member states plus Iceland, Norway and Liechtenstein).

Eligible books

In the PLR system each edition of a book is registered and treated as a separate book. A book is eligible for PLR registration provided that:
• it has an eligible author (or co-author);
• it is printed and bound (paperbacks count as bound);
• it has already been published;
• copies of it have been put on sale, i.e. it is not a free handout;

• the authorship is personal, i.e. not a company or association, and the book is not crown copyright;
• it has an ISBN;
• it is not wholly or mainly a musical score;
• it is not a newspaper, magazine, journal or periodical.

Audiobooks. An audiobook is defined as an 'authored text' or 'a work recorded as a sound recording and consisting mainly of spoken words'. Applications can therefore only be accepted to register audiobooks which meet these requirements and are the equivalent of a printed book. Music, dramatisations and live recordings do not qualify for registration. To qualify for UK PLR in an audiobook contributors should be named on the case in which the audiobook is held; or be able to refer to a contract with the publisher; or be named within the audiobook recording.

Ebooks. Previously only ebooks downloaded to fixed terminals in library premises and then taken away on loan on portable devices to be read elsewhere qualified for PLR payment. Information provided by libraries suggested that the vast majority of ebook and digital audio lending was carried out 'remotely' to home PCs and mobile devices, which meant the loan did not qualify for PLR.

On 27 April 2017 the Digital Economy Bill, which included provision to extend the UK PLR legislation to include remote loans of ebooks from public libraries, received Royal Assent. The new arrangements took effect officially from 1 July 2018, and remote ebook loans data is now collected, and the first payments arising from the newly eligible loans were made in February 2020. The PLR website provides updated information on this legislation.

Statements and payment

Authors with an online account may view their statement online. Registered authors without an online account receive a statement posted to their address if a payment is due.

Sampling arrangements

To help minimise the unfairness that arises inevitably from a sampling system, the scheme specifies the eight regions within which authorities and sampling points have to be designated and includes libraries of varying size. Part of the sample drops out by rotation each year to allow fresh libraries to be included. The following library authorities were designated for the year 1 July 2020–30 June 2021 (all are multi-site authorities). This list is based on the nine government regions for England plus Northern Ireland, Scotland and Wales. The composition of the PLR library authority sample changes annually and not all regions have to be represented each year.
• East – no library authorities during 2020/21
• East Midlands – Derbyshire, Rutland
• London – Bromley, Greenwich, Hounslow, Lewisham
• North East – Durham, Northumberland
• North West & Merseyside – Bury, Lancashire, Trafford
• South East – Bracknell Forest, Isle of Wight, Oxfordshire, West Sussex
• South West – Devon, Plymouth, Shropshire, Wiltshire
• West Midlands – Dudley
• Yorkshire & The Humber – Calderdale, Wakefield

• Northern Ireland – The Northern Ireland Library Authority
• Scotland – Falkirk, Fife, Highland, South Lanarkshire
• Wales – Bridgend, Carmarthenshire, Conwy, Newport.

Participating local authorities are reimbursed on an actual cost basis for additional expenditure incurred in providing loans data to the PLR Office. The extra PLR work mostly consists of modifications to computer programs to accumulate loans data in the local authority computer and to transmit the data to the PLR Office.

Reciprocal arrangements

Reciprocal PLR arrangements now exist with the German, Dutch, Austrian and other European PLR schemes. Authors can apply for overseas PLR for most of these countries through the ALCS (Authors' Licensing and Collecting Society; see page 431). The exception to this rule is Ireland. Authors should now register for Irish PLR through the UK PLR Office. Further information on PLR schemes internationally and recent developments within the EC towards wider recognition of PLR is available from the PLR Office or on the international PLR website.

Glossary of publishing terms

advance

Money paid by a publisher to an author before a book is published which will be covered by future royalties. A publishing contract often allows an author an advance payment against future royalties; the author will not receive any further royalties until the amount paid in advance has been earned by sales of the book.

advance information (AI) sheet

A document that is put together by a publishing company to provide sales and marketing information about a book before publication and can be sent several months before publication to sales representatives. It can incorporate details of the format and contents of the book, key selling points and information about intended readership, as well as information about promotions and reviews.

backlist

The range of books already published by a publisher that are still in print.

blad (book layout and design)

A pre-publication sales and marketing tool. It is often a printed booklet that contains sample pages, images and front and back covers which acts as a preview for promotional use or for sales teams to show to potential retailers, customers or reviewers.

blurb

A short piece of writing or a paragraph that praises and promotes a book, which usually appears on the back or inside cover of the book and may be used in sales and marketing material.

book club edition

An edition of a book specially printed and bound for a book club for sale to its members.

co-edition

The publication of a book by two publishing companies in different countries, where the first company has originated the work and then sells sheets to the second publisher (or licenses the second publisher to reprint the book locally).

commissioning editor

A person who asks authors to write books for the part of the publisher's list for which he or she is responsible or who takes on an author who approaches them direct or via an agent with a proposal. Also called acquisitions editor or acquiring editor (more commonly in the USA). A person who signs-up writers (commissions them to write) an article for a magazine or newspaper.

copy-editor

A person whose job is to check material ready for printing for accuracy, clarity of message and writing style and consistency of typeface, punctuation and layout. Sometimes called a desk editor.

copyright

The legal right, which the creator of an original work has, to only allow copying of the work with permission and sometimes on payment of royalties or a copyright fee. An amendment to the Copyright, Designs and Patents Act (1988) states that in the UK most works are protected for 70 years from the creator's death. The 'copyright page' at the start of a book asserts copyright ownership and author identification.

distributor

Acts as a link between the publisher and retailer. The distributor can receive orders from retailers, ship books, invoice, collect revenue and deal with returns. Distributors often handle books from several publishers. Digital distributors handle ebook distribution.

double-page spread

Two facing pages of an illustrated book.

editor

A person in charge of publishing a newspaper or magazine who makes the final decisions about the content and format. A person in book publishing who has responsibility for the content of a book and can be variously a senior person (editor-in-chief) or day-to-day contact for authors (copy-editor, development editor, commissioning editor, etc).

endmatter

Material at the end of the main body of a book which may be useful to the reader, including references, appendices, indexes and bibliography. Also called back matter.

extent

The number of pages in a book.

folio

A large sheet of paper folded twice across the middle and trimmed to make four pages of a book. Also a page number.

frontlist

New books just published (generally in their first year of publication) or about to be published by a publisher. Promotion of the frontlist is heavy, and the frontlist carries most of a publisher's investment. On the other hand, a backlist which continues to sell is usually the most profitable part of a publisher's list.

imprint

The publisher's or printer's name which appears on the title page of a book or in the bibliographical details; a brand name under which a book is published within a larger publishing company, usually representing a specialised subject area.

inspection copy

A copy of a publication sent or given with time allowed for a decision to purchase or return it. In academic publishing, lecturers can request inspection copies to decide whether to make a book/textbook recommended reading or adopt it as a core textbook for their course.

ISBN

International Standard Book Number.

ISSN

International Standard Serial Number. An international system used on periodicals, magazines, learned journals, etc. The ISSN is formed of eight digits, which refer to the country in which the magazine is published and the title of the publication.

literary agent

Somebody whose job is to negotiate publishing contracts, involving royalties, advances and rights sales on behalf of an author and who earns commission on the proceeds of the sales they negotiate.

moral right

The right of people such as editors, authors or illustrators to have some say in the publication of a work to which they have contributed, even if they do not own the copyright.

out of print or o.p.

Relating to a book of which the publisher has no copies left and which is not going to be reprinted. Print on demand technology, however, means that a book can be kept 'in print' indefinitely.

packager

A company that creates a finished book for a publisher.

PDF/pdf

Portable Document Format. A data file generated from PostScript that is platform-independent, application-independent and font-independent. Acrobat is Adobe's suite of software used to generate, edit and view pdf files.

picture researcher

A person who looks for pictures relevant to a particular topic, so that they can be used as illustrations in, for example, a book, newspaper or TV programme.

prelims

The initial pages of a book, including the title page and table of contents, which precede the main text. Also called front matter.

pre-press

Before a book goes to press.

print on demand or POD

The facility to print and bind a small number of books at short notice, without the need for a large print run, using digital technology. When an order comes through, a digital file of the book can be printed individually and automatically.

production controller

A person in the production department of a publishing company who deals with printers and other suppliers.

proofreader

A person whose job is to proofread texts to check typeset page presentation and text for errors and to mark up corrections.

publisher

A person or company that publishes books, magazines and/or newspapers.

publisher's agreement

A contract between a publisher and the copyright holder, author, agent or another publisher, which lays down the terms under which the publisher will publish the book for the copyright holder.

publishing contract

An agreement between a publisher and an author by which the author grants the publisher the right to publish the work against payment of a fee, usually in the form of a royalty.

reading fee

Money paid to somebody for reading a manuscript and commenting on it.

recto

Relating to the right-hand page of a book, usually given an odd number.

reprint

Copies of a book made from the original, but with a note in the publication details of the date of reprinting and possibly a new title page and cover design.

rights

The legal right to publish something such as a book, picture or extract from a text.

rights manager

A person who negotiates and coordinates rights sales (e.g. for subsidiary, translation or foreign rights). Often travels to book fairs to negotiate rights sales.

royalty

Money paid to a writer for the right to use his or her property, usually a percentage of sales or an agreed amount per sale.

royalty split

The way in which a royalty is divided between several authors or between author and illustrator.

royalty statement

A printed statement from a publisher showing how much royalty is due to an author.

sans serif

A style of printing letters with all lines of equal thickness and no serifs. Sans faces are less easy to read than seriffed faces and they are rarely used for continuous text, although some magazines use them for text matter.

sensitivity reader

Assesses a manuscript with a particular issue of representation in mind, usually one that they have personal experience of.

serialisation

Publication of a book in parts in a magazine or newspaper.

serif

A small decorative line added to letters in some fonts; a font that uses serifs, such as Times. The addition of serifs keeps the letters apart while at the same time making it possible to link one letter to the next, and makes the letters distinct, in particular the top parts which the reader recognises when reading.

slush pile

Unsolicited manuscripts which are sent to publishers or agents, and which may never be read.

style sheet

A guide listing all the rules of house style for a publishing company which has to be followed by authors and editors.

sub-editor

A person who corrects and checks articles in a newspaper before they are printed.

subsidiary rights

Rights other than the right to publish a book in its first form, e.g. paperback rights; rights to adapt the book; rights to serialise it in a magazine; film and TV rights; audio, ebook, foreign and translation rights.

territory

Areas of the world where the publisher has the rights to publish or can make foreign rights deals.

trade discount

A reduction in price given to a customer in the same trade, as by a publisher to another publisher or to a bookseller.

trade paperback (B format)

A paperback edition of a book that is superior in production quality to a mass-market paperback edition and is similar to a hardback in size 198 x 129mm.

trim size or trimmed size

The measurements of a page of a book after it has been cut, or of a sheet of paper after it has been cut to size.

typesetter

A person or company that 'sets' text and prepares the final layout of the page for printing. It can also now involve XML tagging for ebook creation.

typographic error or typo

A mistake made when keying text or typesetting.

verso

The left-hand page of a book, usually given an even number.

volume rights

The right to publish the work in hardback or paperback (this can now sometimes include ebook).

XML tagging

Inserting tags into the text that can allow it to be converted for ebooks or for use in electronic formats.

Copyright and contracts
Author–Publisher contracts

Publishing contracts can be lengthy, it's helpful to know what types of clauses they are likely to include and why they are there.

If you have an agent, he or she will negotiate your publishing contract on your behalf. Organisations such as the of the Society of Authors (see page 349) and WGGB (see page 352) offer contract review services. A contract is a legal agreement between two parties and exists to protect both author and publisher. It includes clauses on rights and obligations to avoid ambiguity as to the responsibilities of both parties. The clauses in your publishing contract are likely to include those listed below.

Definitions used throughout the contract will often be included at the beginning or in an appendix, and might include terms such as 'Net receipts', 'Hybrid Product', 'First Serial', 'Territory', and 'Electronic Book'.

Legal operation and enforcement of the contract is covered by a few standard clauses, such as those relating to 'Interpretation', 'Arbitration', 'Confidentiality', 'Notices' and 'Entire Agreement'.

Free to publish

The author confirms that she is able to enter into the agreement and that the book she is writing is a unique, new property, her own work and will not contain any legally compromising material. Note that the first example below indicates the style of legalese in which your contract is likely to be couched:

Exclusivity 'The Author hereby grants to the Publishers during the legal term of copyright the sole and exclusive licence to publish the said work in volume form.'

Warranty and indemnity are confirmed, meaning the author states that she is freely able to enter into the agreement, is the sole author, owns the rights in the 'work' and that it is unique, i.e. has not been published elsewhere previously and does not contain any libellous or defamatory material or content that isn't hers to include, i.e. that is someone else's copyright and that the author has cleared permissions with the copyright holder for any part of somebody else's work being reproduced in the book. The author agrees to cover any legal costs, other fees or losses if she is in any way in breach of the warranty.

Territory

This is the geographical areas where the book can be sold, for example UK and Europe, or North American, or World territories.

Rights

Legal Term is the period that the contract covers, from date of signature of the contract by both parties or until rights are reverted to the author.

Granting and Reversion An author agrees that the publisher is allowed to publish their Work during the legal term. Rights might revert (back to the author) automatically when sales dip below a minimum annual level, of say fifty copies. An author may negotiate to have rights in their book reverted and will be able to purchase any remaining stock. At that stage the contract is also formally terminated.

Termination might also occur if either party breaches any of the terms of the contract, for example if the author fails to deliver a manuscript of the quality expected on time and if it is found to be plagiarised. Late delivery alone would not usually be grounds for termination, but an author should always inform the agent or publisher if a contracted delivery date cannot be fulfilled.

Copyright Notice and Infringement This covers how the author's name will appear in the book, i.e. © name of author, 20XX. These clauses confirm that copyright in the Work is the property of the author. They will also make it clear that, if the publisher decides to protect the copyright of a book insofar as it threatens the value of the rights sold to a publisher, the author will assist the publisher (at the publisher's expense).

Subsidiary rights include:
• Anthology and quotation rights
• Broadcast reading and audiobook rights
• Digital and electronic rights
• Dramatisation, film, documentary, television sound broadcasting video or other mechanical reproduction rights
• English language rights (royalty exclusive)
• First serial rights (first place e.g. in a magazine where an extract from an original Work is serialised or published)
• Large print, educational, reprint or paperback rights licensed to a book club or to another publisher
• Micrography reprography, merchandising and manufacturing rights
• Second serial rights (rights sold subsequent to the first serial rights, see above)
• Single-extract or digest or book condensation rights
• Translation rights (royalty exclusive)
• US rights (royalty exclusive)

Each set of rights will be subject to a royalty percentage, payable to the author when these rights have been exercised. Some rights are held back or retained by an agent or author, so they might be exploited at another time and be subject to negotiation with a third party after publication. These tend to be the potentially more lucrative rights if exploited, such as dramatisation and film, translation or audio. Some 'hybrid' authors will license print rights to a publisher but retain digital book rights to allow them to self-publish in that format; a contract would make clear in which territories each edition might be sold.

Practicalities

Delivery – this will include a realistic delivery date and the specifications as to what will be delivered in what format (e.g. complete digital manuscript), to what extent (70,000 words including any endmatter) and accompanied by any material (extracts, quotations) for which copyright might need to be cleared.

Payments

Advances The advance is an example of financial goodwill, a pact that author and editor have cemented through the contract to agree to work together and to make money from the activity. It is usually paid in two or three equal tranches, payable on signature of the contract, on delivery and approval of the final manuscript, and on first publication. The advance against royalties means a payment made before any actual revenue from sales of your book have been received.

Royalties are the fees paid to an author on the sale of copies of their book and are subject to sliding scales, so that as a book becomes more successful an author benefits more. As more and more copies are sold the investment the publisher made in producing the first print run will be recouped; subsequent runs might become very profitable for the publisher and rightly an agent will argue for an author to profit from this success too. Such rising royalty rates for a published price contract might look something like this:

• **on home sales**: 7.5 per cent of the published price on the first ten thousand (10,000) copies sold; 10 per cent of the published price up to twenty thousand (20,000) copies sold and 12.5 per cent of the published price on all copies sold thereafter, such royalty not to be deemed a precedent between the Publishers and Author or agent;

• **on home sales where the discount is 52.5 per cent or more**: four-fifths (4/5ths) of the prevailing royalty; on home sales where the discount is 60 per cent or more: three-fifths (3/5ths) of the prevailing rate.

Free and presentation copies will be provided to the author (anywhere between six and fifteen free copies) on publication and to potential reviewers as part of a promotional campaign; royalty payments are not made against these gratis copies. Authors may purchase copies of their own book at discount.

Payment process, accounting periods and other details about how and when the publisher will remunerate the author (or their agent on the author's behalf) will be included.

Publishing process

Author corrections and their proofreading responsibilities might be clearly laid out, covering what checking tasks an author will be expected to undertake and when and which might be carried out and paid for by the publisher, such as having an index prepared or clearing permissions for images or quotations. It might also include a clause in which the publisher 'reserves the right to charge the Author' for the cost of author corrections to page proofs if these are over and above the usual level of alterations. Such costs might be debited against the author's royalty account.

Promotion clauses advise that a publisher shall advertise, promote and market the Work as they deem appropriate 'in their sole discretion'. If you feel strongly as an author that you wish to be consulted about any aspect of promotion or cover design you could ask for such clauses to be modified. The most you are likely to get is an amendment that agrees an author will be 'consulted' and asked to 'agree' to the publisher's plan and that their agreement 'will not be unreasonably withheld'.

Publication date might not be firmly set when the contract is signed but the publisher's commissioning editor should have a clear idea of what quarter they would like the book to appear in. An agreement would usually stipulate that the book should be published within twelve months of date of delivery and acceptance 'unless prevented by circumstances over which they have no control or unless mutually agreed'.

New and updated editions for non-fiction titles might be referred to, defining what would constitute a 'new' rather than a 'revised' edition and how much new content it might include, say at least 10 per cent new material. The author would be offered first refusal on preparing a new edition, but the publisher would want to include a clause to allow them to ask another writer to complete such a project if they perceived there was a market for it, but the original author was unable or unwilling to take on the commission.

The contract should not daunt an author. It is supposed to be a joint declaration and not biased in favour of one party or the other.

By **Alysoun Owen**, Editor of the *Writers' & Artists' Yearbook* and author of the *Writers' & Artists' Guide to Getting Published* (Bloomsbury 2019).

Copyright Licensing Agency Ltd

The Copyright Licensing Agency (CLA) is a non-profit body established to help organisations to legally copy and share extracts from published works.

It is recognised by the government (www.gov.uk/copyright-licensing-agency-licence) as the collective licensing body for the reuse of text and images from books, journals and magazines.More information on collective licensing bodies can be found at: www.gov.uk/guidance/licensing-bodies-and-collective-management-organisations.

It licenses on behalf of its four members: ALCS (the Authors' Licensing and Collecting Society), PLS (Publishers' Licensing Services), DACS (The Design and Copyright Society) and PICSEL (Picture Industry Collecting Society for Effective Licensing).

CLA's licences permit limited copying, including photocopying, scanning and emailing of articles and extracts from books, journals and magazines, as well as digital copying from electronic publications, online titles and websites. CLA issues its licences to schools, further and higher education, businesses and government bodies. The money collected is distributed to the copyright owners to ensure that they are fairly rewarded for the use of their intellectual property. It gives licensees protection against the risk of copyright infringement and includes an indemnity against legal action, offering a simple solution to copyright compliance.

How CLA helps creators and users of copyright work

CLA provides content users with access to millions of titles worldwide. In return, CLA ensures that creators, artists, photographers and writers, along with publishers, are paid royalties for the copying, sharing and re-use of limited extracts of their published work.

> **Further information**
>
> **The Copyright Licensing Agency Ltd**
> 5th Floor, Shackleton House,
> 4 Battle Bridge Lane, London SE1 2HX
> *tel* 020-7400 3100
> *email* cla@cla.co.uk
> *website* www.cla.co.uk

Through this collective licensing system CLA provides users with the simplest and most cost-effective means of obtaining authorisation for the use of their work.

CLA has licences which enable digitisation of existing print material, enabling users to scan and electronically send extracts from print copyright works as well as copy digital electronic and online publications, including websites.

Who is licensed?

CLA offers licences to three principal sectors:
• education (schools, further and higher education);
• government (central departments, local authorities, public bodies); and
• business (businesses, industry and the professions).

The licences meet the specific needs of each sector and user groups within each sector. Depending upon the requirement, there are both blanket and transactional licences available. Every licence allows copying from most print and digital books, journals, magazines and periodicals published in the UK.

The international dimension

Many countries have established equivalents to CLA and the number of such agencies is set to grow. Nearly all these agencies, including CLA, are members of the International Federation of Reproduction Rights Organisations (IFRRO).

Through reciprocal arrangements covering 38 overseas territories, including the USA, Canada and most EU countries, CLA's licences allow copying from an expanding list of international publications. CLA receives monies from these territories for the copying of UK material abroad, passing it on to UK rights holders.

Distribution of licence fees

The fees collected from licensees are forwarded to ALCS, PLS, DACS and PISCEL for distribution to publishers, writers and visual artists. The allocation of fees is based on subscriptions, library holdings and detailed surveys of copying activity (see www.cla.co.uk/who-we-represent and read the 'Distribution Model Report'). CLA has collected and distributed over £1.45 billion as royalties to copyright owners since 1983. For the year 2019/20, £76.8 million was paid to creators and publishers in the UK and abroad.

Copyright. Made simple

The CLA exists to simplify copyright for content users and copyright owners. They help their customers to legally access, copy and share published content while making sure copyright owners are paid royalties for the use of their work.

Their rights, licences and innovative digital services (including the Digital Content Store for Higher Education; and the Education Platform for UK schools) make it easy for content users to use and manage digitalised content and digital versions of books. By doing so they simplify access to the work of 100,000 authors, 25,000 visual artists and 3,500 publishers and play an important part in supporting the creative industries.

Authors' Licensing and Collecting Society

ALCS is the rights management society for UK writers.

ALCS is the largest writers' organisation in the UK with a membership of over 100,000. In the financial year of 2019/20, it paid 110,000 writers over £36.8 million (net) in royalties. Once you've paid your £36 lifetime membership fee, whatever you've earned in secondary royalties is paid into your bank account during twice yearly distributions. You can be part of this organisation which is committed to ensuring that writers' intellectual and moral rights are fully respected and fairly rewarded. ALCS represents all types of writers and includes educational, research and academic authors drawn from the professions - scriptwriters, adapters, playwrights, poets, editors and freelance journalists, across the print and broadcast media.

Established in 1977, ALCS (a non-profit company) was set up in the wake of the campaign to establish a Public Lending Right (see page 417) to help writers protect and exploit their collective rights. The organisation now represents the interests of all UK writers and aims to ensure that they are fairly compensated for any works that are copied, broadcast or recorded.

Internationally recognised as a leading authority on copyright matters and authors' interests, ALCS is committed to fostering an awareness of intellectual property issues among the writing community. It maintains a close watching brief on all matters affecting copyright, both in the UK and internationally, and makes regular representations to the UK government and the European Union.

ALCS collects fees that are difficult, time-consuming or legally impossible for writers and their representatives to claim on an individual basis, money that is nonetheless due to them. To date, it has distributed over £500 million in secondary royalties to writers. Over the years, ALCS has developed highly specialised knowledge and sophisticated systems that can track writers and their works against any secondary use for which they are due payment. A network of international contacts and reciprocal agreements with foreign collecting societies also ensures that UK writers are compensated for any similar use overseas.

The primary sources of fees due to writers are secondary royalties from the following:

Membership

Authors' Licensing and Collecting Society Ltd
5th Floor, Shackleton House,
4 Battle Bridge Lane, London SE1 2HX
tel 020-7264 5700
email alcs@alcs.co.uk
website www.alcs.co.uk
Chief Executive Owen Atkinson

Membership is open to all writers and successors to their estates at a one-off fee of £36. Members of the Society of Authors, the Writers' Guild of Great Britain, National Union of Journalists, Chartered Institute of Journalists and British Association of Journalists have free membership of ALCS. Operations are primarily funded through a commission levied on distributions and membership fees. The commission on funds generated for Ordinary members is currently 9.5%. Most writers will find that this, together with a number of other membership benefits, provides good value.

Photocopying and scanning

The single largest source of income, this is administered by the Copyright Licensing Agency (CLA; see page 429). Created in 1982 by ALCS and the Publishers' Licensing Services (PLS), CLA grants licences to users for copying books and serials. This includes schools, colleges, universities, central and local government departments, as well as the British Library, businesses and other institutions. Licence fees are based on the number of people who benefit and the number of copies made. The revenue from this is then split between the rights holders: authors, publishers and artists. Money due to authors is transferred to ALCS for distribution. ALCS also receives photocopying payments from foreign sources.

Foreign Public Lending Right

The Public Lending Right (PLR) system pays authors whose books are borrowed from public libraries. Through reciprocal agreements, ALCS members receive payment through a number of overseas Public Lending Right (PLR) schemes, currently from Germany, Belgium, the Netherlands, France, Austria, Estonia and Ireland. Please note that ALCS does not administer the UK Public Lending Right; this is managed directly by the UK PLR Office (see page 417).

Simultaneous cable retransmission

This involves the simultaneous showing of one country's television signals in another country, via a cable network. Cable companies pay a central collecting organisation a percentage of their subscription fees, which must be collectively administered. This sum is then divided by the rights holders. ALCS receives the writers' share for British programmes containing literary and dramatic material and distributes it to them.

Educational recording

ALCS, together with the main broadcasters and rights holders, set up the Educational Recording Agency (ERA) in 1989 to offer licences to educational establishments. ERA collects fees from the licensees and pays ALCS the amount due to writers for their literary works.

Other sources of income include a blank tape levy and small, miscellaneous literary rights.

Tracing authors

ALCS is dedicated to protecting and promoting authors' rights and enabling writers to maximise their income. It is committed to ensuring that royalties due to writers are efficiently collected and speedily distributed to them. One of its greatest challenges is finding some of the writers for whom it holds funds and ensuring that they claim their money.

Any published author or broadcast writer could have some funds held by ALCS for them. It may be a nominal sum or it could run into several thousand pounds. Either call or visit the ALCS website – see **Membership** box for contact details.

DACS (Design and Artists Copyright Society)

Established by artists for artists, DACS is the UK's leading visual artists' rights management organisation.

As a not-for-profit organisation, DACS translates rights into revenues and recognition for a wide spectrum of visual artists. It collects and distributes royalties to visual artists and their estates through its different services, including Payback, Artist's Resale Right, Copyright Licensing and

Contact details

DACS
33 Old Bethnal Green Road, London E2 6AA
tel 020-7336 8811
email info@dacs.org.uk
website www.dacs.org.uk

Artimage – in addition to lobbying, advocacy and legal advice for visual artists.

DACS is part of an international network of rights management organisations. Today DACS acts as a trusted broker for over 100,000 artists worldwide and in 2018 it distributed £18 million in royalties to artists and estates. See website for more information about DACS and its services.

Payback

Each year DACS pays a share of royalties to visual artists whose work has been reproduced in UK magazines and books or broadcast on UK television channels. DACS operates this service for situations where it would be impractical or near impossible for an artist to license their rights on an individual basis, for example when a university student wants to photocopy pages from a book that features their work.

Artist's Resale Right

The Artist's Resale Right entitles artists to a royalty each time their work is resold for €1,000 or more by an auction house, gallery or dealer. DACS ensures artists receive their royalties from qualifying sales not just in the UK but also from other countries in the European Economic Area (EEA). Since 1 January 2012 in the UK, artists' heirs and beneficiaries can now benefit from these royalties. (See website for details of eligibility criteria.)

Copyright Licensing

This service benefits artists and their estates when their work is reproduced for commercial purposes, for example on t-shirts or greetings cards, in a book or on a website. DACS can take care of everything on behalf of the artist, ensuring terms, fees and contractual arrangements are all in order and in their best interests. Artists who use this service are also represented globally through the DACS international network of rights management organisations.

Copyright facts

• Copyright is a right granted to visual artists under law.
• Copyright in all artistic works is established from the moment of creation – the only qualification is that the work must be original.

• There is no registration system in the UK; copyright comes into operation automatically and lasts the lifetime of the visual artist plus a period of 70 years after their death.

• After death, copyright is usually transferred to the visual artist's heirs or beneficiaries. When the 70-year period has expired, the work then enters the public domain and no longer benefits from copyright protection.

• The copyright owner has the exclusive right to authorise the reproduction (or copy) of a work in any medium by any other party.

• Any reproduction can only take place with the copyright owner's consent.

• Permission is usually granted in return for a fee, which enables the visual artist to derive some income from other people using his or her work.

• If a visual artist is commissioned to produce a work, he or she will usually retain the copyright unless an agreement is signed which specifically assigns the copyright. When visual creators are employees and create work during the course of their employment, the employer retains the copyright in those works.

Money, tax and benefits
Managing your finances: a guide for writers

Chartered accountants Jonathan and Louise Ford of Writers Tax Limited set out a clear view of the various financial issues that a writer needs to understand and consider at each stage of their writing career, with helpful links and valuable advice.

In some ways the financial issues of being a writer are no different to pursuing any other occupation. You earn money for your skill, you deduct the costs you have incurred earning your money, and you pay tax on what's left. However, there are several factors that, in combination, make the situation of a writer unique; many writers have income from multiple sources, as well as overseas tax issues and matters concerning copyright.

We'll look at the different stages of a writer's career and the financial aspects s/he may need to consider as their career develops: 1) getting started – unpaid writing done for love not money; 2) paid writing often running alongside traditional employed income; 3) paid writing as main source of income; 4) lifelong considerations.

Stage 1: getting started
When you're at an early stage of your writing career and not earning any money from it, there is little you need to do to stay compliant. However, there are still some important things you can consider.

Setting up a dormant limited company
If you are planning to write a book and you would like the royalty income of that book to be held in a limited company, then consider setting up a company even before you start writing. This will allow you to write the book on behalf of your company. If you wait to set the company up until the book is complete, and publishers are interested, then you would have to transfer the copyright of the book to the company at market value; this could cause issues in terms of valuing the copyright and can create a tax problem that

Do I need an accountant?

If your financial situation is straightforward, there may be no need for you to appoint an accountant. If you are employed, then PAYE usually does a reasonable job of collecting the right amount of tax. Your writing income may be quite modest so it should be straightforward to deal with and – if the numbers are not very big – it may not cause too many issues if you get things wrong. To help you as your career develops, a good accountant can do the following:

- Deal with HMRC on your behalf;
- Submit your tax returns on time, so you don't get penalties for being late;
- Make sure you are claiming for the things you can claim for (and not claiming for things you shouldn't);
- Advise you on ways of saving tax legitimately;
- Help you to keep your records accurately;
- Help you to avoid nasty surprises and unexpected tax bills;
- Be on hand for all your tax related questions.

Anybody can call themselves an accountant, even if they have no qualifications or experience. Try to choose someone who is a member of a professional accountancy body, such as ICAEW, ICAS, AAT, ACCA or CIOT. It is also worth getting recommendations from other writers. Social media groups can be a useful source when looking for accountants who act for lots of writers and understand their needs.

could have been avoided. To decide whether this is right for you, you need to weigh up the cost and hassle of having a dormant limited company against the possible future advantages.

Creative averaging

There are a number of conditions you need to satisfy to be eligible for creative averaging; more details are available on HMRC Helpsheet HS234. One such condition is that you cannot use your first year of trading as part of any creative averaging calculation. Using the example given in the box, Theo would need to be submitting information to HMRC about his writing business from the 2018/19 tax year to be able to claim Creative Averaging in 2020/21.

Loss relief against other income

It is possible for a sole trader to make a loss and to set that loss against other income. This can be beneficial for tax reasons. For example, if an author makes a loss of £5,000 and they also have *employed income* of £30,000, they could offset the £5,000 loss against their employed income so that they only have to pay tax on £25,000. To be able to offset losses against other income, you need to be able to show HMRC that the loss has been incurred on a commercial basis with a view to making a profit. A vague idea that one day you might write a book on Greece would not be sufficient evidence to get a tax deduction on the costs of your holiday.

> ### Creative averaging example
>
> Theo earns nothing in the tax year 2019/20 while he is writing his novel.
>
> In 2020/21 his book is published and he makes a profit of £25,000. Without creative averaging his tax bill in 2019/20 would be nothing, but in 2020/21 he would owe £2,500 income tax and £1,553.60 in National Insurance – a total of £4,053.60.
>
> If he elects to use creative averaging, his £25,000 profit would be split across both tax years, giving him a National Insurance bill of £507.12 in 2019/20 and of £428.60 in 2020/21. By choosing to use creative averaging, Theo would have saved £3,117.88 over the two tax years.

Pre-trading expenses

If you haven't been reporting expenditure to HMRC as losses, then it is still possible to get tax relief for 'pre-trading expenditure'. The relief allows you to claim for expenditure incurred within seven years of starting to trade and, in effect, gives tax relief as if it was incurred on the first day of trading. The 'wholly and exclusive' rule will still apply, so it is important to be able to link the expenditure you are claiming to the income you are receiving. The stronger the link, the more likely HMRC are to accept it. In order to maximise any possible pre-trading expenditure claim, it is important to try and keep records and receipts *just in case* you might need them in the future.

Stage 2: paid writing as additional income

Most writers at this stage will still be running their writing business as a sole trader (or freelancer – there is no difference in terms of tax). Legally you don't need to do anything to set up as a sole trader. As soon as you start writing with a view to making a profit, you've become a sole trader. The tax system is very flexible. You can have a part-time employed job, be a partner in a bookshop and be a published author, all at the same time. Important things to consider at this stage are:

Registering with HMRC

If you earn more than £1,000 from self-employment you need to register as a sole trader with HMRC. You can do this at www.gov.uk/register-for-self-assessment/self-employed. You need to register by 5 October in your second tax year (tax years run from 6 April to 5 April).

For example, if you started on 20 November 2020 (tax year 2020/21) then you would need to register with HMRC by 5 October 2021 (tax year 2021/22). You would then get sent a tax return to complete by 31 January 2022 if filing online or 31 October 2021 if filing by paper.

Submitting a tax return

The tax system is called Self Assessment and this means that it is necessary for you to assess what rules and regulations apply to your tax position. There are a range of penalties that HMRC levy and, although it is possible in certain circumstances to appeal the penalties, it is well worth doing all you can to avoid them in the first place.

Keeping records

A self-employed person needs to keep records for at least 5 years from 31 January following the tax year they relate to. For example, if you have transactions in the tax year to 5 April 2021, you need to keep your records until 31 January 2027. You can keep records digitally or on paper. You should keep copies of bank statements, contracts, receipts for expenditure you are claiming for and any invoices you have raised. It is also worth keeping a note of any unusual non-business transactions. If you win £1,000 at the races or get a generous gift from Aunt Ethel, you want to be able to prove this wasn't undeclared income from writing.

It is usually a good idea to have a separate business bank account that you use just for your writing income. This will help to keep things organised and could give you a little more privacy, as your accountant – and possibly HMRC – don't have to look through all your private outgoings.

Money, tax and benefits

HMRC Self Assessment penalties

Late filing

Up to 3 months late £100, plus

after 3 months £10 per day for 90 days, plus

after 3 months penalties accrue at regular intervals based on 5% of the tax due or £300 – whichever is the greater.

You can estimate your penalty at www.gov.uk/estimate-self-assessment-penalties.

Late payment of tax

5% of tax due if not paid within 30 days with further 5% penalties every 6 months.

Interest is also charged (currently 2.7%).

Incorrect returns

Penalties are charged for tax returns that HMRC consider to be incorrect. There is an appeals process. The penalties are all behaviour based and are as follows:

• Careless errors – 0% to 30% of the additional tax due.

• Deliberate errors – 20% to 70% of the additional tax due.

• Deliberate and concealed errors – 30% to 100% of the additional tax due.

Claiming expenses

A writer pays tax on their profit. Profit is income less allowable costs, often referred to as 'expenses'. Sometimes people talk about things being 'tax deductible', which means they can be deducted from your profit before calculating the tax bill, rather than being deducted from your tax bill. For example, if a higher-rate tax payer spends £100 on stationery, this is tax deductible and so it will reduce her profits by £100 and save income tax at 40%, i.e. £40.

Trading allowance

You can claim a £1,000 Trading Allowance against your self-employed income instead of claiming for expenses you have incurred. You cannot claim the Trading Allowance and expenses at the same time. Claiming the Trading Allowance would be suitable when the Trading Allowance is more than the expenses incurred. However, you can't use the Trading Allowance to turn your profit into a loss. There are also restrictions to prevent you from using the Trading Allowance if the income is received from a business controlled by you, or by someone connected to you.

What can you claim for?

The rule is that an expense must be 'wholly and exclusively' for the purpose of your business. Typical costs are:

- Accountancy
- Advertising costs
- Agent commission
- Bank charges
- Computing and IT costs
- Printing, postage and stationery
- Professional subscriptions
- Internet and telephone
- Software subscriptions
- Research costs
- Travel

Some costs may have an element of private use. In this case, HMRC will allow the cost to be apportioned provided you can justify the calculation. For example:

- Motor expenses – may be apportioned according to business use.
- Home as office – apportioned according to rooms and time spent in use.

Alternatively, you may be able to use HMRC Simplified Expenses. You can find more details at www.gov.uk/simpler-income-tax-simplified-expenses.

Cloud bookkeeping

Recent years have seen the development of relatively cheap, simple bookkeeping packages like Xero and Quickbooks. These allow you to link up your business bank account to your accounting records, so you can quickly and accurately keep track of your income and expenditure. They have the advantage of being regularly backed up, less prone to error, and easy to use. You can also store your receipts and paperwork digitally. As the UK moves towards a new system of reporting called Making Tax Digital from April 2023, it will become more important to be able to easily record and report your income.

Prizes and bursaries

There are many prizes and awards open to authors and other creatives, and entering competitions or seeking awards is a normal part of these professions and a good way for them to obtain extra income from their work. Such prizes are usually taxable. However, there are exceptions. When a prize is unsolicited, and awarded as a mark of honour, distinction or public esteem in recognition of outstanding achievement in a particular field, it won't be taxable. For example, if your publisher or agent enters you for a competition without your knowledge or consent, any prize money received should not be taxable.

Payments on account

For self-employed people the tax system can require payments on account of tax to be made every six months. Each payment on account is half of the previous year's tax bill.

For example: Jo's first year of trading is the tax year 2020/21; she owes tax of £4,000 for the 2020/21 tax year which is due for payment by 31 January 2022. Also, on 31 January 2022 she'll need to pay a payment on account of £2,000 towards her 2021/22 tax bill. She'll have to make a further payment of £2,000 in July 2022. Her actual tax bill for 2021/22 is £5,000. In January 2023 her payments will be:

	£
Tax due for tax year 2021/22	5,000
Less:	
Payment on account - paid 31 January 2022	2,000
Payment on account - paid 31 July 2022	2,000
Balance for 2021/22	1,000
Add:	
Payment on account for 2022/23 (50% of £5,000)	2,500
Total due 31 January 2023	3,500

When income is rising, payments on account can catch out the unwary, as each January there is both a shortfall of tax and a new, higher payment on account to pay. A sensible approach is to save for your tax throughout the year and to complete your tax return early in the tax year, so you have plenty of notice if the bill is higher than expected.

When income is falling (or ceasing) then it is possible to make a claim to HMRC to reduce payments on account so that you don't pay tax in advance that is more than necessary. If the payments on account you make are more than your tax bill, these will be offset against your next payments on account or refunded to you.

Setting up a limited company as a 'money box'

If you already have a paid job, then it's possible that your additional income from writing may take your total income into a higher tax band. If you don't need the money now, setting up a limited company could mean that the company pays corporation tax at a lower rate.

For example, Jamie earns £50,000 through his employment; he also receives £1,820 in Child Benefit in respect of his two children. He earns a further £10,000 in profit as a writer. He doesn't need to access the additional money now and is happy to leave it in his company. His tax liability as a sole trader can be compared with that of the limited company as follows:

Sole trader	£
Income tax on £10,000 @ 40%	4,000
High Income Child Benefit Tax Charge	1,820
Total due	5,820

Limited company	£
Corporation tax on £10,000 @ 19%	1,900
Total due	1,900

Although this is an extreme example, it shows that through using a limited company Jamie has saved £3,920 of tax on £10,000 of income. Once Jamie wants to take the money out of the company, it will be taxable on him personally, but he can control the amount paid so that it is covered by his personal allowance entirely or subject to a lower rate of tax than he is paying now. If Jamie's plans are to build up a savings buffer, so that one day he can take the plunge and become a full-time writer, then this could be of real benefit.

Stage 3: writing as main source of income

Typically, a writer at this stage will either be self-employed or trade through a limited company. A limited company has to be 'incorporated' at Companies House and, once it is set up, it exists as a legal entity. It can enter into contracts, have a bank account, and exist without you. It is possible to trade both as a sole trader and through a limited company. It may even be the case that an author has some of their books taxed as a sole trader and other titles taxed within a limited company.

Issues on incorporation

If you do trade through a limited company, it is important to ensure that the underlying paperwork is correct. Here are some issues to bear in mind:
• For a company to receive copyright income, it must be legally entitled to the income. This can be achieved by ensuring the company exists before the book has been written and a service contract is in place between the director (i.e. the author) and the company.
• It isn't sufficient to simply 'bank' any proceeds into your company. All contracts need to be properly drawn up in the company's name.

IR35

IR35 was introduced in April 2000 to stop the practice of employees setting up a limited company (a 'personal service company') and invoicing their employer for their work rather than being paid as an employee. This practice led to a large tax saving for both the employer and the employee.

IR35 only applies to limited companies, so a writer who is trading as a sole trader can ignore it. From April 2021 both public entities and larger private companies will have to look at the status of people working through personal service companies and, if necessary, deduct tax and National Insurance.

For most writers operating through a personal service company, it will be clear that they are not working for anyone as disguised employment. For other writers the situation may be more uncertain. For example, a copywriter with their own company providing weekly content for a client who describes them as their 'Content Manager', pays them a regular salary, expects them to attend meetings on site and doesn't allow a substitute, may be caught by the IR35 rules.

The IR35 rules are complex and, if caught by the rules, your limited company has to pay out most of the money it receives as a salary to the employee – together with Employers National Insurance.

Specialist help should be sought if you think your company may be affected by IR35.

• If you simply give your copyright to your company, it can create a tax issue; HMRC will expect you to pay income tax on the market value of the gift and will also expect the company to pay tax on the income it receives. In effect, the same income could be taxed twice.

• It is possible to sell the copyright to the company. This results in a better tax position, as the company would be able to get some tax relief for the cost of the copyright, but it will require a valuation of the copyright which brings with it costs and some uncertainty.

Sole trader or limited company – the key differences

Sole trader	Limited company
Starting up	
Nothing legal required	Must be incorporated at Companies House
Closing down	
Nothing legal required	Must be formally struck off at Companies House
Legal protection	
None – you and the business are one and the same	Limited liability (but watch out for contracts that pass on liabilities to directors)
If you are sued, then all your assets are at stake	If the company is sued, then only the assets of the company are at stake
Tax on profits	
Income tax paid depending on total earnings from all sources in the year; rates may be 0%, 20%, 40% or 45% depending on income	Corporation tax paid. Rate is currently 19%, although this is due to rise in 2023
Tax on profits extracted	
Not applicable – you pay tax on profit whether extracted or not	Dividend tax due at rates of 0%, 7.5%, 32.5% or 38.1% depending on income
National Insurance	
Pay Class 2 National Insurance and Class 4 National Insurance	Only pay National Insurance on salaries paid to employees if they earn over the limit
Reporting	
Must complete an individual Self Assessment tax return each year	Must file accounts each year with Companies House. Must submit a Confirmation Statement each year to Companies House. Must file a corporation tax return each year with HMRC. May have to run a payroll and report to HMRC. Likely that director/shareholder will have to complete an individual Self Assessment tax return each year
Separate business bank account	
Advisable	Essential
VAT	
Can be VAT registered; it is a person that is VAT registered, not a business, which may have unintended consequences	Can be VAT registered
Creative averaging	
Can be used	Cannot be used
Why choose this one?	
Simple; cheap; you want to take all the money out of business when it's earned, not concerned about legal liability	Save tax if you don't require all the money or are able to take advantage of splitting income; provides legal liability protection

• Once your company owns the copyright, royalty income is 'locked' into being paid to the company. If you wished to own the copyright personally, it would need to be transferred out of the company at a fair value. You may find you have a company for a much longer time than you first anticipate, because it may not be practical to close it down until the copyright has a negligible value.

VAT

VAT (Value Added Tax) is a tax that businesses are required to charge their customers for goods or services. A writer is no different from any other business and therefore must charge VAT when supplying writing services. The standard UK rate of VAT is currently 20%. VAT is a complicated subject and much of it is beyond the scope of this book. However, there are some key things a writer should be aware of.

A VAT-registered business usually submits a quarterly VAT return within one month and seven days of the end of the VAT quarter. Any VAT due is then paid by the same deadline. Being VAT-registered is not entirely bad news; a VAT-registered business has to charge VAT on their relevant services, but they can also claim back VAT on things they buy for their business. For example, in the VAT quarter ending 31 December 2020 a writer gets a publishing deal for £10,000 plus £2,000 of VAT. Their agent charges them £1,500 plus £300 VAT, and they buy a computer for writing for £500 plus £100 VAT. They would submit a VAT return to HMRC by 7 February 2021 and pay over £1,600, as follows:

	£
VAT charged	2,000
Less:	
VAT on agent's fees	300
VAT on computer	100
Paid to HMRC	1,600

Although this may make you feel worse off, especially when you are paying £1,600 to HMRC, you are in fact better off by £400 – this being the difference between the VAT you have been paid and the VAT you have paid out.

VAT registration threshold

A business needs to register for VAT when the level of sales exceeds the VAT threshold. The VAT threshold is currently £85,000 and it applies to the last 12 months. To know whether you need to register or not, you have to look back at your cumulative sales over the last 12 months and, if these exceed the VAT threshold, you must register. You are also required to register if you believe your sales in the next 30 days alone will be more than the VAT threshold – for example if you bag a big publishing deal.

Some writers will make an early 'protective' VAT registration, so that they know they are registered and don't have to worry about tripping over the VAT threshold. It is important to remember that the turnover figure is not necessarily the amount you receive. For example, a writer gets an advance of £10,000; their agent deducts 15% plus their VAT and so the writer only receives £8,200. The figure that counts towards the VAT threshold is £10,000.

Finally, you do not need to include employment income in your turnover calculation or non-UK income (such as royalties from Amazon).

Voluntary registration

You can voluntarily register for VAT even if your sales are under the VAT registration threshold. The reason you may want to do this is to recover the VAT you are being charged – typically by your agent. For example, a writer gets a publishing deal for £25,000; their agent charges 15% commission plus VAT. If they are not VAT-registered, they'll lose the agent VAT of £750 but, if they are VAT-registered, they'd be able to recover this.

Being in the 'VAT club' will allow you to recover VAT on all your other business expenditure, such as computer costs and accountancy fees. Whether it is a good idea to register early depends on your circumstances. If you're not incurring much VAT, then it may not be worth the hassle.

What to include in your sales for VAT

You need to include all your UK sales and any foreign sales collected by your UK publisher. You can exclude any direct foreign sales (such as Amazon self-publishing or sales you or your agent have agreed with a foreign publisher). If you're a sole trader, you can exclude any employed income. But, if you are self-employed as something else too (e.g. you're both a plumber and a writer), you need to aggregate both sets of income. The VAT registration belongs to the *person* not the *business*.

Claiming back VAT

When you first register for VAT, you can reclaim VAT on goods purchased up to four years prior to registration provided those goods are still held when registration takes place. VAT on services supplied in the six months prior to registration may also be reclaimed. To claim VAT you'll need a valid VAT receipt; a credit card receipt isn't enough, and a VAT inspector will disallow any expenditure that you can't produce a valid VAT receipt for – even if it's obvious that you would have paid VAT.

Not all expenditure has VAT charged on it:

Usually has VAT	Usually has no VAT
Agent commission	Trains, planes and taxis
Accountancy fees	Software subscriptions from overseas
Stationery	Postage
Computers and UK software	Entertainment
Internet and mobile phone	Insurance

Withholding tax and double taxation relief

Writers will often receive some or, in the case of an author selling via Amazon Kindle Direct Publishing (KDP), most of their income from an overseas source. Many foreign

Money, tax and benefits

Coronavirus

There is a substantial amount of help and advice through the government website, www.gov.uk/coronavirus. Due to the rapidly changing situation, this should be the place to refer to for up-to-date information.

Government support falls broadly into two categories:

• **Direct grants** – grants (like the Self-Employment Income Support Scheme) are taxable as if they are normal trading income. The grant should be recognised as income in the year it is received.

• **Deferring payment** – many people have struggled to pay their tax bills on time. Various schemes are in place to help and it is best to address the problem with HMRC.

countries will charge a 'withholding tax' on such royalty payments, for example 30% in the case of the USA. Once withholding tax is paid, it is often not cost effective to try to recover it from the country in question, as doing so may require local professional advice and tax returns to be submitted to the country in question.

It is often possible to avoid any withholding tax being deducted in the first instance by completing the information required by the overseas publisher, so they don't have to apply withholding tax. Amazon KDP has an online tax interview to make it as easy as possible for you to comply. Other publishers in other countries will have to follow their own rules and will often ask for a Certificate of Residence to prove you are a UK tax payer. There are more details on applying for a Certificate of Residence at www.gov.uk/guidance/get-a-certificate-of-residence.

If you do suffer withholding tax, then it may be possible to use the foreign tax you have paid to offset against your tax liability on the same income when you complete your tax return. This may give you a worse result, though, as you will pay tax at the highest rate between the two countries. For example, if you are a UK basic rate tax payer and suffer 30% in the US, that will cover the 20% tax you would have to pay in the UK. You would not get a refund of the additional 10%. But, if you are a higher rate tax payer paying 40% tax, you would have to pay the additional 10% tax in the UK.

Stage 4: Lifelong considerations

As a writer's career becomes more established, there are other financial considerations.

Pensions
State Pension

To qualify for the new State Pension, you need a minimum of 10 qualifying years and at least 35 qualifying years to receive the maximum payments. You can check your pension entitlement online at www.gov.uk/check-state-pension. If you have gaps in your pension contribution history, then you can consider making voluntary contributions.

Writers' Guild Pension Fund

For their members writing for TV, radio and film, WGGB (Writers' Guild of Great Britain) have negotiated agreements with the BBC, ITV and PACT so that pension contributions are made to the Writers' Guild Pension Fund. In return for the writer making a contribution to the fund, the production company will also make a contribution, in addition to the writer's fee. More details are available from WGGB (see page 352 for contact details).

Private pensions

If you have been employed, you may have an occupational pension from your employment in place. Most writers who have been self-employed will depend upon their own pension arrangements using 'defined contribution' schemes. Contributions to a private pension by an individual are made net of basic rate income tax. This means that a contribution of £80 actually means the amount invested is £100, with £20 being claimed by the pension company from the Government. A higher-rate tax payer would save another £20 in income tax, making the cost of putting £100 into a pension just £60. There are rules regarding how much you can invest each year and many people will need professional advice as to what scheme they invest in.

Insurances

Being a self-employed writer does mean that you don't have the same safety net that many employees may have. It is sensible to think about how you and your family would manage if you died or, through injury or illness, were unable to continue to earn a living. There are insurance policies that are available to help.

- **Life insurance** can provide a lump sum or a monthly income for a period of time if you die.
- **Critical illness insurance** can provide a lump sum or a monthly income for a period of time if you are diagnosed with a critical illness.
- **Income protection insurance** can provide a monthly income if you are unable to work due to ill health.

Wills

Making a will is important for a number of reasons. Amongst other things, you can specify who inherits your assets, make tax efficient choices, and provide instructions as to who looks after your minor children. A writer also needs to consider what happens with any copyright they hold as part of their estate. Copyright can last up to 70 years after death, so it may represent a valuable asset. You may also have particular instructions as to what happens to your personal papers and unpublished works. It is also worth thinking about what happens with digital assets such as blogs, social media accounts, online videos, and access to cloud storage services like Dropbox. A bit of forward planning may save a lot of trouble for the people dealing with your estate.

Further advice: useful websites

HMRC
www.gov.uk/government/organisations/hm-revenue-customs

Institute of Chartered Accountants in England and Wales
www.icaew.com

Institute of Chartered Accountants Scotland
www.icas.com

These author associations offer support and advice on financial matters to their members.

National Union of Journalists
www.nuj.org.uk

Society of Authors
www.societyofauthors.org (see page 349)

WGGB (Writers' Guild of Great Britain)
https://writersguild.org.uk (see page 352)

Accountancy and business software tools include:

Sage
www.sage.com/en-gb/cp/accounting

Quickbooks
https://quickbooks.intuit.com/uk

Xero
www.xero.com/uk

Money, tax and benefits

Jonathan Ford BSC FCA MSWW and **Louise Ford** BA FCA are the directors of Writers Tax Ltd, a firm of chartered accountants that specialises in helping authors, scriptwriters and other professional writers with their tax and accountancy needs, which they established in 2020. They both qualified as chartered accountants with Price Waterhouse in Liverpool. Jonathan worked at Grant Thornton and later as Financial Controller at Mersey TV before setting up his own company. See their website https://writers.tax for more information.

National Insurance contributions

Sarah Bradford sets out the facts about National Insurance, explaining the principle that underlies it, the various classes of contribution payable by workers, both employed and self-employed, the related benefit entitlements, and information on current rates and earnings thresholds.

Nature of National Insurance contributions

The payment of National Insurance contributions secures access to the state pension and to contributory benefits. This is the contributory principle of National Insurance. National Insurance contributions are payable by employed earners and their employers and also by self-employed earners. People who do not have any earnings or whose earnings are not sufficient to trigger a liability to pay National Insurance contributions can choose to pay National Insurance contributions voluntarily to maintain their contributions record.

If sufficient National Insurance contributions of the right type are paid for a tax year, the year will be a qualifying year for National Insurance purposes. A person needs 35 qualifying years in order to receive the full state pension when they reach state pension age. Where a person has at least ten qualifying years, they will receive a reduced state pension.

Classes of National Insurance

There are various different classes of National Insurance contribution. The class (or classes) that you pay will depend on whether you are an employed earner, a self-employed earner, an employer or a voluntary contributor. Contributions may be earnings-related, payable on profits or payable at a flat rate, depending on the class.

The different classes of contribution are shown in the box below. Class 1, 2 and 4 contributions are only payable once earnings exceed certain thresholds and limits. The rates and thresholds applying for 2021/22 are set out in the box on page 450.

Contributions payable by writers and artists

As for other earners, the class of National Insurance payable by writers and artists depends on whether they are a self-employed earner or an employed earner. This is not something

Classes of National Insurance

Nature of contribution	Payable by
Class 1 Earnings-related	Employed earners (primary Class 1 contributions Employer (secondary Class 1 contributions)
Class 1A Earnings-related	Employer on taxable benefits in kind and taxable termination payments and sporting testimonials
Class 1B Earnings-related	Employer on items included within a PAYE Settlement Agreement and on the tax due under that agreement
Class 2 Flat rate	Self-employed earners
Class 3 Flat rate	Voluntary contributions
Class 3A Variable amount	Payable between 12 October 2015 and 5 April 2017 voluntarily by those who reached state pension age before 6 April 2016 to boost their state pension
Class 4 Profits-related	Self-employed earners

that they can choose – it will depend on the facts of the engagement. It is important that the employment status of the writer or artist is categorised correctly as this will affect not only what class (and therefore how) they pay, but also what benefits they are entitled to.

Categorisation – employed earner v self-employed earner
To ensure that writers and artists pay the correct class of National Insurance contributions, it is important they are correctly categorised. Employed earners will pay Class 1 National Insurance contributions, whereas self-employed earners will pay Class 2 and Class 4 contributions.

A worker's categorisation depends on the characteristics of the engagement. In many cases, it will be clear whether a worker is an employed earner or a self-employed earner. For example, a writer who is employed by a publishing firm and has a contract of employment will be an employed earner and will pay Class 1 National Insurance contributions on their earnings, whereas a freelance writer who undertakes commissions for a variety of people and is paid a fee for each commission will be a self-employed earner and will pay Class 2 and Class 4 contributions.

Characteristics of employment
The following characteristics apply to an engagement where the worker is an employee:
• the person is required to work regularly unless they are unwell or on leave;
• they are expected to work a minimum number of hours a week and expect to be paid for the time that they work;
• a manager or supervisor is responsible for their workload, and will say when a job should be finished or how it should be done;
• they must do the work themselves – they can't send someone else to do it instead;
• the business deducts tax and National Insurance from their pay;
• they are entitled to paid holiday;
• they are entitled to statutory payments;
• they can join the business' pensions scheme;
• they are subject to grievance and disciplinary procedures;
• the contract sets out the procedure applying in the event of redundancy;
• they work at the business premises or at a location specified by the business;
• they only work for that business or, if they have another job, it is completely separate;
• the offer letter and contract refer to the 'employee' and the 'employer'.

For example, a staff writer who is paid a salary and contracted to work 35 hours a week would be an employed earner.

Characteristics of self-employment
The following characteristics indicate that the writer or artist is a self-employed earner:
• they are in business for themselves and are responsible for the success or failure of the business and can make a profit or a loss;
• they decide what work they take on and where and how they do it;
• they can hire someone else to do the work;
• they are responsible for fixing unsatisfactory work in their own time;
• they agree a fixed price for a job – the fee is the same regardless of how long it takes them to do the work;

• they use their own money to buy any equipment needed and to cover the running costs of the business;

• they work for more than one client.

A writer who is commissioned to write specific articles for different publications and who works for a number of publishers, being paid a fee for each article, would be a self-employed earner.

Marginal cases

It will not always be clear whether a writer or artist is an employed earner or a self-employed earner. In this situation, it is necessary to look at the overall picture and see whether, on balance, the writer or artist is employed or self-employed. It should be noted that there is not one single definitive test, rather a question of seeing what characteristics of employment and what characteristics of self-employment are present.

In reaching a decision, the following factors need to be considered:

• The nature of the contract and the written terms – a contract for *services* indicates employment and a contract of *service* indicates self-employment.

• The nature of the engager's business and the nature of the job.

• Right of substitution – a right to send a substitute indicates self-employment.

• Mutuality of obligation – for a contract for services there must be minimum mutual obligations; the employer is obliged to offer work and the employee is obliged to do that work.

• Right of control – a high degree of control (on the part of the employer) over how and where the worker performs the work suggests employment.

• Provision of equipment – the provision by the worker of their own equipment suggests self-employment.

• Financial risk – a person who is self-employed bears a higher degree of financial risk than an employee.

• Opportunity to profit – a person who is self-employed has the opportunity to profit if they do the job quicker or under-budget.

• Length of engagement – while this is not a decisive factor, an open-ended contract is more likely to indicate employment.

• Part and parcel of the organisation – a worker who is seen as 'part and parcel' of the organisation is likely to be an employee.

• Entitlement to benefits – a worker who is entitled to employee-type benefits, such as a pension, is more likely to be an employee.

• Personal factors – a highly skilled worker may not need supervising but may still be an employee.

• Intention – while intention alone cannot determine status, it can be useful in forming an opinion on whether the worker is employed or self-employed.

Check Employment Status for Tax (CEST) tool

HMRC have produced a tool – the Check Employment Status for Tax (CEST) tool – which can be used to reach a decision on whether a writer or artist is employed or self-employed. The tool asks a series of questions on the engagement, which must be answered honestly, in order to reach a decision. As long as the information provided is accurate and represents the reality of the engagement, HMRC will stand by the decision that is reached. The CEST tool is available on the Gov.uk website at www.gov.uk/guidance/check-employment-status-for-tax.

Workers providing their services through a personal service company

Anti-avoidance rules apply where services are provided through a personal limited company or another intermediary to an end client. There are two sets of rules to consider – the off-payroll working rules and the IR35 rules. The rules that apply depend on the nature of the end client.

• Off-payroll working rules

The off-payroll working rules were introduced from 6 April 2017. They apply from the date when services were provided through an intermediary to a private sector body. The rules were extended from 6 April 2021, and from that date they also apply when the end client is a medium or large private sector organisation.

The end client must carry out a status determination to ascertain whether the worker would be an employee of the end client if they provided their services to them directly. Where this is the case, the end client must deduct tax and National Insurance from payments made to the worker's personal company (after adjusting the bill for VAT and the cost of any materials), and report this to HMRC. The worker receives credit for the tax and National Insurance on payment made to them by their personal limited company. They do not need to consider the IR35 rules because the off-payroll working rules apply instead.

• IR35

From 6 April 2021 onwards, the IR35 rules only apply where a worker provides their services to a small private sector organisation through an intermediary, such as a personal service company. The worker's personal service company must determine whether the worker would be an employee of the small private sector organisation if they provided their services directly. If the answer is 'yes' the IR35 rules apply. The intermediary must calculate the deemed employment payment at the end of the tax year, and account for tax and National Insurance on that payment to HMRC.

Employed earners – Class 1 National Insurance

Class 1 National Insurance is payable on the earnings of an employed earner. The employed earner pays primary contributions and the secondary contributor (which is generally the employer) pays secondary contributions. The payment of primary Class 1 National Insurance contributions by the employed earner is the mechanism by which the employed earner earns the right to the state pension and contributory benefits. Secondary Class 1 contributions, payable by the employer, do not earn benefit entitlement – they are akin to a tax on the employee's earnings.

Contributions are calculated by reference to earnings for the earnings period on a non-cumulative basis; no account is taken of earnings previously in the tax year, only those for the earnings period. The earnings period will normally correspond to the pay interval. However, directors have an annual earnings period, regardless of their actual pay frequency. The employer must deduct primary contributions from the employee's pay and pay them over to HMRC together with tax deducted under PAYE and the employer's secondary contributions.

• Primary Class 1 National Insurance

Primary Class 1 National Insurance contributions are payable by employees aged 16 and over until they reach state pension age (which depends on their date of birth). No contributions are payable until earnings reach the *lower earnings limit* (set at £120 per week, £520 per month, £6,240 per year for 2021/22). They are then payable at a notional zero rate until earnings reach the primary threshold. This is important as it secures the year as a qualifying year for National Insurance purposes (as long as earnings are paid above the lower earnings limit for each earnings period in the tax year). Where earnings are below the lower earnings limit, the year is not a qualifying year (although may become one if the worker receives National Insurance credits or pays voluntary contributions).

National Insurance rates and thresholds 2021/22

National Insurance class	Rate or threshold
Class 1	
Lower earnings limit	£120 per week
	£520 per month
	£6,240 per year
Primary threshold	£184 per week
	£797 per month
	£9,568 per year
Secondary threshold	£170 per week
	£737 per month
	£8,840 per year
Upper earnings limit	£967 per week
	£4,189 per month
	£50,270 per year
Upper secondary threshold for under 21s	£967 per week
	£4,189 per month
	£50,270 per year
Apprentice upper secondary threshold	£967 per week
	£4,189 per month
	£50,270 per year
Primary (employee) contributions	
On earnings between the primary threshold and the upper earnings limit	12%
On earnings above the upper earnings limit	2%
Secondary (employer) contributions	
On earnings above the relevant secondary threshold	13.8%
Class 1A and Class 1B	
Contribution rate (employer only)	13.8%
Class 2	
Flat rate contribution	£3.05 per week
Small profits threshold	£6,515 a year
Class 3	
Flat rate contribution	£15.40 per week
Class 4	
Lower profits limit	£9,568 a year
Upper profits limit	£50,270 a year

Contributions are payable on earnings above the *primary threshold* (set at £184 per week, £797 per month, £9,568 per year for 2021/22) at the main primary rate of 12% until earnings reach the *upper earnings limit* (set at £967 per week, £4,189 per month, £50,270 per year for 2021/22). Contributions are payable at the additional primary rate of 2% on earnings above the upper earnings limit.

• Secondary Class 1 contributions

Secondary contributions are payable by the secondary contributor, which in most cases is the employed earner's employer. They are payable on the earnings of an employee aged 16 and above; unlike primary contributions, the secondary liability does not stop when the employed earner reaches state pension age.

Contributions are payable at the secondary rate of 13.8% on earnings in excess of the *secondary threshold* (set at £170 per week, £737 per month, £8,840 per year for 2021/22). A higher threshold applies to the earnings of employees under the age of 21 (the upper secondary threshold for under 21s) and to those of apprentices under the age of 25 (the apprentice upper secondary threshold). Both of these thresholds are aligned with the *upper earnings limit* for primary Class 1 purposes (set at £967 per week, £4,189 per month and £50,270 per year for 2021/22). These thresholds only apply for secondary Class 1 purposes; the employee or apprentice pays the usual primary contributions.

• Earnings for Class 1 purposes

Class 1 contributions are calculated on the earnings for the earnings period. The definition of 'earnings' includes any remuneration or profits derived from the employment. This will include payments of wages and salary, but will also include other items such as statutory sick pay, statutory payments, and certain share-based remuneration. Comprehensive guidance on what to include in earnings for National Insurance purposes can be found in the HMRC guidance CWG2 *Employer further guide to PAYE and National Insurance contributions*. The 2021/22 edition is available on the Gov.uk website at www.gov.uk/government/publications/cwg2-further-guide-to-paye-and-national-insurance-contributions.

• Class 1A National Insurance contributions

Class 1A National Insurance contributions are employer-only contributions payable on taxable benefits in kind and also on taxable termination payments in excess of the £30,000 tax-free threshold and taxable sporting testimonials in excess of the £100,000 tax-free threshold. They are payable at the Class 1A rate of 13.8%.

• Class 1B National Insurance

Class 1B National Insurance contributions are employer-only contributions payable in place of the Class 1 or Class 1A liability that would otherwise arise on items included within a PAYE Settlement Agreement (PSA), and also on the tax due under the PSA.

Self-employed earners – Class 2 and Class 4 National Insurance contributions

Where a writer or artist is a self-employed earner, they will pay Class 2 contributions, and also Class 4 contributions on their profits. Class 2 and Class 4 National Insurance contributions are payable via the Self Assessment system and must be paid by 31 January after the end of the tax year to which they relate (i.e. by 31 January 2023 for 2021/22 contributions).

• Class 2 National Insurance contributions

Class 2 National Insurance contributions are flat-rate contributions payable by self-employed earners whose profits exceed the *small profits threshold*, set at £6,515 for 2021/22. Class 2 National Insurance contributions are payable at the rate of £3.05 per week for 2021/22. The payment of Class 2 contributions is the mechanism by which a self-employed earner earns entitlement to the state pension and contributory benefits. Contributions must be paid for the full year for the year to be a qualifying year. A person whose profits from self-employment are below the small profits threshold can pay Class 2 National Insurance contributions voluntarily. This is a cheap way to build up pension entitlement.

• Class 4 National Insurance contributions

Class 4 National Insurance contributions are payable by self-employed earners on their profits. They do not provide any benefit entitlement, and in effect are a tax on profits. No contributions are payable on profits below the *lower profits threshold*, set at £9,568 for 2021/22. Class 4 contributions are payable at the rate of 9% on profits between the lower profits limit and the *upper profits limit*, set at £50,270 for 2021/22, and on profits in excess of the upper profits limit, at the additional Class 4 rate of 2%.

Voluntary contributions – Class 3

A person can pay voluntary Class 3 contributions to plug gaps in their contributions record. For 2021/22, Class 3 contributions are payable at the rate of £15.40 per week. Where a person has profits from self-employment below the *small profits threshold* (set at £6,515 for 2021/22), they can instead pay Class 2 contributions voluntarily; at £3.05 per week for 2021/22 this is a much cheaper option.

Maximum contributions

Where a person has more than one job, or is both employed and self-employed, there is a cap on the contributions that are payable for the year. The calculations are complex.

National Insurance credits

National Insurance credits are available in certain circumstances where people are unable to work or because they are ill. There are two types of credit. Class 1 credits count towards state pension and contributory benefits, while Class 3 credits only count towards the state pension. Further detail on National Insurance credits can be found on the Gov.uk website at www.gov.uk/national-insurance-credits.

Benefit entitlement

The payment of National Insurance contributions (and the award of National Insurance credits) earns entitlement to the state pension and certain contributory benefits. Only the payment of primary Class 1, Class 2 and Class 3 contributions confer benefit entitlement. Benefit entitlement depends on the class of contribution paid.

Benefit entitlement

Class of contributions	Benefit entitlement
Primary Class 1 (employed earner)	State Pension, contribution-based Jobseeker's Allowance, contribution-based Employment and Support Allowance, Maternity Allowance and Bereavement Payment, Bereavement Allowance, Widowed Parent's Allowance, Bereavement Support Payment.
Class 2 (self-employed earners)	State Pension, contribution-based Employment and Support Allowance, Maternity Allowance and Bereavement Allowance.
Class 3 (voluntary contributions)	State Pension and Bereavement Payment, Bereavement Allowance, Widowed Parent's Allowance.

Sarah Bradford BA (Hons), FCA CTA (Fellow) is the director of Writetax Ltd and WriteTax Consultancy Services Ltd, and the author of *National Insurance Contributions 2021/22* (and earlier editions) published by Bloomsbury Professional. She writes widely on tax and National Insurance contributions.

Index

Writers &Artists

A FREE WRITING PLATFORM TO CALL YOUR OWN

- Share your writing
- Build reward points
- Free writing advice articles
- Publishing guidance
- Save margin notes
- Exclusive discounts

REGISTER NOW

WWW.WRITERSANDARTISTS.CO.UK